International Financial Management
ABRIDGED 10TH EDITION

JEFF MADURA
Florida Atlantic University

SOUTH-WESTERN
CENGAGE Learning

Australia • Brazil • Japan • Korea • Mexico • Singapore • Spain • United Kingdom • United States

SOUTH-WESTERN
CENGAGE Learning

**International Financial Management,
Abridged 10th Edition
Jeff Madura**

VP of Editorial, Business: Jack W. Calhoun

Publisher: Joe Sabatino

Executive Editor: Michael R. Reynolds

Developmental Editor: Kendra Brown

Sr. Marketing Comm. Manager: Jim Overly

Marketing Coordinator: Suellen Ruttkay

Marketing Manager: Nate Anderson

Content Project Manager: Scott Dillon

Manager of Technology, Editorial:
Matt McKinney

Manager of Media, Editorial: John Barans

Sr. Media Editor: Scott Fidler

Sr. Frontlist Buyer, Manufacturing: Kevin Kluck

Production Service/Compositor: Integra

Copyeditor: Ann Whetstone

Proofreader: Pat Lewis

Sr. Editorial Assistant: Adele Scholtz

Sr. Art Director: Michelle Kunkler

Internal/Cover Design: Joe Devine/Red Hangar
Design, LLC

Cover Image: © Bryan Tighe/iStockphoto

For product information and technology assistance, contact us at
Cengage Learning Customer & Sales Support, 1-800-354-9706

For permission to use material from this text or product,
submit all requests online at **www.cengage.com/permissions**
Further permissions questions can be emailed to
permissionrequest@cengage.com

Library of Congress Control Number: 2010930218

Student Edition ISBN 13: 978-0-538-48221-9
Student Edition ISBN 10: 0-538-48221-4

South-Western Cengage Learning
5191 Natorp Boulevard
Mason, OH 45040
USA

Cengage Learning products are represented in Canada by
Nelson Education, Ltd.

For your course and learning solutions, visit **academic.cengage.com**

Purchase any of our products at your local college store or at our
preferred online store **www.cengagebrain.com**

Printed in Canada
1 2 3 4 5 6 7 14 13 12 11 10

Dedicated to Mary

Brief Contents

Contents

PART 2: Exchange Rate Behavior   169

PART 3: Exchange Rate Risk Management 271

9: FORECASTING EXCHANGE RATES 273

PART 4: Long-Term Asset and Liability Management 395

From the Publisher

International Financial Management: Abridged 10th Edition is our offering of a more course-specific, lower cost alternative to *International Financial Management: 10th Edition* for students and instructors. Based on market research with faculty using *International Financial Management: 10th Edition*, we found that many instructors covered less than the twenty-one chapters contained in that textbook. That same research showed that the chapters contained in this abridged version are those that most professors cover in a one-term course. For those instructors that subscribe to this coverage trend, this abridged version is a more efficient and economical alternative to use with students taking their course.

The approach we have taken with *International Financial Management: Abridged 10th Edition* is to remove whole specific chapters in their entirety, all end-of-chapter appendices, and all end-of-part integrative problems. Pagination of this abridged version is consistent with *International Financial Management: 10th Edition* so that all student-oriented supplements, as well as instructor supplements, will work with either version of the book. A classroom of students using either version of the book will be able to follow along on the same page without need for "translating" page numbers. For those instructors who feel that one or more of the eliminated chapters, chapter appendices, or integrated problems are needed in their course, both instructors and students can freely access PDFs of these chapters or appendices at the textbook's website at **www.cengage.com/finance/madura.**

Preface

Businesses evolve into multinational corporations (MNCs) so that they can capitalize on international opportunities. Their financial managers must be able to assess the international environment, recognize opportunities, implement strategies, assess exposure to risk, and manage the risk. The MNCs that are most capable of responding to changes in the international financial environment will be rewarded. The same can be said for the students today who may become the future managers of MNCs.

INTENDED MARKET

International Financial Management, Abridged Tenth Edition, presumes an understanding of basic corporate finance. It is suitable for both undergraduate and master's level courses in international financial management. For master's courses, the more challenging questions, problems, and cases in each chapter are recommended, along with special projects.

ORGANIZATION OF THE TEXT

International Financial Management, Abridged Tenth Edition, is organized first to provide a background on the international environment and then to focus on the managerial aspects from a corporate perspective. Managers of MNCs will need to understand the environment before they can manage within it.

The first two parts of the text provide the macroeconomic framework for the text. Part 1 (Chapters 1 through 5) introduces the major markets that facilitate international business. Part 2 (Chapters 6 through 8) describes relationships between exchange rates and economic variables and explains the forces that influence these relationships.

The remainder of the text provides a microeconomic framework, with a focus on the managerial aspects of international financial management. Part 3 (Chapters 9 through 12) explains the measurement and management of exchange rate risk. Part 4 (Chapters 13 through 16) describes the management of long-term assets and liabilities, including motives for direct foreign investment, multinational capital budgeting, and country risk analysis.

Each chapter is self-contained so that professors can use classroom time to focus on the more comprehensive topics and rely on the text to cover the other concepts. The management of long-term assets (chapters on direct foreign investment, multinational capital budgeting, multinational restructuring, and country risk analysis) is covered before the management of long-term liabilities (chapters on capital structure and long-term financing), because the financing decisions are dependent on the investments. Nevertheless, concepts are explained with an emphasis on how management of long-term assets and long-term liabilities is integrated. For example, the multinational capital budgeting analysis demonstrates how the feasibility of a foreign project may be dependent on the financing mix. Some professors may prefer to teach the chapters on managing long-term liabilities before the chapters on managing long-term assets.

The strategic aspects such as motives for direct foreign investment are covered before the operational aspects such as short-term financing or investment. For professors who prefer to cover the MNC's management of short-term assets and liabilities before the management of long-term assets and liabilities, the parts can be rearranged because they are self-contained.

Professors may limit their coverage of chapters in some sections where they believe the text concepts are covered by other courses or do not need additional attention beyond what is in the text. For example, they may give less attention to the chapters in Part 2 (Chapters 6 through 8) if their students take a course in international economics. If professors focus on the main principles, they may limit their coverage of Chapters 5, 15, and 16.

APPROACH OF THE TEXT

International Financial Management, Abridged Tenth Edition, focuses on management decisions that maximize the value of the firm. It is designed in recognition of the fact that each instructor has a unique way of reinforcing key concepts. Thus, the text offers a variety of methods of reinforcing these concepts so that instructors can select the methods and features that fit their teaching styles.

- *Part-Opening Diagram.* A diagram is provided at the beginning of each part to illustrate how the key concepts covered in that part are related. This offers some information about the organization of chapters in that part.

- *Objectives.* A bulleted list at the beginning of each chapter identifies the key concepts in that chapter.

- *Examples.* The key concepts are thoroughly described in the chapter and supported by examples.

- *Governance.* This feature is integrated throughout the text in recognition of its increasing popularity and use in explaining concepts in international financial management.

- *International Credit Crisis.* Coverage of the international credit crisis is provided in each chapter where applicable.

- *Term Paper on the International Credit Crisis.* Suggested assignments for a term paper on the international credit crisis are provided at the end of Chapter 1.

- *Web Links.* Websites that offer useful related information regarding key concepts are provided in each chapter and online at www.cengage.com/finance/madura.

- *Summary.* A bulleted list at the end of each chapter summarizes the key concepts. This list corresponds to the list of objectives at the beginning of the chapter.

- *Point/Counter-Point.* A controversial issue is introduced, along with opposing arguments, and students are asked to determine which argument is correct and explain why.

- *Self-Test Questions.* A "Self-Test" at the end of each chapter challenges students on the key concepts. The answers to these questions are provided in Appendix A.

- *Questions and Applications.* Many of the questions and other applications at the end of each chapter test the student's knowledge of the key concepts in the chapter.

- *"Blades, Inc." Continuing Case.* At the end of each chapter, the continuing case allows students to use the key concepts to solve problems experienced by a firm called Blades, Inc. (a producer of roller blades). By working on cases related to the same MNC over a school term, students recognize how an MNC's decisions are integrated.

- *Small Business Dilemma.* The Small Business Dilemma at the end of each chapter places students in a position where they must use concepts introduced in the chapter to make decisions about a small MNC called Sports Exports Company.

- *Internet/Excel Exercises.* At the end of each chapter, there are exercises that expose the students to applicable information available at various websites, enable the application of Excel to related topics, or a combination of these. For example, students learn how to obtain exchange rate information online and apply Excel to measure the value at risk.

- *Midterm and Final Examinations.* A midterm self-exam is provided at the end of Chapter 8, which focuses on international macro and market conditions (Chapters 1 through 8). A final self-exam is provided at the end of Chapter 16, which focuses on the managerial chapters (Chapters 9 through 16). Students can compare their answers to those in the answer key provided.

- *Supplemental Cases.* Supplemental cases allow students to apply chapter concepts to a specific situation of an MNC. All supplemental cases are located in Appendix B at the end of the text. Supplemental case content for online-only Chapters 17–21 is available at www.cengage.com/finance/madura.

- *Running Your Own MNC.* This project (provided at www.cengage.com/finance/madura) allows each student to create a small international business and apply key concepts from each chapter to run the business throughout the school term.

- *International Investing Project.* This project (in Appendix D and also provided at www.cengage.com/finance/madura) allows students to simulate investing in stocks of MNCs and foreign companies and requires them to assess how the values of these stocks change during the school term in response to international economic conditions.

- *Discussion in the Boardroom.* This project (in Appendix E and also provided at www.cengage.com/finance/madura) allows students to play the role of managers or board members of a small MNC that they created and make decisions about that firm.

- *References.* References to related readings are provided for every chapter.

The variety of end-of-chapter and end-of-part exercises and cases offer many opportunities for students to engage in teamwork, decision making, and communication.

SUPPLEMENTAL RESOURCES

The text website at www.cengage.com/finance/madura provides additional instructor resources:

- *Instructor's Manual.* The Instructor's Manual contains the chapter theme, topics to stimulate class discussion, and answers to end-of-chapter Questions, Case Problems, Continuing Cases (Blades, Inc.), Small Business Dilemmas, Integrative Problems, and Supplemental Cases. The Instructor's Manual is available on the text website and also the Instructor's Resource CD (IRCD).

- *PowerPoint Presentation Slides.* Revised by Nivine Richie of the University of North Carolina (Wilmington) for this edition, the PowerPoint slides are intended to enhance lectures and provide a guide for student note-taking. Basic Lecture Slides are included on both the text website and IRCD, while supplemental Exhibit Slides can be downloaded from the text website.

- *Test Bank.* An expanded Test Bank contains a large set of questions in multiple choice or true/false format, including content questions as well as problems. The Test Bank is available on the text website and the IRCD.

- *ExamView™ Test Bank.* The ExamView computerized testing program contains all of the questions in the Test Bank. It is easy-to-use test creation software that is compatible with Microsoft® Windows. Instructors can add or edit questions, instructions, and answers and select questions by previewing them on the screen. Instructors can also create and administer quizzes online, whether over the Internet, a local area network (LAN), or a wide area network (WAN). ExamView™ is available on the IRCD only.

ACKNOWLEDGMENTS

Several people have contributed to this textbook. First, the motivation to write the textbook was primarily due to encouragement by Professors Robert L. Conn (Miami University of Ohio), E. Joe Nosari and William Schrode (Florida State University), Anthony E. Scaperlanda (Northern Illinois University), and Richard A. Zuber (University of North Carolina at Charlotte).

Many of the revisions and expanded sections contained in this edition are due to comments and suggestions from students who used previous editions. In addition, many professors reviewed various editions of the text and had a major influence on its content and organization. All are acknowledged in alphabetical order:

Raj Aggarwal, John Carroll University
Alan Alford, Northeastern University
H. David Arnold, Auburn University
Robert Aubey, University of Wisconsin
Bruce D. Bagamery, Central Washington University
James C. Baker, Kent State University
Gurudutt Baliga, University of Delaware
Laurence J. Belcher, Stetson University
Richard Benedetto, Merrimack College
Bharat B. Bhalla, Fairfield University
Rahul Bishnoi, Hofstra University
Rita Biswas, State University of New York–Albany
Steve Borde, University of Central Florida
Sarah Bryant, George Washington University
Francisco Carrada-Bravo, American Graduate School of International Management
Andreas C. Christofi, Azusa Pacific University
Ronnie Clayton, Jacksonville State University
Thomas S. Coe, Quinnipiac University
Alan Cook, Baylor University
W. P. Culbertson, Louisiana State University
Maria deBoyrie, New Mexico State University
Andrea L. DeMaskey, Villanova University
Mike Dosal, SunTrust Bank (Orlando)
Robert Driskill, Ohio State University
Anne M. Drougas, Dominican University

Milton Esbitt, Dominican University
Larry Fauver, University of Miami
Paul Fenton, Bishop's University
Robert G. Fletcher, California State University–Bakersfield
Stuart Fletcher, Appalachian State University
Jennifer Foo, Stetson University
Robert D. Foster, American Graduate School of International Management
Hung-Gay Fung, University of Baltimore
Juli-Ann E. Gasper, Texas A&M University
Farhad F. Ghannadian, Mercer University
Wafica Ghoul, Haigazian University
Joseph F. Greco, California State University–Fullerton
Deborah W. Gregory, Bentley College
Nicholas Gressis, Wright State University
Indra Guertler, Babson College
Ann M. Hackert, Idaho State University
John M. Harris, Jr., Clemson University
Andrea J. Heuson, University of Miami
Ghassem Homaifar, Middle Tennessee State University
James A. Howard, University of Maryland
Nathaniel Jackendoff, Temple University
Pankaj Jain, University of Memphis
Kurt R. Jesswein, Texas A&M International
Steve A. Johnson, University of Texas–El Paso
Manuel L. Jose, University of Akron

Dr. Joan C. Junkus, DePaul University
Rauv Kalra, Morehead State University
Ho-Sang Kang, University of Texas–Dallas
Frederick J. Kelly, Seton Hall University
Robert Kemp, University of Virginia
Coleman S. Kendall, University of Illinois–Chicago
Dara Khambata, American University
Doseong Kim, University of Akron
Elinda F. Kiss, University of Maryland
Thomas J. Kopp, Siena College
Suresh Krishman, Pennsylvania State University
Merouane Lakehal-Ayat, St. John Fisher College
Boyden E. Lee, New Mexico State University
Jeong W. Lee, University of North Dakota
Richard Lindgren, Graceland University
Charmen Loh, Rider University
Carl Luft, DePaul University
K. Christopher Ma, KCM Investment Co.
Davinder K. Malhotra, Philadelphia University
Richard D. Marcus, University of Wisconsin–Milwaukee
Anna D. Martin, Fairfield University
Leslie Mathis, University of Memphis
Ike Mathur, Southern Illinois University
Wendell McCulloch, Jr., California State University–Long Beach
Carl McGowan, University of Michigan–Flint
Fraser McHaffie, Marietta College
Stuart Michelson, Stetson University
Penelope E. Nall, Gardner-Webb University
Vivian Okere, Providence College
Edward Omberg, San Diego State University
Prasad Padmanabhan, San Diego State University
Ali M. Parhizgari, Florida International University
Anne Perry, American University
Rose M. Prasad, Central Michigan University
Larry Prather, East Tennessee State University
Abe Qastin, Lakeland College
Frances A. Quinn, Merrimack College

S. Ghon Rhee, University of Rhode Island
William J. Rieber, Butler University
Ashok Robin, Rochester Institute of Technology
Tom Rosengarth, Westminster College
Kevin Scanlon, Notre Dame University
Michael Scarlatos, CUNY–Brooklyn College
Jacobus T. Severiens, Kent State University
Vivek Sharma, The University of Michigan–Dearborn
Peter Sharp, California State University–Sacramento
Dilip K. Shome, Virginia Tech University
Joseph Singer, University of Missouri–Kansas City
Naim Sipra, University of Colorado–Denver
Jacky So, Southern Illinois University–Edwardsville
Luc Soenen, California Polytechnic State University–San Luis Obispo
Ahmad Sohrabian, California State Polytechnic University–Pomona
Caroline Spencer, Dowling College
Angelo Tarallo, Ramapo College
Amir Tavakkol, Kansas State University
Stephen G. Timme, Georgia State University
Eric Tsai, Temple University
C. Joe Ueng, University of St. Thomas
Mahmoud S. Wahab, University of Hartford
Ralph C. Walter III, Northeastern Illinois University
Elizabeth Webbink, Rutgers University
Ann Marie Whyte, University of Central Florida
Marilyn Wiley, Florida Atlantic University
Rohan Williamson, Georgetown University
Larry Wolken, Texas A&M University
Glenda Wong, De Paul University
Mike Yarmuth, Sullivan University
Yeomin Yoon, Seton Hall University
David Zalewski, Providence College
Emilio Zarruk, Florida Atlantic University
Stephen Zera, California State University–San Marcos

Beyond the suggestions provided by reviewers, this edition also benefited from the input of the many people I have met outside the United States who have been willing to share their views about international financial management. In addition, I thank my colleagues at Florida Atlantic University, including John Bernardin, Kim Gleason, Marek Marciniak, and Jurica Susnjara. I also thank Victor Kalafa (Cross Country Staffing), Thanh Ngo (University of Texas–Pan American), and Oliver Schnusenberg (University of North Florida), for their suggestions.

I acknowledge the help and support from the people at South-Western, including Mike Reynolds (Executive Editor), Nathan Anderson (Marketing Manager), Kendra Brown (Developmental Editor), Adele Scholtz (Senior Editorial Assistant), and Suellen Ruttkay (Marketing Coordinator). A special thanks is due to Scott Dillon (Content Project Manager) and Ann Whetstone (Copyeditor) for their efforts to ensure a quality final product.

Jeff Madura
Florida Atlantic University

About the Author

Jeff Madura is the SunTrust Bank Professor of Finance at Florida Atlantic University. He received his Ph.D. from Florida State University and has written several highly regarded textbooks, including *Financial Markets and Institutions*. His research on international finance has been published in numerous journals, including the *Journal of Financial and Quantitative Analysis; Journal of Money, Credit and Banking; Financial Management; Journal of Financial Research;* and *Financial Review*. He has received multiple awards for excellence in teaching and research and has served as a consultant for international banks, securities firms, and other multinational corporations. He has also served as director for the Southern Finance Association and Eastern Finance Association and as president of the Southern Finance Association.

PART 1

The International Financial Environment

Part 1 (Chapters 1 through 5) provides an overview of the multinational corporation (MNC) and the environment in which it operates. Chapter 1 explains the goals of the MNC, along with the motives and risks of international business. Chapter 2 describes the international flow of funds between countries. Chapter 3 describes the international financial markets and how these markets facilitate ongoing operations. Chapter 4 explains how exchange rates are determined, while Chapter 5 provides background on the currency futures and options markets. Managers of MNCs must understand the international environment described in these chapters in order to make proper decisions.

1

Multinational Financial Management: An Overview

Multinational corporations (MNCs) are defined as firms that engage in some form of international business. Their managers conduct international financial management, which involves international investing and financing decisions that are intended to maximize the value of the MNC. The goal of their managers is to maximize the value of the firm, which is similar to the goal of managers employed by domestic companies.

Initially, firms may merely attempt to export products to a particular country or import supplies from a foreign manufacturer. Over time, however, many of them recognize additional foreign opportunities and eventually establish subsidiaries in foreign countries. Dow Chemical, IBM, Nike, and many other firms have more than half of their assets in foreign countries. Some businesses, such as ExxonMobil, Fortune Brands, and Colgate-Palmolive, commonly generate more than half of their sales in foreign countries.

Even smaller U.S. firms commonly generate more than 20 percent of their sales in foreign markets, including Ferro (Ohio), and Medtronic (Minnesota). Seventy-five percent of U.S. firms that export have fewer than 100 employees.

International financial management is important even to companies that have no international business because these companies must recognize how their foreign competitors will be affected by movements in exchange rates, foreign interest rates, labor costs, and inflation. Such economic characteristics can affect the foreign competitors' costs of production and pricing policies.

This chapter provides background on the goals, motives, and valuation of an MNC.

MANAGING THE MNC

The commonly accepted goal of an MNC is to maximize shareholder wealth. Managers employed by the MNC are expected to make decisions that will maximize the stock price and therefore serve the shareholders. Some publicly traded MNCs based outside the United States may have additional goals, such as satisfying their respective governments, creditors, or employees. However, these MNCs now place more emphasis on satisfying shareholders so that they can more easily obtain funds from shareholders to support their operations. Even in developing countries such as Bulgaria and Vietnam that have only recently encouraged the development of business enterprise, managers of firms must serve shareholder interests so that they can obtain funds from them. If firms announced that they were going to issue stock so that they could use the proceeds to pay excessive salaries to managers or invest in unprofitable business projects, they would not attract demand for their stock. The focus in this text is on the U.S.-based MNC and its shareholders, but the concepts commonly apply to MNCs based in other countries.

The focus of this text is on MNCs whose parents wholly own any foreign subsidiaries, which means that the U.S. parent is the sole owner of the subsidiaries. This is the most common form of ownership of U.S.-based MNCs, and it enables financial managers throughout the MNC to have a single goal of maximizing the value of the entire MNC instead of maximizing the value of any particular foreign subsidiary.

Facing Agency Problems

Managers of an MNC may make decisions that conflict with the firm's goal to maximize shareholder wealth. For example, a decision to establish a subsidiary in one location versus another may be based on the location's appeal to a particular manager rather than on its potential benefits to shareholders. A decision to expand a subsidiary may be motivated by a manager's desire to receive more compensation rather than to enhance the value of the MNC. This conflict of goals between a firm's managers and shareholders is often referred to as the **agency problem.**

The costs of ensuring that managers maximize shareholder wealth (referred to as *agency costs*) are normally larger for MNCs than for purely domestic firms for several reasons. First, MNCs with subsidiaries scattered around the world may experience larger agency problems because monitoring managers of distant subsidiaries in foreign countries is more difficult. Second, foreign subsidiary managers raised in different cultures may not follow uniform goals. Third, the sheer size of the larger MNCs can also create large agency problems. Fourth, some non-U.S. managers tend to downplay the short-term effects of decisions, which may result in decisions for foreign subsidiaries of the U.S.-based MNCs that maximize subsidiary values or pursue other goals. This can be a challenge, especially in countries where some people may perceive that the first priority of corporations should be to serve their respective employees.

EXAMPLE   Two years ago, Seattle Co. (based in the United States) established a subsidiary in Singapore so that it could expand its business there. It hired a manager in Singapore to manage the subsidiary. During the last two years, the sales generated by the subsidiary have not grown. Yet, the manager of the subsidiary has hired several employees to do the work that he was assigned. The managers of the parent company in the United States have not closely monitored the subsidiary because they trusted the manager of the subsidiary and because the subsidiary is so far away. Now they realize that there is an agency problem. The subsidiary is experiencing losses every quarter, so they need to more closely monitor the management of the subsidiary. ●

Parent Control of Agency Problems. The parent corporation of an MNC may be able to prevent agency problems with proper governance. It should clearly communicate the goals for each subsidiary to ensure that all subsidiaries focus on maximizing the value of the MNC rather than their respective subsidiary values. The parent can oversee the subsidiary decisions to check whether the subsidiary managers are satisfying the MNC's goals. The parent can also implement compensation plans that reward the subsidiary managers who satisfy the MNC's goals. A common incentive is to provide managers with the MNC's stock (or options to buy the stock at a fixed price) as part of their compensation so that they benefit directly from a higher stock price when they make decisions that enhance the MNC's value.

When Seattle Co. (from the previous example) recognized the agency problems with its Singapore subsidiary, it created incentives for the manager of the subsidiary that were aligned with the parent's goal of maximizing shareholder wealth. Specifically, it set up a compensation system so that the annual bonus paid to the manager would be based on the level of earnings at the subsidiary. ●

Corporate Control of Agency Problems. In the example of Seattle Co., the agency problems occurred because the subsidiary's management goals were not focused on maximizing shareholder wealth. In some cases, agency problems can occur because the goals of the entire management of the MNC are not focused on maximizing shareholder wealth. Various forms of corporate control can also help prevent these agency problems and therefore ensure that managers make decisions to satisfy the MNC's shareholders. If the MNC's managers make poor decisions that reduce its value, another firm may be able to acquire the MNC at a low price and will probably remove the weak managers. In addition, institutional investors such as mutual funds or pension funds that have large holdings of an MNC's stock have some influence over management because they can complain to the board of directors if managers are making poor decisions. They may attempt to enact changes in a poorly performing MNC, such as the removal of high-level managers or even board members. The institutional investors may also work together when demanding changes in an MNC because an MNC would not want to lose all of its major shareholders.

How SOX Improved Corporate Governance of MNCs. One limitation of the corporate control process is that investors rely on the reporting by the firm's managers for information. If managers are serving themselves rather than the investors, they may exaggerate their performance. There are many well-known examples (such as Enron and WorldCom) in which large MNCs were able to alter their financial reporting so that investors would not be aware of their financial problems.

Enacted in 2002, the Sarbanes-Oxley Act (SOX) ensures a more transparent process for managers to report on the productivity and financial condition of their firm. It requires firms to implement an internal reporting process that can be easily monitored by executives and the board of directors. Some of the common methods used by MNCs to improve their internal control process are:

- Establishing a centralized database of information
- Ensuring that all data are reported consistently among subsidiaries
- Implementing a system that automatically checks data for unusual discrepancies relative to norms
- Speeding the process by which all departments and all subsidiaries have access to the data that they need
- Making executives more accountable for financial statements by personally verifying their accuracy

These systems made it easier for a firm's board members to monitor the financial reporting process. Therefore, SOX reduced the likelihood that managers of a firm can manipulate the reporting process and therefore improved the accuracy of financial information for existing and prospective investors.

Management Structure of an MNC

The magnitude of agency costs can vary with the management style of the MNC. A centralized management style, as illustrated in the top section of Exhibit 1.1, can reduce agency costs because it allows managers of the parent to control foreign subsidiaries and therefore reduces the power of subsidiary managers. However, the parent's managers may make poor decisions for the subsidiary if they are not as informed as subsidiary managers about the financial characteristics of the subsidiary.

Alternatively, an MNC can use a decentralized management style, as illustrated in the bottom section of Exhibit 1.1. This style is more likely to result in higher agency costs because subsidiary managers may make decisions that do not focus on maximizing the value of the entire MNC. Yet, this style gives more control to those managers who are closer to the subsidiary's operations and environment. To the extent that subsidiary managers recognize the goal of maximizing the value of the overall MNC and are compensated in accordance with that goal, the decentralized management style may be more effective.

Given the obvious tradeoff between centralized and decentralized management styles, some MNCs attempt to achieve the advantages of both styles. That is, they allow subsidiary managers to make the key decisions about their respective operations, but the parent's management monitors the decisions to ensure that they are in the best interests of the entire MNC.

How the Internet Facilitates Management Control. The Internet is making it easier for the parent to monitor the actions and performance of its foreign subsidiaries.

EXAMPLE

Recall the example of Seattle Co., which has a subsidiary in Singapore. The Internet allows the foreign subsidiary to e-mail updated information in a standardized format to avoid language problems and to send images of financial reports and product designs. The parent can easily track inventory, sales, expenses, and earnings of each subsidiary on a weekly or monthly basis. Thus, use of the Internet can reduce agency costs due to international business. ●

WHY FIRMS PURSUE INTERNATIONAL BUSINESS

The commonly held theories as to why firms become motivated to expand their business internationally are (1) the theory of comparative advantage, (2) the imperfect markets theory, and (3) the product cycle theory. The three theories overlap to a degree and can complement each other in developing a rationale for the evolution of international business.

Theory of Comparative Advantage

Multinational business has generally increased over time. Part of this growth is due to the heightened realization that specialization by countries can increase production efficiency. Some countries, such as Japan and the United States, have a technology advantage, while other countries, such as Jamaica, China, and Malaysia, have an advantage in the cost of basic labor. Since these advantages cannot be easily transported, countries tend to use their advantages to specialize in the production of goods that can be produced with relative efficiency. This explains why countries such as Japan and the United States are large producers of computer components, while countries such as Jamaica and Mexico are large producers of agricultural and handmade goods. MNCs such as Oracle, Intel, and IBM have grown substantially in foreign countries because of their technology advantage.

When a country specializes in some products, it may not produce other products, so trade between countries is essential. This is the argument made by the classical theory of **comparative advantage.** Comparative advantages allow firms to penetrate foreign markets. Many of the Virgin Islands, for example, specialize in tourism and rely completely on international trade for most products. Although these islands could produce some goods, it

Exhibit 1.1 Management Styles of MNCs

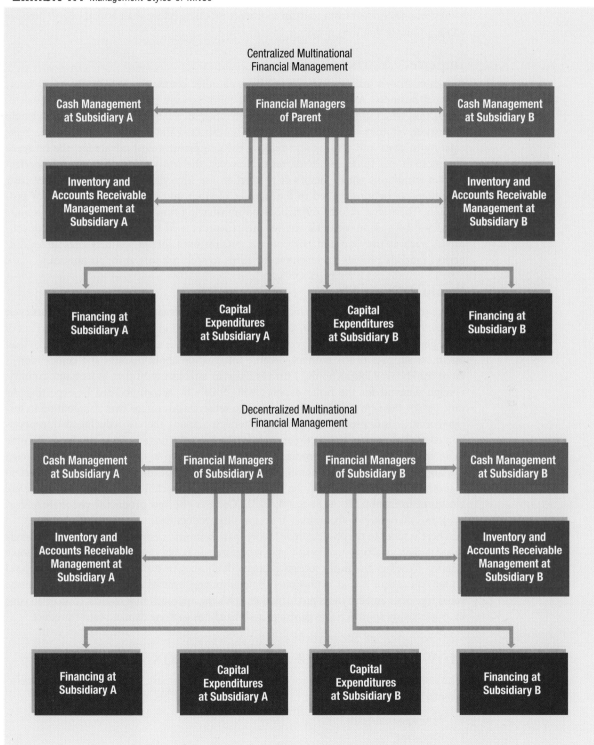

is more efficient for them to specialize in tourism. That is, the islands are better off using some revenues earned from tourism to import products rather than attempting to produce all the products that they need.

Imperfect Markets Theory

If each country's markets were closed from all other countries, there would be no international business. At the other extreme, if markets were perfect so that the factors of production (such as labor) were easily transferable, then labor and other resources would flow wherever they were in demand. The unrestricted mobility of factors would create equality in costs and returns and remove the comparative cost advantage, the rationale for international trade and investment. However, the real world suffers from **imperfect market** conditions where factors of production are somewhat immobile. There are costs and often restrictions related to the transfer of labor and other resources used for production. There may also be restrictions on transferring funds and other resources among countries. Because markets for the various resources used in production are "imperfect," MNCs such as the Gap and Nike often capitalize on a foreign country's resources. Imperfect markets provide an incentive for firms to seek out foreign opportunities.

Product Cycle Theory

One of the more popular explanations as to why firms evolve into MNCs is the **product cycle theory.** According to this theory, firms become established in the home market as a result of some perceived advantage over existing competitors, such as a need by the market for at least one more supplier of the product. Because information about markets and competition is more readily available at home, a firm is likely to establish itself first in its home country. Foreign demand for the firm's product will initially be accommodated by exporting. As time passes, the firm may feel the only way to retain its advantage over competition in foreign countries is to produce the product in foreign markets, thereby reducing its transportation costs. The competition in the foreign markets may increase as other producers become more familiar with the firm's product. The firm may develop strategies to prolong the foreign demand for its product. A common approach is to attempt to differentiate the product so that other competitors cannot offer exactly the same product. These phases of the cycle are illustrated in Exhibit 1.2. As an example, 3M Co. uses one new product to penetrate foreign markets. After entering the market, it expands its product line.

There is more to the product cycle theory than is summarized here. This discussion merely suggests that, as a firm matures, it may recognize additional opportunities outside its home country. Whether the firm's foreign business diminishes or expands over time will depend on how successful it is at maintaining some advantage over its competition. The advantage could represent an edge in its production or financing approach that reduces costs or an edge in its marketing approach that generates and maintains a strong demand for its product.

How Firms Engage in International Business

Firms use several methods to conduct international business. The most common methods are these:

- International trade
- Licensing
- Franchising
- Joint ventures
- Acquisitions of existing operations
- Establishing new foreign subsidiaries

Exhibit 1.2 International Product Life Cycle

Each method is discussed in turn, with some emphasis on its risk and return characteristics.

WEB

www.ita.doc.gov/td/
industry/otea
Outlook of international
trade conditions for
each of several
industries.

International Trade

International trade is a relatively conservative approach that can be used by firms to penetrate markets (by exporting) or to obtain supplies at a low cost (by importing). This approach entails minimal risk because the firm does not place any of its capital at risk. If the firm experiences a decline in its exporting or importing, it can normally reduce or discontinue this part of its business at a low cost.

Many large U.S.-based MNCs, including Boeing, DuPont, General Electric, and IBM, generate more than $4 billion in annual sales from exporting. Nonetheless, small businesses account for more than 20 percent of the value of all U.S. exports.

How the Internet Facilitates International Trade. Many firms use their websites to list the products that they sell, along with the price for each product. This allows them to easily advertise their products to potential importers anywhere in the world without mailing brochures to various countries. In addition, a firm can add to its product line or change prices by simply revising its website. Thus, importers need only monitor an exporter's website periodically to keep abreast of its product information.

Firms can also use their websites to accept orders online. Some products such as software can be delivered directly to the importer over the Internet in the form of a file that lands in the importer's computer. Other products must be shipped, but the Internet makes it easier to track the shipping process. An importer can transmit its order for products via e-mail to the exporter. The exporter's warehouse fills orders. When the warehouse ships the products, it can send an e-mail message to the importer and to the exporter's headquarters. The warehouse may even use technology to monitor its inventory of products so that suppliers are automatically notified to send more supplies once the inventory is reduced to a specific level. If the exporter uses multiple warehouses, the Internet allows them to work as a network so that if one warehouse cannot fill an order, another warehouse will.

Licensing

Licensing obligates a firm to provide its technology (copyrights, patents, trademarks, or trade names) in exchange for fees or some other specified benefits. Starbucks has licensing agreements with SSP (an operator of food and beverages in Europe) to sell Starbucks products in train stations and airports throughout Europe. Sprint Nextel Corp. has a licensing agreement to develop telecommunications services in the United Kingdom. Eli Lilly & Co. has a licensing agreement to produce drugs for foreign countries. IGA, Inc., which operates more than 3,000 supermarkets in the United States, has a licensing agreement to operate supermarkets in China and Singapore. Licensing allows firms to use their technology in foreign markets without a major investment in foreign countries and without the transportation costs that result from exporting. A major disadvantage of licensing is that it is difficult for the firm providing the technology to ensure quality control in the foreign production process.

Franchising

Franchising obligates a firm to provide a specialized sales or service strategy, support assistance, and possibly an initial investment in the franchise in exchange for periodic fees. For example, McDonald's, Pizza Hut, Subway Sandwiches, Blockbuster Video, and Dairy Queen have franchises that are owned and managed by local residents in many foreign countries. Like licensing, franchising allows firms to penetrate foreign markets without a major investment in foreign countries. The recent relaxation of barriers in countries throughout Eastern Europe and South America has resulted in numerous franchising arrangements.

Joint Ventures

A **joint venture** is a venture that is jointly owned and operated by two or more firms. Many firms penetrate foreign markets by engaging in a joint venture with firms that reside in those markets. Most joint ventures allow two firms to apply their respective comparative advantages in a given project. For example, General Mills, Inc., joined in a venture with Nestlé SA so that the cereals produced by General Mills could be sold through the overseas sales distribution network established by Nestlé.

Xerox Corp. and Fuji Co. (of Japan) engaged in a joint venture that allowed Xerox Corp. to penetrate the Japanese market and allowed Fuji to enter the photocopying business. Sara Lee Corp. and AT&T have engaged in joint ventures with Mexican firms to gain entry to Mexico's markets. Joint ventures between automobile manufacturers are numerous, as each manufacturer can offer its technological advantages. General Motors has ongoing joint ventures with automobile manufacturers in several different countries, including the former Soviet states.

Acquisitions of Existing Operations

Firms frequently acquire other firms in foreign countries as a means of penetrating foreign markets. Acquisitions allow firms to have full control over their foreign businesses and to quickly obtain a large portion of foreign market share.

Google, Inc., has made major international acquisitions to expand its business and to improve its technology. It has acquired businesses in Australia (search engines), Brazil (search engines), Canada (mobile browser), China (search engines), Finland (micro-blogging), Germany (mobile software), Russia (online advertising), South Korea (weblog software), Spain (photo sharing), and Sweden (videoconferencing). ●

An acquisition of an existing corporation is subject to the risk of large losses, however, because of the large investment required. In addition, if the foreign operations perform poorly, it may be difficult to sell the operations at a reasonable price.

Some firms engage in partial international acquisitions in order to obtain a stake in foreign operations. This requires a smaller investment than full international acquisitions and therefore exposes the firm to less risk. On the other hand, the firm will not have complete control over foreign operations that are only partially acquired.

Establishing New Foreign Subsidiaries

Firms can also penetrate foreign markets by establishing new operations in foreign countries to produce and sell their products. Like a foreign acquisition, this method requires a large investment. Establishing new subsidiaries may be preferred to foreign acquisitions because the operations can be tailored exactly to the firm's needs. In addition, a smaller investment may be required than would be needed to purchase existing operations. However, the firm will not reap any rewards from the investment until the subsidiary is built and a customer base established

Summary of Methods

The methods of increasing international business extend from the relatively simple approach of international trade to the more complex approach of acquiring foreign firms or establishing new subsidiaries. Any method of increasing international business that requires a direct investment in foreign operations normally is referred to as a **direct foreign investment (DFI).** International trade and licensing usually are not considered to be DFI because they do not involve direct investment in foreign operations. Franchising and joint ventures tend to require some investment in foreign operations, but to a limited degree. Foreign acquisitions and the establishment of new foreign subsidiaries require substantial investment in foreign operations and represent the largest portion of DFI.

Many MNCs use a combination of methods to increase international business. Motorola and IBM, for example, have substantial direct foreign investment but also derive some of their foreign revenue from various licensing agreements, which require less DFI to generate revenue.

The evolution of Nike began in 1962 when Phil Knight, a business student at Stanford's business school, wrote a paper on how a U.S. firm could use Japanese technology to break the German dominance of the athletic shoe industry in the United States. After graduation, Knight visited the Unitsuka Tiger shoe company in Japan. He made a licensing agreement with that company to produce a shoe that he sold in the United States under the name Blue Ribbon Sports (BRS). In 1972, Knight exported his shoes to Canada. In 1974, he expanded his operations into Australia. In 1977, the firm licensed factories in Taiwan and Korea to produce athletic shoes and then sold the shoes in Asian countries. In 1978, BRS became Nike, Inc., and began to export shoes to Europe and South America. As a result of its exporting and its direct foreign investment, Nike's international sales reached $1 billion by 1992 and now exceed $8 billion per year. ●

The manner by which an MNC's international business affects its cash flows is illustrated in Exhibit 1.3. In general, the cash outflows associated with international business by the U.S. parent are to pay for imports, to comply with its international arrangements,

Exhibit 1.3 Cash Flow Diagrams for MNCs

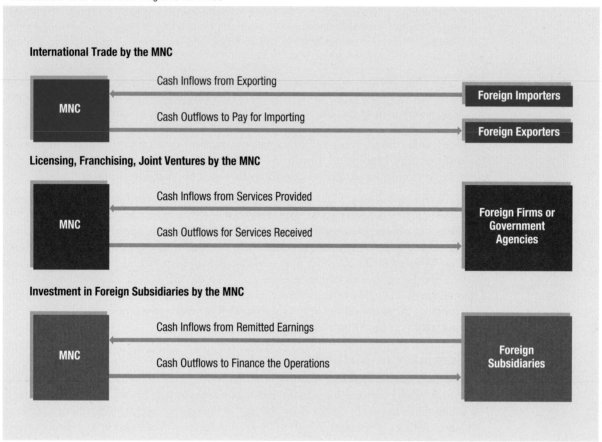

or to support the creation or expansion of foreign subsidiaries. Conversely, an MNC receives cash flows in the form of payment for its exports, fees for the services it provides within international arrangements, and remitted funds from the foreign subsidiaries. The first diagram in this exhibit reflects an MNC that engages in international trade. Thus, its international cash flows result from either paying for imported supplies or receiving payment in exchange for products that it exports.

The second diagram reflects an MNC that engages in some international arrangements (which can include international licensing, franchising, or joint ventures). Any of these international arrangements can require cash outflows by the MNC in foreign countries to comply with the arrangement, such as the expenses incurred from transferring technology or funding partial investment in a franchise or joint venture. These arrangements generate cash flows to the MNC in the form of fees for services (such as technology or support assistance) it provides.

The third diagram reflects an MNC that engages in direct foreign investment. This type of MNC has one or more foreign subsidiaries. There can be cash outflows from the U.S. parent to its foreign subsidiaries in the form of invested funds to help finance the operations of the foreign subsidiaries. There are also cash flows from the foreign subsidiaries to the U.S. parent in the form of remitted earnings and fees for services provided by the parent, which can all be classified as remitted funds from the foreign subsidiaries.

Valuation Model for an MNC

The value of an MNC is relevant to its shareholders and its debtholders. When managers make decisions that maximize the value of the firm, they maximize shareholder wealth (assuming that the decisions are not intended to maximize the wealth of debtholders at the expense of shareholders). Since international financial management should be conducted with the goal of increasing the value of the MNC, it is useful to review some basics of valuation. There are numerous methods of valuing an MNC, and some methods will lead to the same valuation. The valuation method described in this section can be used to understand the key factors that affect an MNC's value in a general sense.

Domestic Model

Before modeling an MNC's value, consider the valuation of a purely domestic firm that does not engage in any foreign transactions. The value (V) of a purely domestic firm in the United States is commonly specified as the present value of its expected cash flows,

$$V = \sum_{t=1}^{n} \left\{ \frac{[E(CF_{\$,t})]}{(1+k)^t} \right\}$$

where $E(CF_{\$,t})$ represents expected cash flows to be received at the end of period t, n represents the number of periods into the future in which cash flows are received, and k represents the weighted average cost of capital, and also the required rate of return by investors and creditors who provide funds to the MNC.

Dollar Cash Flows. The dollar cash flows in period t represent funds received by the firm minus funds needed to pay expenses or taxes, or to reinvest in the firm (such as an investment to replace old computers or machinery). The expected cash flows are estimated from knowledge about various existing projects as well as other projects that will be implemented in the future. A firm's decisions about how it should invest funds to expand its business can affect its expected future cash flows and therefore can affect the firm's value. Holding other factors constant, an increase in expected cash flows over time should increase the value of the firm.

Cost of Capital. The required rate of return (k) in the denominator of the valuation equation represents the cost of capital (including both the cost of debt and the cost of equity) to the firm and is essentially a weighted average of the cost of capital based on all of the firm's projects. As the firm makes decisions that affect its cost of debt or its cost of equity for one or more projects, it affects the weighted average of its cost of capital and therefore affects the required rate of return. For example, if the firm's credit rating is suddenly lowered, its cost of capital will probably increase and so will its required rate of return. Holding other factors constant, an increase in the firm's required rate of return will reduce the value of the firm because expected cash flows must be discounted at a higher interest rate. Conversely, a decrease in the firm's required rate of return will increase the value of the firm because expected cash flows are discounted at a lower required rate of return.

Valuing International Cash Flows

An MNC's value can be specified in the same manner as a purely domestic firm's. However, consider that the expected cash flows generated by a U.S.-based MNC's parent in period t may be coming from various countries and may therefore be denominated in different foreign currencies. The cash flows to the MNC parent occur as a result of the different types of international business described earlier. The MNC's parent may receive foreign currency cash flows due to exporting or to licensing agreements. In addition, it may receive remitted earnings from its foreign subsidiaries.

The foreign currency cash flows will be converted into dollars. Thus, the expected dollar cash flows to be received at the end of period t are equal to the sum of the products of cash flows denominated in each currency j times the expected exchange rate at which currency j could be converted into dollars by the MNC at the end of period t.

$$E(CF_{\$,t}) = \sum_{j=1}^{m}[E(CF_{j,t}) \times E(S_{j,t})]$$

where $CF_{j,t}$ represents the amount of cash flow denominated in a particular foreign currency j at the end of period t, and $S_{j,t}$ represents the exchange rate at which the foreign currency (measured in dollars per unit of the foreign currency) can be converted to dollars at the end of period t.

Valuation of an MNC That Uses Two Currencies.

An MNC that does business in two currencies could measure its expected dollar cash flows in any period by multiplying the expected cash flow in each currency times the expected exchange rate at which that currency could be converted to dollars and then summing those two products.

It may help to think of an MNC as a portfolio of currency cash flows, one for each currency in which it conducts business. The expected dollar cash flows derived from each of those currencies can be combined to determine the total expected dollar cash flows in the given period. It is easier to derive an expected dollar cash flow value for each currency before combining the cash flows among currencies within a given period, because each currency's cash flow amount must be converted to a common unit (the dollar) before combining the amounts.

EXAMPLE Carolina Co. has expected cash flows of $100,000 from local business and 1 million Mexican pesos from business in Mexico at the end of period t. Assuming that the peso's value is expected to be $.09 when converted into dollars, the expected dollar cash flows are:

$$
\begin{aligned}
E(CF_{\$,t}) &= \sum_{j=1}^{m}[E(CF_{j,t}) \times E(S_{j,t})] \\
&= (\$100,000) + [1,000,000 \text{ pesos} \times (\$.09)] \\
&= (\$100,000) + (\$90,000) \\
&= \$190,000.
\end{aligned}
$$

The cash flows of $100,000 from U.S. business were already denominated in U.S. dollars and therefore did not have to be converted. ●

Valuation of an MNC That Uses Multiple Currencies.

The same process described above can be used to value an MNC that uses many foreign currencies. The general formula for estimating the dollar cash flows to be received by an MNC from multiple currencies in one period can be written as:

$$E(CF_{\$,t}) = \sum_{j=1}^{m}[E(CF_{j,t}) \times E(S_{j,t})]$$

EXAMPLE Assume that Yale Co. will receive cash in 15 different countries at the end of the next period. To estimate the value of Yale Co., the first step is to estimate the amount of cash flows that Yale will receive at the end of the period in each currency (such as 2 million euros, 8 million Mexican pesos, etc.). Second, obtain a forecast of the currency's exchange rate for cash flows that will arrive at the end of the period for each of the 15 currencies (such as euro forecast = $1.40, peso forecast = $.12, etc.). The existing exchange rate might be used as a forecast for the exchange rate in the future, but there are many alternative methods (as explained in Chapter 9). Third, multiply the amount of each foreign currency to be received by the forecasted exchange rate of that currency in order to estimate the dollar cash flows to be received due to each currency. Fourth, add the estimated dollar cash flows for all 15 currencies in order to determine the total expected dollar cash flows in the period. The equation above represents the four steps described here. When applying that equation to this example, $m = 15$ because there are 15 different currencies. ●

Valuation of an MNC's Cash Flows over Multiple Periods. The entire process described in the example for a single period is not adequate for valuation because most MNCs have cash flows beyond that period. However, the process can be easily adapted in order to estimate the total dollar cash flows for all future periods. First, the same process that was described for a single period needs to be applied to all future periods in which the MNC will receive cash flows. This will generate an estimate of total dollar cash flows to be received in every period in the future. Second, discount the estimated total dollar cash flow for each period at the weighted cost of capital (k), and sum these discounted cash flows to estimate the value of this MNC.

The process for valuing an MNC receiving multiple currencies over multiple periods can be written in equation form as follows:

$$V = \sum_{t=1}^{n} \left\{ \frac{\sum_{j=1}^{m} [E(CF_{j,t}) \times E(S_{j,t})]}{(1 + k)^t} \right\}$$

where $CF_{j,t}$ represents the cash flow denominated in a particular currency (including dollars), and $S_{j,t}$ represents the exchange rate at which the MNC can convert the foreign currency at the end of period t.

Since the management of an MNC should be focused on maximizing its value, the equation for valuing an MNC is very important. Notice from this valuation equation that the value (V) will increase in response to managerial decisions that increase the amount of its cash flows in a particular currency (CF_j), or to conditions that increase the exchange rate at which that currency is converted into dollars (S_j).

To avoid double-counting, cash flows of the MNC's subsidiaries are considered in the valuation model only when they reflect transactions with the U.S. parent. Thus, any expected cash flows received by foreign subsidiaries should not be counted in the valuation equation until they are expected to be remitted to the parent.

The denominator of the valuation model for the MNC remains unchanged from the original valuation model for the purely domestic firm. However, recognize that the weighted average cost of capital for the MNC is based on funding some projects that reflect business in different countries. Thus, any decision by the MNC's parent that affects the cost of its capital supporting projects in a specific country can affect its weighted average cost of capital (and its required rate of return) and therefore can affect its value.

Uncertainty Surrounding an MNC's Cash Flows

The MNC's future cash flows (and therefore its valuation) are subject to uncertainty because of its exposure to international economic conditions, political conditions, and exchange rate risk, as explained next. Exhibit 1.4 complements the discussion.

Exposure to International Economic Conditions. The amount of consumption in any country is influenced by the income earned by consumers in that country. If economic conditions weaken, the income of consumers becomes relatively low, consumer purchases of products decline, and an MNC's sales in that country may be lower than expected. This results in a reduction in the MNC's cash flows, and therefore in its value.

Exhibit 1.4 How an MNC's Valuation Is Exposed to Uncertainty (Risk)

Uncertain foreign currency cash flows
due to uncertain foreign economic
and political conditions

Uncertainty surrounding
future exchange rates

$$V = \sum_{t=1}^{n} \left\{ \frac{\sum_{j=1}^{m} [E(CF_{j,t}) \times E(S_{j,t})]}{(1 + k)^t} \right\}$$

Uncertainty Surrounding an MNC's Valuation:

Exposure to Foreign Economies: If $[CF_{j,t} < E(CF_{j,t})] \rightarrow V\downarrow$

Exposure to Political Risk: If $[CF_{j,t} < E(CF_{j,t})] \rightarrow V\downarrow$

Exposure to Exchange Rate Risk: If $[S_{j,t} < E(S_{j,t})] \rightarrow V\downarrow$

EXAMPLE

In October 2008, the credit crisis intensified. Investors were concerned that the economic conditions in the United States and in many other countries would deteriorate. This resulted in expectations of a reduced demand for exports produced by U.S. firms. In addition, it resulted in expectations of reduced earnings of foreign subsidiaries (because of a reduced local demand for the subsidiary's products), and therefore a reduction in remitted earnings to the MNC's parent. These revised expectations reflected a reduction in cash flows to be received by the parent, and therefore caused reduced valuations of MNCs. Stock prices of many U.S.-based MNCs declined by more than 20 percent during the October 6–10 period in 2008. ●

Exposure to International Political Risk.
Political risk in any country can affect the level of an MNC's sales. A foreign government may increase taxes or impose barriers on the MNC's subsidiary. Alternatively, consumers in a foreign country may boycott the MNC if there is friction between the government of their country and the MNC's home country. Political actions like these can reduce the cash flows of the MNC.

Exposure to Exchange Rate Risk.
If the foreign currencies to be received by a U.S.-based MNC suddenly weaken against the dollar, the MNC will receive a lower amount of dollar cash flows than was expected. This may reduce the cash flows of the MNC.

EXAMPLE

Missouri Co. has a foreign subsidiary in Canada that generates earnings (in Canadian dollars) each year. Before the subsidiary remits earnings to the parent, it converts Canadian dollars to U.S. dollars. The managers of Missouri expect that because of a recent government policy in Canada, the Canadian dollar will weaken substantially against the U.S. dollar over time. Consequently, the expected U.S. dollar cash flows to be received by the parent are reduced, so the valuation of Missouri Co. is reduced. ●

Many MNCs have cash outflows in one or more foreign currencies because they import supplies or materials from companies in other countries. When an MNC has future cash outflows in foreign currencies, it is exposed to exchange rate movements, but in the opposite direction. If these foreign currencies strengthen, the MNC will need a larger amount of dollars to obtain the foreign currencies that it needs to make its payments. This reduces the MNC's dollar cash flows (on a net basis) overall, and therefore reduces its value.

Uncertainty of an MNC's Cost of Capital

An MNC's cost of capital is influenced by the return required by its investors. If there is suddenly more uncertainty surrounding its future cash flows, investors may only be willing to invest in the MNC if they can expect to receive a higher rate of return. Consequently, the higher level of uncertainty increases the return on investment required by investors (which reflects an increase in the MNC's cost of obtaining capital), and the MNC's valuation decreases.

EXAMPLE

Reconsider the example in which the expected cash flows of U.S.-based MNCs were reduced during October 6–10, 2008, due to the credit crisis. The crisis also increased the uncertainty surrounding the future cash flows, meaning that that there was greater downside risk (that the cash flows could be much worse than expected). MNCs experienced a higher cost of capital, and therefore a higher required rate of return. Consequently, expected cash flows were discounted at a higher rate, which reduced the valuation of the MNCs. This offers an additional explanation for the large stock price decline of U.S.-based MNCs during this period. ●

ORGANIZATION OF THE TEXT

The organization of the chapters in this text is shown in Exhibit 1.5. Chapters 2 through 8 discuss international markets and conditions from a macroeconomic perspective, focusing on external forces that can affect the value of an MNC. Though financial managers may

Exhibit 1.5 Organization of Chapters

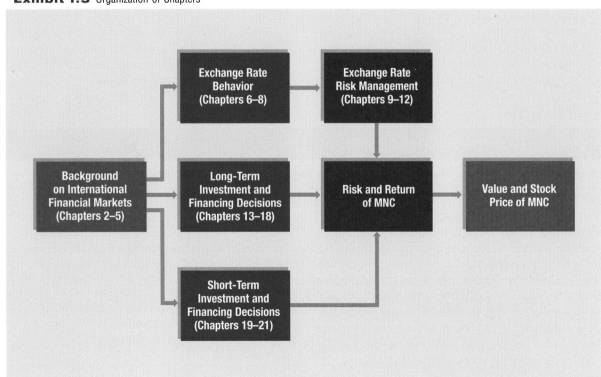

not have control over these forces, they do have some control over their degree of exposure to these forces. These macroeconomic chapters provide the background necessary to make financial decisions.

Chapters 9 through 21 take a microeconomic perspective and focus on how the financial management of an MNC can affect its value. Financial decisions by MNCs are commonly classified as either investing decisions or financing decisions. In general, investing decisions by an MNC tend to affect the numerator of the valuation model because such decisions affect expected cash flows. In addition, if investing decisions by the MNC's parent alter the firm's weighted average cost of capital, they may also affect the denominator of the valuation model. Long-term financing decisions by an MNC's parent tend to affect the denominator of the valuation model because they affect the MNC's cost of capital.

SUMMARY

- The main goal of an MNC is to maximize shareholder wealth. When managers are tempted to serve their own interests instead of those of shareholders, an agency problem exists.
- International business is justified by three key theories. The theory of comparative advantage suggests that each country should use its comparative advantage to specialize in its production and rely on other countries to meet other needs. The imperfect markets theory suggests that because of imperfect markets, factors of production are immobile, which encourages countries to specialize based on the resources they have. The product cycle theory suggests that after firms are established in their home countries, they commonly expand their product specialization in foreign countries.

- The most common methods by which firms conduct international business are international trade, licensing, franchising, joint ventures, acquisitions of foreign firms, and formation of foreign subsidiaries. Methods such as licensing and franchising involve little capital investment but distribute some of the profits to other parties. The acquisition of foreign firms and formation of foreign subsidiaries require substantial capital investments but offer the potential for large returns.
- The valuation model of an MNC shows that the MNC valuation is favorably affected when its foreign cash inflows increase, the currencies denominating those cash inflows increase, or the MNC's required rate of return decreases.

POINT COUNTER-POINT

Should an MNC Reduce Its Ethical Standards to Compete Internationally?

Point Yes. When a U.S.-based MNC competes in some countries, it may encounter some business norms there that are not allowed in the United States. For example, when competing for a government contract, firms might provide payoffs to the government officials who will make the decision. Yet, in the United States, a firm will sometimes take a client on an expensive golf outing or provide skybox tickets to events. This is no different than a payoff. If the payoffs are bigger in some foreign countries, the MNC can compete only by matching the payoffs provided by its competitors.

Counter-Point No. A U.S.-based MNC should maintain a standard code of ethics that applies to any country, even if it is at a disadvantage in a foreign country that allows activities that might be viewed as unethical. In this way, the MNC establishes more credibility worldwide.

Who Is Correct? Use the Internet to learn more about this issue. Which argument do you support? Offer your own opinion on this issue.

SELF-TEST

Answers are provided in Appendix A at the back of the text.

1. What are typical reasons why MNCs expand internationally?

2. Explain why unfavorable economic or political conditions affect the MNC's cash flows, required rate of return, and valuation.

3. Identify the more obvious risks faced by MNCs that expand internationally.

QUESTIONS AND APPLICATIONS

1. Agency Problems of MNCs.

a. Explain the agency problem of MNCs.

b. Why might agency costs be larger for an MNC than for a purely domestic firm?

2. Comparative Advantage.

a. Explain how the theory of comparative advantage relates to the need for international business.

b. Explain how the product cycle theory relates to the growth of an MNC.

3. Imperfect Markets.

a. Explain how the existence of imperfect markets has led to the establishment of subsidiaries in foreign markets.

b. If perfect markets existed, would wages, prices, and interest rates among countries be more similar or less similar than under conditions of imperfect markets? Why?

4. International Opportunities.

a. Do you think the acquisition of a foreign firm or licensing will result in greater growth for an MNC? Which alternative is likely to have more risk?

b. Describe a scenario in which the size of a corporation is not affected by access to international opportunities.

c. Explain why MNCs such as Coca-Cola and PepsiCo, Inc., still have numerous opportunities for international expansion.

5. International Opportunities Due to the Internet.

a. What factors cause some firms to become more internationalized than others?

b. Offer your opinion on why the Internet may result in more international business.

6. Impact of Exchange Rate Movements. Plak Co. of Chicago has several European subsidiaries that remit earnings to it each year. Explain how appreciation of the euro (the currency used in many European countries) would affect Plak's valuation.

7. Benefits and Risks of International Business. As an overall review of this chapter, identify possible reasons for growth in international business. Then, list the various disadvantages that may discourage international business.

8. Valuation of an MNC. Hudson Co., a U.S. firm, has a subsidiary in Mexico, where political risk has recently increased. Hudson's best guess of its future peso cash flows to be received has not changed. However, its valuation has declined as a result of the increase in political risk. Explain.

9. Centralization and Agency Costs. Would the agency problem be more pronounced for Berkely Corp., which has its parent company make most major decisions for its foreign subsidiaries, or Oakland Corp., which uses a decentralized approach?

10. Global Competition. Explain why more standardized product specifications across countries can increase global competition.

11. Exposure to Exchange Rates. McCanna Corp., a U.S. firm, has a French subsidiary that produces wine and exports to various European countries. All of the countries where it sells its wine use the euro as their currency, which is the same currency used in France. Is McCanna Corp. exposed to exchange rate risk?

12. Macro versus Micro Topics. Review the Table of Contents and indicate whether each of the chapters from Chapter 2 through Chapter 21 has a macro or micro perspective.

13. **Methods Used to Conduct International Business.** Duve, Inc., desires to penetrate a foreign market with either a licensing agreement with a foreign firm or by acquiring a foreign firm. Explain the differences in potential risk and return between a licensing agreement with a foreign firm and the acquisition of a foreign firm.

14. **International Business Methods.** Snyder Golf Co., a U.S. firm that sells high-quality golf clubs in the United States, wants to expand internationally by selling the same golf clubs in Brazil.

a. Describe the tradeoffs that are involved for each method (such as exporting, direct foreign investment, etc.) that Snyder could use to achieve its goal.

b. Which method would you recommend for this firm? Justify your recommendation.

15. **Impact of Political Risk.** Explain why political risk may discourage international business.

16. **Impact of September 11.** Following the terrorist attack on the United States, the valuations of many MNCs declined by more than 10 percent. Explain why the expected cash flows of MNCs were reduced, even if they were not directly hit by the terrorist attacks.

Advanced Questions

17. **International Joint Venture.** Anheuser-Busch, the producer of Budweiser and other beers, expanded into Japan by engaging in a joint venture with Kirin Brewery, the largest brewery in Japan. The joint venture enabled Anheuser-Busch to have its beer distributed through Kirin's distribution channels in Japan. In addition, it could utilize Kirin's facilities to produce beer that would be sold locally. In return, Anheuser-Busch provided information about the American beer market to Kirin.

a. Explain how the joint venture enabled Anheuser-Busch to achieve its objective of maximizing shareholder wealth.

b. Explain how the joint venture limited the risk of the international business.

c. Many international joint ventures are intended to circumvent barriers that normally prevent foreign competition. What barrier in Japan did Anheuser-Busch circumvent as a result of the joint venture? What barrier in the United States did Kirin circumvent as a result of the joint venture?

d. Explain how Anheuser-Busch could have lost some of its market share in countries outside Japan as a result of this particular joint venture.

18. **Impact of Eastern European Growth.** The managers of Loyola Corp. recently had a meeting to discuss new opportunities in Europe as a result of the recent integration among Eastern European countries. They decided not to penetrate new markets because of their present focus on expanding market share in the United States. Loyola's financial managers have developed forecasts for earnings based on the 12 percent market share (defined here as its percentage of total European sales) that Loyola currently has in Eastern Europe. Is 12 percent an appropriate estimate for next year's Eastern European market share? If not, does it likely overestimate or underestimate the actual Eastern European market share next year?

19. **Valuation of an MNC.** Birm Co., based in Alabama, is considering several international opportunities in Europe that could affect the value of its firm. The valuation of its firm is dependent on four factors: (1) expected cash flows in dollars, (2) expected cash flows in euros that are ultimately converted into dollars, (3) the rate at which it can convert euros to dollars, and (4) Birm's weighted average cost of capital. For each opportunity, identify the factors that would be affected.

a. Birm plans a licensing deal in which it will sell technology to a firm in Germany for $3 million; the payment is invoiced in dollars, and this project has the same risk level as its existing businesses.

b. Birm plans to acquire a large firm in Portugal that is riskier than its existing businesses.

c. Birm plans to discontinue its relationship with a U.S. supplier so that it can import a small amount of supplies (denominated in euros) at a lower cost from a Belgian supplier.

d. Birm plans to export a small amount of materials to Ireland that are denominated in euros.

20. **Assessing Motives for International Business.** Fort Worth, Inc., specializes in manufacturing some basic parts for sports utility vehicles (SUVs) that are produced and sold in the United States. Its main advantage in the United States is that its production is efficient and less costly than that of some other unionized manufacturers. It has a substantial market share in the United States. Its manufacturing process is labor intensive. It pays relatively low wages compared to U.S. competitors, but has guaranteed the local workers that their job positions will not be eliminated for the next 30 years. It hired a consultant to determine whether it should set up a subsidiary in Mexico, where the parts would be produced. The consultant suggested

that Fort Worth should expand for the following reasons. Offer your opinion on whether the consultant's reasons are logical.

a. Theory of Competitive Advantage: There are not many SUVs sold in Mexico, so Fort Worth, Inc., would not have to face much competition there.

b. Imperfect Markets Theory: Fort Worth cannot easily transfer workers to Mexico, but it can establish a subsidiary there in order to penetrate a new market.

c. Product Cycle Theory: Fort Worth has been successful in the United States. It has limited growth opportunities because it already controls much of the U.S. market for the parts it produces. Thus, the natural next step is to conduct the same business in a foreign country.

d. Exchange Rate Risk: The exchange rate of the peso has weakened recently, so this would allow Fort Worth to build a plant at a very low cost (by exchanging dollars for the cheap pesos to build the plant).

e. Political Risk: The political conditions in Mexico have stabilized in the last few months, so Fort Worth should attempt to penetrate the Mexican market now.

21. Valuation of Wal-Mart's International Business. In addition to all of its stores in the United States, Wal-Mart has 13 stores in Argentina, 302 stores in Brazil, 289 stores in Canada, 73 stores in China, 889 stores in Mexico, and 335 stores in the United Kingdom. Overall, it has 2,750 stores in foreign countries. Consider the value of Wal-Mart as being composed of two parts, a U.S. part (due to business in the United States) and a non-U.S. part (due to business in other countries). Explain how to determine the present value (in dollars) of the non-U.S. part assuming that you had access to all the details of Wal-Mart businesses outside the United States.

22. Impact of International Business on Cash Flows and Risk. Nantucket Travel Agency specializes in tours for American tourists. Until recently, all of its business was in the United States. It just established a subsidiary in Athens, Greece, which provides tour services in the Greek islands for American tourists. It rented a shop near the port of Athens. It also hired residents of Athens who could speak English and provide tours of the Greek islands. The subsidiary's main costs are rent and salaries for its employees and the lease of a few large boats in Athens that it uses for tours. American tourists pay for the entire tour in dollars at Nantucket's main U.S. office before they depart for Greece.

a. Explain why Nantucket may be able to effectively capitalize on international opportunities such as the Greek island tours.

b. Nantucket is privately owned by owners who reside in the United States and work in the main office. Explain possible agency problems associated with the creation of a subsidiary in Athens, Greece. How can Nantucket attempt to reduce these agency costs?

c. Greece's cost of labor and rent are relatively low. Explain why this information is relevant to Nantucket's decision to establish a tour business in Greece.

d. Explain how the cash flow situation of the Greek tour business exposes Nantucket to exchange rate risk. Is Nantucket favorably or unfavorably affected when the euro (Greece's currency) appreciates against the dollar? Explain.

e. Nantucket plans to finance its Greek tour business. Its subsidiary could obtain loans in euros from a bank in Greece to cover its rent, and its main office could pay off the loans over time. Alternatively, its main office could borrow dollars and would periodically convert dollars to euros to pay the expenses in Greece. Does either type of loan reduce the exposure of Nantucket to exchange rate risk? Explain.

f. Explain how the Greek island tour business could expose Nantucket to country risk.

23. Valuation of an MNC. Yahoo! has expanded its business by establishing portals in numerous countries, including Argentina, Australia, China, Germany, Ireland, Japan, and the United Kingdom. It has cash outflows associated with the creation and administration of each portal. It also generates cash inflows from selling advertising space on its website. Each portal results in cash flows in a different currency. Thus, the valuation of Yahoo! is based on its expected future net cash flows in Argentine pesos after converting them into U.S. dollars, its expected net cash flows in Australian dollars after converting them into U.S. dollars, and so on. Explain how and why the valuation of Yahoo! would change if most investors suddenly expected that the dollar would weaken against most currencies over time.

24. Uncertainty Surrounding an MNC's Valuation. Carlisle Co. is a U.S. firm that is about to purchase a large company in Switzerland at a purchase price of

$20 million. This company produces furniture and sells it locally (in Switzerland), and it is expected to earn large profits every year. The company will become a subsidiary of Carlisle and will periodically remit its excess cash flows due to its profits to Carlisle Co. Assume that Carlisle Co. has no other international business. Carlisle has $10 million that it will use to pay for part of the Swiss company and will finance the rest of its purchase with borrowed dollars. Carlisle Co. can obtain supplies from either a U.S. supplier or a Swiss supplier (in which case the payment would be made in Swiss francs). Both suppliers are very reputable and there would be no exposure to country risk when using either supplier. Is the valuation of the total cash flows of Carlisle Co. more uncertain if it obtains its supplies from a U.S. firm or a Swiss firm? Explain briefly.

25. Impact of Exchange Rates on MNC Value.
Olmsted Co. has small computer chips assembled in Poland and transports the final assembled products to the parent, where they are sold by the parent in the United States. The assembled products are invoiced in dollars. Olmsted Co. uses Polish currency (the zloty) to produce these chips and assemble them in Poland. The Polish subsidiary pays the employees in the local currency (zloty), and Olmsted Co. finances its subsidiary operations with loans from a Polish bank (in zloty). The parent of Olmsted will send sufficient monthly payments (in dollars) to the subsidiary in order to repay the loan and other expenses incurred by the subsidiary. If the Polish zloty depreciates against the dollar over time, will that have a favorable, unfavorable, or neutral effect on the value of Olmsted Co.? Briefly explain.

26. Impact of Uncertainty on MNC Value.
Minneapolis Co. is a major exporter of products to Canada. Today, an event occurred that has increased the uncertainty surrounding the Canadian dollar's future value over the long term. Explain how this event can affect the valuation of Minneapolis Co.

27. Exposure of MNCs to Exchange Rate Movements.
Arlington Co. expects to receive 10 million euros in each of the next 10 years. It will need to obtain 2 million Mexican pesos in each of the next 10 years. The euro exchange rate is presently valued at $1.38 and is expected to depreciate by 2 percent each year over time. The peso is valued at $.13 and is expected to

depreciate by 2 percent each year over time. Review the valuation equation for an MNC. Do you think that the exchange rate movements will have a favorable or unfavorable effect on the MNC?

28. Impact of the Credit Crisis on MNC Value.
Much of the attention to the credit crisis was focused on its adverse effects on financial institutions. Yet, many other types of firms were affected as well. Explain why the numerator of the MNC valuation equation was affected during the October 6–10, 2008, period. Explain how the denominator of the MNC valuation equation was affected during this period.

29. Exposure of MNCs to Exchange Rate Movements.
Because of the low labor costs in Thailand, Melnick Co. (based in the United States) recently established a major research and development subsidiary there that it owns. The subsidiary was created to improve new products that the parent of Melnick can sell in the United States (denominated in dollars) to U.S. customers. The subsidiary pays its local employees in baht (the Thai currency). The subsidiary has a small amount of sales denominated in baht, but its expenses are much larger than its revenue. It has just obtained a large loan denominated in baht that will be used to expand its subsidiary. The business that the parent of Melnick Co. conducts in the United States is not exposed to exchange rate risk. If the Thai baht weakens over the next 3 years, will the value of Melnick Co. be favorably affected, unfavorably affected, or not affected? Briefly explain.

30. Shareholder Rights of Investors in MNCs.
MNCs tend to expand more when they can more easily access funds by issuing stock. In some countries, shareholder rights are very limited, and the MNCs have limited ability to raise funds by issuing stock. Explain why access to funding is more severe for MNCs based in countries where shareholder rights are limited.

Discussion in the Boardroom
This exercise can be found in Appendix E at the back of this textbook.

Running Your Own MNC
This exercise can be found on the *International Financial Management* text companion website located at www.cengage.com/finance/madura.

BLADES, INC. CASE

Decision to Expand Internationally

Blades, Inc., is a U.S.-based company that has been incorporated in the United States for 3 years. Blades is a relatively small company, with total assets of only $200 million. The company produces a single type of product, roller blades. Due to the booming roller blade market in the United States at the time of the company's establishment, Blades has been quite successful. For example, in its first year of operation, it reported a net income of $3.5 million. Recently, however, the demand for Blades' "Speedos," the company's primary product in the United States, has been slowly tapering off, and Blades has not been performing well. Last year, it reported a return on assets of only 7 percent. In response to the company's annual report for its most recent year of operations, Blades' shareholders have been pressuring the company to improve its performance; its stock price has fallen from a high of $20 per share 3 years ago to $12 last year. Blades produces high-quality roller blades and employs a unique production process, but the prices it charges are among the top 5 percent in the industry.

In light of these circumstances, Ben Holt, the company's chief financial officer (CFO), is contemplating his alternatives for Blades' future. There are no other cost-cutting measures that Blades can implement in the United States without affecting the quality of its product. Also, production of alternative products would require major modifications to the existing plant setup. Furthermore, and because of these limitations, expansion within the United States at this time seems pointless.

Ben Holt is considering the following: If Blades cannot penetrate the U.S. market further or reduce costs here, why not import some parts from overseas and/or expand the company's sales to foreign countries? Similar strategies have proved successful for numerous companies that expanded into Asia in recent years to increase their profit margins. The CFO's initial focus is on Thailand. Thailand has recently experienced weak economic conditions, and Blades could purchase components there at a low cost. Ben Holt is aware that many of Blades' competitors have begun importing production components from Thailand.

Not only would Blades be able to reduce costs by importing rubber and/or plastic from Thailand due to the low costs of these inputs, but it might also be able to augment weak U.S. sales by exporting to Thailand, an economy still in its infancy and just beginning to appreciate leisure products such as roller blades. While several of Blades' competitors import components from Thailand, few are exporting to the country. Long-term decisions would also eventually have to be made; maybe Blades, Inc., could establish a subsidiary in Thailand and gradually shift its focus away from the United States if its U.S. sales do not rebound. Establishing a subsidiary in Thailand would also make sense for Blades due to its superior production process. Ben Holt is reasonably sure that Thai firms could not duplicate the high-quality production process employed by Blades. Furthermore, if the company's initial approach of exporting works well, establishing a subsidiary in Thailand would preserve Blades' sales before Thai competitors are able to penetrate the Thai market.

As a financial analyst for Blades, Inc., you are assigned to analyze international opportunities and risk resulting from international business. Your initial assessment should focus on the barriers and opportunities that international trade may offer. Ben Holt has never been involved in international business in any form and is unfamiliar with any constraints that may inhibit his plan to export to and import from a foreign country. Mr. Holt has presented you with a list of initial questions you should answer.

1. What are the advantages Blades could gain from importing from and/or exporting to a foreign country such as Thailand?
2. What are some of the disadvantages Blades could face as a result of foreign trade in the short run? In the long run?
3. Which theories of international business described in this chapter apply to Blades, Inc., in the short run? In the long run?
4. What long-range plans other than establishment of a subsidiary in Thailand are an option for Blades and may be more suitable for the company?

SMALL BUSINESS DILEMMA

Developing a Multinational Sporting Goods Corporation

In every chapter of this text, some of the key concepts are illustrated with an application to a small sporting goods firm that conducts international business. These "Small Business Dilemma" features allow students to recognize the dilemmas and possible decisions that firms (such as this sporting goods firm) may face in a global environment. For this chapter, the application is on the development of the sporting goods firm that would conduct international business.

Last month, Jim Logan completed his undergraduate degree in finance and decided to pursue his dream of managing his own sporting goods business. Jim had worked in a sporting goods shop while going to college, and he had noticed that many customers wanted to purchase a low-priced football. However, the sporting goods store where he worked, like many others, sold only top-of-the-line footballs. From his experience, Jim was aware that top-of-the-line footballs had a high markup and that a low-cost football could possibly penetrate the U.S. market. He also knew how to produce footballs. His goal was to create a firm that would produce low-priced footballs and sell them on a wholesale basis to various sporting goods stores in the United States. Unfortunately, many sporting goods stores began to sell low-priced footballs just before Jim was about to start his business. The firm that began to produce the low-cost footballs already provided many other products to sporting goods stores in the United States and therefore had already established a business relationship with these stores. Jim did not believe that he could compete with this firm in the U.S. market.

Rather than pursue a different business, Jim decided to implement his idea on a global basis. While football (as it is played in the United States) has not been a traditional sport in foreign countries, it has become more popular in some foreign countries in recent years. Furthermore, the expansion of cable networks in foreign countries would allow for much more exposure to U.S. football games in those countries in the future. To the extent that this would increase the popularity of football (U.S. style) as a hobby in the foreign countries, it would result in a demand for footballs in foreign countries. Jim asked many of his foreign friends from college days if they recalled seeing footballs sold in their home countries. Most of them said they rarely noticed footballs being sold in sporting goods stores but that they expected the demand for footballs to increase in their home countries. Consequently, Jim decided to start a business of producing low-priced footballs and exporting them to sporting goods distributors in foreign countries. Those distributors would then sell the footballs at the retail level. Jim planned to expand his product line over time once he identified other sports products that he might sell to foreign sporting goods stores. He decided to call his business "Sports Exports Company." To avoid any rent and labor expenses, Jim planned to produce the footballs in his garage and to perform the work himself. Thus, his main business expenses were the cost of the materials used to produce footballs and expenses associated with finding distributors in foreign countries who would attempt to sell the footballs to sporting goods stores.

1. Is Sports Exports Company a multinational corporation?
2. Why are the agency costs lower for Sports Exports Company than for most MNCs?
3. Does Sports Exports Company have any comparative advantage over potential competitors in foreign countries that could produce and sell footballs there?
4. How would Jim Logan decide which foreign markets he would attempt to enter? Should he initially focus on one or many foreign markets?
5. The Sports Exports Company has no immediate plans to conduct direct foreign investment. However, it might consider other less costly methods of establishing its business in foreign markets. What methods might the Sports Exports Company use to increase its presence in foreign markets by working with one or more foreign companies?

INTERNET/EXCEL EXERCISES

The website address of the Bureau of Economic Analysis is www.bea.gov.

1. Use this website to assess recent trends in direct foreign investment (DFI) abroad by U.S. firms. Compare the DFI in the United Kingdom with the DFI in France. Offer a possible reason for the large difference.

2. Based on the recent trends in DFI, are U.S.-based MNCs pursuing opportunities in Asia? In Eastern Europe? In Latin America?

REFERENCES

Baker, Ted, Eric Gedajlovic, and Michael Lubatkin, Sep 2005, A Framework for Comparing Entrepreneurship Processes across Nations, *Journal of International Business Studies*, pp. 492–504.

Buckley, Peter J., and Pervez N. Ghauri, Mar 2004, Globalisation, Economic Geography and the Strategy of Multinational Enterprises, *Journal of International Business Studies*, pp. 81–98.

Fawcett, David, Sep/Oct 2008, The Need for International Valuation Standards, *Valuation Strategies*, pp. 34–37.

Ghemawat, Pankaj, Dec 2005, Regional Strategies for Global Leadership, *Harvard Business Review*, pp. 98–10.

Lieberthal, Kenneth, and Geoffrey Lieberthal, Oct 2003, The Great Transition, *Harvard Business Review*, pp. 70–81.

Meyer, Klaus E., July 2004, Perspectives on Multinational Enterprises in Emerging Economies, *Journal of International Business Studies*, pp. 259–276.

Meyer, Klaus E., and Mike W. Peng, Nov 2005, Probing Theoretically into Central and Eastern Europe: Transactions, Resources, and Institutions, *Journal of International Business Studies*, pp. 600–621.

Moore, Fiona, Nov 2005, Local Players in Global Games: The Strategic Constitution of a Multinational Corporation, *Journal of International Business Studies*, pp. 719–721.

Term Paper on the International Credit Crisis

Write a term paper on one of the topics below or one that is assigned by your professor. Details such as deadline date and length of the paper will be provided by your professor.

Each of the ideas listed below can be easily researched because much media attention has been given to the topics. While this text offers a brief summary of each topic, much more information is available on the Internet by inserting a few key terms or phrases into a search engine.

1. Impact on a Selected Country. Select one country (except the United States) and describe why that country was affected by the international credit crisis. For example, did its financial institutions invest heavily in mortgage-related securities? Did its MNCs suffer from limited liquidity because they relied on credit from other countries during the international credit crunch? Did the country's economy suffer because it relies heavily on exports? Was the country adversely affected because of how the international credit crisis affected its currency's value?

2. Impact on a Selected Company. Select one MNC based in the United States or in any other country. Compare its financial performance in 2007 and in the first two quarters of 2008 to its performance since July 2008 when the crisis intensified. Explain why this MNC's performance was affected by the international credit crisis. Was its revenue reduced due to weak global economic conditions? Was the MNC adversely affected because of how the international credit crisis affected exchange rates? Was it adversely affected because of problems in obtaining credit?

3. International Impact of Lehman Brothers' Bankruptcy. Explain how the bankruptcy of Lehman Brothers had adverse effects on countries outside the United States. Some effects may be indirect, while others are more direct.

4. International Impact of AIG's Financial Problems. Explain how the financial problems of American International Group (AIG) had adverse effects on countries outside the United States. Some effects may be indirect, while others are more direct.

5. Government Response to Crisis. Select a country (except the United States) that was adversely affected by the international credit crisis, and explain how that country's government responded to the crisis. Offer your opinions on whether that government's response to the crisis was more effective than the policies used by the U.S. government.

6. Impact on Exchange Rates. Describe the trend of exchange rates before the credit crisis, during the credit crisis, and after the crisis. Offer insight on why the exchange rates of particular currencies changed as they did as a result of the crisis.

2

International Flow of Funds

CHAPTER OBJECTIVES

The specific objectives of this chapter are to:

- explain the key components of the balance of payments,

- explain how international trade flows are influenced by economic factors and other factors, and

- explain how international capital flows are influenced by country characteristics.

International business is facilitated by markets that allow for the flow of funds between countries. The transactions arising from international business cause money flows from one country to another. The balance of payments is a measure of international money flows and is discussed in this chapter.

Financial managers of MNCs monitor the balance of payments so that they can determine how the flow of international transactions is changing over time. The balance of payments can indicate the volume of transactions between specific countries and may even signal potential shifts in specific exchange rates.

BALANCE OF PAYMENTS

The **balance of payments** is a summary of transactions between domestic and foreign residents for a specific country over a specified period of time. It represents an accounting of a country's international transactions for a period, usually a quarter or a year. It accounts for transactions by businesses, individuals, and the government.

A balance-of-payments statement can be broken down into various components. Those that receive the most attention are the current account and the capital account. The **current account** represents a summary of the flow of funds between one specified country and all other countries due to purchases of goods or services, or the provision of income on financial assets. The **capital account** represents a summary of the flow of funds resulting from the sale of assets between one specified country and all other countries over a specified period of time. Thus, it compares the new foreign investments made by a country with the foreign investments within a country over a particular time period. Transactions that reflect inflows of funds generate positive numbers (credits) for the country's balance, while transactions that reflect outflows of funds generate negative numbers (debits) for the country's balance.

Current Account

The main components of the current account are payments for (1) merchandise (goods) and services, (2) factor income, and (3) transfers.

Payments for Merchandise and Services. Merchandise exports and imports represent tangible products, such as computers and clothing, that are transported between countries. Service exports and imports represent tourism and other services, such as legal, insurance, and consulting services, provided for customers based in other countries. Service exports by the United States result in an inflow of funds to the United States, while service imports by the United States result in an outflow of funds.

The difference between total exports and imports is referred to as the **balance of trade.** A deficit in the balance of trade means that the value of merchandise and services exported by the United States is less than the value of merchandise and services imported by the United States. Before 1993, the balance of trade focused on only merchandise exports and imports. In 1993, it was redefined to include service exports and imports as well. The value of U.S. service exports usually exceeds the value of U.S. service imports. However, the value of U.S. merchandise exports is typically much smaller than the value of U.S. merchandise imports. Overall, the United States normally has a negative balance of trade.

Factor Income Payments. A second component of the current account is **factor income,** which represents income (interest and dividend payments) received by investors on foreign investments in financial assets (securities). Thus, factor income received by U.S. investors reflects an inflow of funds into the United States. Factor income paid by the United States reflects an outflow of funds from the United States.

Transfer Payments. A third component of the current account is transfer payments, which represent aid, grants, and gifts from one country to another.

Examples of Payment Entries. Exhibit 2.1 shows several examples of transactions that would be reflected in the current account. Notice in the exhibit that every transaction that generates a U.S. cash inflow (exports and income receipts by the United States) represents a credit to the current account, while every transaction that generates a U.S. cash outflow (imports and income payments by the United States) represents a debit to the current account. Therefore, a large current account deficit indicates that the United States is sending more cash abroad to buy goods and services or to pay income than it is receiving for those same reasons.

Actual Current Account Balance. The U.S. current account balance in the year 2007 is summarized in Exhibit 2.2. Notice that the exports of merchandise were valued at $1,148 billion, while imports of merchandise by the United States were valued at $1,967 billion. Total U.S. exports of merchandise and services and income receipts amounted to $2,463 billion, while total U.S. imports and income payments amounted to $3,082 billion. The bottom of the exhibit shows that net transfers (which include grants and gifts provided to other countries) were –$112 billion. The negative number for net transfers represents a cash outflow from the United States. Overall, the current account balance was –$731 billion, which is primarily attributed to the excess in U.S. payments sent for imports beyond the payments received from exports.

Exhibit 2.2 shows that the current account balance (line 10) can be derived as the difference between total U.S. exports and income receipts (line 4) and the total U.S. imports and income payments (line 8), with an adjustment for net transfer payments (line 9). This is logical, since the total U.S. exports and income receipts represent U.S. cash inflows while the total U.S. imports and income payments and the net transfers represent U.S. cash outflows. The negative current account balance means that the United States spent more on trade, income, and transfer payments than it received.

Capital and Financial Accounts

The capital account category has been changed to separate it from the financial account, which is described next. The capital account includes the value of financial assets transferred across country borders by people who move to a different country. It also includes

Exhibit 2.1 Examples of Current Account Transactions

INTERNATIONAL TRADE TRANSACTION	U.S. CASH FLOW POSITION	ENTRY ON U.S. BALANCE-OF-PAYMENTS ACCOUNT
J.C. Penney purchases stereos produced in Indonesia that it will sell in its U.S. retail stores.	U.S. cash outflow	Debit
Individuals in the United States purchase CDs over the Internet from a firm based in China.	U.S. cash outflow	Debit
The Mexican government pays a U.S. consulting firm for consulting services provided by the firm.	U.S. cash inflow	Credit
IBM headquarters in the United States purchases computer chips from Singapore that it uses in assembling computers.	U.S. cash outflow	Debit
A university bookstore in Ireland purchases textbooks produced by a U.S. publishing company.	U.S. cash inflow	Credit
INTERNATIONAL INCOME TRANSACTION	**U.S. CASH FLOW POSITION**	**ENTRY ON U.S. BALANCE-OF-PAYMENTS ACCOUNT**
A U.S. investor receives a dividend payment from a French firm in which she purchased stock.	U.S. cash inflow	Credit
The U.S. Treasury sends an interest payment to a German insurance company that purchased U.S. Treasury bonds 1 year ago.	U.S. cash outflow	Debit
A Mexican company that borrowed dollars from a bank based in the United States sends an interest payment to that bank.	U.S. cash inflow	Credit
INTERNATIONAL TRANSFER TRANSACTION	**U.S. CASH FLOW POSITION**	**ENTRY ON U.S. BALANCE-OF-PAYMENTS ACCOUNT**
The United States provides aid to Costa Rica in response to a flood in Costa Rica.	U.S. cash outflow	Debit
Switzerland provides a grant to U.S. scientists to work on cancer research.	U.S. cash inflow	Credit

the value of nonproduced nonfinancial assets that are transferred across country borders, such as patents and trademarks. The sale of patent rights by a U.S. firm to a Canadian firm reflects a credit to the U.S. balance-of-payments account, while a U.S. purchase of patent rights from a Canadian firm reflects a debit to the U.S. balance-of-payments account. The capital account items are relatively minor compared to the financial account items.

The key components of the financial account are payments for (1) direct foreign investment, (2) portfolio investment, and (3) other capital investment.

Direct Foreign Investment. Direct foreign investment represents the investment in fixed assets in foreign countries that can be used to conduct business operations. Examples of direct foreign investment include a firm's acquisition of a foreign company, its construction of a new manufacturing plant, or its expansion of an existing plant in a foreign country.

Portfolio Investment. Portfolio investment represents transactions involving long-term financial assets (such as stocks and bonds) between countries that do not affect the transfer of control. Thus, a purchase of Heineken (Netherlands) stock by a U.S. investor is classified as portfolio investment because it represents a purchase of foreign financial assets

Exhibit 2.2 Summary of Current Account in the Year 2008 (in billions of $)

(1)	U.S. exports of merchandise	+	$1,148
+ (2)	U.S. exports of services	+	497
+ (3)	U.S. income receipts	+	818
= (4)	Total U.S. exports and income receipts	=	$2,463
(5)	U.S. imports of merchandise	–	$1,967
+ (6)	U.S. imports of services	–	378
+ (7)	U.S. income payments	–	737
= (8)	Total U.S. imports and income payments	=	$3,082
(9)	Net transfers by the United States	–	$112
(10)	Current account balance = (4) – (8) – (9)	–	$731

without changing control of the company. If a U.S. firm purchased all of Heineken's stock in an acquisition, this transaction would result in a transfer of control and therefore would be classified as direct foreign investment instead of portfolio investment.

Other Capital Investment. A third component of the financial account consists of other capital investment, which represents transactions involving short-term financial assets (such as money market securities) between countries. In general, direct foreign investment measures the expansion of firms' foreign operations, whereas portfolio investment and other capital investment measure the net flow of funds due to financial asset transactions between individual or institutional investors.

Errors and Omissions and Reserves. If a country has a negative current account balance, it should have a positive capital and financial account balance. This implies that while it sends more money out of the country than it receives from other countries for trade and factor income, it receives more money from other countries than it spends for capital and financial account components, such as investments. In fact, the negative balance on the current account should be offset by a positive balance on the capital and financial account. However, there is not normally a perfect offsetting effect because measurement errors can occur when attempting to measure the value of funds transferred into or out of a country. For this reason, the balance-of-payments account includes a category of errors and omissions.

WEB

www.bea.gov/
Update of the current account balance and international trade balance.

INTERNATIONAL TRADE FLOWS

Canada, France, Germany, and other European countries rely more heavily on trade than the United States does. Canada's trade volume of exports and imports per year is valued at more than 50 percent of its annual gross domestic product (GDP). The trade volume of European countries is typically between 30 and 40 percent of their respective GDPs. The trade volume of the United States and Japan is typically between 10 and 20 percent of their respective GDPs. Nevertheless, for all countries, the volume of trade has grown over time. As of 2008, exports represented about 15 percent of U.S. GDP.

WEB

www.ita.doc.gov/td/
industry/otea
The international trade conditions outlook for each of several industries.

Distribution of U.S. Exports and Imports

The dollar value of U.S. exports to various countries during 2008 is shown in Exhibit 2.3. The amounts of U.S. exports are rounded to the nearest billion. For example, exports to Canada were valued at $264 billion.

Exhibit 2.3 Distribution of U.S. Exports across Countries (in billions of $)

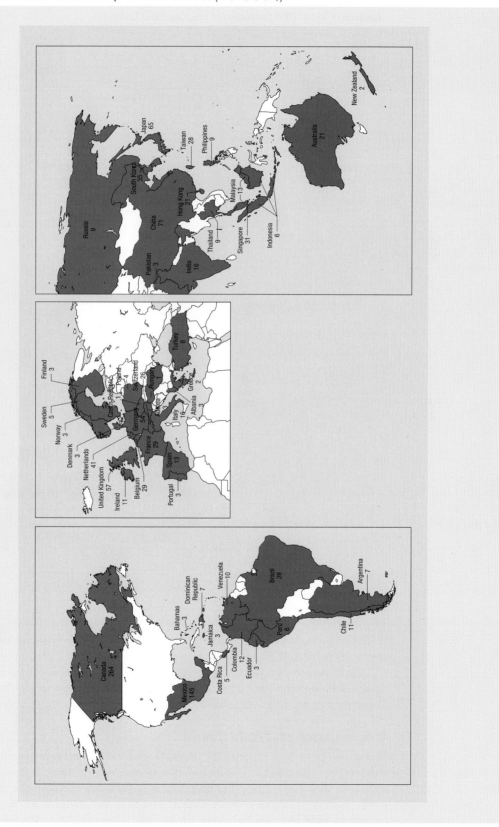

Source: *U.S. Census Bureau, 2009.*

Exhibit 2.4 2008 Distribution of U.S. Exports and Imports

Distribution of Exports

France 2%
South Korea 3%
United Kingdom 4%
Mexico 12%
China 5%
Japan 5%
Germany 4%
Canada 20%
Other 45%

Distribution of Imports

United Kingdom 3%
France 2%
South Korea 2%
Mexico 10%
China 16%
Japan 7%
Germany 5%
Canada 16%
Other 39%

Source: *Federal Reserve, 2009.*

The proportion of total U.S. exports to various countries is shown at the top of Exhibit 2.4. About 20 percent of all U.S. exports are to Canada, while 12 percent are to Mexico.

The proportion of total U.S. imports from various countries is shown at the bottom of Exhibit 2.4. Canada, China, Mexico, and Japan are the key exporters to the United States: Together, they are responsible for about half of the value of all U.S. imports.

U.S. Balance-of-Trade Trend

Recent trends for U.S. exports, U.S. imports, and the U.S. balance of trade are shown in Exhibit 2.5. Notice that the value of U.S. exports and U.S. imports has grown substantially over time. Since 1976, the value of U.S. imports has exceeded the value of U.S. exports, causing a balance-of-trade deficit. Much of the trade deficit is due to a trade imbalance with just two countries, China and Japan. In 2008, U.S. exports to China

Exhibit 2.5 U.S. Balance of Trade over Time

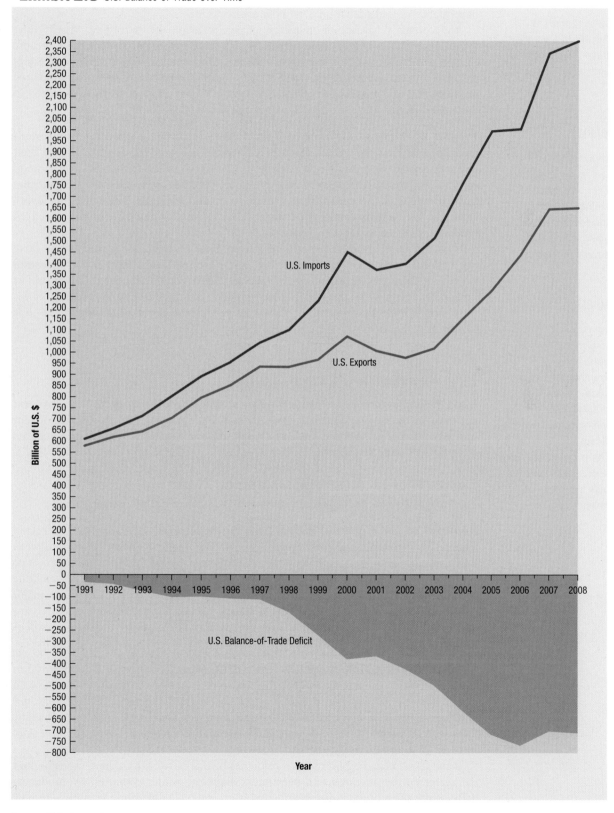

Source: *U.S. Census Bureau, 2009.*

WEB

www.ita.doc.gov
Access to a variety of
trade-related country
and sector statistics.

WEB

www.census.gov/
foreign-trade/balance
Click on a specific
country. The balance of
trade with the country
you specify is shown for
several recent years.

WEB

www.census.gov/
foreign-trade/www/
press.html
Trend of the U.S. bal-
ance of trade in ag-
gregate. Click on U.S.
International Trade in
Goods and Services.
There are several links
here to additional de-
tails about the U.S.
balance of trade.

were about $71 billion, but imports from China were about $337 billion, which resulted in a balance-of-trade deficit of $266 billion with China.

Any country's balance of trade can change substantially over time. Shortly after World War II, the United States experienced a large balance-of-trade surplus because Europe relied on U.S. exports as it was rebuilt. During the last decade, the United States has experienced balance-of-trade deficits because of strong U.S. demand for imported products that are produced at a lower cost than similar products can be produced in the United States.

Impact of a Huge Balance-of-Trade Deficit. If firms, individuals, or government agencies from the United States purchased all their products from U.S. firms, their payments would have resulted in revenue to U.S. firms, which would also contribute to earnings for the shareholders. In addition, if the purchases were directed at U.S. firms, these firms would need to produce more products and could hire more employees. Thus, the U.S. unemployment rate might be lower if U.S. purchases were focused on products produced within the United States.

However, there are some benefits of international trade for the United States. First, international trade has created some jobs in the United States, especially in industries where U.S. firms have a technology advantage. International trade has caused a shift of production to countries that can produce products more efficiently. In addition, it ensures more competition among the firms that produce products, which forces the firms to keep their prices low.

INTERNATIONAL TRADE ISSUES

Given the importance of international trade and the potential impact that a government can have on trade, governments continually seek trade policies that are fair to all countries. Much progress has been made as a result of several events that have either reduced or eliminated trade restrictions.

Events That Increased International Trade

The following events reduced trade restrictions and increased international trade.

Removal of the Berlin Wall. In 1989, the Berlin Wall separating East Germany from West Germany was torn down. This was symbolic of new relations between East Germany and West Germany and was followed by the reunification of the two countries. It encouraged free enterprise in all Eastern European countries and the privatization of businesses that were owned by the government. It also led to major reductions in trade barriers in Eastern Europe. Many MNCs began to export products there, while others capitalized on the cheap labor costs by importing supplies from there.

Single European Act. In the late 1980s, industrialized countries in Europe agreed to make regulations more uniform and to remove many taxes on goods traded between these countries. This agreement, supported by the Single European Act of 1987, was followed by a series of negotiations among the countries to achieve uniform policies by 1992. The act allows firms in a given European country greater access to supplies from firms in other European countries.

Many firms, including European subsidiaries of U.S.-based MNCs, have capitalized on the agreement by attempting to penetrate markets in border countries. By producing more of the same product and distributing it across European countries, firms are now better able to achieve economies of scale. Best Foods (now part of Unilever) was one of many MNCs that increased efficiency by streamlining manufacturing operations as a result of the reduction in barriers.

NAFTA. As a result of the North American Free Trade Agreement (NAFTA) of 1993, trade barriers between the United States and Mexico were eliminated. Some U.S. firms attempted to capitalize on this by exporting goods that had previously been restricted by barriers to Mexico. Other firms established subsidiaries in Mexico to produce their goods at a lower cost than was possible in the United States and then sell the goods in the United States. The removal of trade barriers essentially allowed U.S. firms to penetrate product and labor markets that previously had not been accessible.

The removal of trade barriers between the United States and Mexico allows Mexican firms to export some products to the United States that were previously restricted. Thus, U.S. firms that produce these goods are now subject to competition from Mexican exporters. Given the low cost of labor in Mexico, some U.S. firms have lost some of their market share. The effects are most pronounced in the labor-intensive industries.

GATT. Within a month after the NAFTA accord, the momentum for free trade continued with a GATT (General Agreement on Tariffs and Trade) accord. This accord was the conclusion of trade negotiations from the so-called Uruguay Round that had begun 7 years earlier. It called for the reduction or elimination of trade restrictions on specified imported goods over a 10-year period across 117 countries. The accord has generated more international business for firms that had previously been unable to penetrate foreign markets because of trade restrictions.

Inception of the Euro. In 1999, several European countries adopted the euro as their currency for business transactions between these countries. The euro was phased in as a currency for other transactions during 2001 and completely replaced the currencies of the participating countries on January 1, 2002. Consequently, only the euro is used for transactions in these countries, and firms (including European subsidiaries of U.S.-based MNCs) no longer face the costs and risks associated with converting one currency to another. The single currency system in most of Western Europe encouraged more trade among European countries.

Expansion of the European Union. In 2004, Cyprus, the Czech Republic, Estonia, Hungary, Latvia, Lithuania, Malta, Poland, Slovakia, and Slovenia were admitted to the European Union (EU) followed by Bulgaria and Romania in 2007. Slovenia adopted the euro as its currency in 2007, while Cyprus and Malta adopted it as their currency in 2008. The other new members continue to use their own currencies, but may be able to adopt the euro as their currency in the future if they meet specified guidelines regarding budget deficits and other financial conditions. Nevertheless, their admission into the EU is relevant because restrictions on their trade with Western Europe are reduced. Since wages in these countries are substantially lower than in Western European countries, many MNCs have established manufacturing plants there to produce products and export them to Western Europe.

Other Trade Agreements. In June 2003, the United States and Chile signed a free trade agreement to remove tariffs on products traded between the two countries. In 2006, the Central American Trade Agreement (CAFTA) was implemented, allowing for lower tariffs and regulations among the United States, the Dominican Republic, and four Central American countries. In addition, there is an initiative for Caribbean nations to create a single market in which there is free flow of trade, capital, and workers across countries.

The United States has also established trade agreements with many other countries, including Singapore (2004), Bahrain (2006), Morocco (2006), Oman (2006), and Peru (2007).

Trade Friction

International trade policies partially determine which firms get most of the market share within an industry. These policies affect each country's unemployment level, income level, and economic growth. Even though trade treaties have reduced tariffs and quotas over time, most countries still impose some type of trade restrictions on particular products in order to protect local firms.

An easy way to start an argument among students (or professors) is to ask what they think the international trade policy should be. People whose job prospects are highly influenced by international trade tend to have very strong opinions on this subject. On the surface, most people agree that free trade can be beneficial because it encourages more intense competition among firms, and thus enables consumers to obtain the highest quality and lowest priced products. Free trade should cause a shift in production to those countries where it can be done most efficiently. Each country's government wants to increase its exports because more exports result in a higher level of production and income, and may create jobs. However, a job created in one country may be lost in another, which causes countries to battle for a greater share of the world's exports.

People disagree on the strategies a government should be allowed to use to increase its share of the global market. They may agree that a tariff or quota on imported goods prevents free trade and gives local firms an unfair advantage in their own market. Yet they disagree on whether governments should be allowed to use other, more subtle trade restrictions against foreign firms or provide incentives that give local firms an unfair advantage in the battle for global market share. Consider the following situations that commonly occur:

1. The firms based in one country are not subject to environmental restrictions and, therefore, can produce at a lower cost than firms in other countries.
2. The firms based in one country are not subject to child labor laws and are able to produce products at a lower cost than firms in other countries by relying mostly on children to produce the products.
3. The firms based in one country are allowed by their government to offer bribes to large customers when pursuing business deals in a particular industry. They have a competitive advantage over firms in other countries that are not allowed to offer bribes.
4. The firms in one country receive subsidies from the government, as long as they export the products. The exporting of products that were produced with the help of government subsidies is commonly referred to as **dumping.** These firms may be able to sell their products at a lower price than any of their competitors in other countries.
5. The firms in one country receive tax breaks if they are in specific industries. This practice is not necessarily a subsidy, but it still is a form of government financial support.

In all of these situations, firms in one country may have an advantage over firms in other countries. Every government uses some strategies that may give its local firms an advantage in the fight for global market share. Thus, the playing field in the battle for global market share is probably not even across all countries. Yet, there is no formula that will ensure a fair battle for market share. Regardless of the progress of international trade treaties, governments will always be able to find strategies that can give their local firms an edge in exporting. Suppose, as an extreme example, that a new international treaty outlawed all of the strategies described above. One country's government could still try to give its local firms a trade advantage by attempting to maintain a relatively weak currency. This strategy can increase foreign demand for products produced locally because products denominated in a weak currency can be purchased at a low price.

Using the Exchange Rate as a Policy. At any given point in time, a group of exporters may claim that they are being mistreated and lobby their government to adjust the currency so that their exports will not be so expensive for foreign purchasers. In 2004, European exporters claimed that they were at a disadvantage because the euro was too strong. Meanwhile, U.S. exporters still claimed that they could not compete with China because the Chinese currency (yuan) was maintained at an artificially weak level. In July 2005, China revalued the yuan by 2.1 percent against the dollar in response to criticism. It also implemented a new system in which the yuan could float within narrow boundaries based on a set of major currencies. In May 2007, China widened the band so that the yuan could deviate by as much as .5 percent within a day. This had a very limited effect on the relative pricing of Chinese versus U.S. products and, therefore, on the balance of trade between the two countries.

Outsourcing. One of the most recent issues related to trade is the outsourcing of services. For example, technical support for computer systems used in the United States may be outsourced to India, Bulgaria, China, or other countries where labor costs are low. Outsourcing affects the balance of trade because it means that a service is purchased in another country. This form of international trade allows MNCs to conduct operations at a lower cost. However, it shifts jobs to other countries and is criticized by the people who lose their jobs due to this practice. Many people have opinions about outsourcing that are inconsistent with their own behavior.

EXAMPLE

As a U.S. citizen, Rick says he is embarrassed by U.S. firms that outsource their labor services to other countries as a means of increasing their value because this practice eliminates jobs in the United States. Rick is president of Atlantic Co. and says the company will never outsource its services. Atlantic Co. imports most of its materials from a foreign company. It also owns a factory in Mexico, and the materials produced there are exported to the United States.

Rick recognizes that outsourcing may replace jobs in the United States, but he does not realize that importing materials or operating a factory in Mexico may also replace U.S. jobs. If questioned about his use of foreign labor markets for materials and production, he would probably explain that the high manufacturing wages in the United States force him to rely on lower-cost labor in foreign countries. Yet the same argument could be used by other U.S. firms that outsource services.

Rick owns a Toyota, a Nokia cell phone, a Toshiba computer, and Adidas clothing. He argues that these non-U.S. products are a better value for the money than equivalent U.S. products. His friend Nicole suggests that Rick's consumption choices are inconsistent with his "create U.S. jobs" philosophy. She explains that she only purchases U.S. products. She owns a Ford (produced in Mexico), a Motorola telephone (components produced in Asia), a Compaq computer (produced in China), and Nike clothing (produced in Indonesia). ●

GOVERNANCE

Managerial Decisions about Outsourcing. Managers of a U.S.-based MNC may argue that they produce their products in the United States to create jobs for U.S. workers. However, when the same products can be easily duplicated in foreign markets for one-fifth of the cost, shareholders may pressure the managers to establish a foreign subsidiary or to engage in outsourcing. Shareholders may suggest that the managers are not maximizing the MNC's value as a result of their commitment to creating U.S. jobs. The MNC's board of directors governs the major managerial decisions and could pressure the managers to have some of the production moved outside the United States. The board should consider the potential savings that could occur as a result of having products produced outside the United States. However, it must also consider the possible adverse effects due to bad publicity or to bad morale that could occur among the U.S. workers. If the production cost could be substantially reduced outside the United States without a loss in quality, a possible compromise is to allow foreign production to accommodate any growth in its business. In this way, the strategy would not adversely affect the existing employees involved in production.

Using Trade Policies for Security Reasons.

Some U.S. politicians have argued that international trade and foreign ownership should be restricted when U.S. security is threatened. While the general opinion has much support, there is disagreement regarding the specific business transactions in which U.S. businesses deserve protection from foreign competition. Consider the following questions:

1. Should the United States purchase military planes only from a U.S. producer, even when Brazil could produce the same planes for half the price? The tradeoff involves a larger budget deficit for increased security. Is the United States truly safer with planes produced in the United States? Are technology secrets safer when the production is in the United States by a U.S. firm?

2. If you think military planes should be produced only by a U.S. firm, should there be any restrictions on foreign ownership of the firm? Foreign investors own a proportion of most large publicly traded companies in the United States.

3. Should foreign ownership restrictions be imposed only on investors based in some countries? Or is there a concern that owners based in any foreign country should be banned from doing business transactions when U.S. security is threatened? What is the threat? Is it that the owners could sell technology secrets to enemies? If so, isn't such a threat also possible for U.S. owners? If some foreign owners are acceptable, what countries would be acceptable?

4. What products should be viewed as a threat to U.S. security? For example, even if military planes had to be produced by U.S. firms, what about all the components that are used in the production of the planes? Some of the components used in U.S. military plane production are produced in China and imported by the plane manufacturers.

To realize the degree of disagreement about these issues, try to get a consensus answer on any of these questions from your fellow students in a single classroom. If students without hidden agendas cannot agree on the answer, consider the level of disagreement among owners or employees of U.S. and foreign firms that have much to gain (or lose) from the international trade and investment policy that is implemented. It is difficult to distinguish between a trade or investment restriction that is enhancing national security versus one that is unfairly protecting a U.S. firm from foreign competition. The same dilemma regarding international trade and investment policies to protect national security in the United States also applies to all other countries.

Using Trade Policies for Political Reasons.

International trade policy issues have become even more contentious over time as people have come to expect that trade policies will be used to punish countries for various actions. People expect countries to restrict imports from countries that fail to enforce environmental laws or child labor laws, initiate war against another country, or are unwilling to participate in a war against an unlawful dictator of another country. Every international trade convention now attracts a large number of protesters, all of whom have their own agendas. International trade may not even be the focus of each protest, but it is often thought to be the potential solution to the problem (at least in the mind of that protester). Although all of the protesters are clearly dissatisfied with existing trade policies, there is no consensus as to what trade policies should be. These different views are similar to the disagreements that occur between government representatives when they try to negotiate international trade policy.

The managers of each MNC cannot be responsible for resolving these international trade policy conflicts. However, they should at least recognize how a particular international trade policy affects their competitive position in the industry and how changes in policy could affect their position in the future.

FACTORS AFFECTING INTERNATIONAL TRADE FLOWS

Because international trade can significantly affect a country's economy, it is important to identify and monitor the factors that influence it. The most influential factors are:

- Inflation
- National income
- Government policies
- Exchange rates

Impact of Inflation

If a country's inflation rate increases relative to the countries with which it trades, its current account will be expected to decrease, other things being equal. Consumers and corporations in that country will most likely purchase more goods overseas (due to high local inflation), while the country's exports to other countries will decline.

Impact of National Income

If a country's income level (national income) increases by a higher percentage than those of other countries, its current account is expected to decrease, other things being equal. As the real income level (adjusted for inflation) rises, so does consumption of goods. A percentage of that increase in consumption will most likely reflect an increased demand for foreign goods.

Impact of the Credit Crisis on Trade. The credit crisis weakened the economies (and national incomes) of many different countries. Consequently, the amount of spending, including spending for imported products, declined. MNCs cut back on their plans to boost exports as they lowered their estimates for economic growth in their foreign markets. As they reduced their expansion plans, they also reduced their demand for imported supplies. Thus, international trade flows were reduced in response to the credit crisis.

A related reason for the decline in international trade is that some MNCs could not obtain financing. International trade is commonly facilitated by letters of credit, which are issued by commercial banks on behalf of importers promising to make payment upon delivery. Exporters tend to trust that commercial banks would follow through on their obligation even if they did not trust the importers. However, because many banks experienced financial problems during the credit crisis, exporters were less willing to accept letters of credit.

Impact of Government Policies

A country's government can have a major effect on its balance of trade by its policies on subsidizing exporters, restrictions on imports, or lack of enforcement on piracy.

Subsidies for Exporters. Some governments offer subsidies to their domestic firms so that those firms can produce products at a lower cost than their global competitors. Thus, the demand for the exports produced by those firms is higher as a result of subsidies.

EXAMPLE

Many firms in China commonly receive free loans or free land from the government. They thus incur a lower cost of operations and are able to price their products lower as a result. Lower prices enable them to capture a larger share of the global market. ●

Some subsidies are more obvious than others. It could be argued that every government provides subsidies in some form.

WEB

www.commerce.gov
General information about import restrictions and other trade-related information.

Restrictions on Imports. A country's government can also prevent or discourage imports from other countries. By imposing such restrictions, the government disrupts trade flows. Among the most commonly used trade restrictions are tariffs and quotas.

If a country's government imposes a tax on imported goods (often referred to as a **tariff**), the prices of foreign goods to consumers are effectively increased. Tariffs imposed by the U.S. government are on average lower than those imposed by other governments. Some industries, however, are more highly protected by tariffs than others. American apparel products and farm products have historically received more protection against foreign competition through high tariffs on related imports.

WEB

www.treas.gov/offices/
enforcement/ofac/
An update of sanctions imposed by the U.S. government on specific countries.

In addition to tariffs, a government can reduce its country's imports by enforcing a **quota,** or a maximum limit that can be imported. Quotas have been commonly applied to a variety of goods imported by the United States and other countries.

Lack of Restrictions on Piracy. In some cases, a government can affect international trade flows by its lack of restrictions on piracy.

EXAMPLE

In China, piracy is very common. Individuals (called pirates) manufacture CDs and DVDs that look almost exactly like the original product produced in the United States and other countries. They sell the CDs and DVDs on the street at a price that is lower than the original product. They even sell the CDs and DVDs to retail stores. Consequently, local consumers obtain copies of imports rather than actual imports. According to the U.S. film industry 90 percent of the DVDs that were the intellectual property of U.S. firms and purchased in China may be pirated. It has been estimated that U.S. producers of film, music, and software lose $2 billion in sales per year due to piracy in China. The Chinese government has periodically stated that it would attempt to crack down, but piracy is still prevalent. ●

As a result of piracy, China's demand for imports is lower. Piracy is one reason why the United States has a large balance-of-trade deficit with China. However, even if piracy were eliminated, the U.S. trade deficit with China would still be large.

Impact of Exchange Rates

Each country's currency is valued in terms of other currencies through the use of exchange rates. Currencies can then be exchanged to facilitate international transactions. The values of most currencies fluctuate over time because of market and government forces (as discussed in detail in Chapter 4). If a country's currency begins to rise in value against other currencies, its current account balance should decrease, other things being equal. As the currency strengthens, goods exported by that country will become more expensive to the importing countries. As a consequence, the demand for such goods will decrease.

EXAMPLE

A tennis racket that sells in the United States for $100 will require a payment of C$125 by the Canadian importer if the Canadian dollar is valued at C$1 = $.80. If C$1 = $.70, it would require a payment of C$143, which might discourage the Canadian demand for U.S. tennis rackets. A strong local currency is expected to reduce the current account balance if the traded goods are **price-elastic** (sensitive to price changes). ●

Using the tennis racket example above, consider the possible effects if currencies of several countries depreciate simultaneously against the dollar (the dollar strengthens). The U.S. balance of trade can decline substantially.

In the fall of 2008, exchange rates of the European currencies such as the euro, British pound, Hungarian forint, and Swiss franc declined substantially against the dollar, which caused the prices of European products to decline from the perspective of consumers in the United States. In addition, the prices of American products increased from the perspective of consumers in Europe. This trend was a reversal of the exchange rate movements in 2006–2007. ●

Interaction of Factors

While exchange rate movements can have a significant impact on prices paid for U.S. exports or imports, the effects can be offset by other factors. For example, as a high U.S. inflation rate reduces the current account, it places downward pressure on the value of the dollar (as discussed in detail in Chapter 4). Because a weaker dollar can improve the current account, it may partially offset the impact of inflation on the current account.

CORRECTING A BALANCE-OF-TRADE DEFICIT

A balance-of-trade deficit is not necessarily a problem. It may enable a country's consumers to benefit from imported products that are less expensive than locally produced products. However, the purchase of imported products implies less reliance on domestic production in favor of foreign production. Thus, it may be argued that a large balance-of-trade deficit causes a transfer of jobs to some foreign countries. Consequently, a country's government may attempt to correct a balance-of-trade deficit.

By reconsidering some of the factors that affect the balance of trade, it is possible to develop some common methods for correcting a deficit. Any policy that will increase foreign demand for the country's goods and services will improve its balance-of-trade position. Foreign demand may increase if export prices become more attractive. This can occur when the country's inflation is low or when its currency's value is reduced, thereby making the prices cheaper from a foreign perspective.

A floating exchange rate could possibly correct any international trade imbalances in the following way. A deficit in a country's balance of trade suggests that the country is spending more funds on foreign products than it is receiving from exports to foreign countries. Because it is selling its currency (to buy foreign goods) in greater volume than the foreign demand for its currency, the value of its currency should decrease. This decrease in value should encourage more foreign demand for its goods in the future.

While this theory seems rational, it does not always work as just described. It is possible that, instead, a country's currency will remain stable or appreciate even when the country has a balance-of-trade deficit.

The United States normally experiences a large balance-of-trade deficit, which should place downward pressure on the value of the dollar when holding other factors constant. Yet in many periods there are more financial flows into the United States to purchase securities than there are financial outflows. These forces can offset the downward pressure on the dollar's value caused by the trade imbalance. Thus, the value of the dollar will not necessarily decline when there is a large balance-of-trade deficit in the United States. ●

Limitations of a Weak Home Currency Solution

Even if a country's home currency weakens, its balance-of-trade deficit will not necessarily be corrected for the following reasons.

Counterpricing by Competitors. When a country's currency weakens, its prices become more attractive to foreign customers, so many foreign companies lower their prices to remain competitive with the country's firms.

Impact of Other Weak Currencies. The currency does not necessarily weaken against all currencies at the same time.

EXAMPLE

Even if the dollar weakens against European currencies, the dollar's exchange rates with Asian currencies may remain more stable. As some U.S. firms reduce their demand for supplies produced in European countries, they tend to increase their demand for goods produced in Asian countries. Consequently, the dollar's weakness in European countries causes a change in international trade behavior but does not eliminate the U.S. trade deficit. ●

Prearranged International Transactions. Many international trade transactions are prearranged and cannot be immediately adjusted. Thus, exporters and importers are committed to continue the international transactions that they agreed to complete. Over time, non-U.S. firms may begin to take advantage of the weaker dollar by purchasing U.S. imports, if they believe that the weakness will continue. The lag time between the dollar's weakness and the non-U.S. firms' increased demand for U.S. products has sometimes been estimated to be 18 months or even longer.

The U.S. balance of trade may actually deteriorate in the short run as a result of dollar depreciation because U.S. importers need more dollars to pay for the imports they contracted to purchase. The U.S. balance of trade only improves when U.S. and non-U.S. importers respond to the change in purchasing power that is caused by the weaker dollar. This pattern is called the **J-curve effect,** and it is illustrated in Exhibit 2.6. The further decline in the trade balance before a reversal creates a trend that can look like the letter J.

Exhibit 2.6 J-Curve Effect

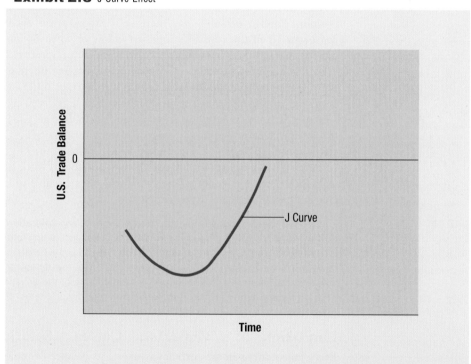

Intracompany Trade. A fourth reason why a weak currency will not always improve a country's balance of trade is that importers and exporters that are under the same ownership have unique relationships. Many firms purchase products that are produced by their subsidiaries in what is referred to as **intracompany trade.** This type of trade makes up more than 50 percent of all international trade. The trade between the two parties will normally continue regardless of exchange rate movements. Thus, the impact of exchange rate movements on intracompany trade patterns is limited.

INTERNATIONAL CAPITAL FLOWS

One of the most important types of capital flows is direct foreign investment. Firms commonly attempt to engage in direct foreign investment so that they can reach additional consumers or can rely on low-cost labor. Exhibit 2.7 identifies the countries that heavily engage in direct foreign investment. MNCs based in the United States engage in DFI more than any other country. MNCs in the United Kingdom, France, and Germany also frequently engage in DFI. Notice that European countries in aggregate account for more than half of the total DFI in other countries. This is not surprising since the MNCs there commonly pursue DFI among other European countries.

The countries in Exhibit 2.7 that are most heavily involved in pursuing DFI also attract much DFI. In particular, the United States attracts about one-sixth of all DFI, which is more than any other country. European countries in aggregate attract more than half of all DFI, more than three times the DFI in the United States.

Exhibit 2.7 Distribution of Global DFI across Regions in 2007–2008

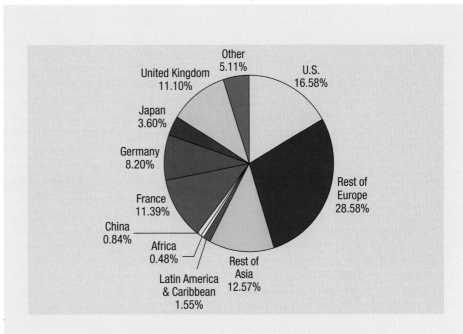

Source: The World Factbook, *Central Intelligence Agency, 2009.*

Distribution of DFI by U.S. Firms

Many U.S.-based MNCs have recently increased their DFI in foreign countries. For example, ExxonMobil, IBM, and Hewlett-Packard have at least 50 percent of their assets in foreign countries. The United Kingdom and Canada are the biggest targets. Europe as a whole receives more than 50 percent of all DFI by U.S. firms. Another 30 percent of DFI is focused on Latin America and Canada, while about 15 percent is concentrated in the Asia and Pacific region. The DFI by U.S. firms in Latin American and Asian countries has increased substantially as these countries have opened their markets to U.S. firms.

Distribution of DFI in the United States

Just as U.S. firms have used DFI to enter markets outside the United States, non-U.S. firms have penetrated the U.S. market. Much of the DFI in the United States comes from the United Kingdom, Japan, the Netherlands, Germany, and Canada. Seagram, Food Lion, and some other foreign-owned MNCs generate more than half of their revenue from the United States. Many well-known firms that operate in the United States are owned by foreign companies, including Shell Oil (Netherlands), Citgo Petroleum (Venezuela), Canon (Japan), and Fireman's Fund (Germany). Many other firms operating in the United States are partially or wholly owned by foreign companies, including MCI Communications (United Kingdom) and Energy East (Spain). While U.S.-based MNCs consider expanding in other countries, they must also compete with foreign firms in the United States.

Factors Affecting DFI

Capital flows resulting from DFI change whenever conditions in a country change the desire of firms to conduct business operations there. Some of the more common factors that could affect a country's appeal for DFI are identified here.

Changes in Restrictions. During the 1990s, many countries lowered their restrictions on DFI, thereby opening the way to more DFI in those countries. Many U.S.-based MNCs, including Bausch & Lomb, Colgate-Palmolive, and General Electric, have been penetrating less developed countries such as Argentina, Chile, Mexico, India, China, and Hungary. New opportunities in these countries have arisen from the removal of government barriers.

WEB

www.privatization.org
Information about privatizations around the world, commentaries, and related publications.

Privatization. Several national governments have recently engaged in **privatization,** or the selling of some of their operations to corporations and other investors. Privatization is popular in Brazil and Mexico, in Eastern European countries such as Poland and Hungary, and in such Caribbean territories as the Virgin Islands. It allows for greater international business as foreign firms can acquire operations sold by national governments.

Privatization was used in Chile to prevent a few investors from controlling all the shares and in France to prevent a possible reversion to a more nationalized economy. In the United Kingdom, privatization was promoted to spread stock ownership across investors, which allowed more people to have a direct stake in the success of British industry.

The primary reason that the market value of a firm may increase in response to privatization is the anticipated improvement in managerial efficiency. Managers in a privately owned firm can focus on the goal of maximizing shareholder wealth, whereas in a state-owned business, the state must consider the economic and social ramifications of any business decision. Also, managers of a privately owned enterprise are more motivated to ensure profitability because their careers may depend on it. For these reasons, privatized firms will search for local and global opportunities that could enhance their value. The trend toward privatization will undoubtedly create a more competitive global marketplace.

Potential Economic Growth. Countries that have greater potential for economic growth are more likely to attract DFI because firms recognize that they may be able to capitalize on that growth by establishing more business there.

Tax Rates. Countries that impose relatively low tax rates on corporate earnings are more likely to attract DFI. When assessing the feasibility of DFI, firms estimate the after-tax cash flows that they expect to earn.

Exchange Rates. Firms typically prefer to pursue DFI in countries where the local currency is expected to strengthen against their own. Under these conditions, they can invest funds to establish their operations in a country while that country's currency is relatively cheap (weak). Then, earnings from the new operations can periodically be converted back to the firm's currency at a more favorable exchange rate.

Factors Affecting International Portfolio Investment

The desire by individual or institutional investors to direct international portfolio investment to a specific country is influenced by the following factors.

Tax Rates on Interest or Dividends. Investors normally prefer to invest in a country where the taxes on interest or dividend income from investments are relatively low. Investors assess their potential after-tax earnings from investments in foreign securities.

Interest Rates. Portfolio investment can also be affected by interest rates. Money tends to flow to countries with high interest rates, as long as the local currencies are not expected to weaken.

Exchange Rates. When investors invest in a security in a foreign country, their return is affected by (1) the change in the value of the security and (2) the change in the value of the currency in which the security is denominated. If a country's home currency is expected to strengthen, foreign investors may be willing to invest in the country's securities to benefit from the currency movement. Conversely, if a country's home currency is expected to weaken, foreign investors may decide to purchase securities in other countries.

WEB

www.worldbank.org
Information on capital flows and international transactions.

Impact of International Capital Flows

The United States relies heavily on foreign capital in many ways. First, there is foreign investment in the United States to build manufacturing plants, offices, and other buildings. Second, foreign investors purchase U.S. debt securities issued by U.S. firms and therefore serve as creditors to these firms. Third, foreign investors purchase Treasury debt securities and therefore serve as creditors to the U.S. government.

Foreign investors are especially attracted to the U.S. financial markets when the interest rate in their home country is substantially lower than that in the United States. For example, Japan's annual interest rate has been close to 1 percent for several years because the supply of funds in its credit market has been very large. At the same time, Japan's economy has been stagnant, so the demand for funds to support business growth has been limited. Given the low interest rates in Japan, many Japanese investors invested their funds in the United States to earn a higher interest rate.

The impact of international capital flows on the U.S. economy is shown in Exhibit 2.8. At a given point in time, the long-term interest rate in the United States is determined by the interaction between the supply of funds available in U.S. credit markets and the amount of funds demanded there. The supply curve S_1 in the left graph reflects the supply of funds from domestic sources. If the United States relied solely on domestic sources for its supply,

Exhibit 2.8 Impact of the International Flow of Funds on U.S. Interest Rates and Business Investment in the United States

S_1 includes only domestic funds
S_2 includes domestic and foreign funds
 supplied to the United States

Amount of Business Investment
in the United States

its equilibrium interest rate would be i_1 and the level of business investment in the United States (shown in the right graph) would be BI_1. But since the supply curve also includes the supply of funds from foreign sources (as shown in S_2), the equilibrium interest rate is i_2. Because of the large amount of international capital flows that are provided to the U.S. credit markets, interest rates in the United States are lower than they would be otherwise. This allows for a lower cost of borrowing and therefore a lower cost of using capital. Consequently, the equilibrium level of business investment is BI_2. Because of the lower interest rate, there are more business opportunities that deserve to be funded.

Consider the long-term rate shown here as the cost of borrowing by the most creditworthy firms. Other firms would have to pay a premium above that rate. Without the international capital flows, there would be less funding available in the United States across all risk levels, and the cost of funding would be higher regardless of the firm's risk level. This would reduce the amount of feasible business opportunities in the United States.

U.S. Reliance on Foreign Funds.
If Japan and China stopped investing in U.S. debt securities, the U.S. interest rates would possibly rise, and investors from other countries would be attracted to the relatively high U.S. interest rate. Thus, the United States would still be able to obtain funding for its debt, but its interest rates (cost of borrowing) may be higher.

In general, access to international funding has allowed more growth in the U.S. economy over time, but it also makes the United States more reliant on foreign investors for funding. The United States should be able to rely on substantial foreign funding in the future as long as the U.S. government and firms are still perceived to be creditworthy. If that trust were ever weakened, the U.S. government and firms would only be able to obtain foreign funding if they paid a higher interest rate to compensate for the risk (a risk premium).

AGENCIES THAT FACILITATE INTERNATIONAL FLOWS

A variety of agencies have been established to facilitate international trade and financial transactions. These agencies often represent a group of nations. A description of some of the more important agencies follows.

International Monetary Fund

The United Nations Monetary and Financial Conference held in Bretton Woods, New Hampshire, in July 1944 was called to develop a structured international monetary system. As a result of this conference, the **International Monetary Fund (IMF)** was formed. The major objectives of the IMF, as set by its charter, are to (1) promote cooperation among countries on international monetary issues, (2) promote stability in exchange rates, (3) provide temporary funds to member countries attempting to correct imbalances of international payments, (4) promote free mobility of capital funds across countries, and (5) promote free trade. It is clear from these objectives that the IMF's goals encourage increased internationalization of business.

The IMF is overseen by a Board of Governors, composed of finance officers (such as the head of the central bank) from each of the 185 member countries. It also has an executive board composed of 24 executive directors representing the member countries. This board is based in Washington, D.C., and meets at least three times a week to discuss ongoing issues.

One of the key duties of the IMF is its **compensatory financing facility (CFF),** which attempts to reduce the impact of export instability on country economies. Although it is available to all IMF members, this facility is used mainly by developing countries. A country experiencing financial problems due to reduced export earnings must demonstrate that the reduction is temporary and beyond its control. In addition, it must be willing to work with the IMF in resolving the problem.

Each member country of the IMF is assigned a quota based on a variety of factors reflecting that country's economic status. Members are required to pay this assigned quota. The amount of funds that each member can borrow from the IMF depends on its particular quota.

The financing by the IMF is measured in **special drawing rights (SDRs).** The SDR is not a currency but simply a unit of account. It is an international reserve asset created by the IMF and allocated to member countries to supplement currency reserves. The SDR's value fluctuates in accordance with the value of major currencies.

The IMF played an active role in attempting to reduce the adverse effects of the Asian crisis. In 1997 and 1998, it provided funding to various Asian countries in exchange for promises from the respective governments to take specific actions intended to improve economic conditions.

Funding Dilemma of the IMF. The IMF typically specifies economic reforms that a country must satisfy to receive IMF funding. In this way, the IMF attempts to ensure that the country uses the funds properly. However, some countries want funding without adhering to the economic reforms required by the IMF.

For example, the IMF may require that a government reduce its budget deficit as a condition for receiving funding. Some governments have failed to implement the reforms required by the IMF.

IMF Funding during the Credit Crisis. In 2008, the IMF used $100 billion to provide short-term loans for temporary funding for developing countries that were devastated by the credit crisis. These funds represented 50 percent of the IMF's total resources. The IMF organized a $25 billion package of loans for Hungary and a $16 billion loan for Ukraine. It also provided funding to some other Eastern European countries and to Brazil, Mexico, and South Korea. The governments of Eastern Europe had borrowed from European banks, and had they defaulted on their loans, more problems might have been created for those banks that had provided loans.

World Bank

The **International Bank for Reconstruction and Development (IBRD),** also referred to as the **World Bank,** was established in 1944. Its primary objective is to make loans to countries to enhance economic development. For example, the World Bank recently extended a loan to Mexico for about $4 billion over a 10-year period for environmental projects to facilitate industrial development near the U.S. border. Its main source of funds is the sale of bonds and other debt instruments to private investors and governments. The World Bank has a profit-oriented philosophy. Therefore, its loans are not subsidized but are extended at market rates to governments (and their agencies) that are likely to repay them.

A key aspect of the World Bank's mission is the **Structural Adjustment Loan (SAL),** established in 1980. The SALs are intended to enhance a country's long-term economic growth. For example, SALs have been provided to Turkey and to some less developed countries that are attempting to improve their balance of trade.

Because the World Bank provides only a small portion of the financing needed by developing countries, it attempts to spread its funds by entering into **cofinancing agreements.** Cofinancing is performed in the following ways:

- *Official aid agencies.* Development agencies may join the World Bank in financing development projects in low-income countries.
- *Export credit agencies.* The World Bank cofinances some capital-intensive projects that are also financed through export credit agencies.
- *Commercial banks.* The World Bank has joined with commercial banks to provide financing for private-sector development. In recent years, more than 350 banks from all over the world have participated in cofinancing, including Bank of America, J.P. Morgan Chase, and Citigroup.

The World Bank recently established the **Multilateral Investment Guarantee Agency (MIGA),** which offers various forms of political risk insurance. This is an additional means (along with its SALs) by which the World Bank can encourage the development of international trade and investment.

The World Bank is one of the largest borrowers in the world; its borrowings have amounted to the equivalent of $70 billion. Its loans are well diversified among numerous currencies and countries, and it has received the highest credit rating (AAA) possible.

World Trade Organization

The **World Trade Organization (WTO)** was created as a result of the Uruguay Round of trade negotiations that led to the GATT accord in 1993. This organization was established to provide a forum for multilateral trade negotiations and to settle trade disputes related to the GATT accord. It began its operations in 1995 with 81 member countries, and more countries have joined since then. Member countries are given voting rights that are used to make judgments about trade disputes and other issues.

International Financial Corporation

In 1956 the **International Financial Corporation (IFC)** was established to promote private enterprise within countries. Composed of a number of member nations, the IFC works to promote economic development through the private rather than the government sector. It not only provides loans to corporations but also purchases stock, thereby becoming part owner in some cases rather than just a creditor. The IFC typically provides 10 to 15 percent of the necessary funds in the private enterprise projects in which it invests, and the remainder of the project must be financed through other sources. Thus, the IFC acts as a catalyst, as opposed to a sole supporter, for private enterprise development projects. It traditionally has obtained financing from the World Bank but can borrow in the international financial markets.

International Development Association

The **International Development Association (IDA)** was created in 1960 with country development objectives somewhat similar to those of the World Bank. Its loan policy is more appropriate for less prosperous nations, however. The IDA extends loans at low interest rates to poor nations that cannot qualify for loans from the World Bank.

Bank for International Settlements

WEB

www.bis.org
Information on the role of the BIS and the various activities in which it is involved.

The **Bank for International Settlements (BIS)** attempts to facilitate cooperation among countries with regard to international transactions. It also provides assistance to countries experiencing a financial crisis. The BIS is sometimes referred to as the "central banks' central bank" or the "lender of last resort." It played an important role in supporting some of the less developed countries during the international debt crisis in the early and mid-1980s. It commonly provides financing for central banks in Latin American and Eastern European countries.

OECD

WEB

www.oecd.org
Summarizes the role and activities of the OECD.

The Organization for Economic Cooperation and Development (OECD) facilitates governance in governments and corporations of countries with market economics. It has 30 member countries and has relationships with numerous countries. The OECD promotes international country relationships that lead to globalization.

Regional Development Agencies

Several other agencies have more regional (as opposed to global) objectives relating to economic development. These include, for example, the Inter-American Development Bank (focusing on the needs of Latin America), the Asian Development Bank (established to enhance social and economic development in Asia), and the African Development Bank (focusing on development in African countries).

In 1990, the European Bank for Reconstruction and Development was created to help the Eastern European countries adjust from communism to capitalism. Twelve Western European countries hold a 51 percent interest, while Eastern European countries hold a 13.5 percent interest. The United States is the biggest shareholder, with a 10 percent interest. There are 40 member countries in aggregate.

How Trade Affects an MNC's Value

An MNC's value can be affected by international trade in several ways. The cash flows (and therefore the value) of an MNC's subsidiaries that export to a specific country are typically expected to increase in response to a higher inflation rate (causing local substitutes to be more expensive) or a higher national income (which increases the level of spending) in that country. The expected cash flows of the MNC's subsidiaries that export or import may increase as a result of country trade agreements that reduce tariffs or other trade barriers.

Cash flows to a U.S.-based MNC that occur in the form of payments for exports manufactured in the United States are expected to increase as a result of a weaker dollar because the demand for its dollar-denominated exports should increase. However, cash flows of

U.S.-based importers may be reduced by a weaker dollar because it will take more dollars (increased cash outflows) to purchase the imports. A stronger dollar will have the opposite effects on cash flows of U.S.-based MNCs involved in international trade.

SUMMARY

- The key components of the balance of payments are the current account and the capital account. The current account is a broad measure of the country's international trade balance. The capital account is a measure of the country's long-term and short-term capital investments, including direct foreign investment and investment in securities (portfolio investment).

- A country's international trade flows are affected by inflation, national income, government restrictions, and exchange rates. High inflation, a high national income, low or no restrictions on imports, and a strong local currency tend to result in a strong de-

mand for imports and a current account deficit. Although some countries attempt to correct current account deficits by reducing the value of their currencies, this strategy is not always successful.

- A country's international capital flows are affected by any factors that influence direct foreign investment or portfolio investment. Direct foreign investment tends to occur in those countries that have no restrictions and much potential for economic growth. Portfolio investment tends to occur in those countries where taxes are not excessive, where interest rates are high, and where the local currencies are not expected to weaken.

POINT COUNTER-POINT

Should Trade Restrictions Be Used to Influence Human Rights Issues?

Point Yes. Some countries do not protect human rights in the same manner as the United States. At times, the United States should threaten to restrict U.S. imports from or investment in a particular country if it does not correct human rights violations. The United States should use its large international trade and investment as leverage to ensure that human rights violations do not occur. Other countries with a history of human rights violations are more likely to honor human rights if their economic conditions are threatened.

Counter-Point No. International trade and human rights are two separate issues. International trade should not be used as the weapon to enforce human rights. Firms engaged in international trade should not be penalized by

the human rights violations of a government. If the United States imposes trade restrictions to enforce human rights, the country will retaliate. Thus, the U.S. firms that export to that foreign country will be adversely affected. By imposing trade sanctions, the U.S. government is indirectly penalizing the MNCs that are attempting to conduct business in specific foreign countries. Trade sanctions cannot solve every difference in beliefs or morals between the more developed countries and the developing countries. By restricting trade, the United States will slow down the economic progress of developing countries.

Who Is Correct? Use the Internet to learn more about this issue. Which argument do you support? Offer your own opinion on this issue.

SELF-TEST

Answers are provided in Appendix A at the back of the text.

1. Briefly explain how changes in various economic factors affect the U.S. current account balance.

2. Explain why U.S. tariffs will not necessarily reduce a U.S. balance-of-trade deficit.

3. Explain why a global recession like that in 2008–2009 might encourage some governments to impose more trade restrictions.

QUESTIONS AND APPLICATIONS

1. Balance of Payments.

a. Of what is the current account generally composed?

b. Of what is the capital account generally composed?

2. Inflation Effect on Trade.

a. How would a relatively high home inflation rate affect the home country's current account, other things being equal?

b. Is a negative current account harmful to a country? Discuss.

3. Government Restrictions. How can government restrictions affect international payments among countries?

4. IMF.

a. What are some of the major objectives of the IMF?

b. How is the IMF involved in international trade?

5. Exchange Rate Effect on Trade Balance. Would the U.S. balance-of-trade deficit be larger or smaller if the dollar depreciates against all currencies, versus depreciating against some currencies but appreciating against others? Explain.

6. Demand for Exports. A relatively small U.S. balance-of-trade deficit is commonly attributed to a strong demand for U.S. exports. What do you think is the underlying reason for the strong demand for U.S. exports?

7. Change in International Trade Volume. Why do you think international trade volume has increased over time? In general, how are inefficient firms affected by the reduction in trade restrictions among countries and the continuous increase in international trade?

8. Effects of the Euro. Explain how the existence of the euro may affect U.S. international trade.

9. Currency Effects. When South Korea's export growth stalled, some South Korean firms suggested that South Korea's primary export problem was the weakness in the Japanese yen. How would you interpret this statement?

10. Effects of Tariffs. Assume a simple world in which the United States exports soft drinks and beer to France and imports wine from France. If the United States imposes large tariffs on the French wine, explain the likely impact on the values of the U.S. beverage firms, U.S. wine producers, the French beverage firms, and the French wine producers.

Advanced Questions

11. Free Trade. There has been considerable momentum to reduce or remove trade barriers in an effort to achieve "free trade." Yet, one disgruntled executive of an exporting firm stated, "Free trade is not conceivable; we are always at the mercy of the exchange rate. Any country can use this mechanism to impose trade barriers." What does this statement mean?

12. International Investments. U.S.-based MNCs commonly invest in foreign securities.

a. Assume that the dollar is presently weak and is expected to strengthen over time. How will these expectations affect the tendency of U.S. investors to invest in foreign securities?

b. Explain how low U.S. interest rates can affect the tendency of U.S.-based MNCs to invest abroad.

c. In general terms, what is the attraction of foreign investments to U.S. investors?

13. Exchange Rate Effects on Trade.

a. Explain why a stronger dollar could enlarge the U.S. balance-of-trade deficit. Explain why a weaker dollar could affect the U.S. balance-of-trade deficit.

b. It is sometimes suggested that a floating exchange rate will adjust to reduce or eliminate any current account deficit. Explain why this adjustment would occur.

c. Why does the exchange rate not always adjust to a current account deficit?

Discussion in the Boardroom

This exercise can be found in Appendix E at the back of this textbook.

Running Your Own MNC

This exercise can be found on the *International Financial Management* text companion website located at www.cengage.com/finance/madura.

BLADES, INC. CASE

Exposure to International Flow of Funds

Ben Holt, chief financial officer (CFO) of Blades, Inc., has decided to counteract the decreasing demand for Speedos roller blades by exporting this product to Thailand. Furthermore, due to the low cost of rubber and plastic in Southeast Asia, Holt has decided to import some of the components needed to manufacture Speedos from Thailand. Holt feels that importing rubber and plastic components from Thailand will provide Blades with a cost advantage (the components imported from Thailand are about 20 percent cheaper than similar components in the United States). Currently, approximately $20 million, or 10 percent, of Blades' sales are contributed by its sales in Thailand. Only about 4 percent of Blades' cost of goods sold is attributable to rubber and plastic imported from Thailand.

Blades faces little competition in Thailand from other U.S. roller blades manufacturers. Those competitors that export roller blades to Thailand invoice their exports in U.S. dollars. Currently, Blades follows a policy of invoicing in Thai baht (Thailand's currency). Ben Holt felt that this strategy would give Blades a competitive advantage since Thai importers can plan more easily when they do not have to worry about paying differing amounts due to currency fluctuations. Furthermore, Blades' primary customer in Thailand (a retail store) has committed itself to purchasing a certain amount of Speedos annually if Blades will invoice in baht for a period of 3 years. Blades' purchases of components from Thai exporters are currently invoiced in Thai baht.

Ben Holt is rather content with current arrangements and believes the lack of competitors in Thailand, the quality of Blades' products, and its approach to pricing will ensure Blades' position in the Thai roller blade market in the future. Holt also feels that Thai importers will prefer Blades over its competitors because Blades invoices in Thai baht.

You, Blades' financial analyst, have doubts as to Blades' "guaranteed" future success. Although you believe Blades' strategy for its Thai sales and imports is sound, you are concerned about current expectations for the Thai economy. Current forecasts indicate a high level of anticipated inflation, a decreasing level of national income, and a continued depreciation of the Thai baht. In your opinion, all of these future developments could affect Blades financially given the company's current arrangements with its suppliers and with the Thai importers. Both Thai consumers and firms might adjust their spending habits should certain developments occur.

In the past, you have had difficulty convincing Ben Holt that problems could arise in Thailand. Consequently, you have developed a list of questions for yourself, which you plan to present to the company's CFO after you have answered them. Your questions are listed here:

1. How could a higher level of inflation in Thailand affect Blades (assume U.S. inflation remains constant)?
2. How could competition from firms in Thailand and from U.S. firms conducting business in Thailand affect Blades?
3. How could a decreasing level of national income in Thailand affect Blades?
4. How could a continued depreciation of the Thai baht affect Blades? How would it affect Blades relative to U.S. exporters invoicing their roller blades in U.S. dollars?
5. If Blades increases its business in Thailand and experiences serious financial problems, are there any international agencies that the company could approach for loans or other financial assistance?

SMALL BUSINESS DILEMMA

Identifying Factors That Will Affect the Foreign Demand at the Sports Exports Company

Recall from Chapter 1 that Jim Logan planned to pursue his dream of establishing his own business (called the Sports Exports Company) of exporting footballs to one or more foreign markets. Jim has decided to initially pursue the market in the United Kingdom because British citizens appear to have some interest in football as a possible hobby, and no other firm has capitalized on this idea in the United Kingdom. (The sporting goods shops in the United Kingdom do not sell footballs but might be willing to sell them.) Jim has contacted one sporting goods distributor that has agreed to purchase footballs on a monthly basis and distribute (sell) them to sporting goods stores throughout the United Kingdom. The distributor's demand for footballs is ultimately influenced by the demand for footballs by British citizens who shop in British sporting goods stores. The Sports Exports Company will receive British pounds when it sells the footballs to the distributor and will then convert the pounds into dollars. Jim recognizes that products (such as the footballs his firm will produce) exported from U.S. firms to foreign countries can be affected by various factors.

Identify the factors that affect the current account balance between the United States and the United Kingdom. Explain how each factor may possibly affect the British demand for the footballs that are produced by the Sports Exports Company.

INTERNET/EXCEL EXERCISES

The website address of the Bureau of Economic Analysis is www.bea.gov.

1. Use this website to assess recent trends in exporting and importing by U.S. firms. How has the balance of trade changed over the last 12 months?

2. Offer possible reasons for this change in the balance of trade.

3. Go to www.census.gov/foreign-trade/balance/ and obtain monthly balance-of-trade data for the last 24 months between the United States and the United Kingdom or a country specified by your professor. Create an electronic spreadsheet in which the first column is the month of concern, and the second column is the trade balance. (See Appendix C for help with conducting analyses with Excel.) Use a compute statement to derive the percentage change in the trade balance in the third column. Then go to www.oanda .com/convert/fxhistory. Obtain the direct exchange rate (dollars per currency unit) of the British pound (or the local currency of the foreign country you select). Obtain the direct exchange rate of the currency at the beginning of each month and insert the data in column 4. Use a compute statement to derive the percentage change in the currency value from one month to the next in column 5. Then apply regression analysis in which the percentage change in the trade balance is the dependent variable and the percentage change in the exchange rate is the independent variable. Is there a significant relationship between the two variables? Is the direction of the relationship as expected? If you think that the exchange rate movements affect the trade balance with a lag (because the transactions of importers and exporters may be booked a few months in advance), you can reconfigure your data to assess that relationship (match each monthly percentage change in the balance of trade with the exchange rate movement that occurred a few months earlier).

REFERENCES

Brealey, R. A., and E. Kaplanis, Mar 2004, The Impact of IMF Programs on Asset Values, *Journal of International Money and Finance*, pp. 253–270.

Cavallari, Lilia, Apr 2004, Optimal Monetary Rules and Internationalized Production, *International Journal of Finance & Economics*, pp. 175–186.

Champy, Jim, and Ellen M. Heffes, Jan/Feb 2008, Is Global Trade a Threat or Opportunity? *Financial Executive*, pp. 36–41.

Eichengreen, Barry, Kenneth Kletzer, and Ashoka Mody, May 2006, The IMF in a World of Private Capital Markets, *Journal of Banking & Finance*, pp. 1335–1357.

Feils, Dorothee J., and Manzur Rahman, Spring 2008, Regional Economic Integration and Foreign Direct Investment: The Case of NAFTA, *Management International Review*, pp. 147–163.

Kelkar, Vijay L., Praveen K. Chaudhry, and Marta Vanduzer-Snow, Mar 2005, Time for Change at the IMF, *Finance & Development*, pp. 46–48.

Koudal, Peter, Mar 2005, Global Manufacturers at a Crossroads, *Harvard Business Review*, pp. 20–21.

Maniam, Balasundram, Spring 2007, An Empirical Investigation of U.S. FDI in Latin America, *Journal of International Business Research*, pp. 1–15.

Miller, Norman, Apr 2005, Can Exchange Rate Variations or Trade Policy Alter the Equilibrium Current Account? *Journal of International Money and Finance*, pp. 465–480.

Mohsen, Bahmani-Oskooee, and Artatrana Ratha, Spring 2004, The J-Curve Dynamics of U.S. Bilateral Trade, *Journal of Economics and Finance*, pp. 32–39.

Rajan, Raghuram, Mar 2005, Rules versus Discretion, *Finance & Development*, pp. 56–57.

3

International Financial Markets

CHAPTER OBJECTIVES

The specific objectives of this chapter are to describe the background and corporate use of the following international financial markets:

- foreign exchange market,
- international money market,
- international credit market,
- international bond market, and
- international stock markets.

Due to growth in international business over the last 30 years, various international financial markets have been developed. Financial managers of MNCs must understand the various international financial markets that are available so that they can use those markets to facilitate their international business transactions.

FOREIGN EXCHANGE MARKET

The **foreign exchange market** allows for the exchange of one currency for another. Large commercial banks serve this market by holding inventories of each currency so that they can accommodate requests by individuals or MNCs. Individuals rely on the foreign exchange market when they travel to foreign countries. People from the United States exchange dollars for Mexican pesos when they visit Mexico, or euros when they visit Italy, or Japanese yen when they visit Japan. Some MNCs based in the United States exchange dollars for Mexican pesos when they purchase supplies in Mexico that are denominated in pesos, or euros when they purchase supplies from Italy that are denominated in euros. Other MNCs based in the United States receive Japanese yen when selling products to Japan and may wish to convert the yen to dollars.

For one currency to be exchanged for another currency, there needs to be an exchange rate that specifies the rate at which one currency can be exchanged for another. The exchange rate of the Mexican peso will determine how many dollars you need to stay in a hotel in Mexico City that charges 500 Mexican pesos per night. The exchange rate of the Mexican peso will also determine how many dollars an MNC will need to purchase supplies that are invoiced at 1 million pesos. The system for establishing exchange rates has changed over time, as described below.

History of Foreign Exchange

The system used for exchanging foreign currencies has evolved from the gold standard, to an agreement on fixed exchange rates, to a floating rate system.

Gold Standard. From 1876 to 1913, exchange rates were dictated by the gold standard. Each currency was convertible into gold at a specified rate. Thus, the exchange rate between two currencies was determined by their relative convertibility rates per ounce of gold. Each country used gold to back its currency.

When World War I began in 1914, the gold standard was suspended. Some countries reverted to the gold standard in the 1920s but abandoned it as a result of a banking panic in the United States and Europe during the Great Depression. In the 1930s, some countries attempted to peg their currency to the dollar or the British pound, but there were frequent revisions. As a result of the instability in the foreign exchange market and the severe restrictions on international transactions during this period, the volume of international trade declined.

Agreements on Fixed Exchange Rates.
In 1944, an international agreement (known as the **Bretton Woods Agreement**) called for fixed exchange rates between currencies. This agreement lasted until 1971. During this period, governments would intervene to prevent exchange rates from moving more than 1 percent above or below their initially established levels.

By 1971, the U.S. dollar appeared to be overvalued; the foreign demand for U.S. dollars was substantially less than the supply of dollars for sale (to be exchanged for other currencies). Representatives from the major nations met to discuss this dilemma. As a result of this conference, which led to the **Smithsonian Agreement,** the U.S. dollar was devalued relative to the other major currencies. The degree to which the dollar was devalued varied with each foreign currency. Not only was the dollar's value reset, but exchange rates were also allowed to fluctuate by 2.25 percent in either direction from the newly set rates. This was the first step in letting market forces (supply and demand) determine the appropriate price of a currency.

Floating Exchange Rate System.
Even after the Smithsonian Agreement, governments still had difficulty maintaining exchange rates within the stated boundaries. By March 1973, the more widely traded currencies were allowed to fluctuate in accordance with market forces, and the official boundaries were eliminated.

Foreign Exchange Transactions

The foreign exchange market should not be thought of as a specific building or location where traders exchange currencies. Companies normally exchange one currency for another through a commercial bank over a telecommunications network. It is an over-the-counter market where many transactions occur through a telecommunications network. While the largest foreign exchange trading centers are in London, New York, and Tokyo, foreign exchange transactions occur on a daily basis in all cities around the world. **Foreign exchange dealers** serve as intermediaries in the foreign exchange market by exchanging currencies desired by MNCs or individuals. Large foreign exchange dealers include CitiFX (a subsidiary of Citigroup), J.P. Morgan Chase, and Deutsche Bank (Germany). Dealers such as these have branches in most major cities, and also facilitate foreign exchange transactions with an online trading service. Other dealers such as FX Connect (a subsidiary of State Street Corporation), OANDA, and ACM rely exclusively on an online trading service to facilitate foreign exchange transactions. Customers establish an online account and can interact with the foreign exchange dealer website to transmit their foreign exchange order.

The average daily trading volume in the foreign exchange market is about $4 trillion, with the U.S. dollar involved in about 40 percent of the transactions. Currencies from emerging countries are involved in about 20 percent of the transactions. Most currency transactions between two non-U.S. countries do not involve the U.S. dollar: A Canadian MNC that purchases supplies from a Mexican MNC exchanges its Canadian dollars for Mexican pesos. A Japanese MNC that invests funds in a British bank exchanges its Japanese yen for British pounds.

Spot Market.
The most common type of foreign exchange transaction is for immediate exchange. The market where these transactions occur is known as the **spot market.**

The exchange rate at which one currency is traded for another in the spot market is known as the **spot rate.**

Spot Market Structure. Commercial transactions in the spot market are often done electronically, and the exchange rate at the time determines the amount of funds necessary for the transaction.

EXAMPLE

Indiana Co. purchases supplies priced at 100,000 euros (€) from Belgo, a Belgian supplier, on the first day of every month. Indiana instructs its bank to transfer funds from its account to Belgo's account on the first day of each month. It only has dollars in its account, whereas Belgo's account is in euros. When payment was made 1 month ago, the euro was worth $1.08, so Indiana Co. needed $108,000 to pay for the supplies (€100,000 × $1.08 = $108,000). The bank reduced Indiana's account balance by $108,000, which was exchanged at the bank for €100,000. The bank then sent the €100,000 electronically to Belgo by increasing Belgo's account balance by €100,000. Today, a new payment needs to be made. The euro is currently valued at $1.12, so the bank will reduce Indiana's account balance by $112,000 (€100,000 × $1.12 = $112,000) and exchange it for €100,000, which will be sent electronically to Belgo.

The bank not only executes the transactions but also serves as the foreign exchange dealer. Each month the bank receives dollars from Indiana Co. in exchange for the euros it provides. In addition, the bank facilitates other transactions for MNCs in which it receives euros in exchange for dollars. The bank maintains an inventory of euros, dollars, and other currencies to facilitate these foreign exchange transactions. If the transactions cause it to buy as many euros as it sells to MNCs, its inventory of euros will not change. If the bank sells more euros than it buys, however, its inventory of euros will be reduced. ●

If a bank begins to experience a shortage in a particular foreign currency, it can purchase that currency from other banks. This trading between banks occurs in what is often referred to as the **interbank market.**

Some other financial institutions such as securities firms can provide the same services described in the previous example. In addition, most major airports around the world have foreign exchange centers, where individuals can exchange currencies. In many cities, there are retail foreign exchange offices where tourists and other individuals can exchange currencies.

Use of the Dollar in the Spot Market. The U.S. dollar is commonly accepted as a medium of exchange by merchants in many countries, especially in countries such as Bolivia, Indonesia, Russia, and Vietnam where the home currency may be weak or subject to foreign exchange restrictions. Many merchants accept U.S. dollars because they can use them to purchase goods from other countries.

Spot Market Time Zones. Although foreign exchange trading is conducted only during normal business hours in a given location, these hours vary among locations due to different time zones. Thus, at any given time on a weekday, somewhere around the world a bank is open and ready to accommodate foreign exchange requests.

When the foreign exchange market opens in the United States each morning, the opening exchange rate quotations are based on the prevailing rates quoted by banks in London and other locations where the foreign exchange markets have opened earlier. Suppose the quoted spot rate of the British pound was $1.80 at the previous close of the U.S. foreign exchange market, but by the time the market opens the following day, the opening spot rate is $1.76. News occurring in the morning before the U.S. market opened could have changed the supply and demand conditions for British pounds in the London foreign exchange market, reducing the quoted price for the pound.

Several U.S. banks have established night trading desks. The largest banks initiated night trading to capitalize on foreign exchange movements at night and to accommodate corporate requests for currency trades. Even some medium-sized banks now offer night trading to accommodate corporate clients.

Spot Market Liquidity. The spot market for each currency can be described by its liquidity, which reflects the level of trading activity. The more buyers and sellers there are, the more liquid a market is. The spot markets for heavily traded currencies such as the euro, the British pound, and the Japanese yen are very liquid. Conversely, the spot markets for currencies of less developed countries are less liquid. A currency's liquidity affects the ease with which an MNC can obtain or sell that currency. If a currency is illiquid, the number of willing buyers and sellers is limited, and an MNC may be unable to quickly purchase or sell that currency at a reasonable exchange rate.

Attributes of Banks That Provide Foreign Exchange. The following characteristics of banks are important to customers in need of foreign exchange:

1. *Competitiveness of quote.* A savings of 1¢ per unit on an order of 1 million units of currency is worth $10,000.
2. *Special relationship with the bank.* The bank may offer cash management services or be willing to make a special effort to obtain even hard-to-find foreign currencies for the corporation.
3. *Speed of execution.* Banks may vary in the efficiency with which they handle an order. A corporation needing the currency will prefer a bank that conducts the transaction promptly and handles any paperwork properly.
4. *Advice about current market conditions.* Some banks may provide assessments of foreign economies and relevant activities in the international financial environment that relate to corporate customers.
5. *Forecasting advice.* Some banks may provide forecasts of the future state of foreign economies and the future value of exchange rates.

This list suggests that a corporation needing a foreign currency should not automatically choose a bank that will sell that currency at the lowest price. Most corporations that often need foreign currencies develop a close relationship with at least one major bank in case they need various foreign exchange services from a bank.

Foreign Exchange Quotations

Spot Market Interaction among Banks. At any given point in time, the exchange rate between two currencies should be similar across the various banks that provide foreign exchange services. If there is a large discrepancy, customers or other banks will purchase large amounts of a currency from whatever bank quotes a relatively low price and immediately sell it to whatever bank quotes a relatively high price. Such actions cause adjustments in the exchange rate quotations that eliminate any discrepancy.

Bid/Ask Spread of Banks. Commercial banks charge fees for conducting foreign exchange transactions. At any given point in time, a bank's **bid** (buy) quote for a foreign currency will be less than its **ask** (sell) quote. The **bid/ask spread** represents the differential between the bid and ask quotes and is intended to cover the costs involved in accommodating requests to exchange currencies. The bid/ask spread is normally expressed as a percentage of the ask quote.

EXAMPLE

To understand how a bid/ask spread could affect you, assume you have $1,000 and plan to travel from the United States to the United Kingdom. Assume further that the bank's bid rate for the British pound is $1.52 and its ask rate is $1.60. Before leaving on your trip, you go

WEB

www.everbank.com
Individuals can open an FDIC-insured CD account in a foreign currency.

WEB

www.xe.com/fx
Allows individuals to buy and sell currencies.

to this bank to exchange dollars for pounds. Your $1,000 will be converted to 625 pounds (£), as follows:

$$\frac{\text{Amount of U.S. dollars to be converted}}{\text{Price charged by bank per pound}} = \frac{\$1,000}{\$1.60} = £625$$

Now suppose that because of an emergency you cannot take the trip, and you reconvert the £625 back to U.S. dollars, just after purchasing the pounds. If the exchange rate has not changed, you will receive

$$£625 \times (\text{Bank's bid rate of \$1.52 per pound}) = \$950$$

Due to the bid/ask spread, you have $50 (5 percent) less than what you started with. Obviously, the dollar amount of the loss would be larger if you originally converted more than $1,000 into pounds. ●

Comparison of Bid/Ask Spread among Currencies.
The differential between a bid quote and an ask quote will look much smaller for currencies that have a smaller value. This differential can be standardized by measuring it as a percentage of the currency's spot rate.

Charlotte Bank quotes a bid price for yen of $.007 and an ask price of $.0074. In this case, the nominal bid/ask spread is $.0074 – $.007, or just four-hundredths of a penny. Yet, the bid/ask spread in percentage terms is actually slightly higher for the yen in this example than for the pound in the previous example. To prove this, consider a traveler who sells $1,000 for yen at the bank's ask price of $.0074. The traveler receives about ¥135,135 (computed as $1,000/$.0074). If the traveler cancels the trip and converts the yen back to dollars, then, assuming no changes in the bid/ask quotations, the bank will buy these yen back at the bank's bid price of $.007 for a total of about $946 (computed by ¥135,135 × $.007), which is $54 (or 5.4 percent) less than what the traveler started with. This spread exceeds that of the British pound (5 percent in the previous example). ●

A common way to compute the bid/ask spread in percentage terms follows:

$$\text{Bid/ask spread} = \frac{\text{Ask rate} - \text{Bid rate}}{\text{Ask rate}}$$

Using this formula, the bid/ask spreads are computed in Exhibit 3.1 for both the British pound and the Japanese yen.

Notice that these numbers coincide with those derived earlier. Such spreads are common for so-called retail transactions serving consumers. For larger so-called wholesale transactions between banks or for large corporations, the spread will be much smaller. The bid/ask spread for small retail transactions is commonly in the range of 3 to 7 percent; for wholesale transactions requested by MNCs, the spread is between .01 and .03 percent. The spread is normally larger for illiquid currencies that are less frequently traded. Commercial banks are normally exposed to more exchange rate risk when maintaining these currencies.

The bid/ask spread as defined here represents the discount in the bid rate as a percentage of the ask rate. An alternative bid/ask spread uses the bid rate as the

Exhibit 3.1 Computation of the Bid/Ask Spread

CURRENCY	BID RATE	ASK RATE	ASK RATE – BID RATE / ASK RATE	=	BID/ASK PERCENTAGE SPREAD
British pound	$1.52	$1.60	$\frac{\$1.60 - \$1.52}{\$1.60}$	=	.05 *or* 5%
Japanese yen	$.0070	$.0074	$\frac{\$.0074 - \$.007}{\$.0074}$	=	.054 *or* 5.4%

denominator instead of the ask rate and measures the percentage markup of the ask rate above the bid rate. The spread is slightly higher when using this formula because the bid rate used in the denominator is always less than the ask rate.

In the following discussion and in examples throughout much of the text, the bid/ask spread will be ignored. That is, only one price will be shown for a given currency to allow you to concentrate on understanding other relevant concepts. These examples depart slightly from reality because the bid and ask prices are, in a sense, assumed to be equal. Although the ask price will always exceed the bid price by a small amount in reality, the implications from examples should nevertheless hold, even though the bid/ask spreads are not accounted for. In particular examples where the bid/ask spread can contribute significantly to the concept, it will be accounted for.

To conserve space, some quotations show the entire bid price followed by a slash and then only the last two or three digits of the ask price.

EXAMPLE   Assume that the prevailing quote for wholesale transactions by a commercial bank for the euro is $1.0876/78. This means that the commercial bank is willing to pay $1.0876 per euro. Alternatively, it is willing to sell euros for $1.0878. The bid/ask spread in this example is:

$$\text{Bid/ask spread} = \frac{\$1.0878 - \$1.0876}{\$1.0878}$$

$$= \text{about } .000184 \text{ or } .0184\% \qquad \bullet$$

Factors That Affect the Spread. The spread on currency quotations is influenced by the following factors:

$$\text{Spread} = f(\underset{+}{\text{Order costs}}, \underset{+}{\text{Inventory costs}}, \underset{-}{\text{Competition}}, \underset{-}{\text{Volume}}, \underset{+}{\text{Currency risk}})$$

- *Order costs.* Order costs are the costs of processing orders, including clearing costs and the costs of recording transactions.
- *Inventory costs.* Inventory costs are the costs of maintaining an inventory of a particular currency. Holding an inventory involves an opportunity cost because the funds could have been used for some other purpose. If interest rates are relatively high, the opportunity cost of holding an inventory should be relatively high. The higher the inventory costs, the larger the spread that will be established to cover these costs.
- *Competition.* The more intense the competition, the smaller the spread quoted by intermediaries. Competition is more intense for the more widely traded currencies because there is more business in those currencies.
- *Volume.* More liquid currencies are less likely to experience a sudden change in price. Currencies that have a large trading volume are more liquid because there are numerous buyers and sellers at any given time. This means that the market has sufficient depth that a few large transactions are unlikely to cause the currency's price to change abruptly.
- *Currency risk.* Some currencies exhibit more volatility than others because of economic or political conditions that cause the demand for and supply of the currency to change abruptly. For example, currencies in countries that have frequent political crises are subject to abrupt price movements. Intermediaries that are willing to buy or sell these currencies could incur large losses due to an abrupt change in the values of these currencies.

EXAMPLE   There are a limited number of banks or other financial institutions that serve as foreign exchange dealers for Russian rubles. The volume of exchange of dollars for rubles is very limited, which implies an illiquid market. Thus, some dealers may not be able to accommodate requests of large exchange transactions for rubles, and the ruble's market value could change abruptly in response to some larger transactions. The ruble's value has been volatile in recent years, which means that dealers that have an inventory of rubles to serve foreign exchange transactions are exposed to the possibility of a pronounced depreciation of the ruble. Given these conditions, dealers are likely to quote a relatively large bid/ask spread for the Russian ruble. ●

Interpreting Foreign Exchange Quotations

Exchange rate quotations for widely traded currencies are published in the *Wall Street Journal* and in business sections of many newspapers on a daily basis. With some exceptions, each country has its own currency. In 1999, several European countries, including Germany, France, and Italy, adopted the euro as their new currency. Currently, the Eurozone encompasses 16 European countries.

Direct versus Indirect Quotations.

The quotations of exchange rates for currencies normally reflect the ask prices for large transactions. Since exchange rates change throughout the day, the exchange rates quoted in a newspaper reflect only one specific point in time during the day. Quotations that represent the value of a foreign currency in dollars (number of dollars per currency) are referred to as **direct quotations.** Conversely, quotations that represent the number of units of a foreign currency per dollar are referred to as indirect quotations. The **indirect quotation** is the reciprocal of the corresponding direct quotation.

EXAMPLE   The spot rate of the euro is quoted this morning at $1.031. This is a direct quotation, as it represents the value of the foreign currency in dollars. The indirect quotation of the euro is the reciprocal of the direct quotation:

$$\text{Indirect quotation} = 1/\text{Direct quotation}$$
$$= 1/\$1.031$$
$$= .97, \text{ which means } .97 \text{ euros} = \$1$$

If you initially received the indirect quotation, you can take the reciprocal of it to obtain the direct quote. Since the indirect quotation for the euro is $.97, the direct quotation is:

$$\text{Direct quotation} = 1/\text{Indirect quotation}$$
$$= 1/.97$$
$$= \$1.031 \qquad\qquad ●$$

A comparison of direct and indirect exchange rates for two points in time appears in Exhibit 3.2. Columns 2 and 3 provide quotes at the beginning of the semester, while

Exhibit 3.2 Direct and Indirect Exchange Rate Quotations

(1) CURRENCY	(2) DIRECT QUOTATION AS OF BEGINNING OF SEMESTER	(3) INDIRECT QUOTATION (NUMBER OF UNITS PER DOLLAR) AS OF BEGINNING OF SEMESTER	(4) DIRECT QUOTATION AS OF END OF SEMESTER	(5) INDIRECT QUOTATION (NUMBER OF UNITS PER DOLLAR) AS OF END OF SEMESTER
Canadian dollar	$.66	1.51	$.70	1.43
Euro	$1.031	.97	$1.064	.94
Japanese yen	$.009	111.11	$.0097	103.09
Mexican peso	$.12	8.33	$.11	9.09
Swiss franc	$.62	1.61	$.67	1.49
U.K. pound	$1.50	.67	$1.60	.62

columns 4 and 5 provide quotes at the end of the semester. For each currency, the indirect quotes at the beginning and end of the semester (columns 3 and 5) are the reciprocals of the direct quotes at the beginning and end of the semester (columns 2 and 4).

Exhibit 3.2 demonstrates that for any currency, the indirect exchange rate at a given point in time is the inverse of the direct exchange rate at that point in time. Exhibit 3.2 also shows the relationship between the movements in the direct exchange rate and movements in the indirect exchange rate of a particular currency.

EXAMPLE

Based on Exhibit 3.2, the Canadian dollar's direct quotation changed from $.66 to $.70 over the semester. This change reflects an appreciation of the Canadian dollar, as the currency's value increased over the semester. Notice that the Canadian dollar's indirect quotation decreased from 1.51 to 1.43 over the semester. This means that it takes fewer Canadian dollars to obtain a U.S. dollar at the end of the semester than it took at the beginning. This change also confirms that the Canadian dollar's value has strengthened, but it can be confusing because the decline in the indirect quote over time reflects an appreciation of the currency.

Notice that the Mexican peso's direct quotation changed from $.12 to $.11 over the semester. This reflects a depreciation of the peso. The indirect quotation increased over the semester, which means that it takes more pesos at the end of the semester to obtain a U.S. dollar than it took at the beginning. This change also confirms that the peso has depreciated over the semester. ●

Interpreting Changes in Exchange Rates. Exhibit 3.3 illustrates the time series relationship between a direct and indirect exchange rate, by showing a trend of the euro's value against the dollar. The direct and indirect exchange rates of the euro are shown over time. Notice that when the euro is appreciating against the dollar (based on an upward movement of the direct exchange rate of the euro), the indirect exchange rate of the euro is declining. That is, when the value of the euro rises, a smaller amount of that currency is needed to obtain a dollar.

When the euro is depreciating (based on a downward movement of the direct exchange rate) against the dollar, the indirect exchange rate is rising. That is, when the value of the euro declines, a larger amount of that currency is needed to obtain a dollar.

If you are doing an extensive analysis of exchange rates, convert all exchange rates into direct quotations. In this way, you can more easily compare currencies and are less likely to make a mistake in determining whether a currency is appreciating or depreciating over a particular period.

Discussions of exchange rate movements can be confusing if some comments refer to direct quotations while others refer to indirect quotations. For consistency, this text uses direct quotations unless an example can be clarified by the use of indirect quotations.

Source of Exchange Rate Quotations. Updated currency quotations are provided for several major currencies on Yahoo's website (http://finance.yahoo.com/currency). You can select any currency for which you want an exchange rate quotation. You can also view a trend of the historical exchange rate movements for any currency. Trends are available for various periods, such as 1 day, 5 days, 1 month, 3 months, 6 months, 1 year, and 5 years. As you review a trend of exchange rates, be aware of whether the exchange rate quotation is direct (value in dollars) or indirect (number of currency per dollar) so that you can properly interpret the trend. The trend not only indicates the direction of the exchange rate, but also the degree to which the currency has changed over time. The trend also indicates the range of exchange rates within a particular period. When a currency's exchange rate is very sensitive to economic conditions, it moves within a wider range.

Exhibit 3.3 Relationship between the Direct and Indirect Exchange Rates over Time

Exchange rate quotations are also provided by many other online sources, including www.federalreserve.gov/releases/ and at www.oanda.com. Some sources provide direct exchange rate quotations for specific currencies and indirect exchange rates for others, so be careful to check which type of quotation is used for any particular currency.

Cross Exchange Rates. Most tables of exchange rate quotations express currencies relative to the dollar, but in some instances, a firm will be concerned about the exchange rate between two nondollar currencies. For example, if a Canadian firm needs Mexican pesos to buy Mexican goods, it wants to know the Mexican peso value relative to the Canadian dollar. The type of rate desired here is known as a **cross exchange rate**, because it reflects the amount of one foreign currency per unit of another foreign currency. Cross exchange rates can be easily determined with the use of foreign exchange quotations. The value of any nondollar currency in terms of another is its value in dollars divided by the other currency's value in dollars.

EXAMPLE

If the peso is worth $.07, and the Canadian dollar is worth $.70, the value of the peso in Canadian dollars (C$) is calculated as follows:

$$\text{Value of peso in C\$} = \frac{\text{Value of peso in \$}}{\text{Value of C\$ in \$}} = \frac{\$.07}{\$.70} = \text{C\$.10}$$

Thus, a Mexican peso is worth C$.10. The exchange rate can also be expressed as the number of pesos equal to one Canadian dollar. This figure can be computed by taking the reciprocal: .70/.07 = 10.0, which indicates that a Canadian dollar is worth 10.0 pesos according to the information provided. ●

Source of Cross Exchange Rate Quotations. Cross exchange rates are provided for several major currencies on Yahoo's website (http://finance.yahoo.com/currency-investing). You can also view the recent trend of a particular cross exchange rate for periods such as 1 day, 5 days, 1 month, 3 months, or 1 year. The trend indicates the volatility of a cross exchange rate over a particular period. Two non-dollar currencies may exhibit high volatility against the U.S. dollar, but if their movements are very highly correlated against the dollar, the cross exchange rate between these currencies would be relatively stable over time.

Forward, Futures, and Options Markets

Forward Contracts. In some cases, an MNC may prefer to lock in an exchange rate at which it can obtain a currency for a future point in time. A **forward contract** is an agreement between a foreign exchange dealer and an MNC that specifies the currencies to be exchanged, the exchange rate, and the date at which the transaction will occur. The **forward rate** is the exchange rate specified within the forward contract at which the currencies will be exchanged. MNCs commonly request forward contracts to hedge future payments that they expect to make or receive in a foreign currency. In this way, they do not have to worry about fluctuations in the spot rate until the time of their future payments.

EXAMPLE

Memphis Co. has ordered supplies from European countries that are denominated in euros. It expects the euro to increase in value over time and therefore desires to hedge its payables in euros. Memphis buys forward contracts on euros to lock in the price that it will pay for euros at a future point in time. Meanwhile, it will receive Mexican pesos in the future and wants to hedge these receivables. Memphis sells forward contracts on pesos to lock in the dollars that it will receive when it sells the pesos at a specified point in the future. ●

The **forward market** represents the market in which the forward contracts are traded. It is an over-the-counter market, and its main participants are the foreign exchange dealers and the MNCs that wish to obtain a forward contract. For example, at any given point in time, Google, Inc., normally has forward contracts in place that are valued at more than $1 billion.

The liquidity of the forward market varies among currencies. The forward market for euros is very liquid because many MNCs take forward positions to hedge their future payments in euros. In contrast, the forward markets for Latin American and Eastern European currencies are less liquid because there is less international trade with those countries and therefore MNCs take fewer forward positions. For some currencies, there is no forward market.

Some quotations of exchange rates include forward rates for the most widely traded currencies. Other forward rates are not quoted in business newspapers but are quoted by the banks that offer forward contracts in various currencies.

Currency Futures Contracts. Futures contracts are somewhat similar to forward contracts except that they are sold on an exchange instead of over the counter. A **currency futures contract** specifies a standard volume of a particular currency to be exchanged on a specific settlement date. Some MNCs involved in international trade use the currency futures markets to hedge their positions. The **futures rate** represents the exchange rate at which one can purchase or sell a specified currency on the settlement date in accordance with the futures contract. Thus, the role of the futures rate within a futures contract is similar to the role of the forward rate within a forward contract.

At this point, it is important to distinguish between the futures rate and the term "future spot rate." The future spot rate is the spot rate that exists at a future point in time. It is uncertain as of today. If a U.S. firm needs Japanese yen in 90 days and if it expects that the future spot rate 90 days from now will exceed the prevailing 90-day futures rate (from a futures contract) or 90-day forward rate (from a forward contract), the firm may seriously consider hedging with a futures or forward contract.

Additional details on futures contracts, including other differences from forward contracts, are provided in Chapter 5.

Currency Options Contracts. Currency options contracts can be classified as calls or puts. A **currency call option** provides the right to buy a specific currency at a specific price (called the **strike price** or **exercise price**) within a specific period of time. It is used to hedge future payables. A **currency put option** provides the right to sell a specific currency at a specific price within a specific period of time. It is used to hedge future receivables.

Currency call and put options can be purchased on an exchange. They offer more flexibility than forward or futures contracts because they do not require any obligation. That is, the firm can elect not to exercise the option.

Currency options have become a popular means of hedging. The Coca-Cola Co. has replaced about 30 to 40 percent of its forward contracting with currency options. While most MNCs commonly use forward contracts, many of them also use currency options. Additional details about currency options, including other differences from futures and forward contracts, are provided in Chapter 5.

INTERNATIONAL MONEY MARKET

In most countries, local corporations commonly need to borrow short-term funds to support their operations. Country governments may also need to borrow short-term funds to finance their budget deficits. Individuals or local institutional investors in those countries provide funds through short-term deposits at commercial banks. In addition, corporations and governments may issue short-term securities that are purchased by local investors. Thus, a domestic money market in each country serves to transfer short-term funds denominated in the local currency from local surplus units (savers) to local deficit units (borrowers).

The growth in international business has caused corporations or governments in a particular country to need short-term funds denominated in a currency that is different from their home currency. First, they may need to borrow funds to pay for imports denominated in a foreign currency. Second, even if they need funds to support local operations, they may consider borrowing in a currency in which the interest rate is lower. This strategy is especially desirable if the firms will have receivables denominated in that currency in the future. Third, they may consider borrowing in a currency that will depreciate against their home currency, as they would be able to repay the loan at a more favorable exchange rate over time. Thus, the actual cost of borrowing would be less than the interest rate of that currency.

Meanwhile, there are some corporations and institutional investors that have motives to invest in a foreign currency rather than their home currency. First, the interest rate that they would receive from investing in their home currency may be lower than what they could earn on short-term investments denominated in some other currencies. Second, they may consider investing in a currency that will appreciate against their home currency because they would be able to convert that currency into their home currency at a more favorable exchange rate at the end of the investment period. Thus, the actual return on their investment would be higher than the quoted interest rate on that foreign currency.

The preferences of corporations and governments to borrow in foreign currencies and of investors to make short-term investments in foreign currencies resulted in the creation of the international money market.

Origins and Development

The international money market includes large banks in countries around the world. Two other important components of the international money market are the European money market and the Asian money market.

European Money Market. The origins of the European money market can be traced to the Eurocurrency market that developed during the 1960s and 1970s. As MNCs expanded their operations during that period, international financial intermediation emerged to accommodate their needs. Because the U.S. dollar was widely used even by foreign countries as a medium for international trade, there was a consistent need for dollars in Europe and elsewhere. To conduct international trade with European countries, corporations in the United States deposited U.S. dollars in European banks. The banks were willing to accept the deposits because they could lend the dollars to corporate customers based in Europe. These dollar deposits in banks in Europe (and on other continents as well) came to be known as **Eurodollars,** and the market for Eurodollars came to be known as the **Eurocurrency market.** ("Eurodollars" and "Eurocurrency" should not be confused with the "euro," which is the currency of many European countries today.)

The growth of the Eurocurrency market was stimulated by regulatory changes in the United States. For example, when the United States limited foreign lending by U.S. banks in 1968, foreign subsidiaries of U.S.-based MNCs could obtain U.S. dollars from banks in Europe via the Eurocurrency market. Similarly, when ceilings were placed on the interest rates paid on dollar deposits in the United States, MNCs transferred their funds to European banks, which were not subject to the ceilings.

The growing importance of the Organization of Petroleum Exporting Countries (OPEC) also contributed to the growth of the Eurocurrency market. Because OPEC generally requires payment for oil in dollars, the OPEC countries began to use the Eurocurrency market to deposit a portion of their oil revenues. These dollar-denominated deposits are sometimes known as **petrodollars.** Oil revenues deposited in banks have sometimes been lent to oil-importing countries that are short of cash. As these countries purchase more oil, funds are again transferred to the oil-exporting countries, which in turn create new deposits. This recycling process has been an important source of funds for some countries.

Today, the term "Eurocurrency market" is not used as often as in the past because several other international financial markets have been developed. The European money market is still an important part of the network of international money markets, however.

Asian Money Market. Like the European money market, the Asian money market originated as a market involving mostly dollar-denominated deposits. Hence, it was originally known as the **Asian dollar market.** The market emerged to accommodate the needs of businesses that were using the U.S. dollar (and some other foreign currencies) as a medium of exchange for international trade. These businesses could not rely on banks in Europe because of the distance and different time zones. Today, the Asian money market, as it is now called, is centered in Hong Kong and Singapore, where large banks accept deposits and make loans in various foreign currencies.

The major sources of deposits in the Asian money market are MNCs with excess cash and government agencies. Manufacturers are major borrowers in this market. Another function is interbank lending and borrowing. Banks that have more qualified loan applicants than they can accommodate use the interbank market to obtain additional funds. Banks in the Asian money market commonly borrow from or lend to banks in the European market.

Money Market Interest Rates among Currencies

The quoted money market interest rates for various currencies are shown for a recent point in time in Exhibit 3.4. Notice how the money market rates vary substantially among some currencies. This is due to differences in the interaction of the total supply of short-term funds available (bank deposits) in a specific country versus the total demand for short-term funds by borrowers in that country. If there is a large supply of savings relative to the demand for short-term funds, the interest rate for that country will be relatively low. Japan's short-term interest rates are typically very low for this reason. Conversely, if there is a strong demand to borrow a currency and a low supply of savings in that currency, the interest rate will be relatively high. Interest rates in developing countries are typically higher than rates in other countries.

Exhibit 3.4 Comparison of International Money Market Interest Rates

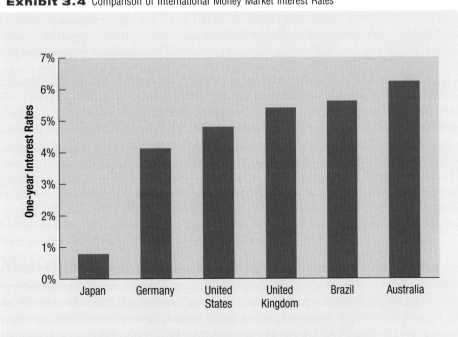

Standardizing Global Bank Regulations

Regulations contributed to the development of the international money market because they imposed restrictions on some local markets, thereby encouraging local investors and borrowers to circumvent the restrictions in local markets. Differences in regulations among countries allowed banks in some countries to have comparative advantages over banks in other countries. Over time, international banking regulations have become more standardized, which allows for more competitive global banking. Three of the more significant regulatory events allowing for a more competitive global playing field are (1) the Single European Act, (2) the Basel Accord, and (3) the Basel II Accord.

Single European Act. One of the most significant events affecting international banking was the **Single European Act,** which was phased in by 1992 throughout the European Union (EU) countries. The following are some of the more relevant provisions of the Single European Act for the banking industry:

- Capital can flow freely throughout Europe.
- Banks can offer a wide variety of lending, leasing, and securities activities in the EU.
- Regulations regarding competition, mergers, and taxes are similar throughout the EU.
- A bank established in any one of the EU countries has the right to expand into any or all of the other EU countries.

As a result of this act, banks have expanded across European countries. Efficiency in the European banking markets has increased because banks can more easily cross countries without concern for country-specific regulations that prevailed in the past.

Another key provision of the act is that banks entering Europe receive the same banking powers as other banks there. Similar provisions apply to non-U.S. banks that enter the United States.

Basel Accord. Before 1987, capital standards imposed on banks varied across countries, which allowed some banks to have a comparative global advantage over others. As an example, suppose that banks in the United States were required to maintain more capital than foreign banks. Foreign banks would grow more easily, as they would need a relatively small amount of capital to support an increase in assets. Despite their low capital, such banks were not necessarily perceived as too risky because the governments in those countries were likely to back banks that experienced financial problems. Therefore, some non-U.S. banks had globally competitive advantages over U.S. banks, without being subject to excessive risk. In December 1987, 12 major industrialized countries attempted to resolve the disparity by proposing uniform bank standards. In July 1988, in the **Basel Accord**, central bank governors of the 12 countries agreed on standardized guidelines. Under these guidelines, banks must maintain capital equal to at least 4 percent of their assets. For this purpose, banks' assets are weighted by risk. This essentially results in a higher required capital ratio for riskier assets. Off-balance sheet items are also accounted for so that banks cannot circumvent capital requirements by focusing on services that are not explicitly shown as assets on a balance sheet.

Basel II Accord. Banking regulators that form the so-called Basel Committee are completing a new accord (called Basel II) to correct some inconsistencies that still exist. For example, banks in some countries have required better collateral to back their loans. The Basel II Accord is attempting to account for such differences among banks. In addition, this accord encourages banks to improve their techniques for controlling operational risk, which could reduce failures in the banking system. The Basel Committee also plans to require banks to provide more information to existing and prospective shareholders about their exposure to different types of risk.

INTERNATIONAL CREDIT MARKET

Multinational corporations and domestic firms sometimes obtain medium-term funds through term loans from local financial institutions or through the issuance of notes (medium-term debt obligations) in their local markets. However, MNCs also have access to medium-term funds through banks located in foreign markets. Loans of one year or longer extended by banks to MNCs or government agencies in Europe are commonly called Eurocredits or **Eurocredit loans.** These loans are provided in the so-called **Eurocredit market.** The loans can be denominated in dollars or many other currencies and commonly have a maturity of 5 years.

Because banks accept short-term deposits and sometimes provide longer-term loans, their asset and liability maturities do not match. This can adversely affect a bank's performance during periods of rising interest rates, since the bank may have locked in a rate on its longer-term loans while the rate it pays on short-term deposits is rising over time. To avoid this risk, banks commonly use floating rate loans. The loan rate floats in accordance with the movement of some market interest rate, such as the **London Interbank Offer Rate (LIBOR),** which is the rate commonly charged for loans between banks. For example, a Eurocredit loan may have a loan rate that adjusts every 6 months and is set at "LIBOR plus 3 percent." The premium paid above LIBOR will depend on the credit risk of the borrower. The LIBOR varies among currencies because the market supply of and demand for funds vary among currencies. Because of the creation of the euro as the currency for many European countries, the key currency for interbank transactions in most of Europe is the euro. Thus, the term "euro-bor" is widely used to reflect the interbank offer rate on euros.

The international credit market is well developed in Asia and is developing in South America. Periodically, some regions are affected by an economic crisis, which increases the credit risk. Financial institutions tend to reduce their participation in those markets when credit risk increases. Thus, even though funding is widely available in many markets, the funds tend to move toward the markets where economic conditions are strong and credit risk is tolerable.

Syndicated Loans

Sometimes a single bank is unwilling or unable to lend the amount needed by a particular corporation or government agency. In this case, a **syndicate** of banks may be organized. Each bank within the syndicate participates in the lending. A lead bank is responsible for negotiating terms with the borrower. Then the lead bank organizes a group of banks to underwrite the loans. The syndicate of banks is usually formed in about 6 weeks, or less if the borrower is well known, because then the credit evaluation can be conducted more quickly.

Borrowers that receive a syndicated loan incur various fees besides the interest on the loan. Front-end management fees are paid to cover the costs of organizing the syndicate and underwriting the loan. In addition, a commitment fee of about .25 or .50 percent is charged annually on the unused portion of the available credit extended by the syndicate.

Syndicated loans can be denominated in a variety of currencies. The interest rate depends on the currency denominating the loan, the maturity of the loan, and the creditworthiness of the borrower. Interest rates on syndicated loans are commonly adjustable according to movements in an interbank lending rate, and the adjustment may occur every 6 months or every year.

Syndicated loans not only reduce the default risk of a large loan to the degree of participation for each individual bank, but they can also add an extra incentive for the borrower to repay the loan. If a government defaults on a loan to a syndicate, word will quickly spread among banks, and the government will likely have difficulty obtaining future loans. Borrowers are therefore strongly encouraged to repay syndicated loans promptly. From the perspective of the banks, syndicated loans increase the probability of prompt repayment.

Impact of the Credit Crisis on the Credit Market

In 2008, the United States experienced a credit crisis that was triggered by the substantial defaults on so-called subprime (lower quality) mortgages. This led to a halt in housing development, which reduced income, spending, and jobs. Financial institutions holding the mortgages or securities representing the mortgages experienced major losses. As the U.S. economy weakened, investors feared that more firms might default, and they shifted their funds out of risky debt securities. Financial institutions in some other countries such as the United Kingdom also offered subprime mortgage loans, and also experienced high default rates. Because of the global integration of financial markets, the problems in the U.S. and U.K. financial markets spread to other markets. Some financial institutions based in Asia and Europe were common purchasers of subprime mortgages that were originated in the United States and United Kingdom. Furthermore, the weakness of the U.S. and European economies caused a reduction in their demand for imports from other countries. Thus, the U.S. credit crisis blossomed into an international credit crisis.

As the credit crisis intensified, many financial institutions became more cautious with their funds. They were less willing to provide credit to MNCs directly or through syndicated loans.

INTERNATIONAL BOND MARKET

Although MNCs, like domestic firms, can obtain long-term debt by issuing bonds in their local markets, MNCs can also access long-term funds in foreign markets. MNCs may choose to issue bonds in the international bond markets for three reasons. First, issuers recognize that they may be able to attract a stronger demand by issuing their bonds in a particular foreign country rather than in their home country. Some countries have a limited investor base, so MNCs in those countries seek financing elsewhere. Second, MNCs may prefer to finance a specific foreign project in a particular currency and therefore may attempt to obtain funds where that currency is widely used. Third, financing in a foreign currency with a lower interest rate may enable an MNC to reduce its cost of financing, although it may be exposed to exchange rate risk (as explained in later chapters). Institutional investors such as commercial banks, mutual funds, insurance companies, and pension funds from many countries are major participants in the international bond market. Some institutional investors prefer to invest in international bond markets rather than their respective local markets when they can earn a higher return on bonds denominated in foreign currencies.

International bonds are typically classified as either foreign bonds or Eurobonds. A **foreign bond** is issued by a borrower foreign to the country where the bond is placed. For example, a U.S. corporation may issue a bond denominated in Japanese yen, which is sold to investors in Japan. In some cases, a firm may issue a variety of bonds in various countries. The currency denominating each type of bond is determined by the country where it is sold. These foreign bonds are sometimes specifically referred to as **parallel bonds.**

Eurobond Market

Eurobonds are bonds that are sold in countries other than the country of the currency denominating the bonds. The emergence of the Eurobond market was partially the result of the **Interest Equalization Tax (IET)** imposed by the U.S. government in 1963 to discourage U.S. investors from investing in foreign securities. Thus, non-U.S. borrowers that historically had sold foreign securities to U.S. investors began to look elsewhere for funds. Further impetus to the market's growth came in 1984 when the U.S. government abolished a withholding tax that it had formerly imposed on some non-U.S. investors and allowed U.S. corporations to issue bearer bonds directly to non-U.S. investors.

Eurobonds have become very popular as a means of attracting funds, perhaps in part because they circumvent registration requirements. U.S.-based MNCs such as McDonald's and Walt Disney commonly issue Eurobonds. Non-U.S. firms such as Guinness, Nestlé, and Volkswagen also use the Eurobond market as a source of funds.

In recent years, governments and corporations from emerging markets such as Croatia, Ukraine, Romania, and Hungary have frequently utilized the Eurobond market. New corporations that have been established in emerging markets rely on the Eurobond market to finance their growth. They have to pay a risk premium of at least 3 percentage points annually above the U.S. Treasury bond rate on dollar-denominated Eurobonds.

Features of Eurobonds. Eurobonds have several distinctive features. They are usually issued in bearer form, which means that there are no records kept regarding ownership. Coupon payments are made yearly. Some Eurobonds carry a convertibility clause allowing them to be converted into a specified number of shares of common stock. An advantage to the issuer is that Eurobonds typically have few, if any, protective covenants. Furthermore, even short-maturity Eurobonds include call provisions. Some Eurobonds, called **floating rate notes (FRNs),** have a variable rate provision that adjusts the coupon rate over time according to prevailing market rates.

Denominations. Eurobonds are commonly denominated in a number of currencies. Although the U.S. dollar is used most often, denominating 70 to 75 percent of Eurobonds, the euro will likely also be used to a significant extent in the future. Recently, some firms have issued debt denominated in Japanese yen to take advantage of Japan's extremely low interest rates. Because interest rates for each currency and credit conditions change constantly, the popularity of particular currencies in the Eurobond market changes over time.

Underwriting Process. Eurobonds are underwritten by a multinational syndicate of investment banks and simultaneously placed in many countries, providing a wide spectrum of fund sources to tap. The underwriting process takes place in a sequence of steps. The multinational managing syndicate sells the bonds to a large underwriting crew. In many cases, a special distribution to regional underwriters is allocated before the bonds finally reach the bond purchasers. One problem with the distribution method is that the second- and third-stage underwriters do not always follow up on their promise to sell the bonds. The managing syndicate is therefore forced to redistribute the unsold bonds or to sell them directly, which creates "digestion" problems in the market and adds to the distribution cost. To avoid such problems, bonds are often distributed in higher volume to underwriters that have fulfilled their commitments in the past at the expense of those that have not. This has helped the Eurobond market maintain its desirability as a bond placement center.

Secondary Market. Eurobonds also have a secondary market. The market makers are in many cases the same underwriters who sell the primary issues. A technological advance called **Euro-clear** helps to inform all traders about outstanding issues for sale, thus allowing a more active secondary market. The intermediaries in the secondary market are based in 10 different countries, with those in the United Kingdom dominating the action. They can act not only as brokers but also as dealers that hold inventories of Eurobonds.

Before the adoption of the euro in much of Europe, MNCs in European countries commonly preferred to issue bonds in their own local currency. The market for bonds in each currency was limited. Now, with the adoption of the euro, MNCs from many different countries can issue bonds denominated in euros, which allows for a much larger and more liquid market. MNCs have benefited because they can more easily obtain debt by issuing bonds, as investors know that there will be adequate liquidity in the secondary market.

Development of Other Bond Markets

Bond markets have developed in Asia and South America. Government agencies and MNCs in these regions use international bond markets to issue bonds when they believe they can reduce their financing costs. Investors in some countries use international bond markets because they expect their local currency to weaken in the future and prefer to invest in bonds denominated in a strong foreign currency. The South American bond market has experienced limited growth because the interest rates in some countries there are usually high. MNCs and government agencies in those countries are unwilling to issue bonds when interest rates are so high, so they rely heavily on short-term financing.

WEB

www.stock markets
.com/
Information about
stock markets around
the world.

INTERNATIONAL STOCK MARKETS

MNCs and domestic firms commonly obtain long-term funding by issuing stock locally. Yet, MNCs can also attract funds from foreign investors by issuing stock in international markets. The stock offering may be more easily digested when it is issued in several markets. In addition, the issuance of stock in a foreign country can enhance the firm's image and name recognition there.

Issuance of Stock in Foreign Markets

Some U.S. firms issue stock in foreign markets to enhance their global image. The existence of various markets for new issues provides corporations in need of equity with a choice. This competition among various new-issues markets should increase the efficiency of new issues.

The locations of an MNC's operations can influence the decision about where to place its stock, as the MNC may desire a country where it is likely to generate enough future cash flows to cover dividend payments. The stocks of some U.S.-based MNCs are widely traded on numerous stock exchanges around the world. This enables non-U.S. investors to have easy access to some U.S. stocks.

MNCs need to have their stock listed on an exchange in any country where they issue shares. Investors in a foreign country are only willing to purchase stock if they can easily sell their holdings of the stock locally in the secondary market. The stock is denominated in the currency of the country where it is placed.

EXAMPLE   Dow Chemical Co., a large U.S.-based MNC, does much business in Japan. It has supported its operations in Japan by issuing stock to investors in Japan, which is denominated in Japanese yen. Thus, it can use the yen proceeds in order to finance the expansion in Japan, and does not need to convert dollars to yen. In order to ensure that the Japanese investors can easily sell the stock that they purchased, Dow Chemical Co. listed its stock on the Tokyo exchange. In addition, Japanese investors can obtain the stock locally rather than incurring the higher transaction costs of purchasing the stock from the New York Stock Exchange. Since the stock listed on the Tokyo exchange is denominated in Japanese yen, Japanese investors who are buying or selling this stock do not need to convert to or from dollars. If Dow plans to expand its business in Japan, it may consider a secondary offering of stock in Japan. Since it already has its stock listed in Japan, it may be able to easily place additional shares in that market in order to raise equity funding for its expansion. ●

Impact of the Euro. The recent conversion of many European countries to a single currency (the euro) has resulted in more stock offerings in Europe by U.S.- and European-based MNCs. In the past, an MNC needed a different currency in every country where it conducted business and therefore borrowed currencies from local banks in those countries. Now, it can use the euro to finance its operations across several European countries and may be able to obtain all the financing it needs with one stock offering in which the stock is denominated in euros. The MNCs can then use a portion of the revenue (in euros) to pay dividends to shareholders who have purchased the stock.

Issuance of Foreign Stock in the United States

Non-U.S. corporations that need large amounts of funds sometimes issue stock in the United States (these are called **Yankee stock offerings**) due to the liquidity of its new-issues market. In other words, a foreign corporation may be more likely to sell an entire issue of stock in the U.S. market, whereas in other, smaller markets, the entire issue may not necessarily sell.

When a non-U.S. firm issues stock in its own country, its shareholder base is quite limited. A few large institutional investors may own most of the shares. By issuing stock in the United States, such a firm diversifies its shareholder base, which can reduce share price volatility caused when large investors sell shares.

The U.S. investment banks commonly serve as underwriters of the stock targeted for the U.S. market and receive underwriting fees representing about 7 percent of the value of stock issued. Since many financial institutions in the United States purchase non-U.S. stocks as investments, non-U.S. firms may be able to place an entire stock offering within the United States.

Many of the recent stock offerings in the United States by non-U.S. firms have resulted from privatization programs in Latin America and Europe. Thus, businesses that were previously government owned are being sold to U.S. shareholders. Given the large size of some of these businesses, the local stock markets are not large enough to digest the stock offerings. Consequently, U.S. investors are financing many privatized businesses based in foreign countries.

Firms that issue stock in the United States typically are required to satisfy stringent disclosure rules on their financial condition. However, they are exempt from some of these rules when they qualify for a Securities and Exchange Commission guideline (called Rule 144a) through a direct placement of stock to institutional investors.

American Depository Receipts. Non-U.S. firms also obtain equity financing by using **American depository receipts (ADRs),** which are certificates representing bundles of stock. The use of ADRs circumvents some disclosure requirements imposed on stock offerings in the United States, yet enables non-U.S. firms to tap the U.S. market for funds. The ADR market grew after businesses were privatized in the early 1990s, as some of these businesses issued ADRs to obtain financing. Examples of ADRs include Cemex (ticker symbol is CX, based in Mexico), China Telecom Corp. (CHA, China), Nokia (NOK, Finland), Heinekin (HINKY, Netherlands), and Credit Suisse Group (CS, Switzerland).

Since ADR shares can be traded just like shares of a stock, the price of an ADR changes each day in response to demand and supply conditions. Over time, however, the value of an ADR should move in tandem with the value of the corresponding stock that is listed on the foreign stock exchange, after adjusting for exchange rate effects. The formula for calculating the price of an ADR is:

$$P_{ADR} = P_{FS} \times S$$

where P_{ADR} represents the price of the ADR, P_{FS} represents the price of the foreign stock measured in foreign currency, and S is the spot rate of the foreign currency. Holding the price of the foreign stock constant, the ADR price should move proportionately with the movement in the currency denominating the foreign stock against the dollar. ADRs are especially attractive to U.S. investors who expect that the foreign stock will perform well and that the currency denominating the foreign stock will appreciate against the dollar.

EXAMPLE

A share of the ADR of the French firm Pari represents one share of this firm's stock that is traded on a French stock exchange. The share price of Pari was 20 euros when the French market closed. As the U.S. stock market opens, the euro is worth $1.05, so the ADR price should be:

$$P_{ADR} = P_{FS} \times S$$
$$= 20 \times \$1.05$$
$$= \$21$$

●

WEB

www.wall-street.com/
foreign.html
Provides links to many
stock markets.

If there is a discrepancy between the ADR price and the price of the foreign stock (after adjusting for the exchange rate), investors can use arbitrage to capitalize on the discrepancy between the prices of the two assets. The act of arbitrage should realign the prices.

EXAMPLE

Assume no transaction costs. If $P_{ADR} < (P_{FS} \times S)$, then ADR shares will flow back to France. They will be converted to shares of the French stock and will be traded in the French market. Investors can engage in arbitrage by buying the ADR shares in the United States, converting them to shares of the French stock, and then selling those shares on the French stock exchange where the stock is listed.

The arbitrage will (1) reduce the supply of ADRs traded in the U.S. market, thereby putting upward pressure on the ADR price, and (2) increase the supply of the French shares traded in the French market, thereby putting downward pressure on the stock price in France. The arbitrage will continue until the discrepancy in prices disappears. ●

The preceding example assumed a conversion rate of one ADR share per share of stock. Some ADRs are convertible into more than one share of the corresponding stock. Under these conditions, arbitrage will occur only if:

$$P_{ADR} = Conv \times P_{FS} \times S$$

where *Conv* represents the number of shares of foreign stock that can be obtained for the ADR.

EXAMPLE

If the Pari ADR from the previous example is convertible into two shares of stock, the ADR price should be:

$$P_{ADR} = 2 \times 20 \times \$1.05$$
$$= \$42$$

In this case, the ADR shares will be converted into shares of stock only if the ADR price is less than $42. ●

In reality, some transaction costs are associated with converting ADRs to foreign shares. Thus, arbitrage will occur only if the potential arbitrage profit exceeds the transaction costs. ADR price quotations are provided on various websites, such as www.adr.com. Many of the websites that provide stock prices for ADRs are segmented by country.

Listing Non-U.S. Firms on U.S. Exchanges

Non-U.S. firms that issue stock in the United States have their shares listed on the New York Stock Exchange or the Nasdaq market. By listing their stock on a U.S. stock exchange, the shares placed in the United States can easily be traded in the secondary market.

Effect of Sarbanes-Oxley Act on Foreign Stock Listings.

In 2002, the U.S. Congress passed the Sarbanes-Oxley Act, requiring firms whose stock is listed on U.S. stock exchanges to provide more complete financial disclosure. The act was the result of financial scandals involving U.S.-based MNCs such as Enron and WorldCom that had used misleading financial statements to hide their weak financial condition from investors. Investors then overestimated the value of the stocks of these companies and eventually lost most or all of their investment. Sarbanes-Oxley was intended to ensure that financial reporting was more accurate and complete, but the cost for complying with the act was estimated to be more than $1 million per year for some firms. Consequently, many non-U.S. firms decided to place new issues of their stock in the United Kingdom instead of in the United States so that they would not have to comply with the law. Some U.S. firms that went public also decided to place their stock in the United Kingdom for the same reason.

Investing in Foreign Stock Markets

Just as some MNCs issue stock outside their home country, many investors purchase stocks outside of the home country. First, they may expect that economic conditions will be very favorable in a particular country and invest in stocks of the firms in that country. Second, investors may consider investing in stocks denominated in currencies that they expect will strengthen over time, since that would enhance the return on their investment. Third, some investors invest in stocks of other countries as a means of diversifying their portfolio. Thus, their investment is less sensitive to possible adverse stock market conditions in their home country. More details about investing in international stock markets are provided in the appendix to this chapter.

Comparison of Stock Markets.

Exhibit 3.5 provides a summary of the major stock markets, but there are numerous other exchanges. Some foreign stock markets are much smaller than the U.S. markets because their firms have relied more on debt financing than equity financing in the past. Recently, however, firms outside the United States have been issuing stock more frequently, which has resulted in the growth of non-U.S. stock markets. The percentage of individual versus institutional ownership of shares varies across stock markets. Financial institutions and other firms own a large proportion of the shares outside the United States, while individual investors own a relatively small proportion of shares.

Large MNCs have begun to float new stock issues simultaneously in various countries. Investment banks underwrite stocks through one or more syndicates across countries. The global distribution of stock can reach a much larger market, so greater quantities of stock can be issued at a given price.

In 2000, the Amsterdam, Brussels, and Paris stock exchanges merged to create the Euronext market. Since then, the Lisbon stock exchange has joined as well. In 2007, the NYSE joined Euronext to create NYSE Euronext, the largest global exchange. It represents a major step in creating a global stock exchange and will likely lead to more consolidation of stock exchanges across countries in the future. Most of the largest firms based in Europe have listed their stock on the Euronext market. This market is likely to grow over time as other stock exchanges may join. A single European stock market with similar guidelines for all stocks regardless of their home country would make it easier for those investors who prefer to do all of their trading in one market.

Exhibit 3.5 Comparison of Stock Exchanges (as of 2008)

COUNTRY	MARKET CAPITALIZATION IN BILLIONS OF DOLLARS	NUMBER OF LISTED COMPANIES
Argentina	$57	111
Australia	1,298	1,998
Brazil	1,369	404
Chile	212	241
China	4,478	1,530
Greece	264	283
Hong Kong	2,654	1,241
Hungary	46	41
Japan	4,330	2,414
Mexico	3,977	367
Norway	353	248
Russia	211	375
Slovenia	29	87
Spain	1,799	3,537
Switzerland	1,271	341
Taiwan	663	703
United Kingdom	3,851	3,307
United States	19,664	5,965

Source: *World Federation of Exchanges.*

In recent years, many new stock markets have been developed. These so-called emerging markets enable foreign firms to raise large amounts of capital by issuing stock. These markets may enable U.S. firms doing business in emerging markets to raise funds by issuing stock there and listing their stock on the local stock exchanges. Market characteristics such as the amount of trading relative to market capitalization and the applicable tax rates can vary substantially among emerging markets.

How Market Characteristics Vary among Countries. In general, stock market participation and trading activity are higher in countries where managers of firms are encouraged to make decisions that serve shareholder interests, and where there is greater transparency so that investors can more easily monitor firms. If investors believe that the money they invest in firms will not be used to serve their interests or that the firms do not provide transparent reporting of their condition or operations, they will probably not invest in that country's stocks. An active stock market requires the trust of the local investors. When there is more trust, there is more participation and trading.

GOVERNANCE

Exhibit 3.6 identifies some of the specific factors that can allow stronger governance and therefore increase the trading activity in stock markets. Shareholders in some countries have more rights than in other countries. For example, shareholders have more voting power in some countries than others, and they can have influence on a wider variety of management issues in some countries.

Second, the legal protection of shareholders varies substantially among countries. Shareholders in some countries may have more power to effectively sue publicly traded

Exhibit 3.6 Impact of Governance on Stock Market Participation and Trading Activity

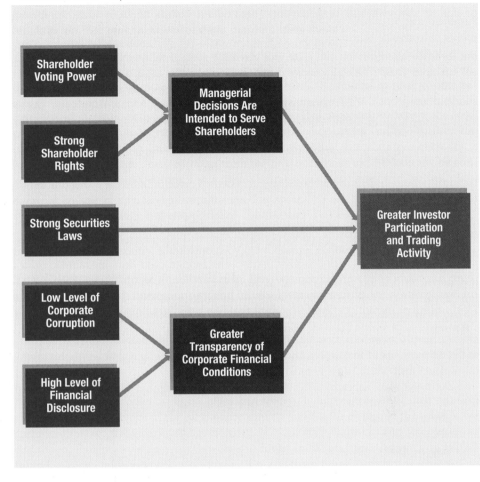

firms if their executives or directors commit financial fraud. In general, common law countries such as the United States, Canada, and the United Kingdom allow for more legal protection than civil law countries such as France or Italy. Managers are more likely to serve shareholder interests if shareholders have more legal protection.

Third, government enforcement of securities laws varies among countries. A country could have laws to protect shareholders but no enforcement of the laws, which means that shareholders are not protected. Fourth, some countries tend to have less corporate corruption than others. Shareholders in these countries are less susceptible to major losses due to agency problems whereby managers use shareholder money for their own benefit. Securities laws are not sufficient to eliminate some forms of corporate corruption. Some cultures discourage corruption more than others, and encourage more transparency.

Fifth, the degree of financial information that must be provided by public companies varies among countries. The variation may be due to the accounting laws set by the government for public companies or reporting rules enforced by local stock exchanges. Shareholders are less susceptible to losses due to a lack of information if the public companies are required to be more transparent in their financial reporting.

In general, stock markets that allow more voting rights for shareholders, more legal protection, more enforcement of the laws, less corruption, and more stringent accounting requirements attract more investors who are willing to invest in stocks. This allows for more confidence in the stock market and greater pricing efficiency (since there is a large enough set of investors who monitor each firm). In addition, companies are attracted to the stock market when there are many investors because they can easily raise funds in the market under these conditions. Conversely, if a stock market does not attract investors, it will not attract companies that need to raise funds. These companies will either need to rely on stock markets in other countries or credit markets (such as bank loans) to raise funds.

Impact of the Credit Crisis on Stock Markets. As the credit crisis spread across industries and countries in 2008, stock markets throughout the world experienced major losses. The credit crisis created fear that many firms could go bankrupt. It reduced the economic outlook in many countries. It also limited the ability of some firms to obtain the financing that they needed for their operations. In the week of October 6–10, 2008, stock prices in the United States declined 18 percent on average, which is the largest weekly decline ever in the United States. Some other stock markets experienced more substantial price declines.

HOW FINANCIAL MARKETS SERVE MNCS

Exhibit 3.7 illustrates the foreign cash flow movements of a typical MNC. These cash flows can be classified into four corporate functions, all of which generally require use of the foreign exchange markets. The spot market, forward market, currency

Exhibit 3.7 Foreign Cash Flow Chart of an MNC

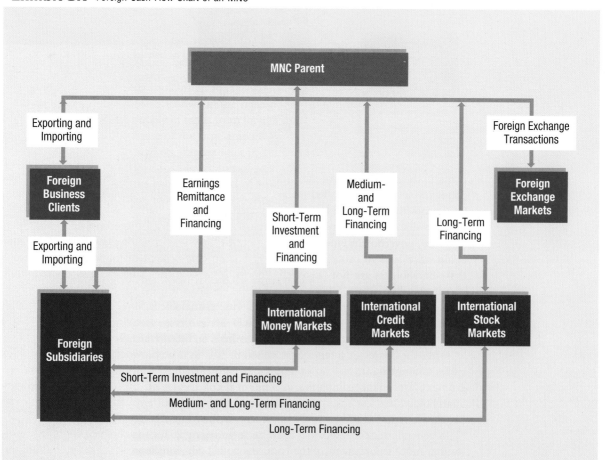

futures market, and currency options market are all classified as foreign exchange markets.

The first function is foreign trade with business clients. Exports generate foreign cash inflows, while imports require cash outflows. A second function is direct foreign investment, or the acquisition of foreign real assets. This function requires cash outflows but generates future inflows through remitted earnings back to the MNC parent or the sale of these foreign assets. A third function is short-term investment or financing in foreign securities. A fourth function is longer-term financing in the international bond or stock markets. An MNC's parent may use international money or bond markets to obtain funds at a lower cost than they can be obtained locally.

SUMMARY

- The foreign exchange market allows currencies to be exchanged in order to facilitate international trade or financial transactions. Commercial banks serve as financial intermediaries in this market. They stand ready to exchange currencies for immediate delivery in the spot market. In addition, they are also willing to negotiate forward contracts with MNCs that wish to buy or sell currencies at a future point in time.

- The international money markets are composed of several large banks that accept deposits and provide short-term loans in various currencies. This market is used primarily by governments and large corporations. The European market is a part of the international money market.

- The international credit markets are composed of the same commercial banks that serve the international money market. These banks convert some of the deposits received into loans (for medium-term periods) to governments and large corporations.

- The international bond markets facilitate international transfers of long-term credit, thereby enabling governments and large corporations to borrow funds from various countries. The international bond market is facilitated by multinational syndicates of investment banks that help to place the bonds. Institutional investors such as mutual funds, banks, and pension funds are the major purchasers of bonds in the international bond market.

- International stock markets enable firms to obtain equity financing in foreign countries. Thus, these markets help MNCs finance their international expansion. Institutional investors such as pension funds and mutual funds are the major purchasers of newly issued stock.

POINT COUNTER-POINT

Should Firms That Go Public Engage in International Offerings?

Point Yes. When a U.S. firm issues stock to the public for the first time in an initial public offering (IPO), it is naturally concerned about whether it can place all of its shares at a reasonable price. It will be able to issue its stock at a higher price by attracting more investors. It will increase its demand by spreading the stock across countries. The higher the price at which it can issue stock, the lower is its cost of using equity capital. It can also establish a global name by spreading stock across countries.

Counter-Point No. If a U.S. firm spreads its stock across different countries at the time of the IPO, there will be less publicly traded stock in the United States.

Thus, it will not have as much liquidity in the secondary market. Investors desire stocks that they can easily sell in the secondary market, which means that they require that the stocks have liquidity. To the extent that a firm reduces its liquidity in the United States by spreading its stock across countries, it may not attract sufficient U.S. demand for the stock. Thus, its efforts to create global name recognition may reduce its name recognition in the United States.

Who Is Correct? Use the Internet to learn more about this issue. Which argument do you support? Offer your own opinion on this issue.

SELF-TEST

Answers are provided in Appendix A at the back of the text.

1. Stetson Bank quotes a bid rate of $.784 for the Australian dollar and an ask rate of $.80. What is the bid/ask percentage spread?

2. Fullerton Bank quotes an ask rate of $.190 for the Peruvian currency (new sol) and a bid rate of $.188. Determine the bid/ask percentage spread.

3. Briefly explain how MNCs can make use of each international financial market described in this chapter.

QUESTIONS AND APPLICATIONS

1.   Motives for Investing in Foreign Money Markets. Explain why an MNC may invest funds in a financial market outside its own country.

2.   Motives for Providing Credit in Foreign Markets. Explain why some financial institutions prefer to provide credit in financial markets outside their own country.

3.   Exchange Rate Effects on Investing. Explain how the appreciation of the Australian dollar against the U.S. dollar would affect the return to a U.S. firm that invested in an Australian money market security.

4.   Exchange Rate Effects on Borrowing. Explain how the appreciation of the Japanese yen against the U.S. dollar would affect the return to a U.S. firm that borrowed Japanese yen and used the proceeds for a U.S. project.

5.   Bank Services. List some of the important characteristics of bank foreign exchange services that MNCs should consider.

6.   Bid/Ask Spread. Utah Bank's bid price for Canadian dollars is $.7938 and its ask price is $.81. What is the bid/ask percentage spread?

7.   Bid/Ask Spread. Compute the bid/ask percentage spread for Mexican peso retail transactions in which the ask rate is $.11 and the bid rate is $.10.

8.   Forward Contract. The Wolfpack Corp. is a U.S. exporter that invoices its exports to the United Kingdom in British pounds. If it expects that the pound will appreciate against the dollar in the future, should it hedge its exports with a forward contract? Explain.

9.   Euro. Explain the foreign exchange situation for countries that use the euro when they engage in international trade among themselves.

10. Indirect Exchange Rate. If the direct exchange rate of the euro is worth $1.25, what is the indirect rate of the euro? That is, what is the value of a dollar in euros?

11. Cross Exchange Rate. Assume Poland's currency (the zloty) is worth $.17 and the Japanese yen is worth $.008. What is the cross rate of the zloty with respect to yen? That is, how many yen equal a zloty?

12. Syndicated Loans. Explain how syndicated loans are used in international markets.

13. Loan Rates. Explain the process used by banks in the Eurocredit market to determine the rate to charge on loans.

14. International Markets. What is the function of the international money markets? Briefly describe the reasons for the development and growth of the European money market. Explain how the international money, credit, and bond markets differ from one another.

15. Evolution of Floating Rates. Briefly describe the historical developments that led to floating exchange rates as of 1973.

16. International Diversification. Explain how the Asian crisis would have affected the returns to a U.S. firm investing in the Asian stock markets as a means of international diversification. (See the chapter appendix.)

17. Eurocredit Loans.

a.   With regard to Eurocredit loans, who are the borrowers?

b.   Why would a bank desire to participate in syndicated Eurocredit loans?

c.   What is LIBOR, and how is it used in the Eurocredit market?

18. Foreign Exchange. You just came back from Canada, where the Canadian dollar was worth $.70. You still have C$200 from your trip and could exchange them for dollars at the airport, but the airport foreign exchange desk will only buy them for $.60. Next week, you will be going to Mexico and will need pesos. The airport foreign exchange desk will sell you pesos for $.10 per peso. You met a tourist at the airport who is from Mexico and is on his way to Canada. He is willing to buy your C$200 for 1,300 pesos. Should you accept the offer or cash the Canadian dollars in at the airport? Explain.

19. Foreign Stock Markets. Explain why firms may issue stock in foreign markets. Why might U.S. firms issue more stock in Europe since the conversion to the euro in 1999?

20. Financing with Stock. Chapman Co. is a privately owned MNC in the United States that plans to engage in an initial public offering (IPO) of stock so that it can finance its international expansion. At the present time, world stock market conditions are very weak but are expected to improve. The U.S. market tends to be weak in periods when the other stock markets around the world are weak. A financial manager of Chapman Co. recommends that it wait until the world stock markets recover before it issues stock. Another manager believes that Chapman Co. could issue its stock now even if the price would be low, since its stock price should rise later once world stock markets recover. Who is correct? Explain.

Advanced Questions

21. Effects of September 11. Why do you think the terrorist attack on the United States was expected to cause a decline in U.S. interest rates? Given the expectations for a decline in U.S. interest rates and stock prices, how were capital flows between the United States and other countries likely affected?

22. International Financial Markets. Recently, Wal-Mart established two retail outlets in the city of Shanzen, China, which has a population of 3.7 million. These outlets are massive and contain products purchased locally as well as imports. As Wal-Mart generates earnings beyond what it needs in Shanzen, it may remit those earnings back to the United States.

Wal-Mart is likely to build additional outlets in Shanzen or in other Chinese cities in the future.

a. Explain how the Wal-Mart outlets in China would use the spot market in foreign exchange.

b. Explain how Wal-Mart might utilize the international money markets when it is establishing other Wal-Mart stores in Asia.

c. Explain how Wal-Mart could use the international bond market to finance the establishment of new outlets in foreign markets.

23. Interest Rates. Why do interest rates vary among countries? Why are interest rates normally similar for those European countries that use the euro as their currency? Offer a reason why the government interest rate of one country could be slightly higher than the government interest rate of another country, even though the euro is the currency used in both countries.

24. Interpreting Exchange Rate Quotations. Today you notice the following exchange rate quotations: (a) $1 = 3.00 Argentine pesos and (b) 1 Argentine peso = .50 Canadian dollars. You need to purchase 100,000 Canadian dollars with U.S. dollars. How many U.S. dollars will you need for your purchase?

25. Pricing ADRs. Today, the stock price of Genevo Co. (based in Switzerland) is priced at SF80 per share. The spot rate of the Swiss franc (SF) is $.70. During the next year, you expect that the stock price of Genevo Co. will decline by 3 percent. You also expect that the Swiss franc will depreciate against the U.S. dollar by 8 percent during the next year. You own American depository receipts (ADRs) that represent Genevo stock. Each share that you own represents one share of the stock traded on the Swiss stock exchange. What is the estimated value of the ADR per share in one year?

26. Explaining Variation in Bid-Ask Spreads. Go to the currency converter at http://finance.yahoo.com/currency and determine the bid-ask spread for the euro. Then determine the bid-ask spread for a currency in a less developed country. What do you think is the main reason for the difference in the bid-ask spreads between these two currencies?

27. Direct versus Indirect Exchange Rates. Assume that during this semester, the euro appreciated against the dollar. Did the direct exchange rate of the euro increase or decrease? Did the indirect exchange rate of the euro increase or decrease?

28. Transparency and Stock Trading Activity. Explain the relationship between transparency of firms and investor participation (or trading activity) among stock markets. Based on this relationship, how can governments of countries increase the amount of trading activity (and therefore liquidity) of their stock markets?

29. How Governance Affects Stock Market Liquidity. Identify some of the key factors that can allow for stronger governance and therefore increase participation and trading activity in a stock market.

30. International Impact of the Credit Crisis. Explain how the international integration of financial markets caused the credit crisis to spread across many countries.

31. Issuing Stock in Foreign Markets. Bloomington Co. is a large U.S.-based MNC with large subsidiaries in Germany. It has issued stock in Germany in order to establish its business. It could have issued stock in the United States and then used the proceeds in order to support the growth in Europe. What is a possible advantage of issuing the stock in Germany to finance German operations? Also, why might the German investors prefer to purchase the stock that was issued in Germany rather than purchase the stock of Bloomington on a U.S. stock exchange?

Discussion in the Boardroom

This exercise can be found in Appendix E at the back of this textbook.

Running Your Own MNC

This exercise can be found on the *International Financial Management* text companion website located at www.cengage.com/finance/madura.

BLADES, INC. CASE

Decisions to Use International Financial Markets

As a financial analyst for Blades, Inc., you are reasonably satisfied with Blades' current setup of exporting "Speedos" (roller blades) to Thailand. Due to the unique arrangement with Blades' primary customer in Thailand, forecasting the revenue to be generated there is a relatively easy task. Specifically, your customer has agreed to purchase 180,000 pairs of Speedos annually, for a period of 3 years, at a price of THB4,594 (THB = Thai baht) per pair. The current direct quotation of the dollar-baht exchange rate is $0.024.

The cost of goods sold incurred in Thailand (due to imports of the rubber and plastic components from Thailand) runs at approximately THB2,871 per pair of Speedos, but Blades currently only imports materials sufficient to manufacture about 72,000 pairs of Speedos. Blades' primary reasons for using a Thai supplier are the high quality of the components and the low cost, which has been facilitated by a continuing depreciation of the Thai baht against the U.S. dollar. If the dollar cost of buying components becomes more expensive in Thailand than in the United States, Blades is contemplating providing its U.S. supplier with the additional business.

Your plan is quite simple; Blades is currently using its Thai-denominated revenues to cover the cost of goods sold incurred there. During the last year, excess revenue was converted to U.S. dollars at the prevailing exchange rate. Although your cost of goods sold is not fixed contractually as the Thai revenues are, you expect them to remain relatively constant in the near future. Consequently, the baht-denominated cash inflows are fairly predictable each year because the Thai customer has committed to the purchase of 180,000 pairs of Speedos at a fixed price. The excess dollar revenue resulting from the conversion of baht is used either to support the U.S. production of Speedos if needed or to invest in the United States. Specifically, the revenues are used to cover cost of goods sold in the U.S. manufacturing plant, located in Omaha, Nebraska.

Ben Holt, Blades' CFO, notices that Thailand's interest rates are approximately 15 percent (versus 8 percent in the United States). You interpret the high interest rates in Thailand as an indication of the uncertainty resulting from Thailand's unstable economy. Holt asks you to assess the feasibility of investing Blades' excess funds from Thailand operations in Thailand at an interest rate of 15 percent. After you express your opposition to his plan, Holt asks you to detail the reasons in a detailed report.

1. One point of concern for you is that there is a trade-off between the higher interest rates in Thailand and the delayed conversion of baht into dollars. Explain what this means.

2. If the net baht received from the Thailand operation are invested in Thailand, how will U.S. operations be affected? (Assume that Blades is currently paying 10 percent on dollars borrowed and needs more financing for its firm.)

3. Construct a spreadsheet to compare the cash flows resulting from two plans. Under the first plan, net baht-denominated cash flows (received today) will be invested in Thailand at 15 percent for a one-year period, after which the baht will be converted to dollars. The expected spot rate for the baht in one year is about

$.022 (Ben Holt's plan). Under the second plan, net baht-denominated cash flows are converted to dollars immediately and invested in the United States for one year at 8 percent. For this question, assume that all baht-denominated cash flows are due today. Does Holt's plan seem superior in terms of dollar cash flows available after one year? Compare the choice of investing the funds versus using the funds to provide needed financing to the firm.

SMALL BUSINESS DILEMMA

Use of the Foreign Exchange Markets by the Sports Exports Company

Each month, the Sports Exports Company (a U.S. firm) receives an order for footballs from a British sporting goods distributor. The monthly payment for the footballs is denominated in British pounds, as requested by the British distributor. Jim Logan, owner of the Sports Exports Company, must convert the pounds received into dollars.

1. Explain how the Sports Exports Company could utilize the spot market to facilitate the exchange of currencies. Be specific.

2. Explain how the Sports Exports Company is exposed to exchange rate risk and how it could use the forward market to hedge this risk.

INTERNET/EXCEL EXERCISES

The Bloomberg website provides quotations of various exchange rates and stock market indexes. Its website address is www.bloomberg.com.

1. Go to the Yahoo site for exchange rate data (http://finance.yahoo.com/currency).

a. What is the prevailing direct exchange rate of the Japanese yen?

b. What is the prevailing direct exchange rate of the euro?

c. Based on your answers to questions a and b, show how to determine the number of yen per euro.

d. One euro is equal to how many yen according to the table in Yahoo?

e. Based on your answer to question d, show how to determine how many euros are equal to one Japanese yen.

f. Click on the euro in the first column in order to generate a historical trend of the direct exchange rate of the euro. Click on 5y to review the euro's exchange rate over the last 5 years. Briefly explain this trend (whether it is mostly upward or downward), and the point(s) at which there was an abrupt shift in the opposite direction.

g. Click on the euro in the column heading in order to generate a historical trend of the indirect exchange rate of the euro. Click on 5y to review the euro's exchange rate over the last 5 years. Briefly explain this trend, and the point(s) at which there was an abrupt shift in the opposite direction. How does this trend of the indirect exchange rate compare to the trend of the direct exchange rate?

h. Based on the historical trend of the direct exchange rate of the euro, what is the approximate percentage change in the euro over the last full year?

i. Just above the foreign exchange table in Yahoo, there is a currency converter. Use this table to convert euros into Canadian dollars. A historical trend is provided. Explain whether the euro generally appreciated or depreciated against the Canadian dollar over this period.

j. Notice from the currency converter that bid and ask exchange rates are provided. What is the percentage bid/ask spread based on the information?

2. Go to the section on currencies within the website. First, identify the direct exchange rates of foreign currencies from the U.S. perspective. Then, identify the indirect exchange rates. What is the direct exchange rate of the euro? What is the indirect exchange rate of the euro? What is the relationship between the direct and indirect exchange rates of the euro?

3. Use the Bloomberg website to determine the cross exchange rate between the Japanese yen and the Aus-

tralian dollar. That is, determine how many yen must be converted to an Australian dollar for Japanese importers that purchase Australian products today. How many Australian dollars are equal to a Japanese yen? What is the relationship between the exchange rate measured as number of yen per Australian dollar and the exchange rate measured as number of Australian dollars per yen?

REFERENCES

Bamrud, Joachim, Jul/Aug 2005, Brazil's Trailblazers Continue to Drive Innovation in ADR Market, *Global Finance*, pp. 32–36.

Bellalah, Mondher, and Sofiane Aboura, Summer 2007, Information Asymmetry in the French Market around Crises, *International Journal of Business*, pp. 301–309.

Champagne, Claudia, and Lawrence Kryzanowski, Autumn 2008, The Impact of Past Syndicate Alliances on the Consolidation of Financial Institutions, *Financial Management*, pp. 535–569.

Cipriani, Marco, and Graciela L. Kaminsky, Apr 2007, Volatility in International Financial Market Issuance: The Role of the Financial Center, *Open Economies Review*, pp. 157–176.

Eleswarapu, Venkat R., and Kumar Venkataraman, Fall 2006, The Impact of Legal and Political Institutions on Equity Trading Costs: A Cross-Country Analysis, *The Review of Financial Studies*, pp. 1081–1112.

Esty, B.C., and W.L. Megginson, 2003, Creditor Rights, Enforcement, and Debt Ownership Structure: Evidence from the Global Syndicated Loan Market, *Journal of Financial and Quantitative Analysis*, pp. 37–59.

Kohers, Gerald, Ninon Kohers, and Theodor Kohers, Winter 2006, Recent Changes in Major European Stock Market Linkages, *Journal of International Business Research*, pp. 63–72.

Melnik, Arie, and Doron Nissim, Jan 2006, Issue Costs in the Eurobond Market: The Effects of Market Integration, *Journal of Banking & Finance*, pp. 157–177.

Moshirian, Fariborz, and Giorgio Szego, Jun 2003, Markets and Institutions: Global Perspectives, *Journal of Banking & Finance*, pp. 1213–1218.

Moshirian, Fariborz, Apr 2006, Aspects of International Financial Services, *Journal of Banking & Finance*, pp. 1057–1064.

Murphy, Austin, Nov 2003, An Empirical Analysis of the Structure of Credit Risk Premiums in the Eurobond Market, *Journal of International Money and Finance*, pp. 865–885.

Tumpel-Gugerell, Gertrude, Jul 2007, The Competitiveness of European Financial Markets, *Business Economics*, pp. 14–20.

Wongswan, Jon, Winter 2006, Transmission of Information across International Equity Markets, *The Review of Financial Studies*, pp. 1157–1189.

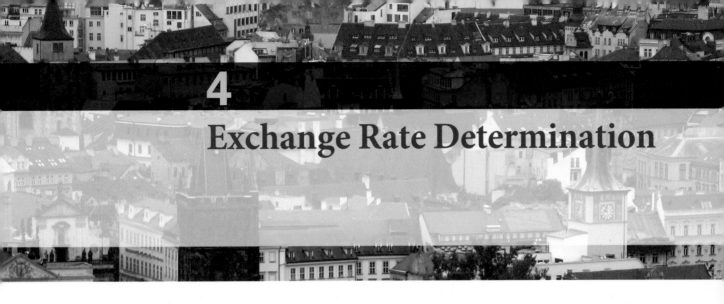

4

Exchange Rate Determination

CHAPTER OBJECTIVES

The specific objectives of this chapter are to:

- explain how exchange rate movements are measured,

- explain how the equilibrium exchange rate is determined,

- examine factors that affect the equilibrium exchange rate, and

- explain the movements in cross exchange rates.

WEB

www.xe.com/ict/

Real-time exchange rate quotations.

Financial managers of MNCs that conduct international business must continuously monitor exchange rates because their cash flows are highly dependent on them. They need to understand what factors influence exchange rates so that they can anticipate how exchange rates may change in response to specific conditions. This chapter provides a foundation for understanding how exchange rates are determined.

MEASURING EXCHANGE RATE MOVEMENTS

Exchange rate movements affect an MNC's value because they can affect the amount of cash inflows received from exporting or from a subsidiary and the amount of cash outflows needed to pay for imports. An exchange rate measures the value of one currency in units of another currency. As economic conditions change, exchange rates can change substantially. A decline in a currency's value is often referred to as **depreciation.** When the British pound depreciates against the U.S. dollar, this means that the U.S. dollar is strengthening relative to the pound. The increase in a currency value is often referred to as **appreciation.**

When a foreign currency's spot rates at two specific points in time are compared, the spot rate at the more recent date is denoted as S and the spot rate at the earlier date is denoted as S_{t-1}. The percentage change in the value of the foreign currency is computed as follows:

$$\text{Percent } \Delta \text{ in foreign currency value} = \frac{S - S_{t-1}}{S_{t-1}}$$

A positive percentage change indicates that the foreign currency has appreciated, while a negative percentage change indicates that it has depreciated. The values of some currencies have changed as much as 5 percent over a 24-hour period.

On some days, most foreign currencies appreciate against the dollar, although by different degrees. On other days, most currencies depreciate against the dollar, but by different degrees. There are also days when some currencies appreciate while others depreciate against the dollar; the media describe this scenario by stating that "the dollar was *mixed* in trading."

EXAMPLE

Exchange rates for the Canadian dollar and the euro are shown in the second and fourth columns of Exhibit 4.1 for the months from January 1 to July 1. First, notice that the direction of the movement may persist for consecutive months in some cases or may not persist in other cases. The magnitude of the movement tends to vary every month, although the range of percentage movements over these months may be a reasonable indicator of the range of percentage movements in future months. A comparison of the movements in these two currencies suggests that they appear to move independently of each other.

Exhibit 4.1 How Exchange Rate Movements and Volatility Are Measured

	VALUE OF CANADIAN DOLLAR (C$)	MONTHLY % CHANGE IN C$	VALUE OF EURO	MONTHLY % CHANGE IN EURO
Jan. 1	$.70	—	$1.18	—
Feb. 1	$.71	+1.43%	$1.16	−1.69%
March 1	$.703	−0.99%	$1.15	−0.86%
April 1	$.697	−0.85%	$1.12	−2.61%
May 1	$.692	−0.72%	$1.11	−0.89%
June 1	$.695	+0.43%	$1.14	+2.70%
July 1	$.686	−1.29%	$1.17	+2.63%
Standard deviation of monthly changes		1.04%		2.31%

WEB

www.bis.org/statistics/eer/index.htm
Information on how each currency's value has changed against a broad index of currencies.

The movements in the euro are typically larger (regardless of direction) than movements in the Canadian dollar. This means that from a U.S. perspective, the euro is a more volatile currency. The standard deviation of the exchange rate movements for each currency (shown at the bottom of the table) verifies this point. The standard deviation should be applied to percentage movements (not the values) when comparing volatility among currencies. ●

Foreign exchange rate movements tend to be larger for longer time horizons. Thus, if yearly exchange rate data were assessed, the movements would be more volatile for each currency than what is shown here, but the euro's movements would still be more volatile. If daily exchange rate movements were assessed, the movements would be less volatile for each currency than what is shown here, but the euro's movements would still be more volatile. A review of daily exchange rate movements is important to an MNC that will need to obtain a foreign currency in a few days and wants to assess the possible degree of movement over that period. A review of annual exchange movements would be more appropriate for an MNC that conducts foreign trade every year and wants to assess the possible degree of movements on a yearly basis. Many MNCs review exchange rates based on short-term and long-term horizons because they expect to engage in international transactions in the near future and in the distant future.

EXCHANGE RATE EQUILIBRIUM

WEB

www.federalreserve.gov/releases/
Current and historic exchange rates.

Although it is easy to measure the percentage change in the value of a currency, it is more difficult to explain why the value changed or to forecast how it may change in the future. To achieve either of these objectives, the concept of an **equilibrium exchange rate** must be understood, as well as the factors that affect the equilibrium rate.

Before considering why an exchange rate changes, realize that an exchange rate at a given point in time represents the *price* of a currency, or the rate at which one currency can be exchanged for another. While the exchange rate always involves two currencies, our focus is from the U.S. perspective. Thus, the exchange rate of any currency refers to the rate at which it can be exchanged for U.S. dollars, unless specified otherwise.

Like any other product sold in markets, the price of a currency is determined by the demand for that currency relative to supply. Thus, for each possible price of a British pound, there is a corresponding demand for pounds and a corresponding supply of pounds for sale. At any point in time, a currency should exhibit the price at which the demand for that currency is equal to supply, and this represents the equilibrium exchange rate. Of course, conditions can change over time, causing the supply or demand for a given currency to adjust, and thereby causing movement in the currency's price. This topic is more thoroughly discussed in this section.

Demand for a Currency

The British pound is used here to explain exchange rate equilibrium. The United Kingdom has not adopted the euro as its currency and continues to use the pound. Exhibit 4.2 shows a hypothetical number of pounds that would be demanded under various possibilities for the exchange rate. At any one point in time, there is only one exchange rate. The exhibit shows the quantity of pounds that would be demanded at various exchange rates at a specific point in time. The demand schedule is downward sloping because corporations and individuals in the United States will be encouraged to purchase more British goods when the pound is worth less, as it will take fewer dollars to obtain the desired amount of pounds. Conversely, if the pound's exchange rate is high, corporations and individuals in the United States are less willing to purchase British goods, as they may obtain goods at a lower price in the United States or other countries.

Supply of a Currency for Sale

Up to this point, only the U.S. demand for pounds has been considered, but the British demand for U.S. dollars must also be considered. This can be referred to as a British *supply of pounds for sale,* since pounds are supplied in the foreign exchange market in exchange for U.S. dollars.

A supply schedule of pounds for sale in the foreign exchange market can be developed in a manner similar to the demand schedule for pounds. Exhibit 4.3 shows the quantity of pounds for sale (supplied to the foreign exchange market in exchange for

Exhibit 4.2 Demand Schedule for British Pounds

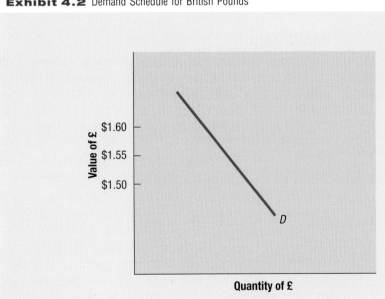

Exhibit 4.3 Supply Schedule of British Pounds for Sale

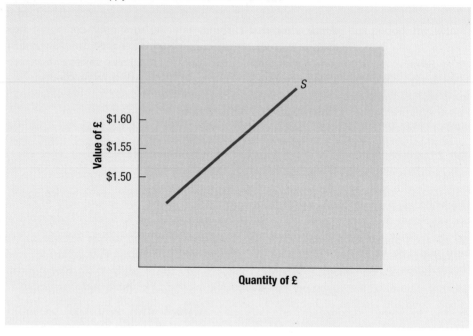

dollars) corresponding to each possible exchange rate at a given point in time. Notice from the supply schedule in Exhibit 4.3 that there is a positive relationship between the value of the British pound and the quantity of British pounds for sale (supplied), which can be explained as follows. When the pound is valued high, British consumers and firms are more likely to purchase U.S. goods. Thus, they supply a greater number of pounds to the market, to be exchanged for dollars. Conversely, when the pound is valued low, the supply of pounds for sale is smaller, reflecting less British desire to obtain U.S. goods.

Equilibrium

The demand and supply schedules for British pounds are combined in Exhibit 4.4. At an exchange rate of $1.50, the quantity of pounds demanded would exceed the supply of pounds for sale. Consequently, the banks that provide foreign exchange services would experience a shortage of pounds at that exchange rate. At an exchange rate of $1.60, the quantity of pounds demanded would be less than the supply of pounds for sale. Therefore, banks providing foreign exchange services would experience a surplus of pounds at that exchange rate. According to Exhibit 4.4, the equilibrium exchange rate is $1.55 because this rate equates the quantity of pounds demanded with the supply of pounds for sale.

Impact of Liquidity. For all currencies, the equilibrium exchange rate is reached through transactions in the foreign exchange market, but for some currencies, the adjustment process is more volatile than for others. The liquidity of a currency affects the sensitivity of the exchange rate to specific transactions. If the currency's spot market is liquid, its exchange rate will not be highly sensitive to a single large purchase or sale of the currency. Therefore, the change in the equilibrium exchange rate will be relatively small. With many willing buyers and sellers of the currency, transactions can be easily accommodated. Conversely, if the currency's spot market is illiquid, its exchange rate

Exhibit 4.4 Equilibrium Exchange Rate Determination

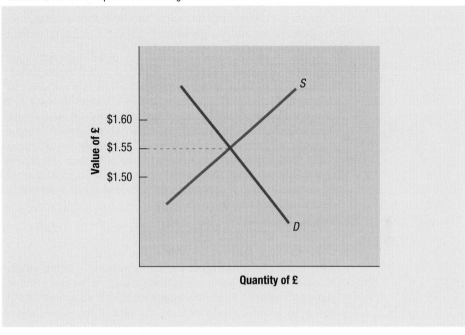

may be highly sensitive to a single large purchase or sale transaction. There are not sufficient buyers or sellers to accommodate a large transaction, which means that the price of the currency must change to rebalance the supply and demand for the currency. Consequently, illiquid currencies tend to exhibit more volatile exchange rate movements, as the equilibrium prices of their currencies adjust to even minor changes in supply and demand conditions.

FACTORS THAT INFLUENCE EXCHANGE RATES

The equilibrium exchange rate will change over time as supply and demand schedules change. The factors that cause currency supply and demand schedules to change are discussed here by relating each factor's influence to the demand and supply schedules graphically displayed in Exhibit 4.4. The following equation summarizes the factors that can influence a currency's spot rate:

$$e = f(\Delta INF, \Delta INT, \Delta INC, \Delta GC, \Delta EXP)$$

where

e = percentage change in the spot rate

ΔINF = change in the differential between U.S. inflation and the foreign country's inflation

ΔINT = change in the differential between the U.S. interest rate and the foreign country's interest rate

ΔINC = change in the differential between the U.S. income level and the foreign country's income level

ΔGC = change in government controls

ΔEXP = change in expectations of future exchange rates

Relative Inflation Rates

Changes in relative inflation rates can affect international trade activity, which influences the demand for and supply of currencies and therefore influences exchange rates.

EXAMPLE

Consider how the demand and supply schedules displayed in Exhibit 4.4 would be affected if U.S. inflation suddenly increased substantially while British inflation remained the same. (Assume that both British and U.S. firms sell goods that can serve as substitutes for each other.) The sudden jump in U.S. inflation should cause an increase in the U.S. demand for British goods and therefore also cause an increase in the U.S. demand for British pounds.

In addition, the jump in U.S. inflation should reduce the British desire for U.S. goods and therefore reduce the supply of pounds for sale. These market reactions are illustrated in Exhibit 4.5. At the previous equilibrium exchange rate of $1.55, there will be a shortage of pounds in the foreign exchange market. The increased U.S. demand for pounds and the reduced supply of pounds for sale place upward pressure on the value of the pound. According to Exhibit 4.5, the new equilibrium value is $1.57. ●

If British inflation increased (rather than U.S. inflation), the opposite forces would occur.

EXAMPLE

Assume there is a sudden and substantial increase in British inflation while U.S. inflation is low. Based on this information, answer the following questions: (1) How is the demand schedule for pounds affected? (2) How is the supply schedule of pounds for sale affected? (3) Will the new equilibrium value of the pound increase, decrease, or remain unchanged? Based on the information given, the answers are (1) the demand schedule for pounds should shift inward, (2) the supply schedule of pounds for sale should shift outward, and (3) the new equilibrium value of the pound will decrease. Of course, the actual amount by which the pound's value will decrease depends on the magnitude of the shifts. There is not enough information to determine their exact magnitude. ●

In reality, the actual demand and supply schedules, and therefore the true equilibrium exchange rate, will reflect several factors simultaneously. The point of the preceding example is to demonstrate how to logically work through the mechanics of the effect that higher inflation in a country can have on an exchange rate. Each factor is assessed one at a time to

Exhibit 4.5 Impact of Rising U.S. Inflation on the Equilibrium Value of the British Pound

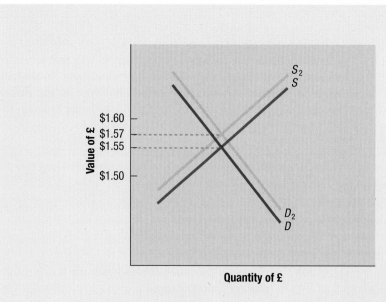

Exhibit 4.6 Impact of Rising U.S. Interest Rates on the Equilibrium Value of the British Pound

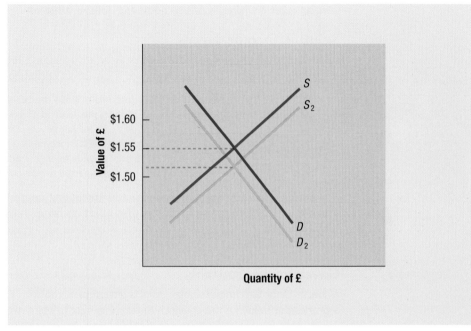

determine its separate influence on exchange rates, holding all other factors constant. Then, all factors can be tied together to fully explain why an exchange rate moves the way it does.

Relative Interest Rates

Changes in relative interest rates affect investment in foreign securities, which influences the demand for and supply of currencies and therefore influences exchange rates.

EXAMPLE

Assume that U.S. interest rates rise while British interest rates remain constant. In this case, U.S. investors will likely reduce their demand for pounds, since U.S. rates are now more attractive relative to British rates, and there is less desire for British bank deposits.

Because U.S. rates will now look more attractive to British investors with excess cash, the supply of pounds for sale by British investors should increase as they establish more bank deposits in the United States. Due to an inward shift in the demand for pounds and an outward shift in the supply of pounds for sale, the equilibrium exchange rate should decrease. This is graphically represented in Exhibit 4.6. If U.S. interest rates decreased relative to British interest rates, the opposite shifts would be expected. ●

Real Interest Rates. Although a relatively high interest rate may attract foreign inflows (to invest in securities offering high yields), the relatively high interest rate may reflect expectations of relatively high inflation. Because high inflation can place downward pressure on the local currency, some foreign investors may be discouraged from investing in securities denominated in that currency. For this reason, it is helpful to consider the real interest rate, which adjusts the nominal interest rate for inflation:

$$\text{Real interest rate} \cong \text{Nominal interest rate} - \text{Inflation rate}$$

This relationship is sometimes called the Fisher effect.

The real interest rate is commonly compared among countries to assess exchange rate movements because it combines nominal interest rates and inflation, both of which influence exchange rates. Other things held constant, a high U.S. real rate of interest relative to other countries tends to boost the dollar's value.

Relative Income Levels

A third factor affecting exchange rates is relative income levels. Because income can affect the amount of imports demanded, it can affect exchange rates.

EXAMPLE

Assume that the U.S. income level rises substantially while the British income level remains unchanged. Consider the impact of this scenario on (1) the demand schedule for pounds, (2) the supply schedule of pounds for sale, and (3) the equilibrium exchange rate. First, the demand schedule for pounds will shift outward, reflecting the increase in U.S. income and therefore increased demand for British goods. Second, the supply schedule of pounds for sale is not expected to change. Therefore, the equilibrium exchange rate of the pound is expected to rise, as shown in Exhibit 4.7. ●

This example presumes that other factors (including interest rates) are held constant. In reality, changing income levels can also affect exchange rates indirectly through their effects on interest rates. When this effect is considered, the impact may differ from the theory presented here, as will be explained shortly.

Government Controls

A fourth factor affecting exchange rates is government controls. The governments of foreign countries can influence the equilibrium exchange rate in many ways, including (1) imposing foreign exchange barriers, (2) imposing foreign trade barriers, (3) intervening (buying and selling currencies) in the foreign exchange markets, and (4) affecting macro variables such as inflation, interest rates, and income levels. Chapter 6 covers these activities in detail.

EXAMPLE

Recall the example in which U.S. interest rates rose relative to British interest rates. The expected reaction was an increase in the British supply of pounds for sale to obtain more U.S. dollars (in order to capitalize on high U.S. money market yields). Yet, if the British government placed a heavy tax on interest income earned from foreign investments, this could discourage the exchange of pounds for dollars. ●

Exhibit 4.7 Impact of Rising U.S. Income Levels on the Equilibrium Value of the British Pound

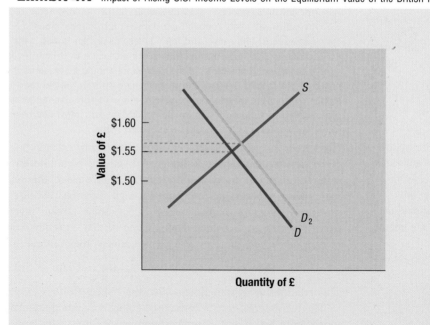

Expectations

A fifth factor affecting exchange rates is market expectations of future exchange rates. Like other financial markets, foreign exchange markets react to any news that may have a future effect. News of a potential surge in U.S. inflation may cause currency traders to sell dollars, anticipating a future decline in the dollar's value. This response places immediate downward pressure on the dollar.

Many institutional investors (such as commercial banks and insurance companies) take currency positions based on anticipated interest rate movements in various countries.

EXAMPLE

Investors may temporarily invest funds in Canada if they expect Canadian interest rates to increase. Such a rise may cause further capital flows into Canada, which could place upward pressure on the Canadian dollar's value. By taking a position based on expectations, investors can fully benefit from the rise in the Canadian dollar's value because they will have purchased Canadian dollars before the change occurred. Although the investors face an obvious risk here that their expectations may be wrong, the point is that expectations can influence exchange rates because they commonly motivate institutional investors to take foreign currency positions. ●

Just as speculators can place upward pressure on a currency's value when they expect that the currency will appreciate, they can place downward pressure on a currency when they expect it to depreciate.

EXAMPLE

In the period from 2006 to 2008, there were substantial capital flows from the United States to Europe (U.S. demand for euros), which placed continuous upward pressure on the euro's value. However, as the credit crisis intensified in September 2008, there were signals that Europe's economy would weaken in the near future. Speculators anticipated that a weaker economy in Europe would cause a reduction in the capital inflows in Europe. Thus, they began to unwind their positions by moving their money out of euros and into dollars. This caused a large increase in the supply of euros for sale (in exchange for dollars) in the foreign exchange market, which caused the euro to depreciate by 20 percent within 2 months. ●

WEB

www.ny.frb.org
Links to information on economic conditions that affect foreign exchange rates and potential speculation in the foreign exchange market.

Impact of Signals on Currency Speculation. Day-to-day speculation on future exchange rate movements is commonly driven by signals of future interest rate movements, but it can also be driven by other factors. Signals of the future economic conditions that affect exchange rates can change quickly, so the speculative positions in currencies may adjust quickly, causing unclear patterns in exchange rates. It is not unusual for the dollar to strengthen substantially on a given day, only to weaken substantially on the next day. This can occur when speculators overreact to news on one day (causing the dollar to be overvalued), which results in a correction on the next day. Overreactions occur because speculators are commonly taking positions based on signals of future actions (rather than the confirmation of actions), and these signals may be misleading.

When speculators speculate on currencies in emerging markets, they can have a substantial impact on exchange rates. Those markets have a smaller amount of foreign exchange trading for other purposes (such as international trade) and therefore are less liquid than the larger markets.

EXAMPLE

The market for the Russian currency (the ruble) is not very active, which means that the volume of rubles purchased or sold in the foreign exchange market is small. Consequently, when news encourages speculators to take positions by purchasing rubles, there can be a major imbalance between the U.S. demand for rubles and the supply of rubles to be exchanged for dollars. So, when U.S. speculators rush to invest in Russia, they can cause an abrupt increase in the value of the ruble. Conversely, there can be an abrupt decline in the value of the ruble when the U.S. speculators attempt to withdraw their investments and exchange rubles back for dollars. ●

Interaction of Factors

Transactions within the foreign exchange markets facilitate either trade or financial flows. Trade-related foreign exchange transactions are generally less responsive to news. Financial flow transactions are very responsive to news, however, because decisions to hold securities denominated in a particular currency are often dependent on anticipated changes in currency values. Sometimes trade-related factors and financial factors interact and simultaneously affect exchange rate movements.

Exhibit 4.8 separates payment flows between countries into trade-related and finance-related flows and summarizes the factors that affect these flows. Over a particular period, some factors may place upward pressure on the value of a foreign currency while other factors place downward pressure on the currency's value.

EXAMPLE Assume the simultaneous existence of (1) a sudden increase in U.S. inflation and (2) a sudden increase in U.S. interest rates. If the British economy is relatively unchanged, the increase in U.S. inflation will place upward pressure on the pound's value because of its impact on international trade. Yet, the increase in U.S. interest rates places downward pressure on the pound's value because of its impact on capital flows. ●

The sensitivity of an exchange rate to these factors is dependent on the volume of international transactions between the two countries. If the two countries engage in a large volume of international trade but a very small volume of international capital flows, the relative inflation rates will likely be more influential. If the two countries engage in a large volume of capital flows, however, interest rate fluctuations may be more influential.

EXAMPLE Assume that Morgan Co., a U.S.-based MNC, commonly purchases supplies from Venezuela and Japan and therefore desires to forecast the direction of the Venezuelan bolivar and the Japanese yen. Morgan's financial analysts have developed the following one-year projections for economic conditions:

Exhibit 4.8 Summary of How Factors Can Affect Exchange Rates

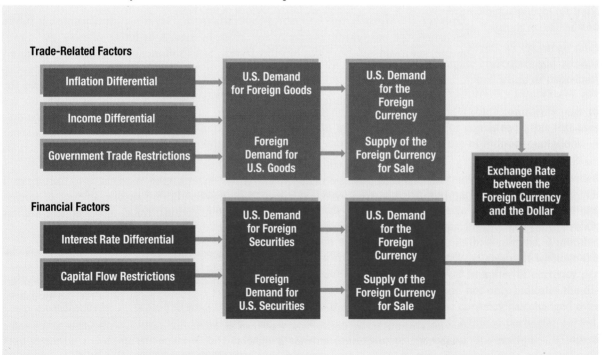

FACTOR	UNITED STATES	VENEZUELA	JAPAN
Change in interest rates	–1%	–2%	–4%
Change in inflation	+2%	–3%	–6%

Assume that the United States and Venezuela conduct a large volume of international trade but engage in minimal capital flow transactions. Also assume that the United States and Japan conduct very little international trade but frequently engage in capital flow transactions. What should Morgan expect regarding the future value of the Venezuelan bolivar and the Japanese yen?

The bolivar should be influenced most by trade-related factors because of Venezuela's assumed heavy trade with the United States. The expected inflationary changes should place upward pressure on the value of the bolivar. Interest rates are expected to have little direct impact on the bolivar because of the assumed infrequent capital flow transactions between the United States and Venezuela.

The Japanese yen should be most influenced by interest rates because of Japan's assumed heavy capital flow transactions with the United States. The expected interest rate changes should place downward pressure on the yen. The inflationary changes are expected to have little direct impact on the yen because of the assumed infrequent trade between the two countries. ●

Capital flows have become larger over time and can easily overwhelm trade flows. For this reason, the relationship between the factors (such as inflation and income) that affect trade and exchange rates is not always as strong as one might expect.

An understanding of exchange rate equilibrium does not guarantee accurate forecasts of future exchange rates because that will depend in part on how the factors that affect exchange rates change in the future. Even if analysts fully realize how factors influence exchange rates, they may not be able to predict how those factors will change.

Influence of Factors across Multiple Currency Markets

Each exchange rate has its own market, meaning its own demand and supply conditions. The value of the British pound in dollars is influenced by the U.S. demand for pounds and the amount of pounds supplied to the market (by British consumers and firms) in exchange for dollars. The value of the Swiss franc in dollars is influenced by the U.S. demand for francs and the amount of francs supplied to the market (by Swiss consumers and firms) in exchange for dollars.

In some periods, most currencies move in the same direction against the dollar. This is typically because of a particular underlying factor in the United States that is having a somewhat similar impact on the demand and supply conditions across all currencies in that period.

EXAMPLE

Assume that interest rates are unusually low in the United States in a particular period, which causes U.S. firms and individual investors with excess short-term cash to invest their cash in various foreign currencies where interest rates are higher. This results in an increased U.S. demand for British pounds, Swiss francs, euros, and other currencies where the interest rate is relatively high compared to the United States and where economic conditions are generally stable. Consequently, there is upward pressure on each of these currencies against the dollar.

Now assume that in the following period, U.S. interest rates rise and are above the interest rates of European countries. This could cause the opposite flow of funds, as investors from European countries invest in dollars in order to capitalize on the higher U.S. interest rates. Consequently, there is an increased supply of British pounds, Swiss francs, and euros for sale by European investors in exchange for dollars. The excess supply of these currencies in the foreign exchange market places downward pressure on their values against the dollar. ●

It is somewhat common for these European currencies to move in the same direction against the dollar because their economic conditions tend to change over time in a somewhat similar manner. However, it is possible for one of the countries to experience different economic conditions in a particular period, which may cause its currency's movement against the dollar to deviate from the movements of the other European currencies.

EXAMPLE

Continuing with the previous example, assume that the U.S. interest rates remain relatively high compared to the European countries, but that the Swiss government suddenly imposes a special tax on interest earned by Swiss firms and consumers on investments in foreign countries. This will reduce the Swiss investment in the United States (and therefore reduce the supply of Swiss francs to be exchanged for dollars), which may stabilize the Swiss franc's value. Meanwhile, investors in other parts of Europe continue to exchange their euros for dollars to capitalize on high U.S. interest rates, which causes the euro to depreciate against the dollar. ●

MOVEMENTS IN CROSS EXCHANGE RATES

The value of the British pound in Swiss francs (from a U.S. perspective, this is a cross exchange rate) is influenced by the Swiss demand for pounds and the supply of pounds to be exchanged (by British consumers and firms) for Swiss francs. The movement in a cross exchange rate over a particular period can be measured as its percentage change in that period, just like any currency's movement against the dollar. You can measure the percentage change in a cross exchange rate over a time period even if you do not have cross exchange rate quotations, as shown here:

EXAMPLE

Today, you notice that the euro is valued at $1.33 while the Mexican peso is valued at $.10. One year ago, the euro was valued at $1.40, and the Mexican peso was worth $.09. This information allows you to determine how the euro changed against the Mexican peso over the last year:

$$\text{Cross rate of euro today} = 1.33/.10 \text{ [One euro} = 13.33 \text{ pesos.]}$$
$$\text{Cross rate of euro one year ago} = 1.40/.09 \text{ [One euro} = 15.55 \text{ pesos.]}$$
$$\text{Percentage change} = (13.33 - 15.55)/15.55 = -14.3\%.$$

Thus, the euro depreciated against the peso by 14.3 percent over the last year. ●

The cross exchange rate changes when either currency's value changes against the dollar. You can use intuition to recognize the following relationships for two nondollar currencies called currency A and currency B:

- When currencies A and B move by the same degree against the dollar, there is no change in the cross exchange rate.
- When currency A appreciates against the dollar by a greater degree than currency B appreciates against the dollar, then currency A appreciates against currency B.
- When currency A appreciates against the dollar by a smaller degree than currency B appreciates, then currency A depreciates against currency B.
- When currency A appreciates against the dollar, while currency B is unchanged against the dollar, currency A appreciates against currency B by the same degree as it appreciated against the dollar.
- When currency A depreciates against the dollar while currency B appreciates against the dollar, then currency A depreciates against currency B.

Exhibit 4.9 shows the movements in the British pound, the euro, and the cross exchange rate of the pound in euros (number of euros per pound). Notice that the pound and euro values commonly move in the same direction against the dollar. The relationships described above are reinforced by this exhibit.

Exhibit 4.9 Trends in the Pound, Euro, and Pound/Euro

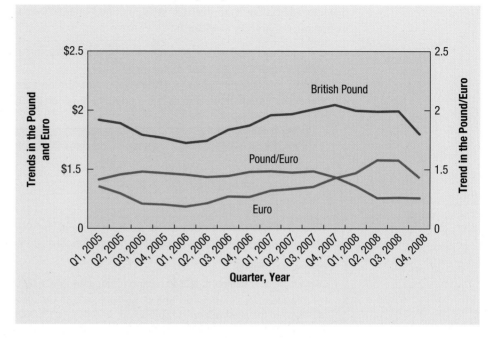

Explaining Movements in Cross Exchange Rates

There are unique international trade and financial flows between every pair of countries. These flows dictate the unique supply and demand conditions for the currencies of the two countries, which affect the movement in the equilibrium exchange rate between the two currencies. A change in the equilibrium cross exchange rate over time is due to the same types of forces identified earlier in the chapter that affect the demand and supply conditions between the two currencies, as illustrated next.

EXAMPLE

Assume that the interest rates in Switzerland and the United Kingdom were similar, but today the Swiss interest rates increased, while British interest rates remain unchanged. If British investors wish to capitalize on the high Swiss interest rates, this reflects an increase in the British demand for Swiss francs. Assuming that the supply of Swiss francs to be exchanged for pounds is unchanged, the increased British demand for Swiss francs should cause the value of the Swiss franc to appreciate against the British pound. ●

ANTICIPATION OF EXCHANGE RATE MOVEMENTS

Some large commercial banks closely monitor exchange rates in the foreign exchange market. They can attempt to anticipate how the equilibrium exchange rate will change in the near future based on existing economic conditions identified in this chapter. They may take a position in the currency in order to benefit from their expectations. They need to consider the prevailing interest rates at which they can invest or borrow, along with their expectations of exchange rates, in order to determine whether to take a speculative position in a foreign currency.

Bank Speculation Based on Expected Appreciation

When commercial banks believe that a particular currency is presently valued lower than it should be in the foreign exchange market, they may consider investing in that currency now before it appreciates. They would hope to liquidate their investment in that currency after it appreciates so that they benefit from selling the currency for a higher price than they paid for it.

- Chicago Bank expects the exchange rate of the New Zealand dollar (NZ$) to appreciate from its present level of $.50 to $.52 in 30 days.
- Chicago Bank is able to borrow $20 million on a short-term basis from other banks.
- Present short-term interest rates (annualized) in the interbank market are as follows:

CURRENCY	LENDING RATE	BORROWING RATE
U.S. dollars	6.72%	7.20%
New Zealand dollars (NZ$)	6.48%	6.96%

Because brokers sometimes serve as intermediaries between banks, the lending rate differs from the borrowing rate. Given this information, Chicago Bank could

1. Borrow $20 million.
2. Convert the $20 million to NZ$40 million (computed as $20,000,000/$.50).
3. Lend the New Zealand dollars at 6.48 percent annualized, which represents a .54 percent return over the 30-day period [computed as 6.48% × (30/360)]. After 30 days, the bank will receive NZ$40,216,000 [computed as NZ$40,000,000 × (1 + .0054)].
4. Use the proceeds from the New Zealand dollar loan repayment (on day 30) to repay the U.S. dollars borrowed. The annual interest on the U.S. dollars borrowed is 7.2 percent, or .6 percent over the 30-day period [computed as 7.2% × (30/360)]. The total U.S. dollar amount necessary to repay the U.S. dollar loan is therefore $20,120,000 [computed as $20,000,000 × (1 + .006)].

Assuming that the exchange rate on day 30 is $.52 per New Zealand dollar as anticipated, the number of New Zealand dollars necessary to repay the U.S. dollar loan is NZ$38,692,308 (computed as $20,120,000/$.52 per New Zealand dollar).

Given that the bank accumulated NZ$40,216,000 from lending New Zealand dollars, it would earn a speculative profit of NZ$1,523,692, which is the equivalent of $792,320 (given a spot rate of $.52 per New Zealand dollar on day 30). The bank would earn this speculative profit without using any funds from deposit accounts because the funds would have been borrowed through the interbank market. ●

Keep in mind that the computations in the example measure the expected profits from the speculative strategy. There is a risk that the actual outcome will be less favorable if the currency appreciates to a smaller degree or depreciates.

Bank Speculation Based on Expected Depreciation

If commercial banks believe that a particular currency is presently valued higher than it should be in the foreign exchange market, they may borrow funds in that currency now (and convert to their local currency now) before the currency's value declines to its proper level. They would hope to repay the loan in that currency after the currency depreciates, so that they would be able to buy that currency for a lower price than the price at which they initially converted that currency to their own currency.

Assume that Carbondale Bank expects an exchange rate of $.48 for the New Zealand dollar on day 30. It can borrow New Zealand dollars, convert them to U.S. dollars, and lend the U.S. dollars out. On day 30, it will close out these positions. Using the rates quoted in the previous example, and assuming the bank can borrow NZ$40 million, the bank takes the following steps:

1. Borrow NZ$40 million.

2. Convert the NZ$40 million to $20 million (computed as NZ$40,000,000 × $.50).

3. Lend the U.S. dollars at 6.72 percent, which represents a .56 percent return over the 30-day period. After 30 days, the bank will receive $20,112,000 [computed as $20,000,000 × (1 + .0056)].

4. Use the proceeds of the U.S. dollar loan repayment (on day 30) to repay the New Zealand dollars borrowed. The annual interest on the New Zealand dollars borrowed is 6.96 percent, or .58 percent over the 30-day period [computed as 6.96% × (30/360)]. The total New Zealand dollar amount necessary to repay the loan is therefore NZ$40,232,000 [computed as NZ$40,000,000 × (1 + .0058)].

Assuming that the exchange rate on day 30 is $.48 per New Zealand dollar as anticipated, the number of U.S. dollars necessary to repay the NZ$ loan is $19,311,360 (computed as NZ $40,232,000 × $.48 per New Zealand dollar). Given that the bank accumulated $20,112,000 from its U.S. dollar loan, it would earn a speculative profit of $800,640 without using any of its own money (computed as $20,112,000 − $19,311,360). ●

Most money center banks continue to take some speculative positions in foreign currencies. In fact, some banks' currency trading profits have exceeded $100 million per quarter.

The potential returns from foreign currency speculation are high for banks that have large borrowing capacity. Nevertheless, foreign exchange rates are very volatile, and a poor forecast could result in a large loss. One of the best-known bank failures, Franklin National Bank in 1974, was primarily attributed to massive speculative losses from foreign currency positions. In September 2008, Citic Pacific (based in Hong Kong) experienced a loss of $2 billion due to speculation in the foreign exchange market. Some other types of firms such as Aracruz (Brazil), and Cemex (Mexico) also incurred large losses in 2008 due to speculation in the foreign exchange market.

Speculation by Individuals

Even individuals whose career has nothing to do with foreign exchange markets speculate in foreign currencies. They can take positions in the currency futures market or options market, as discussed in detail in Chapter 5. Alternatively, they can set up an account at many different foreign exchange trading websites such as FXCM.com with an initial amount as small as $300. They can move their money into one or more foreign currencies. In addition, they can establish a margin account on some websites whereby they may finance a portion of their investment with borrowed funds in order to take positions in a foreign currency.

Many of the websites have a demonstration (demo) that allows prospective speculators to simulate the process of speculating in the foreign exchange market. Thus, speculators can determine how much they would have earned or lost by pretending to take a position with an assumed investment and borrowed funds. The use of borrowed funds to complement their investment increases the potential return and risk on the investment. That is, a speculative gain will be magnified when the position is partially funded with borrowed money, but a speculative loss will also be magnified when the position is partially funded with borrowed money.

Individual speculators quickly realize that the foreign exchange market is very active even when financial markets in their own country close. Consequently, the value of a currency can change substantially overnight while other local financial markets are closed or have very limited trading. Individuals are attracted by the potential for large gains. Yet, as with other forms of gambling, there is a risk that they could lose their entire investment. In this case, they would still be liable for any debt created from borrowing money to support their speculative position.

WEB

www.forex.com
Individuals can open a foreign exchange trading account for a minumum of only $250.

WEB

www.fxcom.com/
Facilitates the trading of foreign currencies.

WEB

www.hedgestreet.com
Facilitates the trading of foreign currencies.

SUMMARY

- Exchange rate movements are commonly measured by the percentage change in their values over a specified period, such as a month or a year. MNCs closely monitor exchange rate movements over the period in which they have cash flows denominated in the foreign currencies of concern.

- The equilibrium exchange rate between two currencies at any point in time is based on the demand and supply conditions. Changes in the demand for a currency or the supply of a currency for sale will affect the equilibrium exchange rate.

- The key economic factors that can influence exchange rate movements through their effects on demand and supply conditions are relative inflation rates, interest rates, and income levels, as well as government controls. As these factors cause a change in international trade or financial flows, they affect the demand for a currency or the supply of currency for sale and therefore affect the equilibrium exchange rate.

- The two factors that are most closely monitored by foreign exchange market participants are relative inflation and interest rates:

  If a foreign country experiences high inflation (relative to the United States), its exports to the United States should decrease (U.S. demand for its currency decreases), its imports should increase (supply of its currency to be exchanged for dollars increases), and there is downward pressure on its currency's equilibrium value.

  If a foreign country experiences an increase in interest rates (relative to U.S. interest rates), the inflow of U.S. funds to purchase its securities should increase (U.S. demand for its currency increases), the outflow of its funds to purchase U.S. securities should decrease (supply of its currency to be exchanged for U.S. dollars decreases), and there is upward pressure on its currency's equilibrium value.

- All relevant factors must be considered simultaneously to assess the likely movement in a currency's value.

- There are unique international trade and financial flows between every pair of countries. These flows dictate the unique supply and demand conditions for the currencies of the two countries, which affect the equilibrium cross exchange rate between the two currencies. The movement in the exchange rate between two nondollar currencies can be determined by considering the movement in each currency against the dollar and applying intuition.

POINT COUNTER-POINT

How Can Persistently Weak Currencies Be Stabilized?

Point The currencies of some Latin American countries depreciate against the U.S. dollar on a consistent basis. The governments of these countries need to attract more capital flows by raising interest rates and making their currencies more attractive. They also need to insure bank deposits so that foreign investors who invest in large bank deposits do not need to worry about default risk. In addition, they could impose capital restrictions on local investors to prevent capital outflows.

Counter-Point Some Latin American countries have had high inflation, which encourages local firms and consumers to purchase products from the United States instead. Thus, these countries could relieve the downward pressure on their local currencies by reducing inflation. To reduce inflation, a country may have to reduce economic growth temporarily. These countries should not raise their interest rates in order to attract foreign investment, because they will still not attract funds if investors fear that there will be large capital outflows upon the first threat of continued depreciation.

Who Is Correct? Use the Internet to learn more about this issue. Which argument do you support? Offer your own opinion on this issue.

SELF-TEST

Answers are provided in Appendix A at the back of the text.

1. Briefly describe how various economic factors can affect the equilibrium exchange rate of the Japanese yen's value with respect to that of the dollar.

2. A recent shift in the interest rate differential between the United States and Country A had a large effect on the value of Currency A. However, the same shift in the interest rate differential between the United States and Country B had no effect on the value of Currency B. Explain why the effects may vary.

3. Smart Banking Corp. can borrow $5 million at 6 percent annualized. It can use the proceeds to invest in Canadian dollars at 9 percent annualized over a six-day period. The Canadian dollar is worth $.95 and is expected to be worth $.94 in six days. Based on this information, should Smart Banking Corp. borrow U.S. dollars and invest in Canadian dollars? What would be the gain or loss in U.S. dollars?

QUESTIONS AND APPLICATIONS

1. Percentage Depreciation. Assume the spot rate of the British pound is $1.73. The expected spot rate one year from now is assumed to be $1.66. What percentage depreciation does this reflect?

2. Inflation Effects on Exchange Rates. Assume that the U.S. inflation rate becomes high relative to Canadian inflation. Other things being equal, how should this affect the (a) U.S. demand for Canadian dollars, (b) supply of Canadian dollars for sale, and (c) equilibrium value of the Canadian dollar?

3. Interest Rate Effects on Exchange Rates. Assume U.S. interest rates fall relative to British interest rates. Other things being equal, how should this affect the (a) U.S. demand for British pounds, (b) supply of pounds for sale, and (c) equilibrium value of the pound?

4. Income Effects on Exchange Rates. Assume that the U.S. income level rises at a much higher rate than does the Canadian income level. Other things being equal, how should this affect the (a) U.S. demand for Canadian dollars, (b) supply of Canadian dollars for sale, and (c) equilibrium value of the Canadian dollar?

5. Trade Restriction Effects on Exchange Rates. Assume that the Japanese government relaxes its controls on imports by Japanese companies. Other things being equal, how should this affect the (a) U.S. demand for Japanese yen, (b) supply of yen for sale, and (c) equilibrium value of the yen?

6. Effects of Real Interest Rates. What is the expected relationship between the relative real interest rates of two countries and the exchange rate of their currencies?

7. Speculative Effects on Exchange Rates. Explain why a public forecast by a respected economist about future interest rates could affect the value of the dollar today. Why do some forecasts by well-respected economists have no impact on today's value of the dollar?

8. Factors Affecting Exchange Rates. What factors affect the future movements in the value of the euro against the dollar?

9. Interaction of Exchange Rates. Assume that there are substantial capital flows among Canada, the United States, and Japan. If interest rates in Canada decline to a level below the U.S. interest rate, and inflationary expectations remain unchanged, how could this affect the value of the Canadian dollar against the U.S. dollar? How might this decline in Canada's interest rates possibly affect the value of the Canadian dollar against the Japanese yen?

10. Trade Deficit Effects on Exchange Rates.
Every month, the U.S. trade deficit figures are announced. Foreign exchange traders often react to this announcement and even attempt to forecast the figures before they are announced.

a. Why do you think the trade deficit announcement sometimes has such an impact on foreign exchange trading?

b. In some periods, foreign exchange traders do not respond to a trade deficit announcement, even when the announced deficit is very large. Offer an explanation for such a lack of response.

11. Comovements of Exchange Rates. Explain why the value of the British pound against the dollar will not always move in tandem with the value of the euro against the dollar.

12. Factors Affecting Exchange Rates. In the 1990s, Russia was attempting to import more goods but had little to offer other countries in terms of potential exports. In addition, Russia's inflation rate was high. Explain the type of pressure that these factors placed on the Russian currency.

13. National Income Effects. Analysts commonly attribute the appreciation of a currency to expectations that economic conditions will strengthen. Yet, this chapter suggests that when other factors are held constant, increased national income could increase imports and cause the local currency to weaken. In reality, other factors are not constant. What other factor is likely to be affected by increased economic growth and could place upward pressure on the value of the local currency?

14. Factors Affecting Exchange Rates. If the Asian countries experience a decline in economic growth (and experience a decline in inflation and interest rates as a result), how will their currency values (relative to the U.S. dollar) be affected?

15. Impact of Crises. Why do you think most crises in countries (such as the Asian crisis) cause the local currency to weaken abruptly? Is it because of trade or capital flows?

16. Impact of September 11. The terrorist attacks on the United States on September 11, 2001, were expected to weaken U.S. economic conditions and reduce U.S. interest rates. How do you think the weaker U.S. economic conditions would have affected trade flows? How would this have affected the value of the dollar (holding other factors constant)? How do you think the lower U.S. interest rates would have affected the value of the U.S. dollar (holding other factors constant)?

Advanced Questions

17. Measuring Effects on Exchange Rates. Tarheel Co. plans to determine how changes in U.S. and Mexican real interest rates will affect the value of the U.S. dollar. (See Appendix C for the basics of regression analysis.)

a. Describe a regression model that could be used to achieve this purpose. Also explain the expected sign of the regression coefficient.

b. If Tarheel Co. thinks that the existence of a quota in particular historical periods may have affected ex-

change rates, how might this be accounted for in the regression model?

18. Factors Affecting Exchange Rates. Mexico tends to have much higher inflation than the United States and also much higher interest rates than the United States. Inflation and interest rates are much more volatile in Mexico than in industrialized countries. The value of the Mexican peso is typically more volatile than the currencies of industrialized countries from a U.S. perspective; it has typically depreciated from one year to the next, but the degree of depreciation has varied substantially. The bid/ask spread tends to be wider for the peso than for currencies of industrialized countries.

a. Identify the most obvious economic reason for the persistent depreciation of the peso.

b. High interest rates are commonly expected to strengthen a country's currency because they can encourage foreign investment in securities in that country, which results in the exchange of other currencies for that currency. Yet, the peso's value has declined against the dollar over most years even though Mexican interest rates are typically much higher than U.S. interest rates. Thus, it appears that the high Mexican interest rates do not attract substantial U.S. investment in Mexico's securities. Why do you think U.S. investors do not try to capitalize on the high interest rates in Mexico?

c. Why do you think the bid/ask spread is higher for pesos than for currencies of industrialized countries? How does this affect a U.S. firm that does substantial business in Mexico?

19. Aggregate Effects on Exchange Rates. Assume that the United States invests heavily in government and corporate securities of Country K. In addition, residents of Country K invest heavily in the United States. Approximately $10 billion worth of investment transactions occur between these two countries each year. The total dollar value of trade transactions per year is about $8 million. This information is expected to also hold in the future.

Because your firm exports goods to Country K, your job as international cash manager requires you to forecast the value of Country K's currency (the "krank") with respect to the dollar. Explain how each of the following conditions will affect the value of the krank, holding other things equal. Then, aggregate all of these impacts to develop an overall forecast of the krank's movement against the dollar.

a. U.S. inflation has suddenly increased substantially, while Country K's inflation remains low.

b. U.S. interest rates have increased substantially, while Country K's interest rates remain low. Investors of both countries are attracted to high interest rates.

c. The U.S. income level increased substantially, while Country K's income level has remained unchanged.

d. The United States is expected to impose a small tariff on goods imported from Country K.

e. Combine all expected impacts to develop an overall forecast.

20. Speculation. Blue Demon Bank expects that the Mexican peso will depreciate against the dollar from its spot rate of $.15 to $.14 in 10 days. The following interbank lending and borrowing rates exist:

CURRENCY	LENDING RATE	BORROWING RATE
U.S. dollar	8.0%	8.3%
Mexican peso	8.5%	8.7%

Assume that Blue Demon Bank has a borrowing capacity of either $10 million or 70 million pesos in the interbank market, depending on which currency it wants to borrow.

a. How could Blue Demon Bank attempt to capitalize on its expectations without using deposited funds? Estimate the profits that could be generated from this strategy.

b. Assume all the preceding information with this exception: Blue Demon Bank expects the peso to appreciate from its present spot rate of $.15 to $.17 in 30 days. How could it attempt to capitalize on its expectations without using deposited funds? Estimate the profits that could be generated from this strategy.

21. Speculation. Diamond Bank expects that the Singapore dollar will depreciate against the U.S. dollar from its spot rate of $.43 to $.42 in 60 days. The following interbank lending and borrowing rates exist:

CURRENCY	LENDING RATE	BORROWING RATE
U.S. dollar	7.0%	7.2%
Singapore dollar	22.0%	24.0%

Diamond Bank considers borrowing 10 million Singapore dollars in the interbank market and investing the funds in U.S. dollars for 60 days. Estimate the profits (or losses) that could be earned from this strategy. Should Diamond Bank pursue this strategy?

22. Relative Importance of Factors Affecting Exchange Rate Risk. Assume that the level of capital flows between the United States and the country of Krendo is negligible (close to zero) and will continue to be negligible. There is a substantial amount of trade between the United States and the country of Krendo and no capital flows. How will high inflation and high interest rates affect the value of the kren (Krendo's currency)? Explain.

23. Assessing the Euro's Potential Movements. You reside in the United States and are planning to make a one-year investment in Germany during the next year. Since the investment is denominated in euros, you want to forecast how the euro's value may change against the dollar over the one-year period. You expect that Germany will experience an inflation rate of 1 percent during the next year, while all other European countries will experience an inflation rate of 8 percent over the next year. You expect that the United States will experience an annual inflation rate of 2 percent during the next year. You believe that the primary factor that affects any exchange rate is the inflation rate. Based on the information provided in this question, will the euro appreciate, depreciate, or stay at about the same level against the dollar over the next year? Explain.

24. Weighing Factors That Affect Exchange Rates. Assume that the level of capital flows between the United States and the country of Zeus is negligible (close to zero) and will continue to be negligible. There is a substantial amount of trade between the United States and the country of Zeus. The main import by the United States is basic clothing purchased by U.S. retail stores from Zeus, while the main import by Zeus is special computer chips that are only made in the United States and are needed by many manufacturers in Zeus. Suddenly, the U.S. government decides to impose a 20 percent tax on the clothing imports. The Zeus government immediately retaliates by imposing a 20 percent tax on the computer chip imports. Second, the Zeus government immediately imposes a 60 percent tax on any interest income that would be earned by Zeus investors if they buy U.S. securities. Third, the Zeus central bank raises its local interest rates so that they are now higher than interest rates in the United States. Do you think the currency of Zeus (called the zee) will appreciate or depreciate against the dollar as a result of all the government actions described above? Explain.

25. How Factors Affect Exchange Rates. The country of Luta has large capital flows with the United States. It has no trade with the United States and will not have trade with the United States in the future. Its interest rate is 6 percent, the same as the U.S. interest rate. Its rate of inflation is 5 percent, the same as the U.S. inflation rate. You expect that the inflation rate in Luta will rise to 8 percent this coming year, while the U.S. inflation rate will remain at 5 percent. You expect that Luta's interest rate will rise to 9 percent during the next year. You expect that the U.S. interest rate will remain at 6 percent this year. Do you think Luta's currency will appreciate, depreciate, or remain unchanged against the dollar? Briefly explain.

26. Speculation on Expected Exchange Rates. Kurnick Co. expects that the pound will depreciate from $1.70 to $1.68 in one year. It has no money to invest, but it could borrow money to invest. A bank allows it to borrow either 1 million dollars or 1 million pounds for one year. It can borrow dollars at 6 percent or British pounds at 5 percent for 1 year. It can invest in a risk-free dollar deposit at 5 percent for 1 year or a risk-free British deposit at 4 percent for 1 year. Determine the expected profit or loss (in dollars) if Kurnick Co. pursues a strategy to capitalize on the expected depreciation of the pound.

27. Assessing Volatility of Exchange Rate Movements. Assume you want to determine whether the monthly movements in the Polish zloty against the dollar are more volatile than monthly movements in some other currencies against the dollar. The zloty was valued at $.4602 on May 1, $.4709 on June 1, $.4888 on July 1, $.4406 on August 1, and $.4260 on September 1. Using Excel or another electronic spreadsheet, compute the standard deviation (a measure of volatility) of the zloty's monthly exchange rate movements. Show your spreadsheet.

28. Impact of Economy on Exchange Rates. Assume that inflation is zero in the United States and in Europe and will remain at zero. United States interest rates are presently the same as in Europe. Assume that the economic growth for the United States is presently similar to Europe. Assume that international capital flows are much larger than international trade flows. Today, there is news that clearly signals economic conditions in Europe will be weakening in the future, while economic conditions in the United States will remain the same. Explain why and how (which direction) the euro's value would change today based on this information.

29. Movements in Cross Exchange Rates. Last year a dollar was equal to 7 Swedish kronor, and a Polish zloty was equal to $.40. Today, the dollar is equal to 8 Swedish kronor, and a Polish zloty is equal to $.44. By what percentage did the cross exchange rate of the Polish zloty in Swedish kronor (that is, the number of kronor that can be purchased with one zloty) change over the last year?

Discussion in the Boardroom

This exercise can be found in Appendix E at the back of this textbook.

Running Your Own MNC

This exercise can be found on the *International Financial Management* text companion website located at www.cengage.com/finance/madura.

BLADES, INC. CASE

Assessment of Future Exchange Rate Movements

As the chief financial officer of Blades, Inc., Ben Holt is pleased that his current system of exporting "Speedos" to Thailand seems to be working well. Blades' primary customer in Thailand, a retailer called Entertainment Products, has committed itself to purchasing a fixed number of Speedos annually for the next 3 years at a fixed price denominated in baht, Thailand's currency. Furthermore, Blades is using a Thai supplier for some of the components needed to manufacture Speedos. Nevertheless, Holt is concerned about recent developments in Asia. Foreign investors from various countries had invested heavily in Thailand to take advantage of the high interest rates there. As a result of the weak economy in Thailand, however, many foreign investors have lost confidence in Thailand and have withdrawn their funds.

Ben Holt has two major concerns regarding these developments. First, he is wondering how these changes in Thailand's economy could affect the value of the Thai baht and, consequently, Blades. More specifically, he is wondering whether the effects on the Thai baht may affect Blades even though its primary Thai customer is committed to Blades over the next 3 years.

Second, Holt believes that Blades may be able to speculate on the anticipated movement of the baht, but he is uncertain about the procedure needed to accomplish this. To facilitate Holt's understanding of exchange rate speculation, he has asked you, Blades' financial analyst, to provide him with detailed illustrations of two scenarios. In the first, the baht would move from a current level of $.022 to $.020 within the next 30 days. Under the second scenario, the baht would move from its current level to $.025 within the next 30 days.

Based on Holt's needs, he has provided you with the following list of questions to be answered:

1. How are percentage changes in a currency's value measured? Illustrate your answer numerically by assuming a change in the Thai baht's value from a value of $.022 to $.026.

2. What are the basic factors that determine the value of a currency? In equilibrium, what is the relationship between these factors?

3. How might the relatively high levels of inflation and interest rates in Thailand affect the baht's value?

(Assume a constant level of U.S. inflation and interest rates.)

4. How do you think the loss of confidence in the Thai baht, evidenced by the withdrawal of funds from Thailand, will affect the baht's value? Would Blades be affected by the change in value, given the primary Thai customer's commitment?

5. Assume that Thailand's central bank wishes to prevent a withdrawal of funds from its country in order to prevent further changes in the currency's value. How could it accomplish this objective using interest rates?

6. Construct a spreadsheet illustrating the steps Blades' treasurer would need to follow in order to speculate on expected movements in the baht's value over the next 30 days. Also show the speculative profit (in dollars) resulting from each scenario. Use both of Ben Holt's examples to illustrate possible speculation. Assume that Blades can borrow either $10 million or the baht equivalent of this amount. Furthermore, assume that the following short-term interest rates (annualized) are available to Blades:

CURRENCY	LENDING RATE	BORROWING RATE
Dollars	8.10%	8.20%
Thai baht	14.80%	15.40%

SMALL BUSINESS DILEMMA

Assessment by the Sports Exports Company of Factors That Affect the British Pound's Value

Because the Sports Exports Company (a U.S. firm) receives payments in British pounds every month and converts those pounds into dollars, it needs to closely monitor the value of the British pound in the future. Jim Logan, owner of the Sports Exports Company, expects that inflation will rise substantially in the United Kingdom, while inflation in the United States will remain low. He also expects that

the interest rates in both countries will rise by about the same amount.

1. Given Jim's expectations, forecast whether the pound will appreciate or depreciate against the dollar over time.

2. Given Jim's expectations, will the Sports Exports Company be favorably or unfavorably affected by the future changes in the value of the pound?

INTERNET/EXCEL EXERCISES

The website of the Federal Reserve Board of Governors provides exchange rate trends of various currencies. Its address is www.federalreserve.gov/releases/.

1. Click on the section "Foreign Exchange Rates–monthly." Use this Web page to determine how exchange rates of various currencies have changed in recent months. Note that most of these currencies (except the British pound) are quoted in units per dollar. In general, have most currencies strengthened or weakened against the dollar over the last 3 months? Offer one or more reasons to explain the recent general movements in currency values against the dollar.

2. Does it appear that the Asian currencies move in the same direction relative to the dollar? Does it appear that the Latin American currencies move

in the same direction against the dollar? Explain.

3. Go to www.oanda.com/convert/fxhistory. Obtain the direct exchange rate ($ per currency unit) of the Canadian dollar for the beginning of each of the last 12 months. Insert this information in a column on an electronic spreadsheet. (See Appendix C for help on conducting analyses with Excel.) Repeat the process to obtain the direct exchange rate of the euro. Compute the percentage change in the value of the Canadian dollar and the euro each month. Determine the standard deviation of the movements (percentage changes) in the Canadian dollar and in the euro. Compare the standard deviation of the euro's movements to the standard deviation of the Canadian dollar's movements. Which currency is more volatile?

REFERENCES

Bahmani-Oskooee, Mohsen, and Scott W. Hegerty, Autumn 2007, Exchange Rate Volatility and Trade Flows: A Review Article, *Journal of Economic Studies*, pp. 211–255.

Egert Balazs, and Laszlo Halpern, May 2006, Equilibrium Exchange Rates in Central and Eastern Europe: A Meta-Regression Analysis, *Journal of Banking & Finance*, pp. 1359–1374.

Froot, Kenneth A., and Tarun Ramadorai, Jun 2005, Currency Returns, Intrinsic Value, and Institutional-Investor Flows, *The Journal of Finance*, pp. 1535–1566.

Morales-Zumaquero, Amalia, Nov 2006, Explaining Real Exchange Rate Fluctuations, *Journal of Applied Economics*, pp. 345–360.

Osler, Carol L., Jan 2006, Macro Lessons from Microstructure, *International Journal of Finance & Economics*, pp. 55–80.

Platt, Gordon, Mar 2006, Rate Differentials Keeping Dollar Strong, *Global Finance*, pp. 52–53.

Platt, Gordon, Sep 2006, Analysts Say China May Accelerate Pace of Its Currency Reforms to Cool an Overheating Economy, *Global Finance*, pp. 55–58.

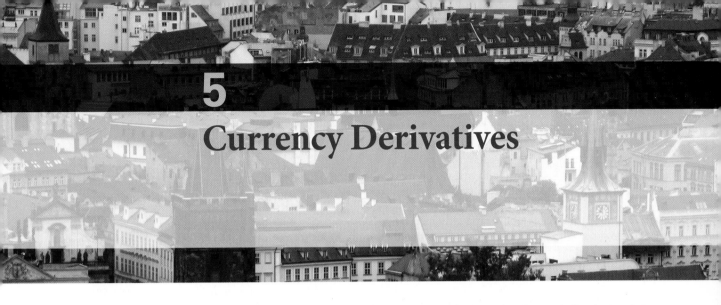

5

Currency Derivatives

A currency derivative is a contract whose price is partially derived from the value of the underlying currency that it represents. Some individuals and financial firms take positions in currency derivatives to speculate on future exchange rate movements. MNCs commonly take positions in currency derivatives to hedge their exposure to exchange rate risk. Their managers must understand how these derivatives can be used to achieve corporate goals.

FORWARD MARKET

The forward market facilitates the trading of forward contracts on currencies. A **forward contract** is an agreement between a corporation and a financial institution (such as a commercial bank) to exchange a specified amount of a currency at a specified exchange rate (called the **forward rate**) on a specified date in the future. When multinational corporations (MNCs) anticipate a future need for or future receipt of a foreign currency, they can set up forward contracts to lock in the rate at which they can purchase or sell a particular foreign currency. Virtually all large MNCs use forward contracts to some degree. Some MNCs have forward contracts outstanding worth more than $100 million to hedge various positions.

Because forward contracts accommodate large corporations, the forward transaction will often be valued at $1 million or more. Forward contracts normally are not used by consumers or small firms. In cases when a bank does not know a corporation well or fully trust it, the bank may request that the corporation make an initial deposit to assure that it will fulfill its obligation. Such a deposit is called a compensating balance and typically does not pay interest.

The most common forward contracts are for 30, 60, 90, 180, and 360 days, although other periods (including longer periods) are available. The forward rate of a given currency will typically vary with the length (number of days) of the forward period.

How MNCs Use Forward Contracts

MNCs use forward contracts to hedge their imports. They can lock in the rate at which they obtain a currency needed to purchase imports.

Turz, Inc., is an MNC based in Chicago that will need 1,000,000 Singapore dollars in 90 days to purchase Singapore imports. It can buy Singapore dollars for immediate delivery at the spot rate of $.50 per Singapore dollar (S$). At this spot rate, the firm would need $500,000 (computed as S$1,000,000 × $.50 per Singapore dollar). However, it does not have the funds right now to exchange for Singapore dollars. It could wait 90 days and then exchange U.S. dollars for Singapore dollars at the spot rate existing at that time. But Turz does not know what the spot rate will be at that time. If the rate rises to $.60 by then, Turz will need $600,000 (computed as S$1,000,000 × $.60 per Singapore dollar), an additional outlay of $100,000 due to the appreciation of the Singapore dollar.

To avoid exposure to exchange rate risk, Turz can lock in the rate it will pay for Singapore dollars 90 days from now without having to exchange U.S. dollars for Singapore dollars immediately. Specifically, Turz can negotiate a forward contract with a bank to purchase S$1,000,000 90 days forward. ●

The ability of a forward contract to lock in an exchange rate can create an opportunity cost in some cases.

EXAMPLE

Assume that in the previous example Turz negotiated a 90-day forward rate of $.50 to purchase S$1,000,000. If the spot rate in 90 days is $.47, Turz will have paid $.03 per unit or $30,000 (1,000,000 units × $.03) more for the Singapore dollars than if it did not have a forward contract. ●

Corporations also use the forward market to lock in the rate at which they can sell foreign currencies. This strategy is used to hedge against the possibility of those currencies depreciating over time.

EXAMPLE

Scanlon, Inc., based in Virginia, exports products to a French firm and will receive payment of €400,000 in 4 months. It can lock in the amount of dollars to be received from this transaction by selling euros forward. That is, Scanlon can negotiate a forward contract with a bank to sell the €400,000 for U.S. dollars at a specified forward rate today. Assume the prevailing 4-month forward rate on euros is $1.10. In 4 months, Scanlon will exchange its €400,000 for $440,000 (computed as €400,000 × $1.10 = $440,000). ●

Bid/Ask Spread. Like spot rates, forward rates have a bid/ask spread. For example, a bank may set up a contract with one firm agreeing to sell the firm Singapore dollars 90 days from now at $.510 per Singapore dollar. This represents the ask rate. At the same time, the firm may agree to purchase (bid) Singapore dollars 90 days from now from some other firm at $.505 per Singapore dollar.

The spread between the bid and ask prices is wider for forward rates of currencies of developing countries, such as Chile, Mexico, South Korea, Taiwan, and Thailand. Because these markets have relatively few orders for forward contracts, banks are less able to match up willing buyers and sellers. This lack of liquidity causes banks to widen the bid/ask spread when quoting forward contracts. The contracts in these countries are generally available only for short-term horizons.

Premium or Discount on the Forward Rate. The difference between the forward rate (F) and the spot rate (S) at a given point in time is measured by the premium:

$$F = S(1 + p)$$

where p represents the forward premium, or the percentage by which the forward rate exceeds the spot rate.

EXAMPLE

If the euro's spot rate is $1.40, and its 1-year forward rate has a forward premium of 2 percent, the 1-year forward rate is:

$$F = S(1 + p)$$
$$= \$1.40(1 + .02)$$
$$= \$1.428$$
●

Given quotations for the spot rate and the forward rate at a given point in time, the premium can be determined by rearranging the above equation:

$$F = S(1 + p)$$
$$F/S = 1 + p$$
$$(F/S) - 1 = p$$

EXAMPLE

If the euro's 1-year forward rate is quoted at $1.428 and the euro's spot rate is quoted at $1.40, the euro's forward premium is:

$$(F/S) - 1 = p$$
$$(\$1.428/\$1.40) - 1 = p$$
$$1.02 - 1 = .02 \text{ or } 2 \text{ percent} \qquad \bullet$$

When the forward rate is less than the prevailing spot rate, the forward premium is negative, and the forward rate exhibits a discount.

EXAMPLE

If the euro's 1-year forward rate is quoted at $1.35 and the euro's spot rate is quoted at $1.40, the euro's forward premium is:

$$(F/S) - 1 = p$$
$$(\$1.35/\$1.40) - 1 = p$$
$$.9643 - 1 = -.0357 \text{ or } -3.57 \text{ percent}$$

Since *p* is negative, the forward rate contains a discount. ●

EXAMPLE

Assume the forward exchange rates of the British pound for various maturities are as shown in the second column of Exhibit 5.1. Based on each forward exchange rate, the forward discount can be computed on an annualized basis, as shown in Exhibit 5.1. ●

In some situations, a firm may prefer to assess the premium or discount on an unannualized basis. In this case, it would not include the fraction that represents the number of periods per year in the formula.

Arbitrage. Forward rates typically differ from the spot rate for any given currency. If the forward rate were the same as the spot rate, and interest rates of the two countries differed, it would be possible for some investors (under certain assumptions) to use **arbitrage** to earn higher returns than would be possible domestically without incurring additional risk (as explained in Chapter 7). Consequently, the forward rate usually contains a premium (or discount) that reflects the difference between the home interest rate and the foreign interest rate.

Movements in the Forward Rate over Time. If the forward rate's premium remained constant, the forward rate would move in perfect tandem with the movements in the corresponding spot rate over time. For example, if the spot rate of the euro increased by 4 percent from a month ago until today, the forward rate would have to increase by 4 percent as well over the same period in order to maintain the same premium. In reality, the forward premium is influenced by the interest rate differential between the two countries (as explained in Chapter 7) and can change over time. Most of the movement in a currency's forward rate over time is due to movements in that currency's spot rate.

Exhibit 5.1 Computation of Forward Rate Premiums or Discounts

TYPE OF EXCHANGE RATE FOR £	VALUE	MATURITY	FORWARD RATE PREMIUM OR DISCOUNT FOR £
Spot rate	$1.681		
30-day forward rate	$1.680	30 days	$\dfrac{\$1.680 - \$1.681}{\$1.681} \times \dfrac{360}{30} = -.71\%$
90-day forward rate	$1.677	90 days	$\dfrac{\$1.677 - \$1.681}{\$1.681} \times \dfrac{360}{90} = -.95\%$
180-day forward rate	$1.672	180 days	$\dfrac{\$1.672 - \$1.681}{\$1.681} \times \dfrac{360}{180} = -1.07\%$

Offsetting a Forward Contract. In some cases, an MNC may desire to offset a forward contract that it previously created.

EXAMPLE

On March 10, Green Bay, Inc., hired a Canadian construction company to expand its office and agreed to pay C$200,000 for the work on September 10. It negotiated a 6-month forward contract to obtain C$200,000 at $.70 per unit, which would be used to pay the Canadian firm in 6 months. On April 10, the construction company informed Green Bay that it would not be able to perform the work as promised. Therefore, Green Bay offset its existing contract by negotiating a forward contract to sell C$200,000 for the date of September 10. However, the spot rate of the Canadian dollar had decreased over the last month, and the prevailing forward contract price for September 10 is $.66. Green Bay now has a forward contract to sell C$200,000 on September 10, which offsets the other contract it has to buy C$200,000 on September 10. The forward rate was $.04 per unit less on its forward sale than on its forward purchase, resulting in a cost of $8,000 (C$200,000 × $.04). ●

If Green Bay in the preceding example negotiates the forward sale with the same bank where it negotiated the forward purchase, it may simply be able to request that its initial forward contract be offset. The bank will charge a fee for this service, which will reflect the difference between the forward rate at the time of the forward purchase and the forward rate at the time of the offset. Thus, the MNC cannot just ignore its obligation, but must pay a fee to offset its original obligation.

Using Forward Contracts for Swap Transactions. A swap transaction involves a spot transaction along with a corresponding forward contract that will ultimately reverse the spot transaction. Many forward contracts are negotiated for this purpose.

EXAMPLE

Soho, Inc., needs to invest 1 million Chilean pesos in its Chilean subsidiary for the production of additional products. It wants the subsidiary to repay the pesos in 1 year. Soho wants to lock in the rate at which the pesos can be converted back into dollars in 1 year, and it uses a 1-year forward contract for this purpose. Soho contacts its bank and requests the following swap transaction:

1. *Today:* The bank should withdraw dollars from Soho's U.S. account, convert the dollars to pesos in the spot market, and transmit the pesos to the subsidiary's account.
2. *In 1 year:* The bank should withdraw 1 million pesos from the subsidiary's account, convert them to dollars at today's forward rate, and transmit them to Soho's U.S. account.

Soho, Inc., is not exposed to exchange rate movements due to the transaction because it has locked in the rate at which the pesos will be converted back to dollars. If the 1-year forward rate exhibits a discount, however, Soho will receive fewer dollars in than it invested in the subsidiary today. It may still be willing to engage in the swap transaction under these circumstances in order to remove uncertainty about the dollars it will receive in 1 year. ●

Non-Deliverable Forward Contracts

A **non-deliverable forward contract (NDF)** is frequently used for currencies in emerging markets. Like a regular forward contract, an NDF represents an agreement regarding a position in a specified amount of a specified currency, a specified exchange rate, and a specified future settlement date. However, an NDF does not result in an actual exchange of the currencies at the future date. That is, there is no delivery. Instead, one party to the agreement makes a payment to the other party based on the exchange rate at the future date.

EXAMPLE

Jackson, Inc., an MNC based in Wyoming, determines as of April 1 that it will need 100 million Chilean pesos to purchase supplies on July 1. It can negotiate an NDF with a local bank as follows. The NDF will specify the currency (Chilean peso), the settlement date (90 days from now), and a so-called reference rate, which identifies the type of exchange rate that will be marked to market at the settlement. Specifically, the NDF will contain the following information:

- Buy 100 million Chilean pesos.
- Settlement date: July 1.
- Reference index: Chilean peso's closing exchange rate (in dollars) quoted by Chile's central bank in 90 days.

Assume that the Chilean peso (which is the reference index) is currently valued at $.0020, so the dollar amount of the position is $200,000 at the time of the agreement. At the time of the settlement date (July 1), the value of the reference index is determined, and a payment is made between the two parties to settle the NDF. For example, if the peso value increases to $.0023 by July 1, the value of the position specified in the NDF will be $230,000 ($.0023 × 100 million pesos). Since the value of Jackson's NDF position is $30,000 higher than when the agreement was created, Jackson will receive a payment of $30,000 from the bank.

Recall that Jackson needs 100 million pesos to buy imports. Since the peso's spot rate rose from April 1 to July 1, Jackson will need to pay $30,000 more for the imports than if it had paid for them on April 1. At the same time, however, Jackson will have received a payment of $30,000 due to its NDF. Thus, the NDF hedged the exchange rate risk.

If the Chilean peso had depreciated to $.0018 instead of rising, Jackson's position in its NDF would have been valued at $180,000 (100 million pesos × $.0018) at the settlement date, which is $20,000 less than the value when the agreement was created. Therefore, Jackson would have owed the bank $20,000 at that time. However, the decline in the spot rate of the peso means that Jackson would pay $20,000 less for the imports than if it had paid for them on April 1. Thus, an offsetting effect would also occur in this example. ●

As these examples show, although an NDF does not involve delivery, it can effectively hedge future foreign currency payments that are anticipated by an MNC.

Since an NDF can specify that any payments between the two parties be in dollars or some other available currency, firms can even use NDFs to hedge existing positions of foreign currencies that are not convertible. Consider an MNC that expects to receive payment in a foreign currency that cannot be converted into dollars. Though the MNC may use the currency to make purchases in the local country of concern, it still may desire to hedge against a decline in the value of the currency over the period before it receives payment. It takes a sell position in an NDF and uses the closing exchange rate of that currency as of the settlement date as the reference index. If the currency depreciates against the dollar over time, the firm will receive the difference between the dollar value of the position when the NDF contract was created and the dollar value of the position as of the settlement date. Thus, it will receive a payment in dollars from the NDF to offset any depreciation in the currency over the period of concern.

CURRENCY FUTURES MARKET

WEB

www.futuresmag.com/
cms/futures/website
Various aspects of derivatives trading such as new products, strategies, and market analyses.

Currency futures contracts are contracts specifying a standard volume of a particular currency to be exchanged on a specific settlement date. Thus, currency futures contracts are similar to forward contracts in terms of their obligation, but differ from forward contracts in the way they are traded. They are commonly used by MNCs to hedge their foreign currency positions. In addition, they are traded by speculators who hope to capitalize on their expectations of exchange rate movements. A buyer of a currency futures contract locks in the exchange rate to be paid for a foreign currency at a future point in time. Alternatively, a seller of a currency futures contract locks in the exchange rate at which a foreign currency can be exchanged for the home currency. In the United States, currency futures contracts are purchased to lock in the amount of dollars needed to obtain a specified amount of a particular foreign currency; they are sold to lock in the amount of dollars to be received from selling a specified amount of a particular foreign currency.

Contract Specifications

Currency futures are commonly traded at the Chicago Mercantile Exchange (CME), which is part of CME Group. Currency futures are available for 19 currencies at the CME. Each contract specifies a standardized number of units, as shown in Exhibit 5.2. Standardized contracts allow for more frequent trading per contract, and therefore greater liquidity. For some currencies, E-mini futures contracts are available at the CME, which specify half the number of units of the typical standardized contract. The CME also offers futures contracts on cross exchange rates (between two non-dollar currencies). The trades are normally executed by the Globex platform.

The typical currency futures contract is based on a currency value in terms of U.S. dollars. However, futures contracts are also available on some cross-rates, such as the exchange rate between the Australian dollar and the Canadian dollar. Thus, speculators who expect that the Australian dollar will move substantially against the Canadian dollar can take a futures position to capitalize on their expectations. In addition, Australian firms that have exposure in Canadian dollars or Canadian firms that have exposure in Australian dollars may use this type of futures contract to hedge their exposure. See www.cme.com for more information about futures on cross exchange rates.

Exhibit 5.2 Currency Futures Contracts Traded on the Chicago Mercantile Exchange

CURRENCY	UNITS PER CONTRACT
Australian dollar	100,000
Brazilian real	100,000
British pound	62,500
Canadian dollar	100,000
Chinese yuan	1,000,000
Czech koruna	4,000,000
Euro	125,000
Hungarian forint	30,000,000
Israeli shekel	1,000,000
Japanese yen	12,500,000
Korean won	125,000,000
Mexican peso	500,000
New Zealand dollar	100,000
Norwegian krone	2,000,000
Polish zloty	500,000
Russian ruble	2,500,000
South African rand	500,000
Swedish krona	2,000,000
Swiss franc	125,000

Currency futures contracts typically specify the third Wednesday in March, June, September, or December as the settlement date. There is also an over-the-counter currency futures market, where financial intermediaries facilitate trading of currency futures contracts with specific settlement dates.

Trading Currency Futures

Firms or individuals can execute orders for currency futures contracts by calling brokerage firms that serve as intermediaries. The order to buy or sell a currency futures contract for a specific currency and a specific settlement date is communicated to the brokerage firm, which in turn communicates the order to the CME.

For example, at a particular point in time, some U.S. firms are purchasing futures contracts on Mexican pesos with a December settlement date in order to hedge their future payables. Meanwhile, other U.S. firms are selling futures contracts on Mexican pesos with a December settlement date in order to hedge their future receivables.

The vast majority of the futures contract orders submitted to the CME are executed by Globex, a computerized platform that matches buy and sell orders for each standardized contract. Globex operates 23 hours a day (is closed from 4 p.m. to 5 p.m.) Monday through Friday.

EXAMPLE

Assume that as of February 10, a futures contract on 62,500 British pounds with a March settlement date is priced at $1.50 per pound. The buyer of this currency futures contract will receive £62,500 on the March settlement date and will pay $93,750 for the pounds (computed as £62,500 × $1.50 per pound plus a commission paid to the broker). The seller of this contract is obligated to sell £62,500 at a price of $1.50 per pound and therefore will receive $93,750 on the settlement date, minus the commission that it owes the broker. ●

Trading Platforms for Currency Futures

There are electronic trading platforms that facilitate the trading of currency futures. These platforms serve as a broker, as they execute the trades desired. The platform typically sets quotes for currency futures based on an ask price at which one can buy a specified currency for a specified settlement date and a bid price at which one can sell a specified currency. Users of the platforms incur a fee in the form of a difference between the bid and ask prices.

Comparison to Forward Contracts

Currency futures contracts are similar to forward contracts in that they allow a customer to lock in the exchange rate at which a specific currency is purchased or sold for a specific date in the future. Nevertheless, there are some differences between currency futures contracts and forward contracts, which are summarized in Exhibit 5.3. Currency futures contracts are sold on an exchange, while each forward contract is negotiated between a firm and a commercial bank over a telecommunications network. Thus, forward contracts can be tailored to the needs of the firm, while currency futures contracts are standardized.

Corporations that have established relationships with large banks tend to use forward contracts rather than futures contracts because forward contracts are tailored to the precise amount of currency to be purchased or sold in the future and the precise forward date that they prefer. Conversely, small firms and individuals who do not have established relationships with large banks or prefer to trade in smaller amounts tend to use currency futures contracts.

Exhibit 5.3 Comparison of the Forward and Futures Markets

	FORWARD	FUTURES
Size of contract	Tailored to individual needs.	Standardized.
Delivery date	Tailored to individual needs.	Standardized.
Participants	Banks, brokers, and multinational companies. Public speculation not encouraged.	Banks, brokers, and multinational companies. Qualified public speculation encouraged.
Security deposit	None as such, but compensating bank balances or lines of credit required.	Small security deposit required.
Clearing operation	Handling contingent on individual banks and brokers. No separate clearinghouse function.	Handled by exchange clearinghouse. Daily settlements to the market price.
Marketplace	Telecommunications network.	Central exchange floor with world-wide communications.
Regulation	Self-regulating.	Commodity Futures Trading Commission; National Futures Association.
Liquidation	Most settled by actual delivery. Some by offset, at a cost.	Most by offset, very few by delivery.
Transaction costs	Set by "spread" between bank's buy and sell prices.	Negotiated brokerage fees.

Source: *Chicago Mercantile Exchange.*

Pricing Currency Futures

The price of currency futures normally will be similar to the forward rate for a given currency and settlement date. This relationship is enforced by the potential arbitrage activity that would occur if there were significant discrepancies.

EXAMPLE Assume that the currency futures price on the British pound is $1.50 and that forward contracts for a similar period are available for $1.48. Firms may attempt to purchase forward contracts and simultaneously sell currency futures contracts. If they can exactly match the settlement dates of the two contracts, they can generate guaranteed profits of $.02 per unit. These actions will place downward pressure on the currency futures price. The futures contract and forward contracts of a given currency and settlement date should have the same price, or else guaranteed profits are possible (assuming no transaction costs). ●

The currency futures price differs from the spot rate for the same reasons that a forward rate differs from the spot rate. If a currency's spot and futures prices were the same and the currency's interest rate was higher than the U.S. rate, U.S. speculators could lock in a higher return than they would receive on U.S. investments. They could purchase the foreign currency at the spot rate, invest the funds at the attractive interest rate, and simultaneously sell currency futures to lock in the exchange rate at which they could reconvert the currency back to dollars. If the spot and futures rates were the same, there would be neither a gain nor a loss on the currency conversion. Thus, the higher foreign interest rate would provide a higher yield on this type of investment. The actions of investors to capitalize on this opportunity would place upward pressure on the spot rate and downward pressure on the currency futures price, causing the futures price to fall below the spot rate.

Credit Risk of Currency Futures Contracts

Each currency futures contract represents an agreement between a client and the exchange clearinghouse, even though the exchange has not taken a position. To illustrate, assume you call a broker to request the purchase of a British pound futures contract with a March settlement date. Meanwhile, another person unrelated to you calls a broker to request the sale of a similar futures contract. Neither party needs to worry about the credit risk of the counterparty. The exchange clearinghouse assures that you will receive whatever is owed to you as a result of your currency futures position.

To minimize its risk in such a guarantee, the CME imposes **margin requirements** to cover fluctuations in the value of a contract, meaning that the participants must make a deposit with their respective brokerage firms when they take a position. The initial margin requirement is typically between $1,000 and $2,000 per currency futures contract. However, if the value of the futures contract declines over time, the buyer may be asked to maintain an additional margin called the "maintenance margin." Margin requirements are not always required for forward contracts due to the more personal nature of the agreement; the bank knows the firm it is dealing with and may trust it to fulfill its obligation.

How Firms Use Currency Futures

Corporations that have open positions in foreign currencies can consider purchasing or selling futures contracts to offset their positions.

Purchasing Futures to Hedge Payables. The purchase of futures contracts locks in the price at which a firm can purchase a currency.

EXAMPLE

Teton Co. orders Canadian goods and upon delivery will need to send C$500,000 to the Canadian exporter. Thus, Teton purchases Canadian dollar futures contracts today, thereby locking in the price to be paid for Canadian dollars at a future settlement date. By holding futures contracts, Teton does not have to worry about changes in the spot rate of the Canadian dollar over time. ●

Selling Futures to Hedge Receivables. The sale of futures contracts locks in the price at which a firm can sell a currency.

EXAMPLE

Karla Co. sells futures contracts when it plans to receive a currency from exporting that it will not need (it accepts a foreign currency when the importer prefers that type of payment). By selling a futures contract, Karla Co. locks in the price at which it will be able to sell this currency as of the settlement date. Such an action can be appropriate if Karla expects the foreign currency to depreciate against Karla's home currency. ●

The use of futures contracts to cover, or **hedge,** a firm's currency positions is described more thoroughly in Chapter 11.

Closing Out a Futures Position

If a firm that buys a currency futures contract decides before the settlement date that it no longer wants to maintain its position, it can close out the position by selling an identical futures contract. The gain or loss to the firm from its previous futures position is dependent on the price of purchasing futures versus selling futures.

The price of a futures contract changes over time in accordance with movements in the spot rate and also with changing expectations about the spot rate's value as of the settlement date.

If the spot rate of a currency increases substantially over a 1-month period, the futures price is likely to increase by about the same amount. In this case, the purchase and subsequent sale of a futures contract would be profitable. Conversely, a decline in the spot rate over time will correspond with a decline in the currency futures price,

Exhibit 5.4 Closing Out a Futures Contract

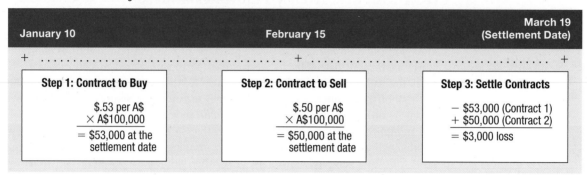

meaning that the purchase and subsequent sale of a futures contract would result in a loss. While the purchasers of the futures contract could decide not to close out their position under such conditions, the losses from that position could increase over time.

On January 10, Tacoma Co. anticipates that it will need Australian dollars (A$) in March when it orders supplies from an Australian supplier. Consequently, Tacoma purchases a futures contract specifying A$100,000 and a March settlement date (which is March 19 for this contract). On January 10, the futures contract is priced at $.53 per A$. On February 15, Tacoma realizes that it will not need to order supplies because it has reduced its production levels. Therefore, it has no need for A$ in March. It sells a futures contract on A$ with the March settlement date to offset the contract it purchased in January. At this time, the futures contract is priced at $.50 per A$. On March 19 (the settlement date), Tacoma has offsetting positions in futures contracts. However, the price when the futures contract was purchased was higher than the price when an identical contract was sold, so Tacoma incurs a loss from its futures positions. Tacoma's transactions are summarized in Exhibit 5.4. Move from left to right along the time line to review the transactions. The example does not include margin requirements. ●

Sellers of futures contracts can close out their positions by purchasing currency futures contracts with similar settlement dates. Most currency futures contracts are closed out before the settlement date.

Speculation with Currency Futures

Currency futures contracts are sometimes purchased by speculators who are simply attempting to capitalize on their expectation of a currency's future movement.

Assume that speculators expect the British pound to appreciate in the future. They can purchase a futures contract that will lock in the price at which they buy pounds at a specified settlement date. On the settlement date, they can purchase their pounds at the rate specified by the futures contract and then sell these pounds at the spot rate. If the spot rate has appreciated by this time in accordance with their expectations, they will profit from this strategy.

Currency futures are often sold by speculators who expect that the spot rate of a currency will be less than the rate at which they would be obligated to sell it.

Assume that as of April 4, a futures contract specifying 500,000 Mexican pesos and a June settlement date is priced at $.09. On April 4, speculators who expect the peso will decline sell futures contracts on pesos. Assume that on June 17 (the settlement date), the spot rate of the peso is $.08. The transactions are shown in Exhibit 5.5 (the margin deposited by the speculators is not considered). The gain on the futures position is $5,000, which represents the difference between the amount received ($45,000) when selling the pesos in accordance with the futures contract versus the amount paid ($40,000) for those pesos in the spot market. ●

Exhibit 5.5 Source of Gains from Buying Currency Futures

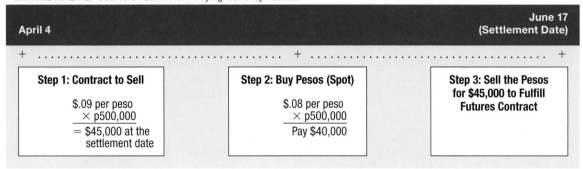

Of course, expectations are often incorrect. It is because of different expectations that some speculators decide to purchase futures contracts while other speculators decide to sell the same contracts at a given point in time.

Currency Futures Market Efficiency. If the currency futures market is efficient, the futures price for a currency at any given point in time should reflect all available information. That is, it should represent an unbiased estimate of the respective currency's spot rate on the settlement date. Thus, the continual use of a particular strategy to take positions in currency futures contracts should not lead to abnormal profits. Some positions will likely result in gains while others will result in losses, but over time, the gains and losses should offset. Research has found that in some years, the futures price has consistently exceeded the corresponding price as of the settlement date, while in other years, the futures price has consistently been below the corresponding price as of the settlement date. This suggests that the currency futures market may be inefficient. However, the patterns are not necessarily observable until after they occur, which means that it may be difficult to consistently generate abnormal profits from speculating in currency futures.

Currency Options Market

Currency options provide the right to purchase or sell currencies at specified prices. They are available for many currencies, including the Australian dollar, British pound, Brazilian real, Canadian dollar, euro, Japanese yen, Mexican peso, New Zealand dollar, Russian ruble, South African rand, and Swiss franc.

Option Exchanges

In late 1982, exchanges in Amsterdam, Montreal, and Philadelphia first allowed trading in standardized foreign currency options. Since that time, options have been offered on the Chicago Mercantile Exchange and the Chicago Board Options Exchange. Currency options are traded through the Globex system at the Chicago Mercantile Exchange, even after the trading floor is closed. Thus, currency options are traded virtually around the clock.

In July 2007, the CME and CBOT merged to form CME Group, which serves international markets for derivative products. The CME and CBOT trading floors were consolidated into a single trading floor at the CBOT. In addition, products of the CME and CBOT were consolidated on a single electronic platform, which reduced the operating and maintenance expenses. Furthermore, the CME Group established a plan of continual innovation of new derivative products in the international marketplace that would be executed by the CME Group's single electronic platform.

The options exchanges in the United States are regulated by the Securities and Exchange Commission. Options can be purchased or sold through brokers for a commission. The commission per transaction is commonly $30 to $60 for a single currency option, but it can be much lower per contract when the transaction involves multiple contracts. Brokers require that a margin be maintained during the life of the contract. The margin is increased for clients whose option positions have deteriorated. This protects against possible losses if the clients do not fulfill their obligations.

Over-the-Counter Market

In addition to the exchanges where currency options are available, there is an over-the-counter market where currency options are offered by commercial banks and brokerage firms. Unlike the currency options traded on an exchange, the over-the-counter market offers currency options that are tailored to the specific needs of the firm. Since these options are not standardized, all the terms must be specified in the contracts. The number of units, desired strike price, and expiration date can be tailored to the specific needs of the client. When currency options are not standardized, there is less liquidity and a wider bid/ask spread.

The minimum size of currency options offered by financial institutions is normally about $5 million. Since these transactions are conducted with a specific financial institution rather than an exchange, there are no credit guarantees. Thus, the agreement made is only as safe as the parties involved. For this reason, financial institutions may require some collateral from individuals or firms desiring to purchase or sell currency options. Currency options are classified as either **calls or puts,** as discussed in the next section.

CURRENCY CALL OPTIONS

A **currency call option** grants the right to buy a specific currency at a designated price within a specific period of time. The price at which the owner is allowed to buy that currency is known as the **exercise price** or **strike price,** and there are monthly expiration dates for each option.

Call options are desirable when one wishes to lock in a maximum price to be paid for a currency in the future. If the spot rate of the currency rises above the strike price, owners of call options can "exercise" their options by purchasing the currency at the strike price, which will be cheaper than the prevailing spot rate. This strategy is somewhat similar to that used by purchasers of futures contracts, but the futures contracts require an obligation, while the currency option does not. The owner can choose to let the option expire on the expiration date without ever exercising it. Owners of expired call options will have lost the premium they initially paid, but that is the most they can lose.

The buyer of a currency call option pays a so-called premium, which reflects the price in order to own the option. The seller of a currency call option receives the premium paid by the buyer. In return, the seller is obligated to accommodate the buyer in accordance with the rights of the currency call option.

Currency options quotations are summarized each day in various financial newspapers. Although currency options typically expire near the middle of the specified month, some of them expire at the end of the specific month and are designated as EOM. Some options are listed as "European Style," which means that they can be exercised only upon expiration.

A currency call option is said to be *in the money* when the present exchange rate exceeds the strike price, *at the money* when the present exchange rate equals the strike price, and *out of the money* when the present exchange rate is less than the strike price. For a given currency and expiration date, an in-the-money call option will require a higher premium than options that are at the money or out of the money.

WEB

www.ino.com

The latest information and prices of options and financial futures as well as the corresponding historic price charts.

Factors Affecting Currency Call Option Premiums

The premium on a call option represents the cost of having the right to buy the underlying currency at a specified price. For MNCs that use currency call options to hedge, the premium reflects a cost of insurance or protection to the MNCs.

The call option premium (referred to as *C*) is primarily influenced by three factors:

$$C = f(\underset{+}{S-X}, \underset{+}{T}, \underset{+}{\sigma})$$

where $S - X$ represents the difference between the spot exchange rate (*S*) and the strike or exercise price *(X)*, *T* represents the time to maturity, and σ represents the volatility of the currency, as measured by the standard deviation of the movements in the currency. The relationships between the call option premium and these factors are summarized next.

- *Spot Price Relative to Strike Price.* The higher the spot rate relative to the strike price, the higher the option price will be. This is due to the higher probability of buying the currency at a substantially lower rate than what you could sell it for. This relationship can be verified by comparing premiums of options for a specified currency and expiration date that have different strike prices.
- *Length of Time Before the Expiration Date.* It is generally expected that the spot rate has a greater chance of rising high above the strike price if it has a longer period of time to do so. A settlement date in June allows two additional months beyond April for the spot rate to move above the strike price. This explains why June option prices exceed April option prices given a specific strike price. This relationship can be verified by comparing premiums of options for a specified currency and strike prices that have different expiration dates.
- *Potential Variability of Currency.* The greater the variability of the currency, the higher the probability that the spot rate can rise above the strike price. Thus, less volatile currencies have lower call option prices. For example, the Canadian dollar is more stable than most other currencies. If all other factors are similar, Canadian call options should be less expensive than call options on other foreign currencies.

The potential volatility in a currency can also vary over time for a particular currency, which can affect the premiums paid on that currency's options. When the credit crisis intensified in the fall of 2008, speculators were quickly moving their money into and out of currencies. This resulted in a higher degree of volatility in the foreign exchange markets. It also caused concerns about future volatility. Consequently, option premiums increased.

How Firms Use Currency Call Options

Corporations with open positions in foreign currencies can sometimes use currency call options to cover these positions.

Using Call Options to Hedge Payables. MNCs can purchase call options on a currency to hedge future payables.

EXAMPLE

When Pike Co. of Seattle orders Australian goods, it makes a payment in Australian dollars to the Australian exporter upon delivery. An Australian dollar call option locks in a maximum rate at which Pike can exchange dollars for Australian dollars. This exchange of currencies at the specified strike price on the call option contract can be executed at any time before the expiration date. In essence, the call option contract specifies the maximum price that Pike must pay to obtain these Australian imports. If the Australian dollar's value remains below the strike price, Pike can purchase Australian dollars at the prevailing spot rate when it needs to pay for its imports and simply let its call option expire. ●

Options may be more appropriate than futures or forward contracts for some situations. Intel Corp. uses options to hedge its order backlog in semiconductors. If an order is canceled, it has the flexibility to let the option contract expire. With a forward contract, it would be obligated to fulfill its obligation even though the order was canceled.

Using Call Options to Hedge Project Bidding. U.S.-based MNCs that bid for foreign projects may purchase call options to lock in the dollar cost of the potential expenses.

EXAMPLE Kelly Co. is an MNC based in Fort Lauderdale that has bid on a project sponsored by the Canadian government. If the bid is accepted, Kelly will need approximately C$500,000 to purchase Canadian materials and services. However, Kelly will not know whether the bid is accepted until 3 months from now. In this case, it can purchase call options with a 3-month expiration date. Ten call option contracts will cover the entire amount of potential exposure. If the bid is accepted, Kelly can use the options to purchase the Canadian dollars needed. If the Canadian dollar has depreciated over time, Kelly will likely let the options expire.

Assume that the exercise price on Canadian dollars is $.70 and the call option premium is $.02 per unit. Kelly will pay $1,000 per option (since there are 50,000 units per Canadian dollar option), or $10,000 for the 10 option contracts. With the options, the maximum amount necessary to purchase the C$500,000 is $350,000 (computed as $.70 per Canadian dollar × C$500,000). The amount of U.S. dollars needed would be less if the Canadian dollar's spot rate were below the exercise price at the time the Canadian dollars were purchased.

Even if Kelly's bid is rejected, it will exercise the currency call option if the Canadian dollar's spot rate exceeds the exercise price before the option expires and would then sell the Canadian dollars in the spot market. Any gain from exercising may partially or even fully offset the premium paid for the options. ●

This type of example is quite common. When Air Products and Chemicals was hired to perform some projects, it needed capital equipment from Germany. The purchase of equipment was contingent on whether the firm was hired for the projects. The company used options to hedge this possible future purchase.

Using Call Options to Hedge Target Bidding. Firms can also use call options to hedge a possible acquisition.

EXAMPLE Morrison Co. is attempting to acquire a French firm and has submitted its bid in euros. Morrison has purchased call options on the euro because it will need euros to purchase the French company's stock. The call options hedge the U.S. firm against the potential appreciation of the euro by the time the acquisition occurs. If the acquisition does not occur and the spot rate of the euro remains below the strike price, Morrison Co. can let the call options expire. If the acquisition does not occur and the spot rate of the euro exceeds the strike price, Morrison Co. can exercise the options and sell the euros in the spot market. Alternatively, Morrison Co. can sell the call options it is holding. Either of these actions may offset part or all of the premium paid for the options. ●

Speculating with Currency Call Options

Because this text focuses on multinational financial management, the corporate use of currency options is more important than the speculative use. The use of options for hedging is discussed in detail in Chapter 11. Speculative trading is discussed here in order to provide more of a background on the currency options market.

Individuals may speculate in the currency options market based on their expectation of the future movements in a particular currency. Speculators who expect that a foreign currency will appreciate can purchase call options on that currency. Once the spot rate of that currency appreciates, the speculators can exercise their options by purchasing that currency at the strike price and then sell the currency at the prevailing spot rate.

Just as with currency futures, for every buyer of a currency call option there must be a seller. A seller (sometimes called a **writer)** of a call option is obligated to sell a specified currency at a specified price (the strike price) up to a specified expiration date. Speculators may sometimes want to sell a currency call option on a currency that they expect will depreciate in the future. The only way a currency call option will be exercised is if the spot rate is higher than the strike price. Thus, a seller of a currency call option will receive the premium when the option is purchased and can keep the entire amount if the option is not exercised. When it appears that an option will be exercised, there will still be sellers of options. However, such options will sell for high premiums due to the high risk that the option will be exercised at some point.

The net profit to a speculator who trades call options on a currency is based on a comparison of the selling price of the currency versus the exercise price paid for the currency and the premium paid for the call option.

EXAMPLE Jim is a speculator who buys a British pound call option with a strike price of $1.40 and a December settlement date. The current spot price as of that date is about $1.39. Jim pays a premium of $.012 per unit for the call option. Assume there are no brokerage fees. Just before the expiration date, the spot rate of the British pound reaches $1.41. At this time, Jim exercises the call option and then immediately sells the pounds at the spot rate to a bank. To determine Jim's profit or loss, first compute his revenues from selling the currency. Then, subtract from this amount the purchase price of pounds when exercising the option, and also subtract the purchase price of the option. The computations follow. Assume one option contract specifies 31,250 units.

	PER UNIT	PER CONTRACT
Selling price of £	$1.41	$44,063 ($1.41 × 31,250 units)
– Purchase price of £	–1.40	–43,750 ($1.40 × 31,250 units)
– Premium paid for option	–.012	–375 ($.012 × 31,250 units)
= Net profit	–$.002	–$62 (–$.002 × 31,250 units)

Assume that Linda was the seller of the call option purchased by Jim. Also assume that Linda would purchase British pounds only if and when the option was exercised, at which time she must provide the pounds at the exercise price of $1.40. Using the information in this example, Linda's net profit from selling the call option is derived here:

	PER UNIT	PER CONTRACT
Selling price of £	$1.40	$43,750 ($1.40 × 31,250 units)
– Purchase price of £	–1.41	–44,063 ($1.41 × 31,250 units)
+ Premium received	+.012	+375 ($.012 × 31,250 units)
= Net profit	$.002	$62 ($.002 × 31,250 units)

As a second example, assume the following information:

- Call option premium on Canadian dollars (C$) = $.01 per unit.
- Strike price = $.70.
- One Canadian dollar option contract represents C$50,000.

A speculator who had purchased this call option decided to exercise the option shortly before the expiration date, when the spot rate reached $.74. The speculator immediately sold the Canadian dollars in the spot market. Given this information, the net profit to the speculator is computed as follows:

	PER UNIT	PER CONTRACT
Selling price of C$	$.74	$37,000 ($.74 × 50,000 units)
– Purchase price of C$	–.70	–35,000 ($.70 × 50,000 units)
– Premium paid for option	–.01	–500 ($.01 × 50,000 units)
= Net profit	$.03	$1,500 ($.03 × 50,000 units)

If the seller of the call option did not obtain Canadian dollars until the option was about to be exercised, the net profit to the seller of the call option was

	PER UNIT	PER CONTRACT
Selling price of C$	$.70	$35,000 ($.70 × 50,000 units)
– Purchase price of C$	–.74	–37,000 ($.74 × 50,000 units)
+ Premium received	+.01	+500 ($.01 × 50,000 units)
= Net profit	–$.03	–$1,500 (–$.03 × 50,000 units)

When brokerage fees are ignored, the currency call purchaser's gain will be the seller's loss. The currency call purchaser's expenses represent the seller's revenues, and the purchaser's revenues represent the seller's expenses. Yet, because it is possible for purchasers and sellers of options to close out their positions, the relationship described here will not hold unless both parties begin and close out their positions at the same time.

An owner of a currency option may simply sell the option to someone else before the expiration date rather than exercising it. The owner can still earn profits since the option premium changes over time, reflecting the probability that the option can be exercised and the potential profit from exercising it.

Break-Even Point from Speculation.
The purchaser of a call option will break even if the revenue from selling the currency equals the payments for (1) the currency (at the strike price) and (2) the option premium. In other words, regardless of the number of units in a contract, a purchaser will break even if the spot rate at which the currency is sold is equal to the strike price plus the option premium.

Based on the information in the previous example, the strike price is $.70 and the option premium is $.01. Thus, for the purchaser to break even, the spot rate existing at the time the call is exercised must be $.71 ($.70 + $.01). Of course, speculators will not purchase a call option if they think the spot rate will only reach the break-even point and not go higher before the expiration date. Nevertheless, the computation of the break-even point is useful for a speculator deciding whether to purchase a currency call option. ●

Speculation by MNCs. Some financial institutions may have a division that uses currency options and other currency derivatives to speculate on future exchange rate movements. However, most MNCs use currency derivatives for hedging rather than for speculation. MNCs should use shareholder and creditor funds to pursue their goal of being market leader in a particular product or service, rather than using the funds to speculate in currency derivatives. An MNC's board of directors attempts to ensure that the MNC's operations are consistent with its goals.

CURRENCY PUT OPTIONS

The owner of a **currency put option** has the right to sell a currency at a specified price (the strike price) within a specified period of time. As with currency call options, the owner of a put option is not obligated to exercise the option. Therefore, the maximum potential loss to the owner of the put option is the price (or premium) paid for the option contract.

The premium of a currency put option reflects the price of the option. The seller of a currency put option receives the premium paid by the buyer (owner). In return, the seller is obligated to accommodate the buyer in accordance with the rights of the currency put option.

A currency put option is said to be *in the money* when the present exchange rate is less than the strike price, *at the money* when the present exchange rate equals the strike price, and *out of the money* when the present exchange rate exceeds the strike price. For a given currency and expiration date, an in-the-money put option will require a higher premium than options that are at the money or out of the money.

Factors Affecting Currency Put Option Premiums

The put option premium (referred to as P) is primarily influenced by three factors:

$$P = f(S - X, T, \sigma)$$
$$-\quad +\ +$$

where $S - X$ represents the difference between the spot exchange rate (S) and the strike or exercise price (X), T represents the time to maturity, and σ represents the volatility of the currency, as measured by the standard deviation of the movements in the currency. The relationships between the put option premium and these factors, which also influence call option premiums as described earlier, are summarized next.

First, the spot rate of a currency relative to the strike price is important. The lower the spot rate relative to the strike price, the more valuable the put option will be, because there is a higher probability that the option will be exercised. Recall that just the opposite relationship held for call options. A second factor influencing the put option premium is the length of time until the expiration date. As with currency call options, the longer the time to expiration, the greater the put option premium will be. A longer period creates a higher probability that the currency will move into a range where it will be feasible to exercise the option (whether it is a put or a call). These relationships can be verified by assessing quotations of put option premiums for a specified currency. A third factor that influences the put option premium is the variability of a currency. As with currency call options, the greater the variability, the greater the put option premium will be, again reflecting a higher probability that the option may be exercised.

Hedging with Currency Put Options

Corporations with open positions in foreign currencies can use currency put options in some cases to cover these positions.

Assume Duluth Co. has exported products to Canada and invoiced the products in Canadian dollars (at the request of the Canadian importers). Duluth is concerned that the Canadian dollars it is receiving will depreciate over time. To insulate itself against possible depreciation, Duluth purchases Canadian dollar put options, which entitle it to sell Canadian dollars at the specified strike price. In essence, Duluth locks in the minimum rate at which it can exchange Canadian dollars for U.S. dollars over a specified period of time. If the Canadian dollar appreciates over this time period, Duluth can let the put options expire and sell the Canadian dollars it receives at the prevailing spot rate. ●

At a given point in time, some put options are deep out of the money, meaning that the prevailing exchange rate is high above the exercise price. These options are cheaper (have a lower premium), as they are unlikely to be exercised because their exercise price is too low. At the same time, other put options have an exercise price that is currently above the prevailing exchange rate and are therefore more likely to be exercised. Consequently, these options are more expensive.

Cisco Systems weighs the tradeoff when using put options to hedge the remittance of earnings from Europe to the United States. It can create a hedge that is cheap, but the options can be exercised only if the currency's spot rate declines substantially. Alternatively, Cisco can create a hedge that can be exercised at a more favorable exchange rate, but it must pay a higher premium for the options. If Cisco's goal in using put options is simply to prevent a major loss if the currency weakens substantially, it may be willing to use an inexpensive put option (low exercise price, low premium). However, if its goal is to ensure that the currency can be exchanged at a more favorable exchange rate, Cisco will use a more expensive put option (high exercise price, high premium). By selecting currency options with an exercise price and premium that fits their objectives, Cisco and other MNCs can increase their value. ●

Speculating with Currency Put Options

Individuals may speculate with currency put options based on their expectations of the future movements in a particular currency. For example, speculators who expect that the British pound will depreciate can purchase British pound put options, which will entitle them to sell British pounds at a specified strike price. If the pound's spot rate depreciates as expected, the speculators can then purchase pounds at the spot rate and exercise their put options by selling these pounds at the strike price.

Speculators can also attempt to profit from selling currency put options. The seller of such options is obligated to purchase the specified currency at the strike price from the owner who exercises the put option. Speculators who believe the currency will appreciate (or at least will not depreciate) may sell a currency put option. If the currency appreciates over the entire period, the option will not be exercised. This is an ideal situation for put option sellers since they keep the premiums received when selling the options and bear no cost.

The net profit to a speculator from trading put options on a currency is based on a comparison of the exercise price at which the currency can be sold versus the purchase price of the currency and the premium paid for the put option.

A put option contract on British pounds specifies the following information:

- Put option premium on British pound (£) = $.04 per unit.
- Strike price = $1.40.
- One option contract represents £31,250.

A speculator who had purchased this put option decided to exercise the option shortly before the expiration date, when the spot rate of the pound was $1.30. The speculator purchased the pounds in the spot market at that time. Given this information, the net profit to the purchaser of the put option is calculated as follows:

	PER UNIT	PER CONTRACT
Selling price of £	$1.40	$43,750 ($1.40 × 31,250 units)
– Purchase price of £	–1.30	–40,625 ($1.30 × 31,250 units)
– Premium paid for option	–.04	–1,250 ($.04 × 31,250 units)
= Net profit	$.06	$1,875 ($.06 × 31,250 units)

Assuming that the seller of the put option sold the pounds received immediately after the option was exercised, the net profit to the seller of the put option is calculated as follows:

	PER UNIT	PER CONTRACT
Selling price of £	$1.30	$40,625 ($1.30 × 31,250 units)
– Purchase price of £	–1.40	–43,750 ($1.40 × 31,250 units)
+ Premium received	+.04	+1,250 ($.04 × 31,250 units)
= Net profit	–$.06	–$1,875 (–$.06 × 31,250 units)

The seller of the put options could simply refrain from selling the pounds (after being forced to buy them at $1.40 per pound) until the spot rate of the pound rises. However, there is no guarantee that the pound will reverse its direction and begin to appreciate. The seller's net loss could potentially be greater if the pound's spot rate continued to fall, unless the pounds were sold immediately.

Whatever an owner of a put option gains, the seller loses, and vice versa. This relationship would hold if brokerage costs did not exist and if the buyer and seller of options entered and closed their positions at the same time. Brokerage fees for currency options exist, however, and are very similar in magnitude to those of currency futures contracts.

Speculating with Combined Put and Call Options.
For volatile currencies, one possible speculative strategy is to create a **straddle,** which uses both a put option and a call option at the same exercise price. This may seem unusual because owning a put option is appropriate for expectations that the currency will depreciate while owning a call option is appropriate for expectations that the currency will appreciate. However, it is possible that the currency will depreciate (at which time the put is exercised) and then reverse direction and appreciate (allowing for profits when exercising the call).

Also, a speculator might anticipate that a currency will be substantially affected by current economic events yet be uncertain of the exact way it will be affected. By purchasing a put option and a call option, the speculator will gain if the currency moves substantially in either direction. Although two options are purchased and only one is exercised, the gains could more than offset the costs.

Currency Options Market Efficiency.
If the currency options market is efficient, the premiums on currency options properly reflect all available information. Under these

conditions, it may be difficult for speculators to consistently generate abnormal profits when speculating in this market. Research has found that the currency options market is efficient after controlling for transaction costs. Although some trading strategies could have generated abnormal gains in specific periods, they would have generated large losses if implemented in other periods. It is difficult to know which strategy would generate abnormal profits in future periods.

CONTINGENCY GRAPHS FOR CURRENCY OPTIONS

A contingency graph for currency options illustrates the potential gain or loss for various exchange rate scenarios.

Contingency Graph for a Purchaser of a Call Option

A contingency graph for a purchaser of a call option compares the price paid for the call option to potential payoffs to be received with various exchange rate scenarios.

EXAMPLE

A British pound call option is available, with a strike price of $1.50 and a call premium of $.02. The speculator plans to exercise the option on the expiration date (if appropriate at that time) and then immediately sell the pounds received in the spot market. Under these conditions, a **contingency graph** can be created to measure the profit or loss per unit (see the upper-left graph in Exhibit 5.6). Notice that if the future spot rate is $1.50 or less, the net gain per unit is –$.02 (ignoring transaction costs). This represents the loss of the premium per unit paid for the option, as the option would not be exercised. At $1.51, $.01 per unit would be earned by exercising the option, but considering the $.02 premium paid, the net gain would be –$.01.

At $1.52, $.02 per unit would be earned by exercising the option, which would offset the $.02 premium per unit. This is the break-even point. At any rate above this point, the gain from exercising the option would more than offset the premium, resulting in a positive net gain. The maximum loss to the speculator in this example is the premium paid for the option. ●

Contingency Graph for a Seller of a Call Option

A contingency graph for the seller of a call option compares the premium received from selling a call option to the potential payoffs made to the buyer of the call option for various exchange rate scenarios.

EXAMPLE

The lower-left graph shown in Exhibit 5.6 provides a contingency graph for a speculator who sold the call option described in the previous example. It assumes that this seller would purchase the pounds in the spot market just as the option was exercised (ignoring transaction costs). At future spot rates of less than $1.50, the net gain to the seller would be the premium of $.02 per unit, as the option would not have been exercised. If the future spot rate is $1.51, the seller would lose $.01 per unit on the option transaction (paying $1.51 for pounds in the spot market and selling pounds for $1.50 to fulfill the exercise request). Yet, this loss would be more than offset by the premium of $.02 per unit received, resulting in a net gain of $.01 per unit.

The break-even point is at $1.52, and the net gain to the seller of a call option becomes negative at all future spot rates higher than that point. Notice that the contingency graphs for the buyer and seller of this call option are mirror images of one another. ●

Contingency Graph for a Buyer of a Put Option

A contingency graph for a buyer of a put option compares the premium paid for the put option to potential payoffs received for various exchange rate scenarios.

Exhibit 5.6 Contingency Graphs for Currency Options

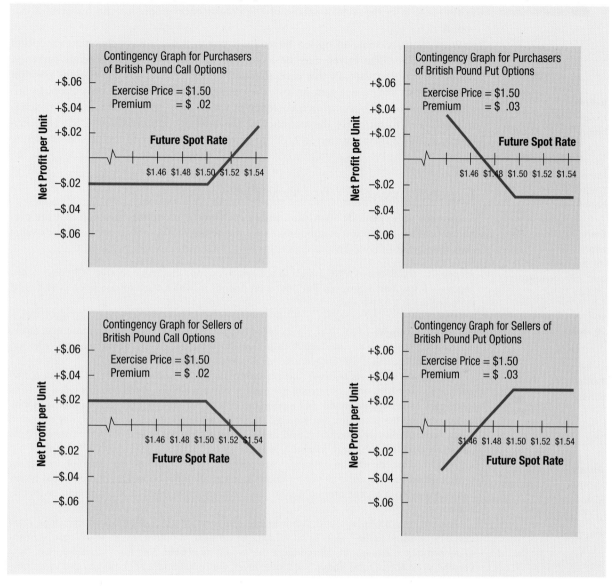

EXAMPLE The upper-right graph in Exhibit 5.6 shows the net gains to a buyer of a British pound put option with an exercise price of $1.50 and a premium of $.03 per unit. If the future spot rate is above $1.50, the option will not be exercised. At a future spot rate of $1.48, the put option will be exercised. However, considering the premium of $.03 per unit, there will be a net loss of $.01 per unit. The break-even point in this example is $1.47, since this is the future spot rate that will generate $.03 per unit from exercising the option to offset the $.03 premium. At any future spot rates of less than $1.47, the buyer of the put option will earn a positive net gain. ●

Contingency Graph for a Seller of a Put Option

A contingency graph for the seller of this put option compares the premium received from selling the option to the possible payoffs made to the buyer of the put option for various exchange rate scenarios. The graph is shown in the lower-right graph in Exhibit 5.6. It is the mirror image of the contingency graph for the buyer of a put option.

For various reasons, an option buyer's net gain will not always represent an option seller's net loss. The buyer may be using call options to hedge a foreign currency, rather than to speculate. In this case, the buyer does not evaluate the options position taken by measuring a net gain or loss; the option is used simply for protection. In addition, sellers of call options on a currency in which they currently maintain a position will not need to purchase the currency at the time an option is exercised. They can simply liquidate their position in order to provide the currency to the person exercising the option.

CONDITIONAL CURRENCY OPTIONS

A currency option can be structured with a conditional premium, meaning that the premium paid for the option is conditioned on the actual movement in the currency's value over the period of concern.

EXAMPLE

Jensen Co., a U.S.-based MNC, needs to sell British pounds that it will receive in 60 days. It can negotiate a traditional currency put option on pounds in which the exercise price is $1.70 and the premium is $.02 per unit.

Alternatively, it can negotiate a conditional currency option with a commercial bank, which has an exercise price of $1.70 and a so-called trigger of $1.74. If the pound's value falls below the exercise price by the expiration date, Jensen will exercise the option, thereby receiving $1.70 per pound, and it will not have to pay a premium for the option.

If the pound's value is between the exercise price ($1.70) and the trigger ($1.74), the option will not be exercised, and Jensen will not need to pay a premium. If the pound's value exceeds the trigger of $1.74, Jensen will pay a premium of $.04 per unit. Notice that this premium may be higher than the premium that would be paid for a basic put option. Jensen may not mind this outcome, however, because it will be receiving a high dollar amount from converting its pound receivables in the spot market.

Jensen must determine whether the potential advantage of the conditional option (avoiding the payment of a premium under some conditions) outweighs the potential disadvantage (paying a higher premium than the premium for a traditional put option on British pounds).

The potential advantage and disadvantage are illustrated in Exhibit 5.7 At exchange rates less than or equal to the trigger level ($1.74), the conditional option results in a larger payment to Jensen by the amount of the premium that would have been paid for the basic option. Conversely, at exchange rates above the trigger level, the conditional option results in a lower payment to Jensen, as its premium of $.04 exceeds the premium of $.02 per unit paid on a basic option. ●

The choice of a basic option versus a conditional option is dependent on expectations of the currency's exchange rate over the period of concern. A firm that was very confident that the pound's value would not exceed $1.74 in the previous example would prefer the conditional currency option.

Conditional currency options are also available for U.S. firms that need to purchase a foreign currency in the near future.

EXAMPLE

A conditional call option on pounds may specify an exercise price of $1.70 and a trigger of $1.67 If the pound's value remains above the trigger of the call option, a premium will not have to be paid for the call option. However, if the pound's value falls below the trigger, a large premium (such as $.04 per unit) will be required. Some conditional options require a premium if the trigger is reached anytime up until the expiration date; others require a premium only if the exchange rate is beyond the trigger as of the expiration date. ●

Exhibit 5.7 Comparison of Conditional and Basic Currency Options

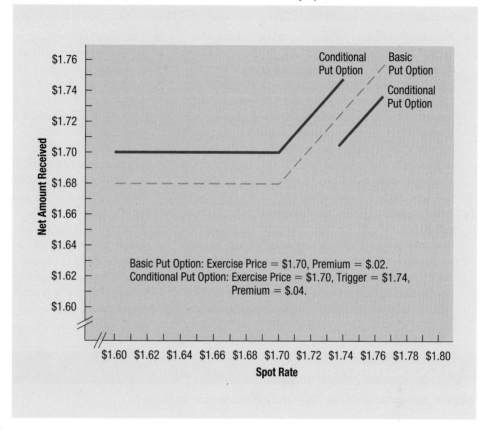

Firms also use various combinations of currency options. For example, a firm may purchase a currency call option to hedge payables and finance the purchase of the call option by selling a put option on the same currency.

EUROPEAN CURRENCY OPTIONS

The discussion of currency options up to this point has dealt solely with American-style options. European-style currency options are also available for speculating and hedging in the foreign exchange market. They are similar to American-style options except that they must be exercised on the expiration date if they are to be exercised at all. Consequently, they do not offer as much flexibility; however, this is not relevant to some situations. For example, firms that purchase options to hedge future foreign currency cash flows will probably not desire to exercise their options before the expiration date anyway. If European-style options are available for the same expiration date as American-style options and can be purchased for a slightly lower premium, some corporations may prefer them for hedging.

SUMMARY

- A forward contract specifies a standard volume of a particular currency to be exchanged on a particular date. Such a contract can be purchased by a firm to hedge payables or sold by a firm to hedge receivables.
- A currency futures contract can be purchased by speculators who expect the currency to appreciate. Conversely, it can be sold by speculators who expect that currency to depreciate. If the currency depreciates, the value of the futures contract declines, allowing those speculators to benefit when they close out their positions.
- Futures contracts on a particular currency can be purchased by corporations that have payables in that currency and wish to hedge against the possible appreciation of that currency. Conversely, these contracts can be sold by corporations that have receivables in that currency and wish to hedge against the possible depreciation of that currency.

- Currency options are classified as call options or put options. Call options allow the right to purchase a specified currency at a specified exchange rate by a specified expiration date. Put options allow the right to sell a specified currency at a specified exchange rate by a specified expiration date.
- Call options on a specific currency can be purchased by speculators who expect that currency to appreciate. Put options on a specific currency can be purchased by speculators who expect that currency to depreciate.
- Currency call options are commonly purchased by corporations that have payables in a currency that is expected to appreciate. Currency put options are commonly purchased by corporations that have receivables in a currency that is expected to depreciate.

POINT COUNTER-POINT

Should Speculators Use Currency Futures or Options?

Point Speculators should use currency futures because they can avoid a substantial premium. To the extent that they are willing to speculate, they must have confidence in their expectations. If they have sufficient confidence in their expectations, they should bet on their expectations without having to pay a large premium to cover themselves if they are wrong. If they do not have confidence in their expectations, they should not speculate at all.

Counter-Point Speculators should use currency options to fit the degree of their confidence. For example, if they are very confident that a currency will appreciate substantially, but want to limit their investment, they can buy deep out-of-the-money op-

tions. These options have a high exercise price but a low premium and therefore require a small investment. Alternatively, they can buy options that have a lower exercise price (higher premium), which will likely generate a greater return if the currency appreciates. Speculation involves risk. Speculators must recognize that their expectations may be wrong. While options require a premium, the premium is worthwhile to limit the potential downside risk. Options enable speculators to select the degree of downside risk that they are willing to tolerate.

Who Is Correct? Use the Internet to learn more about this issue. Which argument do you support? Offer your own opinion on this issue.

SELF-TEST

Answers are provided in Appendix A at the back of the text.

1. A call option on Canadian dollars with a strike price of $.60 is purchased by a speculator for a premium of $.06 per unit. Assume there are 50,000 units

in this option contract. If the Canadian dollar's spot rate is $.65 at the time the option is exercised, what is the net profit per unit and for one contract to the speculator? What would the spot rate need to be at the time the option is exercised for the speculator to break even? What is the net profit per unit to the seller of this option?

2. A put option on Australian dollars with a strike price of $.80 is purchased by a speculator for a premium of $.02. If the Australian dollar's spot rate is $.74 on the expiration date, should the speculator exercise the option on this date or let the option expire? What is the net profit per unit to the speculator? What is the net profit per unit to the seller of this put option?

3. Longer-term currency options are becoming more popular for hedging exchange rate risk. Why do you think some firms decide to hedge by using other techniques instead of purchasing long-term currency options?

4. The spot rate of the New Zealand dollar is $.70. A call option on New Zealand dollars with a 1-year expiration date has an exercise price of $.71 and a premium of $.02. A put option on New Zealand dollars at the money with a 1-year expiration date has a premium of $.03. You expect that the New Zealand dollar's spot rate will rise over time and will be $.75 in 1 year.

a. Today, Jarrod purchased call options on New Zealand dollars with a 1-year expiration date. Estimate the profit or loss per unit for Jarrod at the end of 1 year. [Assume that the options would be exercised on the expiration date or not at all.]

b. Today, Laurie sold put options on New Zealand dollars at the money with a 1-year expiration date. Estimate the profit or loss per unit for Laurie at the end of 1 year. [Assume that the options would be exercised on the expiration date or not at all.]

5. You often take speculative positions in options on euros. One month ago, the spot rate of the euro was $1.49, and the 1-month forward rate was $1.50. At that time, you sold call options on euros at the money. The premium on that option was $.02. Today is when the option will be exercised if it is feasible to do so.

a. Determine your profit or loss per unit on your option position if the spot rate of the euro is $1.55 today.

b. Repeat question a, but assume that the spot rate of the euro today is $1.48.

QUESTIONS AND APPLICATIONS

1. Forward versus Futures Contracts. Compare and contrast forward and futures contracts.

2. Using Currency Futures.

a. How can currency futures be used by corporations?

b. How can currency futures be used by speculators?

3. Currency Options. Differentiate between a currency call option and a currency put option.

4. Forward Premium. Compute the forward discount or premium for the Mexican peso whose 90-day forward rate is $.102 and spot rate is $.10. State whether your answer is a discount or premium.

5. Effects of a Forward Contract. How can a forward contract backfire?

6. Hedging with Currency Options. When would a U.S. firm consider purchasing a call option on euros for hedging? When would a U.S. firm consider purchasing a put option on euros for hedging?

7. Speculating with Currency Options. When should a speculator purchase a call option on Australian dollars? When should a speculator purchase a put option on Australian dollars?

8. Currency Call Option Premiums. List the factors that affect currency call option premiums and briefly explain the relationship that exists for each. Do you think an at-the-money call option in euros has a higher or lower premium than an at-the-money call option in Mexican pesos (assuming the expiration date and the total dollar value represented by each option are the same for both options)?

9. Currency Put Option Premiums. List the factors that affect currency put option premiums and briefly explain the relationship that exists for each.

10. Speculating with Currency Call Options. Randy Rudecki purchased a call option on British pounds for $.02 per unit. The strike price was $1.45, and the spot rate at the time the option was exercised was $1.46. Assume there are 31,250 units in a British pound option. What was Randy's net profit on this option?

11. Speculating with Currency Put Options. Alice Duever purchased a put option on British pounds for $.04 per unit. The strike price was $1.80, and the spot rate at the time the pound option was exercised was $1.59. Assume there are 31,250 units in a British pound option. What was Alice's net profit on the option?

12. Selling Currency Call Options. Mike Suerth sold a call option on Canadian dollars for $.01 per unit. The strike price was $.76, and the spot rate at the time the option was exercised was $.82. Assume Mike did not obtain Canadian dollars until the option was exercised. Also assume that there are 50,000 units in a Canadian dollar option. What was Mike's net profit on the call option?

13. Selling Currency Put Options. Brian Tull sold a put option on Canadian dollars for $.03 per unit. The strike price was $.75, and the spot rate at the time the option was exercised was $.72. Assume Brian immediately sold off the Canadian dollars received when the option was exercised. Also assume that there are 50,000 units in a Canadian dollar option. What was Brian's net profit on the put option?

14. Forward versus Currency Option Contracts. What are the advantages and disadvantages to a U.S. corporation that uses currency options on euros rather than a forward contract on euros to hedge its exposure in euros? Explain why an MNC may use forward contracts to hedge committed transactions and use currency options to hedge contracts that are anticipated but not committed. Why might forward contracts be advantageous for committed transactions, and currency options be advantageous for anticipated transactions?

15. Speculating with Currency Futures. Assume that the euro's spot rate has moved in cycles over time. How might you try to use futures contracts on euros to capitalize on this tendency? How could you determine whether such a strategy would have been profitable in previous periods?

16. Hedging with Currency Derivatives. Assume that the transactions listed in the first column of the table below are anticipated by U.S. firms that have no other foreign transactions. Place an "X" in the table wherever you see possible ways to hedge each of the transactions.

17. Price Movements of Currency Futures. Assume that on November 1, the spot rate of the British pound was $1.58 and the price on a December futures contract was $1.59. Assume that the pound depreciated during November so that by November 30 it was worth $1.51.

a. What do you think happened to the futures price over the month of November? Why?

b. If you had known that this would occur, would you have purchased or sold a December futures contract in pounds on November 1? Explain.

18. Speculating with Currency Futures. Assume that a March futures contract on Mexican pesos was available in January for $.09 per unit. Also assume that forward contracts were available for the same settlement date at a price of $.092 per peso. How could

	FORWARD CONTRACT		FUTURES CONTRACT		OPTIONS CONTRACT	
	FORWARD PURCHASE	FORWARD SALE	BUY FUTURES	SELL FUTURES	PURCHASE A CALL	PURCHASE A PUT
a. Georgetown Co. plans to purchase Japanese goods denominated in yen.						
b. Harvard, Inc., will sell goods to Japan, denominated in yen.						
c. Yale Corp. has a subsidiary in Australia that will be remitting funds to the U.S. parent.						
d. Brown, Inc., needs to pay off existing loans that are denominated in Canadian dollars.						
e. Princeton Co. may purchase a company in Japan in the near future (but the deal may not go through).						

speculators capitalize on this situation, assuming zero transaction costs? How would such speculative activity affect the difference between the forward contract price and the futures price?

19. Speculating with Currency Call Options. LSU Corp. purchased Canadian dollar call options for speculative purposes. If these options are exercised, LSU will immediately sell the Canadian dollars in the spot market. Each option was purchased for a premium of $.03 per unit, with an exercise price of $.75. LSU plans to wait until the expiration date before deciding whether to exercise the options. Of course, LSU will exercise the options at that time only if it is feasible to do so. In the following table, fill in the net profit (or loss) per unit to LSU Corp. based on the listed possible spot rates of the Canadian dollar on the expiration date.

POSSIBLE SPOT RATE OF CANADIAN DOLLAR ON EXPIRATION DATE	NET PROFIT (LOSS) PER UNIT TO LSU CORP.
$.76	
.78	
.80	
.82	
.85	
.87	

20. Speculating with Currency Put Options. Auburn Co. has purchased Canadian dollar put options for speculative purposes. Each option was purchased for a premium of $.02 per unit, with an exercise price of $.86 per unit. Auburn Co. will purchase the Canadian dollars just before it exercises the options (if it is feasible to exercise the options). It plans to wait until the expiration date before deciding whether to exercise the options. In the following table, fill in the net profit (or loss) per unit to Auburn Co. based on the listed possible spot rates of the Canadian dollar on the expiration date.

POSSIBLE SPOT RATE OF CANADIAN DOLLAR ON EXPIRATION DATE	NET PROFIT (LOSS) PER UNIT TO AUBURN CO.
$.76	
.79	
.84	
.87	
.89	
.91	

21. Speculating with Currency Call Options. Bama Corp. has sold British pound call options for speculative purposes. The option premium was $.06 per unit, and the exercise price was $1.58. Bama will purchase the pounds on the day the options are exercised (if the options are exercised) in order to fulfill its obligation. In the following table, fill in the net profit (or loss) to Bama Corp. if the listed spot rate exists at the time the purchaser of the call options considers exercising them.

POSSIBLE SPOT RATE AT THE TIME PURCHASER OF CALL OPTIONS CONSIDERS EXERCISING THEM	NET PROFIT (LOSS) PER UNIT TO BAMA CORP.
$1.53	
1.55	
1.57	
1.60	
1.62	
1.64	
1.68	

22. Speculating with Currency Put Options. Bulldog, Inc., has sold Australian dollar put options at a premium of $.01 per unit, and an exercise price of $.76 per unit. It has forecasted the Australian dollar's lowest level over the period of concern as shown in the following table. Determine the net profit (or loss) per unit to Bulldog, Inc., if each level occurs and the put options are exercised at that time.

	NET PROFIT (LOSS) TO BULLDOG, INC. IF VALUE OCCURS
$.72	
.73	
.74	
.75	
.76	

23. Hedging with Currency Derivatives. A U.S. professional football team plans to play an exhibition game in the United Kingdom next year. Assume that all expenses will be paid by the British government, and that the team will receive a check for 1 million pounds. The team anticipates that the pound will depreciate substantially by the scheduled date of the game. In addition, the National Football League must approve the deal, and approval (or disapproval) will not occur for 3 months. How can the team hedge its position? What is there to lose by waiting 3 months to see if the exhibition game is approved before hedging?

Advanced Questions

24.   Risk of Currency Futures. Currency futures markets are commonly used as a means of capitalizing on shifts in currency values, because the value of a futures contract tends to move in line with the change in the corresponding currency value. Recently, many currencies appreciated against the dollar. Most speculators anticipated that these currencies would continue to strengthen and took large buy positions in currency futures. However, the Fed intervened in the foreign exchange market by immediately selling foreign currencies in exchange for dollars, causing an abrupt decline in the values of foreign currencies (as the dollar strengthened). Participants that had purchased currency futures contracts incurred large losses. One floor broker responded to the effects of the Fed's intervention by immediately selling 300 futures contracts on British pounds (with a value of about $30 million). Such actions caused even more panic in the futures market.

a.   Explain why the central bank's intervention caused such panic among currency futures traders with buy positions.

b.   Explain why the floor broker's willingness to sell 300 pound futures contracts at the going market rate aroused such concern. What might this action signal to other brokers?

c.   Explain why speculators with short (sell) positions could benefit as a result of the central bank's intervention.

d.   Some traders with buy positions may have responded immediately to the central bank's intervention by selling futures contracts. Why would some speculators with buy positions leave their positions unchanged or even increase their positions by purchasing more futures contracts in response to the central bank's intervention?

25.   Estimating Profits from Currency Futures and Options. One year ago, you sold a put option on 100,000 euros with an expiration date of 1 year. You received a premium on the put option of $.04 per unit. The exercise price was $1.22. Assume that 1 year ago, the spot rate of the euro was $1.20, the 1-year forward rate exhibited a discount of 2 percent, and the 1-year futures price was the same as the 1-year forward rate. From 1 year ago to today, the euro depreciated against the dollar by 4 percent. Today the

put option will be exercised (if it is feasible for the buyer to do so).

a.   Determine the total dollar amount of your profit or loss from your position in the put option.

b.   Now assume that instead of taking a position in the put option 1 year ago, you sold a futures contract on 100,000 euros with a settlement date of 1 year. Determine the total dollar amount of your profit or loss.

26.   Impact of Information on Currency Futures and Options Prices. Myrtle Beach Co. purchases imports that have a price of 400,000 Singapore dollars, and it has to pay for the imports in 90 days. It can purchase a 90-day forward contract on Singapore dollars at $.50 or purchase a call option contract on Singapore dollars with an exercise price of $.50. This morning, the spot rate of the Singapore dollar was $.50. At noon, the central bank of Singapore raised interest rates, while there was no change in interest rates in the United States. These actions immediately increased the degree of uncertainty surrounding the future value of the Singapore dollar over the next 3 months. The Singapore dollar's spot rate remained at $.50 throughout the day.

a.   Myrtle Beach Co. is convinced that the Singapore dollar will definitely appreciate substantially over the next 90 days. Would a call option hedge or forward hedge be more appropriate given its opinion?

b.   Assume that Myrtle Beach uses a currency options contract to hedge rather than a forward contract. If Myrtle Beach Co. purchased a currency call option contract at the money on Singapore dollars this afternoon, would its total U.S. dollar cash outflows be more than, less than, or the same as the total U.S. dollar cash outflows if it had purchased a currency call option contract at the money this morning? Explain.

27.   Currency Straddles. Reska, Inc., has constructed a long euro straddle. A call option on euros with an exercise price of $1.10 has a premium of $.025 per unit. A euro put option has a premium of $.017 per unit. Some possible euro values at option expiration are shown in the following table. (See Appendix B in this chapter.)

	VALUE OF EURO AT OPTION EXPIRATION			
	$.90	$1.05	$1.50	$2.00
Call				
Put				
Net				

a. Complete the worksheet and determine the net profit per unit to Reska, Inc., for each possible future spot rate.

b. Determine the break-even point(s) of the long straddle. What are the break-even points of a short straddle using these options?

28. Currency Straddles. Refer to the previous question, but assume that the call and put option premiums are $.02 per unit and $.015 per unit, respectively. (See Appendix B in this chapter.)

a. Construct a contingency graph for a long euro straddle.

b. Construct a contingency graph for a short euro straddle.

29. Currency Option Contingency Graphs. (See Appendix B in this chapter.) The current spot rate of the Singapore dollar (S$) is $.50. The following option information is available:

- Call option premium on Singapore dollar (S$) = $.015.
- Put option premium on Singapore dollar (S$) = $.009.
- Call and put option strike price = $.55.
- One option contract represents S$70,000.

Construct a contingency graph for a short straddle using these options.

30. Speculating with Currency Straddles. Maggie Hawthorne is a currency speculator. She has noticed that recently the euro has appreciated substantially against the U.S. dollar. The current exchange rate of the euro is $1.15. After reading a variety of articles on the subject, she believes that the euro will continue to fluctuate substantially in the months to come. Although most forecasters believe that the euro will depreciate against the dollar in the near future, Maggie thinks that there is also a good possibility of further appreciation. Currently, a call option on euros is available with an exercise price of $1.17 and a premium of $.04. A euro put option with an exercise price of $1.17 and a premium of $.03 is also available. (See Appendix B in this chapter.)

a. Describe how Maggie could use straddles to speculate on the euro's value.

b. At option expiration, the value of the euro is $1.30. What is Maggie's total profit or loss from a long straddle position?

c. What is Maggie's total profit or loss from a long straddle position if the value of the euro is $1.05 at option expiration?

d. What is Maggie's total profit or loss from a long straddle position if the value of the euro at option expiration is still $1.15?

e. Given your answers to the questions above, when is it advantageous for a speculator to engage in a long straddle? When is it advantageous to engage in a short straddle?

31. Currency Strangles. (See Appendix B in this chapter.) Assume the following options are currently available for British pounds (£):

- Call option premium on British pounds = $.04 per unit.
- Put option premium on British pounds = $.03 per unit.
- Call option strike price = $1.56.
- Put option strike price = $1.53.
- One option contract represents £31,250.

a. Construct a worksheet for a long strangle using these options.

b. Determine the break-even point(s) for a strangle.

c. If the spot price of the pound at option expiration is $1.55, what is the total profit or loss to the strangle buyer?

d. If the spot price of the pound at option expiration is $1.50, what is the total profit or loss to the strangle writer?

32. Currency Straddles. Refer to the previous question, but assume that the call and put option premiums are $.035 per unit and $.025 per unit, respectively. (See Appendix B in this chapter.)

a. Construct a contingency graph for a long pound straddle.

b. Construct a contingency graph for a short pound straddle.

33. Currency Strangles. The following information is currently available for Canadian dollar (C$) options (see Appendix B in this chapter):

- Put option exercise price = $.75.
- Put option premium = $.014 per unit.
- Call option exercise price = $.76.
- Call option premium = $.01 per unit.
- One option contract represents C$50,000.

a. What is the maximum possible gain the purchaser of a strangle can achieve using these options?

b. What is the maximum possible loss the writer of a strangle can incur?

c. Locate the break-even point(s) of the strangle.

34. Currency Strangles. For the following options available on Australian dollars (A$), construct a worksheet and contingency graph for a long strangle. Locate the break-even points for this strangle. (See Appendix B in this chapter.)

- Put option strike price = $.67
- Call option strike price = $.65.
- Put option premium = $.01 per unit.
- Call option premium = $.02 per unit.

35. Speculating with Currency Options. Barry Egan is a currency speculator. Barry believes that the Japanese yen will fluctuate widely against the U.S. dollar in the coming month. Currently, 1-month call options on Japanese yen (¥) are available with a strike price of $.0085 and a premium of $.0007 per unit. One-month put options on Japanese yen are available with a strike price of $.0084 and a premium of $.0005 per unit. One option contract on Japanese yen contains ¥6.25 million. (See Appendix B in this chapter.)

a. Describe how Barry Egan could utilize these options to speculate on the movement of the Japanese yen.

b. Assume Barry decides to construct a long strangle in yen. What are the break-even points of this strangle?

c. What is Barry's total profit or loss if the value of the yen in 1 month is $.0070?

d. What is Barry's total profit or loss if the value of the yen in 1 month is $.0090?

36. Currency Bull Spreads and Bear Spreads. A call option on British pounds (£) exists with a strike price of $1.56 and a premium of $.08 per unit. Another call option on British pounds has a strike price of $1.59 and a premium of $.06 per unit. (See Appendix B in this chapter.)

a. Complete the worksheet for a bull spread below.

	VALUE OF BRITISH POUND AT OPTION EXPIRATION			
	$1.50	$1.56	$1.59	$1.65
Call @ $1.56				
Call @ $1.59				
Net				

b. What is the break-even point for this bull spread?

c. What is the maximum profit of this bull spread? What is the maximum loss?

d. If the British pound spot rate is $1.58 at option expiration, what is the total profit or loss for the bull spread?

e. If the British pound spot rate is $1.55 at option expiration, what is the total profit or loss for a bear spread?

37. Bull Spreads and Bear Spreads. Two British pound (£) put options are available with exercise prices of $1.60 and $1.62. The premiums associated with these options are $.03 and $.04 per unit, respectively. (See Appendix B in this chapter.)

a. Describe how a bull spread can be constructed using these put options. What is the difference between using put options versus call options to construct a bull spread?

b. Complete the following worksheet.

	VALUE OF BRITISH POUND AT OPTION EXPIRATION			
	$1.55	$1.60	$1.62	$1.67
Put @ $1.60				
Put @ $1.62				
Net				

c. At option expiration, the spot rate of the pound is $1.60. What is the bull spreader's total gain or loss?

d. At option expiration, the spot rate of the pound is $1.58. What is the bear spreader's total gain or loss?

38. Profits from Using Currency Options and Futures. On July 2, the 2-month futures rate of the Mexican peso contained a 2 percent discount (unannualized). There was a call option on pesos with an exercise price that was equal to the spot rate. There was also a put option on pesos with an exercise price equal to the spot rate. The premium on each of these options was 3 percent of the spot rate at that time. On September 2, the option expired. Go to www.oanda.com (or any website that has foreign exchange rate quotations) and determine the direct quote of the Mexican peso. You exercised the option on this date if it was feasible to do so.

a. What was your net profit per unit if you had purchased the call option?

b. What was your net profit per unit if you had purchased the put option?

c. What was your net profit per unit if you had purchased a futures contract on July 2 that had a settlement date of September 2?

d. What was your net profit per unit if you sold a futures contract on July 2 that had a settlement date of September 2?

39. Uncertainty and Option Premiums. This morning, a Canadian dollar call option contract has a $.71 strike price, a premium of $.02, and expiration date of 1 month from now. This afternoon, news about international economic conditions increased the level of uncertainty surrounding the Canadian dollar. However, the spot rate of the Canadian dollar was still $.71. Would the premium of the call option contract be higher than, lower than, or equal to $.02 this afternoon? Explain.

40. Uncertainty and Option Premiums. At 10:30 a.m., the media reported news that the Mexican government's political problems were reduced, which reduced the expected volatility of the Mexican peso against the dollar over the next month. The spot rate of the Mexican peso was $.13 as of 10 a.m. and remained at that level all morning. At 10 a.m., Hilton Head Co. purchased a call option at the money on 1 million Mexican pesos with an expiration date 1 month from now. At 11:00 a.m., Rhode Island Co. purchased a call option at the money on 1 million pesos with a December expiration date 1 month from now. Did Hilton Head Co. pay more, less, or the same as Rhode Island Co. for the options? Briefly explain.

41. Speculating with Currency Futures. Assume that 1 year ago, the spot rate of the British pound was $1.70. One year ago, the 1-year futures contract of the British pound exhibited a discount of 6 percent. At that time, you sold futures contracts on pounds, representing a total of £1,000,000. From 1 year ago to today, the pound's value depreciated against the dollar by 4 percent. Determine the total dollar amount of your profit or loss from your futures contract.

Discussion in the Boardroom

This exercise can be found in Appendix E at the back of this textbook.

Running Your Own MNC

This exercise can be found on the *International Financial Management* text companion website located at www.cengage.com/finance/madura.

BLADES, INC. CASE

Use of Currency Derivative Instruments

Blades, Inc., needs to order supplies 2 months ahead of the delivery date. It is considering an order from a Japanese supplier that requires a payment of 12.5 million yen payable as of the delivery date. Blades has two choices:

- Purchase two call options contracts (since each option contract represents 6,250,000 yen).
- Purchase one futures contract (which represents 12.5 million yen).

The futures price on yen has historically exhibited a slight discount from the existing spot rate. However, the firm would like to use currency options to hedge payables in Japanese yen for transactions 2 months in advance. Blades would prefer hedging its yen payable position because it is uncomfortable leaving the position open given the historical volatility of the yen. Nevertheless, the firm would be willing to remain unhedged if the yen becomes more stable someday.

Ben Holt, Blades' chief financial officer (CFO), prefers the flexibility that options offer over forward contracts or futures contracts because he can let the options expire if the yen depreciates. He would like to use an exercise price that is about 5 percent above the existing spot rate to ensure that Blades will have to pay no more than 5 percent above the existing spot rate for a transaction 2 months beyond its order date, as long as the option premium is no more than 1.6 percent of the price it would have to pay per unit when exercising the option.

In general, options on the yen have required a premium of about 1.5 percent of the total transaction amount that would be paid if the option is exercised. For example, recently the yen spot rate was $.0072, and the firm purchased a call option with an exercise price of $.00756, which is 5 percent above the existing spot rate. The premium for this option was $.0001134, which is 1.5 percent of the price to be paid per yen if the option is exercised.

A recent event caused more uncertainty about the yen's future value, although it did not affect the spot rate or the forward or futures rate of the yen.

Specifically, the yen's spot rate was still $.0072, but the option premium for a call option with an exercise price of $.00756 was now $.0001512. An alternative call option is available with an expiration date of 2 months from now; it has a premium of $.0001134 (which is the size of the premium that would have existed for the option desired before the event), but it is for a call option with an exercise price of $.00792.

The table below summarizes the option and futures information available to Blades:

	BEFORE EVENT	AFTER EVENT	
Spot rate	$.0072	$.0072	$.0072
Option Information			
Exercise price ($)	$.00756	$.00756	$.00792
Exercise price (% above spot)	5%	5%	10%
Option premium per yen ($)	$.0001134	$.0001512	$.0001134
Option premium (% of exercise price)	1.5%	2.0%	1.5%
Total premium ($)	$1,417.50	$1,890.00	$1,417.50
Amount paid for yen if option is exercised (not including premium)	$94,500	$94,500	$99,000
Futures Contract Information			
Futures price	$.006912	$.006912	

As an analyst for Blades, you have been asked to offer insight on how to hedge. Use a spreadsheet to support your analysis of questions 4 and 6.

1. If Blades uses call options to hedge its yen payables, should it use the call option with the exercise price of $.00756 or the call option with the exercise price of $.00792? Describe the tradeoff.

2. Should Blades allow its yen position to be unhedged? Describe the tradeoff.

3. Assume there are speculators who attempt to capitalize on their expectation of the yen's movement over the 2 months between the order and delivery dates by either buying or selling yen futures now and buying or selling yen at the future spot rate. Given this information, what is the *expectation* on the order date of the yen spot rate by the delivery date? (Your answer should consist of one number.)

4. Assume that the firm shares the market consensus of the future yen spot rate. Given this expectation and given that the firm makes a decision (i.e., option, futures contract, remain unhedged) purely on a cost basis, what would be its optimal choice?

5. Will the choice you made as to the optimal hedging strategy in question 4 definitely turn out to be the lowest-cost alternative in terms of actual costs incurred? Why or why not?

6. Now assume that you have determined that the historical standard deviation of the yen is about $.0005. Based on your assessment, you believe it is highly unlikely that the future spot rate will be more than two standard deviations above the expected spot rate by the delivery date. Also assume that the futures price remains at its current level of $.006912. Based on this expectation of the future spot rate, what is the optimal hedge for the firm?

SMALL BUSINESS DILEMMA

Use of Currency Futures and Options by the Sports Exports Company

The Sports Exports Company receives British pounds each month as payment for the footballs that it exports. It anticipates that the pound will depreciate over time against the U.S. dollar.

1. How can the Sports Exports Company use currency futures contracts to hedge against exchange rate risk? Are there any limitations of using currency futures contracts that would prevent the Sports Exports Company from locking in a specific exchange rate at

which it can sell all the pounds it expects to receive in each of the upcoming months?

2. How can the Sports Exports Company use currency options to hedge against exchange rate risk? Are there any limitations of using currency options contracts that would prevent the Sports Exports Company from locking in a specific exchange rate at which it can sell all the pounds it expects to receive in each of the upcoming months?

3. Jim Logan, owner of the Sports Exports Company, is concerned that the pound may depreciate substantially over the next month, but he also believes that the pound could appreciate substantially if specific situations occur. Should Jim use currency futures or currency options to hedge the exchange rate risk? Is there any disadvantage of selecting this method for hedging?

INTERNET/EXCEL EXERCISES

The website of the Chicago Mercantile Exchange provides information about currency futures and options. Its address is www.cme.com.

1. Use this website to review the prevailing prices of currency futures contracts. Do today's futures prices (for contracts with the closest settlement date) generally reflect an increase or decrease from the day before? Is there any news today that might explain the change in the futures prices?

2. Does it appear that futures prices among currencies (for the closest settlement date) are changing in the same direction? Explain.

3. If you purchase a British pound futures contract with the closest settlement date, what is the futures price? Given that a contract is based on £62,500, what is the dollar amount you will need at the settlement date to fulfill the contract?

4. Go to www.phlx.com/products and obtain the money currency option quotations for the Canadian dollar (the symbol is XCD) and the euro (symbol is XEU) for a similar expiration date. Which currency option has a larger premium? Explain your results.

REFERENCES

Chang, Eric C., and Kit Pong Wong, Sep 2003, Cross-hedging with Currency Options and Futures, *Journal of Financial and Quantitative Analysis*, pp. 555–574.

Cretien, Paul D., Aug 2008, Swaps vs. Eurodollar Spreads, *Futures*, pp. 38–41.

Guay, Wayne, and S. P. Kothari, Dec 2003, How Much Do Firms Hedge with Derivatives? *Journal of Financial Economics*, pp. 423–461.

Kawaller, Ira G., Spring 2008, Hedging Currency Exposures by Multinationals: Things to Consider, *Journal of Applied Finance*, pp. 92–98.

Lien, Donald, and Kit Pong Wong, Sep 2004, Optimal Bidding and Hedging in International Markets, *Journal of International Money and Finance*, pp. 785–798.

Machnes, Yaffa, Nov 2006, Information Embedded in the Trading Volume of Currency Options, Derivatives Use, *Trading & Regulation*, pp. 244–249.

Pukthuanthong-Le, Kuntara, Richard M. Levich, and Lee R. Thomas III, Fall 2007, Do Foreign Exchange Markets Still Trend? *Journal of Portfolio Management*, pp. 114–118.

Pukthuanthong-Le, Kuntara, and Lee R. Thomas III, May/Jun 2008, Weak-Form Efficiency in Currency Markets, *Financial Analysts Journal*, pp. 31–52.

Salcedo, Yesenia, Fall 2006, Trading Options on Currencies, *Futures*, pp. 30–31.

Exchange Rate Behavior

Part 2 (Chapters 6 through 8) focuses on critical relationships pertaining to exchange rates. Chapter 6 explains how governments can influence exchange rate movements and how such movements can affect economic conditions. Chapter 7 explores the relationships among foreign currencies. It also explains how the forward exchange rate is influenced by the differential between interest rates of any two countries. Chapter 8 discusses prominent theories regarding the impact of inflation on exchange rates and the impact of interest rate movements on exchange rates.

6

Government Influence on Exchange Rates

CHAPTER OBJECTIVES

The specific objectives of this chapter are to:

■ describe the exchange rate systems used by various governments,

■ explain how governments can use direct intervention to influence exchange rates,

■ explain how governments can use indirect intervention to influence exchange rates, and

■ explain how government intervention in the foreign exchange market can affect economic conditions.

As explained in Chapter 4, government policies affect exchange rates. Some government policies are specifically intended to affect exchange rates. Other policies are intended to affect economic conditions but indirectly influence exchange rates. Because the performance of an MNC is affected by exchange rates, financial managers need to understand how the government influences exchange rates.

EXCHANGE RATE SYSTEMS

Exchange rate systems can be classified according to the degree by which exchange rates are controlled by the government. Exchange rate systems normally fall into one of the following categories, each of which is discussed in turn:

- Fixed
- Freely floating
- Managed float
- Pegged

Fixed Exchange Rate System

In a **fixed exchange rate system**, exchange rates are either held constant or allowed to fluctuate only within very narrow boundaries. A fixed exchange rate system requires much central bank intervention in order to maintain a currency's value within narrow boundaries. In general, the central bank has to offset any imbalance between demand and supply conditions for its currency in order to prevent its value from changing. The specific details of how central banks intervene are discussed later in this chapter. In some situations, a central bank may reset a fixed exchange rate. That is, it will **devalue** or reduce the value of its currency against other currencies. A central bank's actions to devalue a currency in a fixed exchange rate system are referred to as **devaluation,** while the term *depreciation* represents the decrease in the value of a currency that is allowed to change in response to market conditions. Thus, the term *depreciation* is more commonly used when describing the decrease in values of currencies that are not subject to a fixed exchange rate system.

In a fixed exchange rate system, a central bank may also **revalue** (increase the value of) its currency against other currencies. **Revaluation** refers to an upward adjustment of the exchange rate by the central bank, while the term *appreciation* represents the increase in the value of a currency that is allowed to change in response to market conditions. Thus, the term *appreciation* is more commonly used when describing the increase in values of currencies that are not subject to a fixed exchange rate system.

Bretton Woods Agreement 1944–1971.
From 1944 to 1971, exchange rates were typically fixed according to a system planned at the Bretton Woods conference (held in Bretton Woods, New Hampshire, in 1944) by representatives from various countries. Because this arrangement, known as the **Bretton Woods Agreement,** lasted from 1944 to 1971, that period is sometimes referred to as the Bretton Woods era. Each currency was valued in terms of gold; for example, the U.S. dollar was valued as 1/35 ounce of gold. Since all currencies were valued in terms of gold, their values with respect to each other were fixed. Governments intervened in the foreign exchange markets to ensure that exchange rates drifted no more than 1 percent above or below the initially set rates.

Smithsonian Agreement 1971–1973.
During the Bretton Woods era, the United States often experienced balance-of-trade deficits, an indication that the dollar's value may have been too strong, since the use of dollars for foreign purchases exceeded the demand by foreign countries for dollar-denominated goods. By 1971, it appeared that some currency values would need to be adjusted to restore a more balanced flow of payments between countries. In December 1971, a conference of representatives from various countries concluded with the **Smithsonian Agreement,** which called for a devaluation of the U.S. dollar by about 8 percent against other currencies. In addition, boundaries for the currency values were expanded to within 2.25 percent above or below the rates initially set by the agreement. Nevertheless, international payments imbalances continued, and as of February 1973, the dollar was again devalued. By March 1973, most governments of the major countries were no longer attempting to maintain their home currency values within the boundaries established by the Smithsonian Agreement.

Advantages of Fixed Exchange Rates.
A fixed exchange rate would be beneficial to a country for the following reasons. First, exporters and importers could engage in international trade without concern about exchange rate movements of the currency to which their local currency is linked. Any firms that accept the foreign currency as payment would be insulated from the risk that the currency could depreciate over time. In addition, any firms that need to obtain that foreign currency in the future would be insulated from the risk of the currency appreciating over time. Another benefit is that firms could engage in direct foreign investment, without concern about exchange rate movements of that currency. They would be able to convert their foreign currency earnings into their home currency without concern that the foreign currency denominating their earnings might weaken over time. Thus, the management of an MNC would be much easier.

In addition, investors would be able to invest funds in foreign countries without concern that the foreign currency denominating their investments might weaken over time. A country with a stable exchange rate can attract more funds as investments because the investors would not have to worry about the currency weakening over time. Funds are needed in any country to support economic growth. Countries that attract a large amount of capital flows normally have lower interest rates. This can stimulate their economies.

Disadvantages of Fixed Exchange Rates.
One disadvantage of a fixed exchange rate system is that there is still risk that the government will alter the value of a specific currency. Although an MNC is not exposed to continual movements in an exchange rate, it does face the possibility that its central bank will devalue or revalue its currency.

A second disadvantage is that from a macro viewpoint, a fixed exchange rate system may make each country and its MNCs more vulnerable to economic conditions in other countries.

EXAMPLE Assume that there are only two countries in the world: the United States and the United Kingdom. Also assume a fixed exchange rate system and that these two countries trade frequently with each other. If the United States experiences a much higher inflation rate than the United

Kingdom, U.S. consumers should buy more goods from the United Kingdom and British consumers should reduce their imports of U.S. goods (due to the high U.S. prices). This reaction would force U.S. production down and unemployment up. It could also cause higher inflation in the United Kingdom due to the excessive demand for British goods relative to the supply of British goods produced. Thus, the high inflation in the United States could cause high inflation in the United Kingdom. In the mid- and late 1960s, the United States experienced relatively high inflation and was accused of "exporting" that inflation to some European countries.

Alternatively, a high unemployment rate in the United States will cause a reduction in U.S. income and a decline in U.S. purchases of British goods. Consequently, productivity in the United Kingdom may decrease and unemployment may rise. In this case, the United States may "export" unemployment to the United Kingdom. ●

Freely Floating Exchange Rate System

In a **freely floating exchange rate system,** exchange rate values are determined by market forces without intervention by governments. Whereas a fixed exchange rate system allows no flexibility for exchange rate movements, a freely floating exchange rate system allows complete flexibility. A freely floating exchange rate adjusts on a continual basis in response to demand and supply conditions for that currency.

Advantages of a Freely Floating System. One advantage of a freely floating exchange rate system is that a country is more insulated from the inflation of other countries.

EXAMPLE

Continue with the previous example in which there are only two countries, but now assume a freely floating exchange rate system. If the United States experiences a high rate of inflation, the increased U.S. demand for British goods will place upward pressure on the value of the British pound. As a second consequence of the high U.S. inflation, the reduced British demand for U.S. goods will result in a reduced supply of pounds for sale (exchanged for dollars), which will also place upward pressure on the British pound's value. The pound will appreciate due to these market forces (it was not allowed to appreciate under the fixed rate system). This appreciation will make British goods more expensive for U.S. consumers, even though British producers did not raise their prices. The higher prices will simply be due to the pound's appreciation; that is, a greater number of U.S. dollars are required to buy the same number of pounds as before.

In the United Kingdom, the actual price of the goods as measured in British pounds may be unchanged. Even though U.S. prices have increased, British consumers will continue to purchase U.S. goods because they can exchange their pounds for more U.S. dollars (due to the British pound's appreciation against the U.S. dollar). ●

Another advantage of freely floating exchange rates is that a country is more insulated from unemployment problems in other countries.

EXAMPLE

Under a floating rate system, the decline in U.S. purchases of British goods will reflect a reduced U.S. demand for British pounds. Such a shift in demand can cause the pound to depreciate against the dollar (under the fixed rate system, the pound would not be allowed to depreciate). The depreciation of the pound will make British goods look cheap to U.S. consumers, offsetting the possible reduction in demand for these goods resulting from a lower level of U.S. income. As was true with inflation, a sudden change in unemployment will have less influence on a foreign country under a floating rate system than under a fixed rate system. ●

As these examples illustrate, in a freely floating exchange rate system, problems experienced in one country will not necessarily be contagious. The exchange rate adjustments serve as a form of protection against "exporting" economic problems to other countries.

An additional advantage of a freely floating exchange rate system is that a central bank is not required to constantly maintain exchange rates within specified boundaries. Therefore, it is not forced to implement an intervention policy that may have an unfavorable effect on the economy just to control exchange rates. Furthermore, governments can implement policies without concern as to whether the policies will maintain the exchange rates within specified boundaries. Finally, if exchange rates were not allowed to float, investors would invest funds in whatever country had the highest interest rate. This would likely cause governments in countries with low interest rates to restrict investors' funds from leaving the country. Thus, there would be more restrictions on capital flows, and financial market efficiency would be reduced.

Disadvantages of a Freely Floating Exchange Rate System.
In the previous example, the United Kingdom is somewhat insulated from the problems experienced in the United States due to the freely floating exchange rate system. Although this is an advantage for the country that is protected (the United Kingdom), it can be a disadvantage for the country that initially experienced the economic problems.

EXAMPLE
If the United States experiences high inflation, the dollar may weaken, thereby insulating the United Kingdom from the inflation, as discussed earlier. From the U.S. perspective, however, a weaker U.S. dollar causes import prices to be higher. This can increase the price of U.S. materials and supplies, which will in turn increase U.S. prices of finished goods. In addition, higher foreign prices (from the U.S. perspective) can force U.S. consumers to purchase domestic products. As U.S. producers recognize that their foreign competition has been reduced due to the weak dollar, they can more easily raise their prices without losing their customers to foreign competition. ●

In a similar manner, a freely floating exchange rate system can adversely affect a country that has high unemployment.

EXAMPLE
If the U.S. unemployment rate is rising, U.S. demand for imports will decrease, putting upward pressure on the value of the dollar. A stronger dollar will then cause U.S. consumers to purchase foreign products rather than U.S. products because the foreign products can be purchased cheaply. Yet, such a reaction can actually be detrimental to the United States during periods of high unemployment. ●

As these examples illustrate, a country's economic problems can sometimes be compounded by freely floating exchange rates. Under such a system, MNCs will need to devote substantial resources to measuring and managing exposure to exchange rate fluctuations.

Managed Float Exchange Rate System

The exchange rate system that exists today for some currencies lies somewhere between fixed and freely floating. It resembles the freely floating system in that exchange rates are allowed to fluctuate on a daily basis and there are no official boundaries. It is similar to the fixed rate system in that governments can and sometimes do intervene to prevent their currencies from moving too far in a certain direction. This type of system is known as a **managed float** or "dirty" float (as opposed to a "clean" float where rates float freely without government intervention). The various forms of intervention used by governments to manage exchange rate movements are discussed later in this chapter.

At times, the governments of various countries including Brazil, Russia, South Korea, and Venezuela have imposed bands around their currency to limit its degree of movement. Later, however, they removed the bands when they found that they could not maintain the currency's value within the bands.

Criticism of a Managed Float System.
Critics suggest that a managed float system allows a government to manipulate exchange rates in a manner that can benefit its own country at the expense of others. A government may attempt to weaken its currency

to stimulate a stagnant economy. The increased aggregate demand for products that results from such a policy may reflect a decreased aggregate demand for products in other countries, as the weakened currency attracts foreign demand. Although this criticism is valid, it could apply as well to the fixed exchange rate system, where governments have the power to devalue their currencies.

Pegged Exchange Rate System

Some countries use a **pegged exchange rate** arrangement, in which their home currency's value is pegged to one foreign currency or to an index of currencies. While the home currency's value is fixed in terms of the foreign currency to which it is pegged, it moves in line with that currency against other currencies.

Some governments peg their currency's value to that of a stable currency, such as the dollar, because that forces the value of their currency to be stable. First, this forces their currency's exchange rate with the dollar to be fixed. Second, their currency will move against nondollar currencies by the same degree as the dollar. Since the dollar is more stable than most currencies, it will make their currency more stable than most currencies.

Limitations of a Pegged Exchange Rate. While countries with a pegged exchange rate may attract foreign investment because the exchange rate is expected to remain stable, weak economic or political conditions can cause firms and investors to question whether the peg will hold. If a country suddenly experiences a recession, it may experience capital outflows as some firms and investors withdraw funds because they believe there are better investment opportunities in other countries. These transactions result in an exchange of the local currency for dollars and other currencies, which places downward pressure on the local currency's value. The central bank would need to offset this by intervening in the foreign exchange market (as explained shortly) but might not be able to maintain the peg. If the peg is broken and the exchange rate is dictated by market forces, the local currency's value could decline immediately by 20 percent or more.

If foreign investors fear that a peg may be broken, they quickly sell their investments in that country and convert the proceeds into their home currency. These transactions place more downward pressure on the local currency of that country. Even the local residents may consider selling their local investments and converting their funds to dollars or some other currency if they fear that the peg may be broken. They can exchange their currency for dollars to invest in the United States before the peg breaks. They may leave their investment in the United States until after the peg breaks, and their local currency's value is reduced. Then they can sell their investments in the United States and convert the dollar proceeds back to their currency at a more favorable exchange rate. Their initial actions to convert their money into dollars placed more downward pressure on the local currency.

For the reasons explained here, countries have difficulty maintaining a pegged exchange rate when they are experiencing major political or economic problems. While a country with a stable exchange rate can attract foreign investment, the investors will move their funds to another country if there are concerns that the peg will break. Thus, a pegged exchange rate system could ultimately create more instability in a country's economy. Examples of pegged exchange rate systems follow.

Europe's Snake Arrangement 1972–1979. Several European countries established a pegged exchange rate arrangement in April 1972. Their goal was to maintain their currencies within established limits of each other. This arrangement became known as the **snake.** The snake was difficult to maintain, however, and market pressure caused some currencies to move outside their established limits. Consequently, some members withdrew from the snake arrangement, and some currencies were realigned.

European Monetary System (EMS) 1979–1992.

Due to continued problems with the snake arrangement, the European Monetary System (EMS) was pushed into operation in March 1979. Under the EMS, exchange rates of member countries were held together within specified limits and were also tied to the European Currency Unit (ECU), which was a weighted average of exchange rates of the member countries. Each weight was determined by a member's relative gross national product and activity in intra-European trade. The currencies of these member countries were allowed to fluctuate by no more than 2.25 percent (6 percent for some currencies) from the initially established values.

The method of linking European currency values with the ECU was known as the **exchange rate mechanism (ERM).** The participating governments intervened in the foreign exchange markets to maintain the exchange rates within boundaries established by the ERM.

The European Monetary System forced participating countries to have somewhat similar interest rates, since the currencies were not allowed to deviate much against each other and money would flow to the European country the with the highest interest rate. In 1992, the German government increased its interest rates to prevent excessive spending and inflation. Other European governments, however, were more concerned about stimulating their economies to lower their high unemployment levels, so they wanted to reduce interest rates. They could not achieve their own goals for a stronger economy while their interest rates were so highly influenced by German interest rates. Consequently, some countries suspended their participation in the EMS. European countries realized that a pegged system might work in Europe only if it was set permanently. This provided momentum for the single European currency (the euro), which began in 1999 and is discussed later in this chapter.

Mexico's Pegged System in 1994.

In 1994, Mexico's central bank used a special pegged exchange rate system that linked the peso to the U.S. dollar but allowed the peso's value to fluctuate against the dollar within a band. The Mexican central bank enforced the link through frequent intervention. Mexico experienced a large balance-of-trade deficit in 1994, however, perhaps because the peso was stronger than it should have been and encouraged Mexican firms and consumers to buy an excessive amount of imports.

Many speculators based in Mexico recognized that the peso was being maintained at an artificially high level, and they speculated on its potential decline by investing their funds in the United States. They planned to liquidate their U.S. investments if and when the peso's value weakened so that they could convert the dollars from their U.S. investments into pesos at a favorable exchange rate.

By December 1994, there was substantial downward pressure on the peso. On December 20, 1994, Mexico's central bank devalued the peso by about 13 percent. Mexico's stock prices plummeted, as many foreign investors sold their shares and withdrew their funds from Mexico in anticipation of further devaluation of the peso. On December 22, the central bank allowed the peso to float freely, and it declined by 15 percent. This was the beginning of the so-called Mexican peso crisis. In an attempt to discourage foreign investors from withdrawing their investments in Mexico's debt securities, the central bank increased interest rates, but the higher rates increased the cost of borrowing for Mexican firms and consumers, thereby slowing economic growth.

Mexico's financial problems caused investors to lose confidence in peso-denominated securities, so they liquidated their peso-denominated securities and transferred their funds to other countries. These actions put additional downward pressure on the peso.

In the 4 months after December 20, 1994, the value of the peso declined by more than 50 percent against the dollar. The Mexican crisis might not have occurred if the peso had been allowed to float throughout 1994 because the peso would have gravitated toward its natural level. The crisis illustrates that central bank intervention will not necessarily be able to overwhelm market forces; thus, the crisis may serve as an argument for letting a currency float freely.

China's Pegged Exchange Rate 1996–2005.

From 1996 until 2005, China's yuan was pegged to be worth about $.12 (8.28 yuan per U.S. dollar). During this period, the yuan's value would change against nondollar currencies on a daily basis to the same degree as the dollar. Because of the peg, the yuan's value remained at that level even though the United States was experiencing a trade deficit of more than $100 billion per year with China. U.S. politicians argued that the yuan was being held at a superficially low level by the Chinese government. In response to the growing criticism, China revalued its yuan by 2.1 percent in July 2005. It also agreed to allow its yuan to float subject to a .3 percent limit each day from the previous day's closing value against a set of major currencies. In May 2007, China widened its band so that the yuan's value could float subject to a .5 percent limit each day.

Even though the yuan is now allowed to float (within limits), the huge balance-of-trade deficit will not automatically force appreciation of the yuan. Large net capital flows from China to the United States (purchases of U.S. securities) could offset the trade flows.

Currency Boards Used to Peg Currency Values.

A currency board is a system for pegging the value of the local currency to some other specified currency. The board must maintain currency reserves for all the currency that it has printed. The large amount of reserves may increase the ability of a country's central bank to maintain its pegged currency.

Hong Kong has tied the value of its currency (the Hong Kong dollar) to the U.S. dollar (HK$7.80 = $1.00) since 1983. Every Hong Kong dollar in circulation is backed by a U.S. dollar in reserve. Periodically, economic conditions have caused an imbalance in the U.S. demand for Hong Kong dollars versus the supply of Hong Kong dollars for sale in the foreign exchange market. Under these conditions, the Hong Kong central bank must intervene by making transactions in the foreign exchange market that offset this imbalance. Because it has been successful at maintaining the fixed exchange rate between the Hong Kong dollar and U.S. dollar, firms in the two countries are more willing to do business with each other, without excessive concerns about exchange rate risk. ●

A currency board is effective only if investors believe that it will last. If investors expect that market forces will prevent a government from maintaining the local currency's exchange rate, they will attempt to move their funds to other countries where they expect the local currency to be stronger. When foreign investors withdraw their funds from a country and convert the funds into a different currency, they place downward pressure on the local currency's exchange rate. If the supply of the currency for sale continues to exceed the demand, the government will be forced to devalue its currency.

In 1991, Argentina established a currency board that pegged the Argentine peso to the U.S. dollar. In 2002, Argentina was suffering from major economic problems, and its government was unable to repay its debt. Foreign investors and local investors began to transfer their funds to other countries because they feared that their investments would earn poor returns. These actions required the exchange of pesos into other currencies such as the dollar and caused an excessive supply of pesos for sale in the foreign exchange market. The government could not maintain the exchange rate of 1 peso = 1 dollar because the supply of pesos for sale exceeded the demand at that exchange rate. In March 2002, the government devalued the peso to 1 peso = $.71 (1.4 pesos per dollar). Even at this new exchange rate, the supply of pesos for sale exceeded the demand, so the Argentine government decided to let the peso's value float in response to market conditions rather than set the peso's value. If a currency board is expected to remain in place for a long period, it may reduce fears that the local currency will weaken and thus may encourage investors to maintain their investments within the country. However, a currency board is effective only if the government can convince investors that the exchange rate will be maintained. ●

Interest Rates of Pegged Currencies. A country that uses a currency board does not have complete control over its local interest rates because its rates must be aligned with the interest rates of the currency to which it is tied.

Recall that the Hong Kong dollar is pegged to the U.S. dollar. If Hong Kong lowers its interest rates to stimulate its economy, its interest rate would then be lower than U.S. interest rates. Investors based in Hong Kong would be enticed to exchange Hong Kong dollars for U.S. dollars and invest in the United States where interest rates are higher. Since the Hong Kong dollar is tied to the U.S. dollar, the investors could exchange the proceeds of their investment back to Hong Kong dollars at the end of the investment period without concern about exchange rate risk because the exchange rate is fixed.

If the United States raises its interest rates, Hong Kong would be forced to raise its interest rates (on securities with similar risk as those in the United States). Otherwise, investors in Hong Kong could invest their money in the United States and earn a higher rate. ●

Even though a country may not have control over its interest rate when it establishes a currency board, its interest rate may be more stable than if it did not have a currency board. Its interest rate will move in tandem with the interest rate of the currency to which it is tied. The interest rate may include a risk premium that could reflect either default risk or the risk that the currency board will be discontinued.

Exchange Rate Risk of a Pegged Currency. A currency that is pegged to another currency cannot be pegged against all other currencies. If a currency is pegged to the dollar, then it will move in tandem with the dollar against all other currencies.

While the Argentine peso was pegged to the dollar (in the 1991–2002 period), the dollar commonly strengthened against the Brazilian real and some other currencies in South America; therefore, the Argentine peso also strengthened against those currencies. Many exporting firms in Argentina were adversely affected by the strong Argentine peso, however, because it made their products too expensive for importers. Since Argentina's currency board has been eliminated, the Argentine peso is no longer forced to move in tandem with the dollar against other currencies. ●

Dollarization

Dollarization is the replacement of a foreign currency with U.S. dollars. This process is a step beyond a currency board because it forces the local currency to be replaced by the U.S. dollar. Although dollarization and a currency board both attempt to peg the local currency's value, the currency board does not replace the local currency with dollars. The decision to use U.S. dollars as the local currency cannot be easily reversed because the country no longer has a local currency.

From 1990 to 2000, Ecuador's currency (the sucre) depreciated by about 97 percent against the U.S. dollar. The weakness of the currency caused unstable trade conditions, high inflation, and volatile interest rates. In 2000, in an effort to stabilize trade and economic conditions, Ecuador replaced the sucre with the U.S. dollar as its currency. By November 2000, inflation had declined and economic growth had increased. Thus, it appeared that dollarization had favorable effects. ●

Classification of Exchange Rate Arrangements

Exhibit 6.1 identifies the currencies and exchange rate arrangements used by various countries. Many countries allow the value of their currency to float against others but intervene periodically to influence its value. Some countries in the Middle East such as Qatar, Saudi Arabia, and the United Arab Emirates peg their currencies to the dollar. From 2006 to the summer of 2008, the euro and some other currencies appreciated substantially against the dollar, and therefore against these currencies of the Middle East. Consequently, companies and consumers in the Middle East experienced a reduction in purchasing power when buying foreign products. Many critics suggested that these countries abandon their peg to the dollar. Yet, opinions on this topic always vary, for while importers are adversely affected, exporters can benefit from a weak local currency.

Exhibit 6.1 Exchange Rate Arrangements

FLOATING RATE SYSTEM			
COUNTRY	**CURRENCY**	**COUNTRY**	**CURRENCY**
Afghanistan	new afghani	Norway	krone
Argentina	peso	Paraguay	guarani
Australia	dollar	Peru	new sol
Bolivia	boliviano	Poland	zloty
Brazil	real	Romania	leu
Canada	dollar	Russia	ruble
Chile	peso	Singapore	dollar
Denmark	krone	South Africa	rand
Euro participants	euro	South Korea	won
Hungary	forint	Sweden	krona
India	rupee	Switzerland	franc
Indonesia	rupiah	Taiwan	new dollar
Israel	new shekel	Thailand	baht
Jamaica	dollar	United Kingdom	pound
Japan	yen	Venezuela	bolivar
Mexico	peso		
PEGGED RATE SYSTEM			
The following currencies are pegged to the U.S. dollar.			
COUNTRY	**CURRENCY**	**COUNTRY**	**CURRENCY**
Bahamas	dollar	Qatar	riyal
Barbados	dollar	Saudi Arabia	riyal
Bermuda	dollar	United Arab Emirates	dirham
Hong Kong	dollar		

A SINGLE EUROPEAN CURRENCY

In 1992, the Maastricht Treaty called for the establishment of a single European currency. In January 1999, the euro replaced the national currencies of 11 European countries. Since then, five more countries converted their home currency to the euro. The countries that use the euro as their home currency are: Austria, Belgium, Cyprus, Finland, France, Germany, Greece, Ireland, Italy, Luxembourg, Malta, Netherlands, Portugal, Slovenia, Slovakia, and Spain. The countries that participate in the euro make up a region that is referred to as the *eurozone.* Together, the participating countries produce more than 20 percent of the world's gross domestic product. Their total production exceeds that of the United States. Denmark, Norway, Sweden, Switzerland, and the United Kingdom continue to use their own home currency. The 10 countries in Eastern Europe (including the Czech Republic, Hungary, and Poland) that joined the European Union in 2004 are eligible to participate in the euro if they meet specific economic goals, including a maximum limit on their budget deficit.

Impact on European Monetary Policy

The euro allows for a single money supply throughout much of Europe, rather than a separate money supply for each participating currency. Thus, European monetary policy is consolidated because any effects on the money supply will have an impact on all European countries using the euro as their form of money. The implementation of a common monetary policy may promote more political unity among European countries with similar national defense and foreign policies.

European Central Bank. The **European Central Bank (ECB)** is based in Frankfurt and is responsible for setting monetary policy for all participating European countries. Its objective is to control inflation in the participating countries and to stabilize (within reasonable boundaries) the value of the euro with respect to other major currencies. Thus, the ECB's monetary goals of price stability and currency stability are similar to those of individual countries around the world, but differ in that they are focused on a group of countries instead of a single country.

Implications of a European Monetary Policy. Although a single European monetary policy may allow for more consistent economic conditions across countries, it prevents any individual European country from solving local economic problems with its own unique monetary policy. European governments may disagree on the ideal monetary policy to enhance their local economies, but they must agree on a single European monetary policy. Any given policy used in a particular period may enhance conditions in some countries and adversely affect others. Each participating country is still able to apply its own fiscal policy (tax and government expenditure decisions), however. The use of a common currency may someday create more political harmony among European countries.

Impact on the Valuation of Businesses in Europe

When firms consider acquiring targets in Europe, they can more easily compare the prices (market values) of targets among countries because their values are denominated in the same currency (the euro). In addition, the future currency movements of the target's currency against any non-European currency will be the same. Therefore, U.S. firms can more easily conduct valuations of firms across the participating European countries because when funds are remitted to the U.S. parent from any of the participating countries, the level of appreciation or depreciation will be the same for a particular period and there will be no differences in exchange rate effects.

European firms face more pressure to perform well because they can be measured against all other firms in the same industry throughout the participating countries, not just within their own country. Therefore, these firms are more focused on meeting various performance goals.

Impact on Financial Flows

A single European currency forces the interest rate offered on government securities to be similar across the participating European countries. Any discrepancy in rates would encourage investors within these European countries to invest in the currency with the highest rate, which would realign the interest rates among these countries. However, the rate may still vary between two government securities with the same maturity if they exhibit different levels of credit risk.

Stock prices are now more comparable among the European countries because they are denominated in the same currency. Investors in the participating European countries are now able to invest in stocks throughout these countries without concern about exchange rate risk. Thus, there is more cross-border investing than there was in the past.

Since stock market prices are influenced by expectations of economic conditions, the stock prices among the European countries may become more highly correlated if economies among these countries become more highly correlated. Investors from other countries who invest in European countries may not achieve as much diversification as in the past because of the integration and because the exchange rate effects will be the same for all markets whose stocks are denominated in euros. Stock markets in these European countries are also likely to consolidate over time now that they use the same currency.

Bond investors based in these European countries can now invest in bonds issued by governments and corporations in these countries without concern about exchange rate risk, as long as the bonds are denominated in euros. Some European governments have already issued bonds that are redenominated in euros because the secondary market for some bonds issued in Europe with other currency denominations is now less active. The bond yields in participating European countries are not necessarily similar even though they are now denominated in the same currency; the credit risk may still be higher for issuers in a particular country.

Impact on Exchange Rate Risk

The euro enables residents of participating countries to engage in cross-border trade flows and capital flows throughout the so-called eurozone (of participating countries) without converting to a different currency. The elimination of currency movements among European countries also encourages more long-term business arrangements between firms of different countries, as they no longer have to worry about adverse effects due to currency movements.

Prices of products are now more comparable among European countries, as the exchange rate between the countries is fixed. Thus, buyers can more easily determine where they can obtain products at the lowest cost.

As trade flows between these countries increase, economic conditions in each of these countries should have a larger impact on the other European countries, and economies of these countries may become more integrated.

In addition, foreign exchange transaction costs associated with transactions within the so-called eurozone have been eliminated.

Status Report on the Euro

European countries that participate in the euro are still affected by movements in its value with respect to other currencies such as the dollar. The euro has experienced a

WEB

www.ecb.int/home/
html/index.en.html
Information on the euro
and monetary policy
conducted by the European Central Bank.

volatile ride since it was introduced in 1999. In October 2001, for example, 33 months after it was introduced, its value was $.88, or about 27 percent less than its initial value. The weakness was partially attributed to capital outflows from Europe. By July 2008, the euro was valued at $1.35, or 53 percent above its value in October 2001. The rebound in the euro was triggered by the relatively high European interest rates compared to U.S. interest rates, which attracted capital inflows from the United States. As the credit crisis intensified during the fall of 2008, capital flows to Europe declined, and the euro's value retreated to $1.30, or 16 percent below its peak a few months earlier.

WEB

www.bis.org/cbanks
.htm

Links to websites of central banks around the world; some of the websites are in English.

GOVERNMENT INTERVENTION

Each country has a central bank that may intervene in the foreign exchange markets to control its currency's value. In the United States, for example, the central bank is the Federal Reserve System (the Fed). Central banks have other duties besides intervening in the foreign exchange market. In particular, they attempt to control the growth of the money supply in their respective countries in a way that will favorably affect economic conditions.

Reasons for Government Intervention

The degree to which the home currency is controlled, or "managed," varies among central banks. Central banks commonly manage exchange rates for three reasons:

- To smooth exchange rate movements
- To establish implicit exchange rate boundaries
- To respond to temporary disturbances

Smooth Exchange Rate Movements. If a central bank is concerned that its economy will be affected by abrupt movements in its home currency's value, it may attempt to smooth the currency movements over time. Its actions may keep business cycles less volatile. The central bank may also encourage international trade by reducing exchange rate uncertainty. Furthermore, smoothing currency movements may reduce fears in the financial markets and speculative activity that could cause a major decline in a currency's value.

Establish Implicit Exchange Rate Boundaries. Some central banks attempt to maintain their home currency rates within some unofficial, or implicit, boundaries. Analysts are commonly quoted as forecasting that a currency will not fall below or rise above a particular benchmark value because the central bank would intervene to prevent that. The Federal Reserve periodically intervenes to reverse the U.S. dollar's upward or downward momentum.

Respond to Temporary Disturbances. In some cases, a central bank may intervene to insulate a currency's value from a temporary disturbance. In fact, the stated objective of the Fed's intervention policy is to counter disorderly market conditions.

EXAMPLE   News that oil prices might rise could cause expectations of a future decline in the value of the Japanese yen because Japan exchanges yen for U.S. dollars to purchase oil from oil-exporting countries. Foreign exchange market speculators may exchange yen for dollars in anticipation of this decline. Central banks may therefore intervene to offset the immediate downward pressure on the yen caused by such market transactions. ●

Several studies have found that government intervention does not have a permanent impact on exchange rate movements. In many cases, intervention is overwhelmed by market forces. In the absence of intervention, however, currency movements would be even more volatile.

Direct Intervention

To force the dollar to depreciate, the Fed can intervene directly by exchanging dollars that it holds as reserves for other foreign currencies in the foreign exchange market. By "flooding the market with dollars" in this manner, the Fed puts downward pressure on the dollar. If the Fed desires to strengthen the dollar, it can exchange foreign currencies for dollars in the foreign exchange market, thereby putting upward pressure on the dollar.

WEB

www.ny.frb.org/
markets/foreignex.html
Information on the recent direct intervention in the foreign exchange market by the Federal Reserve Bank of New York.

The effects of direct intervention on the value of the British pound are illustrated in Exhibit 6.2. To strengthen the pound's value (or to weaken the dollar), the Fed exchanges dollars for pounds, which causes an outward shift in the demand for pounds in the foreign exchange market (as shown in the graph on the left). Conversely, to weaken the pound's value (or to strengthen the dollar), the Fed exchanges pounds for dollars, which causes an outward shift in the supply of pounds for sale in the foreign exchange market (as shown in the graph on the right).

Reliance on Reserves. The potential effectiveness of a central bank's direct intervention is the amount of reserves it can use. For example, the central bank of China has a substantial amount of reserves that it can use to intervene in the foreign exchange market. Thus, it can more effectively use direct intervention than many other countries in Asia. If the central bank has a low level of reserves, it may not be able to exert much pressure on the currency's value. Market forces would likely overwhelm its actions.

As foreign exchange activity has grown, central bank intervention has become less effective. The volume of foreign exchange transactions on a single day now exceeds the combined values of reserves at all central banks. Consequently, the number of direct interventions has declined. In 1989, for example, the Fed intervened on 97 different days. Since then, the Fed has not intervened on more than 20 days in any year.

Direct intervention is likely to be more effective when it is coordinated by several central banks. For example, if central banks agree that the euro's market value in dollars is

Exhibit 6.2 Effects of Direct Central Bank Intervention in the Foreign Exchange Market too high, they can engage in coordinated intervention in which they all use euros from their reserves to purchase dollars in the foreign exchange market.

Nonsterilized versus Sterilized Intervention.

When the Fed intervenes in the foreign exchange market without adjusting for the change in the money supply, it is engaging in a **nonsterilized intervention.** For example, if the Fed exchanges dollars for foreign currencies in the foreign exchange markets in an attempt to strengthen foreign currencies (weaken the dollar), the dollar money supply increases.

In a **sterilized intervention,** the Fed intervenes in the foreign exchange market and simultaneously engages in offsetting transactions in the Treasury securities markets. As a result, the dollar money supply is unchanged.

EXAMPLE

If the Fed desires to strengthen foreign currencies (weaken the dollar) without affecting the dollar money supply, it (1) exchanges dollars for foreign currencies and (2) sells some of its holdings of Treasury securities for dollars. The net effect is an increase in investors' holdings of Treasury securities and a decrease in bank foreign currency balances. ●

The difference between nonsterilized and sterilized intervention is illustrated in Exhibit 6.3. In the top section of the exhibit, the Federal Reserve attempts to strengthen the Canadian dollar, and in the bottom section, the Federal Reserve attempts to weaken the Canadian dollar. For each scenario, the graph on the right shows a sterilized intervention involving an exchange of Treasury securities for U.S.

Exhibit 6.3 Forms of Central Bank Intervention in the Foreign Exchange Market

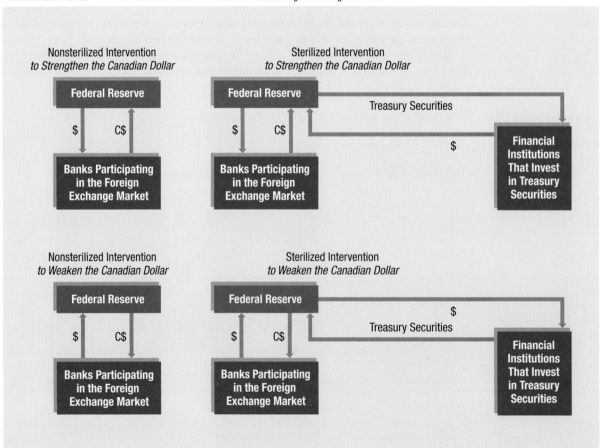

dollars that offsets the U.S. dollar flows resulting from the exchange of currencies. Thus, the sterilized intervention achieves the same exchange of currencies in the foreign exchange market as the nonsterilized intervention, but it involves an additional transaction to prevent adjustments in the U.S. dollar money supply.

Speculating on Direct Intervention. Some traders in the foreign exchange market attempt to determine when Federal Reserve intervention is occurring and the extent of the intervention in order to capitalize on the anticipated results of the intervention effort. Normally, the Federal Reserve attempts to intervene without being noticed. However, dealers at the major banks that trade with the Fed often pass the information to other market participants. Also, when the Fed deals directly with numerous commercial banks, markets are well aware that the Fed is intervening. To hide its strategy, the Fed may pretend to be interested in selling dollars when it is actually buying dollars, or vice versa. It calls commercial banks and obtains both bid and ask quotes on currencies, so the banks will not know whether the Fed is considering purchases or sales of these currencies.

Intervention strategies vary among central banks. Some arrange for one large order when they intervene; others use several smaller orders equivalent to $5 million to $10 million. Even if traders determine the extent of central bank intervention, they still cannot know with certainty what impact it will have on exchange rates.

Indirect Intervention

The Fed can also affect the dollar's value indirectly by influencing the factors that determine it. Recall that the change in a currency's spot rate is influenced by the following factors:

$$e = f(\Delta INF, \Delta INT, \Delta INC, \Delta GC, \Delta EXP)$$

where

e = percentage change in the spot rate

ΔINF = change in the differential between U.S. inflation and the foreign country's inflation

ΔINT = change in the differential between the U.S. interest rate and the foreign country's interest rate

ΔINC = change in the differential between the U.S. income level and the foreign country's income level

ΔGC = change in government controls

ΔEXP = change in expectations of future exchange rates

The central bank can influence all of these variables, which in turn can affect the exchange rate. Since these variables will probably have a more lasting impact on a spot rate than direct intervention, a central bank may use indirect intervention by influencing these variables. Although the central bank can influence all of these variables, it is likely to focus on interest rates or government controls when using indirect intervention.

Government Control of Interest Rates. When central banks of countries increase or reduce interest rates, this may have an indirect effect on the values of their currencies.

When the Federal Reserve reduces U.S. interest rates, U.S. investors may transfer funds to other countries to capitalize on higher interest rates. This action reflects an increase in demand for other currencies and places upward pressure on these currencies against the dollar.

Alternatively, if the Fed raises U.S. interest rates, foreign investors may transfer funds to the United States to capitalize on higher U.S. interest rates (especially if expected inflation in the United States is relatively low). This reflects an increase in supply of foreign currencies to be exchanged for dollars in the foreign exchange market, and places downward pressure on these currencies against the dollar. ●

Central banks have commonly raised their interest rates if their country experiences a currency crisis in order to prevent a major flow of funds out of the country.

EXAMPLE

Russia attracts a large amount of foreign funds from investors who want to capitalize on Russia's growth. However, when the Russian economy weakens, foreign investors flood the foreign exchange market with Russian rubles for other currencies so that they can transfer their money to other countries. The Russian central bank may raise interest rates so that foreign investors would earn a higher yield on securities if they left their funds in Russia. However, if investors still anticipate the major withdrawal of funds from Russia, they will rush to sell their rubles before the ruble's value declines. The actions by investors cause the ruble's value to decline substantially. ●

The example above reflects the situation for many countries that experienced currency crises in the past, including Russia, many Southeast Asian countries, and many Latin American countries. In most cases, the central bank's indirect intervention was not only unsuccessful in preventing the withdrawals of funds, but also increased the financing rate by firms in the country. This can cause the economy to weaken further.

Government Use of Foreign Exchange Controls. Some governments attempt to use foreign exchange controls (such as restrictions on the exchange of the currency) as a form of indirect intervention to maintain the exchange rate of their currency. China has historically used foreign exchange restrictions to control the yuan's exchange rate, but has partially removed these restrictions in recent years.

INTERVENTION AS A POLICY TOOL

The government of any country can implement its own fiscal and monetary policies to control its economy. In addition, it may attempt to influence the value of its home currency in order to improve its economy, weakening its currency under some conditions and strengthening it under others. In essence, the exchange rate becomes a tool, like tax laws and the money supply, that the government can use to achieve its desired economic objectives.

Influence of a Weak Home Currency

A weak home currency can stimulate foreign demand for products. A weak dollar, for example, can substantially boost U.S. exports and U.S. jobs. In addition, it may also reduce U.S. imports. Exhibit 6.4 shows how the Federal Reserve can use either direct or indirect intervention to affect the value of the dollar in order to stimulate the U.S. economy. When the Fed reduces interest rates as a form of indirect intervention, it may stimulate the U.S. economy not only by reducing the value of the dollar, but also by reducing the financing costs of firms and individuals in the United States.

While a weak currency can reduce unemployment at home, it can lead to higher inflation. A weak dollar makes U.S. imports more expensive, and therefore creates a competitive advantage for U.S. firms that are selling products within the United States. Some U.S. firms may increase their prices when the competition from foreign firms is reduced, which results in higher U.S. inflation.

Influence of a Strong Home Currency

A strong home currency can encourage consumers and corporations of that country to buy goods from other countries. This situation intensifies foreign competition and forces domestic producers to refrain from increasing prices. Therefore, the country's overall inflation rate should be lower if its currency is stronger, other things being equal.

Exhibit 6.5 shows how the Federal Reserve can use either direct or indirect intervention to affect the value of the dollar in order to reduce U.S. inflation. When the Fed

Exhibit 6.4 How Central Bank Intervention Can Stimulate the U.S. Economy

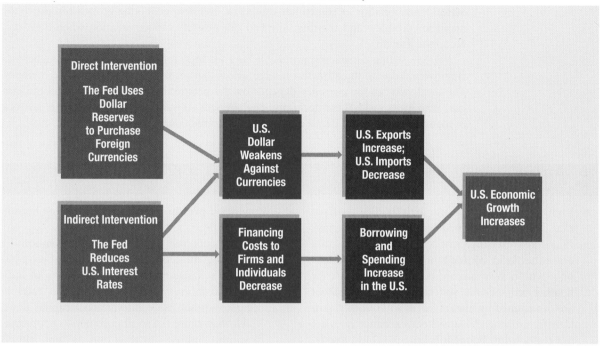

Exhibit 6.5 How Central Bank Intervention Can Reduce Inflation

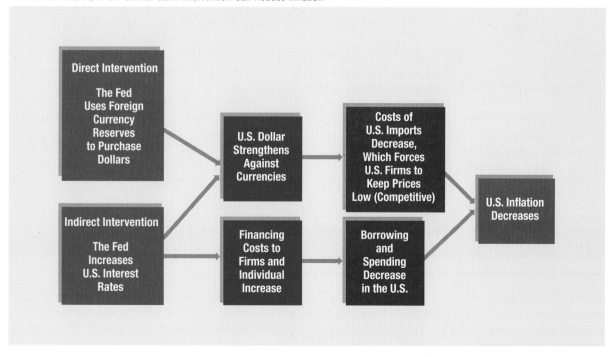

increases interest rates as a form of indirect intervention, it may reduce U.S. inflation not only by increasing the value of the dollar but also by raising the cost of financing. Higher U.S. interest rates result in higher financing costs to firms and individuals in the United

States, which tends to reduce the amount of borrowing and spending in the United States. Since inflation is sometimes caused by excessive economic growth (excessive demand for products and services), the Fed can possibly reduce inflation when it reduces economic growth.

While a strong currency is a possible cure for high inflation, it may cause higher unemployment due to the attractive foreign prices that result from a strong home currency. The ideal value of the currency depends on the perspective of the country and the officials who must make these decisions. The strength or weakness of a currency is just one of many factors that influence a country's economic conditions.

SUMMARY

- Exchange rate systems can be classified as fixed rate, freely floating, managed float, and pegged. In a fixed exchange rate system, exchange rates are either held constant or allowed to fluctuate only within very narrow boundaries. In a freely floating exchange rate system, exchange rate values are determined by market forces without intervention. In a managed float system, exchange rates are not restricted by boundaries but are subject to government intervention. In a pegged exchange rate system, a currency's value is pegged to a foreign currency or a unit of account and moves in line with that currency (or unit of account) against other currencies.

- Governments can use direct intervention by purchasing or selling currencies in the foreign exchange market, thereby affecting demand and supply conditions and, in turn, affecting the equilibrium values of the currencies. When a government purchases a currency in the foreign exchange market, it puts upward pressure on the currency's equilibrium value. When a government sells a currency in the foreign exchange market, it puts downward pressure on the currency's equilibrium value.

- Governments can use indirect intervention by influencing the economic factors that affect equilibrium exchange rates. A common form of indirect intervention is to increase interest rates in order to attract more international capital flows, which may cause the local currency to appreciate. However, indirect intervention is not always effective.

- When government intervention is used to weaken the U.S. dollar, the weak dollar can stimulate the U.S. economy by reducing the U.S. demand for imports and increasing the foreign demand for U.S. exports. Thus, the weak dollar tends to reduce U.S. unemployment, but it can increase U.S. inflation.

  When government intervention is used to strengthen the U.S. dollar, the strong dollar can increase the U.S. demand for imports, thereby intensifying foreign competition. The strong dollar can reduce U.S. inflation but may cause a higher level of U.S. unemployment.

POINT COUNTER-POINT

Should China Be Forced to Alter the Value of Its Currency?

Point U.S. politicians frequently suggest that China needs to increase the value of the Chinese yuan against the U.S. dollar, even though China has allowed the yuan to float (within boundaries). The U.S. politicians claim that the yuan is the cause of the large U.S. trade deficit with China. This issue is periodically raised not only with currencies tied to the dollar but also with currencies that have a floating rate. Some critics argue that the exchange rate can be used as a form of trade protectionism. That is, a country can discourage or prevent imports and encourage exports by keeping the value of its currency artificially low.

Counter-Point China might counter that its large balance-of-trade surplus with the United States has been due to the difference in prices between the two countries and that it should not be blamed for the high

U.S. prices. It might argue that the U.S. trade deficit can be partially attributed to the very high prices in the United States, which are necessary to cover the excessive compensation for executives and other employees at U.S. firms. The high prices in the United States encourage firms and consumers to purchase goods from China. Even if China's yuan is revalued upward, this does not necessarily mean that U.S. firms and con-

sumers will purchase U.S. products. They may shift their purchases from China to Indonesia or other low-wage countries rather than buy more U.S. products. Thus, the underlying dilemma is not China but any country that has lower costs of production than the United States.

Who Is Correct? Use the Internet to learn more about this issue. Which argument do you support? Offer your own opinion on this issue.

SELF-TEST

Answers are provided in Appendix A at the back of the text.

1. Explain why it would be virtually impossible to set an exchange rate between the Japanese yen and the U.S. dollar and to maintain a fixed exchange rate.

2. Assume the Federal Reserve believes that the dollar should be weakened against the Mexican peso. Explain how the Fed could use direct and indirect intervention to weaken the dollar's value with respect to the peso. Assume that future inflation in the United States is expected to be low, regardless of the Fed's actions.

3. Briefly explain why the Federal Reserve may attempt to weaken the dollar.

4. Assume the country of Sluban ties its currency (the slu) to the dollar and the exchange rate will remain

fixed. Sluban has frequent trade with countries in the eurozone and the United States. All traded products can easily be produced by all the countries, and the demand for these products in any country is very sensitive to the price because consumers can shift to wherever the products are relatively cheap. Assume that the euro depreciates substantially against the dollar during the next year.

a. What is the likely effect (if any) of the euro's exchange rate movement on the volume of Sluban's exports to the eurozone? Explain.

b. What is the likely effect (if any) of the euro's exchange rate movement on the volume of Sluban's exports to the United States? Explain.

QUESTIONS AND APPLICATIONS

1. Exchange Rate Systems. Compare and contrast the fixed, freely floating, and managed float exchange rate systems. What are some advantages and disadvantages of a freely floating exchange rate system versus a fixed exchange rate system?

2. Intervention with Euros. Assume that Belgium, one of the European countries that uses the euro as its currency, would prefer that its currency depreciate against the U.S. dollar. Can it apply central bank intervention to achieve this objective? Explain.

3. Direct Intervention. How can a central bank use direct intervention to change the value of a currency? Explain why a central bank may desire to smooth exchange rate movements of its currency.

4. Indirect Intervention. How can a central bank use indirect intervention to change the value of a currency?

5. Intervention Effects. Assume there is concern that the United States may experience a recession. How should the Federal Reserve influence the dollar to prevent a recession? How might U.S. exporters react to this policy (favorably or unfavorably)? What about U.S. importing firms?

6. Currency Effects on Economy. What is the impact of a weak home currency on the home economy, other things being equal? What is the impact of a strong home currency on the home economy, other things being equal?

7. Feedback Effects. Explain the potential feedback effects of a currency's changing value on inflation.

8. Indirect Intervention. Why would the Fed's indirect intervention have a stronger impact on some currencies than others? Why would a central bank's indirect intervention have a stronger impact than its direct intervention?

9. Effects on Currencies Tied to the Dollar.
The Hong Kong dollar's value is tied to the U.S. dollar. Explain how the following trade patterns would be affected by the appreciation of the Japanese yen against the dollar: (a) Hong Kong exports to Japan and (b) Hong Kong exports to the United States.

10. Intervention Effects on Bond Prices.
U.S. bond prices are normally inversely related to U.S. inflation. If the Fed planned to use intervention to weaken the dollar, how might bond prices be affected?

11. Direct Intervention in Europe.
If most countries in Europe experience a recession, how might the European Central Bank use direct intervention to stimulate economic growth?

12. Sterilized Intervention.
Explain the difference between sterilized and nonsterilized intervention.

13. Effects of Indirect Intervention.
Suppose that the government of Chile reduces one of its key interest rates. The values of several other Latin American currencies are expected to change substantially against the Chilean peso in response to the news.

a. Explain why other Latin American currencies could be affected by a cut in Chile's interest rates.

b. How would the central banks of other Latin American countries be likely to adjust their interest rates? How would the currencies of these countries respond to the central bank intervention?

c. How would a U.S. firm that exports products to Latin American countries be affected by the central bank intervention? (Assume the exports are denominated in the corresponding Latin American currency for each country.)

14. Freely Floating Exchange Rates.
Should the governments of Asian countries allow their currencies to float freely? What would be the advantages of letting their currencies float freely? What would be the disadvantages?

15. Indirect Intervention.
During the Asian crisis, some Asian central banks raised their interest rates to prevent their currencies from weakening. Yet, the currencies weakened anyway. Offer your opinion as to why the central banks' efforts at indirect intervention did not work.

Advanced Questions

16. Monitoring of the Fed's Intervention.
Why do foreign market participants attempt to monitor the Fed's direct intervention efforts? How does the Fed attempt to hide its intervention actions? The media frequently report that "the dollar's value strengthened against many currencies in response to the Federal Reserve's plan to increase interest rates." Explain why the dollar's value may change even before the Federal Reserve affects interest rates.

17. Effects of September 11.
Within a few days after the September 11, 2001, terrorist attack on the United States, the Federal Reserve reduced short-term interest rates to stimulate the U.S. economy. How might this action have affected the foreign flow of funds into the United States and affected the value of the dollar? How could such an effect on the dollar have increased the probability that the U.S. economy would strengthen?

18. Intervention Effects on Corporate Performance.
Assume you have a subsidiary in Australia. The subsidiary sells mobile homes to local consumers in Australia, who buy the homes using mostly borrowed funds from local banks. Your subsidiary purchases all of its materials from Hong Kong. The Hong Kong dollar is tied to the U.S. dollar. Your subsidiary borrowed funds from the U.S. parent, and must pay the parent $100,000 in interest each month. Australia has just raised its interest rate in order to boost the value of its currency (Australian dollar, A$). The Australian dollar appreciates against the U.S. dollar as a result. Explain whether these actions would increase, reduce, or have no effect on:

a. The volume of your subsidiary's sales in Australia (measured in A$).

b. The cost to your subsidiary of purchasing materials (measured in A$).

c. The cost to your subsidiary of making the interest payments to the U.S. parent (measured in A$). Briefly explain each answer.

19. Pegged Currencies.
Why do you think a country suddenly decides to peg its currency to the dollar or some other currency? When a currency is unable to maintain the peg, what do you think are the typical forces that break the peg?

20. Impact of Intervention on Currency Option Premiums.
Assume that the central bank of the country Zakow periodically intervenes in the foreign exchange market to prevent large upward or downward fluctuations in its currency (the zak) against the U.S. dollar. Today, the central bank announced that it

would no longer intervene in the foreign exchange market. The spot rate of the zak against the dollar was not affected by this news. Will the news affect the premium on currency call options that are traded on the zak? Will the news affect the premium on currency put options that are traded on the zak? Explain.

21. Impact of Information on Currency Option Premiums. As of 10:00 a.m., the premium on a specific 1-year call option on British pounds is $.04. Assume that the Bank of England had not been intervening in the foreign exchange markets in the last several months. However, it announces at 10:01 a.m. that it will begin to frequently intervene in the foreign exchange market in order to reduce fluctuations in the pound's value against the U.S. dollar over the next year, but it will not attempt to push the pound's value higher or lower than what is dictated by market forces. Also, the Bank of England has no plans to affect economic conditions with this intervention. Most participants who trade currency options did not anticipate this announcement. When they heard the announcement, they expected that the intervention would be successful in achieving its goal. Will this announcement cause the premium on the 1-year call option on British pounds to increase, decrease, or be unaffected? Explain.

22. Speculating Based on Intervention. Assume that you expect that the European Central Bank (ECB) plans to engage in central bank intervention in which it plans to use euros to purchase a substantial amount of U.S. dollars in the foreign exchange market over the next month. Assume that this direct intervention is expected to be successful at influencing the exchange rate.

a. Would you purchase or sell call options on euros today?

b. Would you purchase or sell futures on euros today?

23. Pegged Currency and International Trade. Assume the Hong Kong dollar (HK$) value is tied to the U.S. dollar and will remain tied to the U.S. dollar. Last month, a HK$ = 0.25 Singapore dollars. Today, a HK$ = 0.30 Singapore dollars. Assume that there is much trade in the computer industry among Singapore, Hong Kong, and the United States and that all products are viewed as substitutes for each other and are of about the same quality. Assume that the firms invoice their products in their local currency and do not change their prices.

a. Will the computer exports from the United States to Hong Kong increase, decrease, or remain the same? Briefly explain.

b. Will the computer exports from Singapore to the United States increase, decrease, or remain the same? Briefly explain.

24. Implications of a Revised Peg. The country of Zapakar has much international trade with the United States and other countries as it has no significant barriers on trade or capital flows. Many firms in Zapakar export common products (denominated in zaps) that serve as substitutes for products produced in the United States and many other countries. Zapakar's currency (called the zap) has been pegged at 8 zaps = $1 for the last several years. Yesterday, the government of Zapakar reset the zap's currency value so that it is now pegged at 7 zaps = $1.

a. How should this adjustment in the pegged rate against the dollar affect the volume of exports by Zapakar firms to the United States?

b. Will this adjustment in the pegged rate against the dollar affect the volume of exports by Zapakar firms to non-U.S. countries? If so, explain.

c. Assume that the Federal Reserve significantly raises U.S. interest rates today. Do you think Zapakar's interest rate would increase, decrease, or remain the same?

25. Pegged Currency and International Trade. Assume that Canada decides to peg its currency (the Canadian dollar) to the U.S. dollar and that the exchange rate will remain fixed. Assume that Canada commonly obtains its imports from the United States and Mexico. The United States commonly obtains its imports from Canada and Mexico. Mexico commonly obtains its imports from the United States and Canada. The traded products are always invoiced in the exporting country's currency. Assume that the Mexican peso appreciates substantially against the U.S. dollar during the next year.

a. What is the likely effect (if any) of the peso's exchange rate movement on the volume of Canada's exports to Mexico? Explain.

b. What is the likely effect (if any) of the peso's exchange rate movement on the volume of Canada's exports to the United States? Explain.

Discussion in the Boardroom

This exercise can be found in Appendix E at the back of this textbook.

Running Your Own MNC

This exercise can be found on the *International Financial Management* text companion website located at www.cengage.com/finance/madura.

BLADES, INC. CASE

Assessment of Government Influence on Exchange Rates

Recall that Blades, the U.S. manufacturer of roller blades, generates most of its revenue and incurs most of its expenses in the United States. However, the company has recently begun exporting roller blades to Thailand. The company has an agreement with Entertainment Products, Inc., a Thai importer, for a 3-year period. According to the terms of the agreement, Entertainment Products will purchase 180,000 pairs of "Speedos," Blades' primary product, annually at a fixed price of 4,594 Thai baht per pair. Due to quality and cost considerations, Blades is also importing certain rubber and plastic components from a Thai exporter. The cost of these components is approximately 2,871 Thai baht per pair of Speedos. No contractual agreement exists between Blades, Inc., and the Thai exporter. Consequently, the cost of the rubber and plastic components imported from Thailand is subject not only to exchange rate considerations but to economic conditions (such as inflation) in Thailand as well.

Shortly after Blades began exporting to and importing from Thailand, Asia experienced weak economic conditions. Consequently, foreign investors in Thailand feared the baht's potential weakness and withdrew their investments, resulting in an excess supply of Thai baht for sale. Because of the resulting downward pressure on the baht's value, the Thai government attempted to stabilize the baht's exchange rate. To maintain the baht's value, the Thai government intervened in the foreign exchange market. Specifically, it swapped its baht reserves for dollar reserves at other central banks and then used its dollar reserves to purchase the baht in the foreign exchange market. However, this agreement required Thailand to reverse this transaction by exchanging dollars for baht at a future date. Unfortunately, the Thai government's intervention was unsuccessful, as it was overwhelmed by market forces. Consequently, the Thai government ceased its intervention efforts, and the value of the Thai baht declined substantially against the dollar over a 3-month period.

When the Thai government stopped intervening in the foreign exchange market, Ben Holt, Blades' CFO, was concerned that the value of the Thai baht would continue to decline indefinitely. Since Blades generates net inflow in Thai baht, this would seriously affect the company's profit margin. Furthermore, one of the reasons Blades had expanded into Thailand was to appease the company's shareholders. At last year's annual shareholder meeting, they had demanded that senior management take action to improve the firm's low profit margins. Expanding into Thailand had been Holt's suggestion, and he is now afraid that his career might be at stake. For these reasons, Holt feels that the Asian crisis and its impact on Blades demand his serious attention. One of the factors Holt thinks he should consider is the issue of government intervention and how it could affect Blades in particular. Specifically, he wonders whether the decision to enter into a fixed agreement with Entertainment Products was a good idea under the circumstances. Another issue is how the future completion of the swap agreement initiated by the Thai government will affect Blades. To address these issues and to gain a little more understanding of the process of government intervention, Holt has prepared the following list of questions for you, Blades' financial analyst, since he knows that you understand international financial management.

1. Did the intervention effort by the Thai government constitute direct or indirect intervention? Explain.

2. Did the intervention by the Thai government constitute sterilized or nonsterilized intervention? What is the difference between the two types of intervention? Which type do you think would be more effective in increasing the value of the baht? Why? (Hint: Think about the effect of nonsterilized intervention on U.S. interest rates.)

3. If the Thai baht is virtually fixed with respect to the dollar, how could this affect U.S. levels of inflation? Do you think these effects on the U.S. economy will be more pronounced for companies such as Blades that operate under trade arrangements involving commitments or for firms that do not? How are companies such as Blades affected by a fixed exchange rate?

4. What are some of the potential disadvantages for Thai levels of inflation associated with the floating exchange rate system that is now used in Thailand? Do you think Blades contributes to these disadvantages to a great extent? How are companies such as Blades affected by a freely floating exchange rate?

5. What do you think will happen to the Thai baht's value when the swap arrangement is completed? How will this affect Blades?

SMALL BUSINESS DILEMMA

Assessment of Central Bank Intervention by the Sports Exports Company

Jim Logan, owner of the Sports Exports Company, is concerned about the value of the British pound over time because his firm receives pounds as payment for footballs exported to the United Kingdom. He recently read that the Bank of England (the central bank of the United Kingdom) is likely to intervene directly in the foreign exchange market by flooding the market with British pounds.

1. Forecast whether the British pound will weaken or strengthen based on the information provided.
2. How would the performance of the Sports Exports Company be affected by the Bank of England's policy of flooding the foreign exchange market with British pounds (assuming that it does not hedge its exchange rate risk)?

INTERNET/EXCEL EXERCISES

The website for Japan's central bank, the Bank of Japan, provides information about its mission and its policy actions. Its address is www.boj.or.jp/en.

1. Use this website to review the outline of the Bank of Japan's objectives. Summarize the mission of the Bank of Japan. How does this mission relate to intervening in the foreign exchange market?

2. Review the minutes of recent meetings by Bank of Japan officials. Summarize at least one recent meeting that was associated with possible or actual intervention to affect the yen's value.
3. Why might the foreign exchange intervention strategies of the Bank of Japan be relevant to the U.S. government and to U.S.-based MNCs?

REFERENCES

Arestis, Philip, and Malcolm Sawyer, Sep 2008, A Critical Reconsideration of the Foundations of Monetary Policy in the New Consensus Macroeconomics Framework, *Cambridge Journal of Economics*, pp. 761–779.

Beine, Michel, Charles S. Bos, and Sébastien Laurent, Winter 2007, The Impact of Central Bank FX Interventions on Currency Components, *Journal of Financial Econometrics*, pp. 154–183.

Berg, Ann, Oct 2006, Global Monetary Systems: Then and Now, *Futures*, pp. 62–64.

Fratzscher, Marcel, Feb 2006, On the Long-term Effectiveness of Exchange Rate Communication and Interventions, *Journal of International Money and Finance*, pp. 146–167.

Henning, C. Randall, Jun 2007, Organizing Foreign Exchange Intervention in the Euro Area, *Journal of Common Market Studies*, pp. 315–342.

Koll, Jesper, Sep 2006, Japan Turns Its Back on Reform, *Far Eastern Economic Review*, pp. 33–37.

Orlowski, Lucjan T., Sep 2008, Advancing Inflation Targeting in Central Europe: Strategies, Policy Rules and Empirical Evidence, *Comparative Economic Studies*, pp. 438–459.

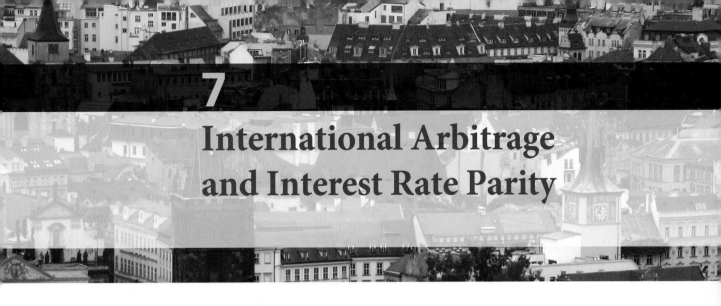

7

International Arbitrage and Interest Rate Parity

CHAPTER OBJECTIVES

The specific objectives of this chapter are to:

■ explain the conditions that will result in various forms of international arbitrage and the realignments that will occur in response, and

■ explain the concept of interest rate parity.

If discrepancies occur within the foreign exchange market, with quoted prices of currencies varying from what the market prices should be, certain market forces will realign the rates. The realignment occurs as a result of international arbitrage. Financial managers of MNCs must understand how international arbitrage realigns exchange rates because it has implications for how they should use the foreign exchange market to facilitate their international business.

INTERNATIONAL ARBITRAGE

Arbitrage can be loosely defined as capitalizing on a discrepancy in quoted prices by making a riskless profit. In many cases, the strategy does not require an investment of funds to be tied up for a length of time and does not involve any risk.

EXAMPLE

Two coin shops buy and sell coins. If Shop A is willing to sell a particular coin for $120, while Shop B is willing to buy that same coin for $130, a person can execute arbitrage by purchasing the coin at Shop A for $120 and selling it to Shop B for $130. The prices at coin shops can vary because demand conditions may vary among shop locations. If two coin shops are not aware of each other's prices, the opportunity for arbitrage may occur. ●

The act of arbitrage will cause prices to realign. In our example, arbitrage would cause Shop A to raise its price (due to high demand for the coin). At the same time, Shop B would reduce its bid price after receiving a surplus of coins as arbitrage occurs. The type of arbitrage discussed in this chapter is primarily international in scope; it is applied to foreign exchange and international money markets and takes three common forms:

- Locational arbitrage
- Triangular arbitrage
- Covered interest arbitrage

Each form will be discussed in turn.

Locational Arbitrage

Commercial banks providing foreign exchange services normally quote about the same rates on currencies, so shopping around may not necessarily lead to a more favorable rate. If the demand and supply conditions for a particular currency vary among banks, the banks may price that currency at different rates, and market forces will force realignment.

When quoted exchange rates vary among locations, participants in the foreign exchange market can capitalize on the discrepancy. Specifically, they can use **locational arbitrage**, which is the process of buying a currency at the location where it is priced cheap and immediately selling it at another location where it is priced higher.

EXAMPLE

Akron Bank and Zyn Bank serve the foreign exchange market by buying and selling currencies. Assume that there is no bid/ask spread. The exchange rate quoted at Akron Bank for a British pound is $1.60, while the exchange rate quoted at Zyn Bank is $1.61. You could conduct locational arbitrage by purchasing pounds at Akron Bank for $1.60 per pound and then selling them at Zyn Bank for $1.61 per pound. Under the condition that there is no bid/ask spread and there are no other costs to conducting this arbitrage strategy, your gain would be $.01 per pound. The gain is risk free in that you knew when you purchased the pounds how much you could sell them for. Also, you did not have to tie your funds up for any length of time. ●

Locational arbitrage is normally conducted by banks or other foreign exchange dealers whose computers can continuously monitor the quotes provided by other banks. If other banks noticed a discrepancy between Akron Bank and Zyn Bank, they would quickly engage in locational arbitrage to earn an immediate risk-free profit. Since banks have a bid/ask spread on currencies, this next example accounts for the spread.

EXAMPLE

The information on British pounds at both banks is revised to include the bid/ask spread in Exhibit 7.1. Based on these quotes, you can no longer profit from locational arbitrage. If you buy pounds from Akron Bank at $1.61 (the bank's ask price) and then sell the pounds at Zyn Bank at its bid price of $1.61, you just break even. As this example demonstrates, even when the bid or ask prices of two banks are different, locational arbitrage will not always be possible. To achieve profits from locational arbitrage, the bid price of one bank must be higher than the ask price of another bank. ●

Gains from Locational Arbitrage. Your gain from locational arbitrage is based on the amount of money that you use to capitalize on the exchange rate discrepancy, along with the size of the discrepancy.

EXAMPLE

The quotations for the New Zealand dollar (NZ$) at two banks are shown in Exhibit 7.2. You can obtain New Zealand dollars from North Bank at the ask price of $.640 and then sell New Zealand dollars to South Bank at the bid price of $.645. This represents one "round-trip" transaction in locational arbitrage. If you start with $10,000 and conduct one round-trip transaction, how many U.S. dollars will you end up with? The $10,000 is initially exchanged for NZ$15,625 ($10,000/$.640 per New Zealand dollar) at North Bank. Then the NZ$15,625 are sold for $.645 each, for a total of $10,078. Thus, your gain from locational arbitrage is $78. ●

Your gain may appear to be small relative to your investment of $10,000. However, consider that you did not have to tie up your funds. Your round-trip transaction could take place over a telecommunications network within a matter of seconds. Also, if you could use a larger sum of money for the transaction, your gains would be larger. Finally, you could continue to repeat your round-trip transactions until North Bank's ask price is no longer less than South Bank's bid price.

This example is not intended to suggest that you can pay for your education through part-time locational arbitrage. As mentioned earlier, foreign exchange dealers compare quotes from banks on computer terminals, which immediately signal any opportunity to employ locational arbitrage.

Exhibit 7.1 Currency Quotes for Locational Arbitrage Example

	AKRON BANK			ZYN BANK	
	BID	**ASK**		**BID**	**ASK**
British pound quote	$1.60	$1.61	British pound quote	$1.61	$1.62

Exhibit 7.2 Locational Arbitrage

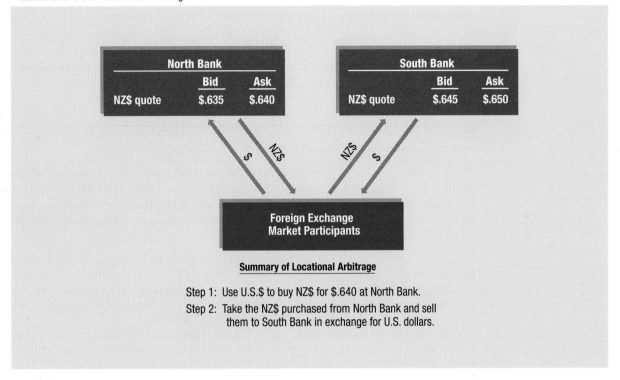

Summary of Locational Arbitrage

Step 1: Use U.S.$ to buy NZ$ for $.640 at North Bank.

Step 2: Take the NZ$ purchased from North Bank and sell them to South Bank in exchange for U.S. dollars.

Realignment due to Locational Arbitrage. Quoted prices will react to the locational arbitrage strategy used by you and other foreign exchange market participants.

EXAMPLE

In the previous example, the high demand for New Zealand dollars at North Bank (resulting from arbitrage activity) will cause a shortage of New Zealand dollars there. As a result of this shortage, North Bank will raise its ask price for New Zealand dollars. The excess supply of New Zealand dollars at South Bank (resulting from sales of New Zealand dollars to South Bank in exchange for U.S. dollars) will force South Bank to lower its bid price. As the currency prices are adjusted, gains from locational arbitrage will be reduced. Once the ask price of North Bank is not any lower than the bid price of South Bank, locational arbitrage will no longer occur. Prices may adjust in a matter of seconds or minutes from the time when locational arbitrage occurs. ●

WEB

http://finance.yahoo
.com/currency?u
Currency converter for
over 100 currencies
with frequent daily for-
eign exchange rate
updates.

The concept of locational arbitrage is relevant in that it explains why exchange rate quotations among banks at different locations normally will not differ by a significant amount. This applies not only to banks on the same street or within the same city but also to all banks across the world. Technology allows banks to be electronically connected to foreign exchange quotations at any time. Thus, banks can ensure that their quotes are in line with those of other banks. They can also immediately detect any discrepancies among quotations as soon as they occur, and capitalize on those discrepancies. Thus, technology enables more consistent prices among banks and reduces the likelihood of significant discrepancies in foreign exchange quotations among locations.

Triangular Arbitrage

Cross exchange rates represent the relationship between two currencies that are different from one's base currency. In the United States, the term *cross exchange rate* refers to the relationship between two nondollar currencies.

EXAMPLE

If the British pound (£) is worth $1.60, while the Canadian dollar (C$) is worth $.80, the value of the British pound with respect to the Canadian dollar is calculated as follows:

$$\text{Value of £ in units of C\$} = \$1.60/\$.80 = 2.0$$

The value of the Canadian dollar in units of pounds can also be determined from the cross exchange rate formula:

$$\text{Value of C\$ in units of £} = \$.80/\$1.60 = .50$$

Notice that the value of a Canadian dollar in units of pounds is simply the reciprocal of the value of a pound in units of Canadian dollars. ●

If a quoted cross exchange rate differs from the appropriate cross exchange rate (as determined by the preceding formula), you can attempt to capitalize on the discrepancy. Specifically, you can use **triangular arbitrage** in which currency transactions are conducted in the spot market to capitalize on a discrepancy in the cross exchange rate between two currencies.

EXAMPLE

Assume that a bank has quoted the British pound (£) at $1.60, the Malaysian ringgit (MYR) at $.20, and the cross exchange rate at £1 = MYR8.1. Your first task is to use the pound value in U.S. dollars and Malaysian ringgit value in U.S. dollars to develop the cross exchange rate that should exist between the pound and the Malaysian ringgit. The cross rate formula in the previous example reveals that the pound should be worth MYR8.0.

When quoting a cross exchange rate of £1 = MYR8.1, the bank is exchanging too many ringgit for a pound and is asking for too many ringgit in exchange for a pound. Based on this information, you can engage in triangular arbitrage by purchasing pounds with dollars, converting the pounds to ringgit, and then exchanging the ringgit for dollars. If you have $10,000, how many dollars will you end up with if you implement this triangular arbitrage strategy? To answer the question, consider the following steps illustrated in Exhibit 7.3:

1. Determine the number of pounds received for your dollars: $10,000 = £6,250, based on the bank's quote of $1.60 per pound.
2. Determine how many ringgit you will receive in exchange for pounds: £6,250 = MYR50,625, based on the bank's quote of 8.1 ringgit per pound.
3. Determine how many U.S. dollars you will receive in exchange for the ringgit: MYR50,625 = $10,125 based on the bank's quote of $.20 per ringgit (5 ringgit to the dollar). The triangular arbitrage strategy generates $10,125, which is $125 more than you started with. ●

Like locational arbitrage, triangular arbitrage does not tie up funds. Also, the strategy is risk free since there is no uncertainty about the prices at which you will buy and sell the currencies.

Accounting for the Bid/Ask Spread. The previous example is simplified in that it does not account for transaction costs. In reality, there is a bid and ask quote for each currency, which means that the arbitrageur incurs transaction costs that can reduce or even eliminate the gains from triangular arbitrage. The following example illustrates how bid and ask prices can affect arbitrage profits.

EXAMPLE

Using the quotations in Exhibit 7.4, you can determine whether triangular arbitrage is possible by starting with some fictitious amount (say, $10,000) of U.S. dollars and estimating the number of dollars you would generate by implementing the strategy. Exhibit 7.4 differs from the previous example only in that bid/ask spreads are now considered.

Recall that the previous triangular arbitrage strategy involved exchanging dollars for pounds, pounds for ringgit, and then ringgit for dollars. Apply this strategy to the bid and ask quotations in Exhibit 7.4. The steps are summarized in Exhibit 7.5.

Exhibit 7.3 Example of Triangular Arbitrage

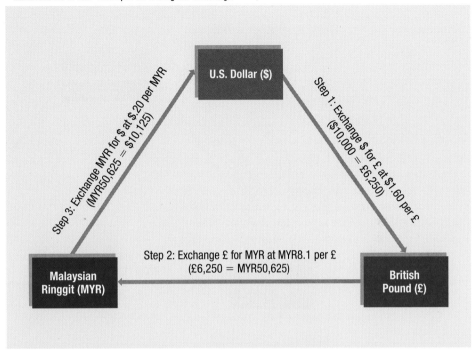

Exhibit 7.4 Currency Quotes for a Triangular Arbitrage Example

	QUOTED BID PRICE	QUOTED ASK PRICE
Value of a British pound in U.S. dollars	$1.60	$1.61
Value of a Malaysian ringgit (MYR) in U.S. dollars	$.200	$.201
Value of a British pound in Malaysian ringgit (MYR)	MYR8.10	MYR8.20

Step 1. Your initial $10,000 will be converted into approximately £6,211 (based on the bank's ask price of $1.61 per pound).

Step 2. Then the £6,211 are converted into MYR50,310 (based on the bank's bid price for pounds of MYR8.1 per pound, £6,211 × 8.1 = MYR50,310).

Step 3. The MYR50,310 are converted to $10,062 (based on the bank's bid price of $.200).

The profit is $10,062 − $10,000 = $62. The profit is lower here than in the previous example because bid and ask quotations are used. ●

Realignment Due to Triangular Arbitrage.

The realignment that results from the triangular arbitrage activity is summarized in the second column of Exhibit 7.6. The realignment will likely occur quickly to prevent continued benefits from triangular arbitrage. The discrepancies assumed here are unlikely to occur within a single bank. More likely, triangular arbitrage would require three transactions at three separate banks.

If any two of these three exchange rates are known, the exchange rate of the third pair can be determined. When the actual cross exchange rate differs from the appropriate cross exchange rate, the exchange rates of the currencies are not in equilibrium. Triangular arbitrage would force the exchange rates back into equilibrium.

Exhibit 7.5 Example of Triangular Arbitrage Accounting for Bid/Ask Spreads

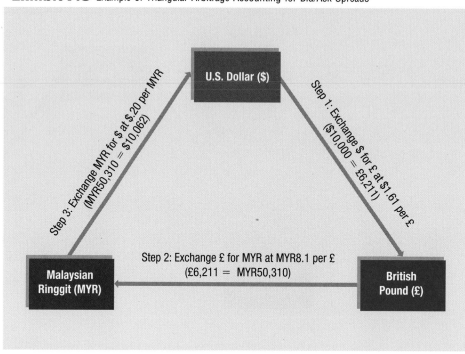

Exhibit 7.6 Impact of Triangular Arbitrage

ACTIVITY	IMPACT
1. Participants use dollars to purchase pounds.	Bank increases its ask price of pounds with respect to the dollar.
2. Participants use pounds to purchase Malaysian ringgit.	Bank reduces its bid price of the British pound with respect to the ringgit; that is, it reduces the number of ringgit to be exchanged per pound received.
3. Participants use Malaysian ringgit to purchase U.S. dollars.	Bank reduces its bid price of ringgit with respect to the dollar.

　　Like locational arbitrage, triangular arbitrage is a strategy that few of us can ever take advantage of because the computer technology available to foreign exchange dealers can easily detect misalignments in cross exchange rates. The point of this discussion is that triangular arbitrage will ensure that cross exchange rates are usually aligned correctly. If cross exchange rates are not properly aligned, triangular arbitrage will take place until the rates are aligned correctly.

Covered Interest Arbitrage

The forward rate of a currency for a specified future date is determined by the interaction of demand for the contract (forward purchases) versus the supply (forward sales). Forward rates are quoted for some widely traded currencies (just below the respective spot rate quotation) in the *Wall Street Journal*. Financial institutions that offer foreign exchange services set the forward rates, but these rates are driven by the market forces (demand and supply conditions). In some cases, the forward rate may be priced at a level that allows investors to engage in arbitrage. Their actions will affect the volume of orders for forward purchases or forward sales of a particular currency, which in turn will affect the equilibrium forward rate. Arbitrage will continue until the forward rate is aligned where it should be, and at that point arbitrage will no longer be feasible. This arbitrage process and its effects on the forward rate are described next.

Steps Involved in Covered Interest Arbitrage. **Covered interest arbitrage** is the process of capitalizing on the interest rate differential between two countries while covering your exchange rate risk with a forward contract. The logic of the term *covered interest arbitrage* becomes clear when it is broken into two parts: "interest arbitrage" refers to the process of capitalizing on the difference between interest rates between two countries; "covered" refers to hedging your position against exchange rate risk.

Covered interest arbitrage is sometimes interpreted to mean that the funds to be invested are borrowed locally. In this case, the investors are not tying up any of their own funds. In another interpretation, however, the investors use their own funds. In this case, the term *arbitrage* is loosely defined since there is a positive dollar amount invested over a period of time. The following discussion is based on this latter meaning of covered interest arbitrage; under either interpretation, however, arbitrage should have a similar impact on currency values.

EXAMPLE

You desire to capitalize on relatively high rates of interest in the United Kingdom and have funds available for 90 days. The interest rate is certain; only the future exchange rate at which you will exchange pounds back to U.S. dollars is uncertain. You can use a forward sale of pounds to guarantee the rate at which you can exchange pounds for dollars at a future point in time.

Assume the following information:

- You have $800,000 to invest.
- The current spot rate of the pound is $1.60.
- The 90-day forward rate of the pound is $1.60.
- The 90-day interest rate in the United States is 2 percent.
- The 90-day interest rate in the United Kingdom is 4 percent.

Based on this information, you should proceed as follows:

1. On day 1, convert the $800,000 to £500,000 and deposit the £500,000 in a British bank.
2. On day 1, sell £520,000 90 days forward. By the time the deposit matures, you will have £520,000 (including interest).
3. In 90 days when the deposit matures, you can fulfill your forward contract obligation by converting your £520,000 into $832,000 (based on the forward contract rate of $1.60 per pound). ●

The steps involved in covered interest arbitrage are illustrated in Exhibit 7.7. The strategy results in a 4 percent return over the 3-month period, which is 2 percent above the return on a U.S. deposit. In addition, the return on this strategy is known on day 1, since you know when you make the deposit exactly how many dollars you will get back from your 90-day investment.

Recall that locational and triangular arbitrage do not tie up funds; thus, any profits are achieved instantaneously. In the case of covered interest arbitrage, the funds are tied up for a period of time (90 days in our example). This strategy would not be advantageous if it earned 2 percent or less, since you could earn 2 percent on a domestic

Exhibit 7.7 Example of Covered Interest Arbitrage

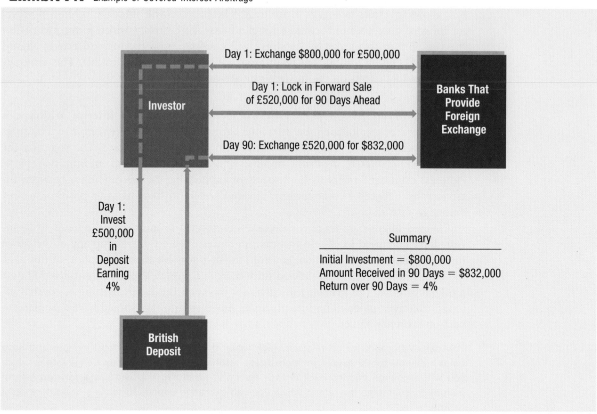

Day 1: Exchange $800,000 for £500,000

Day 1: Lock in Forward Sale
of £520,000 for 90 Days Ahead

Day 90: Exchange £520,000 for $832,000

Investor

**Banks That
Provide
Foreign
Exchange**

Day 1:
Invest
£500,000
in
Deposit
Earning
4%

**British
Deposit**

Summary

Initial Investment = $800,000
Amount Received in 90 Days = $832,000
Return over 90 Days = 4%

deposit. The term *arbitrage* here suggests that you can guarantee a return on your funds that exceeds the returns you could achieve domestically.

Realignment Due to Covered Interest Arbitrage. As with the other forms of arbitrage, market forces resulting from covered interest arbitrage will cause a market realignment. As many investors capitalize on covered interest arbitrage, there is downward pressure on the 90-day forward rate. Once the forward rate has a discount from the spot rate that is about equal to the interest rate advantage, covered interest arbitrage will no longer be feasible. Since the interest rate advantage of the British interest rate over the U.S. interest rate is 2 percent, the arbitrage will no longer be feasible once the forward rate of the pound exhibits a discount of about 2 percent.

Timing of Realignment. The realignment of the forward rate might not be completed until several transactions occur. The realignment does not erase the gains to those U.S. investors who initially engaged in covered interest arbitrage. Recall that they locked in their gain by obtaining a forward contract on the day that they made their investment. But their actions to sell pounds forward placed downward pressure on the forward rate. Perhaps their actions initially would have caused a small discount in the forward rate, such as 1 percent. Under these conditions, U.S. investors would still benefit from covered interest arbitrage, because the 1 percent discount only partially offsets the 2 percent interest rate advantage. While the benefits are not as great as they were initially, covered interest arbitrage should continue until the forward rate exhibits a discount of about 2 percent to offset the 2 percent interest rate advantage. Even though the realignment may not be complete until there are several arbitrage transactions, the realignment will normally be completed quickly, such as within a few minutes.

Realignment Is Focused on the Forward Rate.
In the example above, only the forward rate was affected by the forces of covered interest arbitrage. It is possible that the spot rate could experience upward pressure due to the increased demand. If the spot rate appreciates, then the forward rate would not have to decline by as much in order to achieve the 2 percent forward discount that would offset the 2 percent interest rate differential. But since the forward market is less liquid, the forward rate is more sensitive to shifts in demand or supply conditions caused by covered interest arbitrage, and therefore the forward rate is likely to experience most or all of the necessary adjustment in order to achieve realignment.

EXAMPLE

Assume that as a result of covered interest arbitrage, the 90-day forward rate of the pound declined to $1.5692. Consider the results from using $800,000 (as in the previous example) to engage in covered interest arbitrage after the forward rate has adjusted.

1. Convert $800,000 to pounds:

$$\$800,000/\$1.60 = £500,000$$

2. Calculate accumulated pounds over 90 days at 4 percent:

$$£500,000 \times 1.04 = £520,000$$

3. Reconvert pounds to dollars (at the forward rate of $1.5692) after 90 days:

$$£520,000 \times \$1.5692 = \$815,984$$

4. Determine the yield earned from covered interest arbitrage:

$$(\$815,984 - \$800,000)/\$800,000 = .02, \text{ or } 2\%$$

As this example shows, the forward rate has declined to a level such that future attempts to engage in covered interest arbitrage are no longer feasible. Now the return from covered interest arbitrage is no better than what you can earn domestically. ●

Consideration of Spreads.
Now an example will be provided to illustrate the effects of the spread between the bid and ask quotes and the spread between deposit and loan rates.

EXAMPLE

The following exchange rates and 1-year interest rates exist.

	BID QUOTE	ASK QUOTE
Euro spot	$1.12	$1.13
Euro 1-year forward	1.12	1.13
	DEPOSIT RATE	**LOAN RATE**
Interest rate on dollars	6.0%	9.0%
Interest rate on euros	6.5%	9.5%

You have $100,000 to invest for 1 year. Would you benefit from engaging in covered interest arbitrage?

Notice that the quotes of the euro spot and forward rates are exactly the same, while the deposit rate on euros is .5 percent higher than the deposit rate on dollars. So it may seem that covered interest arbitrage is feasible. However, U.S. investors would be subjected to the ask quote when buying euros (€) in the spot market, versus the bid quote when selling the euros through a 1-year forward contract.

1. Convert $100,000 to euros (ask quote):

$$\$100,000/\$1.13 = €88,496$$

2. Calculate accumulated euros over 1 year at 6.5 percent:

$$€88,496 \times 1.065 = €94,248$$

3. Sell euros for dollars at the forward rate (bid quote):

$$€94,248 \times \$1.12 = \$105,558$$

4. Determine the yield earned from covered interest arbitrage:

$$(\$105,558 - \$100,000)/\$100,000 = .05558, \text{ or } 5.558\%$$

The yield is less than you would have earned if you had invested the funds in the United States. Thus, covered interest arbitrage is not feasible. ●

Covered Interest Arbitrage by Non-U.S. Investors.
In the examples provided up to this point, covered interest arbitrage was conducted as if the United States was the home country for investors. The examples could easily be adapted to make any country the home country for investors.

Assume that the 1-year U.S. interest rate is 5 percent, while the 1-year Japanese interest rate is 4 percent, the spot rate of the Japanese yen is $.01, and the 1-year forward rate of the yen is $.01. Investors based in Japan could benefit from covered interest arbitrage by converting Japanese yen to dollars at the prevailing spot rate, investing the dollars at 5 percent, and simultaneously selling dollars (buying yen) forward. Since they are buying and selling dollars at the same price, they would earn 5 percent on this strategy, which is better than they could earn from investing in Japan.

As Japanese investors engage in covered interest arbitrage, the high Japanese demand to buy yen forward will place upward pressure on the 1-year forward rate of the yen. Once the 1-year forward rate of the Japanese yen exhibits a premium of about 1 percent, new attempts to pursue covered interest arbitrage would not be feasible for Japanese investors because the 1 percent premium paid to buy yen forward would offset the 1 percent interest rate advantage in the United States. ●

The concept of covered interest arbitrage can apply to any two countries as long as there is a spot rate between the two currencies, a forward rate between the two currencies, and risk-free interest rates quoted for both currencies. If investors from Japan wanted to pursue covered interest arbitrage over a 90-day period in France, they would convert Japanese yen to euros in the spot market, invest in a 90-day risk-free security in France, and simultaneously sell euros (buy yen) forward with a 90-day forward contract.

Comparison of Arbitrage Effects

Exhibit 7.8 provides a comparison of the three types of arbitrage. The threat of locational arbitrage ensures that quoted exchange rates are similar across banks in different locations. The threat of triangular arbitrage ensures that cross exchange rates are properly set. The threat of covered interest arbitrage ensures that forward exchange rates are properly set. Any discrepancy will trigger arbitrage, which should eliminate the discrepancy. Thus, arbitrage tends to allow for a more orderly foreign exchange market.

How Arbitrage Reduces Transaction Costs.
Many MNCs engage in transactions amounting to more than $100 million per year. Since the foreign exchange market is

Exhibit 7.8 Comparing Arbitrage Strategies

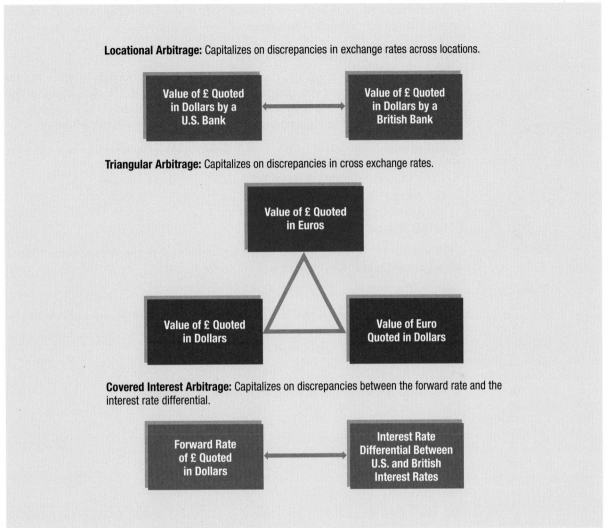

over the counter, there is not one consistently transparent set of exchange quotations. Consequently, managers of an MNC could incur large transaction costs if they consistently paid too much for the currencies that they needed. However, the arbitrage process limits the degree of difference in quotations among currencies. Locational arbitrage limits the differences in a spot exchange rate quotation across locations, while covered interest arbitrage ensures that the forward rate is properly priced. Thus, an MNC's managers should be able to avoid excessive transaction costs.

INTEREST RATE PARITY (IRP)

Once market forces cause interest rates and exchange rates to adjust such that covered interest arbitrage is no longer feasible, there is an equilibrium state referred to as **interest rate parity (IRP).** In equilibrium, the forward rate differs from the spot rate by a sufficient amount to offset the interest rate differential between two currencies. In the previous example, the U.S. investor receives a higher interest rate from the foreign investment, but there is an offsetting effect because the investor must pay more per unit of foreign currency (at the spot rate) than is received per unit when the currency is sold forward (at the forward rate). Recall that when the forward rate is less than the spot rate, this implies that the forward rate exhibits a discount.

Derivation of Interest Rate Parity

The relationship between a forward premium (or discount) of a foreign currency and the interest rates representing these currencies according to IRP can be determined as follows. Consider a U.S. investor who attempts covered interest arbitrage. The investor's return from using covered interest arbitrage can be determined given the following:

- The amount of the home currency (U.S. dollars in our example) that is initially invested (A_h).
- The spot rate (S) in dollars when the foreign currency is purchased.
- The interest rate on the foreign deposit (i_f).
- The forward rate (F) in dollars at which the foreign currency will be converted back to U.S. dollars.

The amount of the home currency received at the end of the deposit period due to such a strategy (called A_n) is:

$$A_n = (A_h/S)(1 + i_f)F$$

Since F is simply S times 1 plus the forward premium (called p), we can rewrite this equation as:

$$A_n = (A_h/S)(1 + i_f)[S(1 + p)]$$
$$= A_h(1 + i_f)(1 + p)$$

The rate of return from this investment (called R) is as follows:

$$R = \frac{A_n - A_h}{A_h}$$
$$= \frac{[A_h(1 + i_f)(1 + p)] - A_h}{A_h}$$
$$= (1 + i_f)(1 + p) - 1$$

If IRP exists, then the rate of return achieved from covered interest arbitrage (R) should be equal to the rate available in the home country. Set the rate that can be achieved from using covered interest arbitrage equal to the rate that can be achieved from an investment in the home country (the return on a home investment is simply the home interest rate called i_h):

$$R = i_h$$

By substituting into the formula the way in which R is determined, we obtain:

$$(1 + i_f)(1 + p) - 1 = i_h$$

By rearranging terms, we can determine what the forward premium of the foreign currency should be under conditions of IRP:

$$(1 + i_f)(1 + p) - 1 = i_h$$
$$(1 + i_f)(1 + p) = 1 + i_h$$
$$1 + p = \frac{1 + i_h}{1 + i_f}$$
$$p = \frac{1 + i_h}{1 + i_f} - 1$$

Thus, given the two interest rates of concern, the forward rate under conditions of IRP can be derived. If the actual forward rate is different from this derived forward rate, there may be potential for covered interest arbitrage.

Determining the Forward Premium

Using the information just presented, the forward premium can be measured based on the interest rate differential under conditions of IRP.

EXAMPLE

Assume that the Mexican peso exhibits a 6-month interest rate of 6 percent, while the U.S. dollar exhibits a 6-month interest rate of 5 percent. From a U.S. investor's perspective, the U.S. dollar is the home currency. According to IRP, the forward rate premium of the peso with respect to the U.S. dollar should be:

$$p = \frac{1 + .05}{1 + .06} - 1$$
$$= -.0094, \text{ or } -.94\% \text{ (not annualized)}$$

Thus, the peso should exhibit a forward discount of about .94 percent. This implies that U.S. investors would receive .94 percent less when selling pesos 6 months from now (based on a forward sale) than the price they pay for pesos today at the spot rate. Such a discount would offset the interest rate advantage of the peso. If the peso's spot rate is $.10, a forward discount of .94 percent means that the 6-month forward rate is as follows:

$$F = S(1 + p)$$
$$= \$.10(1 - .0094)$$
$$= \$.09906$$

●

Influence of the Interest Rate Differential. The relationship between the forward premium (or discount) and the interest rate differential according to IRP is simplified in an approximated form as follows:

$$p = \frac{F - S}{S} \cong i_h - i_f$$

where

p = forward premium (or discount)
F = forward rate in dollars
S = spot rate in dollars
i_h = home interest rate
i_f = foreign interest rate

This approximated form provides a reasonable estimate when the interest rate differential is small. The variables in this equation are not annualized. In our previous example, the U.S. (home) interest rate is less than the foreign interest rate, so the forward rate contains a discount (the forward rate is less than the spot rate). The larger the degree by which the foreign interest rate exceeds the home interest rate, the larger will be the forward discount of the foreign currency specified by the IRP formula.

If the foreign interest rate is less than the home interest rate, the IRP relationship suggests that the forward rate should exhibit a premium.

Implications. If the forward premium is equal to the interest rate differential as explained above, covered interest arbitrage will not be feasible.

EXAMPLE

Use the information on the spot rate, the 6-month forward rate of the peso, and Mexico's interest rate from the preceding example to determine a U.S. investor's return from using covered interest arbitrage. Assume the investor begins with $1,000,000 to invest.

Step 1. On the first day, the U.S. investor converts $1,000,000 into Mexican pesos (MXP) at $.10 per peso:

$$\$1,000,000/\$.10 \text{ per peso} = \text{MXP}10,000,000$$

Step 2. On the first day, the U.S. investor also sells pesos 6 months forward. The number of pesos to be sold forward is the anticipated accumulation of pesos over the 6-month period, which is estimated as:

$$\text{MXP}10,000,000 \times (1 + .06) = \text{MXP}10,600,000$$

Step 3. After 6 months, the U.S. investor withdraws the initial deposit of pesos along with the accumulated interest, amounting to a total of 10,600,000 pesos. The investor converts the pesos into dollars in accordance with the forward contract agreed upon 6 months earlier. The forward rate was $.09906, so the number of U.S. dollars received from the conversion is:

$$\text{MXP}10,600,000 \times (\$.09906 \text{ per peso}) = \$1,050,036$$

In this case, the investor's covered interest arbitrage achieves a return of about 5 percent. Rounding the forward discount to .94 percent causes the slight deviation from the 5 percent return. The results suggest that, in this instance, using covered interest arbitrage generates a return that is about what the investor would have received anyway by simply investing the funds domestically. This confirms that covered interest arbitrage is not worthwhile if IRP exists. ●

Graphic Analysis of Interest Rate Parity

The interest rate differential can be compared to the forward premium (or discount) with the use of a graph. All the possible points that represent interest rate parity are plotted on Exhibit 7.9 by using the approximation expressed earlier and plugging in numbers.

WEB

www.bloomberg.com
Latest information from
financial markets
around the world.

Points Representing a Discount. For all situations in which the foreign interest rate exceeds the home interest rate, the forward rate should exhibit a discount approximately equal to that differential. When the foreign interest rate (i_f) exceeds the home interest rate (i_h) by 1 percent ($i_h - i_f = -1\%$), then the forward rate should exhibit a discount of 1 percent. This is represented by point A on the graph. If the foreign interest rate exceeds the home rate by 2 percent, then the forward rate should exhibit a discount of 2 percent, as represented by point B on the graph, and so on.

Points Representing a Premium. For all situations in which the foreign interest rate is less than the home interest rate, the forward rate should exhibit a premium approximately equal to that differential. For example, if the home interest rate exceeds the foreign rate by 1 percent ($i_h - i_f = 1\%$), then the forward premium should be 1 percent, as represented by point C. If the home interest rate exceeds the foreign rate by 2 percent ($i_h - i_f = 2\%$), then the forward premium should be 2 percent, as represented by point D, and so on.

Exhibit 7.9 can be used whether or not you annualize the rates as long as you are consistent. That is, if you annualize the interest rates to determine the interest rate differential, you should also annualize the forward premium or discount.

Exhibit 7.9 Illustration of Interest Rate Parity

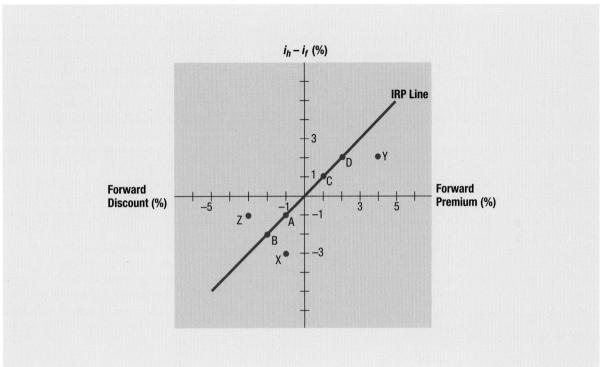

Points Representing IRP. Any points lying on the diagonal line cutting the intersection of the axes represent IRP. For this reason, that diagonal line is referred to as the **interest rate parity (IRP) line.** Covered interest arbitrage is not possible for points along the IRP line.

An individual or corporation can at any time examine all currencies to compare forward rate premiums (or discounts) to interest rate differentials. From a U.S. perspective, interest rates in Japan are usually lower than the home interest rates. Consequently, the forward rate of the Japanese yen usually exhibits a premium and may be represented by points such as C or D or even points above D along the diagonal line in Exhibit 7.9. Conversely, the United Kingdom often has higher interest rates than the United States, so the pound's forward rate often exhibits a discount, represented by point A or B.

A currency representing point B has an interest rate that is 2 percent above the prevailing home interest rate. If the home country is the United States, this means that investors who live in the foreign country and invest their funds in local risk-free securities earn 2 percent more than investors in the United States who invest in risk-free securities in the United States. When IRP exists, even if U.S. investors attempt to use covered interest arbitrage by investing in that foreign currency with the higher interest rate, they will still only earn what they could earn in the United States because the forward rate of that currency would exhibit a 2 percent discount.

A currency representing point D has an interest rate that is 2 percent below the prevailing interest rate. If the home country is the United States, this means that investors who live in the foreign country and invest their funds in local risk-free securities earn 2 percent less than U.S. investors who invest in risk-free securities in the United States. When IRP exists, even if those foreign investors attempt to use covered interest arbitrage by investing in the United States, they will still only earn what they could earn in the

United States because they would have to pay a forward premium of 2 percent when exchanging dollars for their home currency.

Points below the IRP Line. What if a 3-month deposit represented by a foreign currency offers an annualized interest rate of 10 percent versus an annualized interest rate of 7 percent in the home country? Such a scenario is represented on the graph by $i_h - i_f = -3\%$. Also assume that the foreign currency exhibits an annualized forward discount of 1 percent. The combined interest rate differential and forward discount information can be represented by point X on the graph. Since point X is not on the IRP line, we should expect that covered interest arbitrage will be beneficial for some investors. The investor attains an additional 3 percentage points for the foreign deposit, and this advantage is only partially offset by the 1 percent forward discount.

Assume that the annualized interest rate for the foreign currency is 5 percent, as compared to 7 percent for the home country. The interest rate differential expressed on the graph is $i_h - i_f = 2\%$. However, assume that the forward premium of the foreign currency is 4 percent (point Y in Exhibit 7.9). Thus, the high forward premium more than makes up what the investor loses on the lower interest rate from the foreign investment.

If the current interest rate and forward rate situation is represented by point X or Y, home country investors can engage in covered interest arbitrage. By investing in a foreign currency, they will earn a higher return (after considering the foreign interest rate and forward premium or discount) than the home interest rate. This type of activity will place upward pressure on the spot rate of the foreign currency, and downward pressure on the forward rate of the foreign currency, until covered interest arbitrage is no longer feasible.

Points above the IRP Line. Now shift to the left side of the IRP line. Take point Z, for example. This represents a foreign interest rate that exceeds the home interest rate by 1 percent, while the forward rate exhibits a 3 percent discount. This point, like all points to the left of the IRP line, represents a situation in which U.S. investors would achieve a lower return on a foreign investment than on a domestic one. This lower return normally occurs either because (1) the advantage of the foreign interest rate relative to the U.S. interest rate is more than offset by the forward rate discount (reflected by point Z), or because (2) the degree by which the home interest rate exceeds the foreign rate more than offsets the forward rate premium.

For points such as these, however, covered interest arbitrage is feasible from the perspective of foreign investors. Consider British investors in the United Kingdom, whose interest rate is 1 percent higher than the U.S. interest rate, and the forward rate (with respect to the dollar) contains a 3 percent discount (as represented by point Z). British investors will sell their foreign currency in exchange for dollars, invest in dollar-denominated securities, and engage in a forward contract to purchase pounds forward. Though they earn 1 percent less on the U.S. investment, they are able to purchase their home currency forward for 3 percent less than what they initially sold it forward in the spot market. This type of activity will place downward pressure on the spot rate of the pound and upward pressure on the pound's forward rate, until covered interest arbitrage is no longer feasible.

How to Test Whether Interest Rate Parity Exists

An investor or firm can plot all realistic points for various currencies on a graph such as that in Exhibit 7.9 to determine whether gains from covered interest arbitrage can be achieved. The location of the points provides an indication of whether covered interest arbitrage is worthwhile. For points to the right of the IRP line, investors in the home country should consider using covered interest arbitrage, since a return higher than the home interest rate (i_h) is achievable. Of course, as investors and firms take advantage of such opportunities, the point will tend to move toward the IRP line. Covered interest arbitrage should continue until the interest rate parity relationship holds.

Interpretation of Interest Rate Parity

Interest rate parity does not imply that investors from different countries will earn the same returns. It is focused on the comparison of a foreign investment and a domestic investment in risk-free interest-bearing securities by a particular investor.

EXAMPLE

Assume that the United States has a 10 percent interest rate, while the United Kingdom has a 14 percent interest rate. U.S. investors can achieve 10 percent domestically or attempt to use covered interest arbitrage. If they attempt covered interest arbitrage while IRP exists, then the result will be a 10 percent return, the same as they could achieve in the United States. If British investors attempt covered interest arbitrage while IRP exists, then the result will be a 14 percent return, the same as they could achieve in the United Kingdom. Thus, U.S. investors and British investors do *not* achieve the same nominal return here, even though IRP exists. An appropriate summary explanation of IRP is that if IRP exists, investors cannot use covered interest arbitrage to achieve higher returns than those achievable in their respective home countries. ●

Does Interest Rate Parity Hold?

To determine conclusively whether interest rate parity holds, it is necessary to compare the forward rate (or discount) with interest rate quotations occurring at the same time. If the forward rate and interest rate quotations do not reflect the same time of day, then results could be somewhat distorted. Due to limitations in access to data, it is difficult to obtain quotations that reflect the same point in time.

At different points in time, the position of a country may change. For example, if Brazil's interest rate increased while other countries' interest rates stayed the same, Brazil's position would move down along the y axis. Yet, its forward discount would likely be more pronounced (farther to the left along the x axis) as well, since covered interest arbitrage would occur otherwise. Therefore, its new point would be farther to the left but would still be along the 45-degree line.

Numerous academic studies have conducted empirical examination of IRP in several periods. The actual relationship between the forward rate premium and interest rate differentials generally supports IRP. Although there are deviations from IRP, they are often not large enough to make covered interest arbitrage worthwhile, as we will now discuss in more detail.

Considerations When Assessing Interest Rate Parity

If interest rate parity does not hold, covered interest arbitrage deserves consideration. Nevertheless, covered interest arbitrage still may not be worthwhile due to various characteristics of foreign investments, including transaction costs, political risk, and differential tax laws.

Transaction Costs. If an investor wishes to account for transaction costs, the actual point reflecting the interest rate differential and forward rate premium must be farther from the IRP line to make covered interest arbitrage worthwhile. Exhibit 7.10 identifies the areas that reflect potential for covered interest arbitrage *after* accounting for transaction costs. Notice the band surrounding the IRP line. For points not on the IRP line but within this band, covered interest arbitrage is not worthwhile (because the excess return is offset by costs). For points to the right of (or below) the band, investors residing in the home country could gain through covered interest arbitrage. For points to the left of (or above) the band, foreign investors could gain through covered interest arbitrage.

Exhibit 7.10 Potential for Covered Interest Arbitrage When Considering Transaction Costs

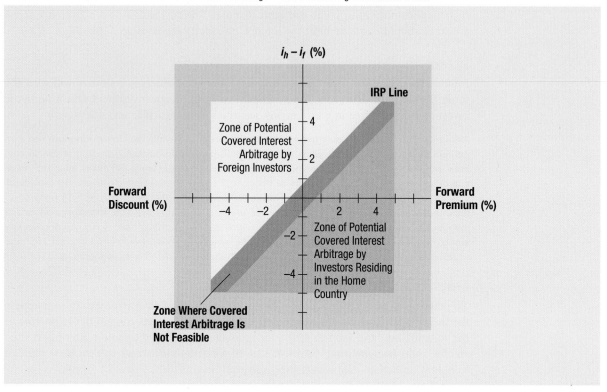

Political Risk. Even if covered interest arbitrage appears feasible after accounting for transaction costs, investing funds overseas is subject to political risk. Though the forward contract locks in the rate at which the foreign funds should be reconverted, there is no guarantee that the foreign government will allow the funds to be reconverted. A crisis in the foreign country could cause its government to restrict any exchange of the local currency for other currencies. In this case, the investor would be unable to use these funds until the foreign government eliminated the restriction.

Investors may also perceive a slight default risk on foreign investments such as foreign Treasury bills, since they may not be assured that the foreign government will guarantee full repayment of interest and principal upon default. Therefore, because of concern that the foreign Treasury bills may default, they may accept a lower interest rate on their domestic Treasury bills rather than engage in covered interest arbitrage in an effort to obtain a slightly higher expected return.

Differential Tax Laws. Because tax laws vary among countries, investors and firms that set up deposits in other countries must be aware of the existing tax laws. Covered interest arbitrage might be feasible when considering before-tax returns but not necessarily when considering after-tax returns. Such a scenario would be due to differential tax rates.

Forward Premiums across Maturity Markets

The yield curve represents the relationship between the annualized yield of risk-free debt and the time to maturity at a given point in time. The shape of the yield curve in the United States commonly has an upward slope, implying that the annualized interest rate is higher for longer terms to maturity. The yield curve of every country has its own unique

Exhibit 7.11 Quoted Interest Rates for Various Times to Maturity

TIME TO MATURITY	U.S. INTEREST (ANNUALIZED) QUOTED TODAY	EURO INTEREST (ANNUALIZED) QUOTED TODAY	INTEREST RATE DIFFERENTIAL (ANNUALIZED) BASED ON TODAY'S QUOTES	APPROXIMATE FORWARD RATE PREMIUM (ANNUALIZED) OF EURO AS OF TODAY IF IRP HOLDS
30 days	4.0%	5.0%	−1.0%	−1.0%
90 days	4.5	5.0	−.5	−.5
180 days	5.0	5.0	.0	.0
1 year	5.5	5.0	+.5	+.5
2 years	6.0	5.0	+1.0	+1.0

shape. Consequently, the annualized interest rate differential between two countries can vary among debt maturities, and so will the annualized forward premiums.

To illustrate, review Exhibit 7.11, which shows today's quoted interest rates for various times to maturity. If you plot a yield curve with the time to maturity on the horizontal axis and the U.S. interest rate on the vertical axis, the U.S. yield curve today is upward sloping. If you repeat the exercise for the interest rate of the euro, the yield curve is flat, as the annualized interest rate in the eurozone is the same regardless of the maturity. For times to maturity of less than 180 days, the euro interest rate is higher than the U.S. interest rate, so the forward rate of the euro would exhibit a discount if IRP holds. For the time to maturity of 180 days, the euro interest rate is equal to the U.S. interest rate, which means that the 180-day forward rate of the euro should be equal to its spot rate (no premium or discount). For times to maturity beyond 180 days, the euro interest rate is lower than the U.S. interest rate, which means that the forward rate of the euro would exhibit a premium if IRP holds. Consider the implications for U.S. firms that hedge future euro payments. A firm that is hedging euro outflow payments for a date of less than 180 days from now will lock in a forward rate for the euro that is lower than the existing spot rate. Conversely, a firm that is hedging euro outflow payments for a date beyond 180 days from now will lock in a forward rate that is above the existing spot rate.

Changes in Forward Premiums

Exhibit 7.12 illustrates the relationship between interest rate differentials and the forward premium over time, when interest rate parity holds. The forward premium must adjust to existing interest rate conditions if interest rate parity holds. In January, the U.S. interest rate is 2 percent above the euro interest rate, so the euro's forward premium must be 2 percent. By February, the U.S. and euro interest rates are the same, so the forward rate must be equal to the spot rate (and therefore have no premium or discount). In March, the U.S. interest rate is 1 percent below the euro interest rate, so the euro must have a forward discount of 1 percent.

Notice that the forward rate of the euro exhibits a premium whenever the U.S. interest rate is higher than the euro interest rate and the size of the premium is about equal to the size of the interest rate differential. Also notice that the forward rate of the euro exhibits a discount whenever the U.S. interest rate is lower than the euro interest rate and the size of the premium is about equal to the size of the interest rate differential.

The comparison of the middle graph and bottom graph is very similar to the points plotted to form the IRP line in Exhibit 7.9. The IRP line in Exhibit 7.9 shows the relationship between the interest rate differential and forward premium for a given point in

Exhibit 7.12 Relationship between the Interest Rate Differential and the Forward Premium

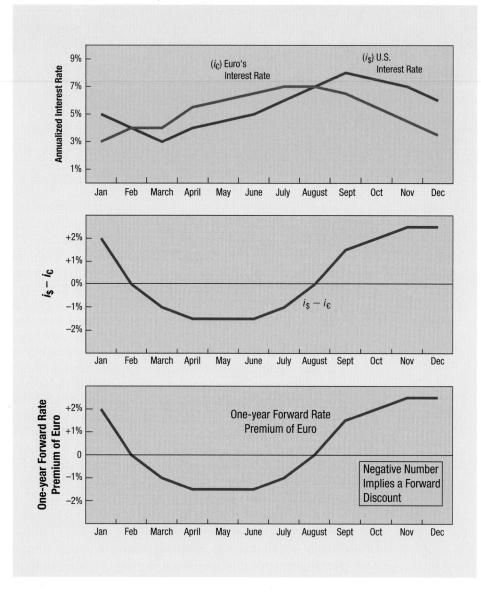

time, while Exhibit 7.12 shows the relationship between the interest rate differential and forward premium over time. Both graphs illustrate that when interest rate parity exists, the forward premium of a foreign currency will be approximately equal to the difference between the U.S. interest rate and the foreign interest rate.

The time series relationship shown in Exhibit 7.12 can be used to determine how the forward rate premium will adjust in response to conditions that affect interest rate movements over time.

EXAMPLE

Assume that interest rate parity exists and will continue to exist. As of this morning, the spot rate of the Canadian dollar was $.80, the 1-year forward rate of the Canadian dollar was $.80, and the 1-year interest rates in Canada and in the United States were 5 percent. Assume that at noon today, the Federal Reserve engaged in monetary policy in which it reduced the 1-year

WEB

www.bmonesbittburns
.com/economics/
fxrates
Forward rates of the
Canadian dollar, British
pound, euro, and Japanese yen for various
periods.

U.S. interest rate to 4 percent. Thus, the 1-year forward rate of the Canadian dollar must change to reflect a 1 percent discount, or else covered interest arbitrage will occur until the forward rate exhibits a 1 percent discount. ●

Explaining Changes in the Forward Rate.
Recall that the forward rate (F) can be written as:

$$F = S(1 + p)$$

The forward rate is indirectly affected by all the factors that can affect the spot rate (S) over time, including inflation differentials, interest rate differentials, etc. The change in the forward rate can also be due to a change in the premium, and the previous section explained how a change in the forward premium is completely dictated by changes in the interest rate differential, assuming that interest rate parity holds. Thus, interest rate movements can affect the forward rate by affecting the spot rate and the forward premium.

EXAMPLE

Assume that as of yesterday, the United States and Canada each had an annual interest rate of 5 percent. Under these conditions, interest rate parity should force the Canadian dollar to have a forward premium of zero. Assume that the annual interest rate in the United States increased to 6 percent today, while the Canadian interest rate remains at 5 percent. To maintain interest rate parity, the forward premium (which was zero yesterday) will be about 1 percent today to reflect the 1 percent interest rate differential between the U.S. and Canadian interest rates today. Thus, the forward rate will be 1 percent above whatever the spot rate is today. As long as the interest rate differential remains at 1 percent, any future movement in the spot rate will result in a similar movement in the forward rate to retain the 1 percent forward premium. ●

Impact of the Credit Crisis on Forward Premiums.
 In October 2008, the Federal Reserve lowered interest rates in the United States in anticipation that the U.S. economy would weaken so that it could encourage borrowing and spending. Central banks in some other countries also reduced their interest rates, but not to the same degree. The U.S. interest rate was already lower than interest rates in most other countries, but the Fed's policy action caused a larger gap. Consequently, the forward discount on most currencies became more pronounced.

SUMMARY

■ Locational arbitrage may occur if foreign exchange quotations differ among banks. The act of locational arbitrage should force the foreign exchange quotations of banks to become realigned, and locational arbitrage will no longer be possible.

■ Triangular arbitrage is related to cross exchange rates. A cross exchange rate between two currencies is determined by the values of these two currencies with respect to a third currency. If the actual cross exchange rate of these two currencies differs from the rate that should exist, triangular arbitrage is possible. The act of triangular arbitrage should force cross exchange rates to become realigned, at which time triangular arbitrage will no longer be possible.

■ Covered interest arbitrage is based on the relationship between the forward rate premium and the interest rate differential. The size of the premium or discount exhibited by the forward rate of a currency should be about the same as the differential between the interest rates of the two countries of concern. In general terms, the forward rate of the foreign currency will contain a discount (premium) if its interest rate is higher (lower) than the U.S. interest rate.

■ If the forward premium deviates substantially from the interest rate differential, covered interest arbitrage is possible. In this type of arbitrage, a foreign short-term investment in a foreign currency is covered by a forward sale of that foreign currency in the future. In this manner, the investor is not exposed to fluctuation in the foreign currency's value.

■ Interest rate parity (IRP) is a theory that states that the size of the forward premium (or discount) should be equal to the interest rate differential between the two countries of concern. When IRP

exists, covered interest arbitrage is not feasible because any interest rate advantage in the foreign country will be offset by the discount on the forward rate. Thus, the act of covered interest arbitrage would generate a return that is no higher than what would be generated by a domestic investment.

POINT COUNTER-POINT

Does Arbitrage Destabilize Foreign Exchange Markets?

Point Yes. Large financial institutions have the technology to recognize when one participant in the foreign exchange market is trying to sell a currency for a higher price than another participant. They also recognize when the forward rate does not properly reflect the interest rate differential. They use arbitrage to capitalize on these situations, which results in large foreign exchange transactions. In some cases, their arbitrage involves taking large positions in a currency and then reversing their positions a few minutes later. This jumping in and out of currencies can cause abrupt price adjustments of currencies and may create more volatility in the foreign exchange market. Regulations should be created that would force financial institutions to maintain their currency positions for at least 1 month. This would result in a more stable foreign exchange market.

Counter-Point No. When financial institutions engage in arbitrage, they create pressure on the price of a

currency that will remove any pricing discrepancy. If arbitrage did not occur, pricing discrepancies would become more pronounced. Consequently, firms and individuals who use the foreign exchange market would have to spend more time searching for the best exchange rate when trading a currency. The market would become fragmented, and prices could differ substantially among banks in a region, or among regions. If the discrepancies became large enough, firms and individuals might even attempt to conduct arbitrage themselves. The arbitrage conducted by banks allows for a more integrated foreign exchange market, which ensures that foreign exchange prices quoted by any institution are in line with the market.

Who Is Correct? Use the Internet to learn more about this issue. Which argument do you support? Offer your own opinion on this issue.

SELF-TEST

Answers are provided in Appendix A at the back of the text.

1. Assume that the following spot exchange rates exist today:

$$£1 = \$1.50$$
$$C\$ = \$.75$$
$$£1 = C\$2$$

Assume no transaction costs. Based on these exchange rates, can triangular arbitrage be used to earn a profit? Explain.

2. Assume the following information:

Spot rate of £ = $1.60
180-day forward rate of £ = $1.56
180-day British interest rate = 4%
180-day U.S. interest rate = 3%

Based on this information, is covered interest arbitrage by U.S. investors feasible (assuming that U.S. investors use their own funds)? Explain.

3. Using the information in the previous question, does interest rate parity exist? Explain.

4. Explain in general terms how various forms of arbitrage can remove any discrepancies in the pricing of currencies.

5. Assume that the British pound's 1-year forward rate exhibits a discount. Assume that interest rate parity continually exists. Explain how the discount on the British pound's 1-year forward discount would change if British 1-year interest rates rose by 3 percentage points while U.S. 1-year interest rates rose by 2 percentage points.

QUESTIONS AND APPLICATIONS

1.   Locational Arbitrage. Explain the concept of locational arbitrage and the scenario necessary for it to be plausible.

2.   Locational Arbitrage. Assume the following information:

	BEAL BANK	YARDLEY BANK
Bid price of New Zealand dollar	$.401	$.398
Ask price of New Zealand dollar	$.404	$.400

Given this information, is locational arbitrage possible? If so, explain the steps involved in locational arbitrage, and compute the profit from this arbitrage if you had $1 million to use. What market forces would occur to eliminate any further possibilities of locational arbitrage?

3.   Triangular Arbitrage. Explain the concept of triangular arbitrage and the scenario necessary for it to be plausible.

4.   Triangular Arbitrage. Assume the following information:

	QUOTED PRICE
Value of Canadian dollar in U.S. dollars	$.90
Value of New Zealand dollar in U.S. dollars	$.30
Value of Canadian dollar in New Zealand dollars	NZ$3.02

Given this information, is triangular arbitrage possible? If so, explain the steps that would reflect triangular arbitrage, and compute the profit from this strategy if you had $1 million to use. What market forces would occur to eliminate any further possibilities of triangular arbitrage?

5.   Covered Interest Arbitrage. Explain the concept of covered interest arbitrage and the scenario necessary for it to be plausible.

6.   Covered Interest Arbitrage. Assume the following information:

Spot rate of Canadian dollar	= $.80
90-day forward rate of Canadian dollar	= $.79
90-day Canadian interest rate	= 4%
90-day U.S. interest rate	= 2.5%

Given this information, what would be the yield (percentage return) to a U.S. investor who used covered interest arbitrage? (Assume the investor invests $1 million.) What market forces would occur to eliminate any further possibilities of covered interest arbitrage?

7.   Covered Interest Arbitrage. Assume the following information:

Spot rate of Mexican peso	= $.100
180-day forward rate of Mexican peso	= $.098
180-day Mexican interest rate	= 6%
180-day U.S. interest rate	= 5%

Given this information, is covered interest arbitrage worthwhile for Mexican investors who have pesos to invest? Explain your answer.

8.   Effects of September 11. The terrorist attack on the United States on September 11, 2001, caused expectations of a weaker U.S. economy. Explain how such expectations could have affected U.S. interest rates and therefore have affected the forward rate premium (or discount) on various foreign currencies.

9. Interest Rate Parity. Explain the concept of interest rate parity. Provide the rationale for its possible existence.

10. Inflation Effects on the Forward Rate. Why do you think currencies of countries with high inflation rates tend to have forward discounts?

11. Covered Interest Arbitrage in Both Directions. Assume that the existing U.S. 1-year interest rate is 10 percent and the Canadian 1-year interest rate is 11 percent. Also assume that interest rate parity exists. Should the forward rate of the Canadian dollar exhibit a discount or a premium? If U.S. investors attempt covered interest arbitrage, what will be their return? If Canadian investors attempt covered interest arbitrage, what will be their return?

12. Interest Rate Parity. Why would U.S. investors consider covered interest arbitrage in France when the interest rate on euros in France is lower than the U.S. interest rate?

13. Interest Rate Parity. Consider investors who invest in either U.S. or British 1-year Treasury bills. Assume zero transaction costs and no taxes.

a. If interest rate parity exists, then the return for U.S. investors who use covered interest arbitrage will be the same as the return for U.S. investors who invest in U.S. Treasury bills. Is this statement true or false? If false, correct the statement.

b. If interest rate parity exists, then the return for British investors who use covered interest arbitrage will be the same as the return for British investors who invest in British Treasury bills. Is this statement true or false? If false, correct the statement.

14. Changes in Forward Premiums. Assume that the Japanese yen's forward rate currently exhibits a premium of 6 percent and that interest rate parity exists. If U.S. interest rates decrease, how must this premium change to maintain interest rate parity? Why might we expect the premium to change?

15. Changes in Forward Premiums. Assume that the forward rate premium of the euro was higher last month than it is today. What does this imply about interest rate differentials between the United States and Europe today compared to those last month?

16. Interest Rate Parity. If the relationship that is specified by interest rate parity does not exist at any period but does exist on average, then covered interest arbitrage should not be considered by U.S. firms. Do you agree or disagree with this statement? Explain.

17. Covered Interest Arbitrage in Both Directions. The 1-year interest rate in New Zealand is 6 percent. The 1-year U.S. interest rate is 10 percent. The spot rate of the New Zealand dollar (NZ$) is $.50. The forward rate of the New Zealand dollar is $.54. Is covered interest arbitrage feasible for U.S. investors? Is it feasible for New Zealand investors? In each case, explain why covered interest arbitrage is or is not feasible.

18. Limitations of Covered Interest Arbitrage. Assume that the 1-year U.S. interest rate is 11 percent, while the 1-year interest rate in Malaysia is 40 percent. Assume that a U.S. bank is willing to purchase the currency of that country from you 1 year from now at a discount of 13 percent. Would covered interest arbitrage be worth considering? Is there any reason why you should not attempt covered interest arbitrage in this situation? (Ignore tax effects.)

19. Covered Interest Arbitrage in Both Directions. Assume that the annual U.S. interest rate is currently 8 percent and Germany's annual interest rate is currently 9 percent. The euro's 1-year forward rate currently exhibits a discount of 2 percent.

a. Does interest rate parity exist?

b. Can a U.S. firm benefit from investing funds in Germany using covered interest arbitrage?

c. Can a German subsidiary of a U.S. firm benefit by investing funds in the United States through covered interest arbitrage?

20. Covered Interest Arbitrage. The South African rand has a 1-year forward premium of 2 percent. One-year interest rates in the United States are 3 percentage points higher than in South Africa. Based on this information, is covered interest arbitrage possible for a U.S. investor if interest rate parity holds?

21. Deriving the Forward Rate. Assume that annual interest rates in the United States are 4 percent, while interest rates in France are 6 percent.

a. According to IRP, what should the forward rate premium or discount of the euro be?

b. If the euro's spot rate is $1.10, what should the 1-year forward rate of the euro be?

22. Covered Interest Arbitrage in Both Directions. The following information is available:

- You have 500,000 to invest.
- The current spot rate of the Moroccan dirham is $.110.

- The 60-day forward rate of the Moroccan dirham is $.108.
- The 60-day interest rate in the United States is 1 percent.
- The 60-day interest rate in Morocco is 2 percent.

a. What is the yield to a U.S. investor who conducts covered interest arbitrage? Did covered interest arbitrage work for the investor in this case?

b. Would covered interest arbitrage be possible for a Moroccan investor in this case?

Advanced Questions

23. Economic Effects on the Forward Rate. Assume that Mexico's economy has expanded significantly, causing a high demand for loanable funds there by local firms. How might these conditions affect the forward discount of the Mexican peso?

24. Differences among Forward Rates. Assume that the 30-day forward premium of the euro is –1 percent, while the 90-day forward premium of the euro is 2 percent. Explain the likely interest rate conditions that would cause these premiums. Does this ensure that covered interest arbitrage is worthwhile?

25. Testing Interest Rate Parity. Describe a method for testing whether interest rate parity exists. Why are transaction costs, currency restrictions, and differential tax laws important when evaluating whether covered interest arbitrage can be beneficial?

26. Deriving the Forward Rate. Before the Asian crisis began, Asian central banks were maintaining a somewhat stable value for their respective currencies. Nevertheless, the forward rate of Southeast Asian currencies exhibited a discount. Explain.

27. Interpreting Changes in the Forward Premium. Assume that interest rate parity holds. At the beginning of the month, the spot rate of the Canadian dollar is $.70, while the 1-year forward rate is $.68. Assume that U.S. interest rates increase steadily over the month. At the end of the month, the 1-year forward rate is higher than it was at the beginning of the month. Yet, the 1-year forward discount is larger (the 1-year premium is more negative) at the end of the month than it was at the beginning of the month. Explain how the relationship between the U.S. interest rate and the Canadian interest rate changed from the beginning of the month until the end of the month.

28. Interpreting a Large Forward Discount. The interest rate in Indonesia is commonly higher than the interest rate in the United States, which reflects a high expected rate of inflation there. Why should Nike consider hedging its future remittances from Indonesia to the U.S. parent even when the forward discount on the currency (rupiah) is so large?

29. Change in the Forward Premium. At the end of this month, you (owner of a U.S. firm) are meeting with a Japanese firm to which you will try to sell supplies. If you receive an order from that firm, you will obtain a forward contract to hedge the future receivables in yen. As of this morning, the forward rate of the yen and spot rate are the same. You believe that interest rate parity holds.

This afternoon, news occurs that makes you believe that the U.S. interest rates will increase substantially by the end of this month, and that the Japanese interest rate will not change. However, your expectations of the spot rate of the Japanese yen are not affected at all in the future. How will your expected dollar amount of receivables from the Japanese transaction be affected (if at all) by the news that occurred this afternoon? Explain.

30. Testing IRP. The 1-year interest rate in Singapore is 11 percent. The 1-year interest rate in the United States is 6 percent. The spot rate of the Singapore dollar (S$) is $.50 and the forward rate of the S$ is $.46. Assume zero transaction costs.

a. Does interest rate parity exist?

b. Can a U.S. firm benefit from investing funds in Singapore using covered interest arbitrage?

31. Implications of IRP. Assume that interest rate parity exists. You expect that the 1-year nominal interest rate in the United States is 7 percent, while the 1-year nominal interest rate in Australia is 11 percent. The spot rate of the Australian dollar is $.60. You will need 10 million Australian dollars in 1 year. Today, you purchase a 1-year forward contract in Australian dollars. How many U.S. dollars will you need in 1 year to fulfill your forward contract?

32. Triangular Arbitrage. You go to a bank and are given these quotes:

You can buy a euro for 14 pesos.

The bank will pay you 13 pesos for a euro.

You can buy a U.S. dollar for .9 euros.

The bank will pay you .8 euros for a U.S. dollar.

You can buy a U.S. dollar for 10 pesos.

The bank will pay you 9 pesos for a U.S. dollar.

You have $1,000. Can you use triangular arbitrage to generate a profit? If so, explain the order of the transactions that you would execute and the profit that you would earn. If you cannot earn a profit from triangular arbitrage, explain why.

33. Triangular Arbitrage. You are given these quotes by the bank:

You can sell Canadian dollars (C$) to the bank for $.70

You can buy Canadian dollars from the bank for $.73.

The bank is willing to buy dollars for 0.9 euros per dollar.

The bank is willing to sell dollars for 0.94 euros per dollar.

The bank is willing to buy Canadian dollars for 0.64 euros per C$.

The bank is willing to sell Canadian dollars for 0.68 euros per C$.

You have $100,000. Estimate your profit or loss if you would attempt triangular arbitrage by converting your dollars to euros, and then convert euros to Canadian dollars and then convert Canadian dollars to U.S. dollars.

34. Movement in Cross Exchange Rates. Assume that cross exchange rates are always proper such that triangular arbitrage is not feasible. While at the Miami airport today, you notice that a U.S. dollar can be exchanged for 125 Japanese yen or 4 Argentine pesos at the foreign exchange booth. Last year, the Japanese yen was valued at $0.01, and the Argentine peso was valued at $.30. Based on this information, the Argentine peso has changed by what percent against the Japanese yen over the last year?

35. Impact of Arbitrage on the Forward Rate. Assume that the annual U.S. interest rate is currently 6 percent and Germany's annual interest rate is currently 8 percent. The spot rate of the euro is $1.10 and the 1-year forward rate of the euro is $1.10. Assume that as covered interest arbitrage occurs, the interest rates are not affected, and the spot rate is not affected. Explain how the 1-year forward rate of the euro will change in order to restore interest rate parity, and why it will change. Your explanation should specify which type of investor (German or U.S.) would be engaging in covered interest arbitrage, whether they are buying or selling euros forward, and how that affects the forward rate of the euro.

36. IRP and Changes in the Forward Rate. Assume that interest rate parity exists. As of this morning, the 1-month interest rate in Canada was lower than the 1-month interest rate in the United States. Assume that as a result of the Fed's monetary policy this afternoon, the 1-month interest rate in the United States declined this afternoon, but was still higher than the Canadian 1-month interest rate. The 1-month interest rate in Canada remained unchanged. Based on the information, the forward rate of the Canadian dollar exhibited a _____ [discount or premium] this morning that _____[increased or decreased] this afternoon. Explain.

37. Deriving the Forward Rate Premium. Assume that the spot rate of the Brazilian real is $.30 today. Assume that interest rate parity exists. Obtain the interest rate data you need from Bloomberg.com to derive the 1-year forward rate premium (or discount), and then determine the 1-year forward rate of the Brazilian real.

38. Change in the Forward Premium over Time. Assume that interest rate parity exists and will continue to exist. As of today, the 1-year interest rate of Singapore is 4 percent versus 7 percent in the United States. The Singapore central bank is expected to decrease interest rates in the future so that as of December 1, you expect that the 1-year interest rate in Singapore will be 2 percent. The U.S. interest rate is not expected to change over time. Based on the information, explain how the forward premium (or discount) is expected to change by December 1.

39. Forward Rates for Different Time Horizons. Assume that interest rate parity (IRP) exists. Assume this information provided by today's *Wall Street Journal*:

Spot rate of British pound = $1.80

6-month forward rate of pound = $1.82

12-month forward rate of pound = $1.78

a. Is the annualized 6-month U.S. risk-free interest rate above, below, or equal to the British risk-free interest rate?

b. Is the 12-month U.S. risk-free interest rate above, below, or equal to the British risk-free interest rate?

40. Interpreting Forward Rate Information. Assume that interest rate parity exists. The 6-month forward rate of the Swiss franc has a premium while the 12-month forward rate of the Swiss franc has a discount. What does this tell you about the relative level of Swiss interest rates versus U.S. interest rates?

41. IRP and Speculation in Currency Futures. Assume that interest rate parity exists. The spot rate of the Argentine peso is $.40. The 1-year interest rate in the United States is 7 percent versus 12 percent in Argentina. Assume the futures price is equal to the forward rate. An investor purchased futures contracts on Argentine pesos, representing a total of 1,000,000 pesos. Determine the total dollar amount of profit or loss from this futures contract based on the expectation that the Argentine peso will be worth $.42 in 1 year.

42. Profit from Covered Interest Arbitrage. Today, the 1-year U.S. interest rate is 4 percent, while the 1-year interest rate in Argentina is 17 percent. The spot rate of the Argentine peso (AP) is $.44. The 1-year forward rate of the AP exhibits a 14 percent discount. Determine the yield (percentage return on investment) to an investor from Argentina who engages in covered interest arbitrage.

43. Assessing Whether IRP Exists. Assume zero transaction costs. As of now, the Japanese 1-year interest rate is 3 percent, and the U.S. 1-year interest rate is 9 percent. The spot rate of the Japanese yen is $.0090 and the 1-year forward rate of the Japanese yen is $.0097.

a. Determine whether interest rate parity exists, or whether the quoted forward rate is too high or too low.
b. Based on the information provided in (a), is covered interest arbitrage feasible for U.S. investors, for Japanese investors, for both types of investors, or for neither type of investor?

44. Change in Forward Rate Due to Arbitrage. Earlier this morning, the annual U.S. interest rate was 6 percent and Mexico's annual interest rate was 8 percent. The spot rate of the Mexican peso was $.16. The 1-year forward rate of the peso was $.15. Assume that as covered interest arbitrage occurred this morning, the interest rates were not affected, and the spot rate was not affected, but the forward rate was affected, and consequently interest rate parity now exists. Explain which type of investor (Mexican or U.S.) engaged in covered interest arbitrage, whether they were buying or selling pesos forward, and how that affected the forward rate of the peso.

45. IRP Relationship. Assume that interest rate parity (IRP) exists. Assume this information provided by today's *Wall Street Journal*:

Spot rate of Swiss franc = $.80

6-month forward rate of Swiss franc = $.78

12-month forward rate of Swiss franc = $.81

Assume that the annualized U.S. interest rate is 7 percent for a 6-month maturity and a 12-month maturity. Do you think the Swiss interest rate for a 6-month maturity is greater than, equal to, or less than the U.S. interest rate for a 6-month maturity? Explain.

46. Impact of Arbitrage on the Forward Rate. Assume that the annual U.S. interest rate is currently 8 percent and Japan's annual interest rate is currently 7 percent. The spot rate of the Japanese yen is $.01. The 1-year forward rate of the Japanese yen is $.01. Assume that as covered interest arbitrage occurs the interest rates are not affected and the spot rate is not affected. Explain how the 1-year forward rate of the yen will change in order to restore interest rate parity, and why it will change. [Your explanation should specify which type of investor (Japanese or U.S.) would be engaging in covered interest arbitrage and whether these investors are buying or selling yen forward, and how that affects the forward rate of the yen.]

47. Profit from Triangular Arbitrage. The bank is willing to buy dollars for 0.9 euros per dollar. It is willing to sell dollars for 0.91 euros per dollar.

You can sell Australian dollars (A$) to the bank for $.72.

You can buy Australian dollars from the bank for $.74.

The bank is willing to buy Australian dollars (A$) for 0.68 euros per A$.

The bank is willing to sell Australian dollars (A$) for 0.70 euros per A$.

You have $100,000. Estimate your profit or loss if you were to attempt triangular arbitrage by converting your dollars to Australian dollars, then converting Australian dollars to euros, and then converting euros to U.S. dollars.

48. Profit from Triangular Arbitrage. Alabama Bank is willing to buy or sell British pounds for

$1.98. The bank is willing to buy or sell Mexican pesos at an exchange rate of 10 pesos per dollar. The bank is willing to purchase British pounds at an exchange rate of 1 peso = .05 British pounds. Show how you can make a profit from triangular arbitrage and what your profit would be if you had $100,000.

Discussion in the Boardroom

This exercise can be found in Appendix E at the back of this textbook.

Running Your Own MNC

This exercise can be found on the *International Financial Management* text companion website located at www.cengage.com/finance/madura.

BLADES, INC. CASE

Assessment of Potential Arbitrage Opportunities

Recall that Blades, a U.S. manufacturer of roller blades, has chosen Thailand as its primary export target for Speedos, Blades' primary product. Moreover, Blades' primary customer in Thailand, Entertainment Products, has committed itself to purchase 180,000 Speedos annually for the next 3 years at a fixed price denominated in baht, Thailand's currency. Because of quality and cost considerations, Blades also imports some of the rubber and plastic components needed to manufacture Speedos from Thailand.

Lately, Thailand has experienced weak economic growth and political uncertainty. As investors lost confidence in the Thai baht as a result of the political uncertainty, they withdrew their funds from the country. This resulted in an excess supply of baht for sale over the demand for baht in the foreign exchange market, which put downward pressure on the baht's value. As foreign investors continued to withdraw their funds from Thailand, the baht's value continued to deteriorate. Since Blades has net cash flows in baht resulting from its exports to Thailand, a deterioration in the baht's value will affect the company negatively.

Ben Holt, Blades' CFO, would like to ensure that the spot and forward rates Blades' bank has quoted are reasonable. If the exchange rate quotes are reasonable, then arbitrage will not be possible. If the quotations are not appropriate, however, arbitrage may be possible. Under these conditions, Holt would like Blades to use some form of arbitrage to take advantage of possible mispricing in the foreign exchange market. Although Blades is not an arbitrageur, Holt believes that arbitrage opportunities could offset the negative impact resulting from the baht's depreciation, which would otherwise seriously affect Blades' profit margins.

Ben Holt has identified three arbitrage opportunities as profitable and would like to know which one of them is the most profitable. Thus, he has asked you, Blades' financial analyst, to prepare an analysis of the arbitrage opportunities he has identified. This would allow Holt to assess the profitability of arbitrage opportunities very quickly.

1. The first arbitrage opportunity relates to locational arbitrage. Holt has obtained spot rate quotations from two banks in Thailand: Minzu Bank and Sobat Bank, both located in Bangkok. The bid and ask prices of Thai baht for each bank are displayed in the table below:

	MINZU BANK	SOBAT BANK
Bid	$.0224	$.0228
Ask	$.0227	$.0229

Determine whether the foreign exchange quotations are appropriate. If they are not appropriate, determine the profit you could generate by withdrawing $100,000 from Blades' checking account and engaging in arbitrage before the rates are adjusted.

2. Besides the bid and ask quotes for the Thai baht provided in the previous question, Minzu Bank has provided the following quotations for the U.S. dollar and the Japanese yen:

	QUOTED BID PRICE	QUOTED ASK PRICE
Value of a Japanese yen in U.S. dollars	$.0085	$.0086
Value of a Thai baht in Japanese yen	¥2.69	¥2.70

Determine whether the cross exchange rate between the Thai baht and Japanese yen is appropriate. If it is not appropriate, determine the profit you could generate for Blades by withdrawing $100,000 from Blades' checking account and engaging in triangular arbitrage before the rates are adjusted.

3. Ben Holt has obtained several forward contract quotations for the Thai baht to determine whether covered interest arbitrage may be possible. He was quoted a forward rate of $.0225 per Thai baht for a 90-day forward contract. The current spot rate is $.0227. Ninety-day interest rates available to Blades in the United States are 2 percent, while 90-day interest rates in Thailand are 3.75 percent (these rates are not annualized). Holt is aware that covered interest arbitrage, unlike locational and triangular arbitrage, requires an investment of funds. Thus, he would like to be able to estimate the dollar profit resulting from arbitrage over and above the dollar amount available on a 90-day U.S. deposit.

Determine whether the forward rate is priced appropriately. If it is not priced appropriately, determine the profit you could generate for Blades by withdrawing $100,000 from Blades' checking account and engaging in covered interest arbitrage. Measure the profit as the excess amount above what you could generate by investing in the U.S. money market.

4. Why are arbitrage opportunities likely to disappear soon after they have been discovered? To illustrate your answer, assume that covered interest arbitrage involving the immediate purchase and forward sale of baht is possible. Discuss how the baht's spot and forward rates would adjust until covered interest arbitrage is no longer possible. What is the resulting equilibrium state called?

SMALL BUSINESS DILEMMA

Assessment of Prevailing Spot and Forward Rates by the Sports Exports Company

As the Sports Exports Company exports footballs to the United Kingdom, it receives British pounds. The check (denominated in pounds) for last month's exports just arrived. Jim Logan (owner of the Sports Exports Company) normally deposits the check with his local bank and requests that the bank convert the check to dollars at the prevailing spot rate (assuming that he did not use a forward contract to hedge this payment). Jim's local bank provides foreign exchange services for many of its business customers who need to buy or sell widely traded currencies. Today, however, Jim decided to check the quotations of the spot rate at other banks before converting the payment into dollars.

1. Do you think Jim will be able to find a bank that provides him with a more favorable spot rate than his local bank? Explain.

2. Do you think that Jim's bank is likely to provide more reasonable quotations for the spot rate of the British pound if it is the only bank in town that provides foreign exchange services? Explain.

3. Jim is considering using a forward contract to hedge the anticipated receivables in pounds next month. His local bank quoted him a spot rate of $1.65 and a 1-month forward rate of $1.6435. Before Jim decides to sell pounds 1 month forward, he wants to be sure that the forward rate is reasonable, given the prevailing spot rate. A 1-month Treasury security in the United States currently offers a yield (not annualized) of 1 percent, while a 1-month Treasury security in the United Kingdom offers a yield of 1.4 percent. Do you believe that the 1-month forward rate is reasonable given the spot rate of $1.65?

INTERNET/EXCEL EXERCISE

The Bloomberg website provides quotations in foreign exchange markets. Its address is www.bloomberg.com.

Use this web page to determine the cross exchange rate between the Canadian dollar and the Japanese yen.

Notice that the value of the pound (in dollars) and the value of the yen (in dollars) are also disclosed. Based on these values, is the cross rate between the Canadian dollar and the yen what you expected it to be? Explain.

REFERENCES

Baillie, Richard T., and Rehim Kilic, Feb 2006, Do Asymmetric and Nonlinear Adjustments Explain the Forward Premium Anomaly? *Journal of International Money and Finance,* pp. 22–47.

Chinn, Menzie D., Feb 2006, The (Partial) Rehabilitation of Interest Rate Parity in the Floating Rate Era: Longer Horizons, Alternative Expectations, and Emerging Markets, *Journal of International Money and Finance,* pp. 7–21.

Ghemawat, Pankaj, Nov 2003, The Forgotten Strategy, *Harvard Business Review,* pp. 76–87.

Shrestha, Keshab, and Kok Hui Tan, Sep 2005, Real Interest Rate Parity: Long-Run and Short-Run Analysis Using Wavelets, *Review of Quantitative Finance and Accounting,* pp. 139–157.

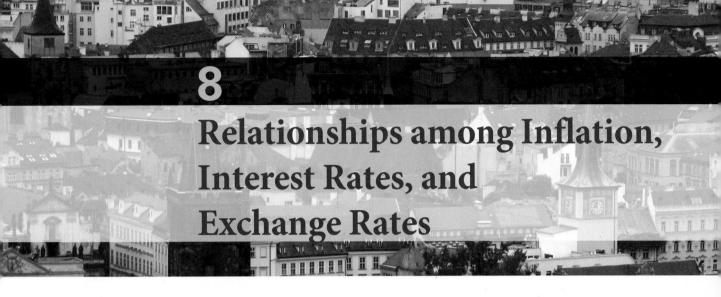

8
Relationships among Inflation, Interest Rates, and Exchange Rates

CHAPTER OBJECTIVES

The specific objectives of this chapter are to:

■ explain the purchasing power parity (PPP) theory and its implications for exchange rate changes,

■ explain the international Fisher effect (IFE) theory and its implications for exchange rate changes, and

■ compare the PPP theory, the IFE theory, and the theory of interest rate parity (IRP), which was introduced in the previous chapter.

Inflation rates and interest rates can have a significant impact on exchange rates (as explained in Chapter 4) and therefore can influence the value of MNCs. Financial managers of MNCs must understand how inflation and interest rates can affect exchange rates so that they can anticipate how their MNCs may be affected. Given their potential influence on MNC values, inflation and interest rates deserve to be studied more closely.

PURCHASING POWER PARITY (PPP)

In Chapter 4, the expected impact of relative inflation rates on exchange rates was discussed. Recall from this discussion that when a country's inflation rate rises, the demand for its currency declines as its exports decline (due to its higher prices). In addition, consumers and firms in that country tend to increase their importing. Both of these forces place downward pressure on the high-inflation country's currency. Inflation rates often vary among countries, causing international trade patterns and exchange rates to adjust accordingly. One of the most popular and controversial theories in international finance is the **purchasing power parity (PPP) theory**, which attempts to quantify the inflation–exchange rate relationship.

Interpretations of Purchasing Power Parity

There are two popular forms of PPP theory, each of which has its own implications.

Absolute Form of PPP. The **absolute form of PPP** is based on the notion that without international barriers, consumers shift their demand to wherever prices are lower. It suggests that prices of the same basket of products in two different countries should be equal when measured in a common currency. If a discrepancy in prices as measured by a common currency exists, the demand should shift so that these prices converge.

EXAMPLE

If the same basket of products is produced by the United States and the United Kingdom, and the price in the United Kingdom is lower when measured in a common currency, the demand for that basket should increase in the United Kingdom and decline in the United States. Both forces would cause the prices of the baskets to be similar when measured in a common currency. ●

Realistically, the existence of transportation costs, tariffs, and quotas may prevent the absolute form of PPP. If transportation costs were high in the preceding example, the demand for the baskets of products might not shift as suggested. Thus, the discrepancy in prices would continue.

234   Part 2: Exchange Rate Behavior

Relative Form of PPP. The **relative form of PPP** accounts for the possibility of market imperfections such as transportation costs, tariffs, and quotas. This version acknowledges that because of these market imperfections, prices of the same basket of products in different countries will not necessarily be the same when measured in a common currency. It does state, however, that the rate of change in the prices of the baskets should be somewhat similar when measured in a common currency, as long as the transportation costs and trade barriers are unchanged.

Assume that the United States and the United Kingdom trade extensively with each other and initially have zero inflation. Now assume that the United States experiences a 9 percent inflation rate, while the United Kingdom experiences a 5 percent inflation rate. Under these conditions, PPP theory suggests that the British pound should appreciate by approximately 4 percent, the differential in inflation rates. Given British inflation of 5 percent and the pound's appreciation of 4 percent, U.S. consumers will be paying about 9 percent more for the British goods than they paid in the initial equilibrium state. This is equal to the 9 percent increase in prices of U.S. goods from the U.S. inflation. The exchange rate should adjust to offset the differential in the inflation rates of the two countries, so that the prices of goods in the two countries should appear similar to consumers. ●

Rationale behind Relative PPP Theory

The rationale behind the relative PPP theory is that exchange rate adjustment is necessary for the relative purchasing power to be the same whether buying products locally or from another country. If the purchasing power is not equal, consumers will shift purchases to wherever products are cheaper until the purchasing power is equal.

Reconsider the previous example, and assume that the pound appreciated by only 1 percent in response to the inflation differential. In this case, the increased price of British goods to U.S. consumers will be approximately 6 percent (5 percent inflation and 1 percent appreciation in the British pound), which is less than the 9 percent increase in the price of U.S. goods to U.S. consumers. Thus, we would expect U.S. consumers to continue to shift their consumption to British goods. Purchasing power parity suggests that the increasing U.S. consumption of British goods by U.S. consumers would persist until the pound appreciated by about 4 percent. Any level of appreciation lower than this would represent more attractive British prices relative to U.S. prices from the U.S. consumer's viewpoint.

From the British consumer's point of view, the price of U.S. goods would have initially increased by 4 percent more than British goods. Thus, British consumers would continue to reduce imports from the United States until the pound appreciated enough to make U.S. goods no more expensive than British goods. Once the pound appreciated by 4 percent, the net effect is that the prices of U.S. goods would increase by approximately 5 percent to British consumers (9 percent inflation minus the 4 percent savings to British consumers due to the pound's 4 percent appreciation). ●

Derivation of Purchasing Power Parity

Assume that the price indexes of the home country (h) and a foreign country (f) are equal. Now assume that over time, the home country experiences an inflation rate of I_h, while the foreign country experiences an inflation rate of I_f. Due to inflation, the price index of goods in the consumer's home country (P_h) becomes

$$P_h(1 + I_h)$$

The price index of the foreign country (P_f) will also change due to inflation in that country:

$$P_f(1 + I_f)$$

If $I_h > I_f$ and the exchange rate between the currencies of the two countries does not change, then the consumer's purchasing power is greater on foreign goods than on home goods. In this case, PPP does not exist. If $I_h < I_f$ and the exchange rate between the currencies of the two countries does not change, then the consumer's purchasing power is greater on home goods than on foreign goods. In this case also, PPP does not exist.

The PPP theory suggests that the exchange rate will not remain constant but will adjust to maintain the parity in purchasing power. If inflation occurs and the exchange rate of the foreign currency changes, the foreign price index from the home consumer's perspective becomes

$$P_f(1 + I_f)(1 + e_f)$$

where e_f represents the percentage change in the value of the foreign currency. According to PPP theory, the percentage change in the foreign currency (e_f) should change to maintain parity in the new price indexes of the two countries. We can solve for e_f under conditions of PPP by setting the formula for the new price index of the foreign country equal to the formula for the new price index of the home country, as follows:

$$P_f(1 + I_f)(1 + e_f) = P_h(1 + I_h)$$

Solving for e_f, we obtain

$$1 + e_f = \frac{P_h(1 + I_h)}{P_f(1 + I_f)}$$

$$e_f = \frac{P_h(1 + I_h)}{P_f(1 + I_f)} - 1$$

Since P_h equals P_f (because price indexes were initially assumed equal in both countries), they cancel, leaving

$$e_f = \frac{1 + I_h}{1 + I_f} - 1$$

This formula reflects the relationship between relative inflation rates and the exchange rate according to PPP. Notice that if $I_h > I_f$, e_f should be positive. This implies that the foreign currency will appreciate when the home country's inflation exceeds the foreign country's inflation. Conversely, if $I_h < I_f$, then e_f should be negative. This implies that the foreign currency will depreciate when the foreign country's inflation exceeds the home country's inflation.

Using PPP to Estimate Exchange Rate Effects

The relative form of PPP can be used to estimate how an exchange rate will change in response to differential inflation rates between countries.

EXAMPLE

Assume that the exchange rate is in equilibrium initially. Then the home currency experiences a 5 percent inflation rate, while the foreign country experiences a 3 percent inflation rate. According to PPP, the foreign currency will adjust as follows:

$$e_f = \frac{1 + I_h}{1 + I_f} - 1$$

$$= \frac{1 + .05}{1 + .03} - 1$$

$$= .0194, \text{ or } 1.94\%$$

●

Thus, according to this example, the foreign currency should appreciate by 1.94 percent in response to the higher inflation of the home country relative to the foreign country. If this exchange rate change does occur, the price index of the foreign country will be as high as the index in the home country from the perspective of home country consumers. Even though inflation is lower in the foreign country, appreciation of the foreign currency pushes the foreign country's price index up from the perspective of consumers in the home country. When considering the exchange rate effect, price indexes of both countries rise by 5 percent from the home country perspective. Thus, consumers' purchasing power is the same for foreign goods and home goods.

EXAMPLE

This example examines the situation when foreign inflation exceeds home inflation. Assume that the exchange rate is in equilibrium initially. Then the home country experiences a 4 percent inflation rate, while the foreign country experiences a 7 percent inflation rate. According to PPP, the foreign currency will adjust as follows:

$$e_f = \frac{1 + I_h}{1 + I_f} - 1$$
$$= \frac{1 + .04}{1 + .07} - 1$$
$$= -.028, \text{or} - 2.8\%$$

Thus, according to this example, the foreign currency should depreciate by 2.8 percent in response to the higher inflation of the foreign country relative to the home country. Even though the inflation is lower in the home country, the depreciation of the foreign currency places downward pressure on the foreign country's prices from the perspective of consumers in the home country. When considering the exchange rate impact, prices of both countries rise by 4 percent. Thus, PPP still exists due to the adjustment in the exchange rate. ●

The theory of purchasing power parity is summarized in Exhibit 8.1. Notice that international trade is the mechanism by which the inflation differential affects the exchange rate according to this theory. This means that PPP is more applicable when the two countries of concern engage in much international trade with each other. If there is very little trade between the countries, the inflation differential should not have a major impact on the trade between the countries, and there is no reason to expect that the exchange rate would change.

Using a Simplified PPP Relationship. A simplified but less precise relationship based on PPP is

$$e_f \cong I_h - I_f$$

That is, the percentage change in the exchange rate should be approximately equal to the differential in inflation rates between the two countries. This simplified formula is appropriate only when the inflation differential is small or when the value of I_f is close to zero.

Graphic Analysis of Purchasing Power Parity

Using PPP theory, we should be able to assess the potential impact of inflation on exchange rates. Exhibit 8.2 is a graphic representation of PPP theory. The points on the exhibit suggest that given an inflation differential between the home and the foreign country of X percent, the foreign currency should adjust by X percent due to that inflation differential.

PPP Line. The diagonal line connecting all these points together is known as the **purchasing power parity (PPP) line.** Point A in Exhibit 8.2 represents our earlier example in which the U.S. (considered the home country) and British inflation rates were

Exhibit 8.1 Summary of Purchasing Power Parity

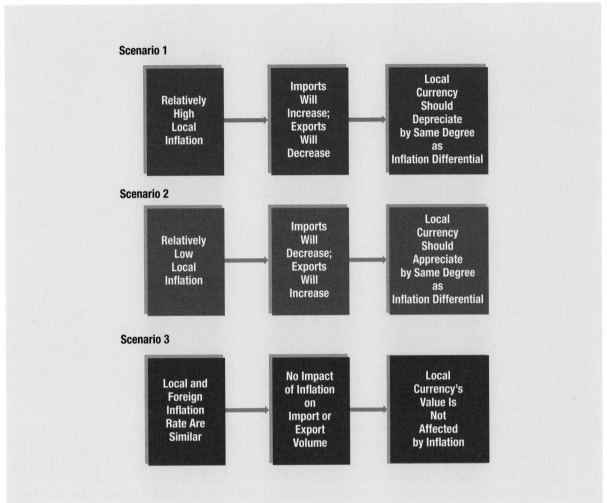

assumed to be 9 and 5 percent, respectively, so that $I_h - I_f = 4\%$. Recall that this led to the anticipated appreciation in the British pound of 4 percent, as illustrated by point A. Point B reflects a situation in which the inflation rate in the United Kingdom exceeds the inflation rate in the United States by 5 percent, so that $I_h - I_f = -5\%$. This leads to anticipated depreciation of the British pound by 5 percent, as illustrated by point B. If the exchange rate does respond to inflation differentials as PPP theory suggests, the actual points should lie on or close to the PPP line.

Purchasing Power Disparity. Exhibit 8.3 identifies areas of purchasing power disparity. Any points off of the PPP line represent purchasing power disparity. Assume an initial equilibrium situation, then a change in the inflation rates of the two countries. If the exchange rate does not move as PPP theory suggests, there is a disparity in the purchasing power of the two countries.

Point C in Exhibit 8.3 represents a situation where home inflation (I_h) exceeds foreign inflation (I_f) by 4 percent. Yet, the foreign currency appreciated by only 1 percent in response to this inflation differential. Consequently, purchasing power disparity exists. Home country consumers' purchasing power for foreign goods has become more favorable relative

Exhibit 8.2 Illustration of Purchasing Power Parity

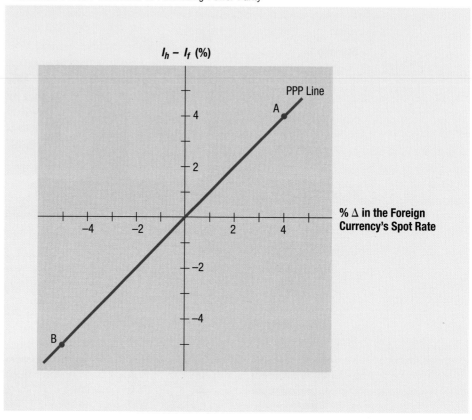

to their purchasing power for the home country's goods. The PPP theory suggests that such a disparity in purchasing power should exist only in the short run. Over time, as the home country consumers take advantage of the disparity by purchasing more foreign goods, upward pressure on the foreign currency's value will cause point C to move toward the PPP line. All points to the left of (or above) the PPP line represent more favorable purchasing power for foreign goods than for home goods.

Point D in Exhibit 8.3 represents a situation where home inflation is 3 percent below foreign inflation. Yet, the foreign currency has depreciated by only 2 percent. Again, purchasing power disparity exists. The purchasing power for foreign goods has become less favorable relative to the purchasing power for the home country's goods. The PPP theory suggests that the foreign currency in this example should have depreciated by 3 percent to fully offset the 3 percent inflation differential. Since the foreign currency did not weaken to this extent, the home country consumers may cease purchasing foreign goods, causing the foreign currency to weaken to the extent anticipated by PPP theory. If so, point D would move toward the PPP line. All points to the right of (or below) the PPP line represent more favorable purchasing power for home country goods than for foreign goods.

Testing the Purchasing Power Parity Theory

The PPP theory not only provides an explanation of how relative inflation rates between two countries can influence an exchange rate, but it also provides information that can be used to forecast exchange rates.

Exhibit 8.3 Identifying Disparity in Purchasing Power

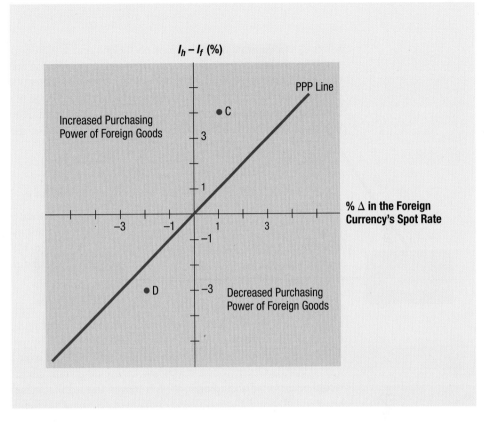

Conceptual Tests of PPP. One way to test the PPP theory is to choose two countries (say, the United States and a foreign country) and compare the differential in their inflation rates to the percentage change in the foreign currency's value during several time periods. Using a graph similar to Exhibit 8.3, we could plot each point representing the inflation differential and exchange rate percentage change for each specific time period and then determine whether these points closely resemble the PPP line as drawn in Exhibit 8.3. If the points deviate significantly from the PPP line, then the percentage change in the foreign currency is not being influenced by the inflation differential in the manner PPP theory suggests.

As an alternative test, several foreign countries could be compared with the home country over a given time period. Each foreign country will exhibit an inflation differential relative to the home country, which can be compared to the exchange rate change during the period of concern. Thus, a point can be plotted on a graph such as Exhibit 8.3 for each foreign country analyzed. If the points deviate significantly from the PPP line, then the exchange rates are not responding to the inflation differentials in accordance with PPP theory. The PPP theory can be tested for any countries on which inflation information is available.

Statistical Test of PPP. A somewhat simplified statistical test of PPP can be developed by applying regression analysis to historical exchange rates and inflation differentials (see Appendix C for more information on regression analysis). To illustrate, let's focus on one particular exchange rate. The quarterly percentage changes in the foreign currency value (e_f) can be regressed against the inflation differential that existed at the beginning of each quarter, as shown here:

$$e_f = a_0 + a_1\left(\frac{1 + I_{U.S.}}{1 + I_f} - 1\right) + \mu$$

where a_0 is a constant, a_1 is the slope coefficient, and μ is an error term. Regression analysis would be applied to quarterly data to determine the regression coefficients. The hypothesized values of a_0 and a_1 are 0 and 1.0, respectively. These coefficients imply that for a given inflation differential, there is an equal offsetting percentage change in the exchange rate, on average. The appropriate t-test for each regression coefficient requires a comparison to the hypothesized value and division by the standard error (s.e.) of the coefficient as follows:

Test for $a_0 = 0$:   Test for $a_1 = 1$:

$$t = \frac{a_0 - 0}{\text{s.e. of } a_0} \qquad t = \frac{a_1 - 1}{\text{s.e. of } a_1}$$

Then the t-table is used to find the critical t-value. If either t-test finds that the coefficients differ significantly from what is expected, the relationship between the inflation differential and the exchange rate differs from that stated by PPP theory. It should be mentioned that the appropriate lag time between the inflation differential and the exchange rate is subject to controversy.

Results of Tests of PPP. Much research has been conducted to test whether PPP exists. Studies by Mishkin, Adler and Dumas, and Abuaf and Jorion[1] found evidence of significant deviations from PPP that persisted for lengthy periods. A related study by Adler and Lehman[2] provided evidence against PPP even over the long term.

Hakkio[3], however, found that when an exchange rate deviated far from the value that would be expected according to PPP, it moved toward that value. Although the relationship between inflation differentials and exchange rates is not perfect even in the long run, it supports the use of inflation differentials to forecast long-run movements in exchange rates.

Tests of PPP for Each Currency. To further examine whether PPP is valid, Exhibit 8.4 illustrates the relationship between relative inflation rates and exchange rate movements over time. The inflation differential shown in each of the four graphs (each graph represents one foreign currency) is measured as the U.S. inflation rate minus the foreign inflation rate. The annual differential in inflation between the United States and each foreign country is represented on the vertical axis. The annual percentage change in the exchange rate of each foreign currency (relative to the U.S. dollar) is represented on the horizontal axis. The annual inflation differentials and percentage changes in exchange rates from 1982 to 2009 are plotted. If PPP existed during the period examined, the points plotted on the graph should be near an imaginary 45-degree line, which would split the axes (like the PPP line shown in Exhibit 8.3).

Although each graph shows different results, some general comments apply to all four graphs. The percentage changes in exchange rates are typically much more volatile than the inflation differentials. Thus, the exchange rates are changing to a greater degree than

[1]Frederic S. Mishkin, "Are Real Interest Rates Equal Across Countries? An Empirical Investigation of International Parity Conditions," *Journal of Finance* (December 1984): 1345–1357; Michael Adler and Bernard Dumas, "International Portfolio Choice and Corporate Finance: A Synthesis," *Journal of Finance* (June 1983): 925–984; Niso Abuaf and Philippe Jorion, "Purchasing Power in the Long Run," *Journal of Finance* (March 1990): 157–174.

[2]Michael Adler and Bruce Lehman, "Deviations from Purchasing Power Parity in the Long Run," *Journal of Finance* (December 1983): 1471–1487.

[3]Craig S. Hakkio, "Interest Rates and Exchange Rates—What Is the Relationship?" *Economic Review*, Federal Reserve Bank of Kansas City (November 1986): 33–43.

Exhibit 8.4 Comparison of Annual Inflation Differentials and Exchange Rate Movements for Four Major Countries

WEB

www.bls.gov/bls/
inflation.htm

Inflation information
provided for various
countries.

PPP theory would predict. In some years, even the direction of a currency could not have been anticipated by PPP theory. The results in Exhibit 8.4 suggest that the relationship between inflation differentials and exchange rate movements often becomes distorted.

Limitation of PPP Tests. A limitation in testing PPP theory is that the results will vary with the base period used. The base period chosen should reflect an equilibrium position since subsequent periods are evaluated in comparison to it. If a base period is used when the foreign currency was relatively weak for reasons other than high inflation, most subsequent periods could show higher appreciation of that currency than what would be predicted by PPP.

Why Purchasing Power Parity Does Not Occur

Purchasing power parity does not consistently occur because of confounding effects and because of a lack of substitutes for some traded goods. These reasons are explained next.

Confounding Effects. The PPP theory presumes that exchange rate movements are driven completely by the inflation differential between two countries. Yet, recall from Chapter 4 that a change in a currency's spot rate is influenced by the following factors:

$$e = f(\Delta INF, \Delta INT, \Delta INC, \Delta GC, \Delta EXP)$$

where

e = percentage change in the spot rate

ΔINF = change in the differential between U.S. inflation and the foreign country's inflation

ΔINT = change in the differential between the U.S. interest rate and the foreign country's interest rate

ΔINC = change in the differential between the U.S. income level and the foreign country's income level

ΔGC = change in government controls

ΔEXP = change in expectations of future exchange rates

Since the exchange rate movement is not driven solely by ΔINF, the relationship between the inflation differential and the exchange rate movement is not as simple as suggested by PPP.

EXAMPLE

Assume that Venezuela's inflation rate is 5 percent above the U.S. inflation rate. From this information, PPP theory would suggest that the Venezuelan bolivar should depreciate by about 5 percent against the U.S. dollar. Yet, if the government of Venezuela imposes trade barriers against U.S. exports, Venezuela's consumers and firms will not be able to adjust their spending in reaction to the inflation differential. Therefore, the exchange rate will not adjust as suggested by PPP. ●

No Substitutes for Traded Goods. The idea behind PPP theory is that as soon as the prices become relatively higher in one country, consumers in the other country will stop buying imported goods and shift to purchasing domestic goods instead. This shift influences the exchange rate. But, if substitute goods are not available domestically, consumers may not stop buying imported goods.

EXAMPLE

Reconsider the previous example in which Venezuela's inflation is 5 percent higher than the U.S. inflation rate. If U.S. consumers do not find suitable substitute goods at home, they may continue to buy the highly priced goods from Venezuela, and the bolivar may not depreciate as expected according to PPP theory. ●

Purchasing Power Parity in the Long Run

Purchasing power parity can be tested over the long run by assessing a "real" exchange rate between two currencies over time. The real exchange rate is the actual exchange rate adjusted for inflationary effects in the two countries of concern. In this way, the exchange rate serves as a measure of purchasing power. If a currency weakens by 10 percent but its home inflation is 10 percent more than inflation in the foreign country, the real exchange rate has not changed. The degree of weakness in the currency is offset by the lower inflationary effects on foreign goods.

WEB

http://finance.yahoo
.com/
Information about anticipated inflation and exchange rates for each country.

If the real exchange rate reverts to some mean level over time, this suggests that it is constant in the long run, and any deviations from the mean are temporary. Conversely, if the real exchange rate moves randomly without any predictable pattern, it does not revert to some mean level and therefore cannot be viewed as constant in the long run. Under these conditions, the notion of PPP is rejected because the movements in the real exchange rate appear to be more than temporary deviations from some equilibrium value.

The study by Abuaf and Jorion,[4] mentioned earlier, tested PPP by assessing the long-run pattern of the real exchange rate. Abuaf and Jorion state that the typical findings rejecting PPP in previous studies are questionable because of limitations in the methods used to test PPP. They suggest that deviations from PPP are substantial in the short run but are reduced by about half in 3 years. Thus, even though exchange rates deviate from the levels predicted by PPP in the short run, their deviations are reduced over the long run.

INTERNATIONAL FISHER EFFECT (IFE)

Along with PPP theory, another major theory in international finance is the **international Fisher effect (IFE)** theory. It uses interest rate rather than inflation rate differentials to explain why exchange rates change over time, but it is closely related to the PPP theory because interest rates are often highly correlated with inflation rates.

The first step in understanding the international Fisher effect is to recognize how a country's nominal interest rate and inflation rate are related. The following example illustrates this relationship by comparing two countries.

Assume that inflation is expected to be very high in Canada during the next year. As a result, the people in Canada will prefer to spend money now rather than save in order to obtain products before prices rise. They will also be more willing to borrow in order to purchase products now before prices increase. Thus, the high expected inflation results in a small supply of loanable funds (savings), a large demand for loanable funds, and a high nominal (quoted) interest rate. Canada's nominal interest rate will need to exceed the expected inflation rate in Canada in order to entice some people to save.

Meanwhile, assume that inflation is expected to be moderate in the United States during the next year. As a result, people in the United States are more willing to save money because they are less concerned with possible price changes due to inflation. Since inflation is not a major concern, there is a large supply of loanable funds, a low demand for loanable funds, and a low nominal interest rate.

The nominal interest rate in the United States should be lower than in Canada because its inflation is lower. ●

The example above illustrates how expected inflation can affect the nominal interest rate. The **Fisher effect** suggests that the nominal interest rate contains two components: (1) expected inflation rate and (2) real rate of interest. This means that the real rate of interest is the nominal interest rate minus the expected inflation rate. The real rate of interest is not directly observable. However, by assuming a specific real rate of return in a country and observing the nominal interest rate, we can derive the expected inflation rate of a country.

The international Fisher effect is the application of the Fisher effect to two countries in order to derive the expected change in the exchange rate. It suggests that nominal interest rates of two countries differ because of the difference in expected inflation between the two countries. In fact, the theory suggests that if the real interest rate is assumed to be the same in the two countries, the difference in the nominal interest rates between two countries is completely attributed to the difference in the expected inflation rates between the two countries. This international Fisher effect is very useful because it only requires data on the nominal risk-free interest rates of the two countries of concern to derive an expected movement in the exchange rate. It also offers very important implications for MNCs whose business operations are affected by exchange rate movements.

Assume that the real interest rate is 2 percent in Canada and is also 2 percent in the United States. The nominal risk-free interest rate of each country is widely publicized and can be easily obtained. Assume the 1-year risk-free interest rate is 13 percent in Canada versus 8 percent in the United

---

[4]Abuaf and Jorion, "Purchasing Power in the Long Run."

States. The expected inflation in Canada is 13% − 2% = 11%. The expected inflation rate in the United States is 8% − 2% = 6%. The difference between expected inflation of the two countries is 11% − 6% = 5%. The international Fisher effect borrows from the theory of purchasing power parity (PPP) to derive an expected exchange rate movement based on the expected inflation rate. Since the expected inflation is 5 percent higher in Canada than the United States, the Canadian dollar is expected to decline against the dollar by about 5 percent. U.S. investors would earn 8 percent on the Canadian investment, which is the same as they could earn in the United States. ●

Implications of the International Fisher Effect

The international Fisher effect (IFE) theory suggests that currencies with high interest rates will have high expected inflation and therefore will be expected to depreciate. Therefore, MNCs and investors based in the United States may not necessarily attempt to invest in interest-bearing securities in those countries because the exchange rate effect could offset the interest rate advantage. The exchange rate effect is not expected to perfectly offset the interest rate advantage in every period. It could be less pronounced in some periods and more pronounced in other periods. But advocates of the IFE would suggest that on average, MNCs and investors that attempt to invest in interest-bearing securities with high interest rates would not benefit because the best guess of the return (after accounting for the exchange rate effect) in any period would be equal to what they could earn domestically.

Implications of the IFE for Foreign Investors

The implications are similar for foreign investors who attempt to capitalize on relatively high U.S. interest rates. The foreign investors will be adversely affected by the effects of a relatively high U.S. inflation rate if they try to capitalize on the high U.S. interest rates.

EXAMPLE

The nominal interest rate is 8 percent in the United States and 5 percent in Japan. The expected real rate of return is 2 percent in each country. The U.S. inflation rate is expected to be 6 percent, while the inflation rate in Japan is expected to be 3 percent.

According to PPP theory, the Japanese yen is expected to appreciate by the expected inflation differential of 3 percent. If the exchange rate changes as expected, Japanese investors who attempt to capitalize on the higher U.S. interest rate will earn a return similar to what they could have earned in their own country. Though the U.S. interest rate is 3 percent higher, the Japanese investors will repurchase their yen at the end of the investment period for 3 percent more than the price at which they sold yen. Therefore, their return from investing in the United States is no better than what they would have earned domestically. ●

The IFE theory can be applied to any exchange rate, even exchange rates that involve two non-U.S. currencies.

EXAMPLE

WEB

www.ny.frb.org/
research/global_
economy/index.html
Exchange rate and in-
terest rate data for
various countries.

Assume that the nominal interest rate is 13 percent in Canada and 5 percent in Japan. Assume the expected real rate of interest is 2 percent in each country. The expected inflation differential between Canada and Japan is 8 percent. According to PPP theory, this inflation differential suggests that the Canadian dollar should depreciate by 8 percent against the yen. Therefore, even though Japanese investors would earn an additional 8 percent interest on a Canadian investment, the Canadian dollar would be valued at 8 percent less by the end of the period. Under these conditions, the Japanese investors would earn a return of about 5 percent by investing in Canada, which is the same as what they would earn on an investment in Japan. ●

These possible investment opportunities, along with some others, are summarized in Exhibit 8.5. Note that wherever investors of a given country invest their funds, the expected nominal return is the same.

Exhibit 8.5 Illustration of the International Fisher Effect (IFE) from Various Investor Perspectives

INVESTORS RESIDING IN	ATTEMPT TO INVEST IN	EXPECTED INFLATION DIFFERENTIAL (HOME INFLATION MINUS FOREIGN INFLATION)	EXPECTED PERCENTAGE CHANGE IN CURRENCY NEEDED BY INVESTORS	NOMINAL INTEREST RATE TO BE EARNED	RETURN TO INVESTORS AFTER CONSIDERING EXCHANGE RATE ADJUSTMENT	INFLATION ANTICIPATED IN HOME COUNTRY	REAL RETURN EARNED BY INVESTORS
Japan	Japan	—	—	5%	5%	3%	2%
	United States	3% − 6% = −3%	−3%	8	5	3	2
	Canada	3% − 11% = −8%	−8	13	5	3	2
United States	Japan	6% − 3% = 3%	3	5	8	6	2
	United States	—	—	8	8	6	2
	Canada	6% − 11% = −5%	−5	13	8	6	2
Canada	Japan	11% − 3% = 8%	8	5	13	11	2
	United States	11% − 6% = 5%	5	8	13	11	2
	Canada	—	—	13	13	11	2

Derivation of the International Fisher Effect

The precise relationship between the interest rate differential of two countries and the expected exchange rate change according to the IFE can be derived as follows. First, the actual return to investors who invest in money market securities (such as short-term bank deposits) in their home country is simply the interest rate offered on those securities. The actual return to investors who invest in a foreign money market security, however, depends on not only the foreign interest rate (i_f) but also the percentage change in the value of the foreign currency (e_f) denominating the security. The formula for the actual or "effective" (exchange-rate-adjusted) return on a foreign bank deposit (or any money market security) is

$$r = (1 + i_f)(1 + e_f) - 1$$

According to the IFE, the effective return on a foreign investment should, on average, be equal to the interest rate on a local money market investment:

$$E(r) = i_h$$

where r is the effective return on the foreign deposit and i_h is the interest rate on the home deposit. We can determine the degree by which the foreign currency must change in order to make investments in both countries generate similar returns. Take the previous formula for what determines r and set it equal to i_h as follows:

$$r = i_h$$
$$(1 + i_f)(1 + e_f) - 1 = i_h$$

Now solve for e_f:

$$(1 + i_f)(1 + e_f) = 1 + i_h$$
$$1 + e_f = \frac{1 + i_h}{1 + i_f}$$
$$e_f = \frac{1 + i_h}{1 + i_f} - 1$$

As verified here, the IFE theory contends that when $i_h > i_f$, e_f will be positive because the relatively low foreign interest rate reflects relatively low inflationary expectations in the foreign country. That is, the foreign currency will appreciate when the foreign interest rate is lower than the home interest rate. This appreciation will improve the foreign return to investors from the home country, making returns on foreign securities similar to returns on home securities. Conversely, when $i_f > i_h$, e_f will be negative. That is, the foreign currency will depreciate when the foreign interest rate exceeds the home interest rate. This depreciation will reduce the return on foreign securities from the perspective of investors in the home country, making returns on foreign securities no higher than returns on home securities.

Numerical Example Based on the Derivation of IFE.

Given two interest rates, the value of e_f can be determined from the formula that was just derived and used to forecast the exchange rate.

EXAMPLE

Assume that the interest rate on a 1-year insured home country bank deposit is 11 percent, and the interest rate on a 1-year insured foreign bank deposit is 12 percent. For the actual returns of these two investments to be similar from the perspective of investors in the home country, the foreign currency would have to change over the investment horizon by the following percentage:

$$e_f = \frac{1 + i_h}{1 + i_f} - 1$$
$$= \frac{1 + .11}{1 + .12} - 1$$
$$= -.0089, \text{ or } -.89\%$$

The implications are that the foreign currency denominating the foreign deposit would need to depreciate by .89 percent to make the actual return on the foreign deposit equal to 11 percent from the perspective of investors in the home country. This would make the return on the foreign investment equal to the return on a domestic investment. ●

The theory of the international Fisher effect is summarized in Exhibit 8.6. Notice that this exhibit is quite similar to the summary of PPP in Exhibit 8.1. In particular, international trade is the mechanism by which the nominal interest rate differential affects the exchange rate according to the IFE theory. This means that the IFE is more applicable when the two countries of concern engage in much international trade with each other. If there is very little trade between the countries, the inflation differential should not have a major impact on the trade

Exhibit 8.6 Summary of International Fisher Effect

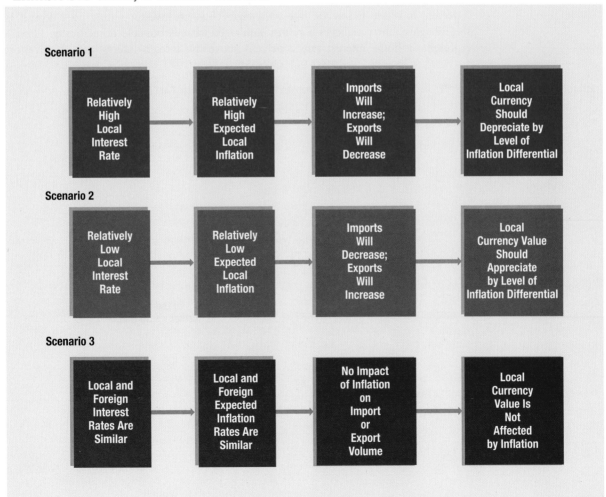

between the countries, and there is no reason to expect that the exchange rate would change in response to the interest rate differential. So even if there was a large interest rate differential between the countries (which signals a large differential in expected inflation), it would have a negligible effect on trade. In this case, investors might be more willing to invest in a foreign country with a high interest rate, although the currency of that country could still weaken for other reasons.

Simplified Relationship. A more simplified but less precise relationship specified by the IFE is

$$e_f \cong i_h - i_f$$

That is, the percentage change in the exchange rate over the investment horizon will equal the interest rate differential between two countries. This approximation provides reasonable estimates only when the interest rate differential is small.

Graphic Analysis of the International Fisher Effect

Exhibit 8.7 displays the set of points that conform to the argument behind IFE theory. For example, point E reflects a situation where the foreign interest rate exceeds the home interest rate by three percentage points. Yet, the foreign currency has depreciated by 3 percent to offset its interest rate advantage. Thus, an investor setting up a deposit in the foreign country achieves a return similar to what is possible domestically. Point F represents a home interest rate 2 percent above the foreign interest rate. If investors

Exhibit 8.7 Illustration of IFE Line (When Exchange Rate Changes Perfectly Offset Interest Rate Differentials)

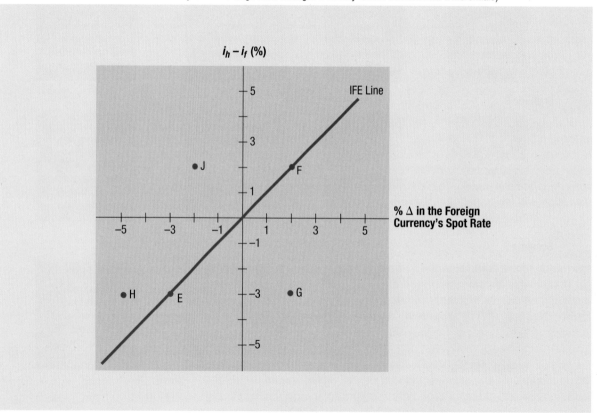

from the home country establish a foreign deposit, they are at a disadvantage regarding the foreign interest rate. However, IFE theory suggests that the currency should appreciate by 2 percent to offset the interest rate disadvantage.

Point F in Exhibit 8.7 also illustrates the IFE from a foreign investor's perspective. The home interest rate will appear attractive to the foreign investor. However, IFE theory suggests that the foreign currency will appreciate by 2 percent, which, from the foreign investor's perspective, implies that the home country's currency denominating the investment instruments will depreciate to offset the interest rate advantage.

Points on the IFE Line. All the points along the so-called **international Fisher effect (IFE) line** in Exhibit 8.7 reflect exchange rate adjustments to offset the differential in interest rates. This means investors will end up achieving the same yield (adjusted for exchange rate fluctuations) whether they invest at home or in a foreign country.

To be precise, IFE theory does not suggest that this relationship will exist continuously over each time period. The point of IFE theory is that if a corporation periodically makes foreign investments to take advantage of higher foreign interest rates, it will achieve a yield that is sometimes above and sometimes below the domestic yield. Periodic investments by a U.S. corporation in an attempt to capitalize on the higher interest rates will, on average, achieve a yield similar to that by a corporation simply making domestic deposits periodically.

Points below the IFE Line. Points below the IFE line generally reflect the higher returns from investing in foreign deposits. For example, point G in Exhibit 8.7 indicates that the foreign interest rate exceeds the home interest rate by 3 percent. In addition, the foreign currency has appreciated by 2 percent. The combination of the higher foreign interest rate plus the appreciation of the foreign currency will cause the foreign yield to be higher than what is possible domestically. If actual data were compiled and plotted, and the vast majority of points were below the IFE line, this would suggest that investors of the home country could consistently increase their investment returns by establishing foreign bank deposits. Such results would refute the IFE theory.

Points above the IFE Line. Points above the IFE line generally reflect returns from foreign deposits that are lower than the returns possible domestically. For example, point H reflects a foreign interest rate that is 3 percent above the home interest rate. Yet, point H also indicates that the exchange rate of the foreign currency has depreciated by 5 percent, more than offsetting its interest rate advantage.

As another example, point J represents a situation in which an investor of the home country is hampered in two ways by investing in a foreign deposit. First, the foreign interest rate is lower than the home interest rate. Second, the foreign currency depreciates during the time the foreign deposit is held. If actual data were compiled and plotted, and the vast majority of points were above the IFE line, this would suggest that investors of the home country would receive consistently lower returns from foreign investments as opposed to investments in the home country. Such results would refute the IFE theory.

Tests of the International Fisher Effect

WEB
www.economagic.com/
fedstl.htm
U.S. inflation and
exchange rate data.

If the actual points (one for each period) of interest rates and exchange rate changes were plotted over time on a graph such as Exhibit 8.7, we could determine whether the points are systematically below the IFE line (suggesting higher returns from foreign investing), above the line (suggesting lower returns from foreign investing), or evenly scattered on both sides (suggesting a balance of higher returns from foreign investing in some periods and lower foreign returns in other periods).

Exhibit 8.8 Illustration of IFE Concept (When Exchange Rate Changes Offset Interest Rate Differentials on Average)

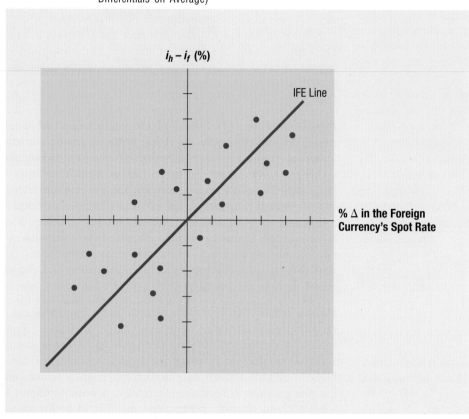

Exhibit 8.8 is an example of a set of points that tend to support the IFE theory. It implies that returns from short-term foreign investments are, on average, about equal to the returns that are possible domestically. Notice that each individual point reflects a change in the exchange rate that does not exactly offset the interest rate differential. In some cases, the exchange rate change does not fully offset the interest rate differential. In other cases, the exchange rate change more than offsets the interest rate differential. Over-all, the results balance out such that the interest rate differentials are, *on average,* offset by changes in the exchange rates. Thus, foreign investments have generated yields that are, on average, equal to those of domestic investments.

If foreign yields are expected to be about equal to domestic yields, a U.S. firm would probably prefer the domestic investments. The firm would know the yield on domestic short-term securities (such as bank deposits) in advance, whereas the yield to be attained from foreign short-term securities would be uncertain because the firm would not know what spot exchange rate would exist at the securities' maturity. Investors generally prefer an investment whose return is known over an investment whose return is uncertain, as-suming that all other features of the investments are similar.

Results from Testing the IFE. Whether the IFE holds in reality depends on the particular time period examined. Although the IFE theory may hold during some time frames, there is evidence that it does not consistently hold. A study by Thomas[5] tested

[5]Lee R. Thomas, "A Winning Strategy for Currency-Futures Speculation," *Journal of Portfolio Management* (Fall 1985): 65–69.

the IFE theory by examining the results of (1) purchasing currency futures contracts of currencies with high interest rates that contained forward discounts (relative to the spot rates) and (2) selling futures on currencies with low interest rates that contained forward premiums. If the high-interest-rate currencies depreciated and the low- interest-rate currencies appreciated to the extent suggested by the IFE theory, this strategy would not generate significant profits. However, 57 percent of the transactions created by this strategy were profitable. In addition, the average gain was much higher than the average loss. This study indicates that the IFE does not hold.

Statistical Test of the IFE. A somewhat simplified statistical test of the IFE can be developed by applying regression analysis to historical exchange rates and the nominal interest rate differential:

$$e_f = a_0 + a_1\left(\frac{1 + i_{U.S.}}{1 + i_f} - 1\right) + \mu$$

where a_0 is a constant, a_1 is the slope coefficient, and μ is an error term. Regression analysis would determine the regression coefficients. The hypothesized values of a_0 and a_1 are 0 and 1.0, respectively.

The appropriate t-test for each regression coefficient requires a comparison to the hypothesized value and then division by the standard error (s.e.) of the coefficients, as follows:

Test for $a_0 = 0$:   Test for $a_1 = 1$:

$$t = \frac{a_0 - 0}{\text{s.e. of } a_0} \qquad t = \frac{a_1 - 1}{\text{s.e. of } a_1}$$

The t-table is then used to find the critical t-value. If either t-test finds that the coefficients differ significantly from what was hypothesized, the IFE is refuted.

Does the International Fisher Effect Hold?

The IFE theory contradicts the concept covered in Chapter 4 regarding how a country with a high interest rate can attract more capital flows and therefore cause the local currency's value to strengthen. The IFE theory also contradicts the point in Chapter 6 about how central banks may purposely try to raise interest rates in order to attract funds and strengthen the value of their local currencies.

In reality, a currency with a high interest rate strengthens in some situations, which is consistent with the points made in Chapters 4 and 6, and contrary to the IFE. Many MNCs commonly invest cash in money market securities in developed countries where they can earn a slightly higher interest rate. They may believe that the higher interest rate in a foreign country does reflect higher expected inflation there. Factors such as demand for loanable funds or monetary policy in that country could have caused the interest rates to be higher there than in the United States. Even if the differential in nominal interest rates accurately reflects the differential in expected inflation rates, an exchange rate is influenced by other factors as well.

While the IFE theory has its limitations, it still offers useful inferences. MNCs that attempt to invest their cash where interest rates are higher should at least consider the possibility that the higher interest rate might reflect a higher expected inflation rate, which could cause depreciation of that currency. MNCs normally avoid investing their cash in less developed countries that have very high interest rates because these countries commonly have very high inflation and their currencies could depreciate substantially in a short period of time.

COMPARISON OF THE **IRP, PPP,** AND **IFE**

At this point, it may be helpful to compare three related theories of international finance: (1) interest rate parity (IRP), discussed in Chapter 7, (2) purchasing power parity (PPP), and (3) the international Fisher effect (IFE). Exhibit 8.9 summarizes the main themes of each theory. Note that although all three theories relate to the determination of exchange rates, they have different implications. The IRP theory focuses on why the forward rate differs from the spot rate and on the degree of difference that should exist. It relates to a specific point in time. In contrast, the PPP theory and IFE theory focus on how a currency's spot rate will change over time. Whereas PPP theory suggests that the spot rate will change in accordance with inflation differentials, IFE theory suggests that it will change in accordance with interest rate differentials. Nevertheless, PPP is related to IFE because expected inflation differentials influence the nominal interest rate differentials between two countries.

Exhibit 8.9 Comparison of the IRP, PPP, and IFE Theories

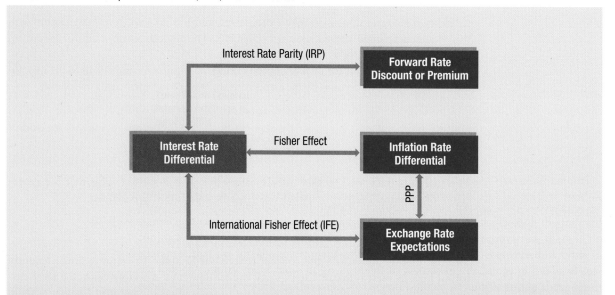

THEORY	KEY VARIABLES OF THEORY		SUMMARY OF THEORY
Interest rate parity (IRP)	Forward rate premium (or discount)	Interest rate differential	The forward rate of one currency with respect to another will contain a premium (or discount) that is determined by the differential in interest rates between the two countries. As a result, covered interest arbitrage will provide a return that is no higher than a domestic return.
Purchasing power parity (PPP)	Percentage change in spot exchange rate	Inflation rate differential	The spot rate of one currency with respect to another will change in reaction to the differential in inflation rates between the two countries. Consequently, the purchasing power for consumers when purchasing goods in their own country will be similar to their purchasing power when importing goods from the foreign country.
International Fisher effect (IFE)	Percentage change in spot exchange rate	Interest rate differential	The spot rate of one currency with respect to another will change in accordance with the differential in interest rates between the two countries. Consequently, the return on uncovered foreign money market securities will, on average, be no higher than the return on domestic money market securities from the perspective of investors in the home country.

Some generalizations about countries can be made by applying these theories. High-inflation countries tend to have high nominal interest rates (due to the Fisher effect). Their currencies tend to weaken over time (because of the PPP and IFE), and the forward rates of their currencies normally exhibit large discounts (due to IRP).

Financial managers that believe in PPP recognize that the exchange rate movement in any particular period will not always move according to the inflation differential between the two countries of concern. Yet, they may still rely on the inflation differential in order to derive their best guess of the expected exchange rate movement. Financial managers that believe in IFE recognize that the exchange rate movement in any particular period will not always move according to the interest rate differential between the two countries of concern. Yet, they may still rely on the interest rate differential in order to derive their best guess of the expected exchange rate movement.

SUMMARY

- Purchasing power parity (PPP) theory specifies a precise relationship between relative inflation rates of two countries and their exchange rate. In inexact terms, PPP theory suggests that the equilibrium exchange rate will adjust by the same magnitude as the differential in inflation rates between two countries. Though PPP continues to be a valuable concept, there is evidence of sizable deviations from the theory in the real world.

- The international Fisher effect (IFE) specifies a precise relationship between relative interest rates of two countries and their exchange rates. It suggests that an investor who periodically invests in foreign interest-bearing securities will, on average, achieve a return similar to what is possible domestically. This implies that the exchange rate of the country with high interest rates will depreciate to offset the interest rate advantage achieved by foreign investments. However, there is evidence that during some periods the IFE does not hold. Thus, investment in foreign short-term securities may achieve a higher return than what is possible domestically. If a firm attempts to achieve this higher return, however, it does incur the risk that the currency denominating the foreign security might depreciate against the investor's home currency during the investment period. In this case, the foreign security could generate a lower return than a domestic security, even though it exhibits a higher interest rate.

- The PPP theory focuses on the relationship between the inflation rate differential and future exchange rate movements. The IFE focuses on the interest rate differential and future exchange rate movements. The theory of interest rate parity (IRP) focuses on the relationship between the interest rate differential and the forward rate premium (or discount) at a given point in time.

POINT COUNTER-POINT

Does PPP Eliminate Concerns about Long-Term Exchange Rate Risk?

Point Yes. Studies have shown that exchange rate movements are related to inflation differentials in the long run. Based on PPP, the currency of a high-inflation country will depreciate against the dollar. A subsidiary in that country should generate inflated revenue from the inflation, which will help offset the adverse exchange effects when its earnings are remitted to the parent. If a firm is focused on long-term performance, the deviations from PPP will offset over time. In some years, the exchange rate effects may exceed the inflation effects, and in other years the inflation effects will exceed the exchange rate effects.

Counter-Point No. Even if the relationship between inflation and exchange rate effects is consistent, this does not guarantee that the effects on the firm will be offsetting. A subsidiary in a high-inflation country will not necessarily be able to adjust its price level to keep up with the increased costs of doing business there. The effects vary with each MNC's situation. Even if the subsidiary can raise its prices to match the rising costs, there are short-term deviations from PPP. The investors who invest in an MNC's stock may be concerned about short-term deviations from PPP because they will not necessarily hold the stock for the long term.

Thus, investors may prefer that firms manage in a manner that reduces the volatility in their performance in short-run and long-run periods.

Who Is Correct? Use the Internet to learn more about this issue. Which argument do you support? Offer your own opinion on this issue.

SELF-TEST

Answers are provided in Appendix A at the back of the text.

1. A U.S. importer of Japanese computer components pays for the components in yen. The importer is not concerned about a possible increase in Japanese prices (charged in yen) because of the likely offsetting effect caused by purchasing power parity (PPP). Explain what this means.

2. Use what you know about tests of PPP to answer this question. Using the information in the first question, explain why the U.S. importer of Japanese computer components should be concerned about its future payments.

3. Use PPP to explain how the values of the currencies of Eastern European countries might change if those countries experience high inflation, while the United States experiences low inflation.

4. Assume that the Canadian dollar's spot rate is $.85 and that the Canadian and U.S. inflation rates are similar. Then assume that Canada experiences 4 percent inflation, while the United States experiences 3 percent inflation. According to PPP, what will be the new value of the Canadian dollar after it adjusts to the inflationary changes? (You may use the approximate formula to answer this question.)

5. Assume that the Australian dollar's spot rate is $.90 and that the Australian and U.S. 1-year interest rates are initially 6 percent. Then assume that the Australian 1-year interest rate increases by 5 percentage points, while the U.S. 1-year interest rate remains unchanged. Using this information and the international Fisher effect (IFE) theory, forecast the spot rate for 1 year ahead.

6. In the previous question, the Australian interest rates increased from 6 to 11 percent. According to the IFE, what is the underlying factor that would cause such a change? Give an explanation based on the IFE of the forces that would cause a change in the Australian dollar. If U.S. investors believe in the IFE, will they attempt to capitalize on the higher Australian interest rates? Explain.

QUESTIONS AND APPLICATIONS

1. PPP. Explain the theory of purchasing power parity (PPP). Based on this theory, what is a general forecast of the values of currencies in countries with high inflation?

2. Rationale of PPP. Explain the rationale of the PPP theory.

3. Testing PPP. Explain how you could determine whether PPP exists. Describe a limitation in testing whether PPP holds.

4. Testing PPP. Inflation differentials between the United States and other industrialized countries have typically been a few percentage points in any given year. Yet, in many years annual exchange rates between the corresponding currencies have changed by 10 percent or more. What does this information suggest about PPP?

5. Limitations of PPP. Explain why PPP does not hold.

6. Implications of IFE. Explain the international Fisher effect (IFE). What is the rationale for the existence of the IFE? What are the implications of the IFE for firms with excess cash that consistently invest in foreign Treasury bills? Explain why the IFE may not hold.

7. Implications of IFE. Assume U.S. interest rates are generally above foreign interest rates. What does this suggest about the future strength or weakness of the dollar based on the IFE? Should U.S. investors invest in foreign securities if they believe in the IFE? Should foreign investors invest in U.S. securities if they believe in the IFE?

8. Comparing Parity Theories. Compare and contrast interest rate parity (discussed in the previous chapter), purchasing power parity (PPP), and the international Fisher effect (IFE).

9. Real Interest Rate. One assumption made in developing the IFE is that all investors in all countries have the same real interest rate. What does this mean?

10. Interpreting Inflationary Expectations. If investors in the United States and Canada require the same real interest rate, and the nominal rate of interest is 2 percent higher in Canada, what does this imply about expectations of U.S. inflation and Canadian inflation? What do these inflationary expectations suggest about future exchange rates?

11. PPP Applied to the Euro. Assume that several European countries that use the euro as their currency experience higher inflation than the United States, while two other European countries that use the euro as their currency experience lower inflation than the United States. According to PPP, how will the euro's value against the dollar be affected?

12. Source of Weak Currencies. Currencies of some Latin American countries, such as Brazil and Venezuela, frequently weaken against most other currencies. What concept in this chapter explains this occurrence? Why don't all U.S.-based MNCs use forward contracts to hedge their future remittances of funds from Latin American countries to the United States if they expect depreciation of the currencies against the dollar?

13. PPP. Japan has typically had lower inflation than the United States. How would one expect this to affect the Japanese yen's value? Why does this expected relationship not always occur?

14. IFE. Assume that the nominal interest rate in Mexico is 48 percent and the interest rate in the United States is 8 percent for 1-year securities that are free from default risk. What does the IFE suggest about the differential in expected inflation in these two countries? Using this information and the PPP theory, describe the expected nominal return to U.S. investors who invest in Mexico.

15. IFE. Shouldn't the IFE discourage investors from attempting to capitalize on higher foreign interest rates? Why do some investors continue to invest overseas, even when they have no other transactions overseas?

16. Changes in Inflation. Assume that the inflation rate in Brazil is expected to increase substantially. How will this affect Brazil's nominal interest rates and the value of its currency (called the real)? If the IFE holds, how will the nominal return to U.S. investors who invest in Brazil be affected by the higher inflation in Brazil? Explain.

17. Comparing PPP and IFE. How is it possible for PPP to hold if the IFE does not?

18. Estimating Depreciation Due to PPP. Assume that the spot exchange rate of the British pound is $1.73. How will this spot rate adjust according to PPP if the United Kingdom experiences an inflation rate of 7 percent while the United States experiences an inflation rate of 2 percent?

19. Forecasting the Future Spot Rate Based on IFE. Assume that the spot exchange rate of the Singapore dollar is $.70. The 1-year interest rate is 11 percent in the United States and 7 percent in Singapore. What will the spot rate be in 1 year according to the IFE? What is the force that causes the spot rate to change according to the IFE?

20. Deriving Forecasts of the Future Spot Rate. As of today, assume the following information is available:

	U.S.	MEXICO
Real rate of interest required by investors	2%	2%
Nominal interest rate	11%	15%
Spot rate	—	$.20
One-year forward rate	—	$.19

a. Use the forward rate to forecast the percentage change in the Mexican peso over the next year.

b. Use the differential in expected inflation to forecast the percentage change in the Mexican peso over the next year.

c. Use the spot rate to forecast the percentage change in the Mexican peso over the next year.

21. Inflation and Interest Rate Effects. The opening of Russia's market has resulted in a highly volatile Russian currency (the ruble). Russia's inflation has commonly exceeded 20 percent per month. Russian interest rates commonly exceed 150 percent, but this is sometimes less than the annual inflation rate in Russia.

a. Explain why the high Russian inflation has put severe pressure on the value of the Russian ruble.

b. Does the effect of Russian inflation on the decline in the ruble's value support the PPP theory? How might the relationship be distorted by political conditions in Russia?

c. Does it appear that the prices of Russian goods will be equal to the prices of U.S. goods from the perspective of Russian consumers (after considering exchange rates)? Explain.

d. Will the effects of the high Russian inflation and the decline in the ruble offset each other for U.S. importers? That is, how will U.S. importers of Russian goods be affected by the conditions?

22. IFE Application to Asian Crisis. Before the Asian crisis, many investors attempted to capitalize on the high interest rates prevailing in the Southeast Asian countries although the level of interest rates primarily reflected expectations of inflation. Explain why investors behaved in this manner. Why does the IFE suggest that the Southeast Asian countries would not have attracted foreign investment before the Asian crisis despite the high interest rates prevailing in those countries?

23. IFE Applied to the Euro. Given the conversion of several European currencies to the euro, explain what would cause the euro's value to change against the dollar according to the IFE.

Advanced Questions

24. IFE. Beth Miller does not believe that the international Fisher effect (IFE) holds. Current 1-year interest rates in Europe are 5 percent, while 1-year interest rates in the United States are 3 percent. Beth converts $100,000 to euros and invests them in Germany. One year later, she converts the euros back to dollars. The current spot rate of the euro is $1.10.

a. According to the IFE, what should the spot rate of the euro in 1 year be?

b. If the spot rate of the euro in 1 year is $1.00, what is Beth's percentage return from her strategy?

c. If the spot rate of the euro in 1 year is $1.08, what is Beth's percentage return from her strategy?

d. What must the spot rate of the euro be in 1 year for Beth's strategy to be successful?

25. Integrating IRP and IFE. Assume the following information is available for the United States and Europe:

	U.S.	EUROPE
Nominal interest rate	4%	6%
Expected inflation	2%	5%
Spot rate	—	$1.13
One-year forward rate	—	$1.10

a. Does IRP hold?

b. According to PPP, what is the expected spot rate of the euro in 1 year?

c. According to the IFE, what is the expected spot rate of the euro in 1 year?

d. Reconcile your answers to parts (a) and (c).

26. IRP. The 1-year risk-free interest rate in Mexico is 10 percent. The 1-year risk-free rate in the United States is 2 percent. Assume that interest rate parity exists. The spot rate of the Mexican peso is $.14.

a. What is the forward rate premium?

b. What is the 1-year forward rate of the peso?

c. Based on the international Fisher effect, what is the expected change in the spot rate over the next year?

d. If the spot rate changes as expected according to the IFE, what will be the spot rate in 1 year?

e. Compare your answers to (b) and (d) and explain the relationship.

27. Testing the PPP. How could you use regression analysis to determine whether the relationship specified by PPP exists on average? Specify the model, and describe how you would assess the regression results to determine if there is a *significant* difference from the relationship suggested by PPP.

28. Testing the IFE. Describe a statistical test for the IFE.

29. Impact of Barriers on PPP and IFE. Would PPP be more likely to hold between the United States and Hungary if trade barriers were completely removed and if Hungary's currency were allowed to float without any government intervention? Would the IFE be more likely to hold between the United States and Hungary if trade barriers were completely removed and if Hungary's currency were allowed to float without any government intervention? Explain.

30. Interactive Effects of PPP. Assume that the inflation rates of the countries that use the euro are very low, while other European countries that have their own currencies experience high inflation. Explain how and why the euro's value could be expected to change against these currencies according to the PPP theory.

31. Applying IRP and IFE. Assume that Mexico has a 1-year interest rate that is higher than the U.S. 1-year interest rate. Assume that you believe in the international Fisher effect (IFE) and interest rate parity. Assume zero transaction costs.

Ed is based in the United States and attempts to speculate by purchasing Mexican pesos today, investing the pesos in a risk-free asset for a year, and then converting the pesos to dollars at the end of 1 year. Ed did not cover his position in the forward market.

Maria is based in Mexico and attempts covered interest arbitrage by purchasing dollars today and simultaneously selling dollars 1 year forward, investing the dollars in a risk-free asset for a year, and then converting the dollars back to pesos at the end of 1 year.

Do you think the rate of return on Ed's investment will be higher than, lower than, or the same as the rate of return on Maria's investment? Explain.

32. Arbitrage and PPP. Assume that locational arbitrage ensures that spot exchange rates are properly aligned. Also assume that you believe in purchasing power parity. The spot rate of the British pound is $1.80. The spot rate of the Swiss franc is 0.3 pounds. You expect that the 1-year inflation rate is 7 percent in the United Kingdom, 5 percent in Switzerland, and 1 percent in the United States. The 1-year interest rate is 6 percent in the United Kingdom, 2 percent in Switzerland, and 4 percent in the United States. What is your expected spot rate of the Swiss franc in 1 year with respect to the U.S. dollar? Show your work.

33. IRP versus IFE. You believe that interest rate parity and the international Fisher effect hold. Assume that the U.S. interest rate is presently much higher than the New Zealand interest rate. You have receivables of 1 million New Zealand dollars that you will receive in 1 year. You could hedge the receivables with the 1-year forward contract. Or, you could decide to not hedge. Is your expected U.S. dollar amount of the receivables in 1 year from hedging higher, lower, or the same as your expected U.S. dollar amount of the receivables without hedging? Explain.

34. IRP, PPP, and Speculating in Currency Derivatives. The U.S. 3-month interest rate (unannualized) is 1 percent. The Canadian 3-month interest rate (unannualized) is 4 percent. Interest rate parity exists. The expected inflation over this period is 5 percent in the United States and 2 percent in Canada. A call option with a 3-month expiration date on Canadian dollars is available for a premium of $.02 and a strike price of $.64. The spot rate of the Canadian dollar is $.65. Assume that you believe in purchasing power parity.

a. Determine the dollar amount of your profit or loss from buying a call option contract specifying C$100,000.

b. Determine the dollar amount of your profit or loss from buying a futures contract specifying C$100,000.

35. Implications of PPP. Today's spot rate of the Mexican peso is $.10. Assume that purchasing power parity holds. The U.S. inflation rate over this year is expected to be 7 percent, while the Mexican inflation over this year is expected to be 3 percent. Wake Forest Co. plans to import from Mexico and will need 20 million Mexican pesos in 1 year. Determine the expected amount of dollars to be paid by the Wake Forest Co. for the pesos in 1 year.

36. Investment Implications of IRP and IFE. The Argentine 1-year CD (deposit) rate is 13 percent, while the Mexican 1-year CD rate is 11 percent and the U.S. 1-year CD rate is 6 percent. All CDs have zero default risk. Interest rate parity holds, and you believe that the international Fisher effect holds.

Jamie (based in the United States) invests in a 1-year CD in Argentina.

Ann (based in the United States) invests in a 1-year CD in Mexico.

Ken (based in the United States) invests in a 1-year CD in Argentina and sells Argentine pesos 1 year forward to cover his position.

Juan (who lives in Argentina) invests in a 1-year CD in the United States.

Maria (who lives in Mexico) invests in a 1-year CD in the United States.

Nina (who lives in Mexico) invests in a 1-year CD in Argentina.

Carmen (who lives in Argentina) invests in a 1-year CD in Mexico and sells Mexican pesos 1 year forward to cover her position.

Corio (who lives in Mexico) invests in a 1-year CD in Argentina and sells Argentine pesos 1 year forward to cover his position.

Based on this information and assuming the international Fisher effect holds, which person will be expected to earn the highest return on the funds invested? If you believe that multiple persons will tie for the highest expected return, name each of them. Explain.

37. Investment Implications of IRP and the IFE.

Today, a U.S. dollar can be exchanged for 3 New Zealand dollars. The 1-year CD (deposit) rate in New Zealand is 7 percent, and the 1-year CD rate in the United States is 6 percent. Interest rate parity exists between the United States and New Zealand. The international Fisher effect exists between the United States and New Zealand. Today a U.S. dollar can be exchanged for 2 Swiss francs. The 1-year CD rate in Switzerland is 5 percent. The spot rate of the Swiss franc is the same as the 1-year forward rate.

Karen (based in the United States) invests in a 1-year CD in New Zealand and sells New Zealand dollars 1 year forward to cover her position.

James (based in the United States) invests in a 1-year CD in New Zealand and does not cover his position.

Brian (based in the United States) invests in a 1-year CD in Switzerland and sells Swiss francs 1 year forward to cover his position.

Eric (who lives in Switzerland) invests in a 1-year CD in Switzerland.

Tonya (who lives in New Zealand) invests in a 1-year CD in the United States and sells U.S. dollars 1 year forward to cover her position.

Based on this information, which person will be expected to earn the highest return on the funds invested? If you believe that multiple persons will tie for the highest expected return, name each of them. Explain.

38. Real Interest Rates, Expected Inflation, IRP, and the Spot Rate.

The United States and the country of Rueland have the same real interest rate of 3 percent. The expected inflation over the next year is 6 percent in the United States versus 21 percent in Rueland. Interest rate parity exists. The 1-year currency futures contract on Rueland's currency (called the ru) is priced at $.40 per ru. What is the spot rate of the ru?

39. PPP and Real Interest Rates.

The nominal (quoted) U.S. 1-year interest rate is 6 percent, while the nominal 1-year interest rate in Canada is 5 percent. Assume you believe in purchasing power parity. You believe the real 1-year interest rate is 2 percent in the United States, and that the real 1-year interest rate is 3 percent in Canada. Today the Canadian dollar spot rate is $.90. What do you think the spot rate of the Canadian dollar will be in 1 year?

40. IFE, Cross Exchange Rates, and Cash Flows.

Assume the Hong Kong dollar (HK$) value is tied to the U.S. dollar and will remain tied to the U.S. dollar. Assume that interest rate parity exists. Today, an Australian dollar (A$) is worth $.50 and HK$3.9. The 1-year interest rate on the Australian dollar is 11 percent, while the 1-year interest rate on the U.S. dollar is 7 percent. You believe in the international Fisher effect.

You will receive A$1 million in 1 year from selling products to Australia, and will convert these proceeds into Hong Kong dollars in the spot market at that time to purchase imports from Hong Kong. Forecast the amount of Hong Kong dollars that you will be able to purchase in the spot market 1 year from now with A$1 million. Show your work.

41. PPP and Cash Flows.

Boston Co. will receive 1 million euros in 1 year from selling exports. It did not hedge this future transaction. Boston believes that the future value of the euro will be determined by purchasing power parity (PPP). It expects that inflation in countries using the euro will be 12 percent next year, while inflation in the United States will be 7 percent next year. Today the spot rate of the euro is $1.46, and the 1-year forward rate is $1.50.

a. Estimate the amount of U.S. dollars that Boston will receive in 1 year when converting its euro receivables into U.S. dollars.

b. Today, the spot rate of the Hong Kong dollar is pegged at $.13. Boston believes that the Hong Kong dollar will remain pegged to the dollar for the next year. If Boston Co. decides to convert its 1 million euros into Hong Kong dollars instead of U.S. dollars at the end of 1 year, estimate the amount of Hong Kong dollars that Boston will receive in 1 year when converting its euro receivables into Hong Kong dollars.

42. PPP and Currency Futures. Assume that you believe purchasing power parity (PPP) exists. You expect that inflation in Canada during the next year will be 3 percent and inflation in the United States will be 8 percent. Today the spot rate of the Canadian dollar is $.90 and the 1-year futures contract of the Canadian dollar is priced at $.88. Estimate the expected profit or loss if an investor sold a 1-year futures contract today on 1 million Canadian dollars and settled this contract on the settlement date.

Discussion in the Boardroom

This exercise can be found in Appendix E at the back of this textbook.

Running Your Own MNC

This exercise can be found on the *International Financial Management* text companion website located at www.cengage.com/finance/madura.

Blades, Inc. Case

Assessment of Purchasing Power Parity

Blades, the U.S.-based roller blades manufacturer, is currently both exporting to and importing from Thailand. The company has chosen Thailand as an export target for its primary product, Speedos, because of Thailand's growth prospects and the lack of competition from both Thai and U.S. roller blade manufacturers in Thailand. Under an existing arrangement, Blades sells 180,000 pairs of Speedos annually to Entertainment Products, Inc., a Thai retailer. The arrangement involves a fixed, baht-denominated price and will last for 3 years. Blades generates approximately 10 percent of its revenue in Thailand.

Blades has also decided to import certain rubber and plastic components needed to manufacture Speedos because of cost and quality considerations. Specifically, the weak economic conditions in Thailand resulting from recent events have allowed Blades to import components from the country at a relatively low cost. However, Blades did not enter into a long-term arrangement to import these components and pays market prices (in baht) prevailing in Thailand at the time of purchase. Currently, Blades incurs about 4 percent of its cost of goods sold in Thailand.

Although Blades has no immediate plans for expansion in Thailand, it may establish a subsidiary there in the future. Moreover, even if Blades does not establish a subsidiary in Thailand, it will continue exporting to and importing from the country for several years. Due to these considerations, Blades' management is very concerned about recent events in Thailand and neighboring countries, as they may affect both Blades' current performance and its future plans.

Ben Holt, Blades' CFO, is particularly concerned about the level of inflation in Thailand. Blades' export arrangement with Entertainment Products, while al-

lowing for a minimum level of revenue to be generated in Thailand in a given year, prevents Blades from adjusting prices according to the level of inflation in Thailand. In retrospect, Holt is wondering whether Blades should have entered into the export arrangement at all. Because Thailand's economy was growing very fast when Blades agreed to the arrangement, strong consumer spending there resulted in a high level of inflation and high interest rates. Naturally, Blades would have preferred an agreement whereby the price per pair of Speedos would be adjusted for the Thai level of inflation. However, to take advantage of the growth opportunities in Thailand, Blades accepted the arrangement when Entertainment Products insisted on a fixed price level. Currently, however, the baht is freely floating, and Holt is wondering how a relatively high level of Thai inflation may affect the baht-dollar exchange rate and, consequently, Blades' revenue generated in Thailand.

Ben Holt is also concerned about Blades' cost of goods sold incurred in Thailand. Since no fixed-price arrangement exists and the components are invoiced in Thai baht, Blades has been subject to increases in the prices of rubber and plastic. Holt is wondering how a potentially high level of inflation will impact the baht-dollar exchange rate and the cost of goods sold incurred in Thailand now that the baht is freely floating.

When Holt started thinking about future economic conditions in Thailand and the resulting impact on Blades, he found that he needed your help. In particular, Holt is vaguely familiar with the concept of purchasing power parity (PPP) and is wondering about this theory's implications, if any, for Blades. Furthermore, Holt also remembers that relatively high interest rates in Thailand will attract capital flows and put upward pressure on the baht.

Because of these concerns, and to gain some insight into the impact of inflation on Blades, Ben Holt has asked you to provide him with answers to the following questions:

1. What is the relationship between the exchange rates and relative inflation levels of the two countries? How will this relationship affect Blades' Thai revenue and costs given that the baht is freely floating? What is the net effect of this relationship on Blades?

2. What are some of the factors that prevent PPP from occurring in the short run? Would you expect PPP to hold better if countries negotiate trade arrangements under which they commit themselves to the

purchase or sale of a fixed number of goods over a specified time period? Why or why not?

3. How do you reconcile the high level of interest rates in Thailand with the expected change of the baht-dollar exchange rate according to PPP?

4. Given Blades' future plans in Thailand, should the company be concerned with PPP? Why or why not?

5. PPP may hold better for some countries than for others. The Thai baht has been freely floating for more than a decade. How do you think Blades can gain insight into whether PPP holds for Thailand? Offer some logic to explain why the PPP relationship may not hold here.

SMALL BUSINESS DILEMMA

Assessment of the IFE by the Sports Exports Company

Every month, the Sports Exports Company receives a payment denominated in British pounds for the footballs it exports to the United Kingdom. Jim Logan, owner of the Sports Exports Company, decides each month whether to hedge the payment with a forward contract for the following month. Now, however, he is questioning whether this process is worth the trouble. He suggests that if the international Fisher effect (IFE) holds, the pound's value should change (on average) by an amount that reflects the differential between the

interest rates of the two countries of concern. Since the forward premium reflects that same interest rate differential, the results from hedging should equal the results from not hedging on average.

1. Is Jim's interpretation of the IFE theory correct?

2. If you were in Jim's position, would you spend time trying to decide whether to hedge the receivables each month, or do you believe that the results would be the same (on average) whether you hedged or not?

INTERNET/EXCEL EXERCISES

The "Market" section of the Bloomberg website provides interest rate quotations for numerous currencies. Its address is www.bloomberg.com.

1. Go to the "Rates and Bonds" section and then click on each foreign country to review its interest rate. Determine the prevailing 1-year interest rate of the Australian dollar, the Japanese yen, and the British pound. Assuming a 2 percent real rate of interest for savers in

any country, determine the expected rate of inflation over the next year in each of these countries that is implied by the nominal interest rate (according to the Fisher effect).

2. What is the approximate expected percentage change in the value of each of these currencies against the dollar over the next year when applying PPP to the inflation level of each of these currencies versus the dollar?

REFERENCES

Acharya, Sankarshan, Mar 2008, Optimal Exchange Rate Beyond Purchase Power Parity, *Journal of American Academy of Business*, pp. 138–144.

Callen, Tim, Mar 2007, PPP versus the Market: Which Weight Matters? *Finance & Development*, pp. 50–51.

Cox, Joe, Sep 2008, Purchasing Power Parity and Cultural Convergence: Evidence from the Global Video Games Market, *Journal of Cultural Economics*, pp. 201–214.

Landon, Stuart, and Constance E. Smith, Mar 2006, Exchange Rates and Investment Good Prices: A Cross-Industry Comparison, *Journal of International Money and Finance*, pp. 237–256.

Palley, Thomas I., Mar 2008, Institutionalism and New Trade Theory: Rethinking Comparative Advantage and Trade Policy, *Journal of Economic Issues*, pp. 195–208.

Sjölander, Pär, Autumn 2007, Unreal Exchange Rates: A Simulation-Based Approach to Adjust Misleading PPP Estimates, *Journal of Economic Studies*, pp. 256–288.

Xu, Zhenhui, Feb 2003, Purchasing Power Parity, Price Indices, and Exchange Rate Forecasts, *Journal of International Money and Finance*, pp. 105–130.

Midterm Self-Exam

MIDTERM REVIEW

You have just completed all the chapters focused on the macro- and market-related concepts. Here is a brief summary of some of the key points in those chapters. Chapter 1 explains the role of financial managers to focus on maximizing the value of the MNC and how that goal can be distorted by agency problems. MNCs use various incentives to ensure that managers serve shareholders rather than themselves. Chapter 1 explains that an MNC's value is the present value of its future cash flows and how a U.S.-based MNC's value is influenced by its foreign cash flows. Its dollar cash flows (and therefore its value) are enhanced when the foreign currencies received appreciate against the dollar, or when foreign currencies of outflows depreciate. The MNC's value is also influenced by its cost of capital, which is influenced by its capital structure and the risk of the projects that it pursues. The valuation is dependent on the environment in which MNCs operate, along with their managerial decisions.

Chapter 2 focuses on international transactions in a global context, with emphasis on international trade and capital flows. International trade flows are sensitive to relative prices of products between countries, while international capital flows are influenced by the potential return on funds invested. They can have a major impact on the economic conditions of each country and the MNCs that operate there. Net trade flows to a country may create more jobs there, while net capital flows to a country can increase the amount of funds that can be channeled to finance projects by firms or government agencies.

Chapter 3 introduces the international money, bond, and stock markets and explains how they facilitate the operations of MNCs. It also explains how the foreign exchange market facilitates international transactions. Chapter 4 explains how a currency's direct exchange rate (value measured in dollars) may rise when its country has relatively low inflation and relatively high interest rates (if expected inflation is low) compared with the United States. Chapter 5 introduces currency derivatives and explains how they can be used by MNCs or individuals to capitalize on expected movements in exchange rates.

Chapter 6 describes the role of central banks in the foreign exchange market and how they can use direct intervention to affect exchange rate movements. They can attempt to raise the value of their home currency by using dollars or another currency in their reserves to purchase their home currency in the foreign exchange market. The central banks can also attempt to reduce the value of their home currency by using their home currency reserves to purchase dollars in the foreign exchange market. Alternatively, they could use indirect intervention by affecting interest rates in a manner that will affect the appeal of their local money market securities relative to other countries. This action affects the supply of their home currency for sale and/or the demand for their home currency in the foreign exchange market and therefore affects the exchange rate.

Chapter 7 explains how the forces of arbitrage allow for parity conditions and more orderly foreign exchange market quotations. Specifically, locational arbitrage ensures that exchange rate quotations are similar among locations. Triangular arbitrage ensures that cross exchange rates are properly aligned. Covered interest arbitrage tends to ensure that the spot and forward exchange rates maintain a relationship that reflects interest rate parity, whereby the forward rate premium reflects the interest rate differential. Chapter 8 gives special attention to the impact of inflation and interest rates on exchange rate movements. Purchasing power parity suggests that a currency will depreciate to offset its country's inflation differential above the United States (or will appreciate if its country's inflation is lower than in the United States). The international Fisher effect suggests that if nominal interest rate differentials reflect the expected inflation differentials (the real interest rate is the same in each country), the exchange rate will move in accordance with purchasing power parity as applied to expected inflation. That is, a currency will depreciate to offset its country's expected inflation differential above the United States (or will appreciate if its country's expected inflation is lower than in the United States).

Midterm Self-Exam

This self-exam allows you to test your understanding of some of the key concepts covered up to this point. Chapters 1 to 8 are macro- and market-oriented, while Chapters 9 to 21 are micro-oriented. This is a good opportunity to assess your understanding of the macro and market concepts, before moving on to the micro concepts in Chapters 9 to 21.

This exam does not replace all the end-of-chapter self-tests, nor does it test all the concepts that have been covered up to this point. It is simply intended to let you test yourself on a general overview of key concepts. Try to simulate taking an exam by answering all questions without using your book and your notes. The answers to this exam are provided just after the exam so that you can grade your exam. If you have any wrong answers, you should reread the related material and then redo any exam questions that you had wrong.

This exam may not necessarily match the level of rigor in your course. Your instructor may offer you specific information about how this Midterm Self-Exam relates to the coverage and rigor of the midterm exam in your course.

1. An MNC's cash flows and therefore its valuation can be affected by expected exchange rate movements (as explained in Chapter 1). Sanoma Co. is a U.S.-based MNC that wants to assess how its valuation is affected by expected exchange rate movements. Given Sanoma's business transactions and its expectations of exchange rates, fill out the table at the top of the next page.

2. The United States has a larger balance-of-trade deficit each year (as explained in Chapter 2). Do you think a weaker dollar would reduce the balance-of-trade deficit? Offer a convincing argument for your answer.

3. Is outsourcing by U.S. firms to foreign countries beneficial to the U.S. economy? Weigh the pros and cons, and offer your conclusions.

4. a. The dollar is presently worth .8 euros. What is the direct exchange rate of the euro?

b. The direct exchange rate of the euro is presently valued higher than it was last month. What does this imply about the movement of the indirect exchange rate of the euro over the last month?

EACH QUARTER DURING THE YEAR, SANOMA'S MAIN BUSINESS TRANS- ACTIONS WILL BE TO:	CURRENCY USED IN TRANSACTION	EXPECTED MOVE- MENT IN CUR- RENCY'S VALUE AGAINST THE U.S. DOLLAR DURING THIS YEAR	HOW THE EXPECTED CURRENCY MOVEMENT WILL AFFECT SANOMA'S NET CASH FLOWS (AND THEREFORE VALUE) THIS YEAR
a. Import materials from Canada	Canadian dollar	Depreciate	
b. Export products to Germany	Euro	Appreciate	
c. Receive remitted earnings from its foreign subsidiary in Argentina	Argentine peso	Appreciate	
d. Receive interest from its Australian cash account	Australian dollar	Depreciate	
e. Make loan payments on a loan provided by a Japanese bank	Japanese yen	Depreciate	

   c. The *Wall Street Journal* quotes the Australian dollar to be worth $.50, while the 1-year forward rate of the Australian dollar is $.51. What is the forward rate premium? What is the expected rate of appreciation (or depreciation) if the 1-year forward rate is used to predict the value of the Australian dollar in 1 year?

5. Assume that the Polish currency (called zloty) is worth $.32. The U.S. dollar is worth .7 euros. A U.S. dollar can be exchanged for 8 Mexican pesos.
   Last year a dollar was valued at 2.9 Polish zloty, and the peso was valued at $.10.

   a. Would U.S. exporters to Mexico that accept pesos as payment be favorably or unfavorably affected by the change in the Mexican peso's value over the last year?

   b. Would U.S. importers from Poland that pay for imports in zloty be favorably or unfavorably affected by the change in the zloty's value over the last year?

   c. What is the percentage change in the cross exchange rate of the peso in zloty over the last year? How would firms in Mexico that sell products to Poland denominated in zloty be affected by the change in the cross exchange rate?

6. Explain how each of the following conditions would be expected to affect the value of the Mexican peso.

SITUATION	EXPECTED IMPACT ON THE EXCHANGE RATE OF THE PESO
a. Mexico suddenly experiences a high rate of inflation.	
b. Mexico's interest rates rise, while its inflation is expected to remain low.	
c. Mexico's central bank intervenes in the foreign exchange market by purchasing dollars with pesos.	
d. Mexico imposes quotas on products imported from the United States.	

7. One year ago, you sold a put option on 100,000 euros with an expiration date of 1 year. You received a premium on the put option of $.05 per unit. The exercise price was $1.22. Assume that 1 year ago, the spot rate of the euro was $1.20. One year ago, the

1-year forward rate of the euro exhibited a discount of 2 percent, and the 1-year futures price of the euro was the same as the 1-year forward rate of the euro. From 1 year ago to today, the euro depreciated against the dollar by 4 percent. Today the put option will be exercised (if it is feasible for the buyer to do so).

a. Determine the total dollar amount of your profit or loss from your position in the put option.

b. One year ago, Rita sold a futures contract on 100,000 euros with a settlement date of 1 year. Determine the total dollar amount of her profit or loss.

8. Assume that the Federal Reserve wants to reduce the value of the euro with respect to the dollar. How could it attempt to use indirect intervention to achieve its goal? What is a possible adverse effect from this type of intervention?

9. Assume that interest rate parity exists. The 1-year nominal interest rate in the United States is 7 percent, while the 1-year nominal interest rate in Australia is 11 percent. The spot rate of the Australian dollar is $.60. Today, you purchase a 1-year forward contract on 10 million Australian dollars. How many U.S. dollars will you need in 1 year to fulfill your forward contract?

10. You go to a bank and are given these quotes:

You can buy a euro for 14 Mexican pesos.
The bank will pay you 13 pesos for a euro.
You can buy a U.S. dollar for .9 euros.
The bank will pay you .8 euros for a U.S. dollar.
You can buy a U.S. dollar for 10 pesos.
The bank will pay you 9 pesos for a U.S. dollar.

You have $1,000. Can you use triangular arbitrage to generate a profit? If so, explain the order of the transactions that you would execute and the profit that you would earn. If you cannot earn a profit from triangular arbitrage, explain why.

11. Today's spot rate of the Mexican peso is $.10. Assume that purchasing power parity holds. The U.S. inflation rate over this year is expected to be 7 percent, while the Mexican inflation over this year is expected to be 3 percent. Carolina Co. plans to import from Mexico and will need 20 million Mexican pesos in 1 year. Determine the expected amount of dollars to be paid by the Carolina Co. for the pesos in 1 year.

12. Tennessee Co. purchases imports that have a price of 400,000 Singapore dollars, and it has to pay for the imports in 90 days. It will use a 90-day forward contract to cover its payables. Assume that interest rate parity exists and will continue to exist. This morning, the spot rate of the Singapore dollar was $.50. At noon, the Federal Reserve reduced U.S. interest rates. There was no change in the Singapore interest rates. The Singapore dollar's spot rate remained at $.50 throughout the day. But the Fed's actions immediately increased the degree of uncertainty surrounding the future value of the Singapore dollar over the next 3 months.

a. If Tennessee Co. locked in a 90-day forward contract this afternoon, would its total U.S. dollar cash outflows be *more than, less than,* or *the same as* the total U.S. dollar cash outflows if it had locked in a 90-day forward contract this morning? Briefly explain.

b. Assume that Tennessee uses a currency options contract to hedge rather than a forward contract. If Tennessee Co. purchased a currency call option contract at the money on Singapore dollars this afternoon, would its total U.S. dollar cash outflows be *more than, less than,* or *the same as* the total U.S. dollar cash outflows if it had purchased a currency call option contract at the money this morning? Briefly explain.

c. Assume that the U.S. and Singapore interest rates were the same as of this morning. Also assume that the international Fisher effect holds. If Tennessee Co. purchased a currency call option contract at the money this morning to hedge its exposure, would you expect that its total U.S. dollar cash outflows would be *more than, less than,* or *the same as* the total U.S. dollar cash outflows if it had negotiated a forward contract this morning? Briefly explain.

13. Today, a U.S. dollar can be exchanged for 3 New Zealand dollars or for 1.6 Canadian dollars. The 1-year CD (deposit) rate is 7 percent in New Zealand, is 6 percent in the United States, and is 5 percent in Canada. Interest rate parity exists between the United States and New Zealand and between the United States and Canada. The international Fisher effect exists between the United States and New Zealand. You expect that the Canadian dollar will be worth $.61 at the end of 1 year.

Karen (based in the United States) invests in a 1-year CD in New Zealand and sells New Zealand dollars 1 year forward to cover her position.

Marcia (who lives in New Zealand) invests in a 1-year CD in the United States and sells U.S. dollars 1 year forward to cover her position.

William (who lives in Canada) invests in a 1-year CD in the United States and does not cover his position.

James (based in the United States) invests in a 1-year CD in New Zealand and does not cover his position.

Based on this information, which person will be expected to earn the highest return on the funds invested? If you believe that multiple people will tie for the highest expected return, name each of them. Briefly explain.

14. Assume that the United Kingdom has an interest rate of 8 percent versus an interest rate of 5 percent in the United States.

a. Explain what the implications are for the future value of the British pound according to the theory in Chapter 4 that a country with high interest rates may attract capital flows versus the theory of the international Fisher effect (IFE) in Chapter 8.

b. Compare the implications of the IFE from Chapter 8 versus interest rate parity (IRP) as related to the information provided here.

ANSWERS TO MIDTERM SELF-EXAM

1. **a.** Increase
   b. Increase
   c. Increase
   d. Decrease
   e. Increase

2. One argument is that a weak dollar will make U.S. products imported by foreign countries cheaper, which will increase the demand for U.S. exports. In addition, a weaker dollar may discourage U.S. firms from importing foreign products because the cost will be higher. Both factors result in a smaller balance-of-trade deficit.

However, a weak dollar might not improve the balance-of-trade deficit because it is unlikely to weaken against all countries simultaneously. Foreign firms may compare the price they would pay for U.S. products to the price paid for similar products in other countries. Even if the dollar weakens, products produced in China or some other countries where there is cheap labor may still be cheaper for customers based in the United States or other countries.

3. Outsourcing can be beneficial to the U.S. economy because it may allow U.S. firms to produce their products at a lower cost and increase their profits (which increases income earned by the U.S. owners of those firms). It also allows U.S. customers to purchase products and services at a lower cost.

However, outsourcing eliminates some jobs in the United States, which reduces or eliminates income for people whose job was outsourced. The overall effect on the U.S. economy is based on a comparison of these two forces. It is possible to make arguments for either side. Also, the effects will vary depending on the location. For example, outsourcing may be more likely in a high-wage city in the United States where firms provide services that can be handled by phone or by electronic interaction. These jobs are easier to outsource than some other jobs.

4. a. A euro = $1.25.
    b. The indirect value of the euro must have declined over the last month.
    c. The forward premium is 2 percent. If the forward rate is used to forecast, the expected degree of appreciation over the next year is ($.51 – $.50)/$.50 = 2%, which is the same as the forward rate premium.

5. a. The peso is valued at $.125 today. Since the peso appreciated, the U.S. exporters are favorably affected.
    b. The zloty was worth about $.345 last year. Since the zloty depreciated, the U.S. importers were favorably affected.
    c. Last year, the cross rate of the peso in zloty = $.10/$.345 = .2898. Today, the cross rate of the peso in zloty = $.125/$.32 = .391. The percentage change is (.391 – .2898)/.2898 = 34.92%.

6. a. Depreciate
    b. Appreciate
    c. Depreciate
    d. Appreciate

7. a. The spot rate depreciated from $1.20 to $1.152. You receive $.05 per unit. The buyer of the put option exercises the option, and you buy the euros for $1.22 and sell them in the spot market for $1.152. Your gain on the put option per unit is ($1.152 – $1.22) + $.05 = –$.018. Total gain = –$.018 × 100,000 = –$1,800.
    b. The futures rate 1 year ago was equal to:
        $1.20 × (1 – .02) = $1.176. So the futures rate is $1.176. The gain per unit is $1.176 – $1.152 = $.024 and the total gain is $.024 × 100,000 = $2,400.

8. The Fed could use indirect intervention by raising U.S. interest rates so that the United States would attract more capital flows, which would place upward pressure on the dollar. However, the higher interest rates could make borrowing too expensive for some firms, and would possibly reduce economic growth.

9. [(1.07)/(1.11)] – 1 = –3.60%. So the 1-year forward rate is $.60 × [1 + (– .036)] = $.5784. You will need 10,000,000 × $.5784 = $5,784,000.

10. Yes, you can generate a profit by converting dollars to euros, and then euros to pesos, and then pesos to dollars. First convert the information to direct quotes:

	BID	ASK
Euro in $	$1.11	$1.25
Pesos in $	$.10	$.11
Euro in pesos	13	14

Use $1,000 to purchase euros: $1,000/$1.25 = 800 euros.

Convert 800 euros to buy pesos: 800 euros × 13 = 10,400 pesos.

Convert the 10,400 pesos to U.S. dollars: 10,400 × $.10 = $1,040.

There is profit of $40 on a $1,000 investment.

The alternative strategy that you could attempt is to first buy pesos:

Use $1,000 to purchase pesos: $1,000/$.11 = 9,090.9 pesos.

Convert 9,090 pesos to euros: 9,090.9/14 = 649.35 euros.

Convert 649.35 euros to dollars: 649.35 euros × $1.11 = $720.78.

This strategy results in a loss.

11. [(1.07)/(1.03)] − 1 = 3.8835%. So the expected future spot rate is $.1038835. Carolina will need to pay $.1038835 × 20 million pesos = $2,077,670.

12. a. Less than because the discount would be more pronounced or the forward premium would be reduced.

b. More than because the option premium increased due to more uncertainty.

c. More than because there is an option premium on the option and the forward rate has no premium in this example, and the expectation is that the future spot rate will be no higher than today's forward rate. The option is at the money, so the exercise price is the same as the expected spot rate but you have to pay the option premium.

13. The expected returns of each person are as follows:

Karen earns 6 percent due to interest rate parity, and earns the same return as that she could earn locally.

Marcia earns 7 percent due to interest rate parity, and earns the same return as that she could earn locally.

William earns 8.6 percent. If he converts, C$ = $.625 today. After 1 year, C$ = $.61. So if William invests C$1,000, it converts to $625. At the end of 1 year, he has $662.50. He converts to C$ and has C$1,086.

James is expected to earn 6 percent, since the international Fisher effect (IFE) suggests that on average, the exchange rate movement will offset the interest rate differential.

14. a. The IFE disagrees with the theory from Chapter 4 that a currency will appreciate if it has a high interest rate (holding other factors such as inflation constant). The IFE says that capital flows will not go to where the interest rate is higher because the higher interest rate reflects a higher expectation of inflation, which means the currency will weaken over time.

If you believe the higher interest rate reflects higher expected inflation, then the IFE makes sense. However, in many cases (such as this case), a higher interest rate may be caused by reasons other than inflation (perhaps the U.K. economy is strong and many firms are borrowing money right now), and if so, then there is no reason to think the currency will depreciate in the future. Therefore, the IFE would not make sense.

The key is that you can see the two different arguments, so that you can understand why a high interest rate may lead to local currency depreciation in some cases and appreciation in other cases.

b. If U.S. investors attempt to capitalize on the higher rate without covering, they do not know what their return will be. However, if they believe in the IFE, then this means that the United Kingdom's higher interest rate of 3 percent above that in the United States reflects a higher expected inflation rate in the United Kingdom of about 3 percent. This implies that the best guess of the change in the pound will be –3 percent for the pound (since the IFE relies on PPP), which means that the best guess of the U.S. investor return is about 5 percent, the same as is possible domestically. It may be better, it may be worse, but on average, it is not expected to be any better than what investors can get locally.

The IFE is focused on situations in which you are trying to anticipate the movement in a currency and you know the interest rate differentials.

Interest rate parity uses interest rate differentials to derive the forward rate. The 1-year forward rate would be exactly equal to the expected future spot rate if you use the IFE to derive a best guess of the future spot rate in 1 year. But if you invest and cover with the forward rate, you know exactly what your outcome will be. If you invest and do not cover, the IFE gives you a prediction of what the outcome will be, but it is just a guess. The result could be 20 percent above or below that guess or even farther away from the guess.

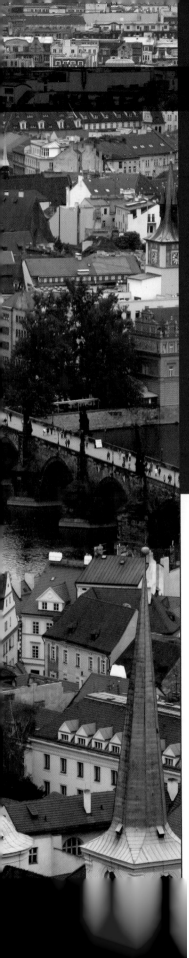

Exchange Rate Risk Management

Part 3 (Chapters 9 through 12) explains the various functions involved in managing exposure to exchange rate risk. Chapter 9 describes various methods used to forecast exchange rates and explains how to assess forecasting performance. Chapter 10 demonstrates how to measure exposure to exchange rate movements. Given a firm's exposure and forecasts of future exchange rates, Chapters 11 and 12 explain how to hedge that exposure.

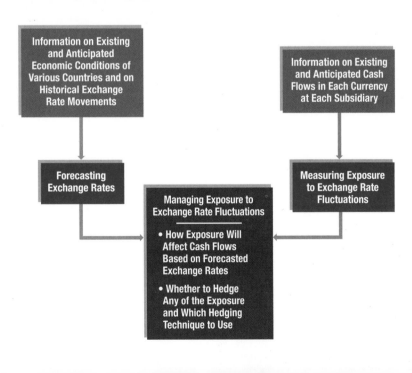

Information on Existing and Anticipated Economic Conditions of Various Countries and on Historical Exchange Rate Movements

Information on Existing and Anticipated Cash Flows in Each Currency at Each Subsidiary

Forecasting Exchange Rates

Measuring Exposure to Exchange Rate Fluctuations

Managing Exposure to Exchange Rate Fluctuations

- How Exposure Will Affect Cash Flows Based on Forecasted Exchange Rates

- Whether to Hedge Any of the Exposure and Which Hedging Technique to Use

9

Forecasting Exchange Rates

CHAPTER OBJECTIVES

The specific objectives of this chapter are to:

■ explain how firms can benefit from forecasting exchange rates,

■ describe the common techniques used for forecasting, and

■ explain how forecasting performance can be evaluated.

The cost of an MNC's operations and the revenue received from operations are affected by exchange rate movements. Therefore, an MNC's forecasts of exchange rate movements can affect the feasibility of its planned projects and might influence its managerial decisions. An MNC's revisions of exchange rate forecasts can change the relative benefits of alternative proposed operations and may cause the MNC to revise its business strategies.

WHY FIRMS FORECAST EXCHANGE RATES

Virtually every operation of an MNC can be influenced by changes in exchange rates. The following are some of the corporate functions for which exchange rate forecasts are necessary:

- *Hedging decision.* MNCs constantly face the decision of whether to hedge future payables and receivables in foreign currencies. Whether a firm hedges may be determined by its forecasts of foreign currency values.

EXAMPLE   Laredo Co., based in the United States, plans to pay for clothing imported from Mexico in 90 days. If the forecasted value of the peso in 90 days is sufficiently below the 90-day forward rate, the MNC may decide not to hedge. Forecasting may enable the firm to make a decision that will increase its cash flows. ●

- *Short-term investment decision.* Corporations sometimes have a substantial amount of excess cash available for a short time period. Large deposits can be established in several currencies. The ideal currency for deposits will (1) exhibit a high interest rate and (2) strengthen in value over the investment period.

EXAMPLE   Lafayette Co. has excess cash and considers depositing the cash into a British bank account. If the British pound appreciates against the dollar by the end of the deposit period when pounds will be withdrawn and exchanged for U.S. dollars, more dollars will be received. Thus, the firm can use forecasts of the pound's exchange rate when determining whether to invest the short-term cash in a British account or a U.S. account. ●

- *Capital budgeting decision.* When an MNC's parent assesses whether to invest funds in a foreign project, the firm takes into account that the project may periodically require the exchange of currencies. The capital budgeting analysis can be completed only when all estimated cash flows are measured in the parent's local currency.

EXAMPLE   Evansville Co. wants to determine whether to establish a subsidiary in Thailand. Forecasts of the future cash flows used in the capital budgeting process will be dependent on the future exchange rate of Thailand's currency (the baht) against the dollar. This dependency can be due to (1) future inflows denominated in baht that will require conversion to dollars and/or (2) the influence of future exchange rates on demand for the subsidiary's products. Accurate forecasts of currency values will improve the estimates of the cash flows and therefore enhance the MNC's decision making. ●

- *Earnings assessment.* The parent's decision about whether a foreign subsidiary should reinvest earnings in a foreign country or remit earnings back to the parent may be influenced by exchange rate forecasts. If a strong foreign currency is expected to weaken substantially against the parent's currency, the parent may prefer to expedite the remittance of subsidiary earnings before the foreign currency weakens.

  Exchange rate forecasts are also useful for forecasting an MNC's earnings. When earnings of an MNC are reported, subsidiary earnings are consolidated and translated into the currency representing the parent firm's home country.

EXAMPLE DuPont has a large amount of business in Europe. Its forecast of consolidated earnings requires a forecast of earnings generated by subsidiaries in each country along with a forecast of the exchange rate at which those earnings will be translated into dollars (in order to consolidate all earnings into a single currency). ●

- *Long-term financing decision.* Corporations that issue bonds to secure long-term funds may consider denominating the bonds in foreign currencies. They prefer that the currency borrowed depreciate over time against the currency they are receiving from sales. To estimate the cost of issuing bonds denominated in a foreign currency, forecasts of exchange rates are required.

EXAMPLE Bryce Co. needs long-term funds to support its U.S. business. It can issue 10-year bonds denominated in Japanese yen at a 1 percent coupon rate, which is 5 percentage points less than the prevailing coupon rate on dollar-denominated bonds. However, Bryce will need to convert dollars to make the coupon or principal payments on the yen-denominated bond, so if the yen's value rises, the yen-denominated bond could be more costly to Bryce than the U.S. bond. Bryce's decision to issue yen-denominated bonds versus dollar-denominated bonds will be dependent on its forecast of the yen's exchange rate over the 10-year period. ●

Most forecasting is applied to currencies whose exchange rates fluctuate continuously, and that is the focus of this chapter. However, some forecasts are also derived for currencies whose exchange rates are pegged. MNCs recognize that a pegged exchange rate today does not necessarily serve as a good forecast for the future.

EXAMPLE The Argentine peso was pegged at 1 U.S. dollar in 2001, but its exchange rate was allowed to fluctuate in the following year, and the peso is now worth less than $.40. If in 2001, MNCs forecasted the Argentine peso's exchange rate for several years ahead based on the pegged exchange rate that existed at that time, their forecasts would have been very poor. ●

An MNC's motives for forecasting exchange rates are summarized in Exhibit 9.1. The motives are distinguished according to whether they can enhance the MNC's value by influencing its cash flows or its cost of capital. The need for accurate exchange rate projections should now be clear. The following section describes the forecasting methods available.

FORECASTING TECHNIQUES

The numerous methods available for forecasting exchange rates can be categorized into four general groups: (1) technical, (2) fundamental, (3) market based, and (4) mixed.

Technical Forecasting

Technical forecasting involves the use of historical exchange rate data to predict future values.

Exhibit 9.1 Corporate Motives for Forecasting Exchange Rates

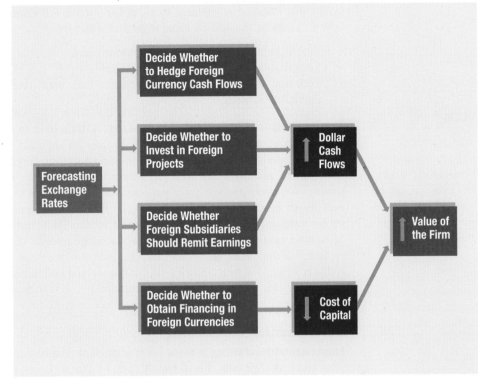

There may be a trend of successive daily exchange rate adjustments in the same direction, which could lead to a continuation of that trend. Alternatively, there may be a trend of the average daily change in the exchange rate per week over several recent weeks. A trend of higher mean daily exchange rate adjustments on a weekly basis may indicate that the exchange rate will continue to appreciate in the future.

Alternatively, there may be some technical indicators that a correction in the exchange rate is likely, which would result in a forecast that the exchange rate will reverse its direction.

Tomorrow Kansas Co. has to pay 10 million Mexican pesos for supplies that it recently received from Mexico. Today, the peso has appreciated by 3 percent against the dollar. Kansas Co. could send the payment today so that it would avoid the effects of any additional appreciation tomorrow. Based on an analysis of historical time series, Kansas has determined that whenever the peso appreciates against the dollar by more than 1 percent, it experiences a reversal of about 60 percent of that change on the following day. That is,

$$e_{t+1} = e_t \times (-60\%) \text{ when } e_t > 1\%$$

Applying this tendency to the current situation in which the peso appreciated by 3 percent today, Kansas Co. forecasts that tomorrow's exchange rate will change by

$$e_{t+1} = e_t \times (-60\%)$$
$$= (3\%) \times (-60\%)$$
$$= -1.8\%$$

Given this forecast that the peso will depreciate tomorrow, Kansas Co. decides that it will make its payment tomorrow instead of today. ●

Technical factors are sometimes cited as the main reason for changing speculative positions that cause an adjustment in the dollar's value. For example, headlines often attribute a change in the dollar's value to technical factors:

- Technical factors overwhelmed economic news.
- Technical factors triggered sales of dollars.
- Technical factors indicated that dollars had been recently oversold, triggering purchases of dollars.

Limitations of Technical Forecasting. MNCs tend to make only limited use of technical forecasting because it typically focuses on the near future, which is not very helpful for developing corporate policies. Most technical forecasts apply to very short-term periods such as 1 day because patterns in exchange rate movements are more systematic over such periods. Since patterns may be less reliable for forecasting long-term movements over a quarter, a year, or 5 years from now, technical forecasts are less useful for forecasting exchange rates in the distant future. Thus, technical forecasting may not be suitable for firms that need to forecast exchange rates in the distant future.

Technical forecasting rarely provides point estimates or a range of possible future values. In addition, a technical forecasting model that has worked well in one particular period will not necessarily work well in another. Unless historical trends in exchange rate movements can be identified, examination of past movements will not be useful for indicating future movements.

Fundamental Forecasting

Fundamental forecasting is based on fundamental relationships between economic variables and exchange rates. Recall from Chapter 4 that a change in a currency's spot rate is influenced by the following factors:

$$e = f(\Delta INF, \Delta INT, \Delta INC, \Delta GC, \Delta EXP)$$

where

e = percentage change in the spot rate

ΔINF = change in the differential between U.S. inflation and the foreign country's inflation

ΔINT = change in the differential between the U.S. interest rate and the foreign country's interest rate

ΔINC = change in the differential between the U.S. income level and the foreign country's income level

ΔGC = change in government controls

ΔEXP = change in expectations of future exchange rates

Given current values of these variables along with their historical impact on a currency's value, corporations can develop exchange rate projections.

A forecast may arise simply from a subjective assessment of the degree to which general movements in economic variables in one country are expected to affect exchange rates. From a statistical perspective, a forecast would be based on quantitatively measured impacts of factors on exchange rates. Although some of the full-blown fundamental models are beyond the scope of this text, a simplified discussion follows.

EXAMPLE

The focus here is on only two of the many factors that affect currency values. Before identifying them, consider that the corporate objective is to forecast the percentage change (rate of appreciation or depreciation) in the British pound with respect to the U.S. dollar during the next quarter. For simplicity, assume the firm's forecast for the British pound is dependent on only two factors that affect the pound's value:

1. Inflation in the United States relative to inflation in the United Kingdom.
2. Income growth in the United States relative to income growth in the United Kingdom (measured as a percentage change).

The first step is to determine how these variables have affected the percentage change in the pound's value based on historical data. This is commonly achieved with regression analysis. First, quarterly data are compiled for the inflation and income growth levels of both the United Kingdom and the United States. The dependent variable is the quarterly percentage change in the British pound value (called *BP*). The independent (influential) variables may be set up as follows:

1. Previous quarterly percentage change in the inflation differential (U.S. inflation rate minus British inflation rate), referred to as INF_{t-1}.
2. Previous quarterly percentage change in the income growth differential (U.S. income growth minus British income growth), referred to as INC_{t-1}.

The regression equation can be defined as

$$BP_t = b_0 + b_1 INF_{t-1} + b_2 INC_{t-1} + \mu_t$$

where b_0 is a constant, b_1 measures the sensitivity of BP_t to changes in INF_{t-1}, b_2 measures the sensitivity of BP_t to changes in INC_{t-1}, and μ_t represents an error term. A set of historical data is used to obtain previous values of *BP, INF,* and *INC.* Using this data set, regression analysis will generate the values of the regression coefficients (b_0, b_1, and b_2). That is, regression analysis determines the direction and degree to which *BP* is affected by each independent variable. The coefficient b_1 will exhibit a positive sign if, when INF_{t-1} changes, BP_t changes in the same direction (other things held constant). A negative sign indicates that BP_t and INF_{t-1} move in opposite directions. In the equation given, b_1 is expected to exhibit a positive sign because when U.S. inflation increases relative to inflation in the United Kingdom, upward pressure is exerted on the pound's value.

The regression coefficient b_2 (which measures the impact of INC_{t-1} on BP_t) is expected to be positive because when U.S. income growth exceeds British income growth, there is upward pressure on the pound's value. These relationships have already been thoroughly discussed in Chapter 4.

Once regression analysis is employed to generate values of the coefficients, these coefficients can be used to forecast. To illustrate, assume the following values: b_0 = .002, b_1 = .8, and b_2 = 1.0. The coefficients can be interpreted as follows. For a one-unit percentage change in the inflation differential, the pound is expected to change by .8 percent in the same direction, other things held constant. For a one-unit percentage change in the income differential, the British pound is expected to change by 1.0 percent in the same direction, other things held constant. To develop forecasts, assume that the most recent quarterly percentage change in INF_{t-1} (the inflation differential) is 4 percent and that INC_{t-1} (the income growth differential) is 2 percent. Using this information along with our estimated regression coefficients, the forecast for BP_t is

$$\begin{aligned} BP_t &= b_0 + b_1 INF_{t-1} + b_2 INC_{t-1} \\ &= .002 + .8(4\%) + 1(2\%) \\ &= .2\% + 3.2\% + 2\% \\ &= 5.4\% \end{aligned}$$

Thus, given the current figures for inflation rates and income growth, the pound should appreciate by 5.4 percent during the next quarter. ●

This example is simplified to illustrate how fundamental analysis can be implemented for forecasting. A full-blown model might include many more than two factors, but the application would still be similar. A large time-series database would be necessary to warrant any confidence in the relationships detected by such a model.

Use of Sensitivity Analysis for Fundamental Forecasting. When a regression model is used for forecasting, and the values of the influential factors have a lagged impact on exchange rates, the actual value of those factors can be used as input for the

forecast. For example, if the inflation differential has a lagged impact on exchange rates, the inflation differential in the previous period may be used to forecast the percentage change in the exchange rate over the future period. Some factors, however, have an instantaneous influence on exchange rates. Since these factors obviously cannot be known, forecasts must be used. Firms recognize that poor forecasts of these factors can cause poor forecasts of the exchange rate movements, so they may attempt to account for the uncertainty by using **sensitivity analysis**, which considers more than one possible outcome for the factors exhibiting uncertainty.

EXAMPLE

Phoenix Corp. develops a regression model to forecast the percentage change in the Mexican peso's value. It believes that the real interest rate differential and the inflation differential are the only factors that affect exchange rate movements, as shown in this regression model:

$$e_t = a_0 + a_1 INT_t + a_2 INF_{t-1} + \mu_t$$

where

e_t = percentage change in the peso's exchange rate over period t

INT_t = real interest rate differential over period t

INF_{t-1} = inflation differential in the previous period t

a_0, a_1, a_2 = regression coefficients

μ_t = error term

Historical data are used to determine values for *e,* along with values for INT_t and INF_{t-1} for several periods (preferably, 30 or more periods are used to build the database). The length of each historical period (quarter, month, etc.) should match the length of the period for which the forecast is needed. The historical data needed per period for the Mexican peso model are (1) the percentage change in the peso's value, (2) the U.S. real interest rate minus the Mexican real interest rate, and (3) the U.S. inflation rate in the previous period minus the Mexican inflation rate in the previous period. Assume that regression analysis has provided the following estimates for the regression coefficients:

REGRESSION COEFFICIENT	ESTIMATE
a_0	.001
a_1	−.7
a_2	.6

The negative sign of a_1 indicates a negative relationship between INT_t and the peso's movements, while the positive sign of a_2 indicates a positive relationship between INF_{t-1} and the peso's movements.

To forecast the peso's percentage change over the upcoming period, INT_t and INF_{t-1} must be estimated. Assume that INF_{t-1} was 1 percent. However, INT_t is not known at the beginning of the period and must therefore be forecasted. Assume that Phoenix Corp. has developed the following probability distribution for INT_t:

PROBABILITY	POSSIBLE OUTCOME
20%	−3%
50%	−4%
30%	−5%
100%	

A separate forecast of e_t can be developed from each possible outcome of INT_t as follows:

FORECAST OF *INT*	FORECAST OF e_t	PROBABILITY
−3%	.1% + (−.7)(−3%) + .6(1%) = 2.8%	20%
−4%	.1% + (−.7)(−4%) + .6(1%) = 3.5%	50%
−5%	.1% + (−.7)(−5%) + .6(1%) = 4.2%	30%

If the firm needs forecasts for other currencies, it can develop the probability distributions of their movements over the upcoming period in a similar manner.

EXAMPLE

Phoenix Corp. can forecast the percentage change in the Japanese yen by regressing historical percentage changes in the yen's value against (1) the differential between U.S. real interest rates and Japanese real interest rates and (2) the differential between U.S. inflation in the previous period and Japanese inflation in the previous period. The regression coefficients estimated by regression analysis for the yen model will differ from those for the peso model. The firm can then use the estimated coefficients along with estimates for the interest rate differential and inflation rate differential to develop a forecast of the percentage change in the yen. Sensitivity analysis can be used to reforecast the yen's percentage change based on alternative estimates of the interest rate differential. ●

Use of PPP for Fundamental Forecasting.
Recall that the theory of purchasing power parity (PPP) specifies the fundamental relationship between the inflation differential and the exchange rate. In simple terms, PPP states that the currency of the relatively inflated country will depreciate by an amount that reflects that country's inflation differential. Recall that according to PPP, the percentage change in the foreign currency's value (e) over a period should reflect the differential between the home inflation rate (I_h) and the foreign inflation rate (I_f) over that period.

EXAMPLE

The U.S. inflation rate is expected to be 1 percent over the next year, while the Australian inflation rate is expected to be 6 percent. According to PPP, the Australian dollar's exchange rate should change as follows:

$$e_f = \frac{1 + I_{U.S.}}{1 + I_f} - 1$$
$$= \frac{1.01}{1.06} - 1$$
$$\cong -4.7\%$$

This forecast of the percentage change in the Australian dollar can be applied to its existing spot rate to forecast the future spot rate at the end of 1 year. If the existing spot rate (S_t) of the Australian dollar is $.50, the expected spot rate at the end of 1 year, $E(S_{t+1})$, will be about $.4765:

$$E(S_{t+1}) = S_t(1 + e_f)$$
$$= \$.50[1 + (-.047)]$$
$$= \$.4765$$ ●

In reality, the inflation rates of two countries over an upcoming period are uncertain and therefore would have to be forecasted when using PPP to forecast the future exchange rate at the end of the period. This complicates the use of PPP to forecast future exchange rates. Even if the inflation rates in the upcoming period were known with certainty, PPP might not be able to forecast exchange rates accurately.

Also, other factors, such as the interest rate differential between countries, can also affect exchange rates. For these reasons, the inflation differential by itself is not sufficient to accurately forecast exchange rate movements. Nevertheless, it should be included in any fundamental forecasting model.

Limitations of Fundamental Forecasting.
Although fundamental forecasting accounts for the expected fundamental relationships between factors and currency values, the following limitations exist:

1. The precise timing of the impact of some factors on a currency's value is not known. It is possible that the full impact of factors on exchange rates will not occur until 2, 3, or 4 quarters later. The regression model would need to be adjusted accordingly.
2. As mentioned earlier, some factors exhibit an immediate impact on exchange rates. They can be usefully included in a fundamental forecasting model only if forecasts can be obtained for them. Forecasts of these factors should be developed for a period that corresponds to the period for which a forecast of exchange rates is necessary. In this case, the accuracy of the exchange rate forecasts will be somewhat dependent on the accuracy of these factors. Even if a firm knows exactly how movements in these factors affect exchange rates, its exchange rate projections may be inaccurate if it cannot predict the values of the factors.
3. Some factors that deserve consideration in the fundamental forecasting process cannot be easily quantified. For example, what if large Australian exporting firms experience an unanticipated labor strike, causing shortages? This will reduce the availability of Australian goods for U.S. consumers and therefore reduce U.S. demand for Australian dollars. Such an event, which would put downward pressure on the Australian dollar value, normally is not incorporated into the forecasting model.
4. Coefficients derived from the regression analysis will not necessarily remain constant over time. In the previous example, the coefficient for INF_{t-1} was .6, suggesting that for a one-unit change in INF_{t-1}, the Mexican peso would appreciate by .6 percent. Yet, if the Mexican or U.S. governments imposed new trade barriers, or eliminated existing barriers, the impact of the inflation differential on trade (and therefore on the Mexican peso's exchange rate) could be affected.

These limitations of fundamental forecasting have been discussed to emphasize that even the most sophisticated forecasting techniques (fundamental or otherwise) cannot provide consistently accurate forecasts. MNCs that develop forecasts must allow for some margin of error and recognize the possibility of error when implementing corporate policies.

WEB

www.cmegroup.com
Quotes on currency futures that can be used to create market-based forecasts.

Market-Based Forecasting

The process of developing forecasts from market indicators, known as **market-based forecasting,** is usually based on either (1) the spot rate or (2) the forward rate.

Use of the Spot Rate.
Today's spot rate may be used as a forecast of the spot rate that will exist on a future date. To see why the spot rate can be a useful market-based forecast, assume the British pound is expected to appreciate against the dollar in the very near future. This expectation will encourage speculators to buy the pound with U.S. dollars today in anticipation of its appreciation, and these purchases can force the pound's value up immediately. Conversely, if the pound is expected to depreciate against the dollar, speculators will sell off pounds now, hoping to purchase them back at a lower

price after they decline in value. Such actions can force the pound to depreciate immediately. Thus, the current value of the pound should reflect the expectation of the pound's value in the very near future. Corporations can use the spot rate to forecast since it represents the market's expectation of the spot rate in the near future. When the spot rate is used as the forecast of the future spot rate, the implication is that the currency will not appreciate or depreciate. In reality, a currency's exchange rate tends to change every day, but the use of the spot rate as a forecast is common when financial managers do not have a strong belief that the currency will appreciate or depreciate. They realize that the currency's value will not remain constant, but use today's spot rate as their best guess of the spot rate at a future point in time.

Use of the Forward Rate. A forward rate quoted for a specific date in the future is commonly used as the forecasted spot rate on that future date. That is, a 30-day forward rate provides a forecast for the spot rate in 30 days, a 90-day forward rate provides a forecast of the spot rate in 90 days, and so on. Recall that the forward rate is measured as

$$F = S(1 + p)$$

where p represents the forward premium. Since p represents the percentage by which the forward rate exceeds the spot rate, it serves as the expected percentage change in the exchange rate:

$$E(e) = p$$
$$= (F/S) - 1 \text{ [by rearranging terms]}$$

EXAMPLE

If the 1-year forward rate of the Australian dollar is $.63, while the spot rate is $.60, the expected percentage change in the Australian dollar is

$$E(e) = p$$
$$= (F/S) - 1$$
$$= (.63/.60) - 1$$
$$= .05, \text{ or } 5\%$$

●

Rationale for Using the Forward Rate. The forward rate should serve as a reasonable forecast for the future spot rate because otherwise speculators would trade forward contracts (or futures contracts) to capitalize on the difference between the forward rate and the expected future spot rate.

EXAMPLE

If many speculators expect the spot rate of the British pound in 30 days to be $1.45, and the prevailing forward rate is $1.40, they might buy pounds 30 days forward at $1.40 and then sell them when received (in 30 days) at the spot rate existing then. As speculators implement this strategy, the substantial demand to purchase pounds 30 days forward will cause the 30-day forward rate to increase. Once the forward rate reaches $1.45 (the expected future spot rate in 30 days), there is no incentive for additional speculation in the forward market. Thus, the forward rate should move toward the market's general expectation of the future spot rate. In this sense, the forward rate serves as a market-based forecast since it reflects the market's expectation of the spot rate at the end of the forward horizon (30 days from now in this example). ●

Although the focus of this chapter is on corporate forecasting rather than speculation, it is speculation that helps to push the forward rate to the level that reflects the general expectation of the future spot rate. If corporations are convinced that the forward rate is a reliable indicator of the future spot rate, they can simply monitor this publicly quoted rate to develop exchange rate projections.

Long-Term Forecasting with Forward Rates.
Long-term exchange rate forecasts can be derived from long-term forward rates.

EXAMPLE
Assume that the spot rate of the euro is currently $1.00, while the 5-year forward rate of the euro is $1.06. This forward rate can serve as a forecast of $1.06 for the euro in 5 years, which reflects a 6 percent appreciation in the euro over the next 5 years. ●

Forward rates are normally available for periods of 2 to 5 years or even longer, but the bid/ask spread is wide because of the limited trading volume. Although such rates are rarely quoted in financial newspapers, the quoted interest rates on risk-free instruments of various countries can be used to determine what the forward rates would be under conditions of interest rate parity.

EXAMPLE
The U.S. 5-year interest rate is currently 10 percent, annualized, while the British 5-year interest rate is 13 percent. The 5-year compounded return on investments in each of these countries is computed as follows:

COUNTRY	FIVE-YEAR COMPOUNDED RETURN
United States	$(1.10)^5 - 1 = 61\%$
United Kingdom	$(1.13)^5 - 1 = 84\%$

Thus, the appropriate 5-year forward rate premium (or discount) of the British pound would be

$$p = \frac{1 + i_{U.S.}}{1 + i_{U.K.}} - 1$$

$$= \frac{1.61}{1.84} - 1$$

$$= -.125, \text{ or } -12.5\%$$

The results of this comparison suggest that the 5-year forward rate of the pound should contain a 12.5 percent discount. That is, the spot rate of the pound is expected to depreciate by 12.5 percent over the 5-year period for which the forward rate is used to forecast. ●

The governments of some emerging markets (such as those in Latin America) do not issue long-term fixed-rate bonds very often. Consequently, long-term interest rates are not available, and long-term forward rates cannot be derived in the manner shown here.

The forward rate is easily accessible and therefore serves as a convenient and free forecast. Like any method of forecasting exchange rates, the forward rate is typically more accurate when forecasting exchange rates for short-term horizons than for long-term horizons. Exchange rates tend to wander farther from expectations over longer periods of time.

Implications of the IFE and IRP for Forecasts.
Recall that if interest rate parity (IRP) holds, the forward rate premium reflects the interest rate differential between two countries. Also recall that if the international Fisher effect (IFE) holds, a currency that has a higher interest rate than the U.S. interest rate should depreciate against the dollar because the higher interest rate implies a higher level of expected inflation in that country than in the United States. Since the forward rate captures the nominal interest rate (and therefore the expected inflation rate) between two countries, it should provide more accurate forecasts for currencies in high-inflation countries than the spot rate.

EXAMPLE
Alves, Inc., is a U.S. firm that does business in Brazil, and it needs to forecast the exchange rate of the Brazilian real for 1 year ahead. It considers using either the spot rate or the forward rate to forecast the real. The spot rate of the Brazilian real is $.40. The 1-year interest rate in

Brazil is 20 percent versus 5 percent in the United States. The 1-year forward rate of the Brazilian real is $.35, which reflects a discount to offset the interest rate differential according to IRP (check this yourself). Alves believes that the future exchange rate of the real will be driven by the inflation differential between Brazil and the United States. It also believes that the real rate of interest in both Brazil and the United States is 3 percent. This implies that the expected inflation rate for next year is 17 percent in Brazil and 2 percent in the United States. The forward rate discount is based on the interest rate differential, which in turn is related to the inflation differential. In this example, the forward rate of the Brazilian real reflects a large discount, which means that it implies a forecast of substantial depreciation of the real. Conversely, using the spot rate of the real as a forecast would imply that the exchange rate at the end of the year will be what it is today. Since the forward rate forecast indirectly captures the differential in expected inflation rates, it is a more appropriate forecast method than the spot rate. ●

Firms may not always believe that the forward rate provides more accurate forecasts than the spot rate. If a firm is forecasting over a very short-term horizon such as a day or a week, the interest rate (and therefore expected inflation) differential may not be as influential. Second, some firms may believe that the interest rate differential may not even be influential in the long run. Third, if the foreign country's interest rate is usually similar to the U.S. rate, the forward rate premium or discount will be close to zero, meaning that the forward rate and spot rate will provide similar forecasts.

Mixed Forecasting

Because no single forecasting technique has been found to be consistently superior to the others, some MNCs prefer to use a combination of forecasting techniques. This method is referred to as **mixed forecasting.** Various forecasts for a particular currency value are developed using several forecasting techniques. The techniques used are assigned weights in such a way that the weights total 100 percent, with the techniques considered more reliable being assigned higher weights. The actual forecast of the currency is a weighted average of the various forecasts developed.

EXAMPLE

College Station, Inc., needs to assess the value of the Mexican peso because it is considering expanding its business in Mexico. The conclusions that would be drawn from each forecasting technique are shown in Exhibit 9.2. Notice that, in this example, the forecasted direction of the peso's value is dependent on the technique used. The fundamental forecast predicts the peso will appreciate, but the technical forecast and the market-based forecast predict it will depreciate. Also, notice that even though the fundamental and market-based forecasts are both driven by the same factor (interest rates), the results are distinctly different. ●

An MNC might decide that only the technical and market-based forecasts are relevant when forecasting in one period, but that the fundamental forecast is the only relevant forecast when forecasting in a later period. Its selection of a forecasting technique may even vary with the currency that it is assessing at a given point in time. For example, it may decide that a market-based forecast provides the best prediction for the pound, while fundamental forecasting generates the best prediction for the New Zealand dollar, and technical forecasting generates the best prediction for the Mexican peso.

 Impact of the Credit Crisis on Forecasts. When the credit crisis intensified in the fall of 2008, many MNCs used subjective judgment to complement their normal forecasting techniques. A common subjective forecast was that that during an international crisis, money flows to the United States because the dollar historically has been stable. Even though the United States was experiencing severe financial problems at that time and its interest rate was not very attractive, money flowed to the United States as expected, and many currencies weakened against the dollar. Partial reliance on subjective judgment improved the forecasting ability during the credit crisis.

Exhibit 9.2 Forecasts of the Mexican Peso Drawn from Each Forecasting Technique

	FACTORS CONSIDERED	SITUATION	FORECAST
Technical Forecast	Recent movement in peso	The peso's value declined below a specific threshold level in the last few weeks.	The peso's value will continue to fall now that it is beyond the threshold level.
Fundamental Forecast	Economic growth, inflation, interest rates	Mexico's interest rates are high, and inflation should remain low.	The peso's value will rise as U.S. investors capitalize on the high interest rates by investing in Mexican securities.
Market-Based Forecast	Spot rate, forward rate	The peso's forward rate exhibits a significant discount, which is attributed to Mexico's relatively high interest rates.	Based on the forward rate, which provides a forecast of the future spot rate, the peso's value will decline.

Reliance on Forecasting Services

Some MNCs hire forecasting services to obtain exchange rate forecasts rather than using their own forecasting techniques. Some forecasting services specialize in technical forecasts, while others specialize in fundamental forecasts. Their services can accommodate a wide range of forecast horizons, such as 1 day from now, 1 year from now, or 10 years from now.

There is no guarantee that MNCs will be able to purchase more accurate exchange rate forecasts than forecasts they could generate on their own. Some MNCs believe that hiring a forecasting service is justified because of other services (such as cash management) that can be provided by the firm. In addition, treasurers of some MNCs recognize the difficulty in generating accurate exchange rate forecasts and prefer not to be directly accountable for the potential error.

Governance of Forecasting Techniques Used

An MNC may benefit from implementing some general guidelines for financial managers that rely on exchange rate forecasts. First, all managers should be using the same forecasts that are endorsed by the MNC. Otherwise, one manager may be making decisions to capitalize on expected appreciation of a currency, while another manager may be making decisions to capitalize on expected depreciation of that currency. Second, if key decisions by an MNC are highly influenced by the exchange rate forecast technique applied, sensitivity analysis should be used to consider alternative forecasts. If the feasibility of a major proposed project is only judged to be feasible when one particular technique is used to forecast exchange rates, the project deserves a closer analysis before it is implemented.

FORECAST ERROR

Regardless of which method is used or which service is hired to forecast exchange rates, it is important to recognize that forecasted exchange rates are rarely perfect. MNCs commonly assess their forecast errors in the past in order to assess the accuracy of their forecasting techniques.

Measurement of Forecast Error

An MNC that forecasts exchange rates must monitor its performance over time to determine whether the forecasting procedure is satisfactory. For this purpose, a measurement of the forecast error is required. There are various ways to compute forecast errors. One popular measurement is discussed here and is defined as follows:

$$\left.\begin{array}{l}\text{Absolute forecast error as a percentage} \\ \text{of the realized value}\end{array}\right\} = \frac{\left|\begin{array}{cc}\text{Forecasted} & \text{Realized} \\ \text{value} & \text{value}\end{array}\right|}{\begin{array}{c}\text{Realized} \\ \text{value}\end{array}}$$

The error is computed using an absolute value because this avoids a possible offsetting effect when determining the mean forecast error. If the forecast error is .05 in the first period and −.05 in the second period (if the absolute value is not taken), the mean error is zero. Yet, that is misleading because the forecast was not perfectly accurate in either period. The absolute value avoids such a distortion.

When comparing a forecasting technique's performance among different currencies, it is often useful to adjust for their relative sizes.

EXAMPLE   Consider the following forecasted and realized values by New Hampshire Co. during one period:

	FORECASTED VALUE	REALIZED VALUE
British pound	$1.35	$1.50
Mexican peso	$ .12	$ .10

In this case, the difference between the forecasted value and the realized value is $.15 for the pound versus $.02 for the peso. This does not necessarily mean that the forecast for the peso is more accurate. When the size of what is forecasted is considered (by dividing the difference by the realized value), one can see that the British pound has been predicted with more accuracy on a percentage basis. With the data given, the forecasting error (as defined earlier) of the British pound is

$$\frac{|\$1.35 - \$1.50|}{\$1.50} = \frac{\$.15}{\$1.50} = .10, \text{ or } 10\%$$

In contrast, the forecast error of the Mexican peso is

$$\frac{|.12 - .10|}{.10} = \frac{.02}{.10} = .20, \text{ or } 20\%$$

Thus, the peso has been predicted with less accuracy. ●

Forecast Errors among Time Horizons

The potential forecast error for a particular currency depends on the forecast horizon. A forecast of the spot rate of the euro for tomorrow will have a relatively small error because tomorrow's spot rate probably will not deviate much from today's spot rate. However, a forecast of the euro in 1 month is more difficult because the euro's value has more time to stray from today's spot rate. A forecast of the euro for 1 year ahead is even more difficult, and a forecast of 10 years ahead will very likely be subject to very large error.

Forecast Errors over Time Periods

The forecast error for a given currency changes over time. In periods when a country is experiencing economic and political problems, its currency is more volatile and more

Exhibit 9.3 Absolute Forecast Error (as % of Realized Value) for the British Pound over Time

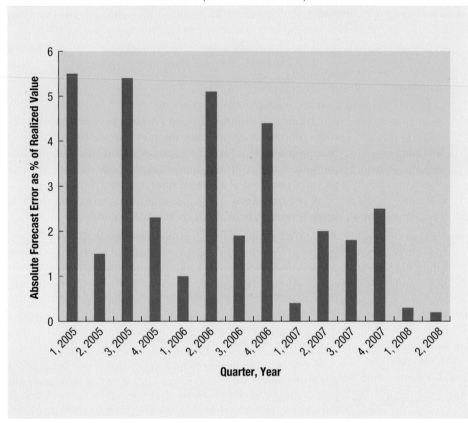

difficult to predict. Exhibit 9.3 shows the magnitude of the absolute errors when the spot rate is used as a predictor for the British pound over time. The size of the errors changes over time, because the errors were larger in periods when the pound's value was more volatile.

Forecast Errors among Currencies

The ability to forecast currency values may vary with the currency of concern. From a U.S. perspective, the Canadian dollar stands out as the currency most accurately predicted. Its mean absolute forecast error is typically less than those of other major currencies because its value is more stable over time. This information is important because it means that a financial manager of a U.S. firm can feel more confident about the number of dollars to be received (or needed) on Canadian transactions. However, even the Canadian dollar has been subject to a large forecast error in recent years.

Exhibit 9.4 shows results from comparing the mean absolute forecast error to the volatility (standard deviation of exchange rate movements) for selected currencies based on quarterly data over the 2005–2008 period. The quarterly forecasts for each currency were derived using the respective currency's prevailing spot rate as the forecast for 1 quarter ahead. Notice that the currencies that have relatively high exchange rate volatility (such as the Brazilian real and the Chilean peso) tend to have higher mean absolute forecast errors. Conversely, currencies that have relatively low volatility (such as the Chinese yuan) have lower mean absolute forecast errors.

Exhibit 9.4 How the Forecast Error Is Influenced by Volatility

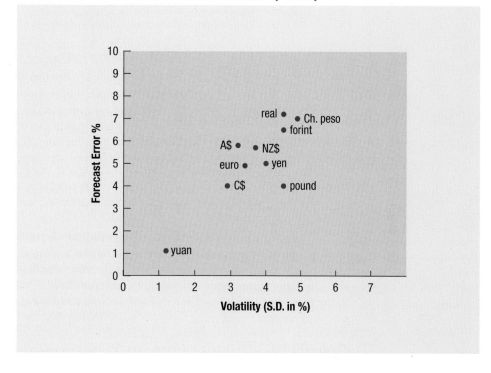

Forecast Bias

The difference between the forecasted and realized exchange rates for a given point in time is a forecast error. Negative errors over time indicate underestimating, while positive errors indicate overestimating. If the errors are consistently positive or negative over time, then a bias in the forecasting procedure does exist. It appears that a bias did exist in distinct periods. During the strong-pound periods, the forecasts underestimated, while in weak-pound periods, the forecasts overestimated.

Statistical Test of Forecast Bias.

If the forward rate is a biased predictor of the future spot rate, this implies that there is a systematic forecast error, which could be corrected to improve forecast accuracy. If the forward rate is unbiased, it fully reflects all available information about the future spot rate. In any case, any forecast errors would be the result of events that could not have been anticipated from existing information at the time of the forecast. A conventional method of testing for a forecast bias is to apply the following regression model to historical data:

$$S_t = a_0 + a_1 F_{t-1} + \mu_t$$

where

S_t = spot rate at time t

F_{t-1} = forward rate at time $t-1$

μ_t = error term

a_0 = intercept

a_1 = regression coefficient

If the forward rate is unbiased, the intercept should equal zero, and the regression coefficient a_1 should equal 1.0. The t-test for a_1 is

$$t = \frac{a_1 - 1}{\text{Standard error of } a_1}$$

If $a_0 = 0$ and a_1 is significantly less than 1.0, this implies that the forward rate is systematically overestimating the spot rate. For example, if $a_0 = 0$ and $a_1 = .90$, the future spot rate is estimated to be 90 percent of the forecast generated by the forward rate.

Conversely, if $a_0 = 0$ and a_1 is significantly greater than 1.0, this implies that the forward rate is systematically underestimating the spot rate. For example, if $a = 0$ and $a_1 = 1.1$, the future spot rate is estimated to be 1.1 times the forecast generated by the forward rate.

When a bias is detected and anticipated to persist in the future, future forecasts may incorporate that bias. For example, if $a_1 = 1.1$, future forecasts of the spot rate may incorporate this information by multiplying the forward rate by 1.1 to create a forecast of the future spot rate.

By detecting a bias, an MNC may be able to adjust for the bias so that it can improve its forecasting accuracy. For example, if the errors are consistently positive, an MNC could adjust today's forward rate downward to reflect the bias. Over time, a forecasting bias can change (from underestimating to overestimating, or vice versa). Any adjustment to the forward rate used as a forecast would need to reflect the anticipated bias for the period of concern.

Graphic Evaluation of Forecast Performance

Forecast performance can be examined with the use of a graph that compares forecasted values with the realized values for various time periods.

EXAMPLE

For eight quarters, Tunek Co. used the 3-month forward rate of Currency Q to forecast value 3 months ahead. The results from this strategy are shown in Exhibit 9.5, and the predicted and realized exchange rate values in Exhibit 9.5 are compared graphically in Exhibit 9.6.

The 45-degree line in Exhibit 9.6 represents perfect forecasts. If the realized value turned out to be exactly what was predicted over several periods, all points would be located on that 45-degree line in Exhibit 9.6. For this reason, the 45-degree line is referred to as the **perfect forecast line**. The closer the points reflecting the eight periods are vertically to the 45-degree line, the better the forecast. The vertical distance between each point and the 45-degree line is

Exhibit 9.5 Evaluation of Forecast Performance

PERIOD	PREDICTED VALUE OF CURRENCY Q FOR END OF PERIOD	REALIZED VALUE OF CURRENCY Q AS OF END OF PERIOD
1	$.20	$.16
2	.18	.14
3	.24	.16
4	.26	.22
5	.30	.28
6	.22	.26
7	.16	.14
8	.14	.10

Exhibit 9.6 Graphic Evaluation of Forecast Performance

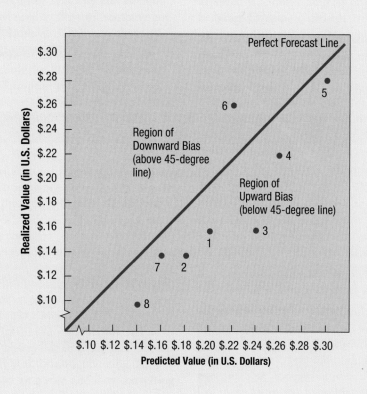

the forecast error. If the point is $.04 above the 45-degree line, this means that the realized spot rate was $.04 higher than the exchange rate forecasted. All points above the 45-degree line reflect underestimation, while all points below the 45-degree line reflect overestimation. ●

If points appear to be scattered evenly on both sides of the 45-degree line, then the forecasts are said to be *unbiased* since they are not consistently above or below the realized values. Whether evaluating the size of forecast errors or attempting to search for a bias, more reliable results are obtained when examining a large number of forecasts.

Graphic Evaluation of Forecast Performance over Subperiods.

Since forecast performance varies over time, it can be assessed across subperiods. Exhibit 9.7 compares the forecast (based on the prevailing spot rate) of the British pound to the future spot rate 1 quarter ahead. The upper left graph of the exhibit covers the period from April 2005 to July 2008. The points are scattered on both sides of the perfect forecast line, suggesting no obvious bias.

However, a more thorough assessment of a forecast bias can be conducted by separating the data into subperiods. The upper right graph shows that in the April 2005 to January 2006 subperiod, the forecasts overestimated the future spot rate because the pound generally depreciated against the dollar. The lower left graph shows that in the January 2006 to October 2007 period, the forecasts underestimated the future spot rate because the pound generally appreciated against the dollar. The lower right graph shows that in the October 2007 to July 2008 period, the forecast slightly overestimated the future spot rate because the pound depreciated slightly against the dollar.

Exhibit 9.7 Graphic Comparison of Forecasted and Realized Spot Rates in Different Subperiods for the British Pound (Using the Forward Rate as the Forecast)

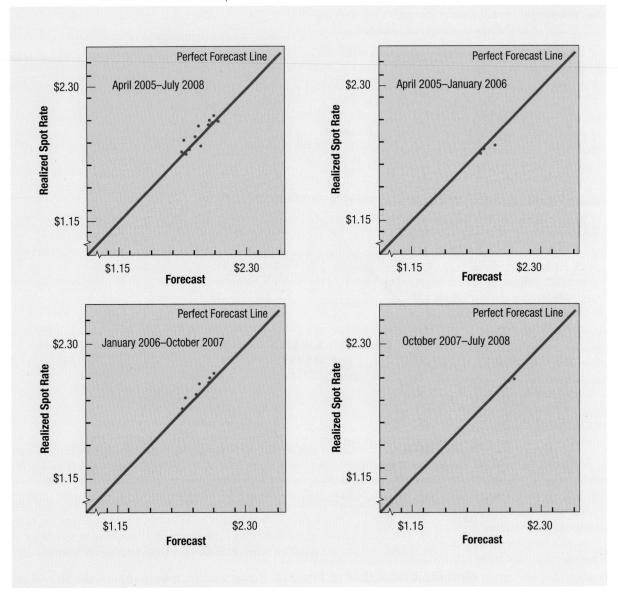

To the extent that a currency's value moves in the same direction, some forms of technical forecasting may derive forecasts that correct for previous forecast errors. However, when a currency's exchange rate reverses its direction, forecasts that correct for recent forecast errors would normally perform poorly.

Comparison of Forecasting Methods

An MNC can compare forecasting methods by plotting the points relating to two methods on a graph similar to Exhibit 9.6. The points pertaining to each method can be distinguished by a particular mark or color. The performance of the two methods can be evaluated by comparing distances of points from the 45-degree line. In some cases, neither forecasting

Exhibit 9.8 Comparison of Forecast Techniques

(1) PERIOD	(2) PREDICTED VALUE OF ZLOTY BY MODEL 1	(3) PREDICTED VALUE OF ZLOTY BY MODEL 2	(4) REALIZED VALUE OF ZLOTY	(5) ABSOLUTE FORECAST ERROR USING MODEL 1	(6) ABSOLUTE FORECAST ERROR USING MODEL 2	(7) = (5) – (6) DIFFERENCE IN ABSOLUTE FORECAST ERRORS (MODEL 1 – MODEL 2)
1	$.20	$.24	$.16	$.04	$.08	$–.04
2	.18	.20	.14	.04	.06	–.02
3	.24	.20	.16	.08	.04	.04
4	.26	.20	.22	.04	.02	.02
5	.30	.18	.28	.02	.10	–.08
6	.22	.32	.26	.04	.06	–.02
7	.16	.20	.14	.02	.06	–.04
8	.14	.24	.10	.04	.14	–.10
				Sum = .32 Mean = .04	Sum = .56 Mean = .07	Sum = –.24 Mean = –.03

method may stand out as superior when compared graphically. If so, a more precise comparison can be conducted by computing the forecast errors for all periods for each method and then comparing these errors.

EXAMPLE

Xavier Co. uses a fundamental forecasting method to forecast the Polish currency (zloty), which it will need to purchase to buy imports from Poland. Xavier also derives a second forecast for each period based on an alternative forecasting model. Its previous forecasts of the zloty, using Model 1 (the fundamental method) and Model 2 (the alternative method), are shown in columns 2 and 3, respectively, of Exhibit 9.8, along with the realized value of the zloty in column 4.

The absolute forecast errors of forecasting with Model 1 and Model 2 are shown in columns 5 and 6, respectively. Notice that Model 1 outperformed Model 2 in six of the eight periods. The mean absolute forecast error when using Model 1 is $.04, meaning that forecasts with Model 1 are off by $.04 on the average. Although Model 1 is not perfectly accurate, it does a better job than Model 2, which had a mean absolute forecast error of $.07. Overall, predictions with Model 1 are on the average $.03 closer to the realized value. ●

For a complete comparison of performance among forecasting methods, an MNC should evaluate as many periods as possible. Only eight periods are used in our example because that is enough to illustrate how to compare forecasting performance. If the MNC has a large number of periods to evaluate, it could statistically test for significant differences in forecasting errors.

Forecasting under Market Efficiency

The efficiency of the foreign exchange market also has implications for forecasting. If the foreign exchange market **is weak-form efficient,** then historical and current exchange rate information is not useful for forecasting exchange rate movements because today's exchange rates reflect all of this information. That is, technical analysis would not be capable of improving forecasts. If the foreign exchange market is **semistrong-form efficient,** then all relevant public information is already reflected in today's exchange rates.

If today's exchange rates fully reflect any historical trends in exchange rate movements, but not other public information on expected interest rate movements, the foreign exchange market is weak-form efficient but not semistrong-form efficient. Much research has tested the efficient market hypothesis for foreign exchange markets. Research suggests that foreign exchange markets appear to be weak-form efficient and semistrong-form efficient. However, there is some evidence of inefficiencies for some currencies in specific periods.

If foreign exchange markets are **strong-form efficient,** then all relevant public and private information is already reflected in today's exchange rates. This form of efficiency cannot be tested because private information is not available.

Even though foreign exchange markets are generally found to be at least semistrong-form efficient, forecasts of exchange rates by MNCs may still be worthwhile. Their goal is not necessarily to earn speculative profits but to use reasonable exchange rate forecasts to implement policies. When MNCs assess proposed policies, they usually prefer to develop their own forecasts of exchange rates over time rather than simply use market-based rates as a forecast of future rates. MNCs are often interested in more than a point estimate of an exchange rate 1 year, 3 years, or 5 years from now. They prefer to develop a variety of scenarios and assess how exchange rates may change for each scenario. Even if today's forward exchange rate properly reflects all available information, it does not indicate to the MNC the possible deviation of the realized future exchange rate from what is expected. MNCs need to determine the range of various possible exchange rate movements in order to assess the degree to which their operating performance could be affected.

USING INTERVAL FORECASTS

It is nearly impossible to predict future exchange rates with perfect accuracy. For this reason, MNCs may specify an interval around their point estimate forecast.

EXAMPLE

Harp, Inc., based in Oklahoma, imports products from Canada. It uses the spot rate of the Canadian dollar (currently $.70) to forecast the value of the Canadian dollar 1 month from now. It also specifies an interval around its forecasts, based on the historical volatility of the Canadian dollar. The more volatile the currency, the more likely it is to wander far from the forecasted value in the future (the larger is the expected forecast error). Harp determines that the standard deviation of the Canadian dollar's movements over the last 12 months is 2 percent. Thus, assuming the movements are normally distributed, it expects that there is a 68 percent chance that the actual value will be within 1 standard deviation (2 percent) of its forecast, which results in an interval from $.686 to $.714. In addition, it expects that there is a 95 percent chance that the Canadian dollar will be within 2 standard deviations (4 percent) of the predicted value, which results in an interval from $.672 to $.728. By specifying an interval, Harp can more properly anticipate how far the actual value of the currency might deviate from its predicted value. If the currency was more volatile, its standard deviation would be larger, and the interval surrounding the point estimate forecast would also be larger. ●

As this example shows, the measurement of a currency's volatility is useful for specifying an interval around a forecast. However, the volatility of a currency can change over time, which means that past volatility levels will not necessarily be the optimal method of establishing an interval around a point estimate forecast. Therefore, MNCs may prefer to forecast exchange rate volatility to determine the interval surrounding their forecast.

The first step in forecasting exchange rate volatility is to determine the relevant period of concern. If an MNC is forecasting the value of the Canadian dollar each day over the next quarter, it may also attempt to forecast the standard deviation of daily exchange rate movements over this quarter. This information could be used along with the point estimate forecast of the Canadian dollar for each day to derive confidence intervals around each forecast.

Methods of Forecasting Exchange Rate Volatility

In order to use an interval forecast, the volatility of exchange rate movements can be forecast from (1) recent exchange rate volatility, (2) historical time series of volatilities, and (3) the implied standard deviation derived from currency option prices.

Use of the Recent Volatility Level.
The volatility of historical exchange rate movements over a recent period can be used to forecast the future. In our example, the standard deviation of monthly exchange rate movements in the Canadian dollar during the previous 12 months could be used to estimate the future volatility of the Canadian dollar over the next month.

Use of a Historical Pattern of Volatilities.
Since historical volatility can change over time, the standard deviation of monthly exchange rate movements in the last 12 months is not necessarily an accurate predictor of the volatility of exchange rate movements in the next month. To the extent that there is a pattern to the changes in exchange rate volatility over time, a series of time periods may be used to forecast volatility in the next period.

EXAMPLE

The standard deviation of monthly exchange rate movements in the Canadian dollar can be determined for each of the last several years. Then, a time-series trend of these standard deviation levels can be used to form an estimate for the volatility of the Canadian dollar over the next month. The forecast may be based on a weighting scheme such as 60 percent times the standard deviation in the last year, plus 30 percent times the standard deviation in the year before that, plus 10 percent times the standard deviation in the year before that. This scheme places more weight on the most recent data to derive the forecast but allows data from the last 3 years to influence the forecast. Normally, the weights that achieved the most accuracy (lowest forecast error) over previous periods would be used when applying this method to forecast exchange rate volatility. ●

WEB

www.fednewyork.org/
markets/impliedvolatility
.html
Implied volatilities of
major currencies. The
implied volatility can be
used to measure the
market's expectations of
a specific currency's
volatility in the future.

Various economic and political factors can cause exchange rate volatility to change abruptly, however, so even sophisticated time-series models do not necessarily generate accurate forecasts of exchange rate volatility. A poor forecast of exchange rate volatility can lead to an improper interval surrounding a point estimate forecast.

Implied Standard Deviation.
A third method for forecasting exchange rate volatility is to derive the exchange rate's implied standard deviation (ISD) from the currency option pricing model. Recall that the premium on a call option for a currency is dependent on factors such as the relationship between the spot exchange rate and the exercise (strike) price of the option, the number of days until the expiration date of the option, and the anticipated volatility of the currency's exchange rate movements.

There is a currency option pricing model for estimating the call option premium based on various factors. The actual values of each of these factors are known, except for the anticipated volatility. By plugging in the prevailing option premium paid by investors for that specific currency option, however, it is possible to derive the market's anticipated volatility for that currency. The volatility is measured by the standard deviation, which can be used to develop a probability distribution surrounding the forecast of the currency's exchange rate.

SUMMARY

- Multinational corporations need exchange rate forecasts to make decisions on hedging payables and receivables, short-term financing and investment, capital budgeting, and long-term financing.
- The most common forecasting techniques can be classified as (1) technical, (2) fundamental, (3) market based, and (4) mixed. Each technique has limitations, and the quality of the forecasts produced varies. Yet due to the high variability in exchange rates, each technique has limited accuracy.

- Forecasting methods can be evaluated by comparing the actual values of currencies to the values predicted by the forecasting method. To be meaningful, this comparison should be conducted over several periods. Two criteria used to evaluate performance of a forecast method are bias and accuracy. When comparing the accuracy of forecasts for two currencies, the absolute forecast error should be divided by the realized value of the currency to control for differences in the relative values of currencies.

POINT COUNTER-POINT

Which Exchange Rate Forecast Technique Should MNCs Use?

Point **Use the spot rate to forecast.** When a U.S.-based MNC firm conducts financial budgeting, it must estimate the values of its foreign currency cash flows that will be received by the parent. Since it is well documented that firms cannot accurately forecast future values, MNCs should use the spot rate for budgeting. Changes in economic conditions are difficult to predict, and the spot rate reflects the best guess of the future spot rate if there are no changes in economic conditions.

Counter-Point **Use the forward rate to forecast.** The spot rates of some currencies do not represent accurate or even unbiased estimates of the future spot rates. Many currencies of developing countries have generally declined over time. These currencies tend to be in countries that have high inflation rates. If the spot rate

had been used for budgeting, the dollar cash flows resulting from cash inflows in these currencies would have been highly overestimated. The expected inflation in a country can be accounted for by using the nominal interest rate. A high nominal interest rate implies a high level of expected inflation. Based on interest rate parity, these currencies will have pronounced discounts. Thus, the forward rate captures the expected inflation differential between countries because it is influenced by the nominal interest rate differential. Since it captures the inflation differential, it should provide a more accurate forecast of currencies, especially those currencies in high-inflation countries.

Who Is Correct? Use the Internet to learn more about this issue. Which argument do you support? Offer your own opinion on this issue.

SELF-TEST

Answers are provided in Appendix A at the back of the text.

1. Assume that the annual U.S. return is expected to be 7 percent for each of the next 4 years, while the annual interest rate in Mexico is expected to be 20 percent. Determine the appropriate 4-year forward rate premium or discount on the Mexican peso, which could be used to forecast the percentage change in the peso over the next 4 years.

2. Consider the following information:

CURRENCY	90-DAY FORWARD RATE	SPOT RATE THAT OCCURRED 90 DAYS LATER
Canadian dollar	$.80	$.82
Japanese yen	$.012	$.011

Assuming the forward rate was used to forecast the future spot rate, determine whether the Canadian dollar or the Japanese yen was forecasted with more accuracy, based on the absolute forecast error as a percentage of the realized value.

3. Assume that the forward rate and spot rate of the Mexican peso are normally similar at a given point in time. Assume that the peso has depreciated consistently and substantially over the last 3 years. Would the forward rate have been biased over this period? If so, would it typically have overestimated or underestimated the future spot rate of the peso (in dollars)? Explain.

4. An analyst has stated that the British pound seems to increase in value over the 2 weeks following announcements by the Bank of England (the British central bank) that it will raise interest rates. If this

statement is true, what are the inferences regarding weak-form or semistrong-form efficiency?

5. Assume that Mexican interest rates are much higher than U.S. interest rates. Also assume that interest rate parity (discussed in Chapter 7) exists. If you use the forward rate of the Mexican peso to forecast the Mexican peso's future spot rate, would you expect the peso to appreciate or depreciate? Explain.

6. Warden Co. is considering a project in Venezuela that will be very profitable if the local currency (bolivar) appreciates against the dollar. If the bolivar depreciates, the project will result in losses. Warden Co. forecasts that the bolivar will appreciate. The bolivar's value historically has been very volatile. As a manager of Warden Co., would you be comfortable with this project? Explain.

QUESTIONS AND APPLICATIONS

1. Motives for Forecasting. Explain corporate motives for forecasting exchange rates.

2. Technical Forecasting. Explain the technical technique for forecasting exchange rates. What are some limitations of using technical forecasting to predict exchange rates?

3. Fundamental Forecasting. Explain the fundamental technique for forecasting exchange rates. What are some limitations of using a fundamental technique to forecast exchange rates?

4. Market-Based Forecasting. Explain the market-based technique for forecasting exchange rates. What is the rationale for using market-based forecasts? If the euro appreciates substantially against the dollar during a specific period, would market-based forecasts have overestimated or underestimated the realized values over this period? Explain.

5. Mixed Forecasting. Explain the mixed technique for forecasting exchange rates.

6. Detecting a Forecast Bias. Explain how to assess performance in forecasting exchange rates. Explain how to detect a bias in forecasting exchange rates.

7. Measuring Forecast Accuracy. You are hired as a consultant to assess a firm's ability to forecast. The firm has developed a point forecast for two different currencies presented in the following table. The firm

asks you to determine which currency was forecasted with greater accuracy.

PERIOD	YEN FORE-CAST	ACTUAL YEN VALUE	POUND FORE-CAST	ACTUAL POUND VALUE
1	$.0050	$.0051	$1.50	$1.51
2	.0048	.0052	1.53	1.50
3	.0053	.0052	1.55	1.58
4	.0055	.0056	1.49	1.52

8. Limitations of a Fundamental Forecast. Syracuse Corp. believes that future real interest rate movements will affect exchange rates, and it has applied regression analysis to historical data to assess the relationship. It will use regression coefficients derived from this analysis along with forecasted real interest rate movements to predict exchange rates in the future. Explain at least three limitations of this method.

9. Consistent Forecasts. Lexington Co. is a U.S.-based MNC with subsidiaries in most major countries. Each subsidiary is responsible for forecasting the future exchange rate of its local currency relative to the U.S. dollar. Comment on this policy. How might Lexington Co. ensure consistent forecasts among the different subsidiaries?

10. **Forecasting with a Forward Rate.** Assume that the 4-year annualized interest rate in the United States is 9 percent and the 4-year annualized interest rate in Singapore is 6 percent. Assume interest rate parity holds for a 4-year horizon. Assume that the spot rate of the Singapore dollar is $.60. If the forward rate is used to forecast exchange rates, what will be the forecast for the Singapore dollar's spot rate in 4 years? What percentage appreciation or depreciation does this forecast imply over the 4-year period?

11. **Foreign Exchange Market Efficiency.** Assume that foreign exchange markets were found to be weak-form efficient. What does this suggest about utilizing technical analysis to speculate in euros? If MNCs believe that foreign exchange markets are strong-form efficient, why would they develop their own forecasts of future exchange rates? That is, why wouldn't they simply use today's quoted rates as indicators about future rates? After all, today's quoted rates should reflect all relevant information.

12. **Forecast Error.** The director of currency forecasting at Champaign-Urbana Corp. says, "The most critical task of forecasting exchange rates is not to derive a point estimate of a future exchange rate but to assess how wrong our estimate might be." What does this statement mean?

13. **Forecasting Exchange Rates of Currencies That Previously Were Fixed.** When some countries in Eastern Europe initially allowed their currencies to fluctuate against the dollar, would the fundamental technique based on historical relationships have been useful for forecasting future exchange rates of these currencies? Explain.

14. **Forecast Error.** Royce Co. is a U.S. firm with future receivables 1 year from now in Canadian dollars and British pounds. Its pound receivables are known with certainty, and its estimated Canadian dollar receivables are subject to a 2 percent error in either direction. The dollar values of both types of receivables are similar. There is no chance of default by the customers involved. Royce's treasurer says that the estimate of dollar cash flows to be generated from the British pound receivables is subject to greater uncertainty than that of the Canadian dollar receivables. Explain the rationale for the treasurer's statement.

15. **Forecasting the Euro.** Cooper, Inc., a U.S.-based MNC, periodically obtains euros to purchase German products. It assesses U.S. and German trade patterns and inflation rates to develop a fundamental forecast for the euro. How could Cooper possibly improve its method of fundamental forecasting as applied to the euro?

16. **Forward Rate Forecast.** Assume that you obtain a quote for a 1-year forward rate on the Mexican peso. Assume that Mexico's 1-year interest rate is 40 percent, while the U.S. 1-year interest rate is 7 percent. Over the next year, the peso depreciates by 12 percent. Do you think the forward rate overestimated the spot rate 1 year ahead in this case? Explain.

17. **Forecasting Based on PPP versus the Forward Rate.** You believe that the Singapore dollar's exchange rate movements are mostly attributed to purchasing power parity. Today, the nominal annual interest rate in Singapore is 18 percent. The nominal annual interest rate in the United States is 3 percent. You expect that annual inflation will be about 4 percent in Singapore and 1 percent in the United States. Assume that interest rate parity holds. Today the spot rate of the Singapore dollar is $.63. Do you think the 1-year forward rate would underestimate, overestimate, or be an unbiased estimate of the future spot rate in 1 year? Explain.

18. **Interpreting an Unbiased Forward Rate.** Assume that the forward rate is an unbiased but not necessarily accurate forecast of the future exchange rate of the yen over the next several years. Based on this information, do you think Raven Co. should hedge its remittance of expected Japanese yen profits to the U.S. parent by selling yen forward contracts? Why would this strategy be advantageous? Under what conditions would this strategy backfire?

Advanced Questions

19. **Probability Distribution of Forecasts.** Assume that the following regression model was applied to historical quarterly data:

$$e_t = a_0 + a_1 INT_t + a_2 INF_{t-1} + \mu_t$$

where

e_t = percentage change in the exchange rate of the Japanese yen in period t

INT_t = average real interest rate differential (U.S. interest rate minus Japanese interest rate) over period t

INF_{t-1} = inflation differential (U.S. inflation rate minus Japanese inflation rate) in the previous period

a_0, a_1, a_2 = regression coefficients

μ_t = error term

Assume that the regression coefficients were estimated as follows:

$$a_0 = .0$$
$$a_1 = .9$$
$$a_2 = .8$$

Also assume that the inflation differential in the most recent period was 3 percent. The real interest rate differential in the upcoming period is forecasted as follows:

INTEREST RATE DIFFERENTIAL	PROBABILITY
0%	30%
1	60
2	10

If Stillwater, Inc., uses this information to forecast the Japanese yen's exchange rate, what will be the probability distribution of the yen's percentage change over the upcoming period?

20. Testing for a Forecast Bias. You must determine whether there is a forecast bias in the forward rate. You apply regression analysis to test the relationship between the actual spot rate and the forward rate forecast (F):

$$S = a_0 + a_1(F)$$

The regression results are as follows:

COEFFICIENT	STANDARD ERROR
$a_0 = .006$	.011
$a_1 = .800$	.05

Based on these results, is there a bias in the forecast? Verify your conclusion. If there is a bias, explain whether it is an overestimate or an underestimate.

21. Effect of September 11 on Forward Rate Forecasts. The September 11, 2001, terrorist attack on the United States was quickly followed by lower interest rates in the United States. How would this affect a fundamental forecast of foreign currencies? How would this affect the forward rate forecast of foreign currencies?

22. Interpreting Forecast Bias Information. The treasurer of Glencoe, Inc., detected a forecast bias when using the 30-day forward rate of the euro to forecast future spot rates of the euro over various periods. He

believes he can use this information to determine whether imports ordered every week should be hedged (payment is made 30 days after each order). Glencoe's president says that in the long run the forward rate is unbiased and that the treasurer should not waste time trying to "beat the forward rate" but should just hedge all orders. Who is correct?

23. Forecasting Latin American Currencies. The value of each Latin American currency relative to the dollar is dictated by supply and demand conditions between that currency and the dollar. The values of Latin American currencies have generally declined substantially against the dollar over time. Most of these countries have high inflation rates and high interest rates. The data on inflation rates, economic growth, and other economic indicators are subject to error, as limited resources are used to compile the data.

a. If the forward rate is used as a market-based forecast, will this rate result in a forecast of appreciation, depreciation, or no change in any particular Latin American currency? Explain.

b. If technical forecasting is used, will this result in a forecast of appreciation, depreciation, or no change in the value of a specific Latin American currency? Explain.

c. Do you think that U.S. firms can accurately forecast the future values of Latin American currencies? Explain.

24. Selecting between Forecast Methods. Bolivia currently has a nominal 1-year risk-free interest rate of 40 percent, which is primarily due to the high level of expected inflation. The U.S. nominal 1-year risk-free interest rate is 8 percent. The spot rate of Bolivia's currency (called the boliviano) is $.14. The 1-year forward rate of the boliviano is $.108. What is the forecasted percentage change in the boliviano if the spot rate is used as a 1-year forecast? What is the forecasted percentage change in the boliviano if the 1-year forward rate is used as a 1-year forecast? Which forecast do you think will be more accurate? Why?

25. Comparing Market-based Forecasts. For all parts of this question, assume that interest rate parity exists, the prevailing 1-year U.S. nominal interest rate is low, and that you expect U.S. inflation to be low this year.

a. Assume that the country Dinland engages in much trade with the United States and the trade involves many different products. Dinland has had a zero trade balance with the United States (the value of exports and imports is about the same) in the past. Assume that you expect a high level of inflation (about 40 percent) in Dinland over the next year be-cause of a large increase in the prices of many products that Dinland produces. Dinland presently has a 1-year risk-free interest rate of more than 40 percent. Do you think that the prevailing spot rate or the 1-year forward rate would result in a more accurate forecast of Dinland's currency (the din) 1 year from now? Explain.

b.   Assume that the country Freeland engages in much trade with the United States and the trade in-volves many different products. Freeland has had a zero trade balance with the United States (the value of exports and imports is about the same) in the past. You expect high inflation (about 40 percent) in Freeland over the next year because of a large increase in the cost of land (and therefore housing) in Freeland. You be-lieve that the prices of products that Freeland produces will not be affected. Freeland presently has a 1-year risk-free interest rate of more than 40 percent. Do you think that the prevailing 1-year forward rate of Free-land's currency (the fre) would overestimate, underes-timate, or be a reasonably accurate forecast of the spot rate 1 year from now? (Presume a direct quotation of the exchange rate, so that if the forward rate underes-timates, it means that its value is less than the realized spot rate in 1 year. If the forward rate overestimates, it means that its value is more than the realized spot rate in 1 year.)

26. IRP and Forecasting. New York Co. has agreed to pay 10 million Australian dollars (A$) in 2 years for equipment that it is importing from Australia. The spot rate of the Australian dollar is $.60. The annualized U.S. interest rate is 4 percent, regardless of the debt maturity. The annualized Australian dollar interest rate is 12 percent regardless of the debt maturity. New York plans to hedge its exposure with a forward contract that it will arrange today. Assume that interest rate parity exists. Determine the amount of U.S. dollars that New York Co. will need in 2 years to make its payment.

27. Forecasting Based on the International Fisher Effect. Purdue Co. (based in the United States) ex-ports cable wire to Australian manufacturers. It in-voices its product in U.S. dollars and will not change its price over the next year. There is intense competition between Purdue and the local cable wire producers based in Australia. Purdue's competitors invoice their products in Australian dollars and will not be changing their prices over the next year. The annualized risk-free interest rate is presently 8 percent in the United States versus 3 percent in Australia. Today the spot rate of the

Australian dollar is $.55. Purdue Co. uses this spot rate as a forecast of the future exchange rate of the Aus-tralian dollar. Purdue expects that revenue from its cable wire exports to Australia will be about $2 million over the next year.

If Purdue decides to use the international Fisher effect rather than the spot rate to forecast the exchange rate of the Australian dollar over the next year, will its expected revenue from its exports be higher, lower, or unaffected? Explain.

28. IRP, Expectations, and Forecast Error. Assume that interest rate parity exists and it will continue to exist in the future. Assume that interest rates of the United States and the United Kingdom vary substantially in many periods. You expect that interest rates at the be-ginning of each month have a major effect on the British pound's exchange rate at the end of each month because you believe that capital flows between the United States and the United Kingdom influence the pound's exchange rate. You expect that money will flow to whichever country has the higher nominal interest rate. At the be-ginning of each month, you will either use the spot rate or the 1-month forward rate to forecast the future spot rate of the pound that will exist at the end of the month. Will the use of the spot rate as a forecast result in smaller, larger, or the same mean absolute forecast error as the forward rate when forecasting the future spot rate of the pound on a monthly basis? Explain.

29. Deriving Forecasts from Forward Rates. As-sume that interest rate parity exists. Today the 1-year U.S. interest rate is equal to 8 percent, while Mexico's 1-year interest rate is equal to 10 percent. Today the 2-year annualized U.S. interest rate is equal to 11 percent, while the 2-year annualized Mexican interest rate is equal to 11 percent. West Virginia Co. uses the forward rate to predict the future spot rate. Based on forward rates for 1 year ahead and 2 years ahead will the peso appreciate or depreciate from the end of year 1 until the end of year 2?

30. Forecast Errors from Forward Rates. Assume that interest rate parity exists. One year ago, the spot rate of the euro was $1.40 and the spot rate of the Japanese yen was $.01. At that time, the 1-year interest rate of the euro and Japanese yen was 3 percent and the 1-year U.S. interest rate was 7 percent. One year ago, you used the 1-year forward rate of the euro to derive a forecast of the future spot rate of the euro and the yen 1 year ahead. Today, the spot rate of the euro is $1.39, while the spot rate of the yen is $.009. Which currency did you forecast more accurately?

31. Forward versus Spot Rate Forecasts. Assume that interest rate parity exists and it will continue to exist in the future. Kentucky Co. wants to forecast the value of the Japanese yen in 1 month. The Japanese interest rate is lower than the U.S. interest rate. Kentucky Co. will either use the spot rate or the 1-month forward rate to forecast the future spot rate of the yen at the end of 1 month. Your opinion is that net capital flows between countries tend to move toward whichever country has the higher nominal interest rate and that these capital flows are the primary factor that affects the value of the currency. Will the forward rate as

a forecast result in a smaller, larger, or the same absolute forecast error as the use of today's spot rate when forecasting the future spot rate of the yen in 1 month? Briefly explain.

Discussion in the Boardroom
This exercise can be found in Appendix E at the back of this textbook.

Running Your Own MNC
This exercise can be found on the *International Financial Management* text companion website located at www.cengage.com/finance/madura.

BLADES, INC. CASE

Forecasting Exchange Rates

Recall that Blades, Inc., the U.S.-based manufacturer of roller blades, is currently both exporting to and importing from Thailand. Ben Holt, Blades' chief financial officer (CFO), and you, a financial analyst at Blades, Inc., are reasonably happy with Blades' current performance in Thailand. Entertainment Products, Inc., a Thai retailer for sporting goods, has committed itself to purchase a minimum number of Blades' Speedos annually. The agreement will terminate after 3 years. Blades also imports certain components needed to manufacture its products from Thailand. Both Blades' imports and exports are denominated in Thai baht. Because of these arrangements, Blades generates approximately 10 percent of its revenue and 4 percent of its cost of goods sold in Thailand.

Currently, Blades' only business in Thailand consists of this export and import trade. Ben Holt, however, is thinking about using Thailand to augment Blades' U.S. business in other ways as well in the future. For example, Holt is contemplating establishing a subsidiary in Thailand to increase the percentage of Blades' sales to that country. Furthermore, by establishing a subsidiary in Thailand, Blades will have access to Thailand's money and capital markets. For instance, Blades could instruct its Thai subsidiary to invest excess funds or to satisfy its short-term needs for funds in the Thai money market. Furthermore, part of the subsidiary's financing could be obtained by utilizing investment banks in Thailand.

Due to Blades' current arrangements and future plans, Ben Holt is concerned about recent developments in Thailand and their potential impact on the company's

future in that country. Economic conditions in Thailand have been unfavorable recently. Movements in the value of the baht have been highly volatile, and foreign investors in Thailand have lost confidence in the baht, causing massive capital outflows from Thailand. Consequently, the baht has been depreciating.

When Thailand was experiencing a high economic growth rate, few analysts anticipated an economic downturn. Consequently, Holt never found it necessary to forecast economic conditions in Thailand even though Blades was doing business there. Now, however, his attitude has changed. A continuation of the unfavorable economic conditions prevailing in Thailand could affect the demand for Blades' products in that country. Consequently, Entertainment Products may not renew its commitment for another 3 years.

Since Blades generates net cash inflows denominated in baht, a continued depreciation of the baht could adversely affect Blades, as these net inflows would be converted into fewer dollars. Thus, Blades is also considering hedging its baht-denominated inflows.

Because of these concerns, Holt has decided to reassess the importance of forecasting the baht-dollar exchange rate. His primary objective is to forecast the baht-dollar exchange rate for the next quarter. A secondary objective is to determine which forecasting technique is the most accurate and should be used in future periods. To accomplish this, he has asked you, a financial analyst at Blades, for help in forecasting the baht-dollar exchange rate for the next quarter.

Holt is aware of the forecasting techniques available. He has collected some economic data and conducted a preliminary analysis for you to use in your analysis. For example, he has conducted a time-series analysis for the exchange rates over numerous quarters. He then used this analysis to forecast the baht's value next quarter. The technical forecast indicates a depreciation of the baht by 6 percent over the next quarter from the baht's current level of $.023 to $.02162. He has also conducted a fundamental forecast of the baht-dollar exchange rate using historical inflation and interest rate data. The fundamental forecast, however, depends on what happens to Thai interest rates during the next quarter and therefore reflects a probability distribution. Based on the inflation and interest rates, there is a 30 percent chance that the baht will depreciate by 2 percent, a 15 percent chance that the baht will depreciate by 5 percent, and a 55 percent chance that the baht will depreciate by 10 percent.

Ben Holt has asked you to answer the following questions:

1. Considering both Blades' current practices and future plans, how can it benefit from forecasting the baht-dollar exchange rate?
2. Which forecasting technique (i.e., technical, fundamental, or market-based) would be easiest to use in forecasting the future value of the baht? Why?
3. Blades is considering using either current spot rates or available forward rates to forecast the future value of

the baht. Available forward rates currently exhibit a large discount. Do you think the spot or the forward rate will yield a better market-based forecast? Why?
4. The current 90-day forward rate for the baht is $.021. By what percentage is the baht expected to change over the next quarter according to a market-based forecast using the forward rate? What will be the value of the baht in 90 days according to this forecast?
5. Assume that the technical forecast has been more accurate than the market-based forecast in recent weeks. What does this indicate about market efficiency for the baht-dollar exchange rate? Do you think this means that technical analysis will always be superior to other forecasting techniques in the future? Why or why not?
6. What is the expected value of the percentage change in the value of the baht during the next quarter based on the fundamental forecast? What is the forecasted value of the baht using the expected value as the forecast? If the value of the baht 90 days from now turns out to be $.022, which forecasting technique is the most accurate? (Use the absolute forecast error as a percentage of the realized value to answer the last part of this question.)
7. Do you think the technique you have identified in question 6 will always be the most accurate? Why or why not?

SMALL BUSINESS DILEMMA

Exchange Rate Forecasting by the Sports Exports Company

The Sports Exports Company converts British pounds into dollars every month. The prevailing spot rate is about $1.65, but there is much uncertainty about the future value of the pound. Jim Logan, owner of the Sports Exports Company, expects that British inflation will rise substantially in the future. In previous years when British inflation was high, the pound depreciated. The prevailing British interest rate is slightly higher than the prevailing U.S. interest rate. The pound has risen slightly over each of the last several months. Jim wants to forecast the value of the pound for each of the next 20 months.

1. Explain how Jim can use technical forecasting to forecast the future value of the pound. Based on the information provided, do you think that a technical

forecast will predict future appreciation or depreciation in the pound?
2. Explain how Jim can use fundamental forecasting to forecast the future value of the pound. Based on the information provided, do you think that a fundamental forecast will predict appreciation or depreciation in the pound?
3. Explain how Jim can use a market-based forecast to forecast the future value of the pound. Do you think the market-based forecast will predict appreciation, depreciation, or no change in the value of the pound?
4. Does it appear that all of the forecasting techniques will lead to the same forecast of the pound's future value? Which technique would you prefer to use in this situation?

Internet/Excel Exercises

The website of the CME Group, which now owns the Chicago Mercantile Exchange among others, provides information about the exchange and the futures contracts offered on the exchange. Its address is www.cmegroup.com.

1. Use the CME Group website to review the historical quotes of futures contracts and obtain a recent quote for the Japanese yen and British pound contracts. Then go to www.oanda.com/convert/fxhistory. Obtain the spot exchange rate for the Japanese yen and British pound on the same date that you have futures contract quotations. Does the Japanese yen futures price reflect a premium or a discount relative to its spot rate? Does the futures price imply appreciation or depreciation of the Japanese yen? Repeat these two questions for the British pound.

2. Go to www.oanda.com/convert/fxhistory and obtain the direct exchange rate of the Canadian dollar at the beginning of each of the last 7 years. Insert this information in a column on an electronic spreadsheet. (See Appendix C for help on conducting analyses with Excel.) Repeat the process to obtain the direct exchange rate of the euro. Assume that you use the spot rate to forecast the future spot rate 1 year ahead. Determine the forecast error (measured as the absolute forecast error as a percentage of the realized value for each year) for the Canadian dollar in each year. Then determine the mean of the annual forecast error over all years. Repeat this process for the euro. Which currency has a lower forecast error on average? Would you have expected this result? Explain.

References

Liu, Shinhua, Jul/Aug 2007, Currency Derivatives and Exchange Rate Forecastability, *Financial Analysts Journal*, pp. 72–78.

Nucci, Francesco, Feb 2003, Cross-Currency, Cross-Maturity Forward Exchange Premiums as Predictors of Spot Rate Changes: Theory and Evidence, *Journal of Banking & Finance*, pp. 183–200.

Pong, Shiuyan, and Mark B. Shackleton, Oct 2004, Forecasting Currency Volatility: A Comparison of Implied Volatilities and AR(FI)MA Models, *Journal of Banking & Finance*, pp. 2541–2563.

10

Measuring Exposure to Exchange Rate Fluctuations

CHAPTER OBJECTIVES

The specific objectives of this chapter are to:

■ discuss the relevance of an MNC's exposure to exchange rate risk,

■ explain how transaction exposure can be measured,

■ explain how economic exposure can be measured, and

■ explain how translation exposure can be measured.

Exchange rate risk can be broadly defined as the risk that a company's performance will be affected by exchange rate movements. Since exchange rate movements can affect an multinational corporation's (MNC's) cash flow, they can affect an MNC's performance and value. Exchange rate movements are volatile, and therefore can have a substantial impact on an MNC's cash flows. MNCs closely monitor their operations to determine how they are exposed to various forms of exchange rate risk. Financial managers must understand how to measure the exposure of their MNCs to exchange rate fluctuations so that they can determine whether and how to protect their operations from that exposure. In this way, they can reduce the sensitivity of their MNC's values to exchange rate movements.

RELEVANCE OF EXCHANGE RATE RISK

Exchange rates are very volatile. Consequently, the dollar value of an MNC's future payables or receivables position in a foreign currency can change substantially in response to exchange rate movements. The following example illustrates how the value of a firm's transactions can change over time in response to exchange rate movements.

EXAMPLE

Consider a U.S. firm whose business is to import products and sell them in the United States. It pays 1 million euros at the beginning of each quarter. If it does not hedge, the dollar value of its payables changes in line with the value of the euro, as shown in Exhibit 10.1. When the euro was weak (such as in 2006), the firm's expenses were low. However, when the euro was strong (such as in 2008), its expenses were high. From the first quarter of 2006 to the second quarter of 2008, the euro appreciated by 34 percent, so the firm's expense (in dollars) to obtain the 1 million euros in order to purchase imports increased by 34 percent. ●

Now change the example by assuming that the U.S. firm was an exporter instead, and received 1 million euros every quarter and converted them to dollars. Exhibit 10.1 would be the same except that the dollars would represent the firm's revenue (in dollars) instead of expenses. This firm would have generated much higher revenue in 2008 when the euro was strong than in 2006 when the euro was weak.

There are some arguments that suggest an MNC's exposure to exchange rate risk is irrelevant. However, for each argument, there is a counterargument, as summarized here.

The Investor Hedge Argument

An argument for exchange rate irrelevance is that investors in MNCs can hedge exchange rate risk on their own. The investor hedge argument assumes that investors

303

Exhibit 10.1 Amount of Dollars Needed to Obtain Imports (transaction value is 1 million euros)

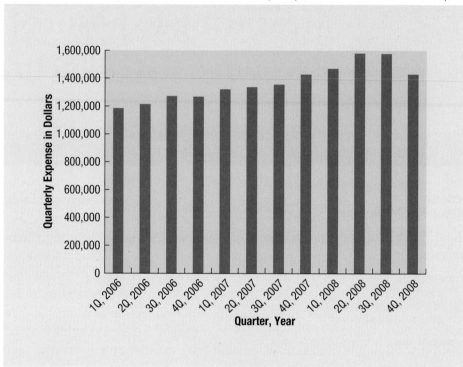

have complete information on corporate exposure to exchange rate fluctuations as well as the capabilities to correctly insulate their individual exposure. To the extent that investors prefer that corporations perform the hedging for them, exchange rate exposure is relevant to corporations. An MNC may be able to hedge at a lower cost than individual investors. In addition, it has more information about its exposure and can more effectively hedge its exposure.

Currency Diversification Argument

Another argument is that if a U.S.-based MNC is well diversified across numerous countries, its value will not be affected by exchange rate movements because of offsetting effects. It is naive, however, to presume that exchange rate effects will offset each other just because an MNC has transactions in many different currencies.

Stakeholder Diversification Argument

Some critics also argue that if stakeholders (such as creditors or stockholders) are well diversified, they will be somewhat insulated against losses experienced by any particular MNC due to exchange rate risk. Many MNCs are similarly affected by exchange rate movements, however, so it is difficult to compose a diversified portfolio of stocks that will be insulated from exchange rate movements.

Response from MNCs

Creditors that provide loans to MNCs can experience large losses if the MNCs experience financial problems. Thus, creditors may prefer that the MNCs maintain low exposure to exchange rate risk. Consequently, MNCs that hedge their exposure to risk may be able to borrow funds at a lower cost.

To the extent that MNCs can stabilize their earnings over time by hedging their exchange rate risk, they may also reduce their general operating expenses over time (by avoiding costs of downsizing and restructuring). Many MNCs, including Colgate-Palmolive, Eastman Kodak, and Merck, have attempted to stabilize their earnings with hedging strategies because they believe exchange rate risk is relevant. Further evidence that MNCs consider exchange rate risk to be relevant can be found in annual reports. The following comments from annual reports of MNCs are typical:

> *The primary purpose of the Company's foreign currency hedging program is to manage the volatility associated with foreign currency purchases of materials and other assets and liabilities created in the normal course of business. Corporate policy prescribes a range of allowable hedging activity.*
>
> *—Procter & Gamble Co.*

> *The Company enters into foreign exchange contracts and options to hedge various currency exposures.... The primary business objective of the activity is to optimize the U.S. dollar value of the Company's assets, liabilities, and future cash flows with respect to exchange rate fluctuations.*
>
> *—Dow Chemical Co.*

Since MNCs recognize that exchange rate risk is relevant, they may consider hedging their positions. They must determine how they are exposed before they can hedge their exposure. Firms are commonly subject to the following forms of exchange rate exposure.

- Transaction exposure
- Economic exposure
- Translation exposure

Each type of exposure will be discussed in turn.

TRANSACTION EXPOSURE

The value of a firm's future contractual transactions in foreign currencies is affected by exchange rate movements. The sensitivity of the firm's contractual transactions in foreign currencies to exchange rate movements is referred to as **transaction exposure.**

To assess transaction exposure, an MNC needs to (1) estimate its net cash flows in each currency and (2) measure the potential impact of the currency exposure.

Estimating "Net" Cash Flows in Each Currency

MNCs tend to focus on transaction exposure over an upcoming short-term period (such as the next month or the next quarter) for which they can anticipate foreign currency cash flows with reasonable accuracy. Since MNCs commonly have foreign subsidiaries spread around the world, they need an information system that can track their expected currency transactions. Subsidiaries should be able to access the same network and provide information on their existing currency positions and their expected transactions for the next month, quarter, or year.

To measure its transaction exposure, an MNC needs to project the consolidated net amount in currency inflows or outflows for all its subsidiaries, categorized by currency. One foreign subsidiary may have expected cash inflows of a foreign currency while another has cash outflows of that same currency. In that case, the MNC's net cash flows of that currency overall may be negligible. If most of the MNC's subsidiaries have future inflows in another currency, however, the net cash flows in that currency could be substantial. Estimating

Exhibit 10.2 Consolidated Net Cash Flow Assessment of Miami Co.

CURRENCY	TOTAL INFLOW	TOTAL OUTFLOW	NET INFLOW OR OUTFLOW	EXPECTED EXCHANGE RATE AT END OF QUARTER	NET INFLOW OR OUTFLOW AS MEASURED IN U.S. DOLLARS
British pound	£17,000,000	£7,000,000	+£10,000,000	$1.50	+$15,000,000
Canadian dollar	C$12,000,000	C$2,000,000	+C$10,000,000	$.80	+$ 8,000,000
Swedish krona	SK20,000,000	SK120,000,000	−SK100,000,000	$.15	−$15,000,000
Mexican peso	MXP90,000,000	MXP10,000,000	+MXP80,000,000	$.10	+$ 8,000,000

Exhibit 10.3 Estimating the Range of Net Inflows or Outflows for Miami Co.

CURRENCY	NET INFLOW OR OUTFLOW	RANGE OF POSSIBLE EXCHANGE RATES AT END OF QUARTER	RANGE OF POSSIBLE NET INFLOWS OR OUTFLOWS IN U.S. DOLLARS (BASED ON RANGE OF POSSIBLE EXCHANGE RATES)
British pound	+£10,000,000	$1.40 to $1.60	+$14,000,000 to +$16,000,000
Canadian dollar	+C$10,000,000	$.79 to $.81	+$ 7,900,000 to +$ 8,100,000
Swedish krona	−SK100,000,000	$.14 to $.16	−$14,000,000 to −$16,000,000
Mexican peso	+MXP80,000,000	$.08 to $.11	+$ 6,400,000 to +$ 8,800,000

the consolidated net cash flows per currency is a useful first step when assessing an MNC's exposure because it helps to determine the MNC's overall position in each currency.

EXAMPLE

Miami Co. conducts its international business in four currencies. Its objective is to first measure its exposure in each currency in the next quarter and then estimate its consolidated cash flows based on expected transactions for 1 quarter ahead, as shown in Exhibit 10.2. For example, Miami expects Canadian dollar inflows of C$12 million and outflows of C$2 million over the next quarter. Thus, Miami expects net inflows of C$10 million. Given an expected exchange rate of $.80 at the end of the quarter, it can convert the expected net inflow of Canadian dollars into an expected net inflow of $8 million (estimated as C$10 million × $.80).

The same process is used to determine the net cash flows of each of the other three currencies. Notice from the last column of Exhibit 10.2 that the expected net cash flows in three of the currencies are positive, while the net cash flows in the Swedish krona are negative (reflecting cash outflows). Thus, Miami will be favorably affected by appreciation of the pound, Canadian dollar, and Mexican peso. Conversely, it will be adversely affected by appreciation of the krona.

The information in Exhibit 10.2 needs to be converted into dollars so that Miami Co. can assess the exposure of each currency by using a standardized measure. For each currency, the net cash flows are converted into dollars to determine the dollar amount of exposure. Notice that Miami has a smaller dollar amount of exposure in Mexican pesos and Canadian dollars than in the other currencies. However, this does not necessarily mean that Miami will be less affected by these exposures, as will be explained shortly.

Recognize that the net inflows or outflows in each foreign currency and the exchange rates at the end of the period are uncertain. Thus, Miami might develop a range of possible exchange rates for each currency, as shown in Exhibit 10.3, instead of a point estimate. In this case, there is a range of net cash flows in dollars rather than a point estimate. Notice that the range of dollar cash flows resulting from Miami's peso transactions is wide, reflecting the high degree of uncertainty surrounding the peso's value over the next quarter. In contrast, the range of dollar cash flows resulting from the Canadian dollar transactions is narrow because the Canadian dollar is expected to be relatively stable over the next quarter. ●

Miami Co. assessed its net cash flow situation for only 1 quarter. It could also derive its expected net cash flows for other periods, such as a week or a month. Some MNCs assess their transaction exposure during several periods by applying the methods just described to each period. The further into the future an MNC attempts to measure its transaction exposure, the less accurate will be the measurement due to the greater uncertainty about inflows or outflows in each foreign currency as well as future exchange rates over periods further into the future. An MNC's overall exposure can be assessed only after considering each currency's variability and the correlations among currencies. The overall exposure of Miami Co. will be assessed after the following discussion of currency variability and correlations.

Exposure of an MNC's Portfolio

The dollar net cash flows of an MNC are generated from a portfolio of currencies. The exposure of the portfolio of currencies can be measured by the standard deviation of the portfolio, which indicates how the portfolio's value may deviate from what is expected. Consider an MNC that will receive payments in two foreign currencies. The risk (as measured by the standard deviation of monthly percentage changes) of a two-currency portfolio (σ_p) can be estimated as follows:

$$\sigma_p = \sqrt{W_X^2 \sigma_X^2 + W_Y^2 \sigma_Y^2 + 2 W_X W_Y \sigma_X \sigma_Y CORR_{XY}}$$

where

W_X = **proportion of total portfolio value that is in currency X**

W_Y = **proportion of total portfolio value that is in currency Y**

σ_X = **standard deviation of monthly percentage changes in currency X**

σ_Y = **standard deviation of monthly percentage changes in currrency Y**

$CORR_{XY}$ = **correlation coefficient of monthly percentage changes between currencies X and Y**

The equation shows that an MNC's exposure to multiple currencies is influenced by the variability of each currency and the correlation of movements between the currencies. The volatility of a currency portfolio is positively related to a currency's volatility and positively related to the correlation between currencies. Each component in the equation that affects a currency portfolio's risk can be measured using a series of monthly movements (percentage changes) in each currency. These components are described in more detail next.

Measurement of Currency Variability. The standard deviation statistic measures the degree of movement for each currency. In any given period, some currencies clearly fluctuate much more than others. For example, the standard deviations of the monthly movements in the Japanese yen and the Swiss franc are typically larger than that of the Canadian dollar. Based on this information, the potential for substantial deviations from the projected future values is greater for the yen and the Swiss franc than for the Canadian dollar (from a U.S. firm's perspective). Some currencies in emerging markets are very volatile.

Exhibit 10.4 compares the volatility (as measured by the standard deviation) of quarterly exchange rate movements against the dollar during the 2005–2008 period. Notice that the Chinese yuan has the lowest volatility level, which is partially attributed to China's efforts to keep the yuan stable. Conversely, the volatility of the Brazilian real, Chilean peso, and Hungarian forint is at least six times the volatility of the yuan. Thus, a U.S.-based MNC would normally be more concerned about exposure to these volatile currencies than to the yuan. The Canadian dollar exhibited relatively low volatility compared to most currencies.

Currency Variability over Time. The variability of a currency will not necessarily remain consistent from one time period to another. Nevertheless, an MNC can at least

Exhibit 10.4 Standard Deviation of Exchange Rate Movements (based on quarterly exchange rates, 2005–2008)

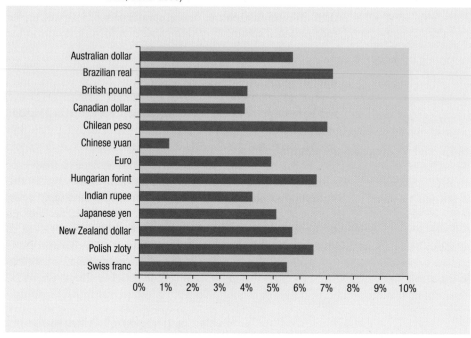

identify currencies whose values are *most likely* to be stable or highly variable in the future. For example, the Canadian dollar typically exhibits lower variability than other currencies, regardless of the period that is assessed.

As the credit crisis intensified in the fall of 2008, there was much uncertainty about the future of foreign economic conditions. The exchange rates of most currencies became very volatile because of the uncertainty. In general, MNCs were subject to a greater degree of risk because of the greater degree of exchange rate volatility. Most of the currencies shown in Exhibit 10.4 had volatility levels in 2008 that were more than twice their volatility levels in 2005–2007.

Measurement of Currency Correlations.
The correlations among currency movements can be measured by their *correlation coefficients,* which indicate the degree to which two currencies move in relation to each other. The extreme case is perfect positive correlation, which is represented by a correlation coefficient equal to 1.00. Correlations can also be negative, reflecting an inverse relationship between individual movements, the extreme case being –1.00.

Exhibit 10.5 shows the correlation coefficients (based on quarterly data) for several currency pairs. It is clear that some currency pairs exhibit a much higher correlation than others. The European currencies are highly correlated, whereas the Canadian dollar has a relatively low correlation with other currencies. Currency correlations are generally positive; this implies that currencies tend to move in the same direction against the U.S. dollar (though by different degrees). The positive correlation may not always occur on a day-to-day basis, but it tends to hold over longer periods of time for most currencies.

Applying Currency Correlations to Net Cash Flows.
The implications of currency correlations for a particular MNC depend on the cash flow characteristics of that MNC.

Exhibit 10.5 Correlations among Movements in Quarterly Exchange Rates

	BRITISH POUND	CANADIAN DOLLAR	EURO	JAPANESE YEN	SWEDISH KRONA
British pound	1.00				
Canadian dollar	.35	1.00			
Euro	.91	.48	1.00		
Japanese yen	.71	.12	.67	1.00	
Swedish krona	.83	.57	.92	.64	1.00

The equation for a portfolio's standard deviation suggests that positive cash flows in highly correlated currencies result in higher exchange rate risk for the MNC. However, many MNCs have negative net cash flow positions in some currencies; in these situations, the correlations can have different effects on the MNC's exchange rate risk. Exhibit 10.6 illustrates some common situations for an MNC that has exposure to only two currencies.

The concept of currency correlations can be applied to the earlier example of Miami Co.'s net cash flows, as displayed in Exhibit 10.3. Recall that Miami Co. anticipates cash inflows in the British pound equivalent to $15 million and cash outflows in the Swedish krona equivalent to $15 million. Thus, if a weak-dollar cycle occurs, Miami will be adversely affected by its exposure to the krona, but favorably affected by its pound exposure. During a strong-dollar cycle, it will be adversely affected by the pound exposure but favorably affected by its krona exposure. If Miami expects that these two currencies will move in the same direction and by about the same degree over the next period, its exposures to these two currencies are partially offset.

Miami may not be too concerned about its exposure to the Canadian dollar's movements because the Canadian dollar is somewhat stable with respect to the U.S. dollar over time; risk of substantial depreciation of the Canadian dollar is low. However, the company should be concerned about its exposure to the Mexican peso's movements because the peso is quite volatile and could depreciate substantially within a short period of time. Miami has no exposure to another currency that will offset the exposure to the peso. Therefore, Miami should seriously consider whether to hedge its expected net cash flow position in pesos. ●

Currency Correlations over Time. An MNC cannot use previous correlations to predict future correlations with perfect accuracy. Nevertheless, some general relationships tend to hold over time. For example, movements in the values of the pound, the euro, and other European currencies against the U.S. dollar tend to be highly correlated in most periods. In addition, the Canadian dollar tends to move independently of other currency movements.

Transaction Exposure Based on Value at Risk

A related method for assessing exposure is the value-at-risk (VAR) method, which measures the potential maximum 1-day loss on the value of positions of an MNC that is exposed to exchange rate movements.

Celia Co. will receive 10 million Mexican pesos (MXP) tomorrow as a result of providing consulting services to a Mexican firm. It wants to determine the maximum 1-day loss due to a potential decline in the value of the peso, based on a 95 percent confidence level. It estimates the standard deviation of daily percentage changes of the Mexican peso to be 1.2 percent over the last 100 days. If these daily percentage changes are normally distributed, the maximum 1-day

Exhibit 10.6 Impact of Cash Flow and Correlation Conditions on an MNC's Exposure

IF THE MNC'S EXPECTED CASH FLOW SITUATION IS:	AND THE CURRENCIES ARE:	THE MNC'S EXPOSURE IS RELATIVELY:
Equal amounts of net inflows in two currencies	Highly correlated	High
Equal amounts of net inflows in two currencies	Slightly positively correlated	Moderate
Equal amounts of net inflows in two currencies	Negatively correlated	Low
A net inflow in one currency and a net outflow of about the same amount in another currency	Highly correlated	Low
A net inflow in one currency and a net outflow of about the same amount in another currency	Slightly positively correlated	Moderate
A net inflow in one currency and a net outflow of about the same amount in another currency	Negatively correlated	High

loss is determined by the lower boundary (the left tail) of a one-tailed probability distribution, which is about 1.65 standard deviations away from the expected percentage change in the peso. Assuming an expected percentage change of 0 percent (implying no expected change in the peso) during the next day, the maximum 1-day loss is

$$\text{Maximum 1-day loss} = E(e_t) - (1.65 \times \sigma_{MXP})$$
$$= 0\% - (1.65 \times 1.2\%)$$
$$= -.0198, \text{ or } -1.98\%$$

Assume the spot rate of the peso is $.09. The maximum 1-day loss of −1.98 percent implies a peso value of

$$\text{Peso value based on maximum 1-day loss} = S \times (1 + \text{max 1-day loss})$$
$$= \$.09 \times [1 + (-.0198)]$$
$$= \$.088218$$

Thus, if the maximum 1-day loss occurs, the peso's value will have declined to $.088218. The dollar value of this maximum 1-day loss is dependent on Celia's position in Mexican pesos. For example, if Celia has MXP10 million, this represents a value of $900,000 (at $.09 per peso), so a decline in the peso's value of −1.98 percent would result in a loss of $900,000 × −1.98% = −$17,820. ●

Factors That Affect the Maximum 1-Day Loss. The maximum 1-day loss of a currency is dependent on three factors. First, it is dependent on the expected percentage change in the currency for the next day. If the expected outcome in the previous example is −.2 percent instead of 0 percent, the maximum loss over the 1-day period is

$$\text{Maximum 1-day loss} = E(e_t) - (1.65 \times \sigma_{MXP})$$
$$= -.2\% - (1.65 \times 1.2\%)$$
$$= -.0218, \text{ or } -2.18\%$$

Second, the maximum 1-day loss is dependent on the confidence level used. A higher confidence level will cause a more pronounced maximum 1-day loss, holding other factors constant. If the confidence level in the example is 97.5 percent instead of 95 percent, the lower boundary is 1.96 standard deviations from the expected percentage change in the peso. Thus, the maximum 1-day loss is

$$\text{Maximum 1-day loss} = E(e_t) - (1.96 \times \sigma_{MXP})$$
$$= 0\% - (1.96 \times 1.2\%)$$
$$= -.02352, \text{or} -2.352\%$$

Third, the maximum 1-day loss is dependent on the standard deviation of the daily percentage changes in the currency over a previous period. If the peso's standard deviation in the example is 1 percent instead of 1.2 percent, the maximum 1-day loss (based on the 95 percent confidence interval) is

$$\text{Maximum 1-day loss} = E(e_t) - (1.65 \times \sigma_{MXP})$$
$$= 0\% - (1.65 \times 1\%)$$
$$= -.0165, \text{or} -1.65\%$$

Applying VAR to Longer Time Horizons. The VAR method can also be used to assess exposure over longer time horizons. The standard deviation should be estimated over the time horizon in which the maximum loss is to be measured.

EXAMPLE

Lada, Inc., expects to receive Mexican pesos in 1 month for products that it exported. It wants to determine the maximum 1-month loss due to a potential decline in the value of the peso, based on a 95 percent confidence level. It estimates the standard deviation of monthly percentage changes of the Mexican peso to be 6 percent over the last 40 months. If these monthly percentage changes are normally distributed, the maximum 1-month loss is determined by the lower boundary (the left tail) of the probability distribution, which is about 1.65 standard deviations away from the expected percentage change in the peso. Assuming an expected percentage change of –1 percent during the next month, the maximum 1-month loss is

$$\text{Maximum 1-month loss} = E(e_t) - (1.65 \times \sigma_{MXP})$$
$$= -1\% - (1.65 \times 6\%)$$
$$= -.109, \text{or} -10.9\%$$ ●

If Lada, Inc., is uncomfortable with the magnitude of the potential loss, it can hedge its position as explained in the next chapter.

Applying VAR to Transaction Exposure of a Portfolio. Since MNCs are commonly exposed to more than one currency, they may apply the VAR method to a currency portfolio. When considering multiple currencies, software packages can be used to perform the computations. An example of applying VAR to a two-currency portfolio is provided here.

EXAMPLE

Benou, Inc., a U.S. exporting firm, expects to receive substantial payments denominated in Indonesian rupiah and Thai baht in 1 month. Based on today's spot rates, the dollar value of the funds to be received is estimated at $600,000 for the rupiah and $400,000 for the baht. Thus, Benou is exposed to a currency portfolio weighted 60 percent in rupiah and 40 percent in baht. Benou wants to determine the maximum expected 1-month loss due to a potential decline in the value of these currencies, based on a 95 percent confidence level. Based on data for the last 20 months, it estimates the standard deviation of monthly percentage changes to be 7 percent for the rupiah and 8 percent for the baht, and a correlation coefficient of .50 between the rupiah and baht. The portfolio's standard deviation is

$$\sigma_p = \sqrt{(.36)(.0049) + (.16)(.0064) + 2(.60)(.40)(.07)(.08)(.50)}$$
$$= \text{about} .0643, \text{or about } 6.43\%$$

If the monthly percentage changes of each currency are normally distributed, the monthly percentage changes of the portfolio should be normally distributed. The maximum 1-month loss of the currency portfolio is determined by the lower boundary (the left tail) of the probability distribution, which is about 1.65 standard deviations away from the expected percentage change in the currency portfolio. Assuming an expected percentage change of 0 percent for each currency during the next month (and therefore an expected change of zero for the portfolio), the maximum 1-month loss is

$$\text{Maximum 1-month loss of currency portfolio} = E(e_t) - (1.65 \times \sigma_p)$$
$$= 0\% - (1.65 \times 6.43\%)$$
$$= \text{about } -.1061, \text{ or about } -10.61\%$$

Compare this maximum 1-month loss to that of the rupiah or the baht:

$$\text{Maximum 1-month loss of rupiah} = 0\% - (1.65 \times 7\%)$$
$$= -.1155, \text{ or } -11.55\%$$
$$\text{Maximum 1-month loss of baht} = 0\% - (1.65 \times 8\%)$$
$$= -.132, \text{ or } -13.2\%$$

Notice that the maximum 1-month loss for the portfolio is lower than the maximum loss for either individual currency, which is attributed to the diversification effects. Even if one currency experiences its maximum loss in a given month, the other currency is not likely to experience its maximum loss in that same month. The lower the correlation between the movements in the two currencies, the greater are the diversification benefits.

Given the maximum losses calculated here, Benou, Inc., may decide to hedge its rupiah position, its baht position, neither position, or both positions. The decision of whether to hedge is discussed in the next chapter. ●

Estimating VAR with an Electronic Spreadsheet. You can easily use Excel or another electronic spreadsheet to facilitate estimates of VAR for a portfolio of currencies:

1. Obtain the series of exchange rates for all relevant dates for each currency of concern and list each currency in its own column.

2. Compute the percentage changes per period (from one date to the next) for each exchange rate in a column.

3. Estimate the standard deviation of the column of percentage changes for each exchange rate.

4. In a separate column, compute the periodic percentage change in the portfolio value by applying weights to the individual currency returns. That is, if the portfolio is equal-weighted (50 percent allocated to each currency), the percentage change in the portfolio value per period is equal to [50 percent times the percentage change in value of one exchange rate] + [50 percent times the percentage change of the other exchange rate].

5. Use a compute statement to determine the standard deviation of the column of percentage changes in the portfolio value.

Once you have determined the standard deviation of percentage changes in the portfolio value, you can estimate the VAR of the portfolio, as explained earlier.

EXAMPLE

Iowa Co. has cash inflows in Swiss francs and Argentine pesos, and its portfolio is weighted 50 percent in Swiss francs and 50 percent in Argentine pesos. It wants to determine the maximum expected loss to its portfolio from exchange rate movements over a 1-month period. (See Exhibit 10.7.) It records monthly exchange rates (shown in Columns 2 and 3) on an electronic spreadsheet so that it can estimate the monthly percentage changes in the exchange rates and in the portfolio, and estimate the standard deviation of the exchange rate movements. Notice that the standard deviation (SD) of the portfolio's movements is substantially lower than the

Exhibit 10.7 Spreadsheet Analysis Used to Apply Value-at-Risk

BEGIN-NING OF MONTH	SWISS FRANC (SF)	ARGENTINE PESO (AP)	% CHANGE IN SF	% CHANGE IN AP	% CHANGE IN EQUAL-WEIGHTED PORTFOLIO
1	$0.60	$0.35	—	—	—
2	$0.64	$0.36	6.67%	2.86%	4.76%
3	$0.60	$0.38	–6.25%	5.56%	–0.35%
4	$0.66	$0.40	10.00%	5.26%	7.63%
5	$0.68	$0.39	3.03%	–2.50%	0.26%
6	$0.72	$0.37	5.88%	–5.13%	0.38%
7	$0.76	$0.36	5.56%	–2.70%	1.43%
			SD of SF = 5.57%	SD of AP = 4.58%	SD of Portfolio = 3.16%

standard deviation of either individual currency's movements. Assuming the expected change of zero for the portfolio over the next month, the maximum 1-month loss of the portfolio is:

$$\text{Maximum 1-month loss} = 0\% - (1.65 \times 3.16\%) = 5.21\%$$ ●

Limitations of VAR. The VAR method presumes that the distribution of exchange rate movements is normal. If the distribution of exchange rate movements is not normal, the estimate of the maximum expected loss is subject to error. In addition, the VAR method assumes that the volatility (standard deviation) of exchange rate movements is stable over time. If exchange rate movements are less volatile in the past than in the future, the estimated maximum expected loss derived from the VAR method will be underestimated.

EXAMPLE

During the credit crisis, exchange rates of many currencies became more volatile. If an MNC applied value at risk in this period using exchange rate data from before the crisis, it would have underestimated volatility levels of the currencies. Therefore, it would have underestimated the maximum expected loss. ●

ECONOMIC EXPOSURE

The value of a firm's cash flows can be affected by exchange rate movements if it executes transactions in foreign currencies, receives revenue from foreign customers, or is subject to foreign competition. The sensitivity of the firm's cash flows to exchange rate movements is referred to as **economic exposure** (also sometimes referred to as operating exposure). Transaction exposure is a subset of economic exposure. But economic exposure also includes other ways in which a firm's cash flows can be affected by exchange rate movements.

EXAMPLE

Intel invoices about 65 percent of its chip exports in U.S. dollars. Although Intel is not subject to transaction exposure for its dollar-denominated exports, it is subject to economic exposure. If the euro weakens against the dollar, the European importers of those chips from Intel will need more euros to pay for them. These importers are subject to transaction exposure and economic exposure. As their costs of importing the chips increase in response to the weak euro, they may decide to purchase chips from European manufacturers instead. Consequently, Intel's cash flows from its exports will be reduced, even though these exports are invoiced in dollars. ●

Exhibit 10.8 Examples That Subject a Firm to Economic Exposure

A U.S. FIRM:	U.S. FIRM'S DOLLAR CASH FLOWS ARE ADVERSELY AFFECTED IF THE:
1. has a contract to export products in which it agreed to accept euros.	euro depreciates.
2. has a contract to import materials that are priced in Mexican pesos.	peso appreciates.
3. exports products to the United Kingdom that are priced in dollars, and competitors are located in the United Kingdom.	pound depreciates (causing some customers to switch to the competitors).
4. sells products to local customers, and its main competitor is based in Belgium.	euro depreciates (causing some customers to switch to the competitors).

Exhibit 10.9 Economic Exposure to Exchange Rate Fluctuations

TRANSACTIONS THAT INFLUENCE THE FIRM'S LOCAL CURRENCY INFLOWS	IMPACT OF LOCAL CURRENCY APPRECIATION ON TRANSACTIONS	IMPACT OF LOCAL CURRENCY DEPRECIATION ON TRANSACTIONS
Local sales (relative to foreign competition in local markets)	Decrease	Increase
Firm's exports denominated in local currency	Decrease	Increase
Firm's exports denominated in foreign currency	Decrease	Increase
Interest received from foreign investments	Decrease	Increase
TRANSACTIONS THAT INFLUENCE THE FIRM'S LOCAL CURRENCY OUTFLOWS		
Firm's imported supplies denominated in local currency	No change	No change
Firm's imported supplies denominated in foreign currency	Decrease	Increase
Interest owed on foreign funds borrowed	Decrease	Increase

Exhibit 10.8 provides examples of how a firm is subject to economic exposure. Consider each example by itself as if the firm had no other international business. Since the first two examples involve contractual transactions in foreign currencies, they reflect transaction exposure. The remaining examples do not involve contractual transactions in foreign currencies and therefore do not reflect transaction exposure. Yet, they do reflect economic exposure because they affect the firm's cash flows. If a firm experienced the exposure described in the third and fourth examples but did not have any contractual transactions in foreign currencies, it would be subject to economic exposure without being subject to transaction exposure.

Some of the more common international business transactions that typically subject an MNC's cash flows to economic exposure are listed in the first column of Exhibit 10.9. The second and third columns of Exhibit 10.9 indicate how each transaction can be affected by the appreciation and depreciation, respectively, of the firm's home (local) currency. The next sections discuss these effects in turn.

Exposure to Local Currency Appreciation

The following discussion is related to the second column of Exhibit 10.9. Local sales (in the firm's home country) are expected to decrease if the local (home) currency appreciates because the firm will face increased foreign competition. Local customers will be able to obtain foreign substitute products cheaply with their strengthened currency.

Cash inflows from exports denominated in the local currency will also likely be reduced as a result of appreciation in that currency because foreign importers will need more of their own currency to pay for these products. Any interest or dividends received from foreign investments will also convert to a reduced amount if the local currency has strengthened.

With regard to the firm's cash outflows, the cost of imported supplies denominated in the local currency will not be directly affected by changes in exchange rates. If the local currency appreciates, however, the cost of imported supplies denominated in the foreign currency will be reduced. In addition, any interest to be paid on financing in foreign currencies will be reduced (in terms of the local currency) if the local currency appreciates because the strengthened local currency will be exchanged for the foreign currency to make the interest payments.

Thus, appreciation in the firm's local currency causes a reduction in both cash inflows and outflows. The impact on a firm's net cash flows will depend on whether the inflow transactions are affected more or less than the outflow transactions. If, for example, the firm is in the exporting business but obtains its supplies and borrows funds locally, its inflow transactions will be reduced by a greater degree than its outflow transactions. In this case, net cash flows will be reduced. Conversely, cash inflows of a firm concentrating its sales locally with little foreign competition will not be severely reduced by appreciation of the local currency. If such a firm obtains supplies and borrows funds overseas, its outflows will be reduced. Overall, this firm's net cash flows will be enhanced by the appreciation of its local currency.

Exposure to Local Currency Depreciation

If the firm's local currency depreciates (see the third column of Exhibit 10.9), its transactions will be affected in a manner opposite to the way they are influenced by appreciation. Local sales should increase due to reduced foreign competition because prices denominated in strong foreign currencies will seem high to the local customers. The firm's exports denominated in the local currency will appear cheap to importers, thereby increasing foreign demand for those products. Even exports denominated in the foreign currency can increase cash flows because a given amount in foreign currency inflows to the firm will convert to a larger amount of the local currency. In addition, interest or dividends from foreign investments will now convert to more of the local currency.

With regard to cash outflows, imported supplies denominated in the local currency will not be directly affected by any change in exchange rates. The cost of imported supplies denominated in the foreign currency will rise, however, because more of the weakened local currency will be required to obtain the foreign currency needed. Any interest payments paid on financing in foreign currencies will increase.

In general, depreciation of the firm's local currency causes an increase in both cash inflows and outflows. A firm that concentrates on exporting and obtains supplies and borrows funds locally will likely benefit from a depreciated local currency. This is the case for Caterpillar, Ford, and DuPont in periods when the dollar weakens substantially against most major currencies. Conversely, a firm that concentrates on local sales, has very little foreign competition, and obtains foreign supplies (denominated in foreign currencies) will likely be hurt by a depreciated local currency.

Economic Exposure of Domestic Firms

Although our focus is on the financial management of MNCs, even purely domestic firms are affected by economic exposure.

Barrington is a U.S. manufacturer of steel that purchases all of its supplies locally and sells all of its steel locally. Because its transactions are solely in the local currency, Barrington is not subject to transaction exposure. It is subject to economic exposure, however, because it faces foreign competition in its local markets. If the exchange rate of the foreign competitor's invoice currency depreciates against the dollar, customers interested in steel products will shift their purchases toward the foreign steel producer. Consequently, demand for Barrington's steel will likely decrease, and so will its net cash inflows. Thus, Barrington is subject to economic exposure even though it is not subject to transaction exposure. ●

Measuring Economic Exposure

Since MNCs are affected by economic exposure, they should assess the potential degree of exposure that exists and then determine whether to insulate themselves against it.

Use of Sensitivity Analysis. One method of measuring an MNC's economic exposure is to separately consider how sales and expense categories are affected by various exchange rate scenarios.

EXAMPLE

Madison Co. is a U.S.-based MNC that purchases most of its materials from Canada and generates a small portion of its sales from exporting to Canada. Its U.S. sales are denominated in U.S. dollars, while its Canadian sales are denominated in Canadian dollars (C$). The estimates of its cash flows are shown in Exhibit 10.10, separated by country. Madison's exchange rate risk is partially due to specific contractual transactions such as purchase orders of products 3 months in advance (transaction exposure). However, most of Madison's business is not based on contractual transactions because its customers typically purchase its products without advance notice. Madison wants to assess its economic exposure, which is the exposure of its total cash flows (whether due to contractual transactions or not) to exchange rate movements.

Assume that Madison Co. expects three possible exchange rates for the Canadian dollar over the period of concern: (1) $.75, (2) $.80, or (3) $.85. These scenarios are separately analyzed in the second, third, and fourth columns of Exhibit 10.11. Row 1 is constant across scenarios since the U.S. business sales are not affected by exchange rate movements. In row 2, the estimated U.S. dollar sales due to the Canadian business are determined by converting the estimated Canadian dollar sales into U.S. dollars. Row 3 is the sum of the U.S. dollar sales in rows 1 and 2.

Row 4 is constant across scenarios since the cost of materials in the United States is not affected by exchange rate movements. In row 5, the estimated U.S. dollar cost of materials due to the Canadian business is determined by converting the estimated Canadian cost of materials into U.S. dollars. Row 6 is the sum of the U.S. dollar cost of materials in rows 4 and 5.

Row 7 is constant across scenarios since the U.S. operating expenses are not affected by exchange rate movements. Row 8 is constant across scenarios since the interest expense on U.S. debt is not affected by exchange rate movements. In row 9, the estimated U.S. dollar interest expense from Canadian debt is determined by converting the estimated Canadian interest expenses into U.S. dollars. Row 10 is the sum of the U.S. dollar interest expenses in rows 8 and 9.

The effect of exchange rates on Madison's revenues and costs can now be reviewed. Exhibit 10.11 illustrates how the dollar value of Canadian sales and Canadian cost of materials would increase as a result of a stronger Canadian dollar. Because Madison's Canadian cost of materials exposure (C$200 million) is much greater than its Canadian sales exposure (C$4 million), a strong Canadian dollar has a negative overall impact on its cash flow. The total amount in U.S. dollars needed to make interest payments is also higher when the Canadian dollar is stronger. In general, Madison Co. would be adversely affected by a stronger Canadian dollar. It would be favorably affected by a weaker Canadian dollar because the reduced value of total sales would be more than offset by the reduced cost of materials and interest expenses. ●

A general conclusion from this example is that firms with more (less) in foreign costs than in foreign revenue will be unfavorably (favorably) affected by a stronger foreign currency. The precise anticipated impact, however, can be determined only by utilizing the procedure described here or some alternative procedure. The example is based on a one-period time horizon. If firms have developed forecasts of sales, expenses, and exchange rates for several periods ahead, they can assess their economic exposure over time. Their economic exposure will be affected by any change in operating characteristics over time.

Exhibit 10.10 Estimated Sales and Expenses for Madison's U.S. and Canadian Business Segments (in Millions)

	U.S. BUSINESS	CANADIAN BUSINESS
Sales	$320	C$4
Cost of materials	$50	C$200
Operating expenses	$60	—
Interest expenses	$3	C$10
Cash flows	$207	−C$206

Exhibit 10.11 Impact of Possible Exchange Rates on Cash Flows of Madison Co. (in Millions)

	EXCHANGE RATE SCENARIO					
	C$1 = $.75		C$1 = $.80		C$1 = $.85	
Sales						
(1) U.S. sales		$320.00		$320.00		$320.00
(2) Canadian sales	C$4 =	$ 3.00	C$4 =	$ 3.20	C$4 =	$ 3.40
(3) Total sales in U.S. $		$323.00		$323.20		$323.40
Cost of Materials and Operating Expenses						
(4) U.S. cost of materials		$ 50.00		$ 50.00		$ 50.00
(5) Canadian cost of materials	C$200 =	$150.00	C$200 =	$160.00	C$200 =	$170.00
(6) Total cost of materials in U.S. $		$200.00		$210.00		$220.00
(7) Operating expenses		$ 60.00		$ 60.00		$ 60.00
Interest Expenses						
(8) U.S. interest expenses		$ 3		$ 3		$ 3
(9) Canadian interest expenses	C$10 =	$ 7.5	C$10 =	$ 8	C$10 =	$ 8.50
(10) Total interest expenses in U.S. $		$ 10.50		$ 11.00		$ 11.50
Cash Flows in U.S. Dollars before Taxes		$ 52.50		$ 42.20		$ 31.90

Use of Regression Analysis. A firm's economic exposure to currency movements can also be assessed by applying regression analysis to historical cash flow and exchange rate data as follows:

$$PCF_t = a_0 + a_1 e_t + \mu_t$$

where

PCF_t = percentage change in inflation-adjusted cash flows measured in the firm's home currency over period t
e_t = percentage change in the direct exchange rate of the currency over period t
μ_t = random error term
a_0 = intercept
a_1 = slope coefficient

The regression coefficient a_1, estimated by regression analysis, indicates the sensitivity of PCF_t to e_t. If the coefficient is positive and significant, this implies that a positive change in the currency's value has a favorable effect on the firm's cash flows. If the coefficient is negative and significant, this implies an inverse relationship between the change in the currency's value and the firm's cash flows. If the firm anticipates no major adjustments in its operating structure, it will expect the sensitivity detected from regression analysis to be somewhat similar in the future.

This regression model can be revised to handle more complex situations. For example, if additional currencies are to be assessed, they can be included in the model as additional independent variables. Each currency's impact is measured by estimating its respective regression coefficient. If an MNC is influenced by numerous currencies, it can measure the sensitivity of PCF_t to an index (or composite) of currencies.

The analysis just described for a single currency can also be extended over separate subperiods, as the sensitivity of a firm's cash flows to a currency's movements may change over time. This would be indicated by a shift in the regression coefficient, which may occur if the firm's exposure to exchange rate movements changes.

Some MNCs may prefer to use their stock price as a proxy for the firm's value and then assess how their stock price changes in response to currency movements. Regression analysis could also be applied to this situation by replacing PCF_t with the percentage change in stock price in the model specified here.

Some researchers, including Adler and Dumas,[1] suggest the use of regression analysis for this purpose. By assigning stock returns as the dependent variable, regression analysis can indicate how the firm's value is sensitive to exchange rate fluctuations.

Some companies may assess the impact of exchange rates on particular corporate characteristics, such as earnings, exports, or sales.

TRANSLATION EXPOSURE

An MNC creates its financial statements by consolidating all of its individual subsidiaries' financial statements. A subsidiary's financial statement is normally measured in its local currency. To be consolidated, each subsidiary's financial statement must be translated into the currency of the MNC's parent. Since exchange rates change over time, the translation of the subsidiary's financial statement into a different currency is affected by exchange rate movements. The exposure of the MNC's consolidated financial statements to exchange rate fluctuations is known as **translation exposure.** In particular, subsidiary earnings translated into the reporting currency on the consolidated income statement are subject to changing exchange rates.

To translate earnings, MNCs use a process established by the Financial Accounting Standards Board (FASB). The prevailing guidelines are set by FASB 52 for translation and by FASB 133 for valuing existing currency derivative contracts.

Does Translation Exposure Matter?

The relevance of translation exposure can be argued based on a cash flow perspective or a stock price perspective.

Cash Flow Perspective. Translation of financial statements for consolidated reporting purposes does not by itself affect an MNC's cash flows. The subsidiary earnings do not actually have to be converted into the parent's currency. If a subsidiary's local currency is currently weak, the earnings could be retained rather than converted and sent to the parent. The earnings could be reinvested in the subsidiary's country if feasible opportunities exist.

---

[1]Michael Adler and Bernard Dumas, "Exposure to Currency Risk: Definition and Measurement," *Financial Management*, 13, no. 2 (Summer 1984).

An MNC's parent, however, may rely on funding from periodic remittances of earnings by the subsidiary. Even if the subsidiary does not need to remit any earnings today, it will remit earnings at some point in the future. To the extent that today's spot rate serves as a forecast of the spot rate that will exist when earnings are remitted, a weak foreign currency today results in a forecast of a weak exchange rate at the time that the earnings are remitted. In this case, the expected future cash flows are affected, so translation exposure is relevant.

Stock Price Perspective. Many investors tend to use earnings when valuing firms, either by deriving estimates of expected cash flows from previous earnings or by applying an industry price-earnings (P/E) ratio to expected annual earnings to derive a value per share of stock. Since an MNC's translation exposure affects its consolidated earnings, it can affect the MNC's valuation.

Determinants of Translation Exposure

Some MNCs are subject to a greater degree of translation exposure than others. An MNC's degree of translation exposure is dependent on the following:

- The proportion of its business conducted by foreign subsidiaries
- The locations of its foreign subsidiaries
- The accounting methods that it uses

Proportion of Business by Foreign Subsidiaries. The greater the percentage of an MNC's business conducted by its foreign subsidiaries, the larger the percentage of a given financial statement item that is susceptible to translation exposure.

EXAMPLE

Locus Co. and Zeuss Co. each generate about 30 percent of their sales from foreign countries. However, Locus Co. generates all of its international business by exporting, whereas Zeuss Co. has a large Mexican subsidiary that generates all of its international business. Locus Co. is not subject to translation exposure (although it is subject to economic exposure), while Zeuss has substantial translation exposure. ●

Locations of Foreign Subsidiaries. The locations of the subsidiaries can also influence the degree of translation exposure because the financial statement items of each subsidiary are typically measured by the home currency of the subsidiary's country.

EXAMPLE

Zeuss Co. and Canton Co. each have one large foreign subsidiary that generates about 30 percent of their respective sales. However, Zeuss Co. is subject to a much higher degree of translation exposure because its subsidiary is based in Mexico, and the peso's value is subject to a large decline. In contrast, Canton's subsidiary is based in Canada, and the Canadian dollar is very stable against the U.S. dollar. ●

Accounting Methods. An MNC's degree of translation exposure can be greatly affected by the accounting procedures it uses to translate when consolidating financial statement data. Many of the important consolidated accounting rules for U.S.-based MNCs are based on FASB 52:

1. The functional currency of an entity is the currency of the economic environment in which the entity operates.

2. The current exchange rate as of the reporting date is used to translate the assets and liabilities of a foreign entity from its functional currency into the reporting currency.

3. The weighted average exchange rate over the relevant period is used to translate revenue, expenses, and gains and losses of a foreign entity from its functional currency into the reporting currency.

4. Translated income gains or losses due to changes in foreign currency values are not recognized in current net income but are reported as a second component of stockholder's equity; an exception to this rule is a foreign entity located in a country with high inflation.

5. Realized income gains or losses due to foreign currency transactions are recorded in current net income, although there are some exceptions.

Under FASB 52, consolidated earnings are sensitive to the functional currency's weighted average exchange rate.

EXAMPLE

A British subsidiary of Providence, Inc., earned £10 million in year 1 and £10 million in year 2. When these earnings are consolidated along with other subsidiary earnings, they are translated into U.S. dollars at the weighted average exchange rate in that year. Assume the weighted average exchange rate is $1.70 in year 1 and $1.50 in year 2. The translated earnings for each reporting period in U.S. dollars are determined as follows:

REPORTING PERIOD	LOCAL EARNINGS OF BRITISH SUBSIDIARY	WEIGHTED AVERAGE EXCHANGE RATE OF POUND OVER THE REPORTING PERIOD	TRANSLATED U.S. DOLLAR EARNINGS OF BRITISH SUBSIDIARY
Year 1	£10,000,000	$1.70	$17,000,000
Year 2	£10,000,000	$1.50	$15,000,000

Notice that even though the subsidiary's earnings in pounds were the same each year, the translated consolidated dollar earnings were reduced by $2 million in year 2. The discrepancy here is due to the change in the weighted average of the British pound exchange rate. The drop in earnings is not the fault of the subsidiary but rather of the weakened British pound that makes its year 2 earnings look small (when measured in U.S. dollars). ●

Examples of Translation Exposure

Consolidated earnings of Black & Decker, The Coca-Cola Co., and other MNCs are very sensitive to exchange rates because more than a third of their assets and sales are overseas. Their earnings in foreign countries are reduced when translated if foreign currencies depreciate against the U.S. dollar.

In the 2002–2007 period, the euro strengthened, which had a favorable translation effect on the consolidated earnings of U.S.-based MNCs that have foreign subsidiaries in the eurozone. In some quarters over this period, more than half of the increase in reported earnings by MNCs was due to the translation effect. Google earned translation gains of $61 million in 2007. In August 2008, some currencies such as the euro and pound began to decline, which reduced the consolidated earnings of U.S.-based MNCs that have foreign subsidiaries.

SUMMARY

■ MNCs with less risk can obtain funds at lower financing costs. Since they may experience more volatile cash flows because of exchange rate movements, exchange rate risk can affect their financing costs. Thus, MNCs recognize the relevance of ex-

change rate risk, and may benefit from hedging their exposure.

■ Transaction exposure is the exposure of an MNC's contractual transactions to exchange rate movements. MNCs can measure their transaction exposure by determining their future payables and receivables positions in various currencies, along with the variability levels and correlations of these currencies. From this information, they can assess how their revenue and costs may change in response to various exchange rate scenarios.

■ Economic exposure is any exposure of an MNC's cash flows (direct or indirect) to exchange rate movements. MNCs can attempt to measure their economic exposure by determining the extent to which their cash flows will be affected by their exposure to each foreign currency.

■ Translation exposure is the exposure of an MNC's consolidated financial statements to exchange rate movements. To measure translation exposure, MNCs can forecast their earnings in each foreign currency and then determine how their earnings could be affected by the potential exchange rate movements of each currency.

POINT COUNTER-POINT

Should Investors Care about an MNC's Translation Exposure?

Point No. The present value of an MNC's cash flows is based on the cash flows that the parent receives. Any impact of the exchange rates on the financial statements is not important unless cash flows are affected. MNCs should focus their energy on assessing the exposure of their cash flows to exchange rate movements and should not be concerned with the exposure of their financial statements to exchange rate movements. Value is about cash flows, and investors focus on value.

Counter-Point Investors do not have sufficient financial data to derive cash flows. They commonly use earnings as a base, and if earnings are distorted, their estimates of cash flows will be also. If they underestimate

cash flows because of how exchange rates affected the reported earnings, they may underestimate the value of the MNC. Even if the value is corrected in the future once the market realizes how the earnings were distorted, some investors may have sold their stock by the time the correction occurs. Investors should be concerned about an MNC's translation exposure. They should recognize that the earnings of MNCs with large translation exposure may be more distorted than the earnings of MNCs with low translation exposure.

Who Is Correct? Use the Internet to learn more about this issue. Which argument do you support? Offer your own opinion on this issues.

SELF-TEST

Answers are provided in Appendix A at the back of the text.

1. Given that shareholders can diversify away an individual firm's exchange rate risk by investing in a variety of firms, why are firms concerned about exchange rate risk?

2. Bradley, Inc., considers importing its supplies from either Canada (denominated in C$) or Mexico (denominated in pesos) on a monthly basis. The quality is the same for both sources. Once the firm completes the agreement with a supplier, it will be obligated to continue using that supplier for at least 3 years. Based on existing exchange rates, the dollar amount to be paid (including transportation costs) will be the same. The firm has no other exposure to exchange rate move-

ments. Given that the firm prefers to have less exchange rate risk, which alternative is preferable? Explain.

3. Assume your U.S. firm currently exports to Mexico on a monthly basis. The goods are priced in pesos. Once material is received from a source, it is quickly used to produce the product in the United States, and then the product is exported. Currently, you have no other exposure to exchange rate risk. You have a choice of purchasing the material from Canada (denominated in C$), from Mexico (denominated in pesos), or from within the United States (denominated in U.S. dollars). The quality and your expected cost are similar across the three sources. Which source is preferable, given that you prefer minimal exchange rate risk?

4. Using the information in the previous question, consider a proposal to price the exports to Mexico in dollars and to use the U.S. source for material. Would this proposal eliminate the exchange rate risk?

5. Assume that the dollar is expected to strengthen against the euro over the next several years. Explain how this will affect the consolidated earnings of U.S.-based MNCs with subsidiaries in Europe.

QUESTIONS AND APPLICATIONS

1.   Transaction versus Economic Exposure. Compare and contrast transaction exposure and economic exposure. Why would an MNC consider examining only its "net" cash flows in each currency when assessing its transaction exposure?

2.   Assessing Transaction Exposure. Your employer, a large MNC, has asked you to assess its transaction exposure. Its projected cash flows are as follows for the next year. Danish krone inflows equal DK50,000,000 while outflows equal DK40,000,000. British pound inflows equal £2,000,000 while outflows equal £1,000,000. The spot rate of the krone is $.15, while the spot rate of the pound is $1.50. Assume that the movements in the Danish krone and the British pound are highly correlated. Provide your assessment as to your firm's degree of transaction exposure (as to whether the exposure is high or low). Substantiate your answer.

3.   Factors That Affect a Firm's Transaction Exposure. What factors affect a firm's degree of transaction exposure in a particular currency? For each factor, explain the desirable characteristics that would reduce transaction exposure.

4.   Currency Correlations. Kopetsky Co. has net receivables in several currencies that are highly correlated with each other. What does this imply about the firm's overall degree of transaction exposure? Are currency correlations perfectly stable over time? What does your answer imply about Kopetsky Co. or any other firm using past data on correlations as an indicator for the future?

5.   Currency Effects on Cash Flows. How should appreciation of a firm's home currency generally affect its cash inflows? How should depreciation of a firm's home currency generally affect its cash outflows?

6.   Transaction Exposure. Fischer, Inc., exports products from Florida to Europe. It obtains supplies and borrows funds locally. How would appreciation of the euro likely affect its net cash flows? Why?

7.   Exposure of Domestic Firms. Why are the cash flows of a purely domestic firm exposed to exchange rate fluctuations?

8.   Measuring Economic Exposure. Memphis Co. hires you as a consultant to assess its degree of economic exposure to exchange rate fluctuations. How would you handle this task? Be specific.

9.   Factors That Affect a Firm's Translation Exposure. What factors affect a firm's degree of translation exposure? Explain how each factor influences translation exposure.

10.   Translation Exposure. Consider a period in which the U.S. dollar weakens against the euro. How will this affect the reported earnings of a U.S.-based MNC with European subsidiaries? Consider a period in which the U.S. dollar strengthens against most foreign currencies. How will this affect the reported earnings of a U.S.-based MNC with subsidiaries all over the world?

11.   Transaction Exposure. Aggie Co. produces chemicals. It is a major exporter to Europe, where its main competition is from other U.S. exporters. All of these companies invoice the products in U.S. dollars. Is Aggie's transaction exposure likely to be significantly affected if the euro strengthens or weakens? Explain. If the euro weakens for several years, can you think of any change that might occur in the global chemicals market?

12.   Economic Exposure. Longhorn Co. produces hospital equipment. Most of its revenues are in the United States. About half of its expenses require outflows in Philippine pesos (to pay for Philippine materials). Most of Longhorn's competition is from U.S. firms that have no international business at all. How will Longhorn Co. be affected if the peso strengthens?

13.   Economic Exposure. Lubbock, Inc., produces furniture and has no international business. Its major competitors import most of their furniture from Brazil and then sell it out of retail stores in the United States. How will Lubbock, Inc., be affected if Brazil's currency (the real) strengthens over time?

14. Economic Exposure. Sooner Co. is a U.S. wholesale company that imports expensive high-quality luggage and sells it to retail stores around the United States. Its main competitors also import high-quality luggage and sell it to retail stores. None of these competitors hedge their exposure to exchange rate movements. Why might Sooner's market share be more volatile over time if it hedges its exposure?

15. PPP and Economic Exposure. Boulder, Inc., exports chairs to Europe (invoiced in U.S. dollars) and competes against local European companies. If purchasing power parity exists, why would Boulder not benefit from a stronger euro?

16. Measuring Changes in Economic Exposure. Toyota Motor Corp. measures the sensitivity of its exports to the yen exchange rate (relative to the U.S. dollar). Explain how regression analysis could be used for such a task. Identify the expected sign of the regression coefficient if Toyota primarily exports to the United States. If Toyota established plants in the United States, how might the regression coefficient on the exchange rate variable change?

17. Impact of Exchange Rates on Earnings. Cieplak, Inc., is a U.S.-based MNC that has expanded into Asia. Its U.S. parent exports to some Asian countries, with its exports denominated in the Asian currencies. It also has a large subsidiary in Malaysia that serves that market. Offer at least two reasons related to exposure to exchange rates that explain why Cieplak's earnings were reduced during the Asian crisis.

Advanced Questions

18. Speculating Based on Exposure. During the Asian crisis in 1998, there were rumors that China would weaken its currency (the yuan) against the U.S. dollar and many European currencies. This caused investors to sell stocks in Asian countries such as Japan, Taiwan, and Singapore. Offer an intuitive explanation for such an effect. What types of Asian firms would have been affected the most?

19. Comparing Transaction and Economic Exposure. Erie Co. has most of its business in the United States, except that it exports to Belgium. Its exports were invoiced in euros (Belgium's currency) last year. It has no other economic exposure to exchange rate risk. Its main competition when selling to Belgium's customers is a company in Belgium that sells similar products, denominated in euros. Starting today, Erie Co. plans to adjust its pricing strategy to invoice

its exports in U.S. dollars instead of euros. Based on the new strategy, will Erie Co. be subject to economic exposure to exchange rate risk in the future? Briefly explain.

20. Using Regression Analysis to Measure Exposure.

a. How can a U.S. company use regression analysis to assess its economic exposure to fluctuations in the British pound?

b. In using regression analysis to assess the sensitivity of cash flows to exchange rate movements, what is the purpose of breaking the database into subperiods?

c. Assume the regression coefficient based on assessing economic exposure was much higher in the second subperiod than in the first subperiod. What does this tell you about the firm's degree of economic exposure over time? Why might such results occur?

21. Transaction Exposure. Vegas Corp. is a U.S. firm that exports most of its products to Canada. It historically invoiced its products in Canadian dollars to accommodate the importers. However, it was adversely affected when the Canadian dollar weakened against the U.S. dollar. Since Vegas did not hedge, its Canadian dollar receivables were converted into a relatively small amount of U.S. dollars. After a few more years of continual concern about possible exchange rate movements, Vegas called its customers and requested that they pay for future orders with U.S. dollars instead of Canadian dollars. At this time, the Canadian dollar was valued at $.81. The customers decided to oblige since the number of Canadian dollars to be converted into U.S. dollars when importing the goods from Vegas was still slightly smaller than the number of Canadian dollars that would be needed to buy the product from a Canadian manufacturer. Based on this situation, has transaction exposure changed for Vegas Corp.? Has economic exposure changed? Explain.

22. Measuring Economic Exposure. Using the cost and revenue information shown for DeKalb, Inc., on the next page, determine how the costs, revenue, and cash flow items would be affected by three possible exchange rate scenarios for the New Zealand dollar (NZ$): (1) NZ$ = $.50, (2) NZ$ = $.55, and (3) NZ$ = $.60. (Assume U.S. sales will be unaffected by the exchange rate.) Assume that NZ$ earnings will be remitted to the U.S. parent at the end of the period. Ignore possible tax effects.

REVENUE AND COST ESTIMATES: DEKALB, INC. (IN MILLIONS OF U.S. DOLLARS AND NEW ZEALAND DOLLARS)		
	U.S. BUSINESS	NEW ZEALAND BUSINESS
Sales	$800	NZ$800
Cost of materials	500	100
Operating expenses	300	0
Interest expense	100	0
Cash flow	−$100	NZ$700

23. Changes in Economic Exposure.
Walt Disney World built an amusement park in France that opened in 1992. How do you think this project has affected Disney's economic exposure to exchange rate movements? Think carefully before you give your final answer. There is more than one way in which Disney's cash flows may be affected. Explain.

24. Lagged Effects of Exchange Rate Movements.
Cornhusker Co. is an exporter of products to Singapore. It wants to know how its stock price is affected by changes in the Singapore dollar's exchange rate. It believes that the impact may occur with a lag of 1 to 3 quarters. How could regression analysis be used to assess the impact?

25. Potential Effects if the United Kingdom Adopted the Euro.
The United Kingdom still has its own currency, the pound. The pound's interest rate has historically been higher than the euro's interest rate. The United Kingdom has considered adopting the euro as its currency. There have been many arguments about whether it should do so.

Use your knowledge and intuition to discuss the likely effects if the United Kingdom adopts the euro. For each of the 10 statements below, insert either *increase* or *decrease* in the first blank and complete the statement by adding a clear, short explanation (perhaps one to three sentences) of why the United Kingdom's adoption of the euro would have that effect.

To help you narrow your focus, follow these guidelines. Assume that the pound is more volatile than the euro. Do not base your answer on whether the pound would have been stronger than the euro in the future. Also, do not base your answer on an unusual change in economic growth in the United Kingdom or in the eurozone if the euro is adopted.

a. The economic exposure of British firms that are heavy exporters to the eurozone would _____ because _____.

b. The translation exposure of firms based in the eurozone that have British subsidiaries would _____ because_____.

c. The economic exposure of U.S. firms that conduct substantial business in the United Kingdom and have no other international business would _____ because _____.

d. The translation exposure of U.S. firms with British subsidiaries would _____ because _____.

e. The economic exposure of U.S. firms that export to the United Kingdom and whose only other international business is importing from firms based in the euro zone would _____ because _____.

f. The discount on the forward rate paid by U.S. firms that periodically use the forward market to hedge payables of British imports would _____ because _____.

g. The earnings of a foreign exchange department of a British bank that executes foreign exchange transactions desired by its European clients would _____ because _____.

h. Assume that the Swiss franc is more highly correlated with the British pound than with the euro. A U.S. firm has substantial monthly exports to the United Kingdom denominated in the British currency and also has substantial monthly imports of Swiss supplies (denominated in Swiss francs). The economic exposure of this firm would _____ because _____.

i. Assume that the Swiss franc is more highly correlated with the British pound than with the euro. A U.S. firm has substantial monthly exports to the United Kingdom denominated in the British currency and also has substantial monthly exports to Switzerland (denominated in Swiss francs). The economic exposure of this firm would _____ because _____.

j. The British government's reliance on monetary policy (as opposed to fiscal policy) as a means of fine-tuning the economy would _____ because _____.

26. Invoicing Policy to Reduce Exposure.
Celtic Co. is a U.S. firm that exports its products to England. It faces competition from many firms in

England. Its price to customers in England has generally been lower than those of the competitors, primarily because the British pound has been strong. It has priced its exports in pounds and then converts the pound receivables into dollars. All of its expenses are in the United States and are paid with dollars. It is concerned about its economic exposure. It considers a change in its pricing policy, in which it will price its products in dollars instead of pounds. Offer your opinion on why this will or will not significantly reduce its economic exposure.

27. Exposure to Cash Flows. Raton Co. is a U.S. company that has net inflows of 100 million Swiss francs and net outflows of 100 million British pounds. The present exchange rate of the Swiss franc is about $.70 while the present exchange rate of the pound is $1.90. Raton Co. has not hedged these positions. The Swiss franc and British pound are highly correlated in their movements against the dollar. Explain whether Raton will be favorably or adversely affected if the dollar weakens against foreign currencies over time.

28. Assessing Exposure. Washington Co. and Vermont Co. have no domestic business. They have a similar dollar equivalent amount of international exporting business. Washington Co. exports all of its products to Canada. Vermont Co. exports its products to Poland and Mexico, with about half of its business in each of these two countries. Each firm receives the currency of the country where it sends its exports. You obtain the end-of-month spot exchange rates of the currencies mentioned above during the end of each of the last 6 months.

END OF MONTH	CANADIAN DOLLAR	MEXICAN PESO	POLISH ZLOTY
1	$.8142	$.09334	$.29914
2	.8176	.09437	.29829
3	.8395	.09241	.30187
4	.8542	.09263	.3088
5	.8501	.09251	.30274
6	.8556	.09448	.30312

You want to assess the data in a logical manner to determine which firm has a higher degree of exchange rate risk. Show your work and write your conclusion.

29. Exposure to Pegged Currency System. Assume that the Mexican peso and the Brazilian currency (the real) have depreciated against the U.S. dollar recently due to the high inflation rates in those countries. Assume that inflation in these two countries is expected to continue and that it will have a major effect on these currencies if they are still allowed to float. Assume that the government of Brazil decides to peg its currency to the dollar and will definitely maintain the peg for the next year. Milez Co. is based in Mexico. Its main business is to export supplies from Mexico to Brazil. It invoices its supplies in Mexican pesos. Its main competition is from firms in Brazil that produce similar supplies and sell them locally. How will the sales volume of Milez Co. be affected (if at all) by the Brazilian government's actions? Explain.

30. Assessing Currency Volatility. Zemart is a U.S. firm that plans to establish international business in which it will export to Mexico (these exports will be denominated in pesos) and to Canada (these exports will be denominated in Canadian dollars) once a month and will therefore receive payments once a month. It is concerned about exchange rate risk. It wants to compare the standard deviation of exchange rate movements of these two currencies against the U.S. dollar on a monthly basis. For this reason, it asks you to:

a. Estimate the standard deviation of the monthly movements in the Canadian dollar against the U.S. dollar over the last 12 months.

b. Estimate the standard deviation of the monthly movements in the Mexican peso against the U.S. dollar over the last 12 months.

c. Determine which currency is less volatile.

You can use the www.oanda.com website (or any legitimate website that has currency data) to obtain the end-of-month direct exchange rate of the peso and the Canadian dollar in order to do your analysis. Show your work. You can use a calculator or a spreadsheet (like Excel) to do the actual computations.

31. Exposure of Net Cash Flows. Each of the following U.S. firms is expected to generate $40 million in net cash flows (after including the estimated cash flows from international sales if there are any) over the next year. Ignore any tax effects. Each firm has the same level of expected earnings. None of the firms has taken any position in exchange rate derivatives to hedge exchange rate risk. All payments for the international trade by each firm will occur 1 year from today.

Sunrise Co. has ordered imports from Austria, and its imports are invoiced in euros. The dollar value of the payables (based on today's exchange rate) from its imports during this year is $10 million. It has no international sales.

Copans Co. has ordered imports from Mexico, and its imports are invoiced in U.S. dollars. The dollar value of the payables from its imports during this year is $15 million. It has no international sales.

Yamato Co. ordered imports from Italy, and its imports are invoiced in euros. The dollar value of the payables (based on today's exchange rate) from its imports during this year is $12 million. In addition, Yamato exports to Portugal, and its exports are denominated in euros. The dollar value of the receivables (based on today's exchange rate) from its exports during this year is $8 million.

Glades Co. ordered imports from Belgium, and these imports are invoiced in euros. The dollar value of the payables (based on today's exchange rate) from its imports during this year is $7 million. Glades also ordered imports from Luxembourg, and these imports are denominated in dollars. The dollar value of these payables is $30 million. Glades has no international sales.

Based on this information, which firm is exposed to the most exchange rate risk? Explain.

32. Cash Flow Sensitivity to Exchange Rate Movements.
The Central Bank of Poland is about to engage in indirect intervention later today in which it will lower Poland's interest rates substantially. This will have an impact on the value of the Polish currency (zloty) against most currencies because it will immediately affect capital flows. Missouri Co. has a subsidiary in Poland that sells appliances. The demand for its appliances is not affected much by the local economy. Most of its appliances produced in Poland are typically invoiced in zloty and are purchased by consumers from Germany. The subsidiary's main competition is from appliance producers in Portugal, Spain, and Italy, which also export appliances to Germany.

a. Explain how the impact on the zloty's value will affect the sales of appliances by the Polish subsidiary.

b. The subsidiary owes a British company 1 million British pounds for some technology that the British company provided. Explain how the impact on the zloty's value will affect the cost of this technology to the subsidiary.

c. The subsidiary plans to take 2 million zloty from its recent earnings and will remit it to the U.S. parent in the near future. Explain how the impact on the zloty's value will affect the amount of dollar cash flows received by the U.S. parent due to this remittance of earnings by the subsidiary.

33. Applying the Value-at-Risk Method.
You use today's spot rate of the Brazilian real to forecast the spot rate of the real for 1 month ahead. Today's spot rate is $.4558. Use the value-at-risk method to determine the maximum percentage loss of the Brazilian real over the next month based on a 95 percent confidence level. Use the spot exchange rates at the end of each of the last 6 months to conduct your analysis. Forecast the exchange rate that would exist under these conditions.

34. Assessing Translation Exposure.
Kanab Co. and Zion Co. are U.S. companies that engage in much business within the United States and are about the same size. They both conduct some international business as well.

Kanab Co. has a subsidiary in Canada that will generate earnings of about C$20 million in each of the next 5 years. Kanab Co. also has a U.S. business that will receive about C$1 million (after costs) in each of the next 5 years as a result of exporting products to Canada that are denominated in Canadian dollars.

Zion Co. has a subsidiary in Mexico that will generate earnings of about 1 million pesos in each of the next 5 years. Zion Co. also has a business in the United States that will receive about 300 million pesos (after costs) in each of the next 5 years as a result of exporting products to Mexico that are denominated in Mexican pesos.

The salvage value of Kanab's Canadian subsidiary and Zion's Mexican subsidiary will be zero in 5 years. The spot rate of the Canadian dollar is $.60 while the spot rate of the Mexican peso is $.10. Assume the Canadian dollar could appreciate or depreciate against the U.S. dollar by about 8 percent in any given year, while the Mexican peso could appreciate or depreciate against the U.S. dollar by about 12 percent in any given year. Which company is subject to a higher degree of translation exposure? Explain.

35. Cross-Currency Relationships.
The Hong Kong dollar (HK$) is presently pegged to the U.S. dollar and is expected to remain pegged. Some Hong Kong firms export products to Australia that are denominated in Australian dollars and have no other business in Australia. The exports are not hedged. The Australian dollar is presently worth .50 U.S. dollars, but

you expect that it will be worth .45 U.S. dollars by the end of the year. Based on your expectations, will the Hong Kong exporters be affected favorably or unfavorably? Briefly explain.

36. Interpreting Economic Exposure.
Spratt Co. (a U.S. firm) attempts to determine its economic exposure to movements in the British pound by applying regression analysis to data over the last 36 quarters:

$$SP = b_0 + b_1e + \mu$$

where SP represents the percentage change in Spratt's stock price per quarter, e represents the percentage change in the pound value per quarter, and μ is an error term. Based on the analysis, the b_0 coefficient is zero and the b_1 coefficient is –.4 and is statistically significant. Assume that interest rate parity exists. Today, the spot rate of the pound is $1.80, the 90-day British interest rate is 3 percent, and the 90-day U.S. interest rate is 2 percent. Assume that the 90-day forward rate is expected to be an accurate forecast of the future spot rate. Would you expect that Spratt's value will be favorably affected, unfavorably affected, or not affected by its economic exposure over the next quarter? Explain.

37. Assessing Translation Exposure.
Assume the euro's spot rate is presently equal to $1.00. All of the following firms are based in New York and are the same size. While these firms concentrate on business in the United States, their entire foreign operations for this quarter are provided here.

Company A expects its exports to cause cash inflows of 9 million euros and imports to cause cash outflows equal to 3 million euros.

Company B has a subsidiary in Portugal that expects revenue of 5 million euros and has expenses of 1 million euros.

Company C expects exports to cause cash inflows of 9 million euros and imports to cause cash outflows of 3 million euros, and will repay the balance of an existing loan equal to 2 million euros.

Company D expects zero exports and imports to cause cash outflows of 11 million euros.

Company E will repay the balance of an existing loan equal to 9 million euros.

Which of the five companies described here has the highest degree of translation exposure?

38. Exchange Rates and Market Share.
Minnesota Co. is a U.S. firm that exports computer parts to Japan. Its main competition is from firms that are based in Japan, which invoice their products in yen. Minnesota's exports are invoiced in U.S. dollars. The prices charged by Minnesota and its competitors will not change during the next year. Will Minnesota's revenue increase, decrease, or be unaffected if the spot rate of the yen appreciates over the next year? Briefly explain.

39. Exchange Rates and Market Share.
Harz Co. (a U.S. firm) has an arrangement with a Chinese company in which it purchases products from them every week at the prevailing spot rate, and then sells the products in the United States invoiced in dollars. All of its competition is from U.S. firms that have no international business. The prices charged by Harz and its competitors will not change over the next year. Will the net cash flows generated by Harz increase, decrease, or be unaffected if the Chinese yuan depreciates over the next year? Briefly explain.

40. IFE and Exposure.
Assume that Maine Co. (a U.S. firm) measures its economic exposure to movements in the British pound by applying regression analysis to data over the last 36 quarters:

$$SP = b_0 + b_1e + \mu$$

where SP represents the percentage change in Maine's stock price per quarter, e represents the percentage change in the British pound value per quarter, and μ is an error term. Based on the analysis, the b_0 coefficient is estimated to be zero and the b_1 coefficient is estimated to be 0.3 and is statistically significant. Maine Co. believes that the movement in the value of the pound over the next quarter will be mostly driven by the international Fisher effect. The prevailing quarterly interest rate in the United Kingdom is lower than the prevailing quarterly interest rate in the United States. Would you expect that Maine's value will be favorably affected, unfavorably affected, or not affected by the pound's movement over the next quarter? Explain.

41. PPP and Exposure.
Layton Co. (a U.S. firm) attempts to determine its economic exposure to movements in the Japanese yen by applying regression analysis to data over the last 36 quarters:

$$SP = b_0 + b_1e + \mu$$

where SP represents the percentage change in Layton's stock price per quarter, e represents the percentage change in the yen value per quarter, and μ is an error term. Based on the analysis, the b_0 coefficient is zero and the b_1 coefficient is 0.4 and is statistically significant. Layton believes that the inflation differential has a major effect on the value of the yen (based on purchasing power parity). The inflation in Japan is expected to rise substantially while the U.S. inflation will remain at a low level. Would you expect that Layton's value will be favorably affected, unfavorably affected, or not affected by its economic exposure over the next quarter? Explain.

42. Exposure to Cash Flows. Lance Co. is a U.S. company that has exposure to the Swiss francs (SF) and Danish kroner (DK). It has net inflows of SF100 million and net outflows of DK500 million. The present exchange rate of the SF is about $.80 while the present exchange rate of the DK is $.10. Lance Co. has not hedged these positions. The SF and DK are highly correlated in their movements against the dollar. Explain whether Lance will be favorably or adversely affected if the dollar strengthens against foreign currencies over time.

43. Assessing Transaction Exposure. Zebra Co. is a U.S. firm that obtains products from a U.S. supplier and then exports them to Canadian firms. Its exports are denominated in U.S. dollars. Its main competitor is a local company in Canada that sells similar products denominated in Canadian dollars. Is Zebra subject to transaction exposure? Briefly explain.

44. Assessing Translation Exposure. Quartz Co. has its entire operations in Miami, Florida, and is an exporter of products to eurozone countries. All of its earnings are derived from its exports. The exports are denominated in euros. Reed Co. (of the United States) is about the same size as Quartz Co. and generates about the same amount of earnings in a typical year. It has a subsidiary in Germany that typically generates about 40 percent of its total earnings. All earnings are reinvested in Germany and therefore not remitted. The rest of Reed's business is in the United States. Which company has a higher degree of translation exposure? Briefly explain.

45. Estimating Value at Risk. Yazoo, Inc., is a U.S. firm that has substantial international business in Japan and has cash inflows in Japanese yen. The spot rate of the yen today is $.01. The yen exchange rate was $.008 three months ago, $.0085 two months ago, and $.009 1 month ago. Yazoo uses today's spot rate of the yen as its forecast of the spot rate in 1 month. However, it wants to determine the maximum expected percentage decline in the value of the Japanese yen in 1 month based on the value-at-risk (VAR) method and a 95 percent probability. Use the exchange rate information provided to derive the maximum expected decline in the yen over the next month.

Discussion in the Boardroom

This exercise can be found in Appendix E at the back of this textbook.

Running Your Own MNC

This exercise can be found on the *International Financial Management* text companion website located at www.cengage.com/finance/madura.

BLADES, INC. CASE

Assessment of Exchange Rate Exposure

Blades, Inc., is currently exporting roller blades to Thailand and importing certain components needed to manufacture roller blades from that country. Under a fixed contractual agreement, Blades' primary customer in Thailand has committed itself to purchase 180,000 pairs of roller blades annually at a fixed price of 4,594 Thai baht (THB) per pair. Blades is importing rubber and plastic components from various suppliers in Thailand at a cost of approximately THB2,871 per pair, although the exact price (in baht) depends on current market prices. Blades imports materials sufficient to manufacture 72,000 pairs of roller blades from Thailand each year. The decision to import materials from Thailand was reached because rubber and plastic components needed to manufacture Blades' products are inexpensive, yet of high quality, in Thailand.

Blades has also conducted business with a Japanese supplier in the past. Although Blades' analysis indicates that the Japanese components are of a lower quality than the Thai components, Blades has occasionally imported components from Japan when the prices were low enough. Currently, Ben Holt, Blades' chief financial officer (CFO), is considering importing components from Japan more frequently. Specifically, he would like to reduce Blades' baht exposure by taking advantage of the recently high correlation between the baht and the yen. Since Blades has net inflows denominated in baht and would have outflows denominated in yen, its net transaction exposure would be reduced if these two currencies were highly correlated. If Blades decides to import components from Japan, it would probably import materials sufficient to manufacture 1,700 pairs of roller blades annually at a price of ¥7,440 per pair.

Holt is also contemplating further expansion into foreign countries. Although he would eventually like to establish a subsidiary or acquire an existing business overseas, his immediate focus is on increasing Blades' foreign sales. Holt's primary reason for this plan is that the profit margin from Blades' imports and exports exceeds 25 percent, while the profit margin from Blades' domestic production is below 15 percent. Consequently, he believes that further foreign expansion will be beneficial to the company's future.

Though Blades' current exporting and importing practices have been profitable, Ben Holt is contemplating extending Blades' trade relationships to countries in different regions of the world. One reason for this decision is that various Thai roller blade manufacturers have recently established subsidiaries in the United States. Furthermore, various Thai roller blade manufacturers have recently targeted the U.S. market by advertising their products over the Internet. As a result of this increased competition from Thailand, Blades is uncertain whether its primary customer in Thailand will renew the current commitment to purchase a fixed number of roller blades annually. The current agreement will terminate in 2 years. Another reason for engaging in transactions with other, non-Asian, countries is that the Thai baht has depreciated substantially recently, which has somewhat reduced Blades' profit margins. The sale of roller blades to other countries with more stable currencies may increase Blades' profit margins.

While Blades will continue exporting to Thailand under the current agreement for the next 2 years, it may also export roller blades to Jogs, Ltd., a British retailer. Preliminary negotiations indicate that Jogs would be willing to commit itself to purchase 200,000 pairs of Speedos, Blades' primary product, for a fixed price of £80 per pair.

Holt is aware that further expansion would increase Blades' exposure to exchange rate fluctuations, but he believes that Blades can supplement its profit margins by expanding. He is vaguely familiar with the different types of exchange rate exposure but has asked you, a financial analyst at Blades, Inc., to help him assess how the contemplated changes would affect Blades' financial position. Among other concerns, Holt is aware that recent economic problems in Thailand have had an effect on Thailand and other Asian countries. Whereas the correlation between Asian currencies such as the Japanese yen and the Thai baht is generally not very high and very unstable, these recent problems have increased the correlation among most Asian currencies. Conversely, the correlation between the British pound and the Asian currencies is quite low.

To aid you in your analysis, Holt has provided you with the following data:

CURRENCY	EXPECTED EXCHANGE RATE	RANGE OF POSSIBLE EXCHANGE RATES
British pound	$1.50	$1.47 to $1.53
Japanese yen	$ .0083	$.0079 to $.0087
Thai baht	$ .024	$.020 to $.028

Holt has asked you to answer the following questions:

1. What type(s) of exposure (i.e., transaction, economic, or translation exposure) is Blades subject to? Why?

2. Using a spreadsheet, conduct a consolidated net cash flow assessment of Blades, Inc., and estimate the range of net inflows and outflows for Blades for the coming year. Assume that Blades enters into the agreement with Jogs, Ltd.

3. If Blades does not enter into the agreement with the British firm and continues to export to Thailand and import from Thailand and Japan, do you think the increased correlations between the Japanese yen and the Thai baht will increase or reduce Blades' transaction exposure?

4. Do you think Blades should import components from Japan to reduce its net transaction exposure in the long run? Why or why not?

5. Assuming Blades enters into the agreement with Jogs, Ltd., how will its overall transaction exposure be affected?

6. Given that Thai roller blade manufacturers located in Thailand have begun targeting the U.S. roller blade market, how do you think Blades' U.S. sales were affected by the depreciation of the Thai baht? How do you think its exports to Thailand and its imports from Thailand and Japan were affected by the depreciation?

SMALL BUSINESS DILEMMA

Assessment of Exchange Rate Exposure by the Sports Exports Company

At the current time, the Sports Exports Company is willing to receive payments in British pounds for the monthly exports it sends to the United Kingdom. While all of its receivables are denominated in pounds, it has no payables in pounds or in any other foreign currency. Jim Logan, owner of the Sports Exports Company, wants to assess his firm's exposure to exchange rate risk.

1. Would you describe the exposure of the Sports Exports Company to exchange rate risk as transaction exposure? Economic exposure? Translation exposure?

2. Jim Logan is considering a change in the pricing policy in which the importer must pay in dollars, so that Jim will not have to worry about converting pounds to dollars every month. If implemented, would this policy eliminate the transaction exposure of the Sports Exports Company? Would it eliminate Sports Exports' economic exposure? Explain.

3. If Jim decides to implement the policy described in the previous question, how would the Sports Exports Company be affected (if at all) by appreciation of the pound? By depreciation of the pound? Would these effects on Sports Exports differ if Jim retained his original policy of pricing the exports in British pounds?

INTERNET/EXCEL EXERCISES

1. Go to www.oanda.com/convert/fxhistory and obtain the direct exchange rate of the Canadian dollar and euro at the beginning of each of the last 7 years.

a. Assume you received C$2 million in earnings from your Canadian subsidiary at the beginning of each year over the last 7 years. Multiply this amount times the direct exchange rate of the Canadian dollar at the beginning of each year to determine how many U.S. dollars you received. Determine the percentage change in the dollar cash flows received from one year to the next. Determine the standard deviation of these percentage changes. This measures the volatility of movements in the dollar earnings resulting from your Canadian business over time.

b. Now assume that you also received 1 million euros at the beginning of each year from your German subsidiary. Repeat the same process for the euro to measure the volatility of movements in the dollar cash flows resulting from your German business over time. Are the movements in dollar cash flows more volatile for the Canadian business or the German business?

c. Now consider the dollar cash flows you received from the Canadian subsidiary and the German subsidiary combined. That is, add the dollar cash flows received from both businesses for each year. Repeat the process to measure the volatility of movements in the dollar cash flows resulting from both businesses over time. Compare the volatility in the dollar cash flows of the portfolio to the volatility in cash flows resulting from the German business. Does it appear that diversification of businesses across two countries results in more stable cash flows than the business in Germany? Explain.

d. Compare the volatility in the dollar cash flows of the portfolio to the volatility in cash flows resulting from the Canadian business. Does it appear that diversification of businesses across two countries results in more stable cash flow movements than the business in Canada? Explain.

2. The following website contains annual reports of many MNCs: www.annualreportservice.com. Review the annual report of your choice. Look for any comments in the report that describe the MNC's transaction exposure, economic exposure, or translation exposure. Summarize the MNC's exposure based on the comments in the annual report.

REFERENCES

Bartram, Söhnke M., and Gordon M. Bodnar, 2007, The Exchange Rate Exposure Puzzle, *Managerial Finance*, pp. 642–666.

Bodnar, Gordon M., and M. H. Franco Wong, Spring 2003, Estimating Exchange Rate Exposures: Issues in Model Structure, *Financial Management*, pp. 35–67.

El-Masry, Ahmed, and Omneya Abdel-Salam, 2007, Exchange Rate Exposure: Do Size and Foreign Operations Matter? *Managerial Finance*, pp. 741–764.

Hyde, Stuart, 2007, The Response of Industry Stock Returns to Market, Exchange Rate and Interest Rate Risks, *Managerial Finance,* pp. 693–709.

Koutmos, Gregory, and Anna D. Martin, Jun 2003, Asymmetric Exchange Rate Exposure: Theory and Evidence, *Journal of International Money and Finance,* pp. 365–383.

Pritamani, Mahesh D. Dilip K. Shome, and Vijay Singal, Jul 2004, Foreign Exchange Exposure of Exporting and Importing Firms, *Journal of Banking & Finance,* pp. 1697–1710.

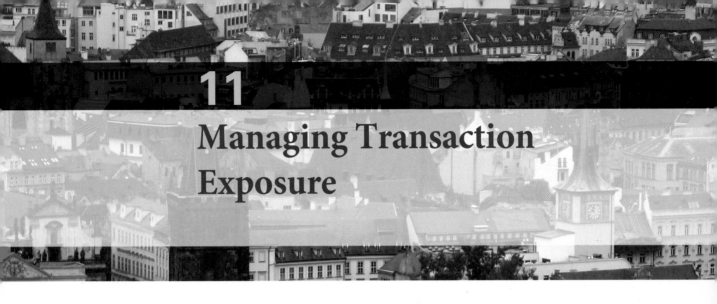

11

Managing Transaction Exposure

CHAPTER
OBJECTIVES

The specific objectives of this chapter are to:

■ compare the techniques commonly used to hedge payables,

■ compare the techniques commonly used to hedge receivables,

■ explain how to hedge long-term transaction exposure, and

■ suggest other methods of reducing exchange rate risk when hedging techniques are not available.

Transaction exposure exists when there are contractual transactions that cause an MNC to either need or receive a specified amount of a foreign currency at a specified point in the future. The dollar value of payables could easily increase by 10 percent or more, and the dollar value of receivables could easily decline by 10 percent or more, which might completely eliminate the profit margin on the sale of the product. For this reason, most MNCs seriously consider the hedging of contractual transactions denominated in foreign currencies. First, an MNC must identify its degree of transaction exposure, as discussed in the previous chapter, Next, it must consider the various techniques to hedge this exposure so that it can decide which hedging technique is optimal and whether to hedge its transaction exposure. By managing transaction exposure, financial managers may be able to increase cash flows and enhance the value of their MNCs.

HEDGING EXPOSURE TO PAYABLES

An MNC may decide to hedge part or all of its known payables transactions so that it is insulated from possible appreciation of the currency. It may select from the following hedging techniques to hedge its payables:

- Futures hedge
- Forward hedge
- Money market hedge
- Currency option hedge

Before selecting a hedging technique, MNCs normally compare the cash flows that would be expected from each technique. The proper hedging technique can vary over time, as the relative advantages of the various techniques may change over time. Each technique is discussed in turn, with examples provided.

Forward or Futures Hedge on Payables

Forward contracts and futures contracts allow an MNC to lock in a specific exchange rate at which it can purchase a specific currency and, therefore, allow it to hedge payables denominated in a foreign currency. A forward contract is negotiated between the firm and a financial institution such as a commercial bank and, therefore, can be tailored to meet the specific needs of the firm. The contract will specify the:

- currency that the firm will pay
- currency that the firm will receive
- amount of currency to be received by the firm
- rate at which the MNC will exchange currencies (called the forward rate)
- future date at which the exchange of currencies will occur

Coleman Co. is a U.S.-based MNC that will need 100,000 euros in 1 year. It could obtain a forward contract to purchase the euros in 1 year. The 1-year forward rate is $1.20, the same rate as currency futures contracts on euros. If Coleman purchases euros 1 year forward, its dollar cost in 1 year is:

$$\text{Cost in \$} = \text{Payables} \times \text{Forward rate}$$
$$= 100{,}000 \text{ euros} \times \$1.20$$
$$= \$120{,}000 \qquad \bullet$$

The same process would apply if futures contracts were used instead of forward contracts. The futures rate is normally very similar to the forward rate, so the main difference would be that the futures contracts are standardized and would be purchased on an exchange, while the forward contract would be negotiated between the MNC and a commercial bank.

Forward contracts are commonly used by large corporations that desire to hedge. DuPont Co. often has the equivalent of $300 million to $500 million in forward contracts at any one time to cover open currency positions, while Union Carbide has more than $100 million in forward contracts.

Money Market Hedge on Payables

A **money market hedge** on payables involves taking a money market position to cover a future payables position. If a firm has excess cash, it can create a simplified money market hedge. However, many MNCs prefer to hedge payables without using their cash balances. A money market hedge can still be used in this situation, but it requires two money market positions: (1) borrowed funds in the home currency and (2) a short-term investment in the foreign currency.

If Coleman Co. needs 100,000 euros in one year, it could convert dollars to euros and deposit the euros in a bank today. Assuming that it could earn 5 percent on this deposit, it would need to establish a deposit of 95,238 euros in order to have 100,000 euros in one year, as shown below:

$$\text{Deposit amount to hedge payables} = \frac{100{,}000 \text{ euros}}{1 + .05} = 95{,}238 \text{ euros}$$

Assuming a spot rate today of $1.18, the dollars needed to make the deposit today are estimated below:

$$\text{Deposit amount in dollars} = 95{,}238 \text{ euros} \times \$1.18 = \$112{,}381$$

Assuming that Coleman can borrow dollars at an interest rate of 8 percent, it would borrow the funds needed to make the deposit, and at the end of the year it would repay the loan:

$$\text{Dollar amount of loan repayment} = \$112{,}381 \times (1 + .08) = \$121{,}371 \qquad \bullet$$

Money Market Hedge versus Forward Hedge. Should an MNC implement a forward contract hedge or a money market hedge? Since the results of both hedges are known beforehand, the firm can implement the one that is more feasible. If interest rate parity (IRP) exists and transaction costs do not exist, the money market hedge will yield the same results as the forward hedge. This is so because the forward premium on the forward rate reflects the interest rate differential between the two currencies. The hedging of future payables with a forward purchase will be similar to borrowing at the home interest rate and investing at the foreign interest rate.

Call Option Hedge on Payables

A currency call option provides the right to buy a specified amount of a particular currency at a specified price (called the *strike price*, or *exercise price*) within a given period of time. Yet, unlike a futures or forward contract, the currency call option *does not obligate* its owner to buy the currency at that price. The MNC has the flexibility to let the option expire and obtain the currency at the existing spot rate when payables are due. However, a firm must assess whether the advantages of a currency option hedge are worth the price (premium) paid for it. Details on currency options are provided in Chapter 5. The following discussion illustrates how they can be used in hedging.

Cost of Call Options Based on a Contingency Graph.

The cost of hedging with call options is not known with certainty at the time that the options are purchased. It is only known once the payables are due and the spot rate at that time is known. For this reason, an MNC attempts to determine what the cost of hedging with call options would be based on various possible spot rates that could exist for the foreign currency at the time that payables are due.

This cost of hedging includes the price paid for the currency, along with the premium paid for the call option. If the spot rate of the currency at the time payables are due is less than the exercise price, the MNC would let the option expire because it could purchase the currency in the foreign exchange market at the spot rate. If the spot rate is equal to or above the exercise price, the MNC would exercise the option and pay the exercise price for the currency.

An MNC can develop a contingency graph that determines the cost of hedging with call options for each of several possible spot rates when payables are due. It may be especially useful when a MNC would like to assess the cost of hedging for a wide range of possible spot rate outcomes.

EXAMPLE

Recall that Coleman Co. considers hedging its payables of 100,000 euros in 1 year. It could purchase call options on 100,000 euros so that it can hedge its payables. Assume that the call options have an exercise price of $1.20, a premium of $.03, and an expiration date of 1 year from now (when the payables are due). Coleman can create a contingency graph for the call option hedge, as shown in Exhibit 11.1. The horizontal axis shows several possible spot rates of the euro that could occur at the time payables are due, while the vertical axis shows the cost of hedging per euro for each of those possible spot rates.

At any spot rate less than the exercise price of $1.20, Coleman would not exercise the call option, so the cost of hedging would be equal to the spot rate at that time, along with the premium. For example, if the spot rate was $1.16 at the time payables were due, Coleman would pay that spot rate along with the $.03 premium per unit. At any spot rate more than or equal to the exercise price of $1.20, Coleman would exercise the call option, and the cost of hedging would be equal to the price paid per euro ($1.20) along with the premium of $.03 per euro. Thus, the cost of hedging is $1.23 for all spot rates beyond the exercise price of $1.20. ●

Exhibit 11.1 illustrates the advantages and disadvantages of a call option for hedging payables. The advantage is that the call option provides an effective hedge, while also allowing the MNC to let the option expire if the spot rate at the time payables are due is lower than the exercise price. However, the obvious disadvantage of the call option is that a premium must be paid for it.

To compare a hedge with a call option to a hedge with a forward contract, recall from a previous example that Coleman Co. could purchase a forward contract on euros for $1.20, which would result in a cost of hedging of $1.20 per euro, regardless of what the spot rate is at the time payables are due because a forward contract, unlike a call option,

Exhibit 11.1 Contingency Graph for Hedging Payables with Call Options

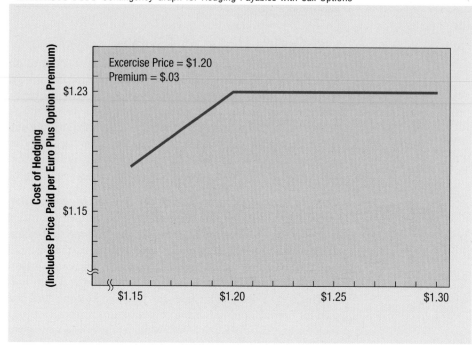

creates an irrevocable obligation to execute. This could be reflected on the same contingency graph in Exhibit 11.1 as a horizontal line beginning at the $1.20 point on the vertical axis and extending straight across for all possible spot rates. In general, the forward rate would result in a lower cost of hedging than currency call options if the spot rate is relatively high at the time payables are due, while currency call options would result in a lower cost of hedging than the forward rate if the spot rate is relatively low at the time payables are due.

Cost of Call Options Based on Currency Forecasts.

While the contingency graph can determine the cost of hedging for various possible spot rates when payables are due, it does not consider an MNC's currency forecasts. Thus, it does not necessarily lead the MNC to a clear decision about whether to hedge with currency options. An MNC may wish to incorporate its own forecasts of the spot rate at the time payables are due, so that it can more accurately estimate the cost of hedging with call options.

EXAMPLE

Recall that Coleman Co. considers hedging its payables of 100,000 euros with a call option that has an exercise price of $1.20, a premium of $.03, and an expiration date of 1 year from now. Also assume that Coleman's forecast for the spot rate of the euro at the time payables are due is as follows:

- $1.16 (20 percent probability)
- $1.22 (70 percent probability)
- $1.24 (10 percent probability)

The effect of each of these scenarios on Coleman's cost of payables is shown in Exhibit 11.2. Columns 1 and 2 simply identify the scenario to be analyzed. Column 3 shows the premium per unit paid on the option, which is the same regardless of the spot rate that occurs when payables are due. Column 4 shows the amount that Coleman would pay per euro for the payables under each scenario, assuming that it owned call options. If Scenario 1 occurs, Coleman will let the options expire and purchase euros in the spot market for $1.16 each.

If Scenario 2 or 3 occurs, Coleman will exercise the options and therefore purchase euros for $1.20 per unit, and it will use the euros to make its payment. Column 5, which is the sum of columns 3 and 4, shows the amount paid per unit when the $.03 premium paid on the call option is included. Column 6 converts column 5 into a total dollar cost, based on the 100,000 euros hedged. ●

Exhibit 11.2 Use of Currency Call Options for Hedging Euro Payables (Exercise Price = $1.20, Premium = $.03)

(1) SCENARIO	(2) SPOT RATE WHEN PAYABLES ARE DUE	(3) PREMIUM PER UNIT PAID ON CALL OPTIONS	(4) AMOUNT PAID PER UNIT WHEN OWNING CALL OPTIONS	(5) = (4) + (3) TOTAL AMOUNT PAID PER UNIT (INCLUDING THE PREMIUM) WHEN OWNING CALL OPTIONS	(6) $ AMOUNT PAID FOR 100,000 EUROS WHEN OWNING CALL OPTIONS
1	$1.16	$.03	$1.16	$1.19	$119,000
2	1.22	.03	1.20	1.23	123,000
3	1.24	.03	1.20	1.23	123,000

Consideration of Alternative Call Options. Several different types of call options may be available, with different exercise prices and premiums for a given currency and expiration date. The tradeoff is that an MNC can obtain a call option with a lower exercise price but would have to pay a higher premium. Alternatively, it can select an option that has a lower premium but then must accept a higher exercise price. Whatever call option is perceived to be most desirable for hedging a particular payables position would be analyzed as explained in the example above, so that it could then be compared to the other hedging techniques.

Summary of Techniques to Hedge Payables

The techniques that can be used to hedge payables are summarized in Exhibit 11.3, with an illustration of how the cost of each hedging technique was measured for Coleman Co. (based on the previous examples). Notice that the cost of the forward hedge or money market hedge can be determined with certainty, while the currency call option hedge has different outcomes depending on the future spot rate at the time payables are due.

Optimal Technique for Hedging Payables

An MNC can select the optimal technique for hedging payables by following these steps. First, since the futures and forward hedge are very similar, the MNC only needs to consider whichever one of these techniques it prefers. Second, when comparing the forward (or futures) hedge to the money market hedge, the MNC can easily determine which hedge is more desirable because the cost of each hedge can be determined with certainty. Once that comparison is completed, the MNC can assess the feasibility of the currency call option hedge. The distribution of the estimated cash outflows resulting from the currency call option hedge can be assessed by estimating its expected value and by determining the likelihood that the currency call option hedge will be less costly than an alternative hedging technique.

EXAMPLE

Recall that Coleman Co. needs to hedge payables of 100,000 euros. Coleman's costs of different hedging techniques can be compared to determine which technique is optimal for hedging the payables. Exhibit 11.4 provides a graphic comparison of the cost of hedging resulting from using different techniques (which were determined in the previous examples in this chapter). For Coleman, the forward hedge is preferable to the money market hedge because it results in a lower cost of hedging payables.

The cost of the call option hedge is described by a probability distribution because it is dependent on the exchange rate at the time that payables are due. The expected value of the cost if using the currency call option hedge is:

$$\text{Expected value of cost} = (\$119{,}000 \times 20\%) + (\$123{,}000 \times 80\%)$$
$$= \$122{,}200$$

Exhibit 11.3 Comparison of Hedging Alternatives for Coleman Co.

Forward Hedge

Purchase euros 1 year forward.

$$\begin{aligned}\text{Dollars needed in 1 year} &= \text{payables in €} \times \text{forward rate of euro}\\ &= 100{,}000 \text{ euros} \times \$1.20\\ &= \$120{,}000\end{aligned}$$

Money Market Hedge

Borrow $, convert to €, invest €, repay $ loan in 1 year.

$$\text{Amount in € to be invested} = \frac{€100{,}000}{1 + .05}$$
$$= 95.238 \text{ euros}$$
$$\text{Amount in \$ needed to convert into € for deposit} = €95{,}238 \times \$1.18$$
$$= \$112{,}381$$
$$\text{Interest and principal owed on \$ loan after 1 year} = \$112{,}381 \times (1 + .08)$$
$$= \$121{,}371$$

Call Option

Purchase call option. (The following computations assume that the option is to be exercised on the day euros are needed, or not at all. Exercise price = $1.20, premium = $.03.)

POSSIBLE SPOT RATE IN 1 YEAR	PREMIUM PER UNIT PAID FOR OPTION	EXERCISE OPTION?	TOTAL PRICE (INCLUDING OPTION PREMIUM) PAID PER UNIT	TOTAL PRICE PAID FOR 100,000 EUROS	PROBABILITY
$1.16	$.03	No	$1.19	$119,000	20%
1.22	.03	Yes	1.23	123,000	70
1.24	.03	Yes	1.23	123,000	10

The probability of the future spot rate being $1.22 (70 percent) and probability of the future spot rate being $1.24 (10 percent) are combined in the calculation because they result in the same cost. The expected value of the cost when hedging with call options exceeds the cost of the forward rate hedge.

When comparing the distribution of the cost of hedging with call options to the cost of the forward hedge, there is a 20 percent chance that the currency call option hedge will be cheaper than the forward hedge. There is an 80 percent chance that the currency call option hedge will be more expensive than the forward hedge. Overall, the forward hedge is the optimal hedge. ●

The optimal technique to hedge payables may vary over time depending on the prevailing forward rate, interest rates, call option premium, and the forecast of the future spot rate at the time payables are due.

Optimal Hedge versus No Hedge on Payables

Even when an MNC knows what its future payables will be, it may decide not to hedge in some cases. It needs to determine the probability distribution of its cost of payables when not hedging as explained next.

EXAMPLE

Coleman Co. has already determined that the forward rate is the optimal hedging technique if it decides to hedge its payables position. Now it wants to compare the forward hedge to no hedge.

Exhibit 11.4 Graphic Comparison of Techniques to Hedge Payables

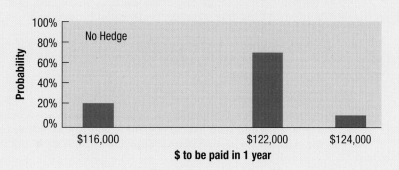

Based on its expectations of the euro's spot rate in 1 year (as described earlier), Coleman Co. can estimate its cost of payables when unhedged:

POSSIBLE SPOT RATE OF EURO IN 1 YEAR	DOLLAR PAYMENTS WHEN NOT HEDGING = 100,000 EUROS × POSSIBLE SPOT RATE	PROBABILITY
$1.16	$116,000	20%
$1.22	$122,000	70%
$1.24	$124,000	10%

This probability distribution of costs when not hedging is shown in the bottom graph of Exhibit 11.4 and can be compared to the cost of the forward hedge in that exhibit.

The expected value of the payables when not hedging is estimated as:

$$\text{Expected value of payables} = (\$116{,}000 \times 20\%) + (\$122{,}000 \times 70\%) + (\$124{,}000 \times 10\%)$$
$$= \$121{,}000$$

This expected value of the payables is $1,000 more than if Coleman uses a forward hedge. In addition, the probability distribution suggests an 80 percent probability that the cost of the payables when unhedged will exceed the cost of hedging with a forward contract. Therefore, Coleman decides to hedge its payables position with a forward contract. ●

Evaluating the Hedge Decision

MNCs can evaluate hedging decisions that they made in the past by estimating the **real cost of hedging payables,** which is measured as:

$$RCH_p = \text{Cost of hedging payables} - \text{Cost of payables if not hedged}$$

After the payables transaction has occurred, an MNC may assess the outcome of its decision to hedge.

EXAMPLE

Recall that Coleman Co. decided to hedge its payables with a forward contract, resulting in a dollar cost of $120,000. Assume that on the day that it makes its payment (one year after it hedged its payables), the spot rate of the euro is $1.18. Notice that this spot rate is different from any of the three possible spot rates that Coleman Co. predicted. This is not unusual, as it is difficult to predict the spot rate, even when creating a distribution of possible outcomes. If Coleman Co. had not hedged, its cost of the payables would have been $118,000 (computed as 100,000 euros × $1.18). Thus, Coleman's real cost of hedging is:

$$RCH_p = \text{Cost of hedging payables} - \text{Cost of payables if not hedged}$$
$$= \$120{,}000 - \$118{,}000$$
$$= \$2{,}000$$

In this example, Coleman's cost of hedging payables turned out to be $2,000 more than if it had not hedged. However, Coleman is not necessarily disappointed in its decision to hedge. That decision allowed it to know exactly how many dollars it would need to cover its payables position and insulated the payment from movements in the euro. ●

HEDGING EXPOSURE TO RECEIVABLES

An MNC may decide to hedge part or all of its receivables transactions denominated in foreign currencies so that it is insulated from the possible depreciation of those currencies. It can apply the same techniques available for hedging payables to hedge receivables. The application of each hedging technique to receivables is discussed next.

Forward or Futures Hedge on Receivables

Forward contracts and futures contracts allow an MNC to lock in a specific exchange rate at which it can sell a specific currency and, therefore, allow it to hedge receivables denominated in a foreign currency.

Viner Co. is a U.S.-based MNC that will receive 200,000 Swiss francs in 6 months. It could obtain a forward contract to sell SF200,000 in 6 months. The 6-month forward rate is $.71, the same rate as currency futures contracts on Swiss francs. If Viner sells Swiss francs 6 months forward, it can estimate the amount of dollars to be received in 6 months:

$$\text{Cash inflow in \$} = \text{Receivables} \times \text{Forward rate}$$
$$= \text{SF200,000} \times \$.71$$
$$= \$142,000 \qquad \bullet$$

The same process would apply if futures contracts were used instead of forward contracts. The futures rate is normally very similar to the forward rate, so the main difference would be that the futures contracts are standardized and would be sold on an exchange, while the forward contract would be negotiated between the MNC and a commercial bank.

Money Market Hedge on Receivables

A money market hedge on receivables involves borrowing the currency that will be received and using the receivables to pay off the loan.

Recall that Viner Co. will receive SF200,000 in 6 months. Assume that it can borrow funds denominated in Swiss francs at a rate of 3 percent over a 6-month period. The amount that it should borrow so that it can use all of its receivables to repay the entire loan in 6 months is:

$$\text{Amount to borrow} = \text{SF200,000}/(1 + .03)$$
$$= \text{SF194,175}$$

If Viner Co. obtains a 6-month loan of SF194,175 from a bank, it will owe the bank SF200,000 in 6 months. It can use its receivables to repay the loan. The funds that it borrowed can be converted to dollars and used to support existing operations. ●

If the MNC does not need any short-term funds to support existing operations, it can still obtain a loan as explained above, convert the funds to dollars, and invest the dollars in the money market.

If Viner Co. does not need any funds to support existing operations, it can convert the Swiss francs that it borrowed into dollars. Assume the spot exchange rate is presently $.70. When Viner Co. converts the Swiss francs, it will receive:

$$\text{Amount of dollars received from loan} = \text{SF194,175} \times \$.70 = \$135,922$$

Then the dollars can be invested in the money market. Assume that Viner Co. can earn 2 percent interest over a 6-month period. In 6 months, the investment will be worth:

$$\$135,922 \times 1.02 = \$138,640$$

Thus, if Viner Co. uses a money market hedge, its receivables will be worth $138,640 in 6 months. ●

Put Option Hedge on Receivables

A put option allows an MNC to sell a specific amount of currency at a specified exercise price by a specified expiration date. An MNC can purchase a put option on the currency denominating its receivables and lock in the minimum amount that it would receive when converting the receivables into its home currency. However, the put option differs from a forward or futures contract in that it is an option and not an obligation. If the currency denominating the receivables is higher than the exercise price at the time of expiration, the MNC can let the put option expire and can sell the currency in the foreign exchange market at the prevailing spot rate. The MNC must also consider the premium that it must pay for the put option.

Cost of Put Options Based on Contingency Graph.

The cost of hedging with put options is not known with certainty at the time that they are purchased. It is only known once the receivables are due and the spot rate at that time is known. For this reason, an MNC attempts to determine the amount of cash it will receive from the put option hedge based on various possible spot rates at the time that receivables arrive.

An estimate of the cash to be received from a put option hedge is the estimated cash received from selling the currency minus the premium paid for the put option. If the spot rate of the currency at the time receivables arrive is less than the exercise price, the MNC would exercise the option and receive the exercise price when selling the currency. If the spot rate at that time is equal to or above the exercise price, the MNC would let the option expire and would sell the currency at the spot rate in the foreign exchange market.

An MNC can develop a contingency graph that determines the cash received from hedging with put options depending on each of several possible spot rates when receivables arrive. It may be especially useful when an MNC would like to estimate the cash received from hedging based on a wide range of possible spot rate outcomes.

Recall that Viner Co. considers hedging its receivables of SF200,000 in 6 months. It could purchase put options on SF200,000, so that it can hedge its receivables. Assume that the put options have an exercise price of $.70, a premium of $.02, and an expiration date of 6 months from now (when the receivables arrive). Viner can create a contingency graph for the put option hedge, as shown in Exhibit 11.5. The horizontal axis shows several possible spot rates of the Swiss franc that could occur at the time receivables arrive, while the vertical axis shows the cash to be received from the put option hedge based on each of those possible spot rates.

At any spot rate less than or equal to the exercise price of $.70, Viner would exercise the put option and would sell the Swiss francs at the exercise price of $.70. After subtracting the $.02 premium per unit, Viner would receive $.68 per unit from selling Swiss francs. At any spot rate more than the exercise price, Viner would let the put option expire and would sell the francs at the spot rate in the foreign exchange market. For example, if the spot rate was $.75 at the time receivables were due, Viner would sell the Swiss francs at that rate. It would receive $.73 after subtracting the $.02 premium per unit. ●

Exhibit 11.5 illustrates the advantages and disadvantages of a put option for hedging receivables. The advantage is that the put option provides an effective hedge, while also allowing the MNC to let the option expire if the spot rate at the time receivables arrive is higher than the exercise price.

However, the obvious disadvantage of the put option is that a premium must be paid for it. Recall from a previous example that Viner Co. could sell a forward contract on Swiss francs for $.71, which would allow it to receive $.71 per Swiss franc, regardless of what the spot rate is at the time receivables arrive. This could be reflected on the same contingency graph in Exhibit 11.5 as a horizontal line beginning at the $.71 point on the vertical axis and extending straight across for all possible spot rates. In general, the forward rate hedge would provide a larger amount of cash than the put option hedge if the spot rate is relatively low at the time Swiss francs are received, while currency put options would provide a larger amount of cash than the forward rate if the spot rate is relatively high at the time Swiss francs are received.

Exhibit 11.5 Contingency Graph for Hedging Receivables with Put Options

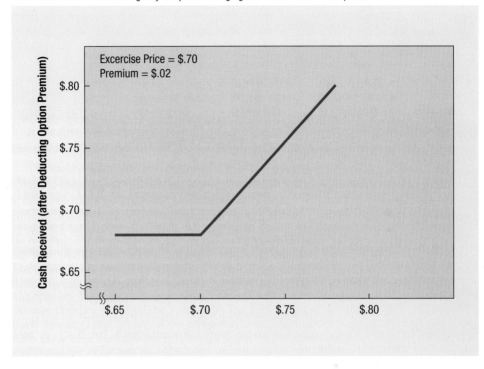

Cost of Put Options Based on Currency Forecasts.

While the contingency graph can determine the cash to be received from hedging based on various possible spot rates when receivables will arrive, it does not consider an MNC's currency forecasts. Thus, it does not necessarily lead the MNC to a clear decision about whether to hedge receivables with currency put options. An MNC may wish to incorporate its own forecasts of the spot rate at the time receivables will arrive, so that it can more accurately estimate the dollar cash inflows to be received when hedging with put options.

EXAMPLE

Viner Co. considers purchasing a put option contract on Swiss francs, with an exercise price of $.72 and a premium of $.02. It has developed the following probability distribution for the spot rate of the Swiss franc in 6 months:

- $.71 (30 percent probability)
- $.74 (40 percent probability)
- $.76 (30 percent probability)

The expected dollar cash flows to be received from purchasing the put options on Swiss francs are shown in Exhibit 11.6. The second column discloses the possible spot rates that may occur in 6 months according to Viner's expectations. The third column shows the option premium that is the same regardless of what happens to the spot rate in the future. The fourth column shows the amount to be received per unit as a result of owning the put options. If the spot rate is $.71 in the future (see the first row), the put option will be exercised at the exercise price of $.72. If the spot rate is more than $.72 in 6 months (as reflected in rows 2 and 3), Viner will not exercise the option, and it will sell the Swiss francs at the prevailing spot rate. Column 5 shows the cash received per unit, which adjusts the figures in column 4 by subtracting the premium paid per unit for the put option. Column 6 shows the amount of dollars to be received, which is equal to cash received per unit (shown in column 5) multiplied by the amount of units (200,000 Swiss francs). ●

Exhibit 11.6 Use of Currency Put Options for Hedging Swiss Franc Receivables (Exercise Price = $.72; Premium = $.02)

(1)	(2)	(3)	(4)	(5) = (4) – (3)	(6)
SCENARIO	SPOT RATE WHEN PAYMENT ON RECEIVABLES IS RECEIVED	PREMIUM PER UNIT ON PUT OPTIONS	AMOUNT RECEIVED PER UNIT WHEN OWNING PUT OPTIONS	NET AMOUNT RECEIVED PER UNIT (AFTER ACCOUNTING FOR PREMIUM PAID)	DOLLAR AMOUNT RECEIVED FROM HEDGING SF200,000 RECEIVABLES WITH PUT OPTIONS
1	$.71	$.02	$.72	$.70	$140,000
2	.74	.02	.74	.72	144,000
3	.76	.02	.76	.74	148,000

Consideration of Alternative Put Options. Several different types of put options may be available, with different exercise prices and premiums for a given currency and expiration date. An MNC can obtain a put option with a higher exercise price, but the tradeoff is that it would have to pay a higher premium. Alternatively, it can select a put option that has a lower premium but then must accept a lower exercise price. Whatever put option is perceived to be most desirable for hedging a particular receivables position would be analyzed as explained in the example above, so that it could then be compared to the other hedging techniques.

Optimal Technique for Hedging Receivables

The techniques that can be used to hedge receivables are summarized in Exhibit 11.7, with an illustration of how the cash inflow from each hedging technique was measured for Viner Co. (based on previous examples).

The optimal technique to hedge receivables may vary over time depending on the specific quotations, such as the forward rate quoted on a forward contract, the interest rates quoted on a money market loan, and the premium quoted on a put option. The optimal technique for hedging a specific receivables position at a future point in time can be determined by comparing the cash to be received among the hedging techniques. First, since the futures and forward hedge are very similar, the MNC only needs to consider whichever one of these techniques it prefers. For our example, the forward hedge will be considered. Second, when comparing the forward (or futures) hedge to the money market hedge, the MNC can easily determine which hedge is more desirable because the cash to be received from either hedge can be determined with certainty.

Once that comparison is completed, the MNC can assess the feasibility of the currency put option hedge. Since the amount of cash to be received from the currency put option is dependent on the spot rate that exists when receivables arrive, this amount can best be described with a probability distribution. This probability distribution of cash to be received when hedging with put options can be assessed by estimating the expected value and determining the likelihood that the currency put option hedge will result in more cash than an alternative hedging technique.

EXAMPLE

Viner Co. can compare the cash to be received as the result of applying different hedging techniques to hedge receivables of SF200,000 in order to determine the optimal technique. Exhibit 11.8 provides a graphic summary of the cash to be received from each hedging technique, based on the previous examples for Viner Co. In this example, the forward hedge is better than the money market hedge because it will generate more cash.

Exhibit 11.7 Comparison of Hedging Alternatives for Viner Co.

Forward Hedge

Sell Swiss francs 6 months forward.

$$\text{Dollars to be received in 6 months} = \text{receivables in SF} \times \text{forward rate of SF}$$
$$= \text{SF200,000} \times \$.71$$
$$= \$142,000$$

Money Market Hedge

Borrow SF, convert to $, invest $, use receivables to pay off loan in 6 months.

$$\text{Amount in SF borrowed} = \frac{\text{SF200,000}}{1 + .03}$$
$$= \text{SF194,175}$$
$$\$ \text{ received from converting SF} = \text{SF194,175} \times \$70 \text{ per SF}$$
$$= \$135,922$$
$$\$ \text{ accumulated after 6 months} = \$135,922 \times (1 + .02)$$
$$= \$138,640$$

Put Option Hedge

Purchase put option. (Assume the options are to be exercised on the day SF are to be received, or not at all. Exercise price = $.72, premium = $.02.)

POSSIBLE SPOT RATE IN 6 MONTHS	PREMIUM PER UNIT PAID FOR OPTION	EXERCISE OPTION?	RECEIVED PER UNIT (AFTER ACCOUNTING FOR THE PREMIUM)	TOTAL DOLLARS RECEIVED FROM CONVERTING SF200,000	PROBABILITY
.71	$.02	Yes	$.70	$140,000	30%
.74	.02	No	.72	144,000	40
.76	.02	No	.74	148,000	30

The graph for the put option hedge shows that the cash to be received is dependent on the exchange rate at the time that receivables are due. The expected value of the cash to be received from the put option hedge is:

$$\text{Expected value of cash to be received} = (\$140,000 \times 30\%)$$
$$+ (\$144,000 \times 40\%)$$
$$+ (\$148,000 \times 30\%)$$
$$= \$144,000$$

The expected value of the cash to be received when hedging with put options exceeds the cash amount that would be received from the forward rate hedge. ●

When comparing the distribution of cash to be received from the put option to the cash when using the forward hedge (see Exhibit 11.8), there is a 30 percent chance that the currency put option hedge will result in less cash than the forward hedge. There is a 70 percent chance that the put option hedge will result in more cash than the forward hedge. Viner decides that the put option hedge is the optimal hedge.

Optimal Hedge versus No Hedge

Even when an MNC knows what its future receivables will be, it may decide not to hedge in some cases. It needs to determine the probability distribution of its revenue from receivables when not hedging as shown in the following example.

Exhibit 11.8 Graph Comparison of Techniques to Hedge Receivables

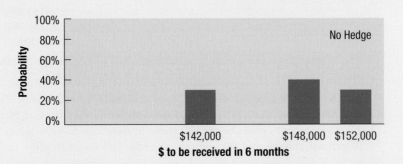

Viner Co. has already determined that the put option hedge is the optimal technique for hedging its receivables position. Now it wants to compare the put option hedge to no hedge. Based on its expectations of the Swiss franc's spot rate in 1 year (as described earlier), Viner Co. can estimate the cash to be received if it remains unhedged:

POSSIBLE SPOT RATE OF SWISS FRANC IN 1 YEAR	DOLLAR PAYMENTS WHEN NOT HEDGING = SF200,000 × POSSIBLE SPOT RATE	PROBABILITY
$.71	$142,000	30%
$.74	$148,000	40%
$.76	$152,000	30%

The expected value of cash that Viner Co. will receive when not hedging is estimated as:

$$\begin{aligned} \text{Expected value of cash to be received} &= (\$142{,}000 \times 30\%) \\ &+ (\$148{,}000 \times 40\%) \\ &+ (\$152{,}000 \times 30\%) \\ &= \$147{,}400 \end{aligned}$$

When comparing this expected value to the expected value of cash that Viner Co. would receive from its put option hedge ($144,000), Viner decides to remain unhedged. In this example, Viner's decision to remain unhedged creates a tradeoff in which it hopes to benefit from the appreciation of the Swiss franc against the U.S. dollar over the next 6 months but is susceptible to adverse effects if the franc depreciates. ●

Evaluating the Hedge Decision

Once the receivables transaction has occurred, an MNC can assess its decision to hedge or not hedge.

Recall that Viner Co. decided not to hedge its receivables. Assume that 6 months later when the receivables arrive, the spot rate of the Swiss franc is $.75. Notice that this spot rate is different from any of the three possible spot rates that Viner Co. predicted. This is not unusual, as it is difficult to predict the spot rate, even when creating a distribution of possible outcomes. Since Viner did not hedge, it receives:

$$\begin{aligned} \text{Cash received} &= \text{Spot rate of SF} \times \text{SF200,000 at time of receivables transaction} \\ &= \$.75 \times \text{SF200,000} \\ &= \$150{,}000 \end{aligned}$$

Now consider what the results would have been if Viner Co. had hedged the receivables position. Recall that Viner would have used the put option hedge if it hedged. Given the spot rate of $.75 when the receivables arrived, Viner would not have exercised the put option. Thus, it would have exchanged the Swiss francs in the spot market for $.75 per unit, minus the $.02 premium per unit that it would have paid for the put option. Its cash received from the put option hedge would have been:

$$\begin{aligned} \text{Cash received} &= \$.73 \times \text{SF200,000} \\ &= \$146{,}000 \end{aligned}$$

●

In this example, Viner's decision to remain unhedged generated $4,000 more than if it had hedged its receivables. The difference of $4,000 is the premium that Viner would have paid to obtain put options. While Viner benefited from remaining unhedged in this example, it recognizes the risk from not hedging.

Exhibit 11.9 Review of Techniques for Hedging Transaction Exposure

HEDGING TECHNIQUE	TO HEDGE PAYABLES	TO HEDGE RECEIVABLES
Futures hedge	Purchase a currency futures contract (or contracts) representing the currency and amount related to the payables.	Sell a currency futures contract (or contracts) representing the currency and amount related to the receivables.
Forward hedge	Negotiate a forward contract to purchase the amount of foreign currency needed to cover the payables.	Negotiate a forward contract to sell the amount of foreign currency that will be received as a result of the receivables.
Money market hedge	Borrow local currency and convert to currency denominating payables. Invest these funds until they are needed to cover the payables.	Borrow the currency denominating the receivables, convert it to the local currency, and invest it. Then pay off the loan with cash inflows from the receivables.
Currency option hedge	Purchase a currency call option (or options) representing the currency and amount related to the payables.	Purchase a currency put option (or options) representing the currency and amount related to the receivables.

Comparison of Hedging Techniques

Each of the hedging techniques is briefly summarized in Exhibit 11.9. When using a futures hedge, forward hedge, or money market hedge, the firm can estimate the funds (denominated in its home currency) that it will need for future payables, or the funds that it will receive after converting foreign currency receivables. The outcome is certain. Thus, it can compare the costs or revenue and determine which of these hedging techniques is appropriate. In contrast, the cash flow associated with the currency option hedge cannot be determined with certainty because the costs of purchasing payables and the revenue generated from receivables are not known ahead of time. Therefore, firms need to forecast cash flows from the option hedge based on possible exchange rate outcomes. A fee (premium) must be paid for the option, but the option offers flexibility because it does not have to be exercised.

Hedging Policies of MNCs

In general, hedging policies vary with the MNC management's degree of risk aversion. An MNC may choose to hedge most of its exposure, to hedge none of its exposure, or to selectively hedge.

WEB

www.ibm.com/us/
The websites of various MNCs provide financial statements such as annual reports that disclose the use of financial derivatives for the purpose of hedging interest rate risk and foreign exchange rate risk.

Hedging Most of the Exposure. Some MNCs hedge most of their exposure so that their value is not highly influenced by exchange rates. MNCs that hedge most of their exposure do not necessarily expect that hedging will always be beneficial. In fact, such MNCs may even use some hedges that will likely result in slightly worse outcomes than no hedges at all, just to avoid the possibility of a major adverse movement in exchange rates. They prefer to know what their future cash inflows or outflows in terms of their home currency will be in each period because this improves corporate planning. A hedge allows the firm to know the future cash flows (in terms of the home currency) that will result from any foreign transactions that have already been negotiated.

Hedging None of the Exposure. MNCs that are well diversified across many countries may consider not hedging their exposure. This strategy may be driven by the view that a diversified set of exposures will limit the actual impact that exchange rates will have on the MNC during any period.

Selective Hedging.

Many MNCs, such as Black & Decker, Eastman Kodak, and Merck choose to hedge only when they believe that it will improve their expected cash flows. Zenith hedges its imports of Japanese components only when it expects the yen to appreciate. Merck has worldwide sales of over $6 billion per year with substantial receivables denominated in foreign currencies as a result of exporting. Since Merck wants to capitalize on the possible appreciation of these foreign currencies (weakening of the dollar), it uses put options to hedge its receivables denominated in foreign currencies. If the dollar weakens, Merck lets the put options expire because the receivables are worth more at the prevailing spot rate. Meanwhile, the put options provide insurance in case the dollar strengthens. If Merck feels very confident that the dollar will strengthen, it uses forward or futures contracts instead of put options because it must pay a premium for the put options.

The following quotations from annual reports illustrate the strategy of selective hedging:

> *The purpose of the Company's foreign currency hedging activities is to reduce the risk that the eventual dollar net cash inflows resulting from sales outside the U.S. will be adversely affected by exchange rates.*
>
> —*The Coca-Cola Co.*

> *Decisions regarding whether or not to hedge a given commitment are made on a case-by-case basis by taking into consideration the amount and duration of the exposure, market volatility, and economic trends.*
>
> —*DuPont Co.*

> *We selectively hedge the potential effect of the foreign currency fluctuations related to operating activities.*
>
> —*General Mills Co.*

Selective hedging implies that the MNC prefers to exercise some control over its exposure and makes decisions based on conditions that may affect the currency's future value.

LIMITATIONS OF HEDGING

Although hedging transaction exposure can be effective, there are some limitations that deserve to be mentioned here.

Limitation of Hedging an Uncertain Amount

Some international transactions involve an uncertain amount of goods ordered and therefore involve an uncertain transaction amount in a foreign currency. Consequently, an MNC may create a hedge for a larger number of units than it will actually need, which causes the opposite form of exposure.

EXAMPLE   Recall the previous example on hedging receivables, which assumed that Viner Co. will receive SF200,000 in 6 months. Now assume that the receivables amount could actually be much lower. If Viner uses the money market hedge on SF200,000 and the receivables amount to only SF120,000, it will have to make up the difference by purchasing SF80,000 in the spot market to achieve the SF200,000 needed to pay off the loan. If the Swiss franc appreciates over the 6-month period, Viner will need a large amount in dollars to obtain the SF80,000. ●

This example shows how **overhedging** (hedging a larger amount in a currency than the actual transaction amount) can adversely affect a firm. A solution to avoid overhedging is to hedge only the minimum known amount in the future transaction. In our example, if the future receivables could be as low as SF120,000, Viner could hedge this amount. Under these conditions, however, the firm may not have completely hedged its position. If the actual transaction amount turns out to be SF200,000 as expected, Viner will be only partially hedged and will need to sell the extra SF80,000 in the spot market.

Alternatively, Viner may consider hedging the minimum level of receivables with a money market hedge and hedging the additional amount of receivables that may occur with a put option hedge. In this way, it is covered if the receivables exceed the minimum amount. It can let the put option expire if the receivables do not exceed the minimum, or if it is better off exchanging the additional Swiss francs received in the spot market.

Firms commonly face this type of dilemma because the precise amount to be received in a foreign currency at the end of a period can be uncertain, especially for firms heavily involved in exporting. Based on this example, it should be clear that most MNCs cannot completely hedge all of their transactions. Nevertheless, by hedging a portion of those transactions that affect them, they can reduce the sensitivity of their cash flows to exchange rate movements.

How the Credit Crisis Affected Uncertainty. During the credit crisis, some international trade agreements were disrupted because some commercial banks failed. Exporters normally rely on commercial banks to make payment on behalf of the importers when products are delivered. But exporters no longer trusted some banks because they were worried that the banks might fail and would therefore not make the payments once the products were delivered. Consequently, the amount of their foreign payables or receivables was more uncertain. This forced some exporters and importers to defer their hedging decisions until they had a definite agreement. By the time they finalized their deals and were ready to hedge their transactions, the exchange rates had already moved and therefore influenced their cash flows.

Limitation of Repeated Short-Term Hedging

The continual hedging of repeated transactions that are expected to occur in the near future has limited effectiveness over the long run.

EXAMPLE Winthrop Co. is a U.S. importer that specializes in importing particular CD players in one large shipment per year and then selling them to retail stores throughout the year. Assume that today's exchange rate of the Japanese yen is $.005 and that the CD players are worth ¥60,000, or $300. The forward rate of the yen generally exhibits a premium of 2 percent. Exhibit 11.10 shows the yen/dollar exchange rate to be paid by the importer over time. As the spot rate changes, the forward rate will often change by a similar amount. Thus, if the spot rate increases by 10 percent over the year, the forward rate may increase by about the same amount, and the importer will pay 10 percent more for next year's shipment (assuming no change in the yen price quoted by the Japanese exporter). The use of a 1-year forward contract during a strong-yen cycle is preferable to no hedge in this case but will still result in subsequent increases in prices paid by the importer each year. This illustrates that the use of short-term hedging techniques does not completely insulate a firm from exchange rate exposure, even if the hedges are used repeatedly over time. ●

If the hedging techniques can be applied to longer-term periods, they can more effectively insulate the firm from exchange rate risk over the long run. That is, Winthrop Co. could, as of time 0, create a hedge for shipments to arrive at the end of each of the next several years. The forward rate for each hedge would be based on the spot rate as of today, as shown in Exhibit 11.11. During a strong-yen cycle, such a strategy would save a substantial amount of money.

This strategy faces a limitation, however, in that the amount in yen to be hedged further into the future is more uncertain because the shipment size will be dependent on economic conditions or other factors at that time. If a recession occurs, Winthrop Co. may reduce the number of CD players ordered, but the amount in yen to be received by the importer is dictated by the forward contract that was created. If the CD player

Exhibit 11.10 Illustration of Repeated Hedging of Foreign Payables When the Foreign Currency Is Appreciating

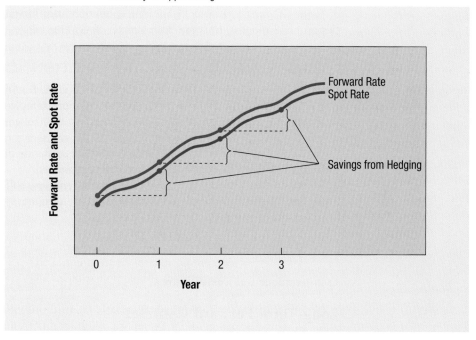

Exhibit 11.11 Long-Term Hedging of Payables When the Foreign Currency Is Appreciating

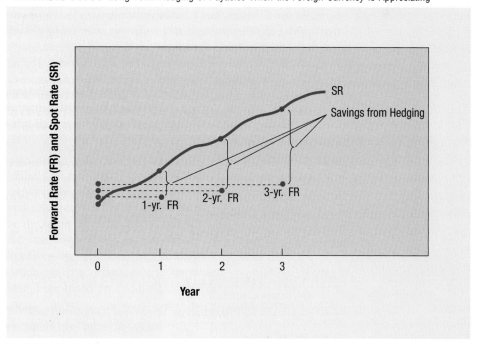

manufacturer goes bankrupt, or simply experiences stockouts, Winthrop Co. is still obligated to purchase the yen, even if a shipment is not forthcoming.

Given the greater uncertainty surrounding the amount of currency to be hedged, some MNCs focus more on hedging receivables or payables that will occur in the near future. Symantec commonly has forward contracts valued at more than $100 million to hedge transaction exposure, and all or most of the contracts have maturities of less than 35 days. Conversely, Procter & Gamble commonly uses forward contracts with maturities up to 18 months. In some cases Procter & Gamble hedges exposure 5 years ahead.

HEDGING LONG-TERM TRANSACTION EXPOSURE

Some MNCs are certain of having cash flows denominated in foreign currencies for several years and attempt to use long-term hedging. For example, Walt Disney Co. hedged its Japanese yen cash flows that will be remitted to the United States (from its Japanese theme park) 20 years ahead. Eastman Kodak Co. and General Electric Co. incorporate foreign exchange management into their long-term corporate planning. Thus, techniques for hedging long-term exchange rate exposure are needed.

Firms that can accurately estimate foreign currency payables or receivables that will occur several years from now commonly use two techniques to hedge such long-term transaction exposure:

- Long-term forward contract
- Parallel loan

Each technique is discussed in turn.

Long-Term Forward Contract

Until recently, **long-term forward contracts**, or long forwards, were seldom used. Today, the long forward is quite popular. Most large international banks routinely quote forward rates for terms of up to 5 years for British pounds, Canadian dollars, Japanese yen, and Swiss francs. Long forwards are especially attractive to firms that have set up fixed-price exporting or importing contracts over a long period of time and want to protect their cash flow from exchange rate fluctuations.

Like a short-term forward contract, the long forward can be tailored to accommodate the specific needs of the firm. Maturities of up to 10 years or more can sometimes be set up for the major currencies. Because a bank is trusting that the firm will fulfill its long-term obligation specified in the forward contract, it will consider only very creditworthy customers.

Parallel Loan

A **parallel loan** (or "back-to-back loan") involves an exchange of currencies between two parties, with a promise to reexchange currencies at a specified exchange rate on a future date. It represents two swaps of currencies, one swap at the inception of the loan contract and another swap at the specified future date. A parallel loan is interpreted by accountants as a loan and is therefore recorded on financial statements. It is covered in more detail in Chapter 18.

ALTERNATIVE HEDGING TECHNIQUES

When a perfect hedge is not available (or is too expensive) to eliminate transaction exposure, the firm should consider methods to at least reduce exposure. Such methods include the following:

- Leading and lagging
- Cross-hedging
- Currency diversification

Each method is discussed in turn.

Leading and Lagging

Leading and lagging strategies involve adjusting the timing of a payment request or disbursement to reflect expectations about future currency movements.

Corvalis Co. is based in the United States and has subsidiaries dispersed around the world. The focus here will be on a subsidiary in the United Kingdom that purchases some of its supplies from a subsidiary in Hungary. These supplies are denominated in Hungary's currency (the forint). If Corvalis Co. expects that the pound will soon depreciate against the forint, it may attempt to expedite the payment to Hungary before the pound depreciates. This strategy is referred to as **leading**.

As a second scenario, assume that the British subsidiary expects the pound to appreciate against the forint soon. In this case, the British subsidiary may attempt to stall its payment until after the pound appreciates. In this way it could use fewer pounds to obtain the forint needed for payment. This strategy is referred to as **lagging**. ●

General Electric and other well-known MNCs commonly use leading and lagging strategies in countries that allow them. In some countries, the government limits the length of time involved in leading and lagging strategies so that the flow of funds into or out of the country is not disrupted. Consequently, an MNC must be aware of government restrictions in any countries where it conducts business before using these strategies.

Cross-Hedging

Cross-hedging is a common method of reducing transaction exposure when the currency cannot be hedged.

Greeley Co., a U.S. firm, has payables in zloty (Poland's currency) 90 days from now. Because it is worried that the zloty may appreciate against the U.S. dollar, it may desire to hedge this position. If forward contracts and other hedging techniques are not possible for the zloty, Greeley may consider cross-hedging. In this case, it needs to first identify a currency that can be hedged and is highly correlated with the zloty. Greeley notices that the euro has recently been moving in tandem with the zloty and decides to set up a 90-day forward contract on the euro. If the movements in the zloty and euro continue to be highly correlated relative to the U.S. dollar (that is, they move in a similar direction and degree against the U.S. dollar), then the exchange rate between these two currencies should be somewhat stable over time. By purchasing euros 90 days forward, Greeley Co. can then exchange euros for the zloty. ●

This type of hedge is sometimes referred to as a *proxy hedge* because the hedged position is in a currency that serves as a proxy for the currency in which the MNC is exposed. The effectiveness of this strategy depends on the degree to which these two currencies are positively correlated. The stronger the positive correlation, the more effective will be the cross-hedging strategy.

Currency Diversification

A third method for reducing transaction exposure is **currency diversification**, which can limit the potential effect of any single currency's movements on the value of an MNC. Some MNCs, such as The Coca-Cola Co., PepsiCo, and Altria, claim that their exposure to exchange rate movements is significantly reduced because they diversify their business among numerous countries.

The dollar value of future inflows in foreign currencies will be more stable if the foreign currencies received are *not* highly positively correlated. The reason is that lower positive correlations or negative correlations can reduce the variability of the dollar value of all foreign currency inflows. If the foreign currencies were highly correlated with each other, diversifying among them would not be a very effective way to reduce risk. If one of the currencies substantially depreciated, the others would do so as well, given that all these currencies move in tandem.

SUMMARY

- To hedge payables, a futures or forward contract on the foreign currency can be purchased. Alternatively, a money market hedge strategy can be used; in this case, the MNC borrows its home currency and converts the proceeds into the foreign currency that will be needed in the future. Finally, call options on the foreign currency can be purchased.

- To hedge receivables, a futures or forward contract on the foreign currency can be sold. Alternatively, a money market hedge strategy can be used. In this case, the MNC borrows the foreign currency to be received and converts the funds into its home currency; the loan is to be repaid by the receivables. Finally, put options on the foreign currency can be purchased.

- Futures contracts and forward contracts normally yield similar results. Forward contracts are more flexible because they are not standardized. The money market hedge yields results similar to those

of the forward hedge if interest rate parity exists. The currency options hedge has an advantage over the other hedging techniques in that the options do not have to be exercised if the MNC would be better off unhedged. A premium must be paid to purchase the currency options, however, so there is a cost for the flexibility they provide.

- Long-term hedging can be accomplished by using long-term forward contracts that match the date of the payables or receivables. Alternatively, a parallel loan involves the exchange of currencies between two parties, with a promise to reexchange currencies at a specified exchange rate on a future date.

- When hedging techniques are not available, there are still some methods of reducing transaction exposure, such as leading and lagging, cross-hedging, and currency diversification.

POINT COUNTER-POINT

Should an MNC Risk Overhedging?

Point Yes. MNCs have some "unanticipated" transactions that occur without any advance notice. They should attempt to forecast the net cash flows in each currency due to unanticipated transactions based on the previous net cash flows for that currency in a previous period. Even though it would be impossible to forecast the volume of these unanticipated transactions per day, it may be possible to forecast the volume on a monthly basis. For example, if an MNC has net cash flows between 3 million and 4 million Philippine pesos every month, it may presume that it will receive at least 3 million pesos in each of the next few months unless conditions change. Thus, it can hedge a position of 3 million in pesos by selling that amount of pesos forward or buying put options on that amount of pesos. Any amount of net cash flows beyond 3 million pesos will not be hedged, but at least the MNC

was able to hedge the minimum expected net cash flows.

Counter-Point No. MNCs should not hedge unanticipated transactions. When they overhedge the expected net cash flows in a foreign currency, they are still exposed to exchange rate risk. If they sell more currency as a result of forward contracts than their net cash flows, they will be adversely affected by an increase in the value of the currency. Their initial reasons for hedging were to protect against the weakness of the currency, but the overhedging described here would cause a shift in their exposure. Overhedging does not insulate an MNC against exchange rate risk. It just changes the means by which the MNC is exposed.

Who Is Correct? Use the Internet to learn more about this issue. Which argument do you support? Offer your own opinion on this issue.

SELF-TEST

Answers are provided in Appendix A at the back of the text.

1. Montclair Co., a U.S. firm, plans to use a money market hedge to hedge its payment of 3 million Australian dollars for Australian goods in 1 year. The U.S. interest rate is 7 percent, while the Australian interest rate is 12 percent. The spot rate of the Australian dollar is $.85, while the 1-year forward rate is $.81. Determine the amount of U.S. dollars needed in 1 year if a money market hedge is used.

2. Using the information in the previous question, would Montclair Co. be better off hedging the payables with a money market hedge or with a forward hedge?

3. Using the information about Montclair from the first question, explain the possible advantage of a currency option hedge over a money market hedge for Montclair Co. What is a possible disadvantage of the currency option hedge?

4. Sanibel Co. purchases British goods (denominated in pounds) every month. It negotiates a 1-month forward contract at the beginning of every month to hedge its payables. Assume the British pound appreciates consistently over the next 5 years. Will Sanibel be affected? Explain.

5. Using the information from question 4, suggest how Sanibel Co. could more effectively insulate itself from the possible long-term appreciation of the British pound.

6. Hopkins Co. transported goods to Switzerland and will receive 2 million Swiss francs in 3 months. It believes the 3-month forward rate will be an accurate forecast of the future spot rate. The 3-month forward rate of the Swiss franc is $.68. A put option is available with an exercise price of $.69 and a premium of $.03. Would Hopkins prefer a put option hedge to no hedge? Explain.

QUESTIONS AND APPLICATIONS

1. Hedging in General. Explain the relationship between this chapter on hedging and the previous chapter on measuring exposure.

2. Money Market Hedge on Receivables. Assume that Stevens Point Co. has net receivables of 100,000 Singapore dollars in 90 days. The spot rate of the S$ is $.50, and the Singapore interest rate is 2 percent over 90 days. Suggest how the U.S. firm could implement a money market hedge. Be precise.

3. Money Market Hedge on Payables. Assume that Vermont Co. has net payables of 200,000 Mexican pesos in 180 days. The Mexican interest rate is 7 percent over 180 days, and the spot rate of the Mexican peso is $.10. Suggest how the U.S. firm could implement a money market hedge. Be precise.

4. Net Transaction Exposure. Why should an MNC identify net exposure before hedging?

5. Hedging with Futures. Explain how a U.S. corporation could hedge net receivables in euros with futures contracts. Explain how a U.S. corporation could hedge net payables in Japanese yen with futures contracts.

6. Hedging with Forward Contracts. Explain how a U.S. corporation could hedge net receivables in Malaysian ringgit with a forward contract. Explain how a U.S. corporation could hedge payables in Canadian dollars with a forward contract.

7. Real Cost of Hedging Payables. Assume that Loras Corp. imported goods from New Zealand and needs 100,000 New Zealand dollars 180 days from now. It is trying to determine whether to hedge this position. Loras has developed the following probability distribution for the New Zealand dollar:

POSSIBLE VALUE OF NEW ZEALAND DOLLAR IN 180 DAYS	PROBABILITY
$.40	5%
.45	10
.48	30
.50	30
.53	20
.55	5

The 180-day forward rate of the New Zealand dollar is $.52. The spot rate of the New Zealand dollar is $.49. Develop a table showing a feasibility analysis for hedging. That is, determine the possible differences between the costs of hedging versus no hedging. What is the probability that hedging will be more costly to the firm than not hedging? Determine the expected value of the additional cost of hedging.

8.   Benefits of Hedging. If hedging is expected to be more costly than not hedging, why would a firm even consider hedging?

9.   Real Cost of Hedging Payables. Assume that Suffolk Co. negotiated a forward contract to purchase 200,000 British pounds in 90 days. The 90-day forward rate was $1.40 per British pound. The pounds to be purchased were to be used to purchase British supplies. On the day the pounds were delivered in accordance with the forward contract, the spot rate of the British pound was $1.44. What was the real cost of hedging the payables for this U.S. firm?

10.   Forward Hedge Decision. Kayla Co. imports products from Mexico, and it will make payment in pesos in 90 days. Interest rate parity holds. The prevailing interest rate in Mexico is very high, which reflects the high expected inflation there. Kayla expects that the Mexican peso will depreciate over the next 90 days. Yet, it plans to hedge its payables with a 90-day forward contract. Why may Kayla believe that it will pay a smaller amount of dollars when hedging than if it remains un hedged?

11.   Forward versus Money Market Hedge on Payables. Assume the following information:

90-day U.S. interest rate	4%
90-day Malaysian interest rate	3%
90-day forward rate of Malaysian ringgit	$.400
Spot rate of Malaysian ringgit	$.404

Assume that the Santa Barbara Co. in the United States will need 300,000 ringgit in 90 days. It wishes to hedge this payables position. Would it be better off using a forward hedge or a money market hedge? Substantiate your answer with estimated costs for each type of hedge.

12.   Forward versus Money Market Hedge on Receivables. Assume the following information:

180-day U.S. interest rate	8%
180-day British interest rate	9%
180-day forward rate of British pound	$1.50
Spot rate of British pound	$1.48

Assume that Riverside Corp. from the United States will receive 400,000 pounds in 180 days. Would it be better off using a forward hedge or a money market hedge? Substantiate your answer with estimated revenue for each type of hedge.

13.   Currency Options. Relate the use of currency options to hedging net payables and receivables. That is, when should currency puts be purchased, and when should currency calls be purchased? Why would Cleveland, Inc., consider hedging net payables or net receivables with currency options rather than forward contracts? What are the disadvantages of hedging with currency options as opposed to forward contracts?

14.   Currency Options. Can Brooklyn Co. determine whether currency options will be more or less expensive than a forward hedge when considering both hedging techniques to cover net payables in euros? Why or why not?

15.   Long-Term Hedging. How can a firm hedge long-term currency positions? Elaborate on each method.

16.   Leading and Lagging. Under what conditions would Zona Co.'s subsidiary consider using a leading strategy to reduce transaction exposure? Under what conditions would Zona Co.'s subsidiary consider using a lagging strategy to reduce transaction exposure?

17.   Cross-Hedging. Explain how a firm can use cross-hedging to reduce transaction exposure.

18.   Currency Diversification. Explain how a firm can use currency diversification to reduce transaction exposure.

19.   Hedging with Put Options. As treasurer of Tucson Corp. (a U.S. exporter to New Zealand), you must decide how to hedge (if at all) future receivables of 250,000 New Zealand dollars 90 days from now. Put options are available for a premium of $.03 per unit and an exercise price of $.49 per New Zealand dollar. The forecasted spot rate of the NZ$ in 90 days follows:

FUTURE SPOT RATE	PROBABILITY
$.44	30%
.40	50
.38	20

Given that you hedge your position with options, create a probability distribution for U.S. dollars to be received in 90 days.

20. Forward Hedge. Would Oregon Co.'s real cost of hedging Australian dollar payables every 90 days have been positive, negative, or about zero on average over a period in which the dollar weakened consistently? What does this imply about the forward rate as an unbiased predictor of the future spot rate? Explain.

21. Implications of IRP for Hedging. If interest rate parity exists, would a forward hedge be more favorable, the same as, or less favorable than a money market hedge on euro payables? Explain.

22. Real Cost of Hedging. Would Montana Co.'s real cost of hedging Japanese yen receivables have been positive, negative, or about zero on average over a period in which the dollar weakened consistently? Explain.

23. Forward versus Options Hedge on Payables. If you are a U.S. importer of Mexican goods and you believe that today's forward rate of the peso is a very accurate estimate of the future spot rate, do you think Mexican peso call options would be a more appropriate hedge than the forward hedge? Explain.

24. Forward versus Options Hedge on Receivables. You are an exporter of goods to the United Kingdom, and you believe that today's forward rate of the British pound substantially underestimates the future spot rate. Company policy requires you to hedge your British pound receivables in some way. Would a forward hedge or a put option hedge be more appropriate? Explain.

25. Forward Hedging. Explain how a Malaysian firm can use the forward market to hedge periodic purchases of U.S. goods denominated in U.S. dollars. Explain how a French firm can use forward contracts to hedge periodic sales of goods sold to the United States that are invoiced in dollars. Explain how a British firm can use the forward market to hedge periodic purchases of Japanese goods denominated in yen.

26. Continuous Hedging. Cornell Co. purchases computer chips denominated in euros on a monthly basis from a Dutch supplier. To hedge its exchange rate risk, this U.S. firm negotiates a 3-month forward contract 3 months before the next order will arrive. In other words, Cornell is always covered for the next three monthly shipments. Because Cornell consistently hedges in this manner, it is not concerned with exchange rate movements. Is Cornell insulated from exchange rate movements? Explain.

27. Hedging Payables with Currency Options. Malibu, Inc., is a U.S. company that imports British goods. It plans to use call options to hedge payables of 100,000 pounds in 90 days. Three call options are available that have an expiration date 90 days from now. Fill in the number of dollars needed to pay for the payables (including the option premium paid) for each option available under each possible scenario in the following table:

SCENARIO	SPOT RATE OF POUND 90 DAYS FROM NOW	EXERCISE PRICE = $1.74; PREMIUM = $.06	EXERCISE PRICE = $1.76; PREMIUM = $.05	EXERCISE PRICE = $1.79; PREMIUM = $.03
1	$1.65			
2	1.70			
3	1.75			
4	1.80			
5	1.85			

If each of the five scenarios had an equal probability of occurrence, which option would you choose? Explain.

28. Forward Hedging. Wedco Technology of New Jersey exports plastics products to Europe. Wedco decided to price its exports in dollars. Telematics International, Inc. (of Florida), exports computer network systems to the United Kingdom (denominated in British pounds) and other countries. Telematics decided to use hedging techniques such as forward contracts to hedge its exposure.

a. Does Wedco's strategy of pricing its materials for European customers in dollars avoid economic exposure? Explain.

b. Explain why the earnings of Telematics International, Inc., were affected by changes in the value of the pound. Why might Telematics leave its exposure unhedged sometimes?

29. The Long-Term Hedge Dilemma. St. Louis, Inc., which relies on exporting, denominates its exports in pesos and receives pesos every month. It expects the peso to weaken over time. St. Louis recognizes the limitation of monthly hedging. It also recognizes that it could remove its transaction exposure by denominating its exports in dollars, but it would still be subject to economic exposure. The long-term hedging techniques are limited, and the firm does not know how many pesos it will receive in the future, so it would have difficulty even if a long-term hedging method was available. How can this business realistically reduce its exposure over the long term?

30. Long-Term Hedging. Since Obisbo, Inc., conducts much business in Japan, it is likely to have cash flows in yen that will periodically be remitted by its Japanese subsidiary to the U.S. parent. What are the limitations of hedging these remittances 1 year in advance over each of the next 20 years? What are the limitations of creating a hedge today that will hedge these remittances over each of the next 20 years?

31. Hedging during the Asian Crisis. Describe how the Asian crisis could have reduced the cash flows of a U.S. firm that exported products (denominated in U.S. dollars) to Asian countries. How could a U.S. firm that exported products (denominated in U.S. dollars) to Asia, and anticipated the Asian crisis before it began, have insulated itself from any currency effects while continuing to export to Asia?

Advanced Questions

32. Comparison of Techniques for Hedging Receivables.

a. Assume that Carbondale Co. expects to receive S$500,000 in 1 year. The existing spot rate of the Singapore dollar is $.60. The 1-year forward rate of the Singapore dollar is $.62. Carbondale created a probability distribution for the future spot rate in 1 year as follows:

FUTURE SPOT RATE	PROBABILITY
$.61	20%
.63	50
.67	30

Assume that 1-year put options on Singapore dollars are available, with an exercise price of $.63 and a premium of $.04 per unit. One-year call options on Singapore dollars are available with an exercise price of $.60 and a premium of $.03 per unit. Assume the following money market rates:

	U.S	SINGAPORE
Deposit rate	8%	5%
Borrowing rate	9	6

Given this information, determine whether a forward hedge, a money market hedge, or a currency options hedge would be most appropriate. Then compare the most appropriate hedge to an unhedged strategy, and decide whether Carbondale should hedge its receivables position.

b. Assume that Baton Rouge, Inc., expects to need S$1 million in 1 year. Using any relevant information in part (a) of this question, determine whether a forward hedge, a money market hedge, or a currency options hedge would be most appropriate. Then, compare the most appropriate hedge to an unhedged strategy, and decide whether Baton Rouge should hedge its payables position.

33. Comparison of Techniques for Hedging Payables.
SMU Corp. has future receivables of 4 million New Zealand dollars (NZ$) in 1 year. It must decide whether to use options or a money market hedge to hedge this position. Use any of the following information to make the decision. Verify your answer by determining the estimate (or probability distribution) of

dollar revenue to be received in 1 year for each type of hedge.

Spot rate of NZ$	$.54	
One-year call option	Exercise price = $.50; premium = $.07	
One-year put option	Exercise price = $.52; premium = $.03	
	U.S.	**NEW ZEALAND**
One-year deposit rate	9%	6%
One-year borrowing rate	11	8
	RATE	**PROBABILITY**
Forecasted spot rate of NZ$	$.50	20%
	.51	50
	.53	30

34. Exposure to September 11. If you were a U.S. importer of products from Europe, explain whether the September 11, 2001, terrorist attacks on the United States would have caused you to hedge your payables (denominated in euros) due a few months later. Keep in mind that the attack was followed by a reduction in U.S. interest rates.

35. Hedging with Forward versus Option Contracts. As treasurer of Tempe Corp., you are confronted with the following problem. Assume the one-year forward rate of the British pound is $1.59. You plan to receive 1 million pounds in 1 year. A one-year put option is available. It has an exercise price of $1.61. The spot rate as of today is $1.62, and the option premium is $.04 per unit. Your forecast of the percentage change in the spot rate was determined from the following regression model:

$$e_t = a_0 + a_1 DINF_{t-1} + a_2 DINT_t + \mu$$

where

e_t = percentage change in British pound value over period t

$DINF_{t-1}$ = differential in inflation between the United States and the United Kingdom in period $t-1$

$DINT_t$ = average differential between U.S. interest rate and British interest rate over period t

a_0, a_1, and a_2 = regression coffiecients

μ = error term

The regression model was applied to historical annual data, and the regression coefficients were estimated as follows:

$$a_0 = 0.0$$
$$a_1 = 1.1$$
$$a_2 = 0.6$$

Assume last year's inflation rates were 3 percent for the United States and 8 percent for the United Kingdom. Also assume that the interest rate differential ($DINT_t$) is forecasted as follows for this year:

FORECAST OF $DINT_t$	PROBABILITY
1%	40%
2	50
3	10

Using any of the available information, should the treasurer choose the forward hedge or the put option hedge? Show your work.

36. Hedging Decision. You believe that IRP presently exists. The nominal annual interest rate in Mexico is 14 percent. The nominal annual interest rate in the United States is 3 percent. You expect that annual inflation will be about 4 percent in Mexico and 5 percent in the United States. The spot rate of the Mexican peso is $.10. Put options on pesos are available with a 1-year expiration date, an exercise price of $.1008, and a premium of $.014 per unit.

You will receive 1 million pesos in 1 year.

a. Determine the expected amount of dollars that you will receive if you use a forward hedge.

b. Determine the expected amount of dollars that you will receive if you do not hedge and believe in purchasing power parity (PPP).

c. Determine the amount of dollars that you will expect to receive if you believe in PPP and use a currency put option hedge. Account for the premium you would pay on the put option.

37. Forecasting with IFE and Hedging. Assume that Calumet Co. will receive 10 million pesos in 15 months. It does not have a relationship with a bank at this time and, therefore, cannot obtain a forward contract to hedge its receivables at this time. However, in 3 months, it will be able to obtain a 1-year (12-month) forward contract to hedge its receivables. Today the 3-month U.S. interest rate is 2 percent (not annualized), the 12-month U.S. interest rate is

8 percent, the 3-month Mexican peso interest rate is 5 percent (not annualized), and the 12-month peso interest rate is 20 percent. Assume that interest rate parity exists.

Assume the international Fisher effect exists. Assume that the existing interest rates are expected to remain constant over time. The spot rate of the Mexican peso today is $.10. Based on this information, estimate the amount of dollars that Calumet Co. will receive in 15 months.

38. Forecasting from Regression Analysis and Hedging. You apply a regression model to annual data in which the annual percentage change in the British pound is the dependent variable, and *INF* (defined as annual U.S. inflation minus U.K. inflation) is the independent variable. Results of the regression analysis show an estimate of 0.0 for the intercept and +1.4 for the slope coefficient. You believe that your model will be useful to predict exchange rate movements in the future.

You expect that inflation in the United States will be 3 percent, versus 5 percent in the United Kingdom. There is an 80 percent chance of that scenario. However, you think that oil prices could rise, and if so, the annual U.S. inflation rate will be 8 percent instead of 3 percent (and the annual U.K. inflation will still be 5 percent). There is a 20 percent chance that this scenario will occur. You think that the inflation differential is the only variable that will affect the British pound's exchange rate over the next year.

The spot rate of the pound as of today is $1.80. The annual interest rate in the United States is 6 percent versus an annual interest rate in the United Kingdom of 8 percent. Call options are available with an exercise price of $1.79, an expiration date of 1 year from today, and a premium of $.03 per unit.

Your firm in the United States expects to need 1 million pounds in 1 year to pay for imports. You can use any one of the following strategies to deal with the exchange rate risk:

a.   Unhedged strategy

b.   Money market hedge

c.   Call option hedge

Estimate the dollar cash flows you will need as a result of using each strategy. If the estimate for a particular strategy involves a probability distribution, show the distribution. Which hedge is optimal?

39. Forecasting Cash Flows and Hedging Decision. Virginia Co. has a subsidiary in Hong Kong and in Thailand. Assume that the Hong Kong dollar is pegged at $.13 per Hong Kong dollar and it

will remain pegged. The Thai baht fluctuates against the U.S. dollar and is presently worth $.03. Virginia Co. expects that during this year, the U.S. inflation rate will be 2 percent, the Thailand inflation rate will be 11 percent, while the Hong Kong inflation rate will be 3 percent. Virginia Co. expects that purchasing power parity will hold for any exchange rate that is not fixed (pegged). The parent of Virginia Co. will receive 10 million Thai baht and 10 million Hong Kong dollars at the end of 1 year from its subsidiaries.

a.   Determine the expected amount of dollars to be received by the U.S. parent from the Thai subsidiary in 1 year when the baht receivables are converted to U.S. dollars.

b.   The Hong Kong subsidiary will send HK$1 million to make a payment for supplies to the Thai subsidiary. Determine the expected amount of baht that will be received by the Thai subsidiary when the Hong Kong dollar receivables are converted to Thai baht.

c.   Assume that interest rate parity exists. Also assume that the real 1-year interest rate in the United States is presumed to be 10 percent, while the real interest rate in Thailand is presumed to be 3.0 percent. Determine the expected amount of dollars to be received by the U.S. parent if it uses a 1-year forward contract today to hedge the receivables of 10 million baht that will arrive in 1 year.

40. Hedging Decision. Chicago Co. expects to receive 5 million euros in 1 year from exports. It can use any one of the following strategies to deal with the exchange rate risk. Estimate the dollar cash flows received as a result of using the following strategies:

a.   Unhedged strategy

b.   Money market hedge

c.   Option hedge

The spot rate of the euro as of today is $1.10. Interest rate parity exists. Chicago uses the forward rate as a predictor of the future spot rate. The annual interest rate in the United States is 8 percent versus an annual interest rate of 5 percent in the eurozone. Put options on euros are available with an exercise price of $1.11, an expiration date of 1 year from today, and a premium of $.06 per unit. Estimate the dollar cash flows it will receive as a result of using each strategy. Which hedge is optimal?

41. Overhedging. Denver Co. is about to order supplies from Canada that are denominated in Canadian dollars (C$). It has no other transactions in Canada and will not have any other transactions in the future. The supplies will arrive in 1 year and payment is due at that time. There is only one supplier in Canada. Denver submits an order for three loads of supplies, which will be priced at C$3 million. Denver Co. purchases C$3 million 1 year forward, since it anticipates that the Canadian dollar will appreciate substantially over the year.

The existing spot rate is $.62, while the 1-year forward rate is $.64. The supplier is not sure if it will be able to provide the full order, so it only guarantees Denver Co. that it will ship one load of supplies. In this case, the supplies will be priced at C$1 million. Denver Co. will not know whether it will receive one load or three loads until the end of the year.

Determine Denver's total cash outflows in U.S. dollars under the scenario that the Canadian supplier only provides one load of supplies and that the spot rate of the Canadian dollar at the end of 1 year is $.59. Show your work.

42. Long-Term Hedging with Forward Contracts. Tampa Co. will build airplanes and export them to Mexico for delivery in 3 years. The total payment to be received in 3 years for these exports is 900 million pesos. Today the peso's spot rate is $.10. The annual U.S. interest rate is 4 percent, regardless of the debt maturity. The annual peso interest rate is 9 percent regardless of the debt maturity. Tampa plans to hedge its exposure with a forward contract that it will arrange today. Assume that interest rate parity exists. Determine the dollar amount that Tampa will receive in 3 years.

43. Timing the Hedge. Red River Co. (a U.S. firm) purchases imports that have a price of 400,000 Singapore dollars, and it has to pay for the imports in 90 days. It will use a 90-day forward contract to cover its payables. Assume that interest rate parity exists. This morning, the spot rate of the Singapore dollar was $.50. At noon, the Federal Reserve reduced U.S. interest rates, while there was no change in interest rates in Singapore. The Fed's actions immediately increased the degree of uncertainty surrounding the future value of the Singapore dollar over the next 3 months. The Singapore dollar's spot rate remained at $.50 throughout the day. Assume that the U.S. and Singapore interest rates were the same as of this morning. Also assume that the international Fisher effect holds. If Red River Co. purchased a currency call option contract at the money this morning to hedge its exposure, would its

total U.S. dollar cash outflows be *more than, less than,* or *the same as* the total U.S. dollar cash outflows if it had negotiated a forward contract this morning? Explain.

44. Hedging with Forward versus Option Contracts. Assume interest rate parity exists. Today, the 1-year interest rate in Canada is the same as the 1-year interest rate in the United States. Utah Co. uses the forward rate to forecast the future spot rate of the Canadian dollar that will exist in 1 year. It needs to purchase Canadian dollars in 1 year. Will the expected cost of its payables be lower if it hedges its payables with a 1-year forward contract on Canadian dollars or a 1-year at-the-money call option contract on Canadian dollars? Explain.

45. Hedging with a Bull Spread. (See the chapter appendix.) Evar Imports, Inc., buys chocolate from Switzerland and resells it in the United States. It just purchased chocolate invoiced at SF62,500. Payment for the invoice is due in 30 days. Assume that the current exchange rate of the Swiss franc is $.74. Also assume that three call options for the franc are available. The first option has a strike price of $.74 and a premium of $.03; the second option has a strike price of $.77 and a premium of $.01; the third option has a strike price of $.80 and a premium of $.006. Evar Imports is concerned about a modest appreciation in the Swiss franc.

a. Describe how Evar Imports could construct a bull spread using the first two options. What is the cost of this hedge? When is this hedge most effective? When is it least effective?

b. Describe how Evar Imports could construct a bull spread using the first option and the third option. What is the cost of this hedge? When is this hedge most effective? When is it least effective?

c. Given your answers to parts (a) and (b), what is the tradeoff involved in constructing a bull spread using call options with a higher exercise price?

46. Hedging with a Bear Spread. (See the chapter appendix.) Marson, Inc., has some customers in Canada and frequently receives payments denominated in Canadian dollars (C$). The current spot rate for the Canadian dollar is $.75. Two call options on Canadian dollars are available. The first option has an exercise price of $.72 and a premium of $.03. The second option has an exercise price of $.74 and a premium of $.01. Marson, Inc., would like to use a bear spread to hedge a receivable position of C$50,000, which is due in

1 month. Marson is concerned that the Canadian dollar may depreciate to $.73 in 1 month.

a. Describe how Marson, Inc., could use a bear spread to hedge its position.

b. Assume the spot rate of the Canadian dollar in 1 month is $.73. Was the hedge effective?

47. Hedging with Straddles. (See the chapter appendix.) Brooks, Inc., imports wood from Morocco. The Moroccan exporter invoices in Moroccan dirham. The current exchange rate of the dirham is $.10. Brooks just purchased wood for 2 million dirham and should pay for the wood in 3 months. It is also possible that Brooks will receive 4 million dirham in 3 months from the sale of refinished wood in Morocco. Brooks is currently in negotiations with a Moroccan importer about the refinished wood. If the negotiations are successful, Brooks will receive the 4 million dirham in 3 months, for a net cash inflow of 2 million dirham. The following option information is available:

- Call option premium on Moroccan dirham = $.003.
- Put option premium on Moroccan dirham = $.002.
- Call and put option strike price = $.098.
- One option contract represents 500,000 dirham.

a. Describe how Brooks could use a straddle to hedge its possible positions in dirham.

b. Consider three scenarios. In the first scenario, the dirham's spot rate at option expiration is equal to the exercise price of $.098. In the second scenario, the dirham depreciates to $.08. In the third scenario, the dirham appreciates to $.11. For each scenario, consider both the case when the negotiations are successful and the case when the negotiations are not successful. Assess the effectiveness of the long straddle in each of these situations by comparing it to a strategy of using long call options to hedge.

48. Hedging with Straddles versus Strangles. (See the chapter appendix.) Refer to the previous problem. Assume that Brooks believes the cost of a long straddle is too high. However, call options with an exercise price of $.105 and a premium of $.002 and put options with an exercise price of $.09 and a premium of $.001 are also available on Moroccan dirham. Describe how Brooks could use a long strangle to hedge its possible dirham positions. What is the tradeoff involved in using a long strangle versus a long straddle to hedge the positions?

49. Comparison of Hedging Techniques. You own a U.S. exporting firm and will receive 10 million Swiss francs in 1 year. Assume that interest parity exists. Assume zero transaction costs. Today, the 1-year interest rate in the United States is 7 percent, and the 1-year interest rate in Switzerland is 9 percent. You believe that today's spot rate of the Swiss franc (which is $.85) is the best predictor of the future spot rate 1 year from now. You consider these alternatives:

- hedge with 1-year forward contract,
- hedge with a money market hedge,
- hedge with at-the-money put options on Swiss francs with a 1-year expiration date, or
- remain unhedged.

Which alternative will generate the highest expected amount of dollars? If multiple alternatives are tied for generating the highest expected amount of dollars, list each of them.

50. PPP and Hedging with Call Options. Visor, Inc. (a U.S. firm), has agreed to purchase supplies from Argentina and will need 1 million Argentine pesos in 1 year. Interest rate parity presently exists. The annual interest rate in Argentina is 19 percent. The annual interest rate in the United States is 6 percent. You expect that annual inflation will be about 11 percent in Argentina and 4 percent in the United States. The spot rate of the Argentine peso is $.30. Call options on pesos are available with a 1-year expiration date, an exercise price of $.29, and a premium of $0.03 per unit. Determine the expected amount of dollars that you will pay from hedging with call options (including the premium paid for the options) if you expect that the spot rate of the peso will change over the next year based on purchasing power parity (PPP).

51. Long-Term Forward Contracts. Assume that interest rate parity exists. The annualized interest rate is presently 5 percent in the United States for any term to maturity, and is 13 percent in Mexico for any term to maturity. Dokar Co. (a U.S. firm) has an agreement in which it will develop and export software to Mexico's government 2 years from now, and will receive 20 million Mexican pesos in 2 years. The spot rate of the peso is $.10. Dokar uses a 2-year forward contract to hedge its receivables in 2 years. How many dollars will Dokar Co. receive in 2 years? Show your work.

52. Money Market versus Put Option Hedge. Narto Co. (a U.S. firm) exports to Switzerland and expects to receive 500,000 Swiss francs in 1 year. The 1-year U.S. interest rate is 5 percent when investing funds and

7 percent when borrowing funds. The 1-year Swiss interest rate is 9 percent when investing funds, and 11 percent when borrowing funds. The spot rate of the Swiss franc is $.80. Narto expects that the spot rate of the Swiss franc will be $.75 in 1 year. There is a put option available on Swiss francs with an exercise price of $.79 and a premium of $.02.

a. Determine the amount of dollars that Narto Co. will receive at the end of 1 year if it implements a money market hedge.

b. Determine the amount of dollars that Narto Co. expects to receive at the end of 1 year (after accounting for the option premium) if it implements a put option hedge.

53. Forward versus Option Hedge. Assume that interest rate parity exists. Today, the 1-year interest rate in Japan is the same as the 1-year interest rate in the United States. You use the international Fisher effect when forecasting how exchange rates will change over the next year. You will receive Japanese yen in 1 year. You can hedge receivables with a 1-year forward contract on Japanese yen or a 1-year at-the-money put option contract on Japanese yen. If you use a forward hedge, will your expected dollar cash flows in 1 year be higher, lower, or the same as if you had used put options? Explain.

54. Long-Term Hedging. Rebel Co. (a U.S. firm) has a contract with the government of Spain and will receive payments of 10,000 euros in exchange for consulting services at the end of each of the next 10 years. The annualized interest rate in the United States is 6 percent regardless of the term to maturity. The annualized interest rate for the euro is 6 percent regardless of the term to maturity. Assume that you expect that the interest rates for the U.S. dollar and for the euro will be the same at any future point in time, regardless of the term to maturity. Assume that interest rate parity exists. Rebel considers two alternative strategies:

Strategy 1 It can use forward hedging 1 year in advance of the receivables, so that at the end of each year, it creates a new 1-year forward hedge for the receivables,

Strategy 2 It can establish a hedge *today* for *all* future receivables (a 1-year forward hedge for receivables in 1 year, a 2-year forward hedge for receivables in 2 years, and so on).

a. Assume that the euro depreciates consistently over the next 10 years. Will strategy 1 result in higher, lower, or the same cash flows for Rebel Co. as strategy 2?

b. Assume that the euro appreciates consistently over the next 10 years. Will strategy 1 result in higher, lower, or the same cash flows for Rebel Co. as strategy 2?

55. Long-Term Hedging. San Fran Co. imports products. It will pay 5 million Swiss francs for imports in 1 year. Mateo Co. will also pay 5 million Swiss francs for imports in 1 year. San Fran Co. and Mateo Co. will also need to pay 5 million Swiss francs for imports arriving in 2 years.

Mateo Co. uses a 1-year forward contract to hedge its payables in 1 year. A year from today, it will use a 1-year forward contract to hedge the payables that it must pay 2 years from today.

Today, San Fran Co. uses a 1-year forward contract to hedge its payables due in 1 year. Today, it also uses a 2-year forward contract to hedge its payables in 2 years.

Assume that interest rate parity exists and it will continue to exist in the future. You expect that the Swiss franc will consistently depreciate over the next 2 years.

Switzerland and the United States have similar interest rates, regardless of their maturity, and they will continue to be the same in the future.

Will the total expected dollar cash outflows that San Fran Co. will pay for the payables be higher, lower, or the same as the total expected dollar cash outflows that Mateo Co. will pay? Explain.

Discussion in the Boardroom

This exercise can be found in Appendix E at the back of this textbook.

Running Your Own MNC

This exercise can be found on the *International Financial Management* text companion website located at www.cengage.com/finance/madura.

BLADES, INC. CASE

Management of Transaction Exposure

Blades, Inc., has recently decided to expand its international trade relationship by exporting to the United Kingdom. Jogs, Ltd., a British retailer, has

committed itself to the annual purchase of 200,000 pairs of Speedos, Blades' primary product, for a price of £80 per pair. The agreement is to last for

2 years, at which time it may be renewed by Blades and Jogs.

In addition to this new international trade relationship, Blades continues to export to Thailand. Its primary customer there, a retailer called Entertainment Products, is committed to the purchase of 180,000 pairs of Speedos annually for another 2 years at a fixed price of 4,594 Thai baht per pair. When the agreement terminates, it may be renewed by Blades and Entertainment Products.

Blades also incurs costs of goods sold denominated in Thai baht. It imports materials sufficient to manufacture 72,000 pairs of Speedos annually from Thailand. These imports are denominated in baht, and the price depends on current market prices for the rubber and plastic components imported.

Under the two export arrangements, Blades sells quarterly amounts of 50,000 and 45,000 pairs of Speedos to Jogs and Entertainment Products, respectively. Payment for these sales is made on the first of January, April, July, and October. The annual amounts are spread over quarters in order to avoid excessive inventories for the British and Thai retailers. Similarly, in order to avoid excessive inventories, Blades usually imports materials sufficient to manufacture 18,000 pairs of Speedos quarterly from Thailand. Although payment terms call for payment within 60 days of delivery, Blades generally pays for its Thai imports upon delivery on the first day of each quarter in order to maintain its trade relationships with the Thai suppliers. Blades feels that early payment is beneficial, as other customers of the Thai supplier pay for their purchases only when it is required.

Since Blades is relatively new to international trade, Ben Holt, Blades' chief financial officer (CFO), is concerned with the potential impact of exchange rate fluctuations on Blades' financial performance. Holt is vaguely familiar with various techniques available to hedge transaction exposure, but he is not certain whether one technique is superior to the others. Holt would like to know more about the forward, money market, and option hedges and has asked you, a financial analyst at Blades, to help him identify the hedging technique most appropriate for Blades. Unfortunately, no options are available for Thailand, but British call and put options are available for £31,250 per option.

Ben Holt has gathered and provided you with the following information for Thailand and the United Kingdom:

	THAILAND	UNITED KINGDOM
Current spot rate	$.0230	$1.50
90-day forward rate	$.0215	$1.49
Put option premium	Not available	$.020 per unit
Put option exercise price	Not available	$1.47
Call option premium	Not available	$.015 per unit
Call option exercise price	Not available	$1.48
90-day borrowing rate (nonannualized)	4%	2%
90-day lending rate (nonannualized)	3.5%	1.8%

In addition to this information, Ben Holt has informed you that the 90-day borrowing and lending rates in the United States are 2.3 and 2.1 percent, respectively, on a nonannualized basis. He has also identified the following probability distributions for the exchange rates of the British pound and the Thai baht in 90 days:

PROBABILITY	SPOT RATE FOR THE BRITISH POUND IN 90 DAYS	SPOT RATE FOR THE THAI BAHT IN 90 DAYS
5%	$1.45	$.0200
20	1.47	$.0213
30	1.48	$.0217
25	1.49	$.0220
15	1.50	$.0230
5	1.52	$.0235

Blades' next sales to and purchases from Thailand will occur 1 quarter from now. If Blades decides to hedge, Holt will want to hedge the entire amount subject to exchange rate fluctuations, even if it requires overhedging (i.e., hedging more than the needed amount). Currently, Holt expects the imported components from Thailand to cost approximately 3,000 baht per pair of Speedos. Holt has asked you to answer the following questions for him:

1. Using a spreadsheet, compare the hedging alternatives for the Thai baht with a scenario under which Blades remains unhedged. Do you think Blades should hedge or remain unhedged? If Blades should hedge, which hedge is most appropriate?

2. Using a spreadsheet, compare the hedging alternatives for the British pound receivables with a scenario under which Blades remains unhedged. Do you think Blades should hedge or remain unhedged? Which hedge is the most appropriate for Blades?

3. In general, do you think it is easier for Blades to hedge its inflows or its outflows denominated in foreign currencies? Why?

4. Would any of the hedges you compared in question 2 for the British pounds to be received in 90 days require Blades to overhedge? Given Blades' exporting arrangements, do you think it is subject to overhedging with a money market hedge?

5. Could Blades modify the timing of the Thai imports in order to reduce its transaction exposure? What is the tradeoff of such a modification?

6. Could Blades modify its payment practices for the Thai imports in order to reduce its transaction exposure? What is the tradeoff of such a modification?

7. Given Blades' exporting agreements, are there any long-term hedging techniques Blades could benefit from? For this question only, assume that Blades incurs all of its costs in the United States.

SMALL BUSINESS DILEMMA

Hedging Decisions by the Sports Exports Company

Jim Logan, owner of the Sports Exports Company, will be receiving about 10,000 British pounds about 1 month from now as payment for exports produced and sent by his firm. Jim is concerned about his exposure because he believes that there are two possible scenarios: (1) the pound will depreciate by 3 percent over the next month or (2) the pound will appreciate by 2 percent over the next month. There is a 70 percent chance that Scenario 1 will occur. There is a 30 percent chance that Scenario 2 will occur.

Jim notices that the prevailing spot rate of the pound is $1.65, and the 1-month forward rate is about $1.645. Jim can purchase a put option over the counter from a securities firm that has an exercise (strike) price of $1.645, a premium of $.025, and an expiration date of 1 month from now.

1. Determine the amount of dollars received by the Sports Exports Company if the receivables to be received in 1 month are not hedged under each of the two exchange rate scenarios.

2. Determine the amount of dollars received by the Sports Exports Company if a put option is used to hedge receivables in 1 month under each of the two exchange rate scenarios.

3. Determine the amount of dollars received by the Sports Exports Company if a forward hedge is used to hedge receivables in 1 month under each of the two exchange rate scenarios.

4. Summarize the results of dollars received based on an unhedged strategy, a put option strategy, and a forward hedge strategy. Select the strategy that you prefer based on the information provided.

INTERNET/EXCEL EXERCISES

1. The following website contains annual reports of many MNCs: www.annualreportservice.com. Review the annual report of your choice. Look for any comments in the report that describe the MNC's hedging of transaction exposure. Summarize the MNC's hedging of transaction exposure based on the comments in the annual report.

2. The following website provides exchange rate movements against the dollar over recent months: www.federalreserve.gov/releases/. Based on the exposure of the MNC you assessed in question 1, determine whether the exchange rate movements of whatever currency (or currencies) it is exposed to moved in a favorable or unfavorable direction over the last few months.

REFERENCES

Brennan, Michael J., Yihong Xia, Fall 2006, International Capital Markets and Foreign Exchange Risk, *The Review of Financial Studies*, pp. 753–795.

Diana, Tom, Apr 2007, How to Hedge Foreign Exchange Risk, *Business Credit*, pp. 60–62.

Ehrlich, Michael, and Asokan Anandarajan, Sep/Oct 2008, Protecting Your Firm from FX Risk, *The Journal of Corporate Accounting & Finance*, pp. 25–34.

Khazeh, Kashi, and Robert C. Winder, Winter 2006, Hedging Transaction Exposure Through Options and Money Markets: Empirical Findings, *Multinational Business Review*, pp. 79–91.

Lien, Donald, and Kit Pong Wong, Dec 2005, Multinationals and Futures Hedging under Liquidity Constraints, *Global Finance Journal*, pp. 210–220.

Makar, Stephen D., and Stephen P. Huffman, Autumn 2008, UK Multinationals' Effective Use of Financial Currency-Hedge Techniques: Estimating and Explaining Foreign Exchange Exposure Using Bilateral Exchange Rates, *Journal of International Financial Management & Accounting*, pp. 219–235.

Martin, Anna D., and Laurence J. Mauer, 2004, Scale Economies in Hedging Foreign Exchange Cash Flow Exposures, *Global Finance Journal*, pp. 17–27.

Yanbo, Jin, and Philippe Jorion, Apr 2006, Firm Value and Hedging: Evidence from U.S. Oil and Gas Producers, *Journal of Finance*, pp. 893–919.

12

Managing Economic Exposure and Translation Exposure

As the previous chapter described, MNCs can manage the exposure of their international contractual transactions to exchange rate movements (referred to as transaction exposure) in various ways. Nevertheless, cash flows of MNCs may still be sensitive to exchange rate movements (economic exposure) even if anticipated international contractual transactions are hedged. Furthermore, the consolidated financial statements of MNCs may still be exposed to exchange rate movements (translation exposure). By managing economic exposure and translation exposure, financial managers may increase the value of their MNCs.

In general, it is more difficult to effectively hedge economic or translation exposure than to hedge transaction exposure, for reasons explained in this chapter.

MANAGING ECONOMIC EXPOSURE

From a U.S. firm's perspective, transaction exposure represents only the exchange rate risk when converting net foreign cash inflows to U.S. dollars or when purchasing foreign currencies to send payments. Economic exposure represents any impact of exchange rate fluctuations on a firm's future cash flows. Corporate cash flows can be affected by exchange rate movements in ways not directly associated with foreign transactions. Thus, firms cannot focus just on hedging their foreign currency payables or receivables but must also attempt to determine how all their cash flows will be affected by possible exchange rate movements.

EXAMPLE

Nike's economic exposure comes in various forms. First, it is subject to transaction exposure because of its numerous purchase and sale transactions in foreign currencies, and this transaction exposure is a subset of economic exposure. Second, any remitted earnings from foreign subsidiaries to the U.S. parent also reflect transaction exposure and therefore reflect economic exposure. Third, a change in exchange rates that affects the demand for shoes at other athletic shoe companies (such as Adidas) can indirectly affect the demand for Nike's athletic shoes. Even if Nike could eliminate its transaction exposure, it cannot perfectly hedge its remaining economic exposure; it is difficult to determine exactly how a specific exchange rate movement will affect the demand for a competitor's athletic shoes and, therefore, how it will indirectly affect the demand for Nike's shoes. ●

The following comments by PepsiCo summarize the dilemma faced by many MNCs that assess economic exposure.

Exhibit 12.1 How Managing Exposure Can Increase an MNC's Value

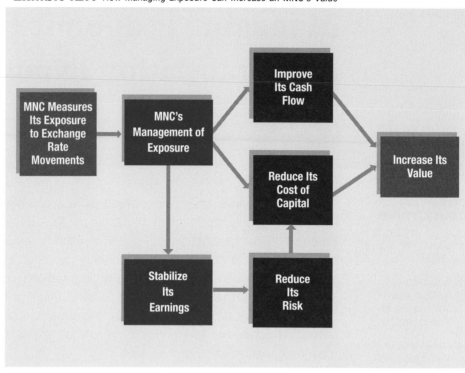

The economic impact of currency exchange rates on us is complex because such changes are often linked to variability in real growth, inflation, interest rates, governmental actions, and other factors. These changes, if material, can cause us to adjust our financing and operating strategies.

—PepsiCo

The means by which an MNC's management of its exposure to exchange rate movements can increase its value are summarized in Exhibit 12.1. It may be able to increase its cash inflows or reduce its cash outflows by properly managing its exposure. Second, it may be able to reduce its financing costs, which lowers its cost of capital. Third, it may be able to stabilize its earnings, which can reduce its risk and therefore reduce its cost of capital.

Assessing Economic Exposure

An MNC must determine how it is subject to economic exposure before it can manage its economic exposure. It must measure its exposure to each currency in terms of its cash inflows and cash outflows. Information for each subsidiary can be used to derive estimates.

EXAMPLE

Recall from Chapter 10 that Madison Co. is subject to economic exposure. Madison can assess its economic exposure to exchange rate movements by determining the sensitivity of its expenses and revenue to various possible exchange rate scenarios. Exhibit 12.2 reproduces Madison's revenue and expense information from Exhibit 10.11. Madison's sales in the United States are not sensitive to exchange rate scenarios. Canadian sales are expected to be C$4 million, but the dollar amount received from these sales will depend on the scenario. The cost of materials purchased in the United States is assumed to be $50 million and insensitive to

Exhibit 12.2 Original Impact of Possible Exchange Rates on Cash Flows of Madison Co. (in Millions)

	EXCHANGE RATE SCENARIO		
	C$1 = $.75	C$1 = $.80	C$1 = .85
Sales			
(1) U.S. sales	$320.00	$320.00	$320.00
(2) Canadian sales	C$4 = 3.00	C$4 = 3.20	C$4 = 3.40
(3) Total sales in U.S. $	$323.00	$323.20	$323.40
Cost of Materials and Operating Expenses			
(4) U.S. cost of materials	$ 50.00	$ 50.00	$ 50.00
(5) Canadian cost of materials	C$200 = 150.00	C$200 = 160.00	C$200 = 170.00
(6) Total cost of materials in U.S. $	$200.00	$210.00	$220.00
(7) Operating expenses	$ 60.00	$ 60.00	$ 60.00
Interest Expenses			
(8) U.S. interest expenses	$ 3	$ 3	$ 3
(9) Canadian interest expenses	C$10 = 7.5	C$10 = 8	C$10 = 8.50
(10) Total interest expenses in U.S. $	$ 10.5	$ 11	$ 11.50
Cash flows in U.S. $ before taxes	$ 52.50	$ 42.20	$ 31.90

exchange rate movements. The cost of materials purchased in Canada is assumed to be C$200 million. The U.S. dollar amount of this cost varies with the exchange rate scenario.

The interest owed to U.S. banks is insensitive to the exchange rate scenario, but the projected amount of dollars needed to pay interest on existing Canadian loans varies with the exchange rate scenario.

Exhibit 12.2 enables Madison to assess how its cash flows before taxes will be affected by different exchange rate movements. A stronger Canadian dollar increases Madison's dollar revenue earned from Canadian sales. However, it also increases Madison's cost of materials purchased from Canada and the dollar amount needed to pay interest on loans from Canadian banks. The higher expenses more than offset the higher revenue in this scenario. Thus, the amount of Madison's cash flows before taxes is inversely related to the strength of the Canadian dollar.

If the Canadian dollar strengthens consistently over the long run, Madison's expenses likely will rise at a higher rate than its U.S. dollar revenue. Consequently, Madison may wish to revise its operations in a manner that either increases Canadian sales or reduces orders of Canadian materials. These actions would allow some offsetting of cash flows and therefore reduce its economic exposure, as explained next. ●

Restructuring to Reduce Economic Exposure

MNCs may restructure their operations to reduce their economic exposure. The restructuring involves shifting the sources of costs or revenue to other locations in order to match cash inflows and outflows in foreign currencies.

EXAMPLE

Reconsider the previous example of Madison Co., which has more cash outflows than cash inflows in Canadian dollars. Madison could create more balance by increasing Canadian sales. It believes that it can achieve Canadian sales of C$20 million if it spends $2 million more on advertising (which is part of Madison's operating expenses). The increased sales will also require an additional expenditure of $10 million on materials from U.S. suppliers. In addition, it plans to reduce its reliance on Canadian suppliers and increase its reliance on U.S. suppliers. Madison anticipates that this strategy will reduce the cost of materials from Canadian suppliers by C$100 million and increase the cost of materials from U.S. suppliers by $80 million (not including the $10 million increase resulting from increased sales to the Canadian market). Furthermore, it plans to borrow additional funds in the United States and retire some existing loans from Canadian banks. The result will be an additional interest expense of $4 million to U.S. banks and a reduction of C$5 million owed to Canadian banks. Exhibit 12.3 shows the anticipated impact of these strategies on Madison's cash flows. For each of the three exchange rate scenarios, the initial projections are in the left column, and the revised projections (as a result of the proposed strategy) are in the right column.

Note first the projected total sales increase in response to Madison's plan to penetrate the Canadian market (see row 2). Second, the U.S. cost of materials is now $90 million higher as a result of the $10 million increase to accommodate increased Canadian sales and the $80 million increase due to the shift from Canadian suppliers to U.S. suppliers (see row 4). The Canadian cost of materials decreases from C$200 million to C$100 million as a result of this shift (see row 5). The revised operating expenses of $62 million include the $2 million increase in advertising expenses necessary to penetrate the Canadian market (see row 7). The interest expenses are revised because of the increased loans from the U.S. banks and reduced loans from Canadian banks (see rows 8 and 9).

If Madison increases its Canadian dollar inflows and reduces its Canadian dollar outflows as proposed, its revenue and expenses will be affected by movements of the Canadian dollar in a somewhat similar manner. Thus, its performance will be less susceptible to movements in the Canadian dollar. Exhibit 12.4 illustrates the sensitivity of Madison's earnings before taxes to the three exchange rate scenarios (derived from Exhibit 12.3). The reduced sensitivity of Madison's proposed restructured operations to exchange rate movements is obvious. ●

The way a firm restructures its operations to reduce economic exposure to exchange rate risk depends on the form of exposure. For Madison Co. future expenses are more sensitive than future revenue to the possible values of a foreign currency. Therefore, it can reduce its economic exposure by increasing the sensitivity of revenue and reducing the sensitivity of expenses to exchange rate movements. Firms that have a greater level of exchange rate–sensitive revenue than expenses, however, would reduce their economic exposure by decreasing the level of exchange rate–sensitive revenue or by increasing the level of exchange rate–sensitive expenses.

Some revenue or expenses may be more sensitive to exchange rates than others. Therefore, simply matching the level of exchange rate–sensitive revenue to the level of exchange rate–sensitive expenses may not completely insulate a firm from exchange rate risk. The firm can best evaluate a proposed restructuring of operations by forecasting various items for various possible exchange rate scenarios (as shown in Exhibit 12.3) and then assessing the sensitivity of cash flows to these different scenarios.

Expediting the Analysis with Computer Spreadsheets.

Determining the sensitivity of cash flows (ignoring tax effects) to alternative exchange rate scenarios can be expedited by using a computer to create a spreadsheet similar to Exhibit 12.3. By revising the input to reflect various possible restructurings, the analyst can determine how each operational structure would affect the firm's economic exposure.

EXAMPLE   Recall that Madison Co. assessed one alternative operational structure in which it increased Canadian sales by C$16 million, reduced its purchases of Canadian materials by C$100 million, and reduced its interest owed to Canadian banks by C$5 million. By using a computerized spreadsheet, Madison can easily assess the impact of alternative strategies, such as increasing Canadian sales by other amounts and/or reducing the Canadian expenses by other amounts. This provides Madison with more information about its economic exposure under various operational structures and enables it to devise the operational structure that will reduce its economic exposure to the degree desired. ●

Exhibit 12.3 Impact of Possible Exchange Rate Movements on Earnings under Two Alternative Operational Structures (in Millions)

	EXCHANGE RATE SCENARIO C$ = $.75		EXCHANGE RATE SCENARIO C$ = $.80		EXCHANGE RATE SCENARIO C$ = $.85	
	ORIGINAL OPERATIONAL STRUCTURE	PROPOSED OPERATIONAL STRUCTURE	ORIGINAL OPERATIONAL STRUCTURE	PROPOSED OPERATIONAL STRUCTURE	ORIGINAL OPERATIONAL STRUCTURE	PROPOSED OPERATIONAL STRUCTURE
Sales						
(1) U.S. sales	$320.0	$320.00	$320.00	$320	$320.00	$320.00
(2) Canadian sales	C$4 = 3.0	C$20 = 15.00	C$4 = 3.20	C$20 = 16	C$4 = 3.40	C$20 = 17.00
(3) Total sales in U.S. $	$323.0	$335.00	$323.20	$336	$323.40	$337.00
Cost of Materials and Operating Expenses						
(4) U.S. cost of materials	$ 50.0	$140.00	$ 50.00	$140	$ 50.00	$140.00
(5) Canadian cost of materials	C$200 = 150.0	C$100 = 75.00	C$200 = 160.00	C$100 = 80	C$200 = 170.00	C$100 = 85.00
(6) Total cost of materials in U.S. $	$200.0	$215.00	$210.00	$220	$220.00	$225.00
(7) Operating expenses	$ 60	$ 62	$ 60	$ 62	$ 60	$ 62
Interest Expenses						
(8) U.S. interest expenses	$ 3.0	$ 7.00	$ 3.00	$ 7	$ 3.00	$ 7.00
(9) Canadian interest expenses	C$10 = 7.5	C$5 = 3.75	C$10 = 8.00	C$5 = 4	C$10 = 8.50	C$5 = 4.25
(10) Total interest expenses in U.S. $	$ 10.5	$ 10.75	$ 11.00	$ 11	$ 11.50	$ 11.25
(11) Cash flows in U.S. $ before taxes	$ 52.5	$ 47.25	$ 42.20	$ 43	$ 31.90	$ 38.75

Exhibit 12.4 Economic Exposure Based on the Original and Proposed Operating Structures

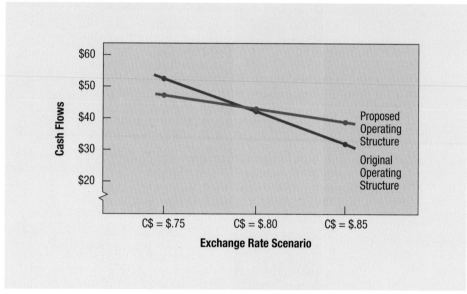

Issues Involved in the Restructuring Decision

Restructuring operations to reduce economic exposure is a more complex task than hedging any single foreign currency transaction, which is why managing economic exposure is normally perceived to be more difficult than managing transaction exposure. By managing economic exposure, however, the firm is developing a long-term solution because once the restructuring is complete, it should reduce economic exposure over the long run. In contrast, the hedging of transaction exposure deals with each upcoming foreign currency transaction separately. Note, however, that it can be very costly to reverse or eliminate restructuring that was undertaken to reduce economic exposure. Therefore, MNCs must be very confident about the potential benefits before they decide to restructure their operations.

When deciding how to restructure operations to reduce economic exposure, one must address the following questions:

• Should the firm attempt to increase or reduce sales in new or existing foreign markets?
• Should the firm increase or reduce its dependency on foreign suppliers?
• Should the firm establish or eliminate production facilities in foreign markets?
• Should the firm increase or reduce its level of debt denominated in foreign currencies?

The first question relates to foreign cash inflows and the remaining ones to foreign cash outflows. Some of the more common solutions to balancing a foreign currency's inflows and outflows are summarized in Exhibit 12.5. Any restructuring of operations that can reduce the periodic difference between a foreign currency's inflows and outflows can reduce the firm's economic exposure to that currency's movements.

MNCs that have production and marketing facilities in various countries may be able to reduce any adverse impact of economic exposure by shifting the allocation of their operations.

EXAMPLE   Deland Co. produces products in the United States, Japan, and Mexico and sells these products (denominated in the currency where they are produced) to several countries. If the Japanese yen strengthens against many currencies, Deland may boost production in Mexico,

Exhibit 12.5 How to Restructure Operations to Balance the Impact of Currency Movements on Cash Inflows and Outflows

TYPE OF OPERATION	RECOMMENDED ACTION WHEN A FOREIGN CURRENCY HAS A GREATER IMPACT ON CASH INFLOWS	RECOMMENDED ACTION WHEN A FOREIGN CURRENCY HAS A GREATER IMPACT ON CASH OUTFLOWS
Sales in foreign currency units	Reduce foreign sales	Increase foreign sales
Reliance on foreign supplies	Increase foreign supply orders	Reduce foreign supply orders
Proportion of debt structure representing foreign debt	Restructure debt to increase debt payments in foreign currency	Restructure debt to reduce debt payments in foreign currency

expecting a decline in demand for the Japanese subsidiary's products. Deland may even transfer some machinery from Japan to Mexico and allocate more marketing funds to the Mexican subsidiary at the expense of the Japanese subsidiary. By following this strategy, however, Deland may have to forgo economies of scale that could be achieved if it concentrated production at one subsidiary while other subsidiaries focused on warehousing and distribution. ●

A CASE ON HEDGING ECONOMIC EXPOSURE

In reality, most MNCs are not able to reduce their economic exposure as easily as Madison Co. in the earlier example. First, an MNC's economic exposure may not be so obvious. An analysis of the income statement for an entire MNC may not necessarily detect its economic exposure. The MNC may be composed of various business units, each of which attempts to achieve high performance for its shareholders. Each business unit may have a unique cost and revenue structure. One unit of an MNC may focus on computer consulting services in the United States and have no exposure to exchange rates. Another unit may also focus on sales of personal computers in the United States, but this unit may be adversely affected by weak foreign currencies because its U.S. customers may buy computers from foreign firms.

Although the MNC is mostly concerned with the effect of exchange rates on its performance and value overall, it can more effectively hedge its economic exposure if it can pinpoint the underlying source of the exposure. Yet, even if the MNC can pinpoint the underlying source of the exposure, there may not be a perfect hedge against that exposure. No textbook formula can provide the perfect solution, but a combination of actions may reduce the economic exposure to a tolerable level, as illustrated in the following example. This example is more difficult than the previous example of Madison Co., but it may be more realistic for many MNCs.

Savor Co.'s Dilemma

Savor Co., a U.S. firm, is primarily concerned with its exposure to the euro. It wants to pinpoint the source of its exposure so that it can determine how to hedge its exposure. Savor has three units that conduct some business in Europe. Because each unit has established a wide variety of business arrangements, it is not obvious whether all three units have a similar exposure. Each unit tends to be independent of the others, and the managers of each unit are compensated according to that unit's performance. Savor may want to hedge its economic exposure, but it must first determine whether it is exposed and the source of the exposure.

Exhibit 12.6 Assessment of Savor Co.'s Cash Flows and the Euro's Movements

(1) QUARTER	(2) % CHANGE IN UNIT A's CASH FLOWS	(3) % CHANGE IN UNIT B's CASH FLOWS	(4) % CHANGE IN UNIT C's CASH FLOWS	(5) % CHANGE IN TOTAL CASH FLOWS	(6) % CHANGE IN THE VALUE OF THE EURO
1	–3	2	1	0	2
2	0	1	3	4	5
3	6	–6	–1	–1	–3
4	–1	1	–1	–1	0
5	–4	0	–1	–5	–2
6	–1	–2	–2	–5	–5
7	1	–3	3	1	4
8	–3	2	1	0	2
9	4	–1	0	3	–4

Assessment of Economic Exposure

Because the exact nature of its economic exposure to the euro is not obvious, Savor attempts to assess the relationship between the euro's movements and each unit's cash flows over the last 9 quarters. A firm may want to use more data, but 9 quarters are sufficient to illustrate the point. The cash flows and movements in the euro are shown in Exhibit 12.6. First, Savor applies regression analysis (as discussed in the previous chapter) to determine whether the percentage change in its total cash flow *(PCF,* shown in column 5) is related to the percentage change in the euro (%Δeuro, shown in column 6) over time:

$$PCF_t = a_0 + a_1(\%\Delta euro)_t + \mu_t$$

Regression analysis derives the values of the constant, a_0, and the slope coefficient, a_1. The slope coefficient represents the sensitivity of PCF_t to movements in the euro. Based on this analysis, the slope coefficient is positive and statistically significant, which implies that the cash flows are positively related to the percentage changes in the euro. That is, a negative change in the euro adversely affects Savor's total cash flows. The R-squared statistic is .31, which suggests that 31 percent of the variation in Savor's cash flows can be explained by movements in the euro. The evidence presented so far strongly suggests that Savor is exposed to exchange rate movements of the euro but does not pinpoint the source of the exposure.

Assessment of Each Unit's Exposure

To determine the source of the exposure, Savor applies the regression model separately to each individual unit's cash flows. The results are shown here (apply the regression analysis yourself as an exercise):

UNIT	SLOPE COEFFICIENT
A	Not significant
B	Not significant
C	Coefficient = .45, which is statistically significant (R-squared = .80)

The results suggest that the cash flows of Units A and B are not subject to economic exposure. However, Unit C is subject to economic exposure. Approximately 80 percent of Unit C's cash flows can be explained by movements in the value of the euro over time. The regression coefficient suggests that for a 1 percent decrease in the value of the euro, the unit's cash flows will decline by about .45 percent. Exhibit 12.6, which shows the euro's exchange rate movements and the cash flows for Savor's individual units, confirms the strong relationship between the euro's movements and Unit C's cash flows.

Identifying the Source of the Unit's Exposure

Now that Savor has determined that one unit is the cause of the exposure, it can pinpoint the characteristics of that unit that cause the exposure. Savor believes that the key components that affect Unit C's cash flows are income statement items such as its U.S. revenue, its cost of goods sold, and its operating expenses. This unit conducts all of its production in the United States.

Savor first determines the value of each income statement item that affected the unit's cash flows in each of the last 9 quarters. It then applies regression analysis to determine the relationship between the percentage change in the euro and each income statement item over those quarters. Assume that it finds:

- A significant positive relationship between Unit C's revenue and the euro's value.
- No relationship between the unit's cost of goods sold and the euro's value.
- No relationship between the unit's operating expenses and the euro's value.

These results suggest that when the euro weakens, the unit's revenue from U.S. customers declines substantially. Its U.S. customers shift their demand to foreign competitors when the euro weakens and they can obtain imports at a low price. Thus, Savor's economic exposure could be due to foreign competition. A firm's economic exposure is not always obvious, however, and regression analysis may detect exposure that was not suspected by the firm or its individual units. Furthermore, regression analysis can be used to provide a more precise estimate of the degree of economic exposure, which can be useful when deciding how to manage the exposure.

Possible Strategies to Hedge Economic Exposure

Now that Savor has identified the source of its economic exposure, it can develop a strategy to reduce that exposure. In general, Savor Co. wants to restructure its business such that it can benefit when the euro weakens in order to offset the adverse effects of a weak euro on its revenue.

Pricing Policy. Savor recognizes that there will be periods in the future when the euro will depreciate against the dollar. Under these conditions, Unit C may attempt to be more competitive by reducing its prices. If the euro's value declines by 10 percent and this reduces the prices that U.S. customers pay for the foreign products by 10 percent, then Unit C can attempt to remain competitive by discounting its prices by 10 percent. Although this strategy can retain market share, the lower prices will result in less revenue and therefore less cash flows. Therefore, this strategy does not completely eliminate Savor's economic exposure. Nevertheless, this strategy may still be feasible, especially if the unit can charge relatively high prices in periods when the euro is strong and U.S. customers have to pay higher prices for European products. In essence, the strategy might allow the unit to generate abnormally high cash flows in a strong-euro period to offset the abnormally low cash flows in a weak-euro period. The adverse effect during a weak-euro period will still occur, however. Given the limitations of this strategy, other strategies should be considered.

Hedging with Forward Contracts. Savor's Unit C could sell euros forward for the period in which it wants to hedge against the adverse effects of the weak euro. Using a forward contract has definite limitations, however. Since the economic exposure is likely to continue indefinitely, the use of a forward contract in the manner described here hedges only for the period of the contract. It does not serve as a continuous long-term hedge against economic exposure. Savor Co. could attempt to sell many forward contracts on euros for different maturities far into the future in order to establish a long-term hedge of its future revenue. However, it does not know what its revenue in euros will be in future periods, especially in the distant future.

Purchasing Foreign Supplies. Another possibility is for the unit to consistently purchase its materials in Europe, a strategy that would reduce its costs (and enhance its cash flows) during a weak-euro period to offset the adverse effects of the weak euro. However, the cost of buying European materials may be higher than the cost of buying local materials, especially when transportation expenses are considered. Savor Co. does not want to use this method to hedge if it is going to significantly increase its operating expenses.

Financing with Foreign Funds. The unit could also reduce its economic exposure by financing a portion of its business with loans in euros. It could convert the loan proceeds to dollars and use the dollars to support its business. It will need to make periodic loan repayments in euros. If the euro weakens, the unit will need fewer dollars to cover the loan repayments. This favorable effect can partially offset the adverse effect of a weak euro on the unit's revenue. If the euro strengthens, the unit will need more dollars to cover the loan repayments, but this adverse effect will be offset by the favorable effect of the strong euro on the unit's revenue. This type of hedge is more effective than the pricing hedge because it can offset the adverse effects of a weak euro in the same period (whereas the pricing policy attempts to make up for lost cash flows once the euro strengthens).

   This strategy also has some limitations. First, the strategy only makes sense if Savor needs some debt financing. It should not borrow funds just for the sake of hedging its economic exposure. Second, Savor might not desire this strategy when the euro has a very high interest rate. Though borrowing in euros can reduce its economic exposure, it may not be willing to enact the hedge at a cost of higher interest expenses than it would pay in the United States.

   Third, this strategy is unlikely to create a perfect hedge against Savor's economic exposure. Even if the company needs debt financing and the interest rate charged on the foreign loan is low, Savor must attempt to determine the amount of debt financing that will hedge its economic exposure. The amount of foreign debt financing necessary to fully hedge the exposure may exceed the amount of funding that Savor needs.

Revising Operations of Other Units. Given the limitations of hedging Unit C's economic exposure by adjusting the unit's operations, Savor may consider modifying the operations of another unit in a manner that will offset the exposure of Unit C. However, this strategy may require changes in another unit that will not necessarily benefit that unit. For example, assume that Unit C could partially hedge its economic exposure by borrowing euros (as explained above) but that it does not need to borrow as much as would be necessary to fully offset its economic exposure. Savor's top management may suggest that Units A and B also obtain their financing in euros, so that the MNC's overall economic exposure is hedged. Thus, a weak euro would still adversely affect Unit C because the adverse effect on its revenue would not be fully offset by the favorable effect on its financing (debt repayments). Yet, if the other units have borrowed euros as well, the combined favorable effects on financing for Savor overall could offset the adverse effects on Unit C.

However, Units A and B will not necessarily desire to finance their operations in euros. Recall that these units are not subject to economic exposure. Also recall that the managers of each unit are compensated according to the performance of that unit. By agreeing to finance in euros, Units A and B could become exposed to movements in the euro. If the euro strengthens, their cost of financing increases. So, by helping to offset the exposure of Unit C, Units A and B could experience weaker performance, and their managers would receive less compensation.

A solution is still possible if Savor's top managers who are not affiliated with any unit can remove the hedging activity from the compensation formula for the units' managers. That is, top management could instruct Units A and B to borrow funds in euros, but could reward the managers of those units based on an assessment of the units' performance that excludes the effect of the euro on financing costs. In this way, the managers will be more willing to engage in a strategy that increases their economic exposure while reducing Savor's.

Savor's Hedging Solution

In summary, Savor's initial analysis of its units determined that only Unit C was highly subject to economic exposure. Unit C could attempt to use a pricing policy that would maintain market share when the euro weakens, but this strategy would not eliminate the economic exposure because its cash flows would still be adversely affected. Borrowing euros can be an effective strategy to hedge Unit C's exposure, but it does not need to borrow the amount of funds necessary to offset its exposure. The optimal solution for Savor Co. is to instruct its other units to do their financing in euros as well. This strategy effectively increases their exposure, but in the opposite manner of Unit C's exposure, so that the MNC's economic exposure overall is reduced. The units' managers should be willing to cooperate if their compensation is not reduced as a result of increasing the exposure of their individual units.

GOVERNANCE   Without proper governance, agency problems could create conflicts of interest and cause each unit's managers to make decisions that are focused only on their own units. Proper governance requires a centralized plan and goals for all subsidiaries, and proper incentives to ensure that the subsidiary managers pursue the centralized goals.

Limitations of Savor's Optimal Hedging Strategy

Even if Savor Co. is able to achieve the hedge described above, the hedge will still not be perfect. The impact of the euro's movements on Savor's cash outflows needed to repay the loans is known with certainty. But the impact of the euro's movements on Savor's cash inflows (revenue) is uncertain and can change over time. If the amount of foreign competition increases, the sensitivity of Unit C's cash flows to exchange rates would increase. To hedge this increased exposure, it would need to borrow a larger amount of euros. An MNC's economic exposure can change over time in response to shifts in foreign competition or other global conditions, so it must continually assess and manage its economic exposure.

HEDGING EXPOSURE TO FIXED ASSETS

Up to this point, the focus has been on how economic exposure can affect periodic cash flows. The effects may extend beyond periodic cash flows, however. When an MNC has fixed assets (such as buildings or machinery) in a foreign country, the dollar cash flows to be received from the ultimate sale of these assets are subject to exchange rate risk.

Wagner Co., a U.S. firm, pursued a 6-year project in Russia. It purchased a manufacturing plant from the Russian government 6 years ago for 500 million rubles. Since the ruble was worth $.16 at the time of the investment, Wagner needed $80 million to purchase the plant. The Russian government guaranteed that it would repurchase the plant for 500 million rubles in 6 years when the project was completed. At that time, however, the ruble was worth only $.034, so Wagner received only $17 million (computed as 500 million x $.034) from selling the plant. Even though the price of the plant in rubles at the time of the sale was the same as the price at the time of the purchase, the sales price of the plant in dollars at the time of the sale was about 79 percent less than the purchase price. ●

A sale of fixed assets can be hedged by selling the currency forward in a long-term forward contract. However, long-term forward contracts may not be available for currencies in emerging markets. An alternative solution is to create a liability in that currency that matches the expected value of the assets at the point in the future when they may be sold. In essence, the sale of the fixed assets generates a foreign currency cash inflow that can be used to pay off the liability that is denominated in the same currency.

In the previous example, Wagner could have financed part of its investment in the Russian manufacturing plant by borrowing rubles from a local bank, with the loan structured to have zero interest payments and a lump-sum repayment value equal to the expected sales price set for the date when Wagner expected to sell the plant. Thus, the loan could have been structured to have a lump-sum repayment value of 500 million rubles in 6 years. ●

The limitations of hedging a sale of fixed assets are that an MNC does not necessarily know the (1) date when it will sell the assets or (2) the price in local currency at which it will sell them. Consequently, it is unable to create a liability that perfectly matches the date and amount of the sale of the fixed assets. Nevertheless, these limitations should not prevent a firm from hedging.

Even if the Russian government would not guarantee a purchase price of the plant, Wagner Co. could create a liability that reflects the earliest possible sales date and the lowest expected sales price. If the sales date turns out to be later than the earliest possible sales date, Wagner might be able to extend its loan period to match the sales date. In this way, it can still rely on the funding from the loan to support operations in Russia until the assets are sold. By structuring the lump-sum loan repayment to match the minimum sales price, Wagner will not be perfectly hedged if the fixed assets turn out to be worth more than the minimum expected amount. Nevertheless, Wagner would at least have reduced its exposure by offsetting a portion of the fixed assets with a liability in the same currency. ●

MANAGING TRANSLATION EXPOSURE

Translation exposure occurs when an MNC translates each subsidiary's financial data to its home currency for consolidated financial statements. Even if translation exposure does not affect cash flows, it is a concern of many MNCs because it can reduce an MNC's consolidated earnings and thereby cause a decline in its stock price.

Columbus Co. is a U.S.-based MNC with a subsidiary in the United Kingdom. The subsidiary typically accounts for about half of the total revenue and earnings generated by Columbus. In the last 3 quarters, the value of the British pound declined, and the reported dollar level of earnings attributable to the British subsidiary was weak simply because of the relatively low rate at which the British earnings were translated into U.S. dollars. During this period, the stock price of Columbus declined because of the decline in consolidated earnings. The high-level managers and the board were criticized in the media for poor performance, even though the only reason for the poor performance was the translation effect on earnings. The employee compensation levels are tied to consolidated earnings and therefore were low this year because of the translation effect. Consequently, Columbus decided that it would attempt to hedge translation exposure in the future. ●

Hedging with Forward Contracts

MNCs can use forward contracts or futures contracts to hedge translation exposure. Specifically, they can sell the currency forward that their foreign subsidiaries receive as earnings. In this way, they create a cash outflow in the currency to offset the earnings received in that currency.

EXAMPLE

Recall that Columbus Co. has one subsidiary based in the United Kingdom. While there is no foreseeable transaction exposure in the near future from the future earnings (since the pounds will remain in the United Kingdom), Columbus is exposed to translation exposure. The subsidiary forecasts that its earnings next year will be £20 million. To hedge its translation exposure, Columbus can implement a forward hedge on the expected earnings by selling £20 million 1 year forward. Assume the forward rate at that time is $1.60, the same as the spot rate. At the end of the year, Columbus can buy £20 million at the spot rate and fulfill its forward contract obligation to sell £20 million. If the pound depreciates during the fiscal year, then Columbus will be able to purchase pounds at the end of the fiscal year to fulfill the forward contract at a cheaper rate than it can sell them ($1.60 per pound). Thus, it will have generated income that can offset the translation loss.

If the pound depreciates over the year such that the average weighted exchange rate is $1.50 over the year, the subsidiary's earnings will be translated as follows:

$$\text{Translated earnings} = \text{Subsidiary earnings} \times \text{Weighted average exchange rate}$$
$$= 20 \text{ million pounds} \times \$1.50$$
$$= \$30 \text{ million}$$

If the exchange rate had not declined over the year, the translated amount of earnings would have been $32 million (computed as 20 million pounds × $1.60), so the exchange rate movements caused the reported earnings to be reduced by $2 million.

However, there is a gain from the forward contract because the spot rate declined over the year. If we assume that the spot rate is worth $1.50 at the end of the year, then the gain on the forward contract would be:

$$\text{Gain on forward contract} = (\text{Amount received from forward sale}) - (\text{Amount paid to fulfill forward contract obligation})$$
$$= (20 \text{ million pounds} \times \$1.60) -$$
$$(20 \text{ million pounds} \times \$1.50)$$
$$= \$32 \text{ million} - \$30 \text{ million}$$
$$= \$2 \text{ million}$$

●

In reality, a perfect offsetting effect is unlikely. However, when there is a relatively large reduction in the weighted average exchange rate, there will likely be a large reduction in the spot rate over that same period. Consequently, the larger the adverse translation effect, the larger the gain on the forward contract. Thus, the forward contract is normally effective in hedging a portion of the translation exposure.

Limitations of Hedging Translation Exposure

There are four limitations in hedging translation exposure.

Inaccurate Earnings Forecasts.

A subsidiary's earnings in a future period are uncertain In the previous example involving Columbus, Inc., British earnings were projected to be £20 million. If the actual earnings turned out to be much higher, and if the pound weakened during the year, the translation loss would likely exceed the gain generated from the forward contract strategy.

Inadequate Forward Contracts for Some Currencies. A second limitation is that forward contracts are not available for all currencies. Thus, an MNC with subsidiaries in some smaller countries may not be able to obtain forward contracts for the currencies of concern.

Accounting Distortions. A third limitation is that the forward rate gain or loss reflects the difference between the forward rate and the future spot rate, whereas the translation gain or loss is caused by the change in the average exchange rate over the period in which the earnings are generated. In addition, the translation losses are not tax deductible, whereas gains on forward contracts used to hedge translation exposure are taxed.

Increased Transaction Exposure. The fourth and most critical limitation with a hedging strategy such as using a forward contract on translation exposure is that the MNC may be increasing its transaction exposure. For example, consider a situation in which the subsidiary's currency appreciates during the fiscal year, resulting in a translation gain. If the MNC enacts a hedge strategy at the start of the fiscal year, this strategy will generate a transaction loss that will somewhat offset the translation gain.

Some MNCs may not be comfortable with this offsetting effect. The translation gain is simply a paper gain; that is, the reported dollar value of earnings is higher due to the subsidiary currency's appreciation. If the subsidiary reinvests the earnings, however, the parent does not receive any more income due to this appreciation. The MNC parent's net cash flow is not affected. Conversely, the loss resulting from a hedge strategy is a *real* loss; that is, the net cash flow to the parent will be reduced due to this loss. Thus, in this situation, the MNC reduces its translation exposure at the expense of increasing its transaction exposure.

Governing the Hedge of Translation Exposure

Many managers of an MNC are granted stock options as part of their compensation. They recognize that the MNC's stock price may change in response to a change in consolidated earnings. They can partially hedge against adverse effects of exchange rate movements on consolidated earnings. To the extent that managers are concerned that any adverse translation effect on consolidated earnings would result in a lower stock price, their own compensation is affected. They may hedge translation exposure to hedge their own exposure to their compensation. In this case, their decisions for the MNC are based on their own situation. An MNC can impose controls to prevent this type of agency problem. For example, it could specify the conditions that are necessary for managers to hedge translation exposure or require board approval.

SUMMARY

- Economic exposure can be managed by balancing the sensitivity of revenue and expenses to exchange rate fluctuations. To accomplish this, however, the firm must first recognize how its revenue and expenses are affected by exchange rate fluctuations. For some firms, revenue is more susceptible. These firms are most concerned that their home currency will appreciate against foreign currencies since the unfavorable effects on revenue will more than off- set the favorable effects on expenses. Conversely, firms whose expenses are more sensitive to exchange rates than their revenue are most concerned that their home currency will depreciate against foreign currencies. When firms reduce their economic exposure, they reduce not only these unfavorable effects but also the favorable effects if the home currency value moves in the opposite direction.

- Translation exposure can be reduced by selling forward the foreign currency used to measure a subsidiary's income. If the foreign currency depreciates against the home currency, the adverse impact on the consolidated income statement can be offset by the gain on the forward sale in that currency. If the foreign currency appreciates over the time period of concern, there will be a loss on the forward sale that is offset by a favorable effect on the reported consolidated earnings. However, many MNCs would not be satisfied with a "paper gain" that offsets a "cash loss."

POINT COUNTER-POINT

Can an MNC Reduce the Impact of Translation Exposure by Communicating?

Point Yes. Investors commonly use earnings to derive an MNC's expected future cash flows. Investors do not necessarily recognize how an MNC's translation exposure could distort their estimates of the MNC's future cash flows. Therefore, the MNC could clearly communicate in its annual report and elsewhere how the earnings were affected by translation gains and losses in any period. If investors have this information, they will not overreact to earnings changes that are primarily attributed to translation exposure.

Counter-Point No. Investors focus on the bottom line and should ignore any communication regarding the translation exposure. Moreover, they may believe that translation exposure should be accounted for anyway. If foreign earnings are reduced because of a weak currency, the earnings may continue to be weak if the currency remains weak.

Who Is Correct? Use the Internet to learn more about this issue. Which argument do you support? Offer your own opinion on this issue.

SELF-TEST

Answers are provided in Appendix A at the back of the text.

1. Salem Exporting Co. purchases chemicals from U.S. sources and uses them to make pharmaceutical products that are exported to Canadian hospitals. Salem prices its products in Canadian dollars and is concerned about the possibility of the long-term depreciation of the Canadian dollar against the U.S. dollar. It periodically hedges its exposure with short-term forward contracts, but this does not insulate against the possible trend of continuing Canadian dollar depreciation. How could Salem offset some of its exposure resulting from its export business?

2. Using the information in question 1, give a possible disadvantage of offsetting exchange rate exposure from the export business.

3. Coastal Corp. is a U.S. firm with a subsidiary in the United Kingdom. It expects that the pound will depreciate this year. Explain Coastal's translation exposure. How could Coastal hedge its translation exposure?

4. Arlington Co. has substantial translation exposure in European subsidiaries. The treasurer of Arlington Co. suggests that the translation effects are not relevant because the earnings generated by the European subsidiaries are not being remitted to the U.S. parent, but are simply being reinvested in Europe. Nevertheless, the vice president of finance of Arlington Co. is concerned about translation exposure because the stock price is highly dependent on the consolidated earnings, which are dependent on the exchange rates at which the earnings are translated. Who is correct?

5. Lincolnshire Co. exports 80 percent of its total production of goods in New Mexico to Latin American countries. Kalafa Co. sells all the goods it produces in the United States, but it has a subsidiary in Spain that usually generates about 20 percent of its total earnings. Compare the translation exposure of these two U.S. firms.

QUESTIONS AND APPLICATIONS

1.   Reducing Economic Exposure. Baltimore, Inc., is a U.S.-based MNC that obtains 10 percent of its supplies from European manufacturers. Sixty percent of its revenues are due to exports to Europe, where its product is invoiced in euros. Explain how Baltimore can attempt to reduce its economic exposure to exchange rate fluctuations in the euro.

2.   Reducing Economic Exposure. UVA Co. is a U.S.-based MNC that obtains 40 percent of its foreign supplies from Thailand. It also borrows Thailand's currency (the baht) from Thai banks and converts the baht to dollars to support U.S. operations. It currently receives about 10 percent of its revenue from Thai customers. Its sales to Thai customers are denominated in baht. Explain how UVA Co. can reduce its economic exposure to exchange rate fluctuations.

3.   Reducing Economic Exposure. Albany Corp. is a U.S.-based MNC that has a large government contract with Australia. The contract will continue for several years and generate more than half of Albany's total sales volume. The Australian government pays Albany in Australian dollars. About 10 percent of Albany's operating expenses are in Australian dollars; all other expenses are in U.S. dollars. Explain how Albany Corp. can reduce its economic exposure to exchange rate fluctuations.

4.   Tradeoffs When Reducing Economic Exposure. When an MNC restructures its operations to reduce its economic exposure, it may sometimes forgo economies of scale. Explain.

5.   Exchange Rate Effects on Earnings. Explain how a U.S.-based MNC's consolidated earnings are affected when foreign currencies depreciate.

6.   Hedging Translation Exposure. Explain how a firm can hedge its translation exposure.

7.   Limitations of Hedging Translation Exposure. Bartunek Co. is a U.S.-based MNC that has European subsidiaries and wants to hedge its translation exposure to fluctuations in the euro's value. Explain some limitations when it hedges translation exposure.

8.   Effective Hedging of Translation Exposure. Would a more established MNC or a less established MNC be better able to effectively hedge its given level of translation exposure? Why?

9.   Comparing Degrees of Economic Exposure. Carlton Co. and Palmer, Inc., are U.S.-based MNCs with subsidiaries in Mexico that distribute medical supplies (produced in the United States) to customers throughout Latin America. Both subsidiaries purchase the products at cost and sell the products at 90 percent markup. The other operating costs of the subsidiaries are very low. Carlton Co. has a research and development center in the United States that focuses on improving its medical technology. Palmer, Inc., has a similar center based in Mexico. The parent of each firm subsidizes its respective research and development center on an annual basis. Which firm is subject to a higher degree of economic exposure? Explain.

10.   Comparing Degrees of Translation Exposure. Nelson Co. is a U.S. firm with annual export sales to Singapore of about S$800 million. Its main competitor is Mez Co., also based in the United States, with a subsidiary in Singapore that generates about S$800 million in annual sales. Any earnings generated by the subsidiary are reinvested to support its operations. Based on the information provided, which firm is subject to a higher degree of translation exposure? Explain.

Advanced Questions

11.   Managing Economic Exposure. St. Paul Co. does business in the United States and New Zealand. In attempting to assess its economic exposure, it compiled the following information.

a.   St. Paul's U.S. sales are somewhat affected by the value of the New Zealand dollar (NZ$), because it faces competition from New Zealand exporters. It forecasts the U.S. sales based on the following three exchange rate scenarios:

EXCHANGE RATE OF NZ$	REVENUE FROM U.S. BUSINESS (IN MILLIONS)
NZ$ = $.48	$100
NZ$ = .50	105
NZ$ = .54	110

b.   Its New Zealand dollar revenues on sales to New Zealand invoiced in New Zealand dollars are expected to be NZ$600 million.

c.   Its anticipated cost of materials is estimated at $200 million from the purchase of U.S. materials and

NZ$100 million from the purchase of New Zealand materials.

d. Fixed operating expenses are estimated at $30 million.

e. Variable operating expenses are estimated at 20 percent of total sales (after including New Zealand sales, translated to a dollar amount).

f. Interest expense is estimated at $20 million on existing U.S. loans, and the company has no existing New Zealand loans.

Forecast net cash flows for St. Paul Co. under each of the three exchange rate scenarios. Explain how St. Paul's net cash flows are affected by possible exchange rate movements. Explain how it can restructure its operations to reduce the sensitivity of its net cash flows to exchange rate movements without reducing its volume of business in New Zealand.

12. Assessing Economic Exposure. Alaska, Inc., plans to create and finance a subsidiary in Mexico that produces computer components at a low cost and exports them to other countries. It has no other international business. The subsidiary will produce computers and export them to Caribbean islands and will invoice the products in U.S. dollars. The values of the currencies in the islands are expected to remain very stable against the dollar. The subsidiary will pay wages, rent, and other operating costs in Mexican pesos. The subsidiary will remit earnings monthly to the parent.

a. Would Alaska's cash flows be favorably or unfavorably affected if the Mexican peso depreciates over time?

b. Assume that Alaska considers partial financing of this subsidiary with peso loans from Mexican banks instead of providing all the financing with its own funds. Would this alternative form of financing increase, decrease, or have no effect on the degree to which Alaska is exposed to exchange rate movements of the peso?

13. Hedging Continual Exposure. Clearlake, Inc., produces its products in its factory in Texas and exports most of the products to Mexico each month. The exports are denominated in pesos. Clearlake recognizes that hedging on a monthly basis does not really protect against long-term movements in exchange rates. It also recognizes that it could eliminate its transaction exposure by denominating the exports in dollars, but that it still would have economic exposure (because Mexican consumers would reduce demand if the peso weakened). Clearlake does not know how many pesos it will receive in the future, so it would have difficulty even if a long-term hedging method were available. How can Clearlake

realistically deal with this dilemma and reduce its exposure over the long term? (There is no perfect solution, but in the real world, there rarely are perfect solutions.)

14. Sources of Supplies and Exposure to Exchange Rate Risk. Laguna Co. (a U.S. firm) will be receiving 4 million British pounds in 1 year. It will need to make a payment of 3 million Polish zloty in 1 year. It has no other exchange rate risk at this time. However, it needs to buy supplies and can purchase them from Switzerland, Hong Kong, Canada, or Ecuador. Another alternative is that it could also purchase one-fourth of the supplies from each of the four countries mentioned in the previous sentence. The supplies will be invoiced in the currency of the country from which they are imported. Laguna Co. believes that none of the sources of the imports would provide a clear cost advantage. As of today, the dollar cost of these supplies would be about $6 million regardless of the source that will provide the supplies.

The spot rates today are as follows:

British pound = $1.80

Swiss franc = $.60

Polish zloty = $.30

Hong Kong dollar = $.14

Canadian dollar = $.60

The movements of the pound and the Swiss franc and the Polish zloty against the dollar are highly correlated. The Hong Kong dollar is tied to the U.S. dollar, and you expect that it will continue to be tied to the dollar. The movements in the value of the Canadian dollar against the U.S. dollar are not correlated with the movements of the other currencies. Ecuador uses the U.S. dollar as its local currency.

Which alternative should Laguna Co. select in order to minimize its overall exchange rate risk?

15. Minimizing Exposure. Lola Co. (a U.S. firm) expects to receive 10 million euros in 1 year. It does not plan to hedge this transaction with a forward contract or other hedging techniques. This is its only international business, and it is not exposed to any other form of exchange rate risk. Lola Co. plans to purchase materials for future operations, and it will send its payment for these materials in 1 year. The value of the materials to be purchased is about equal to the expected value of the receivables. Lola Co. can purchase the materials from Switzerland, Hong Kong, Canada, or the United States. Another alternative is that it could also purchase one-fourth of the materials from each of the four countries mentioned in the previous sentence. The supplies will be invoiced in the currency of the country from which they are imported.

The movements of the euro and the Swiss franc against the dollar are highly correlated and will continue to be highly correlated. The Hong Kong dollar is tied to the U.S. dollar and you expect that it will continue to be tied to the dollar. The movements in the value of Canadian dollar against the U.S. dollar are independent of (not correlated with) the movements of other currencies against the U.S. dollar.

Lola Co. believes that none of the sources of the imports would provide a clear cost advantage.

Which alternative should Lola Co. select for obtaining supplies that will minimize its overall exchange rate risk?

Discussion in the Boardroom

This exercise can be found in Appendix E at the back of this textbook.

Running Your Own MNC

This exercise can be found on the *International Financial Management* text companion website located at www.cengage.com/finance/madura.

BLADES, INC. CASE

Assessment of Economic Exposure

Blades, Inc., has been exporting to Thailand since its decision to supplement its declining U.S. sales by exporting there. Furthermore, Blades has recently begun exporting to a retailer in the United Kingdom. The suppliers of the components needed by Blades for roller blade production (such as rubber and plastic) are located in the United States and Thailand. Blades decided to use Thai suppliers for rubber and plastic components needed to manufacture roller blades because of cost and quality considerations. All of Blades' exports and imports are denominated in the respective foreign currency; for example, Blades pays for the Thai imports in baht.

The decision to export to Thailand was supported by the fact that Thailand had been one of the world's fastest growing economies in recent years. Furthermore, Blades found an importer in Thailand that was willing to commit itself to the annual purchase of 180,000 pairs of Blades' Speedos, which are among the highest quality roller blades in the world. The commitment began last year and will last another 2 years, at which time it may be renewed by the two parties. Due to this commitment, Blades is selling its roller blades for 4,594 baht per pair (approximately $100 at current exchange rates) instead of the usual $120 per pair. Although this price represents a substantial discount from the regular price for a pair of Speedo blades, it still constitutes a considerable markup above cost. Because importers in other Asian countries were not willing to make this type of commitment, this was a decisive factor in the choice of Thailand for exporting purposes. Although Ben Holt, Blades' chief financial officer (CFO), believes the sports product market in Asia has very high future growth potential, Blades has recently begun exporting to Jogs, Ltd., a British retailer.

Jogs has committed itself to purchase 200,000 pairs of Speedos annually for a fixed price of £80 per pair.

For the coming year, Blades expects to import rubber and plastic components from Thailand sufficient to manufacture 80,000 pairs of Speedos, at a cost of approximately 3,000 baht per pair of Speedos.

You, as Blades' financial analyst, have pointed out to Ben Holt that recent events in Asia have fundamentally affected the economic condition of Asian countries, including Thailand. For example, you have pointed out that the high level of consumer spending on leisure products such as roller blades has declined considerably. Thus, the Thai retailer may not renew its commitment with Blades in 2 years. Furthermore, you are worried that the current economic conditions in Thailand may lead to a substantial depreciation of the Thai baht, which would affect Blades negatively.

Despite recent developments, however, Ben Holt remains optimistic; he is convinced that Southeast Asia will exhibit high potential for growth when the impact of recent events in Asia subsides. Consequently, Holt has no doubt that the Thai customer will renew its commitment for another 3 years when the current agreement terminates. In your opinion, Holt is not considering all of the factors that might directly or indirectly affect Blades. Moreover, you are worried that he is ignoring Blades' future in Thailand even if the Thai importer renews its commitment for another 3 years. In fact, you believe that a renewal of the existing agreement with the Thai customer may affect Blades negatively due to the high level of inflation in Thailand.

Since Holt is interested in your opinion and wants to assess Blades' economic exposure in Thailand, he has asked you to conduct an analysis of the impact of the value of the baht on next year's earnings to assess Blades' economic exposure. You have gathered the following information:

- Blades has forecasted sales in the United States of 520,000 pairs of Speedos at regular prices; exports to Thailand of 180,000 pairs of Speedos for 4,594 baht a pair; and exports to the United Kingdom of 200,000 pairs of Speedos for £80 per pair.
- Cost of goods sold for 80,000 pairs of Speedos are incurred in Thailand; the remainder is incurred in the United States, where the cost of goods sold per pair of Speedos runs approximately $70.
- Fixed costs are $2 million, and variable operating expenses other than costs of goods sold represent approximately 11 percent of U.S. sales. All fixed and variable operating expenses other than cost of goods sold are incurred in the United States.
- Recent events in Asia have increased the uncertainty regarding certain Asian currencies considerably, making it extremely difficult to forecast the value of the baht at which the Thai revenues will be converted. The current spot rate of the baht is $.022, and the current spot rate of the pound is

SCENARIO	EFFECT ON THE AVERAGE VALUE OF BAHT	AVERAGE VALUE OF BAHT	AVERAGE VALUE OF POUND
1	No change	$.0220	$1.530
2	Depreciate by 5%	.0209	1.485
3	Depreciate by 10%	.0198	1.500

$1.50. You have created three scenarios and derived an expected value on average for the upcoming year based on each scenario (see the table below):

- Blades currently has no debt in its capital structure. However, it may borrow funds in Thailand if it establishes a subsidiary in the country.

Ben Holt has asked you to answer the following questions:

1. How will Blades be negatively affected by the high level of inflation in Thailand if the Thai customer renews its commitment for another 3 years?

2. Holt believes that the Thai importer will renew its commitment in 2 years. Do you think his assessment is correct? Why or why not? Also, assume that the Thai economy returns to the high growth level that existed prior to the recent unfavorable economic events. Under this assumption, how likely is it that the Thai importer will renew its commitment in 2 years?

3. For each of the three possible values of the Thai baht and the British pound, use a spreadsheet to estimate cash flows for the next year. Briefly comment on the level of Blades' economic exposure. Ignore possible tax effects.

4. Now repeat your analysis in question 3 but assume that the British pound and the Thai baht are perfectly correlated. For example, if the baht depreciates by 5 percent, the pound will also depreciate by 5 percent. Under this assumption, is Blades subject to a greater degree of economic exposure? Why or why not?

5. Based on your answers to the previous three questions, what actions could Blades take to reduce its level of economic exposure to Thailand?

SMALL BUSINESS DILEMMA

Hedging the Sports Exports Company's Economic Exposure to Exchange Rate Risk

Jim Logan, owner of the Sports Exports Company, remains concerned about his exposure to exchange rate risk. Even if Jim hedges his transactions from 1 month to another, he recognizes that a long-term trend of depreciation in the British pound could have a severe impact on his firm. He believes that he must continue to focus on the British market for selling his footballs.

However, he plans to consider various ways in which he can reduce his economic exposure. At the current time, he obtains material from a local manufacturer and uses a machine to produce the footballs, which are then exported. He still uses his garage as a place of production and would like to continue using his garage to maintain low operating expenses.

1. How could Jim adjust his operations to reduce his economic exposure? What is a possible disadvantage of such an adjustment?

2. Offer another solution to hedging the economic exposure in the long run as Jim's business grows. What are the disadvantages of this solution?

INTERNET/EXCEL EXERCISES

1. Review an annual report of an MNC of your choice. Many MNCs provide their annual report on their websites. Look for any comments that relate to the MNC's economic or translation exposure. Does it appear that the MNC hedges its economic exposure or translation exposure? If so, what methods does it use to hedge its exposure?

2. Go to http://finance.yahoo.com and insert the ticker symbol IBM (or use a different MNC if you wish) in the stock quotations box. Then scroll down and click on Historical Prices. Set the date range so that you can access data for least the last 20 quarters. Obtain the stock price of IBM at the beginning of the last 20 quarters and insert the data on your electronic spreadsheet. Compute the percentage change in the stock price of IBM from one quarter to the next. Then go to www.oanda.com/convert/fxhistory and obtain direct exchange rates of the Canadian dollar and the euro that match up with the stock price data. Run a regression analysis with the quarterly percentage

change in IBM's stock price as the dependent variable and the quarterly change in the Canadian dollar's value as the independent variable. (Appendix C explains how Excel can be used to run regression analysis.) Does it appear that IBM's stock price is affected by changes in the value of the Canadian dollar? If so, what is the direction of the relationship? Is the relationship strong? (Check the R-squared statistic.) Based on this relationship, do you think IBM should attempt to hedge its economic exposure to movements in the Canadian dollar?

3. Repeat the process using the euro in place of the Canadian dollar. Does it appear that IBM's stock price is affected by changes in the value of the euro? If so, what is the direction of the relationship? Is the relationship strong? (Check the R-squared statistic.) Based on this relationship, do you think IBM should attempt to hedge its economic exposure to movements in the euro?

REFERENCES

Chiang, Yi-Chein, and Hui-Ju Lin, Autumn 2007, Foreign Exchange Exposures, Financial and Operational Hedge Strategies of Taiwan Firms, *Investment Management & Financial Innovations*, pp. 95–106.

Davis, Joseph H., Mar 2004, Currency Risk and the U.S. Dollar, *Journal of Financial Planning*, pp. 48–56.

Goldberg, Stephen R., and Emily L. Drogt, Jan/Feb 2008, Managing Foreign Exchange Risk, *The Journal of Corporate Accounting & Finance*, pp. 49–57.

Goswami, Gautam, and Milind M. Shrikhande, Fall 2007, Economic Exposure and Currency Swaps, *Journal of Applied Finance*, pp. 62–71.

Hagelin, Nicklas, and Bengt Pramborg, Spring 2004, Hedging Foreign Exchange Exposure: Risk Reduction from Transaction and Translation Hedging, *Journal of International Financial Management & Accounting*, pp. 1–20.

Kroll, Karen, Jun 2007, To Hedge, Or Not to Hedge? *Business Finance*, pp. 29–31.

Maurer, Raimond, and Shohreh Valiani, 2007, Hedging the Exchange Rate Risk in International Portfolio Diversification: Currency Forwards versus Currency Options, *Managerial Finance*, pp. 667–692.

Long-Term Asset and Liability Management

Part 4 (Chapters 13 through 18) focuses on how multinational corporations (MNCs) manage long-term assets and liabilities. Chapter 13 explains how MNCs can benefit from international business. Chapter 14 describes the information MNCs must have when considering multinational projects and demonstrates how the capital budgeting analysis is conducted. Chapter 15 explains the methods by which MNC operations are governed. It also describes how MNCs engage in corporate control and restructuring. Chapter 16 explains how MNCs assess country risk associated with their prevailing projects as well as with their proposed projects. Chapter 17 explains the capital structure decision for MNCs, which affects the cost of financing new projects. Chapter 18 describes the MNC's long-term financing decision.

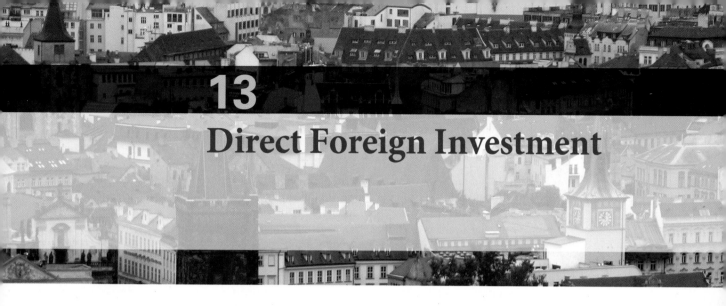

13

Direct Foreign Investment

The specific objectives of this chapter are to:

- describe common motives for initiating direct foreign investment and

- illustrate the benefits of international diversification.

MNCs commonly capitalize on foreign business opportunities by engaging in direct foreign investment (DFI), which is investment in real assets (such as land, buildings, or even existing plants) in foreign countries. They engage in joint ventures with foreign firms, acquire foreign firms, and form new foreign subsidiaries. Financial managers must understand the potential return and risk associated with DFI so that they can make investment decisions that maximize the MNC's value.

MOTIVES FOR DIRECT FOREIGN INVESTMENT

MNCs commonly consider direct foreign investment because it can improve their profitability and enhance shareholder wealth. They are normally focused on investing in real assets such as machinery or buildings that can support operations, rather than financial assets. The direct foreign investment decisions of MNCs normally involve foreign real assets and not foreign financial assets. When MNCs review various foreign investment opportunities, they must consider whether the opportunity is compatible with their operations. In most cases, MNCs engage in DFI because they are interested in boosting revenues, reducing costs, or both.

Revenue-Related Motives

The following are typical motives of MNCs that are attempting to boost revenues:

- *Attract new sources of demand.* A corporation often reaches a stage when growth is limited in its home country, possibly because of intense competition. Even if it faces little competition, its market share in its home country may already be near its potential peak. Thus, the firm may consider foreign markets where there is potential demand. Many developing countries, such as Argentina, Chile, Mexico, Hungary, and China, have been perceived as attractive sources of new demand. Many MNCs have penetrated these countries since barriers have been removed. Because the consumers in some countries have historically been restricted from purchasing goods produced by firms outside their countries, the markets for some goods are not well established and offer much potential for penetration by MNCs.

EXAMPLE   Blockbuster, Inc., has recently established video stores in Australia, Chile, Japan, and several European countries where the video-rental concept is relatively new. With over 2,000 stores in the United States, Blockbuster's growth potential in the United States was limited. China has also attracted MNCs. Motorola recently invested more than $1 billion in joint ventures in China. The Coca-Cola Co. has invested about $500 million in bottling facilities in China, and PepsiCo has invested about $200 million in bottling facilities. Yum Brands has KFC franchises and Pizza Hut franchises in China. Other MNCs such as Ford Motor Co., United Technologies, General Electric, Hewlett-Packard, and IBM have also invested more than $100 million in China to attract demand by consumers there. ●

- *Enter profitable markets.* If other corporations in the industry have proved that superior earnings can be realized in other markets, an MNC may also decide to sell in those markets. It may plan to undercut the prevailing, excessively high prices. A common problem with this strategy is that previously established sellers in a new market may prevent a new competitor from taking away their business by lowering their prices just when the new competitor attempts to break into this market.

- *Exploit monopolistic advantages.* Firms may become internationalized if they possess resources or skills not available to competing firms. If a firm possesses advanced technology and has exploited this advantage successfully in local markets, the firm may attempt to exploit it internationally as well. In fact, the firm may have a more distinct advantage in markets that have less advanced technology.

- *React to trade restrictions.* In some cases, MNCs use DFI as a defensive rather than an aggressive strategy. Specifically, MNCs may pursue DFI to circumvent trade barriers.

EXAMPLE

Japanese automobile manufacturers established plants in the United States in anticipation that their exports to the United States would be subject to more stringent trade restrictions. Japanese companies recognized that trade barriers could be established that would limit or prohibit their exports. By producing automobiles in the United States, Japanese manufacturers could circumvent trade barriers. ●

- *Diversify internationally.* Since economies of countries do not move perfectly in tandem over time, net cash flow from sales of products across countries should be more stable than comparable sales of the products in a single country. By diversifying sales (and possibly even production) internationally, a firm can make its net cash flows less volatile. Thus, the possibility of a liquidity deficiency is less likely. In addition, the firm may enjoy a lower cost of capital as shareholders and creditors perceive the MNC's risk to be lower as a result of more stable cash flows. Potential benefits to MNCs that diversify internationally are examined more thoroughly later in the chapter.

EXAMPLE

Several firms experienced weak sales because of reduced U.S. demand for their products. They responded by increasing their expansion in foreign markets. AT&T and Starbucks pursued new business in China. United Technologies planned substantial expansion in Europe and Asia. IBM increased its presence in China, India, South Korea, and Taiwan. Cisco Systems expanded substantially in China, Japan, and South Korea. Foreign expansion diversifies an MNC's sources of revenue and thus reduces its reliance on the U.S. economy. Wal-Mart has not only diversified internationally but has spread its business into many emerging markets as well. Thus, it is less sensitive to a recession in the more developed countries such as those in Western Europe. ●

Cost-Related Motives

MNCs also engage in DFI in an effort to reduce costs. The following are typical motives of MNCs that are trying to cut costs:

- *Fully benefit from economies of scale.* A corporation that attempts to sell its primary product in new markets may increase its earnings and shareholder wealth due to **economies of scale** (lower average cost per unit resulting from increased production). Firms that utilize much machinery are most likely to benefit from economies of scale.

The removal of trade barriers by the Single European Act allowed MNCs to achieve greater economies of scale. Some U.S.-based MNCs consolidated their European plants because the removal of tariffs between countries in the European Union (EU) enabled firms to achieve economies of scale at a single European plant without incurring excessive exporting costs. The act also enhanced economies of scale by making regulations on television ads, automobile standards, and other products and services uniform across the EU. As a result, Colgate-Palmolive Co. and other MNCs are manufacturing more homogeneous products that can be sold in all EU countries. The adoption of the euro also encouraged consolidation by eliminating exchange rate risk within these countries. ●

- *Use foreign factors of production.* Labor and land costs can vary dramatically among countries. MNCs often attempt to set up production in locations where land and labor are cheap. Due to market imperfections (as discussed in Chapter 1) such as imperfect information, relocation transaction costs, and barriers to industry entry, specific labor costs do not necessarily become equal among markets. Thus, it is worthwhile for MNCs to survey markets to determine whether they can benefit from cheaper costs by producing in those markets.

Many U.S.-based MNCs, including Black & Decker, Eastman Kodak, Ford Motor Co., and General Electric, have established subsidiaries in Mexico to achieve lower labor costs.

Mexico has attracted almost $8 billion in DFI from firms in the automobile industry, primarily because of the low-cost labor. Mexican workers at subsidiaries of automobile plants who manufacture sedans and trucks earn daily wages that are less than the average hourly rate for similar workers in the United States. Ford produces trucks at subsidiaries based in Mexico.

Non-U.S. automobile manufacturers are also capitalizing on the low-cost labor in Mexico. Volkswagen of Germany produces its Beetle in Mexico. Daimler AG of Germany manufactures its 12-wheeler trucks in Mexico, and Nissan Motor Co. of Japan produces some of its wagons in Mexico.

Other Japanese companies are also increasingly using Mexico and other low-wage countries for production. For example, Sony Corp. recently established a plant in Tijuana. Matsushita Electrical Industrial Co. has a large plant in Tijuana.

Baxter International has established manufacturing plants in Mexico and Malaysia to capitalize on lower costs of production (primarily wage rates). Honeywell has joint ventures in countries such as Korea and India where production costs are low. It has also established subsidiaries in countries where production costs are low, such as Mexico, Malaysia, Hong Kong, and Taiwan. ●

- *Use foreign raw materials.* Due to transportation costs, a corporation may attempt to avoid importing raw materials from a given country, especially when it plans to sell the finished product back to consumers in that country. Under such circumstances, a more feasible solution may be to develop the product in the country where the raw materials are located.
- *Use foreign technology.* Corporations are increasingly establishing overseas plants or acquiring existing overseas plants to learn the technology of foreign countries. This technology is then used to improve their own production processes and increase production efficiency at all subsidiary plants around the world.
- *React to exchange rate movements.* When a firm perceives that a foreign currency is undervalued, the firm may consider DFI in that country, as the initial outlay should be relatively low.

A related reason for such DFI is to offset the changing demand for a company's exports due to exchange rate fluctuations. For example, when Japanese automobile manufacturers build plants in the United States, they can reduce exposure to exchange rate fluctuations by incurring dollar costs for their production that offset dollar revenues.

Although MNCs do not engage in large projects simply as an indirect means of speculating on currencies, the feasibility of proposed projects may be dependent on existing and expected exchange rate movements.

Cost-Related Motives in the Expanded European Union.
Several countries that became part of the European Union in 2004 and 2007 were targeted for new DFI by MNCs that wanted to reduce manufacturing costs.

EXAMPLE

Peugot increased its production in the Czech Republic, Toyota expanded its production in Slovakia, Audi expanded in Hungary, and Renault expanded in Romania. Volkswagen recently expanded its capacity in Slovenia and cut some jobs in Spain. While it originally established operations in Spain because the wages were about half of those in Germany, wages in Slovenia are less than half of those in Spain. The expansion of the EU allows new member countries to transport products throughout Europe at reduced tariffs. ●

The shifts to low-wage countries will make manufacturers more efficient and competitive, but the tradeoff is thousands of jobs lost in Western Europe. However, it may be argued that the high unionized wages encouraged the firms to seek growth in productivity elsewhere. European labor unions tend to fight layoffs but recognize that manufacturers might move completely out of the Western European countries where unions have more leverage and move into the low-wage countries in Eastern Europe.

Selfish Managerial Motives for DFI.
In addition to the motives discussed so far, there are other selfish motives for DFI. First, managers may attempt to expand their divisions internationally if their compensation may be increased as a result of expansion. Second, many high-level managers may have large holdings of the MNC's stock and would prefer that the MNC diversify its business internationally in order to reduce risk. This goal will not necessarily satisfy shareholders who want the MNC to focus on increasing its return. However, it will satisfy high-level managers who want to reduce risk, so that the stock price is more stable and the value of their stock holdings is more stable. An MNC's board of directors can attempt to oversee the proposed international projects to ensure that the DFI would serve shareholders.

Comparing Benefits of DFI among Countries

Exhibit 13.1 summarizes the possible benefits of DFI and explains how MNCs can use DFI to achieve those benefits. Most MNCs pursue DFI based on their expectations of capitalizing on one or more of the potential benefits summarized in Exhibit 13.1.

The potential benefits from DFI vary with the country. Countries in Western Europe have well-established markets where the demand for most products and services is large. Thus, these countries may appeal to MNCs that want to penetrate markets because they have better products than those already being offered. Countries in Eastern Europe, Asia, and Latin America tend to have relatively low costs of land and labor. If an MNC desires to establish a low-cost production facility, it would also consider other factors such as the work ethic and skills of the local people, availability of labor, and cultural traits. Although most attempts to increase international business are motivated by one or more of the benefits listed here, some disadvantages are also associated with DFI.

EXAMPLE

Most of Nike's shoe production is concentrated in China, Indonesia, Thailand, and Vietnam. The government regulation of labor in these countries is limited. Thus, if Nike wants to ensure that employees receive fair treatment, it may have to govern the factories itself. Also, because Nike is such a large company, it receives much attention when employees in factories that produce shoes for Nike receive unfair treatment. Nike incurs additional costs of oversight to

GOVERNANCE

WEB

www.morganstanley
.com/views/gef/index
.html
Morgan Stanley's
Global Economic Forum,
which has analyses,
discussions, statistics,
and forecasts related to
non-U.S. economies.

WEB

http://finance.yahoo
.com/
Information about
economic growth and
other macroeconomic
indicators used when
considering direct
foreign investment in
a foreign country.

WEB

www.worldbank.org
Valuable updated
country data that can
be considered when
making DFI decisions.

prevent unfair treatment of employees. While its expenses from having products produced in Asia are still significantly lower than if the products were produced in the United States, it needs to recognize these other expenses when determining where to have its products produced. A country with the lowest wages will not necessarily be the ideal location for production if an MNC will incur very high expenses to ensure that the factories treat local employees fairly. ●

Comparing Benefits of DFI over Time

As conditions change over time, so do possible benefits from pursuing direct foreign investment in various countries. Thus, some countries may become more attractive targets while other countries become less attractive. The choice of target countries for DFI has changed over time. Canada now receives a smaller proportion of total DFI than it received in the past, while Europe, Latin America, and Asia receive a larger proportion than in the past. More than one-half of all DFI by U.S. firms is in European countries. The opening of the Eastern European countries and the expansion of the EU account for some of the increased DFI in Europe, especially Eastern Europe. The increased focus on Latin America is partially attributed to its high economic growth, which has encouraged MNCs to capitalize on new sources of demand for their products. In addition, MNCs have targeted Latin America and Asia to use factors of production that are less expensive in foreign countries than in the United States.

Exhibit 13.1 Summary of Motives for Direct Foreign Investment

	MEANS OF USING DFI TO ACHIEVE THIS BENEFIT
Revenue-Related Motives	
1. Attract new sources of demand.	Establish a subsidiary or acquire a competitor in a new market.
2. Enter markets where superior profits are possible.	Acquire a competitor that has controlled its local market.
3. Exploit monopolistic advantages.	Establish a subsidiary in a market where competitors are unable to produce the identical product; sell products in that country.
4. React to trade restrictions.	Establish a subsidiary in a market where tougher trade restrictions will adversely affect the firm's export volume.
5. Diversify internationally.	Establish subsidiaries in markets whose business cycles differ from those where existing subsidiaries are based.
Cost-Related Motives	
6. Fully benefit from economies of scale.	Establish a subsidiary in a new market that can sell products produced elsewhere; this allows for increased production and possibly greater production efficiency.
7. Use foreign factors of production.	Establish a subsidiary in a market that has relatively low costs of labor or land; sell the finished product to countries where the cost of production is higher.
8. Use foreign raw materials.	Establish a subsidiary in a market where raw materials are cheap and accessible; sell the finished product to countries where the raw materials are more expensive.
9. Use foreign technology.	Participate in a joint venture in order to learn about a production process or other operations.
10. React to exchange rate movements.	Establish a subsidiary in a new market where the local currency is weak but is expected to strengthen over time.

EXAMPLE

Last year Georgia Co. contemplated DFI in Thailand, where it would produce and sell cell phones. It decided that costs were too high. Now it is reconsidering because costs in Thailand have declined. Georgia could lease office space at a low cost. It could also purchase a manufacturing plant at a lower cost because factories that recently failed are standing empty. In addition, the Thai baht has depreciated substantially against the dollar recently, so Georgia Co. could invest in Thailand at a time when the dollar can be exchanged at a favorable exchange rate.

Georgia Co. also discovers, however, that while the cost-related characteristics have improved, the revenue-related characteristics are now less desirable. A new subsidiary in Thailand might not attract new sources of demand due to the country's weak economy. In addition, Georgia might be unable to earn excessive profits there because the weak economy might force existing firms to keep their prices very low in order to survive. Georgia Co. must compare the favorable aspects of DFI in Thailand with the unfavorable aspects by using multinational capital budgeting, which is explained in the following chapter. ●

BENEFITS OF INTERNATIONAL DIVERSIFICATION

An international project can reduce a firm's overall risk as a result of international diversification benefits. The key to international diversification is selecting foreign projects whose performance levels are not highly correlated over time. In this way, the various international projects should not experience poor performance simultaneously.

EXAMPLE

Merrimack Co., a U.S. firm, plans to invest in a new project in either the United States or the United Kingdom. Once the project is completed, it will constitute 30 percent of the firm's total funds invested in itself. The remaining 70 percent of its investment in its business is exclusively in the United States. Characteristics of the proposed project are forecasted for a 5-year period for both a U.S. and a British location, as shown in Exhibit 13.2.

Merrimack Co. plans to assess the feasibility of each proposed project based on expected risk and return, using a 5-year time horizon. Its expected annual after-tax return on investment on its prevailing business is 20 percent, and its variability of returns (as measured by the standard deviation) is expected to be .10. The firm can assess its expected overall performance based on developing the project in the United States and in the United Kingdom. In doing so, it is essentially comparing two portfolios. In the first portfolio, 70 percent of its total funds are invested in its prevailing U.S. business, with the remaining 30 percent invested in a new project located in the United States. In the second portfolio, again 70 percent of the firm's total funds are invested in its prevailing business, but the remaining 30 percent are invested in a new project located in the United Kingdom. Therefore, 70 percent of the portfolios' investments are identical. The difference is in the remaining 30 percent of funds invested.

WEB

www.trade.gov/mas/
Outlook of international
trade conditions for
each of several
industries.

Exhibit 13.2 Evaluation of Proposed Projects in Alternative Locations

	EXISTING BUSINESS	CHARACTERISTICS OF PROPOSED PROJECT	
		IF LOCATED IN THE UNITED STATES	IF LOCATED IN THE UNITED KINGDOM
Mean expected annual return on investment (after taxes)	20%	25%	25%
Standard deviation of expected annual after-tax returns on investment	.10	.09	.11
Correlation of expected annual after-tax returns on investment with after-tax returns of prevailing U.S. business	—	.80	.02

If the new project is located in the United States, the firm's overall expected after-tax return (r_p) is

$r_p =$	[(70%)	×	(20%)]	+	[(30%)	×	(25%)]	=	21.5%
	% of funds invested in prevailing business		Expected return on prevailing business		% of funds invested in new U.S. project		Expected return on new U.S. project		Firm's overall expected return

This computation is based on weighting the returns according to the percentage of total funds invested in each investment.

If the firm calculates its overall expected return with the new project located in the United Kingdom instead of the United States, the results are unchanged. This is because the new project's expected return is the same regardless of the country of location. Therefore, in terms of return, neither new project has an advantage.

With regard to risk, the new project is expected to exhibit slightly less variability in returns during the 5-year period if it is located in the United States (see Exhibit 13.2). Since firms typically prefer more stable returns on their investments, this is an advantage. However, estimating the risk of the individual project without considering the overall firm would be a mistake. The expected correlation of the new project's returns with those of the prevailing business must also be considered. Recall that portfolio variance is determined by the individual variability of each component as well as their pairwise correlations. The variance of a portfolio (σ_p^2) composed of only two investments (A and B) is computed as

$$\sigma_p^2 = w_A^2 \sigma_A^2 + w_B^2 \sigma_B^2 + 2 w_A w_B \sigma_A \sigma_B (CORR_{AB})$$

where w_A and w_B represent the percentage of total funds allocated to investments A and B, respectively; (σ_A) and (σ_B) are the standard deviations of returns on investments A and B, respectively, and $CORR_{AB}$ is the correlation coefficient of returns between investments A and B. This equation for portfolio variance can be applied to the problem at hand. The portfolio reflects the overall firm. First, compute the overall firm's variance in returns assuming it locates the new project in the United States (based on the information provided in Exhibit 13.2). This variance (σ_p^2) is

$$\sigma_p^2 = (.70)^2 (.10)^2 + (.30)^2 (.09)^2 + 2(.70)(.30)(.10)(.09)(.80)$$
$$= (.49)(.01) + (.09)(.0081) + .003024$$
$$= .0049 + .000729 + .003024$$
$$= .008653$$

If Merrimack Co. decides to locate the new project in the United Kingdom instead of the United States, its overall variability in returns will be different because that project differs from the new U.S. project in terms of individual variability in returns and correlation with the prevailing business. The overall variability of the firm's returns based on locating the new project in the United Kingdom is estimated by variance in the portfolio returns (σ_p^2):

$$\sigma_p^2 = (.70)^2 (.10)^2 + (.30)^2 (.11)^2 + 2(.70)(.30)(.10)(.11)(.02)$$
$$= (.49)(.01) + (.09)(.0121) + .0000924$$
$$= .0049 + .001089 + .0000924$$
$$= .0060814$$

Thus, Merrimack will generate more stable returns if the new project is located in the United Kingdom. The firm's overall variability in returns is almost 29.7 percent less if the new project is located in the United Kingdom rather than in the United States.

The variability is reduced when locating in the foreign country because of the correlation of the new project's expected returns with the expected returns of the prevailing business. If the new project is located in Merrimack's home country (the United States), its returns are expected to be more highly correlated with those of the prevailing business than they would be if the project were located in the United Kingdom. When economic conditions of two countries (such as the United States and the United Kingdom) are not highly correlated, then a firm may reduce its risk by diversifying its business in both countries instead of concentrating in just one. ●

Diversification Analysis of International Projects

Like any investor, an MNC with investments positioned around the world is concerned with the risk and return characteristics of the investments. The portfolio of all investments reflects the MNC in aggregate.

EXAMPLE

WEB

www.treasury.gov
Links to international information that should be considered by MNCs that are considering direct foreign investment.

Virginia, Inc., considers a global strategy of developing projects as shown in Exhibit 13.3. Each point on the graph reflects a specific project that either has been implemented or is being considered. The return axis may be measured by potential return on assets or return on equity. The risk may be measured by potential fluctuation in the returns generated by each project.

Exhibit 13.3 shows that Project A has the highest expected return of all the projects. While Virginia, Inc., could devote most of its resources toward this project to attempt to achieve such a high return, its risk is possibly too high by itself. In addition, such a project may not be able to absorb all available capital anyway if its potential market for customers is limited. Thus, Virginia, Inc., develops a portfolio of projects. By combining Project A with several other projects, Virginia, Inc., may decrease its expected return. On the other hand, it may also reduce its risk substantially.

Exhibit 13.3 Risk-Return Analysis of International Projects

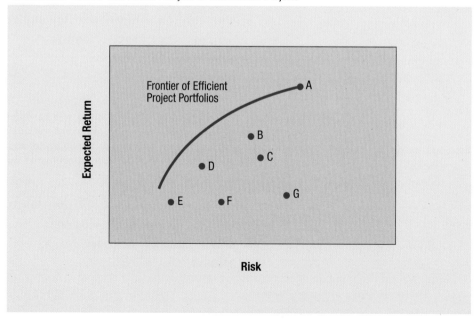

If Virginia, Inc appropriately combines projects, its project portfolio may be able to achieve a risk-return tradeoff exhibited by any of the points on the curve in Exhibit 13.3. This curve represents a frontier of efficient project portfolios that exhibit desirable risk-return characteristics, in that no single project could outperform any of these portfolios. The term *efficient* refers to a minimum risk for a given expected return. Project portfolios outperform the individual projects considered by Virginia, Inc., because of the diversification attributes discussed earlier. The lower, or more negative, the correlation in project returns over time, the lower will be the project portfolio risk. As new projects are proposed, the frontier of efficient project portfolios available to Virginia, Inc., may shift. ●

Comparing Portfolios along the Frontier. Along the frontier of efficient project portfolios, no portfolio can be singled out as "optimal" for all MNCs. This is because MNCs vary in their willingness to accept risk. If the MNC is very conservative and has the choice of any portfolios represented by the frontier in Exhibit 13.3, it will probably prefer one that exhibits low risk (near the bottom of the frontier). Conversely, a more aggressive strategy would be to implement a portfolio of projects that exhibits risk-return characteristics such as those near the top of the frontier.

Comparing Frontiers among MNCs. The actual location of the frontier of efficient project portfolios depends on the business in which the firm is involved. Some MNCs have frontiers of possible project portfolios that are more desirable than the frontiers of other MNCs.

EXAMPLE   Eurosteel, Inc., sells steel solely to European nations and is considering other related projects. Its frontier of efficient project portfolios exhibits considerable risk (because it sells just one product to countries whose economies move in tandem). In contrast, Global Products, Inc., which sells a wide range of products to countries all over the world, has a lower degree of project portfolio risk. Therefore, its frontier of efficient project portfolios is closer to the vertical axis. This comparison is illustrated in Exhibit 13.4. Of course, this comparison assumes that Global Products, Inc., is knowledgeable about all of its products and the markets where it sells. ●

Exhibit 13.4 Risk-Return Advantage of a Diversified MNC

Our discussion suggests that MNCs can achieve more desirable risk-return characteristics from their project portfolios if they sufficiently diversify among products and geographic markets. This also relates to the advantage an MNC has over a purely domestic firm with only a local market. The MNC may be able to develop a more efficient portfolio of projects than its domestic counterpart.

Diversification among Countries

Exhibit 13.5 shows how the stock market values of various countries have changed over time. A country's stock market value reflects the expectations of business opportunities and economic growth. Notice how the changes in stock market values vary among countries, which suggests that business and economic conditions vary among countries. Thus, when an MNC diversifies its business among countries rather than focusing on only one foreign country, it reduces its exposure to any single foreign country. However, economic

Exhibit 13.5 Comparison of Expected Economic Growth among Countries: Annual Stock Market Return

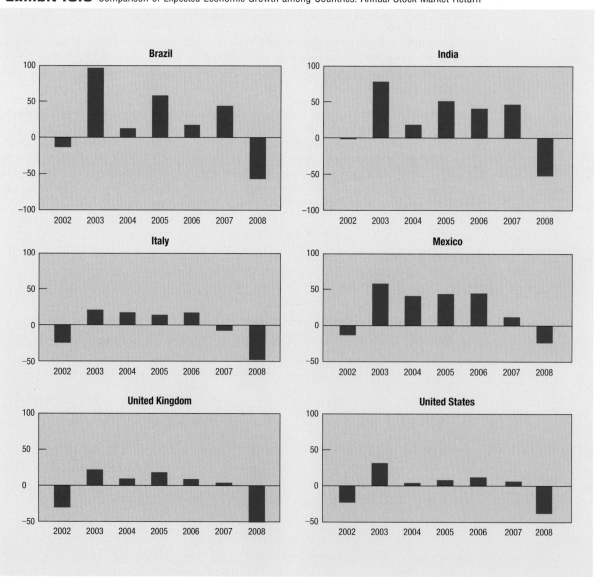

conditions are commonly correlated over time, because the weakness of one country may cause a reduction in imports demanded from other countries. Notice that in 2002 (when the United States experienced a recession), all stock markets in Exhibit 13.5 were weak, reflecting expectations of weak economic conditions in these countries.

In addition, most countries experienced weak economies during the credit crisis in 2008. Thus, diversification across economies may not be so effective when there are global economic conditions that adversely affect most countries.

HOST GOVERNMENT VIEWS OF DFI

Each government must weigh the advantages and disadvantages of direct foreign investment in its country. It may provide incentives to encourage some forms of DFI, barriers to prevent other forms of DFI, and impose conditions on some other forms of DFI.

Incentives to Encourage DFI

The ideal DFI solves problems such as unemployment and lack of technology without taking business away from local firms.

EXAMPLE

WEB

www.pwc.com
Access to country-specific information such as general business rules and regulations, tax environments, and some other useful statistics and surveys.

Consider an MNC that is willing to build a production plant in a foreign country that will use local labor and produce goods that are not direct substitutes for other locally produced goods. In this case, the plant will not cause a reduction in sales by local firms. The host government would normally be receptive toward this type of DFI. Another desirable form of DFI from the perspective of the host government is a manufacturing plant that uses local labor and then exports the products (assuming no other local firm exports such products to the same areas). ●

In some cases, a government will offer incentives to MNCs that consider DFI in its country. Governments are particularly willing to offer incentives for DFI that will result in the employment of local citizens or an increase in technology. Common incentives offered by the host government include tax breaks on the income earned there, rent-free land and buildings, low-interest loans, subsidized energy, and reduced environmental regulations. The degree to which a government will offer such incentives depends on the extent to which the MNC's DFI will benefit that country.

EXAMPLE

The decision by Allied Research Associates, Inc. (a U.S.-based MNC), to build a production facility and office in Belgium was highly motivated by Belgian government subsidies. The Belgian government subsidized a large portion of the expenses incurred by Allied Research Associates and offered tax concessions and favorable interest rates on loans to Allied. ●

While many governments encourage DFI, they use different types of incentives. France has periodically sold government land at a discount, while Finland and Ireland attracted MNCs in the late 1990s by imposing a very low corporate tax rate on specific businesses.

Barriers to DFI

Governments are less anxious to encourage DFI that adversely affects locally owned companies, unless they believe that the increased competition is needed to serve consumers. Therefore, they tend to closely regulate any DFI that may affect local firms, consumers, and economic conditions.

Protective Barriers. When MNCs consider engaging in DFI by acquiring a foreign company, they may face various barriers imposed by host government agencies. All countries have one or more government agencies that monitor mergers and acquisitions. These agencies may prevent an MNC from acquiring companies in their country if they believe it will attempt to lay off employees. They may even restrict foreign ownership of any local firms.

"Red Tape" Barriers. An implicit barrier to DFI in some countries is the "red tape" involved, such as procedural and documentation requirements. An MNC pursuing DFI is subject to a different set of requirements in each country. Therefore, it is difficult for an MNC to become proficient at the process unless it concentrates on DFI within a single foreign country. The current efforts to make regulations uniform across Europe have simplified the paperwork required to acquire European firms.

Industry Barriers. The local firms of some industries in particular countries have substantial influence on the government and will likely use their influence to prevent competition from MNCs that attempt DFI. MNCs that consider DFI need to recognize the influence that these local firms have on the local government.

Environmental Barriers. Each country enforces its own environmental constraints. Some countries may enforce more of these restrictions on a subsidiary whose parent is based in a different country. Building codes, disposal of production waste materials, and pollution controls are examples of restrictions that force subsidiaries to incur additional costs. Many European countries have recently imposed tougher antipollution laws as a result of severe problems.

Regulatory Barriers. Each country also enforces its own regulatory constraints pertaining to taxes, currency convertibility, earnings remittance, employee rights, and other policies that can affect cash flows of a subsidiary established there. Because these regulations can influence cash flows, financial managers must consider them when assessing policies. Also, any change in these regulations may require revision of existing financial policies, so financial managers should monitor the regulations for any potential changes over time. Some countries may require extensive protection of employee rights. If so, managers should attempt to reward employees for efficient production so that the goals of labor and shareholders will be closely aligned.

Ethical Differences. There is no consensus standard of business conduct that applies to all countries. A business practice that is perceived to be unethical in one country may be totally ethical in another. For example, U.S.-based MNCs are well aware that certain business practices that are accepted in some less developed countries would be illegal in the United States. Bribes to governments in order to receive special tax breaks or other favors are common in some countries. If MNCs do not participate in such practices, they may be at a competitive disadvantage when attempting DFI in a particular country.

Political Instability. The governments of some countries may prevent DFI. If a country is susceptible to abrupt changes in government and political conflicts, the feasibility of DFI may be dependent on the outcome of those conflicts. MNCs want to avoid a situation in which they pursue DFI under a government that is likely to be removed after the DFI occurs.

Government-Imposed Conditions to Engage in DFI

Some governments allow international acquisitions but impose special requirements on MNCs that desire to acquire a local firm. For example, the MNC may be required to ensure pollution control for its manufacturing or to structure the business to export the products it produces so that it does not threaten the market share of other local firms. The MNC may even be required to retain all the employees of the target firm so that unemployment and general economic conditions in the country are not adversely affected.

EXAMPLE

Mexico requires that a specified minimum proportion of parts used to produce automobiles there be made in Mexico. The proportion is lower for automobiles that are to be exported.

Spain's government allowed Ford Motor Co. to set up production facilities in Spain only if it would abide by certain provisions. These included limiting Ford's local sales volume to 10 percent of the previous year's local automobile sales. In addition, two-thirds of the total volume of automobiles produced by Ford in Spain must be exported. The idea behind these provisions was to create jobs for workers in Spain without seriously affecting local competitors. Allowing a subsidiary that primarily exports its product achieved this objective. ●

Government-imposed conditions do not necessarily prevent an MNC from pursuing DFI in a specific foreign country, but they can be costly. Thus, MNCs should be willing to consider DFI that requires costly conditions only if the potential benefits outweigh the costs.

SUMMARY

- MNCs may be motivated to initiate direct foreign investment in order to attract new sources of demand or to enter markets where superior profits are possible. These two motives are normally based on opportunities to generate more revenue in foreign markets. Other motives for using DFI are typically related to cost efficiency, such as using foreign factors of production, raw materials, or technology. In addition MNCs may engage in DFI to protect their foreign market share, to react to exchange rate movements, or to avoid trade restrictions.
- International diversification is a common motive for direct foreign investment. It allows an MNC to reduce its exposure to domestic economic conditions. In this way, the MNC may be able to stabilize its cash flows and reduce its risk. Such a goal is desirable because it may reduce the firm's cost of financing. International projects may allow MNCs to achieve lower risk than is possible from only domestic projects without reducing their expected returns. International tends to be better able to reduce risk when the DFI is targeted to countries whose economies are somewhat unrelated to an MNC's home country economy.

POINT COUNTER-POINT

Should MNCs Avoid DFI in Countries with Liberal Child Labor Laws?

Point Yes. An MNC should maintain its hiring standards, regardless of what country it is in. Even if a foreign country allows children to work, an MNC should not lower its standards. Although the MNC forgoes the use of low-cost labor, it maintains its global credibility.

Counter-Point No. An MNC will not only benefit its shareholders, but will create employment for some children who need support. The MNC can provide reasonable working conditions and perhaps may even offer educational programs for its employees.

Who Is Correct? Use the Internet to learn more about this issue. Which argument do you support? Offer your own opinion on this issue.

SELF-TEST

Answers are provided in Appendix A at the back of the text.

1. Offer some reasons why U.S. firms might prefer to engage in direct foreign investment (DFI) in Canada rather than Mexico.

2. Offer some reasons why U.S. firms might prefer to direct their DFI to Mexico rather than Canada.

3. One U.S. executive said that Europe was not considered as a location for DFI because of the euro's value. Interpret this statement.

4. Why do you think U.S. firms commonly use joint ventures as a strategy to enter China?

5. Why would the United States offer a foreign automobile manufacturer large incentives for establishing a production subsidiary in the United States? Isn't this strategy indirectly subsidizing the foreign competitors of U.S. firms?

QUESTIONS AND APPLICATIONS

1. **Motives for DFI.** Describe some potential benefits to an MNC as a result of direct foreign investment (DFI). Elaborate on each type of benefit. Which motives for DFI do you think encouraged Nike to expand its footwear production in Latin America?

2. **Impact of a Weak Currency on Feasibility of DFI.** Packer, Inc., a U.S. producer of computer disks, plans to establish a subsidiary in Mexico in order to penetrate the Mexican market. Packer's executives believe that the Mexican peso's value is relatively strong and will weaken against the dollar over time. If their expectations about the peso's value are correct, how will this affect the feasibility of the project? Explain.

3. **DFI to Achieve Economies of Scale.** Bear Co. and Viking, Inc., are automobile manufacturers that desire to benefit from economies of scale. Bear Co. has decided to establish distributorship subsidiaries in various countries, while Viking, Inc., has decided to establish manufacturing subsidiaries in various countries. Which firm is more likely to benefit from economies of scale?

4. **DFI to Reduce Cash Flow Volatility.** Raider Chemical Co. and Ram, Inc., had similar intentions to reduce the volatility of their cash flows. Raider implemented a long-range plan to establish 40 percent of its business in Canada. Ram, Inc., implemented a long-range plan to establish 30 percent of its business in Europe and Asia, scattered among 12 different countries. Which company will more effectively reduce cash flow volatility once the plans are achieved?

5. **Impact of Import Restrictions.** If the United States imposed long-term restrictions on imports, would the amount of DFI by non-U.S. MNCs in the United States increase, decrease, or be unchanged? Explain.

6. **Capitalizing on Low-Cost Labor.** Some MNCs establish a manufacturing facility where there is a relatively low cost of labor. Yet, they sometimes close the facility later because the cost advantage dissipates. Why do you think the relative cost advantage of these countries is reduced over time? (Ignore possible exchange rate effects.)

7. **Opportunities in Less Developed Countries.** Offer your opinion on why economies of some less developed countries with strict restrictions on international trade and DFI are somewhat independent from economies of other countries. Why would MNCs desire to enter such countries? If these countries relaxed their restrictions, would their economies continue to be independent of other economies? Explain.

8. **Effects of September 11.** In August 2001, Ohio, Inc., considered establishing a manufacturing plant in central Asia, which would be used to cover its exports to Japan and Hong Kong. The cost of labor was very low in central Asia. On September 11, 2001, the terrorist attacks on the United States caused Ohio to reassess the potential cost savings. Why would the estimated expenses of the plant increase after the terrorist attacks?

9. **DFI Strategy.** Bronco Corp. has decided to establish a subsidiary in Taiwan that will produce stereos and sell them there. It expects that its cost of producing these stereos will be one-third the cost of producing them in the United States. Assuming that its production cost estimates are accurate, is Bronco's strategy sensible? Explain.

10. **Risk Resulting from International Business.** This chapter concentrates on possible benefits to a firm that increases its international business.

a. What are some risks of international business that may not exist for local business?

b. What does this chapter reveal about the relationship between an MNC's degree of international business and its risk?

11. **Motives for DFI.** Starter Corp. of New Haven, Connecticut, produces sportswear that is licensed by professional sports teams. It recently decided to expand in Europe. What are the potential benefits for this firm from using DFI?

12. Disney's DFI Motives. What potential benefits do you think were most important in the decision of the Walt Disney Co. to build a theme park in France?

13. DFI Strategy. Once an MNC establishes a subsidiary, DFI remains an ongoing decision. What does this statement mean?

14. Host Government Incentives for DFI. Why would foreign governments provide MNCs with incentives to undertake DFI there?

Advanced Questions

15. DFI Strategy. JCPenney has recognized numerous opportunities to expand in foreign countries and has assessed many foreign markets, including Brazil, Greece, Mexico, Portugal, Singapore, and Thailand. It has opened new stores in Europe, Asia, and Latin America. In each case, the firm was aware that it did not have sufficient understanding of the culture of each country that it had targeted. Consequently, it engaged in joint ventures with local partners who knew the preferences of the local customers.

a. What comparative advantage does JCPenney have when establishing a store in a foreign country, relative to an independent variety store?

b. Why might the overall risk of JCPenney decrease or increase as a result of its recent global expansion?

c. JCPenney has been more cautious about entering China. Explain the potential obstacles associated with entering China.

16. DFI Location Decision. Decko Co. is a U.S. firm with a Chinese subsidiary that produces cell phones in China and sells them in Japan. This subsidiary pays its wages and its rent in Chinese yuan, which is stable relative to the dollar. The cell phones sold to Japan are denominated in Japanese yen. Assume that Decko Co. expects that the Chinese yuan will continue to stay stable against the dollar. The subsidiary's main goal is to generate profits for itself and reinvest the profits. It does not plan to remit any funds to the U.S. parent.

a. Assume that the Japanese yen strengthens against the U.S. dollar over time. How would this be expected to affect the profits earned by the Chinese subsidiary?

b. If Decko Co. had established its subsidiary in Tokyo, Japan, instead of China, would its subsidiary's profits be more exposed or less exposed to exchange rate risk?

c. Why do you think that Decko Co. established the subsidiary in China instead of Japan? Assume no major country risk barriers.

d. If the Chinese subsidiary needs to borrow money to finance its expansion and wants to reduce its exchange rate risk, should it borrow U.S. dollars, Chinese yuan, or Japanese yen?

17. Foreign Investment Decision. Trak Co. (of the United States) presently serves as a distributor of products by purchasing them from other U.S. firms and selling them in Japan. It wants to purchase a manufacturer in India that could produce similar products at a low cost (due to low labor costs in India) and export the products to Japan. The operating expenses would be denominated in Indian rupees. The products would be invoiced in Japanese yen. If Trak Co. can acquire a manufacturer, it will discontinue its existing distributor business. If the yen is expected to appreciate against the dollar, while the rupee is expected to depreciate against the dollar, how would this affect Trak's direct foreign investment?

18. Foreign Investment Strategy. Myzo Co. (based in the United States) sells basic household products that many other U.S. firms produce at the same quality level, and these other U.S. firms have about the same production cost as Myzo. Myzo is considering direct foreign investment. It believes that the market in the United States is saturated and wants to pursue business in a foreign market where it can generate more revenue. It decides to create a subsidiary in Mexico that will produce household products and sell its products only in Mexico. This subsidiary would definitely not export its products to the United States because exports to the United States could reduce the parent's market share and Myzo wants to ensure that its U.S. employees remain employed. The labor costs in Mexico are very low. Myzo will comply with some international labor laws. By complying with the laws, the total costs of Myzo's subsidiary will be 20 percent higher than other Mexican producers of household products in Mexico that are of similar quality. However, Myzo's subsidiary will be able to produce household products at a cost that is 40 percent lower than its cost of producing household products in the United States. Briefly explain whether you think Myzo's strategy for direct foreign investment is feasible.

Discussion in the Boardroom

This exercise can be found in Appendix E at the back of this textbook.

Running Your Own MNC

This exercise can be found on the *International Financial Management* text companion website located at www.cengage.com/finance/madura.

BLADES, INC. CASE

Consideration of Direct Foreign Investment

For the last year, Blades, Inc., has been exporting to Thailand in order to supplement its declining U.S. sales. Under the existing arrangement, Blades sells 180,000 pairs of roller blades annually to Entertainment Products, a Thai retailer, for a fixed price denominated in Thai baht. The agreement will last for another 2 years. Furthermore, to diversify internationally and to take advantage of an attractive offer by Jogs, Ltd., a British retailer, Blades has recently begun exporting to the United Kingdom. Under the resulting agreement, Jogs will purchase 200,000 pairs of Speedos, Blades' primary product, annually at a fixed price of £80 per pair.

Blades' suppliers of the needed components for its roller blade production are located primarily in the United States, where Blades incurs the majority of its cost of goods sold. Although prices for inputs needed to manufacture roller blades vary, recent costs have run approximately $70 per pair. Blades also imports components from Thailand because of the relatively low price of rubber and plastic components and because of their high quality. These imports are denominated in Thai baht, and the exact price (in baht) depends on prevailing market prices for these components in Thailand. Currently, inputs sufficient to manufacture a pair of roller blades cost approximately 3,000 Thai baht per pair of roller blades.

Although Thailand had been among the world's fastest growing economies, recent events in Thailand have increased the level of economic uncertainty. Specifically, the Thai baht, which had been pegged to the dollar, is now a freely floating currency and has depreciated substantially in recent months. Furthermore, recent levels of inflation in Thailand have been very high. Hence, future economic conditions in Thailand are highly uncertain.

Ben Holt, Blades' chief financial officer (CFO), is seriously considering DFI in Thailand. He believes that this is a perfect time to either establish a subsidiary or acquire an existing business in Thailand because the uncertain economic conditions and the depreciation of the baht have substantially lowered the initial costs required for DFI. Holt believes the growth potential in Asia will be extremely high once the Thai economy stabilizes.

Although Holt has also considered DFI in the United Kingdom, he would prefer that Blades invest in Thailand as opposed to the United Kingdom. Forecasts indicate that the demand for roller blades in the United Kingdom is similar to that in the United States; since Blades' U.S. sales have recently declined because of the high prices it charges, Holt expects that DFI in the United Kingdom will yield similar results, especially since the components required to manufacture roller blades are more expensive in the United Kingdom than in the United States. Furthermore, both domestic and foreign roller blade manufacturers are relatively well established in the United Kingdom, so the growth potential there is limited. Holt believes the Thai roller blade market offers more growth potential.

Blades can sell its products at a lower price but generate higher profit margins in Thailand than it can in the United States. This is because the Thai customer has committed itself to purchase a fixed number of Blades' products annually only if it can purchase Speedos at a substantial discount from the U.S. price. Nevertheless, since the cost of goods sold incurred in Thailand is substantially below that incurred in the United States, Blades has managed to generate higher profit margins from its Thai exports and imports than in the United States.

As a financial analyst for Blades, Inc., you generally agree with Ben Holt's assessment of the situation. However, you are concerned that Thai consumers have not been affected yet by the unfavorable economic conditions. You believe that they may reduce their spending on leisure products within the next year. Therefore, you think it would be beneficial to wait until next year, when the unfavorable economic conditions in Thailand may subside, to make a decision regarding DFI in Thailand. However, if economic conditions in Thailand improve over the next year, DFI may become more expensive both because target firms will be more expensive and because the baht may appreciate. You are also aware that several of Blades' U.S. competitors are considering expanding into Thailand in the next year.

If Blades acquires an existing business in Thailand or establishes a subsidiary there by the end of next year, it would fulfill its agreement with Entertainment Products for the subsequent year. The Thai retailer has expressed an interest in renewing the contractual agreement with Blades at that time if Blades establishes operations in Thailand. However, Holt believes that Blades could charge a higher price for its products if it establishes its own distribution channels.

Holt has asked you to answer the following questions:

1. Identify and discuss some of the benefits that Blades, Inc., could obtain from DFI.

2. Do you think Blades should wait until next year to undertake DFI in Thailand? What is the tradeoff if Blades undertakes the DFI now?

3. Do you think Blades should renew its agreement with the Thai retailer for another 3 years? What is the tradeoff if Blades renews the agreement?

4. Assume a high level of unemployment in Thailand and a unique production process employed by Blades, Inc. How do you think the Thai government would view the establishment of a subsidiary in Thailand by firms such as Blades? Do you think the Thai government would be more or less supportive if firms such as Blades acquired existing businesses in Thailand? Why?

SMALL BUSINESS DILEMMA

Direct Foreign Investment Decision by the Sports Exports Company

Jim Logan's business, the Sports Exports Company, continues to grow. His primary product is the footballs he produces and exports to a distributor in the United Kingdom. However, his recent joint venture with a British firm has also been successful. Under this arrangement, a British firm produces other sporting goods for Jim's firm; these goods are then delivered to that distributor. Jim intentionally started his international business by exporting because it was easier and cheaper to export than to establish a place of business in the United Kingdom. However, he is considering establishing a firm in the United Kingdom to produce the footballs there instead of in his garage (in the United States). This firm would also produce the other sporting goods that he now sells, so he would no longer have to rely on another British firm (through the joint venture) to produce those goods.

1. Given the information provided here, what are the advantages to Jim of establishing the firm in the United Kingdom?

2. Given the information provided here, what are the disadvantages to Jim of establishing the firm in the United Kingdom?

INTERNET/EXCEL EXERCISES

IBM has substantial operations in many countries, including the United States, Canada, and Germany. Go to http://finance.yahoo.com/q?s=ibm and click on 1y just below the chart provided.

1. Scroll down and click on Historical Prices. (Or apply this exercise to a different MNC.) Set the date range so that you can obtain quarterly values of the U.S. stock index for the last 20 quarters. Insert the quarterly data on a spreadsheet. Compute the percentage change in IBM's stock price for each quarter. Then go to http://finance.yahoo.com/intlindices?e=americas and click on index GSPC (which represents the U.S. stock market index), so that you can derive the quarterly percentage change in the U.S. stock index over the last 20 quarters. Then run a regression analysis with IBM's quarterly return (percentage change in stock price) as the dependent variable and the quarterly percentage change in the U.S. stock market's value as the independent variable. (Appendix C explains how Excel can be used to run regression analysis.) The slope coefficient serves as an estimate of the sensitivity of IBM's value to the U.S. market returns. Also, check the fit of the relationship based on the R-squared statistic.

2. Go to http://finance.yahoo.com/intlindices?e=europe and click on GDAXI (the German stock market index). Repeat the process so that you can assess IBM's sensitivity to the German stock market. Compare the slope coefficient between the two analyses. Is IBM's value more sensitive to the U.S. market or the German market? Does the U.S. market or the German market explain a higher proportion of the variation in IBM's returns (check the R-squared statistic)? Offer an explanation of your results.

REFERENCES

Harrison, Joan, Jul 2006, Easing Chinese Wariness of Private Equity Investment, *Mergers and Acquisitions*, pp. 22–25.

Jackson, Matt, France Houdard, and Matt Highfield, Jan/Feb 2008, Room to Grow: Business Location, Global Expansion and Resource Deficits, *The Journal of Business Strategy*, pp. 34–39.

Kelley, Eric, and Tracie Woidtke, Sep 2006, Investor Protection and Real Investment by U.S. Multinationals, *Journal of Financial and Quantitative Analysis*, pp. 541–592.

Mataloni, Ray, Nov 2007, Operations of U.S. Multinational Companies in 2005, *Survey of Current Business*, pp. 42–64.

Stulz, Rene M., Aug 2005, The Limits of Financial Globalization, *Journal of Finance,* pp. 1595–1638.

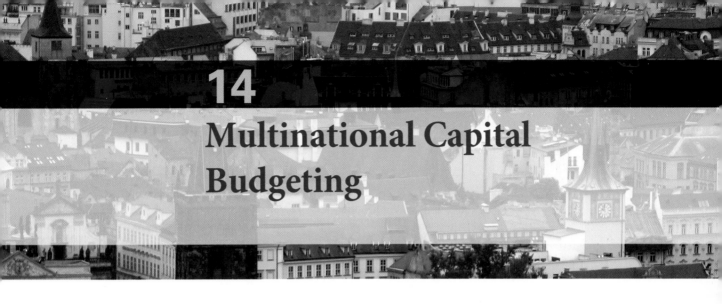

14

Multinational Capital Budgeting

CHAPTER OBJECTIVES

The specific objectives of this chapter are to:

■ compare the capital budgeting analysis of an MNC's subsidiary versus its parent,

■ demonstrate how multinational capital budgeting can be applied to determine whether an international project should be implemented, and

■ explain how the risk of international projects can be assessed.

Multinational corporations (MNCs) evaluate international projects by using multinational capital budgeting, which compares the benefits and costs of these projects. Given that many MNCs spend more than $100 million per year on international projects, multinational capital budgeting is a critical function. Many international projects are irreversible and cannot be easily sold to other corporations at a reasonable price. Proper use of multinational capital budgeting can identify the international projects worthy of implementation.

Special circumstances of international projects that affect the future cash flows or the discount rate used to discount cash flows make multinational capital budgeting more complex. Financial managers must understand how to apply capital budgeting to international projects, so that they can maximize the value of the MNC.

SUBSIDIARY VERSUS PARENT PERSPECTIVE

Normally, MNC decisions should be based on the parent's perspective. Some projects can be feasible for a subsidiary even if they are not feasible for the parent, since net after-tax cash inflows to the subsidiary can differ substantially from those to the parent. Such differences in cash flows between the subsidiary versus parent can be due to several factors, some of which are discussed here.

Tax Differentials

If the earnings due to the project will someday be remitted to the parent, the MNC needs to consider how the parent's government taxes these earnings. If the parent's government imposes a high tax rate on the remitted funds, the project may be feasible from the subsidiary's point of view, but not from the parent's point of view. Under such a scenario, the parent should not consider implementing the project, even though it appears feasible from the subsidiary's perspective.

Restricted Remittances

Consider a potential project to be implemented in a country where government restrictions require that a percentage of the subsidiary earnings remain in the country. Since the parent may never have access to these funds, the project is not attractive to the parent, although it may be attractive to the subsidiary. One possible solution is to let the

WEB

www.kpmg.com
Detailed information on the tax regimes, rates, and regulations of over 75 countries.

subsidiary obtain partial financing for the project within the host country. In this case, the portion of funds not allowed to be sent to the parent can be used to cover the financing costs over time.

Excessive Remittances

Consider a parent that charges its subsidiary very high administrative fees because management is centralized at the headquarters. To the subsidiary, the fees represent an expense. To the parent, the fees represent revenue that may substantially exceed the actual cost of managing the subsidiary. In this case, the project's earnings may appear low from the subsidiary's perspective and high from the parent's perspective. The feasibility of the project again depends on perspective.

Exchange Rate Movements

When earnings are remitted to the parent, they are normally converted from the subsidiary's local currency to the parent's currency. The amount received by the parent is therefore influenced by the existing exchange rate. Therefore, a project that appears to be feasible to the subsidiary may not be feasible to the parent if the subsidiary's currency is expected to weaken over time.

Summary of Factors

Exhibit 14.1 illustrates the process from the time earnings are generated by the subsidiary until the parent receives the remitted funds. The exhibit shows how the cash flows of the subsidiary may be reduced by the time they reach the parent. The subsidiary's earnings are reduced initially by corporate taxes paid to the host government. Then, some of the earnings are retained by the subsidiary (either by the subsidiary's choice or according to the host government's rules), with the residual targeted as funds to be remitted. Those funds that are remitted may be subject to a withholding tax by the host government. The remaining funds are converted to the parent's currency (at the prevailing exchange rate) and remitted to the parent.

Given the various factors shown here that can drain subsidiary earnings, the cash flows actually remitted by the subsidiary may represent only a small portion of the earnings it generates. The feasibility of the project from the parent's perspective is dependent not on the subsidiary's cash flows but on the cash flows that the parent ultimately receives.

The parent's perspective is appropriate in attempting to determine whether a project will enhance the firm's value. Given that the parent's shareholders are its owners, it should make decisions that satisfy its shareholders. Each project, whether foreign or domestic, should ultimately generate sufficient cash flows to the parent to enhance shareholder wealth. Any changes in the parent's expenses should also be included in the analysis. The parent may incur additional expenses for monitoring the new foreign subsidiary's management or consolidating the subsidiary's financial statements. Any project that can create a positive net present value for the parent should enhance shareholder wealth.

One exception to the rule of using a parent's perspective occurs when the foreign subsidiary is not wholly owned by the parent and the foreign project is partially financed with retained earnings of the parent and of the subsidiary. In this case, the foreign subsidiary has a group of shareholders that it must satisfy. Any arrangement made between the parent and the subsidiary should be acceptable to the two entities only if the arrangement enhances the values of both. The goal is to make decisions in the interests of both groups of shareholders and not to transfer wealth from one entity to another.

Exhibit 14.1 Process of Remitting Subsidiary Earnings to the Parent

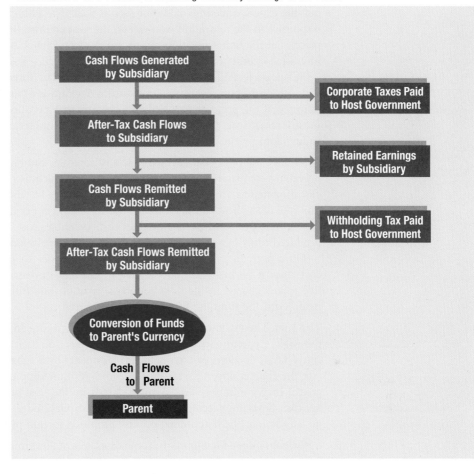

Although this exception occasionally occurs, most foreign subsidiaries of MNCs are wholly owned by the parents. Examples in this text implicitly assume that the subsidiary is wholly owned by the parent (unless noted otherwise) and therefore focus on the parent's perspective.

WEB

http://finance.yahoo
.com/intlindices?u
Information on the re-
cent performance of
country stock indexes.
This is sometimes used
as a general indication
of economic conditions
in various countries
and may be considered
by MNCs that assess
the feasibility of foreign
projects.

INPUT FOR MULTINATIONAL CAPITAL BUDGETING

Regardless of the long-term project to be considered, an MNC will normally require forecasts of the economic and financial characteristics related to the project. Each of these characteristics is briefly described here:

1. *Initial investment.* The parent's initial investment in a project may constitute the major source of funds to support a particular project. Funds initially invested in a project may include not only whatever is necessary to start the project but also additional funds, such as working capital, to support the project over time. Such funds are needed to finance inventory, wages, and other expenses until the project begins to generate revenue. Because cash inflows will not always be sufficient to cover upcoming cash outflows, working capital is needed throughout a project's lifetime.

2. *Price and consumer demand.* The price at which the product could be sold can be forecasted using competitive products in the markets as a comparison. A long-term

capital budgeting analysis requires projections for not only the upcoming period but the expected lifetime of the project as well. The future prices will most likely be responsive to the future inflation rate in the host country (where the project is to take place), but the future inflation rate is not known. Thus, future inflation rates must be forecasted in order to develop projections of the product price over time.

When projecting a cash flow schedule, an accurate forecast of consumer demand for a product is quite valuable, but future demand is often difficult to forecast. For example, if the project is a plant in Germany that produces automobiles, the MNC must forecast what percentage of the auto market in Germany it can pull from prevailing auto producers.

3. *Costs.* Like the price estimate, variable-cost forecasts can be developed from assessing prevailing comparative costs of the components (such as hourly labor costs and the cost of materials). Such costs should normally move in tandem with the future inflation rate of the host country. Even if the variable cost per unit can be accurately predicted, the projected total variable cost (variable cost per unit times quantity produced) may be wrong if the demand is inaccurately forecasted.

On a periodic basis, the fixed cost may be easier to predict than the variable cost since it normally is not sensitive to changes in demand. It is, however, sensitive to any change in the host country's inflation rate from the time the forecast is made until the time the fixed costs are incurred.

4. *Tax laws.* The tax laws on earnings generated by a foreign subsidiary or remitted to the MNC's parent vary among countries. Under some circumstances, the MNC receives tax deductions or credits for tax payments by a subsidiary to the host country (see the chapter appendix for more details). Withholding taxes must also be considered if they are imposed on remitted funds by the host government. Because after-tax cash flows are necessary for an adequate capital budgeting analysis, international tax effects must be determined on any proposed foreign projects.

5. *Restrictions on remitted funds.* In some cases, a host government will prevent a subsidiary from sending its earnings to the parent. This restriction may reflect an attempt to encourage additional local spending or to avoid excessive sales of the local currency in exchange for some other currency. Since the restrictions on fund transfers prevent cash from coming back to the parent, projected net cash flows from the parent's perspective will be affected. If the parent is aware of these restrictions, it can incorporate them when projecting net cash flows. Sometimes, however, the host government adjusts its restrictions over time; in that case, the MNC can only forecast the future restrictions and incorporate these forecasts into the analysis.

6. *Exchange rates.* Any international project will be affected by exchange rate fluctuations during the life of the project, but these movements are often very difficult to forecast. While it is possible to hedge foreign currency cash flows, there is normally much uncertainty surrounding the amount of foreign currency cash flows. Since the MNC can only guess at future costs and revenue due to the project, it may decide not to hedge the projected foreign currency cash flows.

7. *Salvage (liquidation) value.* The after-tax salvage value of most projects is difficult to forecast. It will depend on several factors, including the success of the project and the attitude of the host government toward the project. As an extreme possibility, the host government could take over the project without adequately compensating the MNC.

Some projects have indefinite lifetimes that can be difficult to assess, while other projects have designated specific lifetimes, at the end of which they will be liquidated.

This makes the capital budgeting analysis easier to apply. The MNC does not always have complete control over the lifetime decision. In some cases, political events may force the firm to liquidate the project earlier than planned. The probability that such events will occur varies among countries.

8. *Required rate of return.* Once the relevant cash flows of a proposed project are estimated, they can be discounted at the project's required rate of return, which may differ from the MNC's cost of capital because of that particular project's risk.

   An MNC can estimate its cost of capital in order to decide what return it would require in order to approve proposed projects. The manner by which an MNC determines its cost of capital is discussed in Chapter 17.

WEB

www.weforum.org
Information on global competitiveness and other details of interest to MNCs that implement projects in foreign countries.

Additional considerations will be discussed after a simplified multinational capital budgeting example is provided. In the real world, magic numbers aren't provided to MNCs for insertion into their computers. The challenge revolves around accurately forecasting the variables relevant to the project evaluation. If garbage (inaccurate forecasts) is input into a capital budgeting analysis, the output of an analysis will also be garbage. Consequently, an MNC may take on a project by mistake. Since such a mistake may be worth millions of dollars, MNCs need to assess the degree of uncertainty for any input that is used in the project evaluation. This is discussed more thoroughly later in this chapter.

MULTINATIONAL CAPITAL BUDGETING EXAMPLE

Capital budgeting for the MNC is necessary for all long-term projects that deserve consideration. The projects may range from a small expansion of a subsidiary division to the creation of a new subsidiary. This section presents an example involving the possible development of a new subsidiary. It begins with assumptions that simplify the capital budgeting analysis. Then, additional considerations are introduced to emphasize the potential complexity of such an analysis.

This example illustrates one of many possible methods available that would achieve the same result. Also, keep in mind that a real-world problem may involve more extenuating circumstances than those shown here.

Background

Spartan, Inc., is considering the development of a subsidiary in Singapore that would manufacture and sell tennis rackets locally. Spartan's management has asked various departments to supply relevant information for a capital budgeting analysis. In addition, some Spartan executives have met with government officials in Singapore to discuss the proposed subsidiary. The project would end in 4 years. All relevant information follows.

1. *Initial investment.* An estimated 20 million Singapore dollars (S$), which includes funds to support working capital, would be needed for the project. Given the existing spot rate of $.50 per Singapore dollar, the U.S. dollar amount of the parent's initial investment is $10 million.

2. *Price and demand.* The estimated price and demand schedules during each of the next 4 years are shown here:

	YEAR 1	YEAR 2	YEAR 3	YEAR 4
Price per Racket	S$350	S$350	S$360	S$380
Demand in Singapore	60,000 units	60,000 units	100,000 units	100,000 units

3. *Costs.* The variable costs (for materials, labor, etc.) per unit have been estimated and consolidated as shown here:

	YEAR 1	YEAR 2	YEAR 3	YEAR 4
Variable Costs per Racket	S$200	S$200	S$250	S$260

The expense of leasing extra office space is S$1 million per year. Other annual overhead expenses are expected to be S$1 million per year.

4. *Depreciation.* The Singapore government will allow Spartan's subsidiary to depreciate the cost of the plant and equipment at a maximum rate of S$2 million per year, which is the rate the subsidiary will use.

5. *Taxes.* The Singapore government will impose a 20 percent tax rate on income. In addition, it will impose a 10 percent withholding tax on any funds remitted by the subsidiary to the parent.

The U.S. government will allow a tax credit on taxes paid in Singapore; therefore, earnings remitted to the U.S. parent will not be taxed by the U.S. government.

6. *Remitted funds.* The Spartan subsidiary plans to send all net cash flows received back to the parent firm at the end of each year. The Singapore government promises no restrictions on the cash flows to be sent back to the parent firm but does impose a 10 percent withholding tax on any funds sent to the parent, as mentioned earlier.

7. *Salvage value.* The Singapore government will pay the parent S$12 million to assume ownership of the subsidiary at the end of 4 years. Assume that there is no capital gains tax on the sale of the subsidiary.

8. *Exchange rates.* The spot exchange rate of the Singapore dollar is $.50. Spartan uses the spot rate as its best forecast of the exchange rate that will exist in future periods. Thus, the forecasted exchange rate for all future periods is $.50.

9. *Required rate of return.* Spartan, Inc., requires a 15 percent return on this project.

Analysis

The capital budgeting analysis will be conducted from the parent's perspective, based on the assumption that the subsidiary is intended to generate cash flows that will ultimately be passed on to the parent. Thus, the net present value (*NPV*) from the parent's perspective is based on a comparison of the present value of the cash flows received by the parent to the initial outlay by the parent. As explained earlier in this chapter, an international project's *NPV* is dependent on whether a parent or subsidiary perspective is used. Since the U.S. parent's perspective is used, the cash flows of concern are the dollars ultimately received by the parent as a result of the project.

The required rate of return is based on the cost of capital used by the parent to make its investment, with an adjustment for the risk of the project. For the establishment of the subsidiary to benefit Spartan's parent, the present value of future cash flows (including the salvage value) ultimately received by the parent should exceed the parent's initial outlay.

The capital budgeting analysis to determine whether Spartan, Inc., should establish the subsidiary is provided in Exhibit 14.2 (review this exhibit as you read on). The first step is to incorporate demand and price estimates in order to forecast total revenue (see lines 1 through 3). Then, the expenses are summed up to forecast total expenses (see lines 4 through 9). Next, before-tax earnings are computed (in line 10) by subtracting total

Exhibit 14.2 Capital Budgeting Analysis: Spartan, Inc.

		YEAR 0	YEAR 1	YEAR 2	YEAR 3	YEAR 4
1.	Demand		60,000	60,000	100,000	100,000
2.	Price per unit		S$350	S$350	S$360	S$380
3.	Total revenue = (1) × (2)		S$21,000,000	S$21,000,000	S$36,000,000	S$38,000,000
4.	Variable cost per unit		S$200	S$200	S$250	S$260
5.	Total variable cost = (1) × (4)		S$12,000,000	S$12,000,000	S$25,000,000	S$26,000,000
6.	Annual lease expense		S$1,000,000	S$1,000,000	S$1,000,000	S$1,000,000
7.	Other fixed annual expenses		S$1,000,000	S$1,000,000	S$1,000,000	S$1,000,000
8.	Noncash expense (depreciation)		S$2,000,000	S$2,000,000	S$2,000,000	S$2,000,000
9.	Total expenses = (5) + (6) + (7) + (8)		S$16,000,000	S$16,000,000	S$29,000,000	S$30,000,000
10.	Before-tax earnings of subsidiary = (3) − (9)		S$5,000,000	S$5,000,000	S$7,000,000	S$8,000,000
11.	Host government tax (20%)		S$1,000,000	S$1,000,000	S$1,400,000	S$1,600,000
12.	After-tax earnings of subsidiary		S$4,000,000	S$4,000,000	S$5,600,000	S$6,400,000
13.	Net cash flow to subsidiary = (12) + (8)		S$6,000,000	S$6,000,000	S$7,600,000	S$8,400,000
14.	S$ remitted by subsidiary (100% of net cash flow)		S$6,000,000	S$6,000,000	S$7,600,000	S$8,400,000
15.	Withholding tax on remitted funds (10%)		S$600,000	S$600,000	S$760,000	S$840,000
16.	S$ remitted after withholding taxes		S$5,400,000	S$5,400,000	S$6,840,000	S$7,560,000
17.	Salvage value					S$12,000,000
18.	Exchange rate of S$		$.50	$.50	$.50	$.50
19.	Cash flows to parent		$2,700,000	$2,700,000	$3,420,000	$9,780,000
20.	PV of parent cash flows (15% discount rate)		$2,347,826	$2,041,588	$2,248,706	$5,591,747
21.	Initial investment by parent	$10,000,000				
22.	Cumulative NPV		−$7,652,174	−$5,610,586	−$3,361,880	$2,229,867

expenses from total revenues. Host government taxes (line 11) are then deducted from before-tax earnings to determine after-tax earnings for the subsidiary (line 12).

The depreciation expense is added to the after-tax subsidiary earnings to compute the net cash flow to the subsidiary (line 13). All of these funds are to be remitted by the subsidiary, so line 14 is the same as line 13. The subsidiary can afford to send all net cash flow to the parent since the initial investment provided by the parent includes working capital. The funds remitted to the parent are subject to a 10 percent withholding tax (line 15), so the actual amount of funds to be sent after these taxes is shown in line 16. The salvage value of the project is shown in line 17. The funds to be remitted must first be converted into dollars at the exchange rate (line 18) existing at that time. The parent's cash flow from the subsidiary is shown in line 19. The periodic funds received from the subsidiary are not subject to U.S. corporate taxes since it was assumed that the parent would receive credit for the taxes paid in Singapore that would offset taxes owed to the U.S. government.

Calculation of NPV. Although several capital budgeting techniques are available, a commonly used technique is to estimate the cash flows and salvage value to be received by the parent and compute the *NPV* of the project, as shown here:

$$NPV = -IO + \sum_{t=1}^{n} \frac{CF_t}{(1+k)^t} + \frac{SV_n}{(1+k)^n}$$

where

IO = initial outlay (investment)
CF_t = cash flow in period t
SV_n = salvage value
k = required rate of return on the project
n = lifetime of the project (number of periods)

The net cash flow per period (line 19) is discounted at the required rate of return (15 percent rate in this example) to derive the *present value* (*PV*) of each period's net cash flow (line 20). Finally, the cumulative *NPV* (line 22) is determined by consolidating the discounted cash flows for each period and subtracting the initial investment (in line 21). For example, as of the end of Year 2, the cumulative *NPV* was –$5,610,586. This was determined by consolidating the $2,347,826 in Year 1, the $2,041,588 in Year 2, and subtracting the initial investment of $10,000,000. The cumulative *NPV* in each period measures how much of the initial outlay has been recovered up to that point by the receipt of discounted cash flows. Thus, it can be used to estimate how many periods it will take to recover the initial outlay. For some projects, the cumulative *NPV* remains negative in all periods, which suggests that the discounted cash flows never exceed the initial outlay. That is, the initial outlay is never fully recovered. The critical value in line 22 is the one for the last period because it reflects the *NPV* of the project.

In our example, the cumulative *NPV* as of the end of the last period is $2,229,867 Because the *NPV* is positive, Spartan, Inc., may accept this project if the discount rate of 15 percent has fully accounted for the project's risk. If the analysis has not yet accounted for risk, however, Spartan may decide to reject the project. The way an MNC can account for risk in capital budgeting is discussed shortly.

OTHER FACTORS TO CONSIDER

The example of Spartan, Inc., ignored a variety of factors that may affect the capital budgeting analysis, such as:

- Exchange rate fluctuations
- Inflation
- Financing arrangement
- Blocked funds
- Uncertain salvage value
- Impact of project on prevailing cash flows
- Host government incentives
- Real options

Each of these factors is discussed in turn.

Exchange Rate Fluctuations

Recall that Spartan, Inc., uses the Singapore dollar's current spot rate ($.50) as a forecast for all future periods of concern. The company realizes that the exchange rate will typically change over time, but it does not know whether the Singapore dollar will strengthen or weaken in the future. Though the difficulty in accurately forecasting exchange rates is well known, a multinational capital budgeting analysis could at least incorporate other scenarios for exchange rate movements, such as a pessimistic scenario and an optimistic scenario. From the parent's point of view, appreciation of the Singapore dollar would be favorable since the Singapore dollar inflows would someday be converted to more U.S. dollars. Conversely, depreciation would be unfavorable since the weakened Singapore dollars would convert to fewer U.S. dollars over time.

Exhibit 14.3 illustrates both a weak Singapore dollar (weak-S$) scenario and a strong Singapore dollar (strong-S$) scenario. At the top of the table, the anticipated after-tax Singapore dollar cash flows (including salvage value) are shown for the subsidiary from lines 16 and 17 in Exhibit 14.2. The amount in U.S. dollars that these Singapore dollars convert to depends on the exchange rates existing in the various periods when they are converted. The number of Singapore dollars multiplied by the forecasted exchange rate will determine the estimated number of U.S. dollars received by the parent.

Notice from Exhibit 14.3 how the cash flows received by the parent differ depending on the scenario. A strong Singapore dollar is clearly beneficial, as indicated by the increased U.S. dollar value of the cash flows received. The large differences in cash flows received by the parent in the different scenarios illustrate the impact of exchange rate expectations on the feasibility of an international project.

The *NPV* forecasts based on projections for exchange rates are illustrated in Exhibit 14.4. The estimated *NPV* is highest if the Singapore dollar is expected to strengthen and lowest if it is expected to weaken. The estimated *NPV* is negative for the weak-S$ scenario but positive for the stable-S$ and strong-S$ scenarios. This project's true feasibility would depend on the probability distribution of these three scenarios for the Singapore dollar during the

Exhibit 14.3 Analysis Using Different Exchange Rate Scenarios: Spartan, Inc.

	YEAR 0	YEAR 1	YEAR 2	YEAR 3	YEAR 4
S$ remitted after withholding taxes (including salvage value)		S$5,400,000	S$5,400,000	S$6,840,000	S$19,560,000
Strong-S$ Scenario					
Exchange rate of S$		$.54	$.57	$.61	$.65
Cash flows to parent		$2,916,000	$3,078,000	$4,172,400	$12,714,000
PV of cash flows (15% discount rate)		$2,535,652	$2,327,410	$2,743,421	$7,269,271
Initial investment by parent	$10,000,000				
Cumulative *NPV*		–$7,464,348	–$5,136,938	–$2,393,517	$4,875,754
Weak-S$ Scenario					
Exchange rate of S$		$.47	$.45	$.40	$.37
Cash flows to parent		$2,538,000	$2,430,000	$2,736,000	$7,237,200
PV of cash flows (15% discount rate)		$2,206,957	$1,837,429	$1,798,964	$4,137,893
Initial investment by parent	$10,000,000				
Cumulative *NPV*		–$7,793,043	–$5,955,614	–$4,156,650	–$18,757

Exhibit 14.4 Sensitivity of the Project's *NPV* to Different Exchange Rate Scenarios: Spartan, Inc.

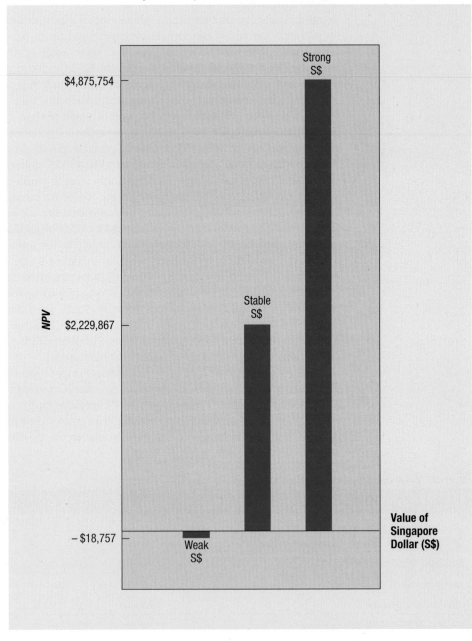

project's lifetime. If there is a high probability that the weak-S$ scenario will occur, this project should not be accepted.

Some U.S.-based MNCs consider projects in countries where the local currency is tied to the dollar. They may conduct a capital budgeting analysis that presumes the exchange rate will remain fixed. It is possible, however, that the local currency will be devalued at some point in the future, which could have a major impact on the cash flows to be received by the parent. Therefore, the MNC may reestimate the project's *NPV* based on a particular devaluation scenario that it believes could possibly occur. If the project is still feasible under this scenario, the MNC may be more comfortable pursuing the project.

Inflation

Capital budgeting analysis implicitly considers inflation since variable cost per unit and product prices generally have been rising over time. In some countries, inflation can be quite volatile from year to year and can therefore strongly influence a project's net cash flows. In countries where the inflation rate is high and volatile, it will be virtually impossible for a subsidiary to accurately forecast inflation each year. Inaccurate inflation forecasts can lead to inaccurate net cash flow forecasts.

Although fluctuations in inflation should affect both costs and revenues in the same direction, the magnitude of their changes may be very different. This is especially true when the project involves importing partially manufactured components and selling the finished product locally. The local economy's inflation will most likely have a stronger impact on revenues than on costs in such cases.

The joint impact of inflation and exchange rate fluctuations on a subsidiary's net cash flows may produce a partial offsetting effect from the viewpoint of the parent. The exchange rates of highly inflated countries tend to weaken over time. Thus, even if subsidiary earnings are inflated, they will be deflated when converted into the parent's home currency (if the subsidiary's currency has weakened). Such an offsetting effect is not exact or consistent, though. Because inflation is only one of many factors that influence exchange rates, there is no guarantee that a currency will depreciate when the local inflation rate is relatively high. Therefore, one cannot ignore the impact of inflation and exchange rates on net cash flows.

Financing Arrangement

Many foreign projects are partially financed by foreign subsidiaries. To illustrate how this foreign financing can influence the feasibility of the project, consider the following revisions in the example of Spartan, Inc.

Subsidiary Financing. Assume that the subsidiary borrows S\$10 million to purchase the offices that are leased in the initial example. Assume that the subsidiary will make interest payments on this loan (of S\$1 million) annually and will pay the principal (S\$10 million) at the end of Year 4, when the project is terminated. Since the Singapore government permits a maximum of S\$2 million per year in depreciation for this project, the subsidiary's depreciation rate will remain unchanged. Assume the offices are expected to be sold for S\$10 million after taxes at the end of Year 4.

Domestic capital budgeting problems would not include debt payments in the measurement of cash flows because all financing costs are captured by the discount rate. Foreign projects are more complicated, however, especially when the foreign subsidiary partially finances the investment in the foreign project. Although consolidating the initial investments made by the parent and the subsidiary simplifies the capital budgeting process, it can cause significant estimation errors. The estimated foreign cash flows that are ultimately remitted to the parent and are subject to exchange rate risk will be overstated if the foreign interest expenses are not explicitly considered as cash outflows for the foreign subsidiary. Thus, a more accurate approach is to separate the investment made by the subsidiary from the investment made by the parent. The capital budgeting analysis can focus on the parent's perspective by comparing the present value of the cash flows received by the parent to the initial investment by the parent.

Given the revised assumptions, the following revisions must be made to the capital budgeting analysis:

1. Since the subsidiary is borrowing funds to purchase the offices, the lease payments of S\$1 million per year will not be necessary. However, the subsidiary will pay interest of S\$1 million per year as a result of the loan. Thus, the annual cash outflows for the subsidiary are still the same.

2. The subsidiary must pay the S$10 million in loan principal at the end of 4 years. However, since the subsidiary expects to receive S$10 million (in 4 years) from the sale of the offices it purchases with the funds provided by the loan, it can use the proceeds of the sale to pay the loan principal.

Since the subsidiary has already taken the maximum depreciation expense allowed by the Singapore government before the offices were considered, it cannot increase its annual depreciation expenses. In this example, the cash flows ultimately received by the parent when the subsidiary obtains financing to purchase offices are similar to the cash flows determined in the original example (when the offices are to be leased). Therefore, the *NPV* under the condition of subsidiary financing is the same as the *NPV* in the original example. If the numbers were not offsetting, the capital budgeting analysis would be repeated to determine whether the *NPV* from the parent's perspective is higher than in the original example.

Parent Financing. Consider one more alternative arrangement, in which, instead of the subsidiary leasing the offices or purchasing them with borrowed funds, the parent uses its own funds to purchase the offices. Thus, its initial investment is $15 million, composed of the original $10 million investment as explained earlier, plus an additional $5 million to obtain an extra S$10 million to purchase the offices. This example illustrates how the capital budgeting analysis changes when the parent takes a bigger stake in the investment. If the parent rather than the subsidiary purchases the offices, the following revisions must be made to the capital budgeting analysis:

1. The subsidiary will not have any loan payments (since it will not need to borrow funds) because the parent will purchase the offices. Since the offices are to be purchased, there will be no lease payments either.

2. The parent's initial investment is $15 million instead of $10 million.

3. The salvage value to be received by the parent is S$22 million instead of S$12 million because the offices are assumed to be sold for S$10 million after taxes at the end of Year 4. The S$10 million to be received from selling the offices can be added to the S$12 million to be received from selling the rest of the subsidiary.

The capital budgeting analysis for Spartan, Inc., under this revised financing strategy in which the parent finances the entire $15 million investment is shown in Exhibit 14.5. This analysis uses our original exchange rate projections of $.50 per Singapore dollar for each period. The numbers that are directly affected by the revised financing arrangement are bracketed. Other numbers are also affected indirectly as a result. For example, the subsidiary's after-tax earnings increase as a result of avoiding interest or lease payments on its offices. The *NPV* of the project under this alternative financing arrangement is positive but less than in the original arrangement. Given the higher initial outlay of the parent and the lower *NPV,* this arrangement is not as feasible as the arrangement in which the subsidiary either leases the offices or purchases them with borrowed funds.

Comparison of Parent versus Subsidiary Financing. One reason that the subsidiary financing is more feasible than complete parent financing is that the financing rate on the loan is lower than the parent's required rate of return on funds provided to the subsidiary. If local loans had a relatively high interest rate, however, the use of local financing would likely not be as attractive.

In general, this revised example shows that the increased investment by the parent increases the parent's exchange rate exposure for the following reasons. First, since the

Exhibit 14.5 Analysis with an Alternative Financing Arrangement: Spartan, Inc.

		YEAR 0	YEAR 1	YEAR 2	YEAR 3	YEAR 4
1.	Demand		60,000	60,000	100,000	100,000
2.	Price per unit		S$350	S$350	S$360	S$380
3.	Total revenue = (1) × (2)		S$21,000,000	S$21,000,000	S$36,000,000	S$38,000,000
4.	Variable cost per unit		S$200	S$200	S$250	S$260
5.	Total variable cost = (1) × (4)		S$12,000,000	S$12,000,000	S$25,000,000	S$26,000,000
6.	Annual lease expense		[S$0]	[S$0]	[S$0]	[S$0]
7.	Other fixed annual expenses		S$1,000,000	S$1,000,000	S$1,000,000	S$1,000,000
8.	Noncash expense (depreciation)		S$2,000,000	S$2,000,000	S$2,000,000	S$2,000,000
9.	Total expenses = (5) + (6) + (7) + (8)		S$15,000,000	S$15,000,000	S$28,000,000	S$29,000,000
10.	Before-tax earnings of subsidiary = (3) − (9)		S$6,000,000	S$6,000,000	S$8,000,000	S$9,000,000
11.	Host government tax (20%)		S$1,200,000	S$1,200,000	S$1,600,000	S$1,800,000
12.	After-tax earnings of subsidiary		S$4,800,000	S$4,800,000	S$6,400,000	S$7,200,000
13.	Net cash flow to subsidiary = (12) + (8)		S$6,800,000	S$6,800,000	S$8,400,000	S$9,200,000
14.	S$ remitted by subsidiary (100% of S$)		S$6,800,000	S$6,800,000	S$8,400,000	S$9,200,000
15.	Withholding tax on remitted funds (10%)		S$680,000	S$680,000	S$840,000	S$920,000
16.	S$ remitted after withholding taxes		S$6,120,000	S$6,120,000	S$7,560,000	S$8,280,000
17.	Salvage value					[S$22,000,000]
18.	Exchange rate of S$		$.50	$.50	$.50	$.50
19.	Cash flows to parent		$3,060,000	$3,060,000	$3,780,000	$15,140,000
20.	PV of parent cash flows (15% discount rate)		$2,660,870	$2,313,800	$2,485,411	$8,656,344
21.	Initial investment by parent	[$15,000,000]				
22.	Cumulative NPV		−$12,339,130	−$10,025,330	−$7,539,919	$1,116,425

parent provides the entire investment, no foreign financing is required. Consequently, the subsidiary makes no interest payments and therefore remits larger cash flows to the parent. Second, the salvage value to be remitted to the parent is larger. Given the larger payments to the parent, the cash flows ultimately received by the parent are more susceptible to exchange rate movements.

The parent's exposure is not as large when the subsidiary purchases the offices because the subsidiary incurs some of the financing expenses. The subsidiary financing essentially shifts some of the expenses to the same currency that the subsidiary will receive and therefore reduces the amount that will ultimately be converted into dollars for remittance to the parent.

Financing with Other Subsidiaries' Retained Earnings. Some foreign projects are completely financed with retained earnings of existing foreign subsidiaries. These projects are difficult to assess from the parent's perspective because their direct effects are normally felt by the subsidiaries. One approach is to view a subsidiary's investment in a project as an opportunity cost, since the funds could be remitted to the parent rather than invested in the foreign project. Thus, the initial outlay from the parent's perspective is the amount of funds it would have received from the subsidiary if the funds had been remitted rather than invested in this project. The cash flows from the parent's perspective reflect those cash flows ultimately received by the parent as a result of the foreign project.

Even if the project generates earnings for the subsidiary that are reinvested by the subsidiary, the key cash flows from the parent's perspective are those that it ultimately receives from the project. In this way, any international factors that will affect the cash flows (such as withholding taxes and exchange rate movements) are incorporated into the capital budgeting process.

Blocked Funds

In some cases, the host country may block funds that the subsidiary attempts to send to the parent. Some countries require that earnings generated by the subsidiary be reinvested locally for at least 3 years before they can be remitted. Such restrictions can affect the accept/reject decision on a project.

EXAMPLE

Reconsider the example of Spartan, Inc., assuming that all funds are blocked until the subsidiary is sold. Thus, the subsidiary must reinvest those funds until that time. Blocked funds penalize a project if the return on the reinvested funds is less than the required rate of return on the project.

Assume that the subsidiary uses the funds to purchase marketable securities that are expected to yield 5 percent annually after taxes. A reevaluation of Spartan's cash flows (from Exhibit 14.2) to incorporate the blocked-funds restriction is shown in Exhibit 14.6. The withholding tax is not applied until the funds are remitted to the parent, which is in Year 4. The original exchange rate

Exhibit 14.6 Capital Budgeting with Blocked Funds: Spartan, Inc.

	YEAR 0	YEAR 1	YEAR 2	YEAR 3	YEAR 4
S$ to be remitted by subsidiary		S$6,000,000	S$6,000,000	S$7,600,000	S$8,400,000
					S$7,980,000
S$ accumulated by reinvesting funds to be remitted					S$6,615,000
					S$6,945,750
					S$29,940,750
Withholding tax (10%)					S$2,994,075
S$ remitted after withholding tax					S$26,946,675
Salvage value					S$12,000,000
Exchange rate					$.50
Cash flows to parent					$19,473,338
PV of parent cash flows (15% discount rate)					$11,133,944
Initial investment by parent	$10,000,000				
Cumulative NPV		−$10,000,000	−$10,000,000	−$10,000,000	$1,133,944

projections are used here. All parent cash flows depend on the exchange rate 4 years from now. The *NPV* of the project with blocked funds is still positive, but it is substantially less than the *NPV* in the original example.

If the foreign subsidiary has a loan outstanding, it may be able to better utilize the blocked funds by repaying the local loan. For example, the S$6 million at the end of Year 1 could be used to reduce the outstanding loan balance instead of being invested in marketable securities, assuming that the lending bank allows early repayment. ●

There may be other situations that deserve to be considered in multinational capital budgeting, such as political conditions in the host country and restrictions that may be imposed by a country's host government. These country risk characteristics are discussed in more detail in Chapter 16.

Uncertain Salvage Value

The salvage value of an MNC's project typically has a significant impact on the project's *NPV*. When the salvage value is uncertain, the MNC may incorporate various possible outcomes for the salvage value and reestimate the *NPV* based on each possible outcome. It may even estimate the break-even salvage value (also called break-even terminal value), which is the salvage value necessary to achieve a zero *NPV* for the project. If the actual salvage value is expected to equal or exceed the break-even salvage value, the project is feasible. The break-even salvage value (called SV_n) can be determined by setting *NPV* equal to zero and rearranging the capital budgeting equation, as follows:

$$NPV = -IO + \sum_{t=1}^{n} \frac{CF_t}{(1+k)^t} + \frac{SV_n}{(1+k)^n}$$

$$0 = -IO + \sum_{t=1}^{n} \frac{CF_t}{(1+k)^t} + \frac{SV_n}{(1+k)^n}$$

$$IO - \sum_{t=1}^{n} \frac{CF_t}{(1+k)^t} = \frac{SV_n}{(1+k)^n}$$

$$\left[IO - \sum_{t=1}^{n} \frac{CF_t}{(1+k)^t} \right] (1+k)^n = SV_n$$

EXAMPLE

Reconsider the Spartan, Inc., example and assume that Spartan is not guaranteed a price for the project. The break-even salvage value for the project can be determined by (1) estimating the present value of future cash flows (excluding the salvage value), (2) subtracting the discounted cash flows from the initial outlay, and (3) multiplying the difference times $(1 + k)^n$. Using the original cash flow information from Exhibit 14.2, the present value of cash flows can be determined:

PV of parent cash flows

$$= \frac{\$2,700,000}{(1.15)^1} + \frac{\$2,700,000}{(1.15)^2} + \frac{\$3,420,000}{(1.15)^3} + \frac{\$3,780,000}{(1.15)^4}$$

$$= \$2,347,826 + \$2,041,588 + \$2,248,706 + \$2,161,227$$

$$= \$8,799,347$$

Given the present value of cash flows and the estimated initial outlay, the break-even salvage value is determined this way:

$$SV_n = \left[IO - \sum \frac{CF_t}{(1+k)^t} \right] (1+k)^n$$

$$= (\$10,000,000 - \$8,799,347)(1.15)^4$$

$$= \$2,099,950$$

Given the original information in Exhibit 14.2, Spartan, Inc., will accept the project only if the salvage value is estimated to be at least $2,099,950 (assuming that the project's required rate of return is 15 percent).

Assuming the forecasted exchange rate of $.50 per Singapore dollar (2 Singapore dollars per U.S. dollar), the project must sell for more than S$4,199,900 (computed as $2,099,950 divided by $.50) to exhibit a positive *NPV* (assuming no taxes are paid on this amount). If Spartan did not have a guarantee from the Singapore government, it could assess the probability that the subsidiary would sell for more than the break-even salvage value and then incorporate this assessment into its decision to accept or reject the project. ●

Impact of Project on Prevailing Cash Flows

Thus far, in our example, we have assumed that the new project has no impact on prevailing cash flows. In reality, however, there may often be an impact.

EXAMPLE

Reconsider the Spartan, Inc., example, assuming this time that (1) Spartan currently exports tennis rackets from its U.S. plant to Singapore; (2) Spartan, Inc., still considers establishing a subsidiary in Singapore because it expects production costs to be lower in Singapore than in the United States; and (3) without a subsidiary, Spartan's export business to Singapore is expected to generate net cash flows of $1 million over the next 4 years. With a subsidiary, these cash flows would be forgone. The effects of these assumptions are shown in Exhibit 14.7. The previously estimated cash flows to the parent from the subsidiary (drawn from Exhibit 14.2) are restated in Exhibit 14.7. These estimates do not account for forgone cash flows since the possible export business was not considered. If the export business is established, however, the forgone cash flows attributable to this business must be considered, as shown in Exhibit 14.7. The adjusted cash flows to the parent account for the project's impact on prevailing cash flows.

The present value of adjusted cash flows and cumulative *NPV* are also shown in Exhibit 14.7. The project's *NPV* is now negative as a result of the adverse effect on prevailing cash flows. Thus, the project will not be feasible if the exporting business to Singapore is eliminated. ●

Some foreign projects may have a favorable impact on prevailing cash flows. For example, if a manufacturer of computer components establishes a foreign subsidiary to manufacture computers, the subsidiary might order the components from the parent. In this case, the sales volume of the parent would increase.

Host Government Incentives

Foreign projects proposed by MNCs may have a favorable impact on economic conditions in the host country and are therefore encouraged by the host government. Any incentives offered by the host government must be incorporated into the capital budgeting

Exhibit 14.7 Capital Budgeting When Prevailing Cash Flows Are Affected: Spartan, Inc.

	YEAR 0	YEAR 1	YEAR 2	YEAR 3	YEAR 4
Cash flows to parent, ignoring impact on prevailing cash flows		$2,700,000	$2,700,000	$3,420,000	$9,780,000
Impact of project on prevailing cash flows		−$1,000,000	−$1,000,000	−$1,000,000	−$1,000,000
Cash flows to parent, incorporating impact on prevailing cash flows		$1,700,000	$1,700,000	$2,420,000	$8,780,000
PV of cash flows to parent (15% discount rate)		$1,478,261	$1,285,444	$1,591,189	$5,019,994
Initial investment	$10,000,000				
Cumulative *NPV*		−$8,521,739	−$7,236,295	−$5,645,106	−$625,112

analysis. For example, a low-rate host government loan or a reduced tax rate offered to the subsidiary will enhance periodic cash flows. If the government subsidizes the initial establishment of the subsidiary, the MNC's initial investment will be reduced.

Real Options

A real option is an option on specified real assets such as machinery or a facility. Some capital budgeting projects contain real options in that they may allow opportunities to obtain or eliminate real assets. Since these opportunities can generate cash flows, they can enhance the value of a project.

EXAMPLE

Reconsider the Spartan example and assume that the government in Singapore promised that if Spartan established the subsidiary to produce tennis rackets in Singapore, it would be allowed to purchase some government buildings at a future point in time at a discounted price. This offer does not directly affect the cash flows of the project that is presently being assessed, but it reflects an implicit call option that Spartan could exercise in the future. In some cases, real options can be very valuable and may encourage MNCs to accept a project that they would have rejected without the real option. ●

The value of a real option within a project is primarily influenced by two factors: (1) the probability that the real option will be exercised and (2) the *NPV* that will result from exercising the real option. In the previous example, Spartan's real option is influenced by (1) the probability that Spartan will capitalize on the opportunity to purchase government buildings at a discount, and (2) the *NPV* that would be generated from this opportunity.

ADJUSTING PROJECT ASSESSMENT FOR RISK

If an MNC is unsure of the estimated cash flows of a proposed project, it needs to incorporate an adjustment for this risk. Three methods are commonly used to adjust the evaluation for risk:

- Risk-adjusted discount rate
- Sensitivity analysis
- Simulation

Each method is described in turn.

Risk-Adjusted Discount Rate

The greater the uncertainty about a project's forecasted cash flows, the larger should be the discount rate applied to cash flows, other things being equal. This risk-adjusted discount rate tends to reduce the worth of a project by a degree that reflects the risk the project exhibits. This approach is easy to use, but it is criticized for being somewhat arbitrary. In addition, an equal adjustment to the discount rate over all periods does not reflect differences in the degree of uncertainty from one period to another. If the projected cash flows among periods have different degrees of uncertainty, the risk adjustment of the cash flows should vary also.

Consider a country where the political situation is slowly destabilizing. The probability of blocked funds, expropriation, and other adverse events is increasing over time. Thus, cash flows sent to the parent are less certain in the distant future than they are in the near future. A different discount rate should therefore be applied to each period in accordance with its corresponding risk. Even so, the adjustment will be subjective and may not accurately reflect the risk.

Despite its subjectivity, the risk-adjusted discount rate is a commonly used technique, perhaps because of the ease with which it can be arbitrarily adjusted. In addition, there is no alternative technique that will perfectly adjust for risk, although in certain cases some others (discussed next) may better reflect a project's risk.

Sensitivity Analysis

Once the MNC has estimated the *NPV* of a proposed project, it may want to consider alternative estimates for its input variables.

EXAMPLE Recall that the demand for the Spartan subsidiary's tennis rackets (in our earlier example) was estimated to be 60,000 in the first 2 years and 100,000 in the next 2 years. If demand turns out to be 60,000 in all 4 years, how will the *NPV* results change? Alternatively, what if demand is 100,000 in all 4 years? Use of such *what-if* scenarios is referred to as **sensitivity analysis**. The objective is to determine how sensitive the *NPV* is to alternative values of the input variables. The estimates of any input variables can be revised to create new estimates for *NPV*. If the *NPV* is consistently positive during these revisions, then the MNC should feel more comfortable about the project. If it is negative in many cases, the accept/reject decision for the project becomes more difficult. ●

The two exchange rate scenarios developed earlier represent a form of sensitivity analysis. Sensitivity analysis can be more useful than simple point estimates because it reassesses the project based on various circumstances that may occur. Many computer software packages are available to perform sensitivity analysis.

GOVERNANCE ## *Managerial Controls over the Use of Sensitivity Analysis*

When managers conduct sensitivity analyses, they may be tempted to exaggerate their estimates of cash inflows in order to ensure that their projects are approved, especially if they are rewarded for the growth of their department. Proper governance can prevent this type of agency problem. First, the estimates of cash flows should be thoroughly examined by the board or by managers outside of the department that wants to implement the project. Second, a project's feasibility can be assessed after it has been implemented to determine whether the estimated cash flows by managers were reasonably accurate. However, many international projects are irreversible, so an ideal control system would assess the proposal closely before investing the funds in the project.

Simulation

Simulation can be used for a variety of tasks, including the generation of a probability distribution for *NPV* based on a range of possible values for one or more input variables. Simulation is typically performed with the aid of a computer package.

EXAMPLE Reconsider Spartan, Inc., and assume that it expects the exchange rate to depreciate by 3 to 7 percent per year (with an equal probability of all values in this range occurring). Unlike a single point estimate, simulation can consider the range of possibilities for the Singapore dollar's exchange rate at the end of each year. It considers all point estimates for the other variables and randomly picks one of the possible values of the Singapore dollar's depreciation level for each of the 4 years. Based on this random selection process, the *NPV* is determined.

The procedure just described represents one iteration. Then the process is repeated: The Singapore dollar's depreciation for each year is again randomly selected (within the range of possibilities assumed earlier), and the *NPV* of the project is computed. The simulation program may be run for, say, 100 iterations. This means that 100 different possible scenarios are created for the possible exchange rates of the Singapore dollar during the 4-year project period. Each iteration reflects a different scenario. The *NPV* of the project based on each scenario is then computed. Thus, simulation generates a distribution of *NPVs* for the project. The major advantage of simulation is that the MNC can examine the range of possible *NPVs* that may occur. From the information, it can determine the probability that the *NPV* will be positive or greater than a particular level. The greater the uncertainty of the exchange rate, the greater will be the uncertainty of the *NPV*. The risk of a project will be greater if it involves transactions in more volatile currencies, other things being equal. ●

In reality, many or all of the input variables necessary for multinational capital budgeting may be uncertain in the future. Probability distributions can be developed for all variables with uncertain future values. The final result is a distribution of possible *NPVs* that might occur for the project. The simulation technique does not put all of its emphasis on any one particular *NPV* forecast but instead provides a distribution of the possible outcomes that may occur.

The project's cost of capital can be used as a discount rate when simulation is performed. The probability that the project will be successful can be estimated by measuring the area within the probability distribution in which the $NPV > 0$. This area represents the probability that the present value of future cash flows will exceed the initial outlay. An MNC can also use the probability distribution to estimate the probability that the project will backfire by measuring the area in which $NPV < 0$.

Simulation is difficult to do manually because of the iterations necessary to develop a distribution of *NPVs*. Computer programs can run 100 iterations and generate results within a matter of seconds. The user of a simulation program must provide the probability distributions for the input variables that will affect the project's *NPV*. As with any model, the accuracy of results generated by simulation will be dependent on the accuracy of the input.

SUMMARY

- Capital budgeting may generate different results and a different conclusion depending on whether it is conducted from the perspective of an MNC's subsidiary or from the perspective of the MNC's parent. The subsidiary's perspective does not consider possible exchange rate and tax effects on cash flows transferred by the subsidiary to the parent. When a parent is deciding whether to implement an international project, it should determine whether the project is feasible from its own perspective.

- Multinational capital budgeting requires any input that will help estimate the initial outlay, periodic cash flows, salvage value, and required rate of return on the project. Once these factors are estimated, the international project's net present value can be estimated, just as if it were a domestic project. However, it is normally more difficult to estimate these factors for an international project.

- Exchange rates create an additional source of uncertainty because they affect the cash flows ultimately received by the parent as a result of the project. Other international conditions that can influence the cash flows ultimately received by the parent include the financing arrangement (parent versus subsidiary financing of the project), blocked funds by the host government, and host government incentives.

- The risk of international projects can be accounted for by adjusting the discount rate used to estimate the project's net present value. However, the adjustment to the discount rate is subjective. An alternative method is to estimate the net present value based on various possible scenarios for exchange rates or any other uncertain factors. This method is facilitated by the use of sensitivity analysis or simulation.

POINT COUNTER-POINT

Should MNCs Use Forward Rates to Estimate Dollar Cash Flows of Foreign Projects?

Point Yes. An MNC's parent should use the forward rate for each year in which it will receive net cash flows in a foreign currency. The forward rate is market determined and serves as a useful forecast for future years.

Counter-Point No. An MNC should use its own forecasts for each year in which it will receive net cash flows in a foreign currency. If the forward rates for future time periods are higher than the MNC's expected spot rates, the MNC may accept a project that it should not accept.

Who Is Correct? Use the Internet to learn more about this issue. Which argument do you support? Offer your own opinion on this issue.

SELF-TEST

Answers are provided in Appendix A at the back of the text.

1. Two managers of Marshall, Inc., assessed a proposed project in Jamaica. Each manager used exactly the same estimates of the earnings to be generated by the project, as these estimates were provided by other employees. The managers agree on the proportion of funds to be remitted each year, the life of the project, and the discount rate to be applied. Both managers also assessed the project from the U.S. parent's perspective. Nevertheless, one manager determined that this project had a large net present value, while the other manager determined that the project had a negative net present value. Explain the possible reasons for such a difference.

2. Pinpoint the parts of a multinational capital budgeting analysis for a proposed sales distribution center in Ireland that are sensitive when the forecast of a stable economy in Ireland is revised to predict a recession.

3. New Orleans Exporting Co. produces small computer components, which are then sold to Mexico. It plans to expand by establishing a plant in Mexico that will produce the components and sell them locally. This plant will reduce the amount of goods that are transported from New Orleans. The firm has determined that the cash flows to be earned in Mexico would yield a positive net present value after accounting for tax and exchange rate effects, converting cash flows to dollars, and discounting them at the proper discount rate. What other major factor must be considered to estimate the project's *NPV*?

4. Explain how the present value of the salvage value of an Indonesian subsidiary will be affected (from the U.S. parent's perspective) by (a) an increase in the risk of the foreign subsidiary and (b) an expectation that Indonesia's currency (rupiah) will depreciate against the dollar over time.

5. Wilmette Co. and Niles Co. (both from the United States) are assessing the acquisition of the same firm in Thailand and have obtained the future cash flow estimates (in Thailand's currency, baht) from the firm. Wilmette would use its retained earnings from U.S. operations to acquire the subsidiary. Niles Co. would finance the acquisition mostly with a term loan (in baht) from Thai banks. Neither firm has any other business in Thailand. Which firm's dollar cash flows would be affected more by future changes in the value of the baht (assuming that the Thai firm is acquired)?

6. Review the capital budgeting example of Spartan, Inc., discussed in this chapter. Identify the specific variables assessed in the process of estimating a foreign project's net present value (from a U.S. perspective) that would cause the most uncertainty about the *NPV*.

QUESTIONS AND APPLICATIONS

1.   MNC Parent's Perspective. Why should capital budgeting for subsidiary projects be assessed from the parent's perspective? What additional factors that normally are not relevant for a purely domestic project deserve consideration in multinational capital budgeting?

2. Accounting for Risk. What is the limitation of using point estimates of exchange rates in the capital budgeting analysis?

List the various techniques for adjusting risk in multinational capital budgeting. Describe any advantages or disadvantages of each technique.

Explain how simulation can be used in multinational capital budgeting. What can it do that other risk adjustment techniques cannot?

3. Uncertainty of Cash Flows. Using the capital budgeting framework discussed in this chapter, explain the sources of uncertainty surrounding a proposed project in Hungary by a U.S. firm. In what ways is the estimated net present value of this project more uncertain than that of a similar project in a more developed European country?

4. Accounting for Risk. Your employees have estimated the net present value of project X to be $1.2 million. Their report says that they have not accounted for risk, but that with such a large *NPV*, the project should be accepted since even a risk-adjusted *NPV* would likely be positive. You have the final decision as to whether to accept or reject the project. What is your decision?

5. Impact of Exchange Rates on *NPV*.

a. Describe in general terms how future appreciation of the euro will likely affect the value (from the parent's perspective) of a project established in Germany today by a U.S.-based MNC. Will the sensitivity of the project value be affected by the percentage of earnings remitted to the parent each year?

b. Repeat this question, but assume the future depreciation of the euro.

6. Impact of Financing on *NPV*. Explain how the financing decision can influence the sensitivity of the net present value to exchange rate forecasts.

7. September 11 Effects on *NPV*. In August 2001, Woodsen, Inc., of Pittsburgh, Pennsylvania, considered the development of a large subsidiary in Greece. In response to the September 11, 2001, terrorist attack on the United States, its expected cash flows and earnings from this acquisition were reduced only slightly. Yet, the firm decided to retract its offer because of an increase in its required rate of return on the project, which caused the *NPV* to be negative. Explain why the required rate of return on its project may have increased after the attack.

8. Assessing a Foreign Project. Huskie Industries, a U.S.-based MNC, considers purchasing a small

manufacturing company in France that sells products only within France. Huskie has no other existing business in France and no cash flows in euros. Would the proposed acquisition likely be more feasible if the euro is expected to appreciate or depreciate over the long run? Explain.

9. Relevant Cash Flows in Disney's French Theme Park. When Walt Disney World considered establishing a theme park in France, were the forecasted revenues and costs associated with the French park sufficient to assess the feasibility of this project? Were there any other "relevant cash flows" that deserved to be considered?

10. Capital Budgeting Logic. Athens, Inc., established a subsidiary in the United Kingdom that was independent of its operations in the United States. The subsidiary's performance was well above what was expected. Consequently, when a British firm approached Athens about the possibility of acquiring the subsidiary, Athens' chief financial officer implied that the subsidiary was performing so well that it was not for sale. Comment on this strategy.

11. Capital Budgeting Logic. Lehigh Co. established a subsidiary in Switzerland that was performing below the cash flow projections developed before the subsidiary was established. Lehigh anticipated that future cash flows would also be lower than the original cash flow projections. Consequently, Lehigh decided to inform several potential acquiring firms of its plan to sell the subsidiary. Lehigh then received a few bids. Even the highest bid was very low, but Lehigh accepted the offer. It justified its decision by stating that any existing project whose cash flows are not sufficient to recover the initial investment should be divested. Comment on this statement.

12. Impact of Reinvested Foreign Earnings on *NPV*. Flagstaff Corp. is a U.S.-based firm with a subsidiary in Mexico. It plans to reinvest its earnings in Mexican government securities for the next 10 years since the interest rate earned on these securities is so high. Then, after 10 years, it will remit all accumulated earnings to the United States. What is a drawback of using this approach? (Assume the securities have no default or interest rate risk.)

13. Capital Budgeting Example. Brower, Inc., just constructed a manufacturing plant in Ghana. The construction cost 9 billion Ghanian cedi. Brower intends to leave the plant open for 3 years. During the 3 years of operation, cedi cash flows are expected to be

3 billion cedi, 3 billion cedi, and 2 billion cedi, respectively. Operating cash flows will begin one year from today and are remitted back to the parent at the end of each year. At the end of the third year, Brower expects to sell the plant for 5 billion cedi. Brower has a required rate of return of 17 percent. It currently takes 8,700 cedi to buy 1 U.S. dollar, and the cedi is expected to depreciate by 5 percent per year.

a. Determine the *NPV* for this project. Should Brower build the plant?

b. How would your answer change if the value of the cedi was expected to remain unchanged from its current value of 8,700 cedi per U.S. dollar over the course of the 3 years? Should Brower construct the plant then?

14. Impact of Financing on *NPV.* Ventura Corp., a U.S.-based MNC, plans to establish a subsidiary in Japan. It is very confident that the Japanese yen will appreciate against the dollar over time. The subsidiary will retain only enough revenue to cover expenses and will remit the rest to the parent each year. Will Ventura benefit more from exchange rate effects if its parent provides equity financing for the subsidiary or if the subsidiary is financed by local banks in Japan? Explain.

15. Accounting for Changes in Risk. Santa Monica Co., a U.S.-based MNC, was considering establishing a consumer products division in Germany, which would be financed by German banks. Santa Monica completed its capital budgeting analysis in August. Then, in November, the government leadership stabilized and political conditions improved in Germany. In response, Santa Monica increased its expected cash flows by 20 percent but did not adjust the discount rate applied to the project. Should the discount rate be affected by the change in political conditions?

16. Estimating the *NPV.* Assume that a less developed country called LDC encourages direct foreign investment (DFI) in order to reduce its unemployment rate, currently at 15 percent. Also assume that several MNCs are likely to consider DFI in this country. The inflation rate in recent years has averaged 4 percent. The hourly wage in LDC for manufacturing work is the equivalent of about $5 per hour. When Piedmont Co. develops cash flow forecasts to perform a capital budgeting analysis for a project in LDC, it assumes a wage rate of $5 in Year 1 and applies a 4 percent increase for each of the next 10 years. The components produced are to be exported to Piedmont's headquarters in the United States, where they will be used in the production of computers. Do you think Piedmont will over-

estimate or underestimate the net present value of this project? Why? (Assume that LDC's currency is tied to the dollar and will remain that way.)

17. PepsiCo's Project in Brazil. PepsiCo recently decided to invest more than $300 million for expansion in Brazil. Brazil offers considerable potential because it has 150 million people and their demand for soft drinks is increasing. However, the soft drink consumption is still only about one-fifth of the soft drink consumption in the United States. PepsiCo's initial outlay was used to purchase three production plants and a distribution network of almost 1,000 trucks to distribute its products to retail stores in Brazil. The expansion in Brazil was expected to make PepsiCo's products more accessible to Brazilian consumers.

a. Given that PepsiCo's investment in Brazil was entirely in dollars, describe its exposure to exchange rate risk resulting from the project. Explain how the size of the parent's initial investment and the exchange rate risk would have been affected if PepsiCo had financed much of the investment with loans from banks in Brazil.

b. Describe the factors that PepsiCo likely considered when estimating the future cash flows of the project in Brazil.

c. What factors did PepsiCo likely consider in deriving its required rate of return on the project in Brazil?

d. Describe the uncertainty that surrounds the estimate of future cash flows from the perspective of the U.S. parent.

e. PepsiCo's parent was responsible for assessing the expansion in Brazil. Yet, PepsiCo already had some existing operations in Brazil. When capital budgeting analysis was used to determine the feasibility of this project, should the project have been assessed from a Brazilian perspective or a U.S. perspective? Explain.

18. Impact of Asian Crisis. Assume that Fordham Co. was evaluating a project in Thailand (to be financed with U.S. dollars). All cash flows generated from the project were to be reinvested in Thailand for several years. Explain how the Asian crisis would have affected the expected cash flows of this project and the required rate of return on this project. If the cash flows were to be remitted to the U.S. parent, explain how the Asian crisis would have affected the expected cash flows of this project.

19. Tax Effects on *NPV.* When considering the implementation of a project in one of various possible countries, what types of tax characteristics should be assessed among the countries? (See the chapter appendix.)

20. Capital Budgeting Analysis. A project in South Korea requires an initial investment of 2 billion South Korean won. The project is expected to generate net cash flows to the subsidiary of 3 billion and 4 billion won in the 2 years of operation, respectively. The project has no salvage value. The current value of the won is 1,100 won per U.S. dollar, and the value of the won is expected to remain constant over the next 2 years.

a. What is the *NPV* of this project if the required rate of return is 13 percent?

b. Repeat the question, except assume that the value of the won is expected to be 1,200 won per U.S. dollar after 2 years. Further assume that the funds are blocked and that the parent company will only be able to remit them back to the United States in 2 years. How does this affect the *NPV* of the project?

21. Accounting for Exchange Rate Risk. Carson Co. is considering a 10-year project in Hong Kong, where the Hong Kong dollar is tied to the U.S. dollar. Carson Co. uses sensitivity analysis that allows for alternative exchange rate scenarios. Why would Carson use this approach rather than using the pegged exchange rate as its exchange rate forecast in every year?

22. Decisions Based on Capital Budgeting. Marathon, Inc., considers a 1-year project with the Belgian government. Its euro revenue would be guaranteed. Its consultant states that the percentage change in the euro is represented by a normal distribution and that based on a 95 percent confidence interval, the percentage change in the euro is expected to be between 0 and 6 percent. Marathon uses this information to create three scenarios: 0, 3, and 6 percent for the euro. It derives an estimated *NPV* based on each scenario and then determines the mean *NPV*. The *NPV* was positive for the 3 and 6 percent scenarios, but was slightly negative for the 0 percent scenario. This led Marathon to reject the project. Its manager stated that it did not want to pursue a project that had a one-in-three chance of having a negative *NPV*. Do you agree with the manager's interpretation of the analysis? Explain.

23. Estimating Cash Flows of a Foreign Project. Assume that Nike decides to build a shoe factory in Brazil; half the initial outlay will be funded by the parent's equity and half by borrowing funds in Brazil. Assume that Nike wants to assess the project from its own perspective to determine whether the project's future cash flows will provide a sufficient return to the parent to warrant the initial investment. Why will the estimated cash flows be different from the estimated cash flows of Nike's shoe factory in New Hampshire? Why will the initial outlay be different? Explain how Nike can conduct multinational capital budgeting in a manner that will achieve its objective.

Advanced Questions

24. Break-even Salvage Value. A project in Malaysia costs $4 million. Over the next 3 years, the project will generate total operating cash flows of $3.5 million, measured in today's dollars using a required rate of return of 14 percent. What is the break-even salvage value of this project?

25. Capital Budgeting Analysis. Zistine Co. considers a 1-year project in New Zealand so that it can capitalize on its technology. It is risk averse but is attracted to the project because of a government guarantee. The project will generate a guaranteed NZ$8 million in revenue, paid by the New Zealand government at the end of the year. The payment by the New Zealand government is also guaranteed by a credible U.S. bank. The cash flows earned on the project will be converted to U.S. dollars and remitted to the parent in 1 year. The prevailing nominal 1-year interest rate in New Zealand is 5 percent, while the nominal 1-year interest rate in the United States is 9 percent. Zistine's chief executive officer believes that the movement in the New Zealand dollar is highly uncertain over the next year, but his best guess is that the change in its value will be in accordance with the international Fisher effect (IFE). He also believes that interest rate parity holds. He provides this information to three recent finance graduates that he just hired as managers and asks them for their input.

a. The first manager states that due to the parity conditions, the feasibility of the project will be the same whether the cash flows are hedged with a forward contract or are not hedged. Is this manager correct? Explain.

b. The second manager states that the project should not be hedged. Based on the interest rates, the IFE suggests that Zistine Co. will benefit from the future exchange rate movements, so the project will generate a higher *NPV* if Zistine does not hedge. Is this manager correct? Explain.

c. The third manager states that the project should be hedged because the forward rate contains a premium and, therefore, the forward rate will generate more U.S. dollar cash flows than the expected amount of dollar cash flows if the firm remains unhedged. Is this manager correct? Explain.

26.   Accounting for Uncertain Cash Flows. Blustream, Inc., considers a project in which it will sell the use of its technology to firms in Mexico. It already has received orders from Mexican firms that will generate MXP3 million in revenue at the end of the next year. However, it might also receive a contract to provide this technology to the Mexican government. In this case, it will generate a total of MXP5 million at the end of the next year. It will not know whether it will receive the government order until the end of the year.

Today's spot rate of the peso is $.14. The 1-year forward rate is $.12. Blustream expects that the spot rate of the peso will be $.13 1 year from now. The only initial outlay will be $300,000 to cover development expenses (regardless of whether the Mexican government purchases the technology). Blustream will pursue the project only if it can satisfy its required rate of return of 18 percent. Ignore possible tax effects. It decides to hedge the maximum amount of revenue that it will receive from the project.

a.   Determine the NPV if Blustream receives the government contract.

b.   If Blustream does not receive the contract, it will have hedged more than it needed to and will offset the excess forward sales by purchasing pesos in the spot market at the time the forward sale is executed. Determine the NPV of the project assuming that Blustream does not receive the government contract.

c.   Now consider an alternative strategy in which Blustream only hedges the minimum peso revenue that it will receive. In this case, any revenue due to the government contract would not be hedged. Determine the NPV based on this alternative strategy and assume that Blustream receives the government contract.

d.   If Blustream uses the alternative strategy of only hedging the minimum peso revenue that it will receive, determine the NPV assuming that it does not receive the government contract.

e.   If there is a 50 percent chance that Blustream will receive the government contract, would you advise Blustream to hedge the maximum amount or the minimum amount of revenue that it may receive? Explain.

f.   Blustream recognizes that it is exposed to exchange rate risk whether it hedges the minimum amount or the maximum amount of revenue it will receive. It considers a new strategy of hedging the minimum amount it will receive with a forward contract and hedging the additional revenue it might receive with a put option on Mexican pesos. The 1-year put option has an exercise price of $.125 and a premium of $.01. Determine the NPV if Blustream uses this strategy and receives the government contract. Also, determine the NPV if Blustream uses this strategy and does not receive the government contract. Given that there is a 50 percent probability that Blustream will receive the government contract, would you use this new strategy or the strategy that you selected in question (e)?

27.   Capital Budgeting Analysis. Wolverine Corp. currently has no existing business in New Zealand but is considering establishing a subsidiary there. The following information has been gathered to assess this project:

- The initial investment required is $50 million in New Zealand dollars (NZ$). Given the existing spot rate of $.50 per New Zealand dollar, the initial investment in U.S. dollars is $25 million. In addition to the NZ$50 million initial investment for plant and equipment, NZ$20 million is needed for working capital and will be borrowed by the subsidiary from a New Zealand bank. The New Zealand subsidiary will pay interest only on the loan each year, at an interest rate of 14 percent. The loan principal is to be paid in 10 years.
- The project will be terminated at the end of Year 3, when the subsidiary will be sold.
- The price, demand, and variable cost of the product in New Zealand are as follows:

YEAR	PRICE	DEMAND	VARIABLE COST
1	NZ$500	40,000 units	NZ$30
2	NZ$511	50,000 units	NZ$35
3	NZ$530	60,000 units	NZ$40

- The fixed costs, such as overhead expenses, are estimated to be NZ$6 million per year.
- The exchange rate of the New Zealand dollar is expected to be $.52 at the end of Year 1, $.54 at the end of Year 2, and $.56 at the end of Year 3.

- The New Zealand government will impose an income tax of 30 percent on income. In addition, it will impose a withholding tax of 10 percent on earnings remitted by the subsidiary. The U.S. government will allow a tax credit on the remitted earnings and will not impose any additional taxes.
- All cash flows received by the subsidiary are to be sent to the parent at the end of each year. The subsidiary will use its working capital to support ongoing operations.
- The plant and equipment are depreciated over 10 years using the straight-line depreciation method. Since the plant and equipment are initially valued at NZ$50 million, the annual depreciation expense is NZ$5 million.
- In 3 years, the subsidiary is to be sold. Wolverine plans to let the acquiring firm assume the existing New Zealand loan. The working capital will not be liquidated but will be used by the acquiring firm that buys the subsidiary. Wolverine expects to receive NZ$52 million after subtracting capital gains taxes. Assume that this amount is not subject to a withholding tax.
- Wolverine requires a 20 percent rate of return on this project.

a. Determine the net present value of this project. Should Wolverine accept this project?

b. Assume that Wolverine is also considering an alternative financing arrangement, in which the parent would invest an additional $10 million to cover the working capital requirements so that the subsidiary would avoid the New Zealand loan. If this arrangement is used, the selling price of the subsidiary (after subtracting any capital gains taxes) is expected to be NZ$18 million higher. Is this alternative financing arrangement more feasible for the parent than the original proposal? Explain.

c. From the parent's perspective, would the *NPV* of this project be more sensitive to exchange rate movements if the subsidiary uses New Zealand financing to cover the working capital or if the parent invests more of its own funds to cover the working capital? Explain.

d. Assume Wolverine used the original financing proposal and that funds are blocked until the subsidiary is sold. The funds to be remitted are reinvested at a rate of 6 percent (after taxes) until the end of Year 3. How is the project's *NPV* affected?

e. What is the break-even salvage value of this project if Wolverine uses the original financing proposal and funds are not blocked?

f. Assume that Wolverine decides to implement the project, using the original financing proposal. Also assume that after 1 year, a New Zealand firm offers Wolverine a price of $27 million after taxes for the subsidiary and that Wolverine's original forecasts for Years 2 and 3 have not changed. Compare the present value of the expected cash flows if Wolverine keeps the subsidiary to the selling price. Should Wolverine divest the subsidiary? Explain.

28. Capital Budgeting with Hedging. Baxter Co. considers a project with Thailand's government. If it accepts the project, it will definitely receive one lump-sum cash flow of 10 million Thai baht in 5 years. The spot rate of the Thai baht is presently $.03. The annualized interest rate for a 5-year period is 4 percent in the United States and 17 percent in Thailand. Interest rate parity exists. Baxter plans to hedge its cash flows with a forward contract. What is the dollar amount of cash flows that Baxter will receive in 5 years if it accepts this project?

29. Capital Budgeting and Financing. Cantoon Co. is considering the acquisition of a unit from the French government. Its initial outlay would be $4 million. It will reinvest all the earnings in the unit. It expects that at the end of 8 years, it will sell the unit for 12 million euros after capital gains taxes are paid. The spot rate of the euro is $1.20 and is used as the forecast of the euro in the future years. Cantoon has no plans to hedge its exposure to exchange rate risk. The annualized U.S. risk-free interest rate is 5 percent regardless of the maturity of the debt, and the annualized risk-free interest rate on euros is 7 percent, regardless of the maturity of the debt. Assume that interest rate parity exists. Cantoon's cost of capital is 20 percent. It plans to use cash to make the acquisition.

a. Determine the *NPV* under these conditions.

b. Rather than use all cash, Cantoon could partially finance the acquisition. It could obtain a loan of 3 million euros today that would be used to cover a portion of the acquisition. In this case, it would have to pay a lump-sum total of 7 million euros at the end of 8 years to repay the loan. There are no interest payments on this debt. The way in which this financing deal is structured, none of the payment is tax deductible. Determine the *NPV* if Cantoon uses the forward rate instead of the spot rate to forecast the future spot rate of the euro, and elects to partially finance the acquisition. You need to derive the 8-year forward rate for this specific question.

30. Sensitivity of *NPV* to Conditions. Burton Co., based in the United States, considers a project in which it has an initial outlay of $3 million and expects to receive 10 million Swiss francs (SF) in 1 year. The spot rate of the franc is $.80. Burton Co. decides to purchase put options on Swiss francs with an exercise price of $.78 and a premium of $.02 per unit to hedge its receivables. It has a required rate of return of 20 percent.

a. Determine the net present value of this project for Burton Co. based on the forecast that the Swiss franc will be valued at $.70 at the end of 1 year.

b. Assume the same information as in part (a), but with the following adjustment. While Burton expected to receive 10 million Swiss francs, assume that there were unexpected weak economic conditions in Switzerland after Burton initiated the project. Consequently, Burton received only 6 million Swiss francs at the end of the year. Also assume that the spot rate of the franc at the end of the year was $.79. Determine the net present value of this project for Burton Co. if these conditions occur.

31. Hedge Decision on a Project. Carlotto Co. (a U.S. firm) will definitely receive 1 million British pounds in 1 year based on a business contract it has with the British government. Like most firms, Carlotto Co. is risk-averse and only takes risk when the potential benefits outweigh the risk. It has no other international business, and is considering various methods to hedge its exchange rate risk. Assume that interest rate parity exists. Carlotto Co. recognizes that exchange rates are very difficult to forecast with accuracy, but it believes that the 1-year forward rate of the pound

yields the best forecast of the pound's spot rate in 1 year. Today the pound's spot rate is $2.00, while the 1-year forward rate of the pound is $1.90. Carlotto Co. has determined that a forward hedge is better than alternative forms of hedging. Should Carlotto Co. hedge with a forward contract or should it remain unhedged? Briefly explain.

32. *NPV* of Partially Hedged Project. Sazer Co. (a U.S. firm) is considering a project in which it produces special safety equipment. It will incur an initial outlay of $1 million for the research and development of this equipment. It expects to receive 600,000 euros in 1 year from selling the products in Portugal where it already does much business. In addition, it also expects to receive 300,000 euros in 1 year from sales to Spain, but these cash flows are very uncertain because it has no existing business in Spain. Today's spot rate of the euro is $1.50 and the 1-year forward rate is $1.50. It expects that the euro's spot rate will be $1.60 in 1 year. It will pursue the project only if it can satisfy its required rate of return of 24 percent. It decides to hedge all the expected receivables due to business in Portugal, and none of the expected receivables due to business in Spain. Estimate the net present value (*NPV*) of the project.

Discussion in the Boardroom

This exercise can be found in Appendix E at the back of this textbook.

Running Your Own MNC

This exercise can be found on the *International Financial Management* text companion website located at www.cengage.com/finance/madura.

BLADES, INC. CASE

Decision by Blades, Inc., to Invest in Thailand

Since Ben Holt, Blades' chief financial officer (CFO), believes the growth potential for the roller blade market in Thailand is very high, he, together with Blades' board of directors, has decided to invest in Thailand. The investment would involve establishing a subsidiary in Bangkok consisting of a manufacturing plant to produce Speedos, Blades' high-quality roller blades. Holt believes that economic conditions in Thailand will be relatively strong in 10 years, when he expects to sell the subsidiary.

Blades will continue exporting to the United Kingdom under an existing agreement with Jogs, Ltd., a British retailer. Furthermore, it will continue its sales in the

United States. Under an existing agreement with Entertainment Products, Inc., a Thai retailer, Blades is committed to selling 180,000 pairs of Speedos to the retailer at a fixed price of 4,594 Thai baht per pair. Once operations in Thailand commence, the agreement will last another year, at which time it may be renewed. Thus, during its first year of operations in Thailand, Blades will sell 180,000 pairs of roller blades to Entertainment Products under the existing agreement whether it has operations in the country or not. If it establishes the plant in Thailand, Blades will produce 108,000 of the 180,000 Entertainment Products Speedos at the plant during the last year of the agreement. Therefore, the new subsidiary would need to import 72,000 pairs of Speedos from the United States so that it can accommodate its agreement with Entertainment Products. It will save the equivalent of 300 baht per pair in variable costs on the 108,000 pairs not previously manufactured in Thailand.

Entertainment Products has already declared its willingness to renew the agreement for another 3 years under identical terms. Because of recent delivery delays, however, it is willing to renew the agreement only if Blades has operations in Thailand. Moreover, if Blades has a subsidiary in Thailand, Entertainment Products will keep renewing the existing agreement as long as Blades operates in Thailand. If the agreement is renewed, Blades expects to sell a total of 300,000 pairs of Speedos annually during its first 2 years of operation in Thailand to various retailers, including 180,000 pairs to Entertainment Products. After this time, it expects to sell 400,000 pairs annually (including 180,000 to Entertainment Products). If the agreement is not renewed, Blades will be able to sell only 5,000 pairs to Entertainment Products annually, but not at a fixed price. Thus, if the agreement is not renewed, Blades expects to sell a total of 125,000 pairs of Speedos annually during its first 2 years of operation in Thailand and 225,000 pairs annually thereafter. Pairs not sold under the contractual agreement with Entertainment Products will be sold for 5,000 Thai baht per pair, since Entertainment Products had required a lower price to compensate it for the risk of being unable to sell the pairs it purchased from Blades.

Ben Holt wishes to analyze the financial feasibility of establishing a subsidiary in Thailand. As a Blades' financial analyst, you have been given the task of analyzing the proposed project. Since future economic conditions in Thailand are highly uncertain, Holt has also asked you to conduct some sensitivity analyses. Fortunately, he has provided most of the information you need to conduct a capital budgeting analysis. This information is detailed here:

- The building and equipment needed will cost 550 million Thai baht. This amount includes additional funds to support working capital.
- The plant and equipment, valued at 300 million baht, will be depreciated using straight-line depreciation. Thus, 30 million baht will be depreciated annually for 10 years.
- The variable costs needed to manufacture Speedos are estimated to be 3,500 baht per pair next year.
- Blades' fixed operating expenses, such as administrative salaries, will be 25 million baht next year.

- The current spot exchange rate of the Thai baht is $.023. Blades expects the baht to depreciate by an average of 2 percent per year for the next 10 years.
- The Thai government will impose a 25 percent tax rate on income and a 10 percent withholding tax on any funds remitted by the subsidiary to Blades. Any earnings remitted to the United States will not be taxed again.
- After 10 years, Blades expects to sell its Thai subsidiary. It expects to sell the subsidiary for about 650 million baht, after considering any capital gains taxes.
- The average annual inflation in Thailand is expected to be 12 percent. Unless prices are contractually fixed, revenue, variable costs, and fixed costs are subject to inflation and are expected to change by the same annual rate as the inflation rate.

Blades could continue its current operations of exporting to and importing from Thailand, which have generated a return of about 20 percent. Blades requires a return of 25 percent on this project in order to justify its investment in Thailand. All excess funds generated by the Thai subsidiary will be remitted to Blades and will be used to support U.S. operations.

Ben Holt has asked you to answer the following questions:

1. Should the sales and the associated costs of 180,000 pairs of roller blades to be sold in Thailand under the existing agreement be included in the capital budgeting analysis to decide whether Blades should establish a subsidiary in Thailand? Should the sales resulting from a renewed agreement be included? Why or why not?

2. Using a spreadsheet, conduct a capital budgeting analysis for the proposed project, assuming that Blades renews the agreement with Entertainment Products. Should Blades establish a subsidiary in Thailand under these conditions?

3. Using a spreadsheet, conduct a capital budgeting analysis for the proposed project assuming that Blades does not renew the agreement with Entertainment Products. Should Blades establish a subsidiary in Thailand under these conditions? Should Blades renew the agreement with Entertainment Products?

4. Since future economic conditions in Thailand are uncertain, Ben Holt would like to know how critical the salvage value is in the alternative you think is most feasible.

5. The future value of the baht is highly uncertain. Under a worst-case scenario, the baht may depreciate by as much as 5 percent annually. Revise your spreadsheet to illustrate how this would affect Blades' decision to establish a subsidiary in Thailand. (Use the capital budgeting analysis you have identified as the most favorable from questions 2 and 3 to answer this question.)

SMALL BUSINESS DILEMMA

Multinational Capital Budgeting by the Sports Exports Company

Jim Logan, owner of the Sports Exports Company, has been pleased with his success in the United Kingdom. He began his business by producing footballs and exporting them to the United Kingdom. While American-style football is still not nearly as popular in the United Kingdom as it is in the United States, his firm controls the market in the United Kingdom. Jim is considering an application of the same business in Mexico. He would produce the footballs in the United States and export them to a distributor of sporting goods in Mexico, who would sell the footballs to retail stores. The distributor likely would want to pay for the product each month in Mexican pesos. Jim would need to hire one full-time employee in the United States to produce the footballs. He would also need to lease one warehouse.

1. Describe the capital budgeting steps that would be necessary to determine whether this proposed project is feasible, as related to this specific situation.

2. Explain why there is uncertainty surrounding the cash flows of this project.

INTERNET/EXCEL EXERCISES

Assume that you invested equity to establish a project in Portugal in January about 7 years ago. At the time the project began, you could have supported it with a 7-year loan either in dollars or in euros. If you borrowed U.S. dollars, your annual loan payment (including principal) would have been $2.5 million. If you borrowed euros, your annual loan payment (including principal) would have been 2 million euros. The project generated 5 million euros per year in revenue.

1. Use an Excel spreadsheet to determine the dollar net cash flows (after making the debt payment) that you would receive at the end of each of the last 7 years if you partially financed the project by borrowing dollars.

2. Determine the standard deviation of the dollar net cash flows that you would receive at the end of each of the last 7 years if you partially financed the project by borrowing dollars.

3. Reestimate the dollar net cash flows and the standard deviation of the dollar net cash flows if you partially financed the project by borrowing euros. (You can obtain the end-of-year exchange rate of the euro for the last 7 years at www.oanda.com or similar websites.) Are the project's net cash flows more volatile if you had borrowed dollars or euros? Explain your results.

REFERENCES

Benassy-Quere, Agnes, Lionel Fontagné, and Amina Lahrèche-Révil, Sep 2005, How Does FDI React to Corporate Taxation? *International Tax and Public Finance,* pp. 583–603.

Doukas, John A., and Ozgur B. Kan, May 2006, Does Global Diversification Destroy Firm Value? *Journal of International Business Studies,* pp. 352–371.

Shackelton, Mark B., Andrianos E. Tsekrekos, and Rafal Wojakowski, Jan 2004, Strategic Entry and Market Leadership in a Two-player Real Options Game, *Journal of Banking & Finance,* pp. 179–201.

15

International Corporate Governance and Control

The specific objectives of this chapter are to:

- describe the common forms of corporate governance by MNCs,

- provide a background on how MNCs use corporate control as a form of governance,

- explain the motives, barriers, and valuation process in international corporate control,

- identify the factors that are considered when valuing a foreign target,

- explain why valuations of a target firm vary among MNCs that consider corporate control strategies, and

- identify other types of international corporate control actions.

When multinational corporations (MNCs) expand internationally, they are subject to various types of agency problems. Many of the agency problems occur because incentives for managers of the parent or its subsidiaries are not properly structured to ensure that managers focus on maximizing the value of the firm (and therefore shareholder wealth). International corporate governance and corporate control can ensure that managerial goals are aligned with those of shareholders.

INTERNATIONAL CORPORATE GOVERNANCE

MNCs commonly use a number of methods to ensure that their foreign subsidiary managers own shares of the firm in order to align their interests with those of the corporation. They may offer bonuses in the form of stock that cannot be sold for a few years, which encourages the managers of foreign subsidiaries to focus on the goal of maximizing the MNC's stock price when making decisions for the subsidiaries. Under these conditions, the high-level managers may properly govern themselves. However, since the stock ownership by high-level managers of an MNC is typically limited, managers' first priority on decision making may be to protect their job even if it reduces the stock price. For example, they may make decisions that will expand their subsidiary in order to justify their position, even if these decisions adversely affect the value of the MNC overall. Furthermore, expansion might improve their potential for more responsibility and therefore a promotion. Thus, governance may be needed to ensure that managerial decisions serve shareholder interests. Common forms of governance of MNCs are described next.

Governance by Board Members

The board of directors is responsible for appointing high-level managers of the firm, including the chief executive officer (CEO). It oversees major decisions of the firm such as restructuring and expansion, and is supposed to make sure that key management decisions are in the best interest of shareholders. However, boards of MNCs are not always effective at governance.

First, some boards of directors allow the firm's chief executive officer to serve as the chair of the board, which may reduce the ability of a board to control management because the chair may have sufficient power to control the board. For example, the chair commonly organizes the agenda for a board meeting and might establish the process in which decisions are made. Second, boards typically contain insiders (managers working for the firm) who might prefer policies that favor managerial power. Boards of MNCs may be more effective if they contain a larger number of outside board members that do not work for the firm. Third, board members who are employees of a foreign subsidiary may attempt to make decisions that maximize the benefits to the subsidiary and not the MNC overall.

Governance by Institutional Investors

Institutional investors such as pension funds, mutual funds, hedge funds, and insurance companies commonly hold a large proportion of a firm's shares. If the firm performs well, its stock will perform well and the institutional investors benefit. However, ownership of 1 or 2 percent of the firm's shares will not necessarily be sufficient to swing an important vote. While institutional investors may contact board members if they are displeased with policies of the firm, their power to enact change is limited. They can show the displeasure by selling the shares that they own, but this does not necessarily solve the problem. In fact, managers who do not want to be monitored might prefer that institutional owners sell their holdings of the stock so that the managers are not subject to close monitoring.

The ability or willingness to enforce governance commonly varies among types of institutional investors. For example, some public pension funds and mutual funds may invest in the stock of companies and plan to hold the stock for a long time. Thus, they do not actively govern the companies in which they invest. Conversely, hedge funds commonly use an investment strategy of investing in companies that have performed poorly (and therefore have a low stock price) but have the potential to improve. The hedge funds will actively govern the companies in which they invest because they only benefit from their investments if these companies improve their performance.

Governance by Shareholder Activists

Some institutional investors or individual shareholders are called blockholders because they hold a large proportion (such as at least 5 percent) of the firm's stock. Blockholders commonly become shareholder activists, that is, they take actions to influence management. Investors do not have to be blockholders to become activists, but there is more motivation for investors to be activists if they have a lot at stake and can possibly influence management with their significant voting power. If shareholder activists dislike a new policy by management, they may contact the board and voice their opinion. They may also engage in proxy contests, in which they attempt to change the composition of the board of directors. They may even attempt to serve on the board if they have sufficient support from other shareholders. In addition, shareholder activists commonly file lawsuits against the firm in an attempt to influence managerial decisions.

INTERNATIONAL CORPORATE CONTROL

Even with the various forms of governance described above, managers may still be able to make decisions that serve themselves rather than shareholders. To the extent that a firm's decisions are focused on serving its managers rather than shareholders, its stock price should be relatively low, reflecting these poor decisions. Consequently, the firm could be subjected to a takeover attempt, that is, it becomes a "target." The target may be contacted by another firm that wants to engage in discussions regarding a takeover. If the target declines this request, the other firm might still acquire it by engaging in a tender offer, whereby it stands willing to purchase shares from the target's shareholders. If the target presently has a low stock price, another firm might hope to acquire it at a very low cost and then restructure it by removing the inefficient managers.

Most countries allow local companies to be acquired by MNCs from other countries. Thus, the international market for corporate control can correct inefficient MNCs wherever they are, which has two important implications. First, MNC managers recognize that if they make decisions that destroy value, the MNC could be subject to a takeover and its managers could lose their jobs. Second, when MNCs are expanding their business globally, they may consider the market for corporate control as a means of achieving their expansion goals.

Motives for International Acquisitions

Many international acquisitions are motivated by the desire to increase global market share or to capitalize on economies of scale through global consolidation. Some MNCs may have a comparative advantage in terms of their technology or image in a foreign market where competition is not as intense as in their domestic market. U.S.-based MNCs such as Oracle Corp., Google, Inc., Borden, Inc., and Dow Chemical Co. have recently engaged in international acquisitions. In general, announcements of acquisitions of foreign targets lead to neutral or slightly favorable stock price effects for acquirers, on average, whereas acquisitions of domestic targets lead to negative effects for acquirers, on average. The publicly traded foreign targets almost always experience a large favorable stock price response at the time of the acquisition, which is attributed to the large premium that the acquirer pays to obtain control of the target.

MNCs may view international acquisitions as a better form of direct foreign investment (DFI) than establishing a new subsidiary. However, there are distinct differences between these two forms of DFI. Through an international acquisition, the firm can immediately expand its international business since the target is already in place.

EXAMPLE

Yahoo! successfully established portals in Europe and Asia. However, it believed that it could improve its presence in Asia by focusing on the Greater China area. China has much potential because of its population base, but it also imposes restrictions that discourage DFI by firms. Meanwhile, Kimo, a privately held company and the leading portal in Taiwan, had 4 million registered users in Taiwan. Yahoo! agreed to acquire Kimo for about $150 million. With this DFI, Yahoo! not only established a presence in Taiwan but also established a link to mainland China. ●

When viewed as a project, the international acquisition usually generates quicker and larger cash flows than the establishment of a new subsidiary, but it also requires a larger initial outlay. International acquisitions also necessitate the integration of the parent's management style with that of the foreign target.

Trends in International Acquisitions

WEB

www.worldbank.org
Data on socioeconomic development and performance indicators as well as links to statistical and project-oriented publications and analyses.

Traditionally, MNCs in various countries tend to focus on specific geographic regions and use stocks or cash to make their purchases depending on shareholder power.

MNCs based in the United States acquire more firms in the United Kingdom than in any other country. British and Canadian firms are the most common acquirers of companies in the United States. In general, Europe has been a popular target for U.S. firms, especially since many European countries adopted the euro and allowed easier entry for firms that want to do business there.

When a U.S. firm attempts to acquire a target firm in a country where shareholder rights are weak, it usually uses stock as a method of payment. The target shareholders are willing to accept stock as payment because they will now own shares of a stock in which they enjoy stronger shareholder rights. However, if a firm in a weak shareholder rights country wants to acquire a U.S. firm, it would likely need to use cash, because the shareholders of the target firm in the United States do not want to hold stock of a firm where shareholder rights are weak.

International acquisitions have generally increased over time. However, the pace slowed during the credit crisis in 2008. MNCs reduced their expansion plans during the credit crisis because of forecasts of a weak global economy. In addition, they could not effectively finance acquisitions. Credit was quite limited during the credit crisis because creditors feared that some MNCs might fail and therefore not repay their loans. Using stock offerings to finance acquisitions was also not a realistic option. If MNCs attempted to issue stock in order to support acquisitions, they would have to issue the stock at about the prevailing market price. Yet because MNCs at that time had low stock prices due to the negative outlook for the global economy, they would have received a relatively small amount of proceeds from a secondary stock offering.

Barriers to International Corporate Control

The international market for corporate control is limited by barriers that a target firm or its host government can implement to protect against a takeover.

Anti-Takeover Amendments Implemented by Target. First, the target may implement an anti-takeover amendment, that requires a large proportion of shareholders to approve the takeover. This type of amendment allows a firm's employees to prevent a takeover.

Poison Pills Implemented by Target. An alternative method of protecting against a takeover is a poison pill, which grants special rights to managers or shareholders under specified conditions. For example, a poison pill might grant existing shareholders of the target additional stock if a takeover is initiated. A poison pill does not require the approval of other shareholders, so it can be easily implemented by the target firm. In some cases, a poison pill is not implemented to prevent a takeover, but as a bargaining tool by the target firm. Since a poison pill can make it very expensive for another firm to acquire the target, it essentially forces the MNC to negotiate with the target's management.

In most cases, the target's management and board will be unwilling to give up control unless an MNC is willing to pay a premium (above the existing share price) of perhaps 30 to 50 percent. For example, if a firm wants to acquire a target that presently has a market value of $100 million (based on today's stock price), it may have to pay $130 to $150 million to obtain control of the target. When an MNC must pay such a high price for the target, its board may decide that the takeover cannot be justified.

Alternatively, an MNC might pursue the takeover anyway, which commonly causes some of its shareholders to sell their shares as a protest against paying such a high premium. Consequently, the share prices of the MNC could decline in response to its announced intentions to take over a target, especially when the premium that it plans to pay is very high.

Host Government Barriers. Governments of some countries restrict foreign firms from taking control of local firms, or they may allow foreign ownership of local firms only if specific guidelines are satisfied. For example, foreign firms might be allowed to acquire a local firm only if they retain all employees in the local target company. If the local firm was an appealing takeover target to foreign firms because it was inefficient and could be acquired at a low price, the inability to reduce its employment level means the foreign firm may be prevented from improving the target. Thus, this type of restriction could serve as a major barrier to international corporate control.

Model for Valuing a Foreign Target

Recall from Chapter 1 that the value of an MNC is based on the present value of expected cash flows to be received. When an MNC engages in restructuring, it affects the

WEB

www.cia.gov
Provides a link to the *World Factbook,* which has valuable information about countries that would be considered by MNCs that may attempt to acquire foreign targets.

structure of its assets, which will ultimately affect the present value of its cash flows. For example, if it acquires a company, it will incur a large initial outlay this year, but its expected annual cash flows will now be larger. An MNC's decision to invest in a foreign company is similar to the decision to invest in other projects in that it is based on a comparison of benefits and costs as measured by net present value. From an MNC's parent's perspective, the foreign target's value can be estimated as the present value of cash flows that it would receive from the target, as the target would become a foreign subsidiary owned by the parent.

The MNC's parent would consider investing in the target only if the estimated present value of the cash flows it would ultimately receive from the target over time exceeds the initial outlay necessary to purchase the target. Thus, capital budgeting analysis can be used to determine whether a firm should be acquired. The net present value of a company from the acquiring firm's perspective (NPV_a) is

$$NPV_a = -IO_a + \sum_{t=1}^{n} \frac{CF_{a,t}}{(1 + k)^t} + \frac{SV_a}{(1 + k)^n}$$

where
$\quad IO_a$ = initial outlay needed by the acquiring firm to acquire the target
$\quad CF_{a,t}$ = cash flow to be generated by the target for the acquiring firm
$\quad\quad k$ = required rate of return on the acquisition of the target
$\quad SV_a$ = salvage value of the target (expected selling price of the target at a point in the future)
$\quad\quad n$ = time when the target will be sold by the acquiring firm

Estimating the Initial Outlay. The initial outlay reflects the price to be paid for the target. When firms acquire publicly traded foreign targets, they commonly pay premiums of at least 30 percent above the prevailing stock price of the target in order to gain ownership. This type of premium is also typical for acquisitions of domestic targets. The main point here is that the estimate of the initial outlay must account for the premium since an MNC normally will not be able to purchase a publicly traded target at the target's prevailing market value.

For an acquisition to be successful, the acquirer must substantially improve the target's cash flows so that it can overcome the large premium it pays for the target. The capital budgeting analysis of a foreign target must also account for the exchange rate of concern. For example, consider a U.S.-based MNC that assesses the acquisition of a foreign company. The dollar initial outlay ($IO_{U.S.}$) needed by the U.S. firm is determined by the acquisition price in foreign currency units (IO_f) and the spot rate of the foreign currency (S):

$$IO_{U.S.} = IO_f(S)$$

Estimating the Cash Flows. The dollar amount of cash flows to the U.S. firm is determined by the foreign currency cash flows ($CF_{f,t}$) per period remitted to the United States and the spot rate at that time (S_t):

$$CF_{a,t} = (CF_{f,t})S_t$$

This ignores any withholding taxes or blocked-funds restrictions imposed by the host government and any income taxes imposed by the U.S. government. Some international acquisitions backfire because the MNC overestimates the net cash flows of the target. That is, the MNC's managers are excessively optimistic when estimating the target's future cash flows, which leads them to make acquisitions that are not feasible.

The dollar amount of salvage value to the U.S. firm is determined by the salvage value in foreign currency units (SV_f) and the spot rate at the time (period n) when it is converted to dollars (S_n):

$$SV_a = (SV_f)S_n$$

Estimating the NPV. The net present value of a foreign target can be derived by substituting the equalities just described in the capital budgeting equation:

$$NPV_a = -IO_a + \sum_{t=1}^{n} \frac{CF_{a,t}}{(1+k)^t} + \frac{SV}{(1+k)^n}$$

$$= -(IO_f)S + \sum_{t=1}^{n} \frac{(CF_{f,t})S_t}{(1+k)^t} + \frac{(SV_f)S_n}{(1+k)^n}$$

Impact of the SOX Act on the Valuation of Targets. In response to some major abuses in financial reporting by some MNCs such as Enron and WorldCom, Congress passed the Sarbanes-Oxley (SOX) Act in 2002. The SOX Act improved the process for reporting profits used by U.S. firms (including U.S.-based MNCs). It requires firms to document an orderly and transparent process for reporting so that they cannot distort their earnings. It also requires more accountability for oversight by executives and the board of directors. This increased accountability has had a direct impact on the process for assessing acquisitions. Executives of MNCs are prompted to conduct a more thorough review of the foreign target's operations and risk (called due diligence). In addition, the board of directors of an MNC conducts a more thorough review of any proposed acquisitions before agreeing to them. MNCs increasingly hire outside advisers (including attorneys and investment banks) to offer their assessment of proposed acquisitions. If an MNC pursues an acquisition, it must ensure that financial information of the target is accurate.

FACTORS AFFECTING TARGET VALUATION

When an MNC estimates the future cash flows that it will ultimately receive after acquiring a foreign target, it considers several factors about the target or its respective country.

Target-Specific Factors

The following characteristics of the foreign target are typically considered when estimating the cash flows that the target will provide to the parent.

Target's Previous Cash Flows. Since the foreign target has been conducting business, it has a history of cash flows that it has generated. The recent cash flows per period may serve as an initial base from which future cash flows per period can be estimated after accounting for other factors. It may also make it easier to estimate the cash flows it will generate than it would be to estimate the cash flows to be generated from a new foreign subsidiary.

A company's previous cash flows are not necessarily an accurate indicator of future cash flows, however, if the target's future cash flows have to be converted into the acquirer's home currency when they are remitted to the parent. Therefore, the MNC needs to carefully consider all the factors that could influence the cash flows that will be generated from a foreign target.

Managerial Talent of the Target. An acquiring firm must assess the target's existing management so that it can determine how the target firm will be managed after the acquisition. The way the acquirer plans to deal with the managerial talent will affect the estimated cash flows to be generated by the target.

If the MNC acquires the target, it may allow the target firm to be managed as it was before the acquisition. Under these conditions, however, the acquiring firm may have less potential for enhancing the target's cash flows.

A second alternative for the MNC is to downsize the target firm after acquiring it. For example, if the acquiring firm introduces new technology that reduces the need for some of the target's employees, it can attempt to downsize the target. Downsizing reduces expenses but may also reduce productivity and revenue, so the effect on cash flows can vary with the situation. In addition, in several countries an MNC may encounter significant barriers to increasing efficiency by downsizing. Governments of some countries are likely to intervene and prevent the acquisition if downsizing is anticipated.

A third alternative for the MNC is to maintain the existing employees of the target but restructure the operations so that labor is used more efficiently. For example, the MNC may infuse its own technology into the target firm and then restructure operations so that many of the employees receive new job assignments. This strategy may cause the acquirer to incur some additional expenses, but there is potential for improved cash flows over time.

Country-Specific Factors

An MNC typically considers the following country-specific factors when estimating the cash flows that will be provided by the foreign target to the parent.

Target's Local Economic Conditions. Potential targets in countries where economic conditions are strong are more likely to experience strong demand for their products in the future and may generate higher cash flows. However, some firms are more sensitive to economic conditions than others. Also, some acquisitions of firms are intended to focus on exporting from the target's home country, so the economic conditions in the target's country may not be as important. Economic conditions are difficult to predict over a long-term period, especially for emerging countries.

Target's Local Political Conditions. Potential targets in countries where political conditions are favorable are less likely to experience adverse shocks to their cash flows. The sensitivity of cash flows to political conditions is dependent on the firm's type of business. Political conditions are also difficult to predict over a long-term period, especially for emerging countries.

If an MNC plans to improve the efficiency of a target by laying off employees that are not needed, it must first make sure that the government would allow layoffs before it makes the acquisition. Some countries protect employees from layoffs, which may cause many local firms to be inefficient. An MNC might not be capable of improving efficiency if it is not allowed to lay off employees.

Target's Industry Conditions. Industry conditions within a country can cause some targets to be more desirable than others. Some industries in a particular country may be extremely competitive while others are not. In addition, some industries exhibit strong potential for growth in a particular country, while others exhibit very little potential. When an MNC assesses targets among countries, it would prefer a country where the growth potential for its industry is high and the competition within the industry is not excessive.

Target's Currency Conditions. If a U.S.-based MNC plans to acquire a foreign target, it must consider how future exchange rate movements may affect the target's local

WEB

http://research
.stlouisfed.org/fred2
Numerous economic
and financial time se-
ries, e.g., on balance-
of-payments statistics,
interest rates, and for-
eign exchange rates.

currency cash flows. It must also consider how exchange rates will affect the conversion of the target's remitted earnings to the U.S. parent. In the typical case, ideally the foreign currency would be weak at the time of the acquisition (so that the MNC's initial outlay is low) but strengthen over time as funds are periodically remitted to the U.S. parent. There can be exceptions to this general statement, but the point is that the MNC forecasts future exchange rates and then applies those forecasts to determine the impact on cash flows.

Target's Local Stock Market Conditions. Potential target firms that are publicly held are continuously valued in the market, so their stock prices can change rapidly. As the target firm's stock price changes, the acceptable bid price necessary to buy that firm will likely change as well. Thus, there can be substantial swings in the purchase price that would be acceptable to a target. This is especially true for publicly traded firms in emerging markets in Asia, Eastern Europe, and Latin America where stock prices commonly change by 5 percent or more in a week. Therefore, an MNC that plans to acquire a target would prefer to make its bid at a time when the local stock market prices are generally low.

Taxes Applicable to the Target. When an MNC assesses a foreign target, it must estimate the expected after-tax cash flows that it will ultimately receive in the form of funds remitted to the parent. Thus, the tax laws applicable to the foreign target are used to derive the after-tax cash flows. First, the applicable corporate tax rates are applied to the estimated future earnings of the target to determine the after-tax earnings. Second, the after-tax proceeds are determined by applying any withholding tax rates to the funds that are expected to be remitted to the parent in each period. Third, if the acquiring firm's government imposes an additional tax on remitted earnings or allows a tax credit, that tax or credit must be applied.

EXAMPLE OF THE VALUATION PROCESS

Lincoln Co. desires to expand in Latin America or Canada. The methods Lincoln uses to initially screen targets in various countries and then to estimate a target's value are discussed next.

International Screening Process

Lincoln Co. considers the factors just described when it conducts an initial screening of prospective targets. It has identified prospective targets in Mexico, Brazil, Colombia, and Canada, as shown in Exhibit 15.1. The target in Mexico has no plans to sell its business and is unwilling to even consider an offer from Lincoln Co. Therefore, this firm is no longer considered. Lincoln anticipates potential political problems that could create barriers to an acquisition in Colombia, even though the Colombian target is willing to be acquired. Stock market conditions are not favorable in Brazil, as the stock prices of most Brazilian companies have recently risen substantially. Lincoln does not want to pay as much as the Brazilian target is now worth based on its prevailing market value.

Based on this screening process, the only foreign target that deserves a closer assessment is the target in Canada. According to Lincoln's assessment, Canadian currency conditions are slightly unfavorable, but this is not a reason to eliminate the target from further consideration. Thus, the next step would be for Lincoln to obtain as much information as possible about the target and conditions in Canada. Then Lincoln can use this information to derive the target's expected cash flows and to determine whether the target's value exceeds the initial outlay that would be required to purchase it, as explained next.

Estimating the Target's Value

Once Lincoln Co. has completed its initial screening of targets, it conducts a valuation of all targets that passed the screening process. Lincoln can estimate the present value of future cash flows that would result from acquiring the target. This estimation is then used to determine whether the target should be acquired.

Continuing with our simplified example, Lincoln's screening process resulted in only one eligible target, a Canadian firm. Assume the Canadian firm has conducted all of its business locally. Assume also that Lincoln expects that it can obtain materials at a lower cost than the target can because of its relationships with some Canadian suppliers and that it also expects to implement a more efficient production process. Lincoln also plans to use its existing managerial talent to manage the target and thereby reduce the administrative and marketing expenses incurred by the target. It also expects that the target's revenue will increase when its products are sold under Lincoln's name. Lincoln expects to maintain prices of the products as they are.

The target's expected cash flows can be measured by first determining the revenue and expense levels in recent years and then adjusting those levels to reflect the changes that would occur after the acquisition.

Revenue. The target's annual revenue has ranged between C$80 million and C$90 million in Canadian dollars (C$) over the last 4 years. Lincoln Co. expects that it can improve sales, and forecasts revenue to be C$100 million next year, C$93.3 million in the following year, and C$121 million in the year after. The cost of goods sold has been about 50 percent of the revenue in the past, but Lincoln expects it will fall to 40 percent of revenue because of improvements in efficiency. The estimates are shown in Exhibit 15.2.

Expenses. Selling and administrative expenses have been about C$20 million annually, but Lincoln believes that through restructuring it can reduce these expenses to C$15 million in each of the next 3 years. Depreciation expenses have been about C$10 million in the past and are expected to remain at that level for the next 3 years. The Canadian tax rate on the target's earnings is expected to be 30 percent.

Earnings and Cash Flows. Given the information assumed here, the after-tax earnings that the target would generate under Lincoln's ownership are estimated in Exhibit 15.2. The cash flows generated by the target are determined by adding the depreciation expenses back to the after-tax earnings. Assume that the target will need C$5 million in cash each year to support existing operations (including the repair of existing machinery) and that the remaining cash flow can be remitted to the U.S. parent. Assume

Exhibit 15.1 Example of Process Used to Screen Foreign Targets

TARGET BASED IN:	IS THE TARGET RECEPTIVE TO AN ACQUISITION?	LOCAL ECONOMIC AND INDUSTRY CONDITIONS	LOCAL POLITICAL CONDITIONS	LOCAL CURRENCY CONDITIONS	PREVAILING STOCK MARKET PRICES	TAX LAWS
Mexico	No	Favorable	OK	OK	OK	May change
Brazil	Maybe	OK	OK	OK	Too high	May change
Colombia	Yes	Favorable	Volatile	Favorable	OK	Reasonable
Canada	Yes	OK	Favorable	Slightly unfavorable	OK	Reasonable

Exhibit 15.2 Valuation of Canadian Target Based on the Assumptions Provided (in Millions of Dollars)

	LAST YEAR	YEAR 1	YEAR 2	YEAR 3
Revenue	C$90	C$100	C$93.3	C$121
Cost of goods sold	C$45	C$40	C$37.3	C$ 48.4
Gross profit	C$45	C$60	C$56	C$ 72.6
Selling & administrative expenses	C$20	C$15	C$15	C$15
Depreciation	C$10	C$10	C$10	C$10
Earnings before taxes	C$15	C$35	C$31	C$47.6
Tax (30%)	C$ 4.5	C$10.5	C$ 9.3	C$14.28
Earnings after taxes	C$10.5	C$24.5	C$21.7	C$33.32
+Depreciation		C$10	C$10	C$10
−Funds to reinvest		C$5	C$5	C$5
Sale of firm after capital gains taxes				C$230
Cash flows in C$		C$29.5	C$26.7	C$268.32
Exchange rate of C$		$ .80	$ .80	$ .80
Cash flows in $		$23.6	$21.36	$214.66
PV (20% discount rate)		$19.67	$14.83	$124.22
Cumulative PV		$19.67	$34.50	$158.72

that the target firm is financially supported only by its equity. It currently has 10 million shares of stock outstanding that are priced at C$17 per share.

Cash Flows to Parent. Since Lincoln's parent wishes to assess the target from its own perspective, it focuses on the dollar cash flows that it expects to receive. Assuming no additional taxes, the expected cash flows generated in Canada that are to be remitted to Lincoln's parent are converted into U.S. dollars at the expected exchange rate at the end of each year. Lincoln uses the prevailing exchange rate of the Canadian dollar (which is $.80) as the expected exchange rate for the Canadian dollar in future years.

Estimating the Target's Future Sales Price. If Lincoln purchases the target, it will sell the target in 3 years, after improving the target's performance. Lincoln expects to receive C$230 million (after capital gains taxes) from the sale. The price at which the target can actually be sold will depend on its expected future cash flows from that point forward, but those expected cash flows are partially dependent on its performance prior to that time. Thus, Lincoln can enhance the sales price by improving the target's performance over the 3 years it plans to own the target.

Valuing the Target Based on Estimated Cash Flows. The expected U.S. dollar cash flows to Lincoln's parent over the next 3 years are shown in Exhibit 15.2. The high cash flow in Year 3 is due to Lincoln's plans to sell the target at that time. Assuming that Lincoln has a required rate of return of 20 percent on this project, the cash flows are discounted at that rate to derive the present value of target cash flows. From Lincoln's perspective, the present value of the target is about $158.72 million.

Given that the target's shares are currently valued at C$17 per share, the 10 million shares are worth C$170 million. At the prevailing exchange rate of $.80 per dollar, the target is currently valued at $136 million by the market (computed as C$170 million × $.80).

Lincoln's valuation of the target of about $159 million is about 17 percent above the market valuation. However, Lincoln will have to pay a premium on the shares to persuade the target's board of directors to approve the acquisition. If Lincoln would have to pay a premium of more than 17 percent to purchase the target, it should not pursue the acquisition.

Sources of Uncertainty. This example shows how the acquisition of a publicly traded foreign firm differs from the creation of a new foreign subsidiary. Although the valuation of a publicly traded foreign firm can utilize information about an existing business, the cash flows resulting from the acquisition are still subject to uncertainty for several reasons, which can be identified by reviewing the assumptions made in the valuation process. First, the growth rate of revenue is subject to uncertainty. If this rate is overestimated (perhaps because Canadian economic growth is overestimated), the earnings generated in Canada will be lower, and cash flows remitted to the U.S. parent will be lower as well.

Second, the cost of goods sold could exceed the assumed level of 40 percent of revenue, which would reduce cash flows remitted to the parent. Third, the selling and administrative expenses could exceed the assumed amount of C$15 million, especially when considering that the annual expenses were C$20 million prior to the acquisition. Fourth, Canada's corporate tax rate could increase, which would reduce the cash flows remitted to the parent. Fifth, the exchange rate of the Canadian dollar may be weaker than assumed, which would reduce the cash flows received by the parent. Sixth, the estimated selling price of the target 3 years from now could be incorrect for any of these five reasons, and this estimate is very influential on the valuation of the target today.

Since one or more of these conditions could occur, the estimated net present value of the target could be overestimated. Consequently, it is possible for Lincoln to acquire the target at a purchase price exceeding its actual value. In particular, the future cash flows are very sensitive to exchange rate movements. This can be illustrated by using sensitivity analysis and reestimating the value of the target based on different scenarios for the exchange rate over time.

Changes in Valuation over Time

If Lincoln Co. decides not to bid for the target at this time, it will need to redo its analysis if it later reconsiders acquiring the target. As the factors that affect the expected cash flows or the required rate of return from investing in the target change, so will the value of the target.

Impact of Stock Market Conditions. A change in stock market conditions affects the price per share of each stock in that market. Thus, the value of publicly traded firms in that market will change. Remember that an acquirer needs to pay a premium above the market valuation to acquire a foreign firm.

Continuing with our example involving Lincoln Co.'s pursuit of a Canadian target, assume that the target firm has a market price of C$17 per share, representing a valuation of C$170 million, but that before Lincoln makes its decision to acquire the target, the Canadian stock market level rises by 20 percent. If the target's stock price rises by this same percentage, the firm is now valued at

$$\text{New stock price} = \text{C\$170 million} \times 1.2$$
$$= \text{C\$204 million}$$

Using the 10 percent premium assumed in the earlier example, Lincoln must now pay C$224.4 million (computed as C$204 million × 1.1) if it wants to acquire the target. This example illustrates how the price paid for the target can change abruptly simply because of a change in the general level of the stock market.

Even if a target is privately held, general stock market conditions will affect the amount that an acquirer has to pay for the target because a privately held company's value is influenced by the market price multiples of related firms in the same country. A simple method of valuing a private company is to apply the price-earnings (P/E) ratios of publicly traded firms in the same industry to the private company's annual earnings. When stock prices rise in a particular country, P/E ratios of publicly traded firms in that country typically rise, and a higher P/E ratio would be applied to value a private firm.

Impact of Credit Availability. The availability of credit greatly impacts the ability of MNCs to make acquisitions. During the credit crisis in 2008, stock market values of many firms weakened substantially. As a result, foreign targets could be purchased at a much lower price. However, this did not encourage more acquisitions. The decline in value reflected the lower cash flow estimates of the companies because economies of most countries were expected to weaken. In fact, foreign acquisitions declined during this period because MNCs did not want to expand while the global economies were weak. Furthermore, credit was limited, which restricted the amount of funding that would be available for MNCs that pursued acquisitions.

Impact of Exchange Rates. Whether a foreign target is publicly traded or private, a U.S. acquirer must convert dollars to the local currency to purchase the target. If the foreign currency appreciates by the time the acquirer makes payment, the acquisition will be more costly. The cost of the acquisition changes in the same proportion as the change in the exchange rate.

Impact of Market Anticipation Regarding the Target. The stock price of the target may increase if investors anticipate that the target will be acquired because they are aware that stock prices of targets rise abruptly after a bid by the acquiring firm. Thus, it is important that Lincoln keep its intentions about acquiring the target confidential.

DISPARITY IN FOREIGN TARGET VALUATIONS

Most MNCs that consider acquiring a specific target will use a somewhat similar process for valuing the target. Nevertheless, their valuations will differ because of differences in the way the MNCs estimate the key determinants of a given target's valuation: (1) cash flows to be generated by the target, (2) exchange rate effects on funds remitted to the MNC's parent, and (3) the required rate of return when investing in the target.

Estimated Cash Flows of the Foreign Target

The target's expected future cash flows will vary among MNCs because the cash flows will be dependent on the MNC's management or oversight of the target's operations. If an MNC can improve the production efficiency of the target without reducing the target's production volume, it can improve the target's cash flows.

Each MNC may have a different plan as to how the target will fit within its structure and how the target will conduct future operations. The target's expected cash flows will be influenced by the way it is utilized. An MNC with production plants in Asia that purchases another Asian production plant may simply be attempting to increase its market share and production capacity. This MNC's cash flows change because of a higher production and sales level. Conversely, an MNC with all of its production plants in the United States may purchase an Asian production plant to shift its production where costs are lower. This MNC's cash flows change because of lower expenses.

Tax laws can create competitive advantages for acquirers based in some countries. Acquirers based in low-tax countries may be able to generate higher cash flows from acquiring a foreign target than acquirers in high-tax countries simply because they are subject to lower taxes on the future earnings remitted by the target (after it is acquired).

Exchange Rate Effects on the Funds Remitted

The valuation of a target can vary among MNCs simply because of differences in the exchange rate effects on funds remitted by the foreign target to the MNC's parent. If the target remits funds frequently in the near future, its value will be partially dependent on the expected exchange rate of the target's local currency in the near future. If the target does not remit funds in the near future, its value is more dependent on its local growth strategy and on exchange rates in the distant future.

Required Return of Acquirer

The valuation of the target could also vary among MNCs because of differences in their required rate of return from investing funds to acquire the target. If an MNC targets a successful foreign company and plans to continue the target's local business in a more efficient manner, the risk of the business will be relatively low. Therefore the MNC's required return from acquiring the target will be relatively low. Conversely, if an MNC targets the company because it plans to turn the company into a major exporter, the risk is much higher. The target has not established itself in foreign markets, so the cash flows that would result from the exporting business are very uncertain. Thus, the required return to acquire the target company will be relatively high as well.

If potential acquirers are based in different countries, their required rates of return from a specific target will vary even if they plan to use the target in similar ways. Recall that an MNC's required rate of return on any project is dependent on the local risk-free interest rate (since that influences the cost of funds for that MNC). Therefore, the required rate of return for MNCs based in countries with relatively high interest rates such as Brazil and Venezuela may differ from MNCs based in low-interest-rate countries such as the United States or Japan. The higher required rate of return for MNCs based in Latin American countries will not necessarily lead to a lower valuation. The target's currency might be expected to appreciate substantially against Latin American currencies (since some Latin American currencies have consistently weakened over time), which would enhance the amount of cash flows received as a result of remitted funds and could possibly offset the effects of the higher required rate of return.

OTHER CORPORATE CONTROL DECISIONS

Besides acquiring foreign firms, MNCs may also pursue international partial acquisitions, acquisitions of privatized businesses, and international divestitures. Each type is described in turn.

International Partial Acquisitions

In many cases, an MNC may consider a partial international acquisition of a firm, in which it purchases part of the existing stock of a foreign firm. A partial international acquisition requires less funds because only a portion of the foreign target's shares are purchased. With this type of investment, the foreign target normally continues operating and may not experience the employee turnover that commonly occurs after a target's ownership changes. Nevertheless, by acquiring a substantial fraction of the shares, the MNC may have some influence on the target's management and is in a position to complete the acquisition in the future. Some MNCs buy substantial stakes in foreign companies to have some control over their operations. For example, Coca-Cola has purchased stakes in many foreign bottling companies that bottle its syrup. In this way, it can ensure that the bottling operations meet its standards.

Valuation Process. When an MNC considers a partial acquisition in which it will purchase sufficient shares so that it can control the firm, the MNC can conduct its valuation of the target in much the same way as when it purchases the entire firm. If the MNC buys only a small proportion of the firm's shares, however, the MNC cannot restructure the firm's operations to make it more efficient. Therefore, its estimates of the firm's cash flows must be made from the perspective of a passive investor rather than as a decision maker for the firm.

International Acquisitions of Privatized Businesses

In recent years, government-owned businesses in many developing countries in Eastern Europe and South America have been sold to individuals or corporations. Many MNCs have capitalized on this wave of so-called privatization by taking control of businesses that are sold by governments. These businesses may be attractive because of the potential for MNCs to increase their efficiency.

Valuation Process. An MNC can conduct a valuation of a foreign business that was owned by the government in a developing country by using capital budgeting analysis, as illustrated earlier. However, the valuation of such businesses is difficult for the following reasons:

- The future cash flows are very uncertain because the businesses were previously operating in environments of little or no competition. Thus, previous sales volume figures may not be useful indicators of future sales.
- Data concerning what businesses are worth are very limited in some countries because there are not many publicly traded firms in their markets and there is limited disclosure of prices paid for targets in other acquisitions. Consequently, there may not be any benchmarks to use when valuing a business.
- Economic conditions in these countries are very uncertain during the transition to a market-oriented economy.
- Political conditions tend to be volatile during the transition because government policies for businesses are sometimes unclear or subject to abrupt changes.
- If the government retains a portion of the firm's equity, it may attempt to exert some control over the firm. Its objectives may be very different from those of the acquirer, a situation that could lead to conflict.

Despite these difficulties, MNCs such as IBM and PepsiCo have acquired privatized businesses as a means of entering new markets. Hungary serves as a model country for privatizations. Hungary's government was quick and efficient at selling off its assets to MNCs. More than 25,000 MNCs have a foreign stake in Hungary's businesses.

International Divestitures

An MNC should periodically reassess its direct foreign investments to determine whether they should be retained or sold (divested). Some foreign projects may no longer be feasible as a result of the MNC's increased cost of capital, increased host government taxes, increased political risk in the host country, or revised projections of exchange rates. Many divestitures occur as a result of a revised assessment of industry or economic conditions. For example,

Exhibit 15.3 Divestiture Analysis: Spartan, Inc.

	END OF YEAR 2 (TODAY)	END OF YEAR 3 (1 YEAR FROM TODAY)	END OF YEAR 4 (2 YEARS FROM TODAY)
S$ remitted after withholding taxes		S$6,840,000	S$19,560,000
Selling price	S$13,000,000		
Exchange rate	$.46	$.44	$.40
Cash flow received from divestiture	$5,980,000		
Cash flows forgone due to divestiture		$3,009,600	$7,824,000
PV of forgone cash flows (15% discount rate)		$2,617,044	$5,916,068

$$NPV_d = \$5,980,000 - (\$2,617,044 + \$5,916,068)$$
$$= \$5,980,000 - \$8,533,112$$
$$= -\$2,553,112$$

Pfizer, Johnson & Johnson, and several other U.S.-based MNCs divested some of their Latin American subsidiaries when economic conditions deteriorated there.

Valuation Process. The valuation of a proposed international divestiture can be determined by comparing the present value of the cash flows if the project is continued to the proceeds that would be received (after taxes) if the project is divested.

EXAMPLE

Reconsider the example from the previous chapter in which Spartan, Inc., considered establishing a Singapore subsidiary. Assume that the Singapore subsidiary was created and, after 2 years, the spot rate of the Singapore dollar (S$) is $.46. In addition, forecasts have been revised for the remaining 2 years of the project, indicating that the Singapore dollar should be worth $.44 in Year 3 and $.40 in the project's final year. Because these forecasted exchange rates have an adverse effect on the project, Spartan, Inc., considers divesting the subsidiary. For simplicity, assume that the original forecasts of the other variables remain unchanged and that a potential acquirer has offered S$13 million (after adjusting for any capital gains taxes) for the subsidiary if the acquirer can retain the existing working capital.

Spartan can conduct a divestiture analysis by comparing the after-tax proceeds from the possible sale of the project (in U.S. dollars) to the present value of the expected U.S. dollar inflows that the project will generate if it is not sold. This comparison will determine the net present value of the divestiture (NPV_d), as illustrated in Exhibit 15.3. Since the present value of the subsidiary's cash flows from Spartan's perspective exceeds the price at which it can sell the subsidiary, the divestiture is not feasible. Thus, Spartan should not divest the subsidiary at the price offered. Spartan may still search for another firm that is willing to acquire the subsidiary for a price that exceeds its present value. ●

CONTROL DECISIONS AS REAL OPTIONS

Some international corporate control decisions by MNCs involve **real options,** or implicit options on real assets (such as buildings, machinery, and other assets used by MNCs to facilitate their production). A real option can be classified as a call option on real assets or a put option on real assets, as explained next.

Call Option on Real Assets

A **call option on real assets** represents a proposed project that contains an option of pursuing an additional venture. Some possible forms of restructuring by MNCs contain a call option on real assets. Multinational capital budgeting can be conducted in a manner to account for the option.

EXAMPLE

Coral, Inc., an Internet firm in the United States, is considering the acquisition of an Internet business in Mexico. Coral estimates and discounts the expected dollar cash flows that would result from acquiring this business and compares them to the initial outlay. At this time, the present value of the future cash flows that are directly attributable to the Mexican business is slightly lower than the initial outlay that would be required to purchase that business, so the business appears to be an infeasible investment.

A Brazilian Internet firm is also for sale, but its owners will only sell the business to a firm that they know and trust, and Coral, Inc., has no relationship with this business. A possible advantage of the Mexican firm that is not measured by the traditional multinational capital budgeting analysis is that it frequently does business with the Brazilian Internet firm and could use its relationship to help Coral acquire the Brazilian firm. Thus, if Coral purchases the Mexican business, it will have an option to also acquire the Internet firm in Brazil. In essence, Coral will have a call option on real assets (of the Brazilian firm) because it will have the option (not the obligation) to purchase the Brazilian firm. The expected purchase price of the Brazilian firm over the next few months serves as the exercise price in the call option on real assets. If Coral acquires the Brazilian firm, it now has a second initial outlay and will generate a second stream of cash flows.

When the call option on real assets is considered, the acquisition of the Mexican Internet firm may now be feasible, even though it was not feasible when considering only the cash flows directly attributable to that firm. The project can be analyzed by segmenting it into two scenarios. In the first scenario, Coral, Inc., acquires the Mexican firm but, after taking a closer look at the Brazilian firm, decides not to exercise its call option (decides not to purchase the Brazilian firm). The net present value in this scenario is simply a measure of the present value of expected dollar cash flows directly attributable to the Mexican firm minus the initial outlay necessary to purchase the Mexican firm. In the second scenario, Coral, Inc., acquires the Mexican firm and then exercises its option by also purchasing the Brazilian firm. In this case, the present value of combined (Mexican firm plus Brazilian firm) cash flow streams (in dollars) would be compared to the combined initial outlays.

If the outlay necessary to acquire the Brazilian firm was made after the initial outlay of the Mexican firm, the outlay for the Brazilian firm should be discounted to determine its present value. If Coral, Inc., knows the probability of the two scenarios, it can determine the probability of each scenario and then determine the expected value of the net present value of the proposed project by summing the products of the probability of each scenario times the respective net present value for that scenario. ●

Put Option on Real Assets

A **put option on real assets** represents a proposed project that contains an option of divesting part or all of the project. As with a call option on real assets, a put option on real assets can be accounted for by multinational capital budgeting.

EXAMPLE

Jade, Inc., an office supply firm in the United States, is considering the acquisition of a similar business in Italy. Jade, Inc., believes that if future economic conditions in Italy are favorable, the net present value of this project is positive. However, given that weak economic conditions in Italy are more likely, the proposed project appears to be infeasible.

Assume now that Jade, Inc., knows that it can sell the Italian firm at a specified price to another firm over the next 4 years. In this case, Jade has an implied put option attached to the project.

The feasibility of this project can be assessed by determining the net present value under both the scenario of strong economic conditions and the scenario of weak economic conditions. The expected value of the net present value of this project can be estimated as the sum of the products of the probability of each scenario times its respective net present value. If economic conditions are favorable, the net present value is positive. If economic conditions are weak, Jade, Inc., may sell the Italian firm at the locked-in sales price (which resembles the exercise price of a put option) and therefore may still achieve a positive net present value over the short time that it owned the Italian firm. Thus, the put option on real assets may turn an infeasible project into a feasible project. ●

SUMMARY

- An MNC's board of directors is responsible for ensuring that its managers focus on maximizing the wealth of the shareholders. A board should typically be more effective if the chair is an outside board member and if the board is dominated by outside members. Institutional investors monitor an MNC, but some institutional investors (such as hedge funds) tend to be more effective monitors than others. Blockholders who have a large stake in the firm may also serve as effective monitors and can influence the management because of their voting power.

- The international market for corporate control serves as another form of governance because if public firms do not serve shareholders they may become subject to takeovers. However, managers of public firms can implement some tactics such as anti-takeover provisions and poison pills in order to protect against takeovers.

- The valuation of a firm's target is influenced by target-specific factors (such as the target's previous cash flows and its managerial talent) and country-specific factors (such as economic conditions, political conditions, currency conditions, and stock market conditions).

- In the typical valuation process, an MNC initially screens prospective targets based on willingness to be acquired and country barriers. Then, each prospective target is valued by estimating its cash flows, based on target-specific characteristics and the target's country characteristics, and by discounting the expected cash flows. Then the perceived value is compared to the target's market value to determine whether the target can be purchased at a price that is below the perceived value from the MNC's perspective.

- Valuations of a foreign target may vary among potential acquirers because of differences in estimates of the target's cash flows or exchange rate movements or differences in the required rate of return among acquirers. These differences may be especially pronounced when the acquirers are from different countries.

- Besides international acquisitions of firms, the more common types of international corporate control transactions include international partial acquisitions, international acquisitions of privatized businesses, and international divestitures. The feasibility of these types of transactions can be assessed by applying multinational capital budgeting.

POINT COUNTER-POINT

Can a Foreign Target Be Assessed Like Any Other Asset?

Point Yes. The value of a foreign target to an MNC is the present value of the future cash flows to the MNC. The process of estimating a foreign target's value is the same as the process of estimating a machine's value. A target has expected cash flows, which can be derived from information about previous cash flows.

Counter-Point No. A target's behavior will change after it is acquired by an MNC. Its efficiency may improve depending on the ability of the MNC to integrate the target with its own operations. The morale of the target employees could either improve or worsen after the acquisition, depending on the treatment by the acquirer. Thus, a proper estimate of cash flows generated by the target must consider the changes in the target due to the acquisition.

Who Is Correct? Use the Internet to learn more about this issue. Which argument do you support? Offer your own opinion on this issue.

SELF-TEST

Answers are provided in Appendix A at the back of the text.

1. Explain why more acquisitions have taken place in Europe in recent years.

2. What are some of the barriers to international acquisitions?

3. Why might a U.S.-based MNC prefer to establish a foreign subsidiary rather than acquire an existing firm in a foreign country?

4. Provo, Inc. (based in Utah), has been considering the divestiture of a Swedish subsidiary that produces ski equipment and sells it locally. A Swedish firm has already offered to acquire this Swedish subsidiary. Assume that the U.S. parent has just revised its projections of the Swedish krona's value downward. Will the proposed divestiture now seem more or less feasible than it did before? Explain.

QUESTIONS AND APPLICATIONS

1. Motives for Restructuring. Why do you think MNCs continuously assess possible forms of multinational restructuring, such as foreign acquisitions or downsizing of a foreign subsidiary?

2. Exposure to Country Regulations. Maude, Inc., a U.S.-based MNC, has recently acquired a firm in Singapore. To eliminate inefficiencies, Maude downsized the target substantially, eliminating two-thirds of the workforce. Why might this action affect the regulations imposed on the subsidiary's business by the Singapore government?

3. Global Expansion Strategy. Poki, Inc., a U.S.-based MNC, is considering expanding into Thailand because of decreasing profit margins in the United States. The demand for Poki's product in Thailand is very strong. However, forecasts indicate that the baht is expected to depreciate substantially over the next 3 years. Should Poki expand into Thailand? What factors may affect its decision?

4. Valuation of a Private Target. Rastell, Inc., a U.S.-based MNC, is considering the acquisition of a Russian target to produce personal computers (PCs) and market them throughout Russia, where demand for PCs has increased substantially in recent years. Assume that the stock prices of most Russian companies rose substantially just prior to Rastell's assessment of the target. If Rastell, Inc., acquires a private target in Russia, will it be able to avoid the impact of the high stock prices on business valuations in Russia?

5. Comparing International Projects. Savannah, Inc., a manufacturer of clothing, wants to increase its market share by acquiring a target producing a popular clothing line in Europe. This clothing line is well established. Forecasts indicate a relatively stable euro over the life of the project. Marquette, Inc., wants to increase its market share in the personal computer market by acquiring a target in Thailand that currently produces radios and converting the operations to produce PCs. Forecasts indicate a depreciation of the baht over the life of the project. Funds resulting from both projects will be remitted to the respective U.S. parent on a regular basis. Which target do you think will result in a higher net present value? Why?

6. Privatized Business Valuations. Why are valuations of privatized businesses previously owned by the governments of developing countries more difficult than valuations of existing firms in developed countries?

7. Valuing a Foreign Target. Blore, Inc., a U.S.-based MNC, has screened several targets. Based on economic and political considerations, only one eligible target remains in Malaysia. Blore would like you to value this target and has provided you with the following information:

- Blore expects to keep the target for 3 years, at which time it expects to sell the firm for 300 million Malaysian ringgit (MYR) after any taxes.
- Blore expects a strong Malaysian economy. The estimates for revenue for the next year are MYR200 million. Revenues are expected to increase by 8 percent in each of the following 2 years.
- Cost of goods sold is expected to be 50 percent of revenue.
- Selling and administrative expenses are expected to be MYR30 million in each of the next 3 years.
- The Malaysian tax rate on the target's earnings is expected to be 35 percent.
- Depreciation expenses are expected to be MYR20 million per year for each of the next 3 years.
- The target will need MYR7 million in cash each year to support existing operations.
- The target's stock price is currently MYR30 per share. The target has 9 million shares outstanding.
- Any remaining cash flows will be remitted by the target to Blore, Inc. Blore uses the prevailing exchange rate of the Malaysian ringgit as the expected exchange rate for the next 3 years. This exchange rate is currently $.25.
- Blore's required rate of return on similar projects is 20 percent.

a. Prepare a worksheet to estimate the value of the Malaysian target based on the information provided.

b. Will Blore, Inc., be able to acquire the Malaysian target for a price lower than its valuation of the target?

8.   Uncertainty Surrounding a Foreign Target. Refer to question 7. What are some of the key sources of uncertainty in Blore's valuation of the target? Identify two reasons why the expected cash flows from an Asian subsidiary of a U.S.-based MNC would be lower if Asia experienced a new crisis.

9.   Divestiture Strategy. The reduction in expected cash flows of Asian subsidiaries as a result of the Asian crisis likely resulted in a reduced valuation of these subsidiaries from the parent's perspective. Explain why a U.S.-based MNC might not have sold its Asian subsidiaries.

10.   Why a Foreign Acquisition May Backfire. Provide two reasons why an MNC's strategy of acquiring a foreign target will backfire. That is, explain why the acquisition might result in a negative *NPV*.

Advanced Questions

11.   Pricing a Foreign Target. Alaska, Inc., would like to acquire Estoya Corp., which is located in Peru. In initial negotiations, Estoya has asked for a purchase price of 1 billion Peruvian new sol. If Alaska completes the purchase, it would keep Estoya's operations for 2 years and then sell the company. In the recent past, Estoya has generated annual cash flows of 500 million new sol per year, but Alaska believes that it can increase these cash flows by 5 percent each year by improving the operations of the plant. Given these improvements, Alaska believes it will be able to resell Estoya in 2 years for 1.2 billion new sol. The current exchange rate of the new sol is $.29, and exchange rate forecasts for the next 2 years indicate values of $.29 and $.27, respectively. Given these facts, should Alaska, Inc., pay 1 billion new sol for Estoya Corp. if the required rate of return is 18 percent? What is the maximum price Alaska should be willing to pay?

12.   Global Strategy. Senser Co. established a subsidiary in Russia 2 years ago. Under its original plans, Senser intended to operate the subsidiary for a total of 4 years. However, it would like to reassess the situation, because exchange rate forecasts for the Russian ruble indicate that it may depreciate from its current level of $.033 to $.028 next year and to $.025 in the following year. Senser could sell the subsidiary today for 5 million rubles to a potential acquirer. If Senser continues to operate the subsidiary, it will generate cash flows of 3 million rubles next year and 4 million rubles in the following year. These cash flows would be remitted back to the parent in the United States. The required rate of return of the project is 16 percent. Should Senser continue operating the Russian subsidiary?

13.   Divestiture Decision. Colorado Springs Co. plans to divest either its Singapore or its Canadian subsidiary. Assume that if exchange rates remain constant, the dollar cash flows each of these subsidiaries would provide to the parent over time would be somewhat similar. However, the firm expects the Singapore dollar to depreciate against the U.S. dollar, and the Canadian dollar to appreciate against the U.S. dollar. The firm can sell either subsidiary for about the same price today. Which one should it sell?

14.   Divestiture Decision. San Gabriel Corp. recently considered divesting its Italian subsidiary and determined that the divestiture was not feasible. The required rate of return on this subsidiary was 17 percent.

In the last week, San Gabriel's required return on that subsidiary increased to 21 percent. If the sales price of the subsidiary has not changed, explain why the divestiture may now be feasible.

15. Divestiture Decision. Ethridge Co. of Atlanta, Georgia, has a subsidiary in India that produces products and sells them throughout Asia. In response to the September 11, 2001, terrorist attack on the United States, Ethridge Co. decided to conduct a capital budgeting analysis to determine whether it should divest the subsidiary. Why might this decision be different after the attack as opposed to before the attack? Describe the general method for determining whether the divestiture is financially feasible.

16. Feasibility of a Divestiture. Merton, Inc., has a subsidiary in Bulgaria that it fully finances with its own equity. Last week, a firm offered to buy the subsidiary from Merton for $60 million in cash, and the offer is still available this week as well. The annualized long-term risk-free rate in the United States increased from 7 to 8 percent this week. The expected monthly cash flows to be generated by the subsidiary have not changed since last week. The risk premium that Merton applies to its projects in Bulgaria was reduced from 11.3 to 10.9 percent this week. The annualized long-term risk-free rate in Bulgaria declined from 23 to 21 percent this week. Would the *NPV* to Merton, Inc., from divesting this unit be more or less than the *NPV* determined last week? Why? (No analysis is necessary, but make sure that your explanation is very clear.)

17. Accounting for Government Restrictions. Sunbelt, Inc., plans to purchase a firm in Indonesia. It believes that it can install its operating procedure in this firm, which would significantly reduce the firm's operating expenses. However, the Indonesian government may approve the acquisition only if Sunbelt does not lay off any workers. How can Sunbelt possibly increase efficiency without laying off workers? How can Sunbelt account for the Indonesian government's position as it assesses the *NPV* of this possible acquisition?

18. Foreign Acquisition Decision. Florida Co. produces software. Its primary business in Boca Raton is expected to generate cash flows of $4 million at the end of each of the next 3 years, and Florida expects that it could sell this business for $10 million (after accounting for capital gains taxes) at the end of 3 years. Florida Co. also has a side business in Pompano Beach that takes the software created in Boca Raton and exports it to Europe. As long as the side business distributes this software to Europe, it is expected to generate $2 million in cash flows at the end of each of the next 3 years. This side business in Pompano Beach is separate from Florida's main business.

Recently, Florida was contacted by Ryne Co. located in Europe, which specializes in distributing software throughout Europe. If Florida acquires Ryne Co., it would rely on Ryne instead of its side business to sell its software in Europe because Ryne could easily reach all of Florida Co.'s existing European customers and additional potential European customers. By acquiring Ryne, Florida would be able to sell much more software in Europe than it can sell with its side business, but it has to determine whether the acquisition would be feasible. The initial investment to acquire Ryne Co. would be $7 million. Ryne would generate 6 million euros per year in profits and would be subject to a European tax rate of 40 percent. All after-tax profits would be remitted to Florida Co. at the end of each year, and the profits would not be subject to any U.S. taxes since they were already taxed in Europe. The spot rate of the euro is $1.10, and Florida Co. believes the spot rate is a reasonable forecast of future exchange rates. Florida Co. expects that it could sell Ryne Co. at the end of 3 years for 3 million euros (after accounting for any capital gains taxes). Florida Co.'s required rate of return on the acquisition is 20 percent. Determine the net present value of this acquisition. Should Florida Co. acquire Ryne Co.?

19. Foreign Acquisition Decision. Minnesota Co. consists of two businesses. Its local business is expected to generate cash flows of $1 million at the end of each of the next 3 years. It also owns a foreign subsidiary based in Mexico, whose business is selling technology in Mexico. This business is expected to generate $2 million in cash flows at the end of each of the next 3 years. The main competitor of the Mexican subsidiary is Perez Co., a privately held firm that is based in Mexico. Minnesota Co. just contacted Perez Co. and wants to acquire it. If it acquires Perez, Minnesota would merge the operations of Perez Co. with its Mexican subsidiary's business. It expects that these merged operations in Mexico would generate a total of $3 million in cash flows at the end of each of the next 3 years. Perez Co. is willing to be acquired for a price of 40 million pesos. The spot rate of the Mexican peso is $.10. The required rate of return on this project is 24 percent. Determine the net present value of this acquisition by Minnesota Co. Should Minnesota Co. pursue this acquisition?

20. Decision to Sell a Business. Kentucky Co. has an existing business in Italy that it is trying to sell. It receives one offer today from Rome Co. for $20 million (after capital gains taxes are paid). Alternatively, Venice Co. wants to buy the business but will not have the funds to make the acquisition until 2 years from now. It is meeting with Kentucky Co. today to negotiate the acquisition price that it will guarantee for Kentucky in 2 years (the price would be backed by a reputable bank so there would be no concern about Venice Co. backing out of the agreement). If Kentucky Co. retains the business for the next 2 years, it expects that the business will generate 6 million euros per year in cash flows (after taxes are paid) at the end of each of the next 2 years, which would be remitted to the United States. The euro is presently $1.20, and that rate can be used as a forecast of future spot rates. Kentucky would only retain the business if it can earn a rate of return of at least 18 percent by keeping the firm for the next 2 years rather than selling it to Rome Co. now. Determine the minimum price in dollars at which Kentucky should be willing to sell its business (after accounting for capital gain taxes paid) to Venice Co. in order to satisfy its required rate of return.

21. Foreign Divestiture Decision. Baltimore Co. considers divesting its six foreign projects as of today. Each project will last 1 year. Its required rate of return on each project is the same. The cost of operations for each project is denominated in dollars and is the same. Baltimore believes that each project will generate the equivalent of $10 million in 1 year based on today's exchange rate. However, each project generates its cash flow in a different currency. Baltimore believes that interest rate parity (IRP) exists. Baltimore forecasts exchange rates as explained in the table below.

a. Based on this information, which project will Baltimore be most likely to divest? Why?

b. Based on this information, which project will Baltimore be least likely to divest? Why?

22. Factors That Affect the *NPV* of a Divestiture. Washington Co. (a U.S. firm) has a subsidiary in Germany that generates substantial earnings in euros each year. One week ago, it received an offer from a company to purchase the subsidiary, and it has not yet responded to this offer.

a. Since last week, the expected stream of euro cash flows has not changed, but the forecasts of the euro's value in future periods have been revised downward. Will the *NPV* of the divestiture be larger or smaller or the same as it was last week? Briefly explain.

b. Since last week, the expected stream of euro cash flows has not changed, but the long-term interest rate in the United States has declined. Will the *NPV* of the divestiture be larger or smaller or the same as it was last week? Briefly explain.

23. Impact of Country Perspective on Target Valuation. Targ Co. of the United States has been targeted by three firms that consider acquiring it: (1) Americo (from the United States), Japino (of Japan), and Canzo (of Canada). These three firms do not have any other international business, have similar risk levels, and have a similar capital structure. Each of the three potential acquirers has derived similar expected dollar cash flow estimates for Targ Co. The long-term risk-free interest rate is 6 percent in the United States, 9 percent in Canada, and 3 percent in Japan. The stock market conditions are similar in each of the countries. There are no potential country risk problems that would result from acquiring Targ Co. All potential acquirers expect that the Canadian dollar will appreciate by 1 percent a year against the U.S. dollar and will be stable against the Japanese yen. Which firm will likely have the highest valuation of Targ Co.? Explain.

24. Valuation of a Foreign Target. Gaston Co. (a U.S. firm) is considering the purchase of a target

PROJECT	COMPARISON OF 1-YEAR U.S. AND FOREIGN INTEREST RATES	FORECAST METHOD USED TO FORECAST THE SPOT RATE 1 YEAR FROM NOW
Country A	U.S. interest rate is higher than currency A's interest rate	Spot rate
Country B	U.S interest rate is higher than currency B's interest rate	Forward rate
Country C	U.S. interest rate is the same as currency C's interest rate	Forward rate
Country D	U.S. interest rate is the same as currency D's interest rate	Spot rate
Country E	U.S. interest rate is lower than currency E's interest rate	Forward rate
Country F	U.S. interest rate is lower than currency F's interest rate	Spot rate

company based in Mexico. The net cash flows to be generated by this target firm are expected to be 300 million pesos at the end of 1 year. The existing spot rate of the peso is $.14, while the expected spot rate in 1 year is $.12. All cash flows will be remitted to the parent at the end of 1 year. In addition, Gaston hopes to sell the company for 800 million pesos (after taxes) at the end of 1 year. The target has 10 million shares outstanding. If Gaston purchases this target, it would require a 25 percent return. The maximum value that Gaston should pay for this target company today is _____ pesos per share. Show your work.

25. Divestiture of a Foreign Subsidiary. Rudecki Co. (a U.S. firm) has a Polish subsidiary that it is considering divesting. This company is completely focused on research and development for Rudecki's other business. Rudecki has cash outflows (paid in zloty, the Polish currency) for the laboratories and scientists in Poland. While the subsidiary does not generate any sales, its research and development lead to new products and higher sales of products that are sold solely in the United States and denominated in dollars. There is no foreign competition. Last week, a firm offered to purchase the subsidiary for $10 million, and the offer is still available. Today Rudecki has revised its forecasts of the zloty upward for all future periods. Will today's adjustment in exchange rate forecasts increase, decrease, or have no effect on the net present value of a divestiture of this subsidiary from Rudecki's perspective? Briefly explain. [Keep in mind that the NPV of the divestiture is not the same as the NPV that results from acquiring a project.]

26. Poison Pills and Takeovers. Explain how a foreign target could use poison pills to prevent a takeover or change the terms of a takeover.

27. Governance of MNCs by Shareholders. Explain the various ways in which large shareholders can attempt to govern an MNC and improve its management.

28. Divestiture of a Foreign Subsidiary. Ved Co. (a U.S. firm) has a subsidiary in Germany that generates substantial earnings in euros each year. It will soon decide whether to divest the subsidiary. One week ago, a company offered to purchase the subsidiary from Ved Co., and Ved has not yet responded to this offer.

a. Since last week, the expected stream of euro cash flows has not changed, but the forecasts of the euro's value in future periods have been revised downward. When deciding whether a divestiture is feasible, Ved Co. estimates the NPV of the divestiture. Will Ved's estimated NPV of the divestiture be larger or smaller or the same as it was last week? Briefly explain.

b. If the long-term interest rate in the United States suddenly declines and all other factors are unchanged, will the NPV of the divestiture be larger, smaller, or the same as it was last week? Briefly explain.

Discussion in the Boardroom

This exercise can be found in Appendix E at the back of this textbook.

Running Your Own MNC

This exercise can be found on the *International Financial Management* text companion website located at www.cengage.com/finance/madura.

BLADES, INC. CASE

Assessment of an Acquisition in Thailand

Recall that Ben Holt, Blades' chief financial officer (CFO), has suggested to the board of directors that Blades proceed with the establishment of a subsidiary in Thailand. Due to the high growth potential of the roller blade market in Thailand, his analysis suggests that the venture will be profitable. Specifically, his view is that Blades should establish a subsidiary in Thailand to manufacture roller blades, whether an existing agreement with Entertainment Products (a Thai retailer) is renewed or not. Under this agreement, Entertainment Products is committed to the purchase of

180,000 pairs of Speedos, Blades' primary product, annually. The agreement was initially for 3 years and will expire 2 years from now. At this time, the agreement may be renewed. Due to delivery delays, Entertainment Products has indicated that it will renew the agreement only if Blades establishes a subsidiary in Thailand. In this case, the price per pair of roller blades would be fixed at 4,594 Thai baht per pair. If Blades decides not to renew the agreement, Entertainment Products has indicated that it would purchase only 5,000 pairs of Speedos annually at prevailing market prices.

According to Ben Holt's analysis, renewing the agreement with Entertainment Products and establishing a subsidiary in Thailand will result in a net present value (*NPV*) of $2,638,735. Conversely, if the agreement is not renewed and a subsidiary is established, the resulting *NPV* is $8,746,688. Consequently, Holt has suggested to the board of directors that Blades establish a subsidiary without renewing the existing agreement with Entertainment Products.

Recently, a Thai roller blade manufacturer called Skates'n'Stuff contacted Holt regarding the potential sale of the company to Blades. Skates'n'Stuff entered the Thai roller blade market a decade ago and has generated a profit in every year of operation. Furthermore, Skates'n'Stuff has established distribution channels in Thailand. Consequently, if Blades acquires the company, it could begin sales immediately and would not require an additional year to build the plant in Thailand. Initial forecasts indicate that Blades would be able to sell 280,000 pairs of roller blades annually. These sales are incremental to the acquisition of Skates'n'Stuff. Furthermore, all sales resulting from the acquisition would be made to retailers in Thailand. Blades' fixed expenses would be 20 million baht annually. Although Holt has not previously considered the acquisition of an existing business, he is now wondering whether acquiring Skates'n'Stuff may be a better course of action than building a subsidiary in Thailand.

Holt is also aware of some disadvantages associated with such an acquisition. Skates'n'Stuff's CFO has indicated that he would be willing to accept a price of 1 billion baht in payment for the company, which is clearly more expensive than the 550 million baht outlay that would be required to establish a subsidiary in Thailand. However, Skates'n'Stuff's CFO has indicated that it is willing to negotiate. Furthermore, Blades employs a high-quality production process, which enables it to charge relatively high prices for roller blades produced in its plants. If Blades acquires Skates'n'Stuff, which uses an inferior production process (resulting in lower quality roller blades), it would have to charge a lower price for the roller blades it produces there. Initial forecasts indicate that Blades will be able to charge a price of 4,500 Thai baht per pair of roller blades without affecting demand. However, because Skates'n'Stuff uses a production process that results in lower quality roller blades than Blades' Speedos, operating costs incurred would be similar to the amount incurred if Blades establishes a subsidiary in Thailand. Thus, Blades estimates that it would incur operating costs of about 3,500 baht per pair of roller blades.

Ben Holt has asked you, a financial analyst for Blades, Inc., to determine whether the acquisition of Skates'n'Stuff is a better course of action for Blades than the establishment of a subsidiary in Thailand. Acquiring Skates'n'Stuff will be more favorable than establishing a subsidiary if the present value of the cash flows generated by the company exceeds the purchase price by more than $8,746,688, the *NPV* of establishing a new subsidiary. Thus, Holt has asked you to construct a spreadsheet that determines the *NPV* of the acquisition.

To aid you in your analysis, Holt has provided the following additional information, which he gathered from various sources, including unaudited financial statements of Skates'n'Stuff for the last 3 years:

- Blades, Inc., requires a return on the Thai acquisition of 25 percent, the same rate of return it would require if it established a subsidiary in Thailand.
- If Skates'n'Stuff is acquired, Blades, Inc., will operate the company for 10 years, at which time Skates'n'Stuff will be sold for an estimated 1.1 million baht.
- Of the 1 billion baht purchase price, 600 million baht constitutes the cost of the plant and equipment. These items are depreciated using straight-line depreciation. Thus, 60 million baht will be depreciated annually for 10 years.
- Sales of 280,000 pairs of roller blades annually will begin immediately at a price of 4,500 baht per pair.
- Variable costs per pair of roller blades will be 3,500 per pair.
- Fixed operating costs, including salaries and administrative expenses, will be 20 million baht annually.
- The current spot rate of the Thai baht is $.023. Blades expects the baht to depreciate by an average of 2 percent per year for the next 10 years.
- The Thai government will impose a 25 percent tax on income and a 10 percent withholding tax on any funds remitted by Skates'n'Stuff to Blades, Inc. Any earnings remitted to the United States will not be taxed again in the United States. All earnings generated by Skates'n'Stuff will be remitted to Blades, Inc.
- The average inflation rate in Thailand is expected to be 12 percent annually. Revenues, variable costs, and fixed costs are subject to inflation and are expected to change by the same annual rate as the inflation rate.

In addition to the information outlined above, Ben Holt has informed you that Blades, Inc., will need to manufacture all of the 180,000 pairs to be delivered to Entertainment Products this year and next year in Thailand. Since Blades previously only used components from Thailand (which are of a lower quality but cheaper than U.S. components) sufficient to manufacture 72,000 pairs annually, it will incur cost savings of 32.4 million baht this year and next year. However, since Blades will sell 180,000 pairs of Speedos annually to Entertainment Products this year and next year whether it acquires Skates'n'Stuff or not, Holt has urged you not to include these sales in your analysis. The agreement with Entertainment Products will not be renewed at the end of next year.

Ben Holt would like you to answer the following questions:

1. Using a spreadsheet, determine the *NPV* of the acquisition of Skates'n'Stuff. Based on your numerical analysis, should Blades establish a subsidiary in Thailand or acquire Skates'n'Stuff?

2. If Blades negotiates with Skates'n'Stuff, what is the maximum amount (in Thai baht) Blades should be willing to pay?

3. Are there any other factors Blades should consider in making its decision? In your answer, you should consider the price Skates'n'Stuff is asking relative to your analysis in question 1, other potential businesses for sale in Thailand, the source of the information your analysis is based on, the production process that will be employed by the target in the future, and the future management of Skates'n'Stuff.

SMALL BUSINESS DILEMMA

Multinational Restructuring by the Sports Exports Company

The Sports Exports Company has been successful in producing footballs in the United States and exporting them to the United Kingdom. Recently, Jim Logan (owner of the Sports Exports Company) has considered restructuring his company by expanding throughout Europe. He plans to export footballs and other sporting goods that were not already popular in Europe to one large sporting goods distributor in Germany; the goods will then be distributed to any retail sporting goods stores throughout Europe that are willing to purchase these goods. This distributor will make payments in euros to the Sports Exports Company.

1. Are there any reasons why the business that has been so successful in the United Kingdom will not necessarily be successful in other European countries?

2. If the business is diversified throughout Europe, will this substantially reduce the exposure of the Sports Exports Company to exchange rate risk?

3. Now that several countries in Europe participate in a single currency system, will this affect the performance of new expansion throughout Europe?

INTERNET/EXCEL EXERCISES

1. Use an online news source to review an international acquisition in the last month. Describe the motive for this acquisition. Explain how the acquirer could benefit from this acquisition.

2. You consider acquiring a target in Argentina, Brazil, or Canada. You realize that the value of a target is partially influenced by stock market conditions in a country. Go to http://finance.yahoo.com/intlindices?e=Americas, and click on index MERV (which represents the Argentina stock market index). Click on 1y just below the chart provided. Then scroll down and click on Historical Prices. Set the date range so that you

can obtain the stock index value as of 3 years ago, 2 years ago, 1 year ago, and as of today. Insert the data on a spreadsheet. Compute the annual percentage change in the stock value. Also compute the annual percentage change in the stock value from 3 years ago until today. Repeat the process for the Brazilian stock index BVSP and the Canadian stock index GSPTSE. Based on this information, in which country have values of corporations increased the most? In which country have the values of corporations increased the least? Why might this information influence your decision on where to pursue a target?

REFERENCES

Chkir, Imed, and Jean-Claude Cosset, Winter 2003, The Effect of International Acquisitions on Firm Leverage, *Journal of Financial Research*, pp. 501–515.

Copeland, Tom, and Peter Tufano, Mar 2004, A Real-World Way to Manage Real Options, *Harvard Business Review*, pp. 90–104.

Doukas, John A., and Ozgur B. Kan, May 2006, Does Global Diversification Destroy Firm Value? *Journal of International Business Studies*, pp. 352–371.

Faccio, Mara, and Ronald W. Masulis, Jun 2005, The Choice of Payment Method in European Mergers and Acquisitions, *Journal of Finance*, p. 1.

Nadolska, Anna, and Harry G. Barkema, Dec 2007, Learning to Internationalize: The Pace and Success of Foreign Acquisitions, in Part Focused Issue: Internationalization—Positions, *Journal of International Business Studies*, pp. 1170–1186.

Reuer, Jeffrey J., Oded Shenkar, and Roberto Ragozzino, Jan 2004, Mitigating Risk in International Mergers and Acquisitions: The Role of Contingent Payouts, *Journal of International Business Studies*, pp. 19–32.

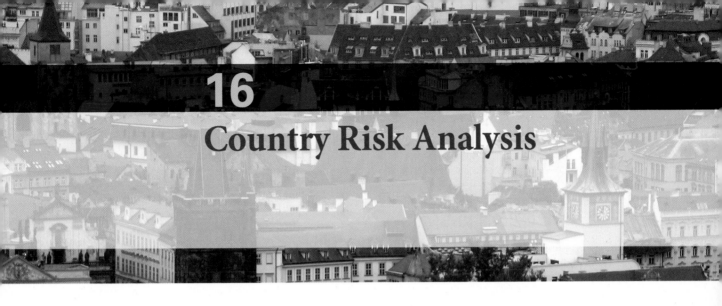

16

Country Risk Analysis

CHAPTER OBJECTIVES

The specific objectives of this chapter are to:

- identify the common factors used by MNCs to measure country risk,

- explain the techniques used to measure country risk,

- explain how to derive an overall measure of country risk,

- explain how MNCs use the assessment of country risk when making financial decisions, and

- explain how MNCs prevent host government takeovers.

An MNC conducts country risk analysis when assessing whether to continue conducting business in a particular country. The analysis can also be used when determining whether to implement new projects in foreign countries. Country risk can be partitioned into the country's political risk and its financial risk. Financial managers must understand how to measure country risk so that they can make investment decisions that maximize their MNC's value.

WHY COUNTRY RISK ANALYSIS IS IMPORTANT

Country risk is the potentially adverse impact of a country's environment on an MNC's cash flows. Country risk analysis can be used to monitor countries where the MNC is currently doing business. If the country risk level of a particular country begins to increase, the MNC may consider divesting its subsidiaries located there. MNCs can also use country risk analysis as a screening device to avoid conducting business in countries with excessive risk. Events that heighten country risk tend to discourage U.S. direct foreign investment in that particular country.

Country risk analysis is not restricted to predicting major crises. An MNC may also use this analysis to revise its investment or financing decisions in light of recent events. In any given week, the following unrelated international events might occur around the world:

- A terrorist attack
- A major labor strike in an industry
- A political crisis due to a scandal within a country
- Concern about a country's banking system that may cause a major outflow of funds
- The imposition of trade restrictions on imports

Any of these events could affect the potential cash flows to be generated by an MNC or the cost of financing projects and therefore affect the value of the MNC.

Even if an MNC reduces its exposure to all such events in a given week, a new set of events will occur in the following week. For each of these events, an MNC must consider whether its cash flows will be affected and whether there has been a change in policy to which it should respond. Country risk analysis is an ongoing process. Most MNCs will not be affected by every event, but they will pay close attention to any events that may have an impact on the industries or countries in which they do business. They also recognize that they cannot eliminate their exposure to all events but may at least attempt to limit their exposure to any single country-specific event.

COUNTRY RISK FACTORS

An MNC must assess country risk not only in countries where it currently does business but also in those where it expects to export or establish subsidiaries. Several risk characteristics of a country may significantly affect performance, and the MNC should be concerned about the likely degree of impact for each.

Political Risk

Political risk factors can impede the performance of a local subsidiary. An extreme form of political risk is the possibility that the host country will take over a subsidiary. In some cases of expropriation, compensation (the amount decided by the host country government) is awarded. In other cases, the assets are confiscated, and no compensation is provided. Expropriation can take place peacefully or by force. The following are some of the more common forms of political risk:

- Attitude of consumers in the host country
- Actions of host government
- Blockage of fund transfers
- Currency inconvertibility
- War
- Inefficient bureaucracy
- Corruption

Each of these characteristics is discussed in turn.

Attitude of Consumers in the Host Country. A mild form of political risk (to an exporter) is a tendency of residents to purchase only locally produced goods. Even if the exporter decides to set up a subsidiary in the foreign country, this philosophy could prevent its success. All countries tend to exert some pressure on consumers to purchase from locally owned manufacturers. (In the United States, consumers are encouraged to look for the "Made in the U.S.A." label.) MNCs that consider entering a foreign market (or have already entered that market) must monitor the general loyalty of consumers toward locally produced products. If consumers are very loyal to local products, a joint venture with a local company may be more feasible than an exporting strategy.

WEB

www.cia.gov
Valuable information about political risk that should be considered by MNCs that engage in direct foreign investment.

Actions of Host Government. Various actions of a host government can affect the cash flow of an MNC. A host government might impose pollution control standards (which affect costs) and additional corporate taxes (which affect after-tax earnings), as well as withholding taxes and fund transfer restrictions (which affect after-tax cash flows sent to the parent).

Some MNCs use turnover in government members or philosophy as a proxy for a country's political risk. While such change can significantly influence the MNC's future cash flows, it alone does not serve as a suitable representation of political risk. A subsidiary will not necessarily be affected by changing governments. Furthermore, a subsidiary can be affected by new policies of the host government or by a changed attitude toward the subsidiary's home country (and therefore the subsidiary), even when the host government has no risk of being overthrown.

A host government can use various means to make an MNC's operations coincide with its own goals. It may, for example, require the use of local employees for managerial positions at a subsidiary. In addition, it may require social facilities (such as an exercise room or nonsmoking areas) or special environmental controls (such as air pollution controls). Furthermore, a host government may require special permits, impose extra taxes, or subsidize competitors. It may also impose restrictions or fines to protect local competition.

In March 2004, antitrust regulators representing European Union countries decided to fine Microsoft about 500 million euros (equivalent to about $610 million at the time) for abusing its monopolistic position in computer software. They also imposed restrictions on how Microsoft could bundle its Windows Media Player (needed to access music or videos) in its personal computers sold in Europe. Microsoft argued that the fine was unfair because it is not subject to such restrictions in its home country, the United States. Some critics argue, however, that the European regulators are not being too strict, but rather that the U.S. regulators are being too lenient. In 2008, European regulators launched new investigations about possible antitrust violations by Microsoft. ●

In some cases, MNCs are adversely affected by a lack of restrictions in a host country, which allows illegitimate business behavior to take market share. One of the most troubling issues for MNCs is the failure by host governments to enforce copyright laws against local firms that illegally copy the MNC's product. For example, local firms in Asia commonly copy software produced by MNCs and sell it to customers at lower prices. Software producers lose an estimated $3 billion in sales annually in Asia for this reason. Furthermore, the legal systems in some countries do not adequately protect a firm against copyright violations or other illegal means of obtaining market share.

Blockage of Fund Transfers. Subsidiaries of MNCs often send funds back to headquarters for loan repayments, purchases of supplies, administrative fees, remitted earnings, or other purposes. In some cases, a host government may block fund transfers, which could force subsidiaries to undertake projects that are not optimal (just to make use of the funds). Alternatively, the MNC may invest the funds in local securities that provide some return while the funds are blocked. But this return may be inferior to what could have been earned on funds remitted to the parent.

Currency Inconvertibility. Some governments do not allow the home currency to be exchanged into other currencies. Thus, the earnings generated by a subsidiary in these countries cannot be remitted to the parent through currency conversion. When the currency is inconvertible, an MNC's parent may need to exchange it for goods to extract benefits from projects in that country.

War. Some countries tend to engage in constant conflicts with neighboring countries or experience internal turmoil. This can affect the safety of employees hired by an MNC's subsidiary or by salespeople who attempt to establish export markets for the MNC. In addition, countries plagued by the threat of war typically have volatile business cycles, which make cash flows generated from such countries more uncertain. MNCs in all countries have some exposure to terrorist attacks, but the exposure is much higher in some than in others. Even if an MNC is not directly damaged due to a war, it may incur costs from ensuring the safety of its employees.

Inefficient Bureaucracy. Another country risk factor is a government's bureaucracy, which can complicate an MNC's business. Although this factor may seem irrelevant, it has been a major deterrent for MNCs that consider projects in various emerging countries. Bureaucracy can delay an MNC's efforts to establish a new subsidiary or expand business in a country. In some cases, the bureaucratic problem is caused by government employees who expect "gifts" before they approve applications by MNCs. In other cases, the problem is caused by a lack of government organization, so the development of a new business is delayed until various applications are approved by different sections of the bureaucracy.

WEB

http://finance.yahoo.com/
Assessments of various political risk characteristics by outside evaluators.

Exhibit 16.1 Corruption Index Ratings for Selected Countries (Maximum rating = 10. High ratings indicate low corruption.)

COUNTRY	INDEX RATING	COUNTRY	INDEX RATING
Finland	9.6	Chile	7.3
New Zealand	9.6	United States	7.3
Denmark	9.5	Spain	6.8
Singapore	9.4	Uruguay	6.4
Sweden	9.2	Taiwan	5.9
Switzerland	9.1	Hungary	5.2
Netherlands	8.9	Malaysia	5.0
Austria	8.6	Italy	4.9
United Kingdom	8.6	Czech Republic	4.8
Canada	8.5	Greece	4.4
Hong Kong	8.3	Brazil	3.9
Germany	8.0	China	3.3
Belgium	7.4	India	3.3
France	7.4	Mexico	3.3
Ireland	7.4	Russia	2.5

Source: *Transparency International, 2009.* Transparency International's Corruption Perceptions Index measures the perceived level of public sector corruption as seen by business people and country analysts; ranging between 10 (highly clean) and 0 (highly corrupt).

WEB

www.heritage.org
Interesting insight into international political risk issues that should be considered by MNCs conducting international business.

Corruption. Corruption can adversely affect an MNC's international business because it can increase the cost of conducting business or reduce revenue. Various forms of corruption can occur at the firm level or with firm–government interactions. For example, an MNC may lose revenue because a government contract is awarded to a local firm that paid off a government official. Laws defining corruption and their enforcement vary among countries, however. For example, in the United States, it is illegal to make a payment to a high-ranking government official in return for political favors, but it is legal for U.S. firms to contribute to a politician's election campaign.

Transparency International has derived a corruption index for most countries (see www.transparency.org). The index for selected countries is shown in Exhibit 16.1.

Financial Risk

Along with political factors, financial factors should be considered when assessing country risk. One of the most obvious financial factors is the current and potential state of the country's economy. An MNC that exports to a country or develops a subsidiary in a country is very concerned about that country's demand for its products. This demand is, of course, strongly influenced by the country's economy. A recession in the country could severely reduce demand for the MNC's exports or for products sold by the MNC's local subsidiary. MNCs such as 3M, DuPont, IBM, and Nike were adversely affected by a weak European economy during the credit crisis of 2008.

Economic Growth. An MNC's sales in a particular country can be highly influenced by economic growth. Recent levels of a country's gross domestic product (GDP) may be used to measure recent economic growth. In some cases, they may be used to forecast future economic growth. A country's economic growth is influenced by interest rates, exchange rates, and inflation. These factors are discussed in turn.

- *Interest rates.* Higher interest rates tend to slow the growth of an economy and reduce demand for the MNC's products. Lower interest rates often stimulate the economy and increase demand for the MNC's products.
- *Exchange rates.* Exchange rates can influence the demand for the country's exports, which in turn affects the country's production and income level. A strong currency may reduce demand for the country's exports, increase the volume of products imported by the country, and therefore reduce the country's production and national income. A very weak currency can cause speculative outflows and reduce the amount of funds available to finance growth by businesses.
- *Inflation.* Inflation can affect consumers' purchasing power and therefore their demand for an MNC's goods. It affects the expenses associated with operations in the country. It may also influence a country's financial condition by influencing the country's interest rates and currency value.

Most financial factors that affect a country's economic conditions are difficult to forecast. Thus, even if an MNC considers them in its country risk assessment, it may still make poor decisions because of an improper forecast of the country's financial factors.

ASSESSMENT OF RISK FACTORS

A **macroassessment of country risk** represents an overall risk assessment of a country and involves consideration of all variables that affect country risk except those unique to a particular firm or industry. This type of assessment is convenient in that it remains the same for a given country, regardless of the firm or industry of concern; however, it excludes relevant information that could improve the accuracy of the assessment. A macroassessment of country risk serves as a foundation that can then be modified to reflect the particular business of the MNC, as explained next.

A **microassessment of country risk** involves the assessment of a country as it relates to the MNC's type of business. It is used to determine how the country risk relates to the specific MNC. The specific impact of a particular form of country risk can affect MNCs in different ways, which is why a microassessment of country risk is needed.

EXAMPLE

Country Z has been assigned a relatively low macroassessment by most experts due to its poor financial condition. Two MNCs are deciding whether to set up subsidiaries in Country Z. Carco, Inc., is considering developing a subsidiary that would produce automobiles and sell them locally, while Milco, Inc., plans to build a subsidiary that would produce military supplies. Carco's plan to build an automobile subsidiary does not appear to be feasible unless Country Z does not have a sufficient number of automobile producers already.

Country Z's government may be committed to purchasing a given amount of military supplies, regardless of how weak the economy is. Thus, Milco's plan to build a military supply subsidiary may still be feasible, even though Country Z's financial condition is poor.

It is possible, however, that Country Z's government will order its military supplies from a locally owned firm because it wants its supply needs to remain confidential. This possibility is an element of country risk because it is a country characteristic (or attitude) that can affect the feasibility of a project. Yet, this specific characteristic is relevant only to Milco, Inc., and not to Carco, Inc. ●

This example illustrates how an appropriate country risk assessment varies with the firm, industry, and project of concern, and therefore why a macroassessment of country risk has limitations. A microassessment is also necessary when evaluating the country risk related to a particular project proposed by a particular firm.

TECHNIQUES TO ASSESS COUNTRY RISK

Once a firm identifies all the macro- and microfactors that deserve consideration in the country risk assessment, it may wish to implement a system for evaluating these factors and determining a country risk rating. Various techniques are available to achieve this objective. The following are some of the more popular techniques:

- Checklist approach
- Delphi technique
- Quantitative analysis
- Inspection visits
- Combination of techniques

Each technique is briefly discussed in turn.

Checklist Approach

A checklist approach involves making a judgment on all the political and financial factors (both macro and micro) that contribute to a firm's assessment of country risk. Ratings are assigned to a list of various financial and political factors, and these ratings are then consolidated to derive an overall assessment of country risk. Some factors (such as real GDP growth) can be measured from available data, while others (such as probability of entering a war) must be subjectively measured.

A substantial amount of information about countries is available on the Internet. This information can be used to develop ratings of various factors used to assess country risk. The factors are then converted to some numerical rating in order to assess a particular country. Those factors thought to have a greater influence on country risk should be assigned greater weights. Both the measurement of some factors and the weighting scheme implemented are subjective.

Delphi Technique

The **Delphi technique** involves the collection of independent opinions without group discussion. As applied to country risk analysis, the MNC could survey specific employees or outside consultants who have some expertise in assessing a specific country's risk characteristics. The MNC receives responses from its survey and may then attempt to determine some consensus opinions (without attaching names to any of the opinions) about the perception of the country's risk. Then, it sends this summary of the survey back to the survey respondents and asks for additional feedback regarding its summary of the country's risk.

Quantitative Analysis

Once the financial and political variables have been measured for a period of time, models for quantitative analysis can attempt to identify the characteristics that influence the level of country risk. For example, regression analysis may be used to assess risk, since it can measure the sensitivity of one variable to other variables. A firm could regress a measure of its business activity (such as its percentage increase in sales) against country characteristics (such as real growth in GDP) over a series of previous months or quarters. Results from such an analysis will indicate the susceptibility of a particular business to a country's economy. This is valuable information to incorporate into the overall evaluation of country risk.

Although quantitative models can quantify the impact of variables on each other, they do not necessarily indicate a country's problems before they actually occur (preferably before the firm's decision to pursue a project in that country). Nor can they evaluate subjective data that cannot be quantified. In addition, historical trends of various country characteristics are not always useful for anticipating an upcoming crisis.

Inspection Visits

Inspection visits involve traveling to a country and meeting with government officials, business executives, and/or consumers. Such meetings can help clarify any uncertain opinions the firm has about a country. Indeed, some variables, such as intercountry relationships, may be difficult to assess without a trip to the host country.

Combination of Techniques

Many MNCs do not have a formal method to assess country risk. This does not mean that they neglect to assess country risk, but rather that there is no proven method that is always most appropriate. Consequently, many MNCs use a combination of techniques to assess country risk.

EXAMPLE

Missouri, Inc., recognizes that it must consider several financial and political factors in its country risk analysis of Mexico, where it plans to establish a subsidiary. Missouri creates a checklist of several factors and assigns a rating to each factor. It uses the Delphi technique to rate various political factors. It uses quantitative analysis to predict future economic conditions in Mexico so that it can rate various financial factors. It conducts an inspection visit to complement its assessment of the financial and political factors. ●

MEASURING COUNTRY RISK

An overall country risk rating using a checklist approach can be developed from separate ratings for political and financial risk. First, the political factors are assigned values within some arbitrarily chosen range (such as values from 1 to 5, where 5 is the best value/lowest risk). Next, these political factors are assigned weights (representing degree of importance), which should add up to 100 percent. The assigned values of the factors times their respective weights can then be summed to derive a political risk rating.

The process is then repeated to derive the financial risk rating. All financial factors are assigned values (from 1 to 5, where 5 is the best value/lowest risk). Then the assigned values of the factors times their respective weights can be summed to derive a financial risk rating.

Once the political and financial ratings have been derived, a country's overall country risk rating as it relates to a specific project can be determined by assigning weights to the political and financial ratings according to their perceived importance. The importance of political risk versus financial risk varies with the intent of the MNC. An MNC considering direct foreign investment to attract demand in that country must be highly concerned about financial risk. An MNC establishing a foreign manufacturing plant and planning to export the goods from there should be more concerned with political risk.

If the political risk is thought to be much more influential on a particular project than the financial risk, it will receive a higher weight than the financial risk rating (together both weights must total 100 percent). The political and financial ratings multiplied by their respective weights will determine the overall country risk rating for a country as it relates to a particular project.

EXAMPLE

Assume that Cougar Co. plans to build a steel plant in Mexico. It has used the Delphi technique and quantitative analysis to derive ratings for various political and financial factors. The discussion here focuses on how to consolidate the ratings to derive an overall country risk rating.

Exhibit 16.2 illustrates Cougar's country risk assessment of Mexico. Notice in Exhibit 16.2 that two political factors and five financial factors contribute to the overall country risk rating in this example. Cougar Co. will consider projects only in countries that have a country risk rating of 3.5 or higher, based on its country risk rating.

Cougar Co. has assigned the values and weights to the factors as shown in Exhibit 16.3. In this example, the company generally assigns the financial factors higher ratings than the political factors. The financial condition of Mexico has therefore been assessed more

Exhibit 16.2 Determining the Overall Country Risk Rating

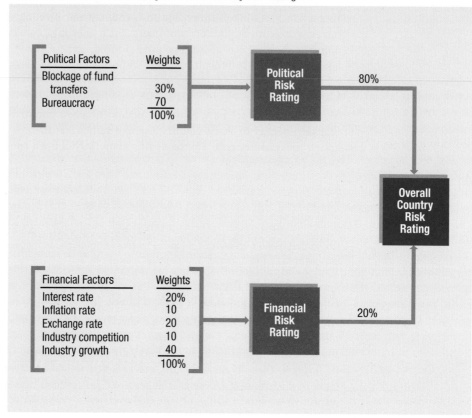

favorably than the political condition. Industry growth is the most important financial factor in Mexico, based on its 40 percent weighting. The bureaucracy is thought to be the most important political factor, based on a weighting of 70 percent; regulation of international fund transfers receives the remaining 30 percent weighting. The political risk rating is estimated at 3.3 by adding the products of the assigned ratings (column 2) and weights (column 3) of the political risk factors.

The financial risk is computed to be 3.9, based on adding the products of the assigned ratings and the weights of the financial risk factors. Once the political and financial ratings are determined, the overall country risk rating can be derived (as shown at the bottom of Exhibit 16.3), given the weights assigned to political and financial risk. Column 3 at the bottom of Exhibit 16.3 indicates that Cougar perceives political risk (receiving an 80 percent weight) to be much more important than financial risk (receiving a 20 percent weight) in Mexico for the proposed project. The overall country risk rating of 3.42 may appear low given the individual category ratings. This is due to the heavy weighting given to political risk, which in this example is critical from the firm's perspective. In particular, Cougar views Mexico's bureaucracy as a critical factor and assigns it a low rating. Given that Cougar considers projects only in countries that have a rating of at least 3.5, it decides not to pursue the project in Mexico. ●

Variation in Methods of Measuring Country Risk

The procedure described here is just one of many that could be used to derive an overall measure of country risk. Most procedures are similar, though, in that they somehow assign ratings and weights to all individual characteristics relevant to country risk assessment.

Exhibit 16.3 Derivation of the Overall Country Risk Rating Based on Assumed Information

(1)	(2)	(3)	(4) = (2) × (3)
POLITICAL RISK FACTORS	RATING ASSIGNED BY COMPANY TO FACTOR (WITHIN A RANGE OF 1–5)	WEIGHT ASSIGNED BY COMPANY TO FACTOR ACCORDING TO IMPORTANCE	WEIGHTED VALUE OF FACTOR
Blockage of fund transfers	4	30%	1.2
Bureaucracy	3	70	2.1
		100%	3.3 = Political risk rating
FINANCIAL RISK FACTORS			
Interest rate	5	20%	1.0
Inflation rate	4	10	.4
Exchange rate	4	20	.8
Industry competition	5	10	.5
Industry growth	3	40	1.2
		100%	3.9 = Financial risk rating

(1)	(2)	(3)	(4) = (2) × (3)
CATEGORY	RATING AS DETERMINED ABOVE	WEIGHT ASSIGNED BY COMPANY TO EACH RISK CATEGORY	WEIGHTED RATING
Political risk	3.3	80%	2.64
Financial risk	3.9	20	.78
		100%	3.42 = Overall country risk rating

The number of relevant factors comprising both the political risk and the financial risk categories will vary with the country being assessed and the type of corporate operations planned for that country. The assignment of values to the factors, along with the degree of importance (weights) assigned to the factors, will also vary with the country being assessed and the type of corporate operations planned for that country.

Comparing Risk Ratings among Countries

An MNC may evaluate country risk for several countries, perhaps to determine where to establish a subsidiary. One approach to comparing political and financial ratings among countries, advocated by some foreign risk managers, is a **foreign investment risk matrix (FIRM)** that displays the financial (or economic) and political risk by intervals ranging across the matrix from "poor" to "good." Each country can be positioned in its appropriate location on the matrix based on its political rating and financial rating.

Actual Country Risk Ratings across Countries

Country risk ratings are shown in Exhibit 16.4. This exhibit is not necessarily applicable to a particular MNC that wants to pursue international business because the risk

Exhibit 16.4 Country Risk Ratings among Countries

Source: Coface, 2007. These ratings measure the likelihood of customers in the country to make payment. They do not measure all other country risk characteristics such as government stability.

assessment here may not focus on the factors that are relevant to that MNC. Nevertheless, the exhibit illustrates how the risk rating can vary substantially among countries.
Many industrialized countries have high ratings, indicating low risk. Emerging countries
tend to have lower ratings. Country risk ratings change over time in response to the factors that influence a country's rating.

Impact of the Credit Crisis. Many countries experienced a decline in their country
risk rating due to the credit crisis in 2008. The decline in housing prices created severe
financial problems for commercial banks and other financial institutions. These institutions then became more cautious when providing credit. The international credit crunch
contributed to the weak global economy. Countries especially reliant on international
credit were adversely affected when credit was difficult to access.

INCORPORATING RISK IN CAPITAL BUDGETING

Some firms may contend that no risk is too high when considering a project. Their reasoning is that if the potential return is high enough, the project is worth undertaking.
When employee safety is a concern, however, the project may be rejected regardless of
its potential return. If the country risk is too high, MNCs do not need to analyze the
feasibility of the proposed project any further.

If the risk of a country is in the tolerable range, any project related to that country
deserves further consideration. Country risk can be incorporated in the capital budgeting
analysis of a proposed project by adjusting the discount rate or by adjusting the estimated cash flows. Each method is discussed here.

Adjustment of the Discount Rate

The discount rate of a proposed project is supposed to reflect the required rate of return
on that project. Thus, the discount rate can be adjusted to account for the country risk.
The lower the country risk rating, the higher the perceived risk and the higher the discount rate applied to the project's cash flows. This approach is convenient in that one
adjustment to the capital budgeting analysis can capture country risk. However, there is
no precise formula for adjusting the discount rate to incorporate country risk. The adjustment is somewhat arbitrary and may therefore cause feasible projects to be rejected
or infeasible projects to be accepted.

Adjustment of the Estimated Cash Flows

Perhaps the most appropriate method for incorporating forms of country risk in a capital budgeting analysis is to estimate how the cash flows would be affected by each form
of risk. For example, if there is a 20 percent probability that the host government will
temporarily block funds from the subsidiary to the parent, the MNC should estimate
the project's net present value (*NPV*) under these circumstances, realizing that there is
a 20 percent chance that this *NPV* will occur.

If there is a chance that a host government takeover will occur, the foreign project's
NPV under these conditions should be estimated. Each possible form of risk has an estimated impact on the foreign project's cash flows and therefore on the project's *NPV*. By
analyzing each possible impact, the MNC can determine the probability distribution of
*NPV*s for the project. Its accept/reject decision on the project will be based on its assessment of the probability that the project will generate a positive *NPV*, as well as the size
of possible *NPV* outcomes. Though this procedure may seem somewhat tedious, it directly incorporates forms of country risk into the cash flow estimates and explicitly illustrates the possible results from implementing the project. The more convenient method

of adjusting the discount rate in accordance with the country risk rating does not indicate the probability distribution of possible outcomes.

Reconsider the example of Spartan, Inc., that was discussed in Chapter 14. Assume for the moment that all the initial assumptions regarding Spartan's initial investment, project life, pricing policy, exchange rate projections, and so on still apply. Now, however, we will incorporate two country risk characteristics that were not included in the initial analysis. First, assume that there is a 30 percent chance that the withholding tax imposed by the Singapore government will be at a 20 percent rate rather than a 10 percent rate. Second, assume that there is a 40 percent chance that the Singapore government will provide Spartan a payment (salvage value) of S$7 million rather than S$12 million. These two possibilities represent a form of country risk.

Assume that these two possible situations are unrelated. To determine how the *NPV* is affected by each of these scenarios, a capital budgeting analysis similar to that shown in Exhibit 14.2 in Chapter 14 can be used. If this analysis is already on a spreadsheet, the *NPV* can easily be estimated by adjusting line items no. 15 (withholding tax on remitted funds) and no. 17 (salvage value). The capital budgeting analysis measures the effect of a 20 percent withholding tax rate in Exhibit 16.5. Since items before line no. 14 are not affected, these items are not shown here. If the 20 percent withholding tax rate is imposed, the *NPV* of the 4-year project is $1,252,160.

Now consider the possibility of the lower salvage value, while using the initial assumption of a 10 percent withholding tax rate. The capital budgeting analysis accounts for the lower salvage value in Exhibit 16.6. The estimated *NPV* is $800,484, based on this scenario.

Finally, consider the possibility that both the higher withholding tax and the lower salvage value occur. The capital budgeting analysis in Exhibit 16.7 accounts for both of these situations. The *NPV* is estimated to be –$177,223.

Once estimates for the *NPV* are derived for each scenario, Spartan, Inc., can attempt to determine whether the project is feasible. There are two country risk variables that are uncertain, and there are four possible *NPV* outcomes, as illustrated in Exhibit 16.8. Given the probability of each possible situation and the assumption that the withholding tax outcome is independent from the salvage value outcome, joint probabilities can be determined for each pair of outcomes by multiplying the probabilities of the two outcomes of concern. Since the probability of a 20 percent withholding tax is 30 percent, the probability of a 10 percent withholding tax is 70 percent. Given that the probability of a lower salvage value is 40 percent, the probability of the initial estimate for the salvage value is 60 percent. Thus, scenario no. 1 (10 percent withholding tax and S$12 million salvage value) created in Chapter 14 has a joint probability (probability that both outcomes will occur) of 70% × 60% = 42%.

Exhibit 16.5 Analysis of Project Based on a 20 Percent Withholding Tax: Spartan, Inc.

	YEAR 0	YEAR 1	YEAR 2	YEAR 3	YEAR 4
14. S$ remitted by subsidiary		S$6,000,000	S$6,000,000	S$7,600,000	S$8,400,000
15. Withholding tax imposed on remitted funds (20%)		S$1,200,000	S$1,200,000	S$1,520,000	S$1,680,000
16. S$ remitted after withholding taxes		S$4,800,000	S$4,800,000	S$6,080,000	S$6,720,000
17. Salvage value					S$12,000,000
18. Exchange rate of S$		$.50	$.50	$.50	$.50
19. Cash flows to parent		$2,400,000	$2,400,000	$3,040,000	$9,360,000
20. *PV* of parent cash flows (15% discount rate)		$2,086,956	$1,814,745	$1,998,849	$5,351,610
21. Initial investment by parent	$10,000,000				
22. Cumulative *NPV*		–$7,913,044	–$6,098,299	–$4,099,450	$1,252,160

Exhibit 16.6 Analysis of Project Based on a Reduced Salvage Value: Spartan, Inc.

	YEAR 0	YEAR 1	YEAR 2	YEAR 3	YEAR 4
14. S$ remitted by subsidiary		S$6,000,000	S$6,000,000	S$7,600,000	S$8,400,000
15. Withholding tax imposed on remitted funds (10%)		S$600,000	S$600,000	S$760,000	S$840,000
16. S$ remitted after withholding taxes		S$5,400,000	S$5,400,000	S$6,840,000	S$7,560,000
17. Salvage value					S$7,000,000
18. Exchange rate of S$		$.50	$.50	$.50	$.50
19. Cash flows to parent		$2,700,000	$2,700,000	$3,420,000	$7,280,000
20. PV of parent cash flows (15% discount rate)		$2,347,826	$2,041,588	$2,248,706	$4,162,364
21. Initial investment by parent	$10,000,000				
22. Cumulative NPV		−$7,652,174	−$5,610,586	−$3,361,880	$800,484

Exhibit 16.7 Analysis of Project Based on a 20 Percent Withholding Tax and a Reduced Salvage Value: Spartan, Inc.

	YEAR 0	YEAR 1	YEAR 2	YEAR 3	YEAR 4
14. S$ remitted by subsidiary		S$6,000,000	S$6,000,000	S$7,600,000	S$8,400,000
15. Withholding tax imposed on remitted funds (20%)		S$1,200,000	S$1,200,000	S$1,520,000	S$1,680,000
16. S$ remitted after withholding taxes		S$4,800,000	S$4,800,000	S$6,080,000	S$6,720,000
17. Salvage value					S$7,000,000
18. Exchange rate of S$		$.50	$.50	$.50	$.50
19. Cash flows to parent		$2,400,000	$2,400,000	$3,040,000	$6,860,000
20. PV of parent cash flows (15% discount rate)		$2,086,956	$1,814,745	$1,998,849	$3,922,227
21. Initial investment by parent	$10,000,000				
22. Cumulative NPV		−$7,913,044	−$6,098,299	−$4,099,450	−$177,223

In Exhibit 16.8, scenario no. 4 is the only scenario in which there is a negative NPV. Since this scenario has a 12 percent chance of occurring, there is a 12 percent chance that the project will adversely affect the value of the firm. Put another way, there is an 88 percent chance that the project will enhance the firm's value. The expected value of the project's NPV can be measured as the sum of each scenario's estimated NPV multiplied by its respective probability across all four scenarios, as shown at the bottom of Exhibit 16.8. Most MNCs would accept the proposed project, given the likelihood that the project will have a positive NPV and the limited loss that would occur under even the worst-case scenario. ●

Using an Electronic Spreadsheet. In the previous example, the initial assumptions for most input variables were used as if they were known with certainty. However, Spartan, Inc., could account for the uncertainty of country risk characteristics (as in our current example) while also allowing for uncertainty in the other variables as well. This process can be facilitated if the analysis is on a computer spreadsheet.

Exhibit 16.8 Summary of Estimated *NPV*s across the Possible Scenarios: Spartan, Inc.

SCENARIO	WITHHOLDING TAX IMPOSED BY SINGAPORE GOVERNMENT	SALVAGE VALUE OF PROJECT	NPV	PROBABILITY
1	10%	S$12,000,000	$2,229,867	(70%)(60%) = 42%
2	20%	S$12,000,000	$1,252,160	(30%)(60%) = 18%
3	10%	S$7,000,000	$800,484	(70%)(40%) = 28%
4	20%	S$7,000,000	−$177,223	(30%)(40%) = 12%
		$E(NPV) = \$2,229,867(42\%)$ $+ \$1,252,160(18\%)$ $+ \$800,484(28\%)$ $- \$177,223(12\%)$ $= \$1,364,801$		

EXAMPLE

If Spartan, Inc., wishes to allow for three possible exchange rate trends, it can adjust the exchange rate projections for each of the four scenarios assessed in the current example. Each scenario will reflect a specific withholding tax outcome, a specific salvage value outcome, and a specific exchange rate trend. There will be a total of 12 scenarios, with each scenario having an estimated *NPV* and a probability of occurrence. Based on the estimated *NPV* and the probability of each scenario, Spartan, Inc., can then measure the expected value of the *NPV* and the probability that the *NPV* will be positive, which leads to a decision regarding whether the project is feasible. ●

GOVERNANCE

Governance of the Country Risk Assessment. Many international projects by MNCs last for 20 years or more. Yet, an MNC's managers may not expect to be employed for such a long period of time. Thus, they do not necessarily feel accountable for the entire lifetime of a project. There are many countries that may have low country risk today but are very fragile. Some countries could easily experience a major shift in the government's economic policy from capitalist to socialist or vice versa. In addition, some countries rely heavily on the production of a specific commodity (such as oil) and could experience major financial problems should the world's market price of that commodity decline.

When managers want to pursue a project because of its potential success during the next few years, they may overlook the potential for increased country risk surrounding the project over time. In their minds, they may no longer be held accountable if the project fails several years from now. Consequently, MNCs need a proper governance system to ensure that managers fully consider country risk when assessing potential projects. One solution is to require that major long-term projects use input from an external source (such as a consulting firm) regarding the country risk assessment of a specific project and that this assessment be directly incorporated in the analysis of the project. In this way, a more unbiased measurement of country risk can be used to determine whether the project is feasible. In addition, the board of directors may attempt to oversee large long-term projects to make sure that country risk is fully incorporated into the analysis.

Assessing Risk of Existing Projects

An MNC should not only consider country risk when assessing a new project but also review the country risk periodically after a project has been implemented. If an MNC has a subsidiary in a country that experiences adverse political conditions, it may need to seriously consider divesting the subsidiary. At this point, the focus would be on determining whether the subsidiary could be sold for a value that exceeds the present value of its future expected cash flows.

PREVENTING HOST GOVERNMENT TAKEOVERS

Although direct foreign investment offers several possible benefits, country risk can offset such benefits. The most severe country risk is a host government takeover. This type of takeover may result in major losses, especially when the MNC does not have any power to negotiate with the host government.

The following are the most common strategies used to reduce exposure to a host government takeover:

- Use a short-term horizon.
- Rely on unique supplies or technology.
- Hire local labor.
- Borrow local funds.
- Purchase insurance.
- Use project finance.

Use a Short-Term Horizon

An MNC may concentrate on recovering cash flow quickly so that in the event of expropriation, losses are minimized. An MNC would also exert only a minimum effort to replace worn-out equipment and machinery at the subsidiary. It may even phase out its overseas investment by selling off its assets to local investors or the government in stages over time. Consequently, there would be little incentive for a host government to take over an MNC's subsidiary.

Rely on Unique Supplies or Technology

If the subsidiary can bring in supplies from its headquarters (or a sister subsidiary) that cannot be duplicated locally, the host government will not be able to take over and operate the subsidiary without those supplies. The MNC can also cut off the supplies if the subsidiary is treated unfairly.

If the subsidiary can hide the technology in its production process, a government takeover will be less likely. A takeover would be successful in this case only if the MNC would provide the necessary technology, and the MNC would do so only under conditions of a friendly takeover that would ensure that it received adequate compensation.

Hire Local Labor

If local employees of the subsidiary would be affected by the host government's takeover, they can pressure their government to avoid such action. However, the government could still keep those employees after taking over the subsidiary. Thus, this strategy has only limited effectiveness in avoiding or limiting a government takeover.

Borrow Local Funds

If the subsidiary borrows funds locally, local banks will be concerned about its future performance. If for any reason a government takeover would reduce the probability that the banks would receive their loan repayments promptly, they might attempt to prevent a takeover by the host government. However, the host government may guarantee repayment to the banks, so this strategy has only limited effectiveness. Nevertheless, it could still be preferable to a situation in which the MNC not only loses the subsidiary but also still owes home country creditors.

Purchase Insurance

Insurance can be purchased to cover the risk of expropriation. For example, the U.S. government provides insurance through the Overseas Private Investment Corporation (OPIC). The insurance premiums paid by a firm depend on the degree of insurance coverage and the risk associated with the firm. Typically, however, any insurance policy will cover only a portion of the company's total exposure to country risk.

Many home countries of MNCs have investment guarantee programs that insure to some extent the risks of expropriation, wars, or currency blockage. Some guarantee programs have a 1-year waiting period or longer before compensation is paid on losses due to expropriation. Also, some insurance policies do not cover all forms of expropriation. Furthermore, to be eligible for such insurance, the subsidiary might be required by the country to concentrate on exporting rather than on local sales. Even if a subsidiary qualifies for insurance, there is a cost. Any insurance will typically cover only a portion of the assets and may specify a maximum duration of coverage, such as 15 or 20 years. A subsidiary must weigh the benefits of this insurance against the cost of the policy's premiums and potential losses in excess of coverage. The insurance can be helpful, but it does not by itself prevent losses due to expropriation.

The World Bank has established an affiliate called the Multilateral Investment Guarantee Agency (MIGA) to provide political insurance for MNCs with direct foreign investment in less developed countries. MIGA offers insurance against expropriation, breach of contract, currency inconvertibility, war, and civil disturbances.

Use Project Finance

Many of the world's largest infrastructure projects are structured as "project finance" deals, which limit the exposure of the MNCs. First, project finance deals are heavily financed with credit. Thus, the MNC's exposure is limited because it invests only a limited amount of equity in the project. Second, a bank may guarantee the payments to the MNC. Third, project finance deals are unique in that they are secured by the project's future revenues from production. That is, the project is separate from the MNC that manages the project. The loans are "nonrecourse" in that the creditor cannot pursue the MNC for payment but only the assets and cash flows of the project itself. Thus, the cash flows of the project are relevant, and not the credit risk of the borrower. Because of the transparency of the process arising from the single purpose and finite plan for termination, project finance allows projects to be financed that otherwise would likely not obtain financing under conventional terms. A host government is unlikely to take over this type of project because it would have to assume the existing liabilities due to the credit arrangement.

SUMMARY

- The factors used by MNCs to measure a country's political risk include the attitude of consumers toward purchasing locally produced goods, the host government's actions toward the MNC, the blockage of fund transfers, currency inconvertibility,

war, bureaucratic problems, and corruption. These factors can increase the costs of international business.

- The factors used by MNCs to measure a country's financial risk are the country's gross domestic product, interest rate, exchange rate, and inflation rate.

■ The techniques typically used by MNCs to measure the country risk are the checklist approach, the Delphi technique, quantitative analysis, and inspection visits. Since no one technique covers all aspects of country risk, a combination of these techniques is commonly used. An overall measure of country risk is essentially a weighted average of the political or financial factors that are perceived to comprise country risk. Each MNC has its own view as to the weights that should be assigned to each factor and its own view about each factor's importance as related to its business. Thus, the overall rating for a country varies among MNCs.

■ Once country risk is measured, it can be incorporated into a capital budgeting analysis by adjusting of the discount rate. The adjustment is somewhat arbitrary, however, and may lead to improper decision making. An alternative method of incorporating country risk analysis into capital budgeting is to explicitly account for each factor that affects country risk. For each possible form of risk, the MNC can recalculate the foreign project's net present value under the condition that the event (such as blocked funds or increased taxes) occurs.

■ MNCs can reduce the likelihood of a host government takeover of their subsidiary by using a short-term horizon for their operations whereby the investment in the subsidiary is limited. In addition, reliance on unique technology (that cannot be copied), local citizens for labor, and local financial institutions for financing may create some protection from the host government.

POINT COUNTER-POINT

Does Country Risk Matter for U.S. Projects?

Point No. U.S.-based MNCs should consider country risk for foreign projects only. A U.S.-based MNC can account for U.S. economic conditions when estimating cash flows of a U.S. project or deriving the required rate of return on a project, but it does not need to consider country risk.

Counter-Point Yes. Country risk should be considered for U.S. projects. Country risk can indirectly affect the cash flows of a U.S. project. Consider a U.S. project in which supplies are produced and sent to a U.S. exporter. The demand for the supplies will be dependent on the demand for the exports over time, and the demand for exports over time may be dependent on country risk.

Who Is Correct? Use the Internet to learn more about this issue. Which argument do you support? Offer your own opinion on this issue.

SELF-TEST

Answers are provided in Appendix A at the back of the text.

1. Key West Co. exports highly advanced phone system components to its subsidiary shops on islands in the Caribbean. The components are purchased by consumers to improve their phone systems. These components are not produced in other countries. Explain how political risk factors could adversely affect the profitability of Key West Co.

2. Using the information in question 1, explain how financial risk factors could adversely affect the profitability of Key West Co.

3. Given the information in question 1, do you expect that Key West Co. is more concerned about the adverse effects of political risk or of financial risk?

4. Explain what types of firms would be most concerned about an increase in country risk as a result of the terrorist attack on the United States on September 11, 2001.

5. Rockford Co. plans to expand its successful business by establishing a subsidiary in Canada. However, it is concerned that after 2 years the Canadian government will either impose a special tax on any income sent back to the U.S. parent or order the subsidiary to be sold at that time. The executives have estimated that either of these scenarios has a 15 percent chance of occurring. They have decided to add four percentage points to the project's required rate of return to in- corporate the country risk that they are concerned about in the capital budgeting analysis. Is there a better way to more precisely incorporate the country risk of concern here?

QUESTIONS AND APPLICATIONS

1.   Forms of Country Risk. List some forms of po- litical risk other than a takeover of a subsidiary by the host government, and briefly elaborate on how each factor can affect the risk to the MNC. Identify common financial factors for an MNC to consider when asses- sing country risk. Briefly elaborate on how each factor can affect the risk to the MNC.

2.   Country Risk Assessment. Describe the steps involved in assessing country risk once all relevant in- formation has been gathered.

3.   Uncertainty Surrounding the Country Risk Assessment. Describe the possible errors involved in assessing country risk. In other words, explain why country risk analysis is not always accurate.

4.   Diversifying Away Country Risk. Why do you think that an MNC's strategy of diversifying projects internationally could achieve low exposure to country risk?

5.   Monitoring Country Risk. Once a project is ac- cepted, country risk analysis for the foreign country involved is no longer necessary, assuming that no other proposed projects are being evaluated for that country. Do you agree with this statement? Why or why not?

6.   Country Risk Analysis. If the potential return is high enough, any degree of country risk can be toler- ated. Do you agree with this statement? Why or why not? Do you think that a proper country risk analysis can replace a capital budgeting analysis of a project considered for a foreign country? Explain.

7.   Country Risk Analysis. Niagara, Inc., has de- cided to call a well-known country risk consultant to conduct a country risk analysis in a small country where it plans to develop a large subsidiary. Niagara prefers to hire the consultant since it plans to use its employees for other important corporate functions. The consultant uses a computer program that has as- signed weights of importance linked to the various factors. The consultant will evaluate the factors for this small country and insert a rating for each factor into the computer. The weights assigned to the factors are not adjusted by the computer, but the factor ratings are adjusted for each country that the consultant assesses. Do you think Niagara, Inc., should use this consultant? Why or why not?

8.   Microassessment. Explain the microassessment of country risk.

9.   Incorporating Country Risk in Capital Bud- geting. How could a country risk assessment be used to adjust a project's required rate of return? How could such an assessment be used instead to adjust a project's estimated cash flows?

10.   Reducing Country Risk. Explain some methods of reducing exposure to existing country risk, while maintaining the same amount of business within a particular country.

11.   Managing Country Risk. Why do some subsidiaries maintain a low profile as to where their parents are located?

12.   Country Risk Analysis. When NYU Corp. con- sidered establishing a subsidiary in Zenland, it per- formed a country risk analysis to help make the decision. It first retrieved a country risk analysis per- formed about 1 year earlier, when it had planned to begin a major exporting business to Zenland firms. Then it updated the analysis by incorporating all cur- rent information on the key variables that were used in that analysis, such as Zenland's willingness to accept exports, its existing quotas, and existing tariff laws. Is this country risk analysis adequate? Explain.

13.   Reducing Country Risk. MNCs such as Alcoa, DuPont, Heinz, and IBM donated products and tech- nology to foreign countries where they had subsidiar- ies. How could these actions have reduced some forms of country risk?

14.   Country Risk Ratings. Assauer, Inc., would like to assess the country risk of Glovanskia. Assauer has identified various political and financial risk factors, as shown below.

POLITICAL RISK FACTOR	ASSIGNED RATING	ASSIGNED WEIGHT
Blockage of fund transfers	5	40%
Bureaucracy	3	60%

FINANCIAL RISK FACTOR	ASSIGNED RATING	ASSIGNED WEIGHT
Interest rate	1	10%
Inflation	4	20%
Exchange rate	5	30%
Competition	4	20%
Growth	5	20%

Assauer has assigned an overall rating of 80 percent to political risk factors and of 20 percent to financial risk factors. Assauer is not willing to consider Glovanskia for investment if the country risk rating is below 4.0. Should Assauer consider Glovanskia for investment?

15. Effects of September 11. Arkansas, Inc., exports to various less developed countries, and its receivables are denominated in the foreign currencies of the importers. It considers reducing its exchange rate risk by establishing small subsidiaries to produce products. By incurring some expenses in the countries where it generates revenue, it reduces its exposure to exchange rate risk. Since September 11, 2001, when terrorists attacked the United States, it has questioned whether it should restructure its operations. Its CEO believes that its cash flows may be less exposed to exchange rate risk but more exposed to other types of risk as a result of restructuring. What is your opinion?

Advanced Questions

16. How Country Risk Affects *NPV*. Hoosier, Inc., is planning a project in the United Kingdom. It would lease space for 1 year in a shopping mall to sell expensive clothes manufactured in the United States. The project would end in 1 year, when all earnings would be remitted to Hoosier, Inc. Assume that no additional corporate taxes are incurred beyond those imposed by the British government. Since Hoosier, Inc., would rent space, it would not have any long-term assets in the United Kingdom and expects the salvage (terminal) value of the project to be about zero.

Assume that the project's required rate of return is 18 percent. Also assume that the initial outlay required by the parent to fill the store with clothes is $200,000. The pretax earnings are expected to be £300,000 at the end of 1 year. The British pound is expected to be worth $1.60 at the end of 1 year, when the after-tax earnings are converted to dollars and remitted to the United States. The following forms of country risk must be considered:

- The British economy may weaken (probability = 30 percent), which would cause the expected pretax earnings to be £200,000.
- The British corporate tax rate on income earned by U.S. firms may increase from 40 to 50 percent (probability = 20 percent).

These two forms of country risk are independent. Calculate the expected value of the project's net present value (*NPV*) and determine the probability that the project will have a negative *NPV*.

17. How Country Risk Affects *NPV*. Explain how the capital budgeting analysis in the previous question would need to be adjusted if there were three possible outcomes for the British pound along with the possible outcomes for the British economy and corporate tax rate.

18. JCPenney's Country Risk Analysis. Recently, JCPenney decided to consider expanding into various foreign countries; it applied a comprehensive country risk analysis before making its expansion decisions. Initial screenings of 30 foreign countries were based on political and economic factors that contribute to country risk. For the remaining 20 countries where country risk was considered to be tolerable, specific country risk characteristics of each country were considered. One of JCPenney's biggest targets is Mexico, where it planned to build and operate seven large stores.

a. Identify the political factors that you think may possibly affect the performance of the JCPenney stores in Mexico.

b. Explain why the JCPenney stores in Mexico and in other foreign markets are subject to financial risk (a subset of country risk).

c. Assume that JCPenney anticipated that there was a 10 percent chance that the Mexican government would temporarily prevent conversion of peso profits into dollars because of political conditions. This event would prevent JCPenney from remitting earnings generated in Mexico and could adversely affect the performance of these stores (from the U.S. perspective).

Offer a way in which this type of political risk could be explicitly incorporated into a capital budgeting analysis when assessing the feasibility of these projects.

d. Assume that JCPenney decides to use dollars to finance the expansion of stores in Mexico. Second, assume that JCPenney decides to use one set of dollar cash flow estimates for any project that it assesses. Third, assume that the stores in Mexico are not subject to political risk. Do you think that the required rate of return on these projects would differ from the required rate of return on stores built in the United States at that same time? Explain.

e. Based on your answer to the previous question, does this mean that proposals for any new stores in the United States have a higher probability of being accepted than proposals for any new stores in Mexico?

19. How Country Risk Affects *NPV*. Monk, Inc., is considering a capital budgeting project in Tunisia. The project requires an initial outlay of 1 million Tunisian dinar; the dinar is currently valued at $.70. In the first and second years of operation, the project will generate 700,000 dinar in each year. After 2 years, Monk will terminate the project, and the expected salvage value is 300,000 dinar. Monk has assigned a discount rate of 12 percent to this project. The following additional information is available:

- There is currently no withholding tax on remittances to the United States, but there is a 20 percent chance that the Tunisian government will impose a withholding tax of 10 percent beginning next year.
- There is a 50 percent chance that the Tunisian government will pay Monk 100,000 dinar after 2 years instead of the 300,000 dinar it expects.
- The value of the dinar is expected to remain unchanged over the next 2 years.

a. Determine the net present value (*NPV*) of the project in each of the four possible scenarios.

b. Determine the joint probability of each scenario.

c. Compute the expected *NPV* of the project and make a recommendation to Monk regarding its feasibility.

20. How Country Risk Affects *NPV*. In the previous question, assume that instead of adjusting the estimated cash flows of the project, Monk had decided to adjust the discount rate from 12 to 17 percent. Reevaluate the *NPV* of the project's expected scenario using this adjusted discount rate.

21. Risk and Cost of Potential Kidnapping. In 2004 during the war in Iraq, some MNCs capitalized on opportunities to rebuild Iraq. However, in April 2004, some employees were kidnapped by local militant groups. How should an MNC account for this potential risk when it considers direct foreign investment (DFI) in any particular country? Should it avoid DFI in any country in which such an event could occur? If so, how would it screen the countries to determine which are acceptable? For whatever countries that it is willing to consider, should it adjust its feasibility analysis to account for the possibility of kidnapping? Should it attach a cost to reflect this possibility or increase the discount rate when estimating the net present value? Explain.

22. Integrating Country Risk and Capital Budgeting. Tovar Co. is a U.S. firm that has been asked to provide consulting services to help Grecia Co. (in Greece) improve its performance. Tovar would need to spend $300,000 today on expenses related to this project. In one year, Tovar will receive payment from Grecia, which will be tied to Grecia's performance during the year. There is uncertainty about Grecia's performance and about Grecia's tendency for corruption.

Tovar expects that it will receive 400,000 euros if Grecia achieves strong performance following the consulting job. However, there are two forms of country risk that are a concern to Tovar Co. There is an 80 percent chance that Grecia will achieve strong performance. There is a 20 percent chance that Grecia will perform poorly, and in this case, Tovar will receive a payment of only 200,000 euros.

While there is a 90 percent chance that Grecia will make its payment to Tovar, there is a 10 percent chance that Grecia will become corrupt, and in this case, Grecia will not submit any payment to Tovar.

Assume that the outcome of Grecia's performance is independent of whether Grecia becomes corrupt. The prevailing spot rate of the euro is $1.30, but Tovar expects that the euro will depreciate by 10 percent in 1 year, regardless of Grecia's performance or whether it is corrupt.

Tovar's cost of capital is 26 percent. Determine the expected value of the project's net present value. Determine the probability that the project's *NPV* will be negative.

23. Capital Budgeting and Country Risk. Wyoming Co. is a nonprofit educational institution that wants to import educational software products from Hong Kong and sell them in the United States. It wants to assess the net present value of this project since any profits it earns will be used for its foundation. It expects to pay HK$5 million for the imports. Assume the existing exchange rate is HK$1 = $.12. It would also incur selling expenses of $1 million to sell the products in the United States. It would be able to sell the products in the United States for $1.7 million. However, it is concerned about two forms of country risk. First, there is a 60 percent chance that the Hong Kong dollar will be revalued to be worth HK$1 = $.16 by the Hong Kong government. Second, there is a 70 percent chance that the Hong Kong government will impose a special tax of 10 percent on the amount that U.S. importers must pay for Hong Kong exports. These two forms of country risk are independent, meaning that the probability that the Hong Kong dollar will be revalued is independent of the probability that the Hong Kong government will impose a special tax. Wyoming's required rate of return on this project is 22 percent. What is the expected value of the project's net present value? What is the probability that the project's *NPV* will be negative?

24. Accounting for Country Risk of a Project.
Kansas Co. wants to invest in a project in China. It would require an initial investment of 5 million yuan. It is expected to generate cash flows of 7 million yuan at the end of 1 year. The spot rate of the yuan is $.12, and Kansas thinks this exchange rate is the best forecast of the future. However, there are two forms of country risk.

First, there is a 30 percent chance that the Chinese government will require that the yuan cash flows earned by Kansas at the end of 1 year be reinvested in China for 1 year before it can be remitted (so that cash would not be remitted until 2 years from today). In this case, Kansas would earn 4 percent after taxes on a bank deposit in China during that second year.

Second, there is a 40 percent chance that the Chinese government will impose a special remittance tax of 400,000 yuan at the time that Kansas Co. remits cash flows earned in China back to the United States.

The two forms of country risk are independent. The required rate of return on this project is 26 percent. There is no salvage value. What is the expected value of the project's net present value?

25. Accounting for Country Risk of a Project.
Slidell Co. (a U.S. firm) considers a foreign project in which it expects to receive 10 million euros at the end of this year. It plans to hedge receivables of 10 million euros with a forward contract. Today, the spot rate of the euro is $1.20, while the 1-year forward rate of the euro is presently $1.24, and the expected spot rate of

the euro in 1 year is $1.19. The initial outlay is $7 million. Slidell has a required return of 18 percent.

There is a 20 percent chance that political problems will cause a reduction in foreign business, such that it would only receive 4 million euros at the end of 1 year. Determine the expected value of the net present value of this project.

26. Political Risk and Currency Derivative Values.
Assume that interest rate parity exists. At 10:30 a.m., the media reported news that the Mexican government's political problems were reduced, which reduced the expected volatility of the Mexican peso against the dollar over the next month. However, this news had no effect on the prevailing 1-month interest rates of the U.S. dollar or Mexican peso, and also had no effect on the expected exchange rate of the Mexican peso in 1 month. The spot rate of the Mexican peso was $.13 as of 10 a.m. and remained at that level all morning.

a. At 10 a.m., Piazza Co. purchased a call option at the money on 1 million Mexican pesos with a December expiration date. At 11:00 a.m., Corradetti Co. purchased a call option at the money on 1 million pesos with a December expiration date. Did Corradetti Co. pay more, less, or the same as Piazza Co. for the options? Briefly explain.

b. Teke Co. purchased futures contracts on 1 million Mexican pesos with a December settlement date at 10 a.m. Malone Co. purchased futures contracts on 1 million Mexican pesos with a December settlement date at 11 a.m. Did Teke Co. pay more, less, or the same as Malone Co. for the futures contracts? Briefly explain.

27. Political Risk and Project *NPV*.
Drysdale Co. (a U.S. firm) is considering a new project that would result in cash flows of 5 million Argentine pesos in 1 year under the most likely economic and political conditions. The spot rate of the Argentina peso in 1 year is expected to be $.40 based on these conditions. However, it wants to also account for the 10 percent probability of a political crisis in Argentina, which would change the expected cash flows to 4 million Argentine pesos in 1 year. In addition, it wants to account for the 20 percent probability that the exchange rate may only be $.36 at the end of 1 year. These two forms of country risk are independent. Drysdale's required rate of return is 25 percent and its initial outlay for this project is $1.4 million. Show the distribution of possible outcomes for the project's net present value (*NPV*).

28. Country Risk and Project *NPV*.
Atro Co. (a U.S. firm) considers a foreign project in which it expects to

receive 10 million euros at the end of 1 year. While it realizes that its receivables are uncertain, it definitely decides to hedge receivables of 10 million euros with a forward contract today. As of today, the spot rate of the euro is $1.20, while the 1-year forward rate of the euro is presently $1.24, and the expected spot rate of the euro in one year is $1.19. The initial outlay of this project is $7 million. Atro has a required return of 18 percent.

a. Estimate the *NPV* of this project based on the expectation of 10 million euros in receivables.

b. Now estimate the *NPV* based on the possibility that country risk could cause a reduction in foreign

business, such that Atro Co. only receives 4 million euros instead of 10 million euros at the end of 1 year. Estimate the net present value of the project if this form of country risk occurs.

Discussion in the Boardroom

This exercise can be found in Appendix E at the back of this textbook.

Running Your Own MNC

This exercise can be found on the *International Financial Management* text companion website located at www.cengage.com/finance/madura.

BLADES, INC. CASE

Country Risk Assessment

Recently, Ben Holt, Blades' chief financial Officer (CFO), has assessed whether it would be more beneficial for Blades to establish a subsidiary in Thailand to manufacture roller blades or to acquire an existing manufacturer, Skates'n'Stuff, which has offered to sell the business to Blades for 1 billion Thai baht. In Holt's view, establishing a subsidiary in Thailand yields a higher net present value (*NPV*) than acquiring the existing business. Furthermore, the Thai manufacturer has rejected an offer by Blades, Inc., for 900 million baht. A purchase price of 900 million baht for Skates'n'Stuff would make the acquisition as attractive as the establishment of a subsidiary in Thailand in terms of *NPV*. Skates'n'Stuff has indicated that it is not willing to accept less than 950 million baht.

Although Holt is confident that the *NPV* analysis was conducted correctly, he is troubled by the fact that the same discount rate, 25 percent, was used in each analysis. In his view, establishing a subsidiary in Thailand may be associated with a higher level of country risk than acquiring Skates'n'Stuff. Although either approach would result in approximately the same level of financial risk, the political risk associated with establishing a subsidiary in Thailand may be higher then the political risk of operating Skates'n'Stuff. If the establishment of a subsidiary in Thailand is associated with a higher level of country risk overall, then a higher discount rate should have been used in the analysis. Based on these considerations, Holt wants to measure the country risk associated with Thailand on both a macro and a micro level and then to reexamine the feasibility of both approaches.

First, Holt has gathered some more detailed political information for Thailand. For example, he believes that consumers in Asian countries prefer to purchase goods produced by Asians, which might prevent a subsidiary in Thailand from being successful. This cultural characteristic might not prevent an acquisition of Skates'n'Stuff from succeeding, however, especially if Blades retains the company's management and employees. Furthermore, the subsidiary would have to apply for various licenses and permits to be allowed to operate in Thailand, while Skates'n'Stuff obtained these licenses and permits long ago. However, the number of licenses required for Blades' industry is relatively low compared to other industries. Moreover, there is a high possibility that the Thai government will implement capital controls in the near future, which would prevent funds from leaving Thailand. Since Blades, Inc., has planned to remit all earnings generated by its subsidiary or by Skates'n'Stuff back to the United States, regardless of which approach to direct foreign investment it takes, capital controls may force Blades to reinvest funds in Thailand.

Ben Holt has also gathered some information regarding the financial risk of operating in Thailand. Thailand's economy has been weak lately, and recent forecasts indicate that a recovery may be slow. A weak economy may affect the demand for Blades' products, roller blades. The state of the economy is of particular concern to Blades since it produces a leisure product. In the case of an economic turndown, consumers will first eliminate these types of purchases. Holt is also worried about the high interest rates in Thailand, which may further slow economic growth if Thai citizens begin saving more. Furthermore, Holt is also aware that inflation levels in Thailand are expected to remain high. These high inflation levels can affect the purchasing power of Thai consumers, who may adjust their spending habits to purchase more essential products than roller blades. However, high levels of inflation also indicate that consumers in Thailand are still spending a relatively high proportion of their earnings.

Another financial factor that may affect Blades' operations in Thailand is the baht-dollar exchange rate. Current forecasts indicate that the Thai baht may depreciate in the future. However, recall that Blades will sell all roller blades produced in Thailand to Thai consumers. Therefore, Blades is not subject to a lower level of U.S. demand resulting from a weak baht. Blades will remit the earnings generated in Thailand back to the United States, however, and a weak baht would reduce the dollar amount of these translated earnings. Based on these initial considerations, Holt feels that the level of political risk of operating may be higher if Blades decides to establish a subsidiary to manufacture roller blades (as opposed to acquiring Skates'n'Stuff). Conversely, the financial risk of operating in Thailand will be roughly the same whether Blades establishes a subsidiary or acquires Skates'n'Stuff. Holt is not satisfied with this initial assessment, however, and would like to have numbers at hand when he meets with the board of directors next week. Thus, he would like to conduct a quantitative analysis of the country risk associated with operating in Thailand. He has asked you, a financial analyst at Blades, to develop a country risk analysis for Thailand and to adjust the discount rate for the riskier venture (i.e., establishing a subsidiary or acquiring Skates'n'Stuff). Holt has provided the following information for your analysis:

- Since Blades produces leisure products, it is more susceptible to financial risk factors than political risk factors. You should use weights of 60 percent for financial risk factors and 40 percent for political risk factors in your analysis.
- You should use the attitude of Thai consumers, capital controls, and bureaucracy as political risk factors in your analysis. Holt perceives capital

controls as the most important political risk factor. In his view, the consumer attitude and bureaucracy factors are of equal importance.
- You should use interest rates, inflation levels, and exchange rates as the financial risk factors in your analysis. In Holt's view, exchange rates and interest rates in Thailand are of equal importance, while inflation levels are slightly less important.
- Each factor used in your analysis should be assigned a rating in a range of 1 to 5, where 5 indicates the most unfavorable rating.

Ben Holt has asked you to provide answers to the following questions for him, which he will use in his meeting with the board of directors:

1. Based on the information provided in the case, do you think the political risk associated with Thailand is higher or lower for a manufacturer of leisure products such as Blades as opposed to, say, a food producer? That is, conduct a microassessment of political risk for Blades, Inc.

2. Do you think the financial risk associated with Thailand is higher or lower for a manufacturer of leisure products such as Blades as opposed to, say, a food producer? That is, conduct a microassessment of financial risk for Blades, Inc. Do you think a leisure product manufacturer such as Blades will be more affected by political or financial risk factors?

3. Without using a numerical analysis, do you think establishing a subsidiary in Thailand or acquiring Skates'n'Stuff will result in a higher assessment of political risk? Of financial risk? Substantiate your answer.

4. Using a spreadsheet, conduct a quantitative country risk analysis for Blades, Inc., using the information Ben Holt has provided for you. Use your judgment to assign weights and ratings to each political and financial risk factor and determine an overall country risk rating for Thailand. Conduct two separate analyses for (a) the establishment of a subsidiary in Thailand and (b) the acquisition of Skates'n'Stuff.

5. Which method of direct foreign investment should utilize a higher discount rate in the capital budgeting analysis? Would this strengthen or weaken the tentative decision of establishing a subsidiary in Thailand?

SMALL BUSINESS DILEMMA

Country Risk Analysis at the Sports Exports Company

The Sports Exports Company produces footballs in the United States and exports them to the United Kingdom. It also has an ongoing joint venture with a British firm that produces some sporting goods for a fee. The Sports Exports Company is considering the establishment of a small subsidiary in the United Kingdom.

1. Under the current conditions, is the Sports Exports Company subject to country risk?

2. If the firm does decide to develop a small subsidiary in the United Kingdom, will its exposure to country risk change? If so, how?

INTERNET/EXCEL EXERCISE

Go to the website of the CIA *World Factbook* at www.cia.gov/library/publications/the-world-factbook/index.html. Select a country and review the information about the country's political conditions. Explain whether these conditions would likely discourage an MNC from engaging in direct foreign investment. Explain how the political conditions could adversely affect the cash flows of the MNC.

REFERENCES

Bekefi, Tamara, and Marc J. Epstein, Feb 2008, Measuring and Managing Social and Political Risk, *Strategic Finance,* pp. 33–41.

Click, Reid W., Sep 2005, Financial and Political Risks in US Direct Foreign Investment, *Journal of International Business Studies,* pp. 559–575.

Clouser, Gary, Mar 2008, Country Risk, Country Reward, *Oil & Gas Investor,* pp. 15–22.

Demirbag, Mehmet Ekrem Tatoglu, and Keith W. Glaister, 2008, Factors Affecting Perceptions of the Choice between Acquisition and Greenfield Entry: The Case of Western FDI in an Emerging Market, *Management International Review,* pp. 5–38.

Diana, Tom, Sep 2006, Combat and Credit—An Unstable Mix for International Sales, *Business Credit,* pp. 52–53.

Markus, Stanislav, Jan 2008, Corporate Governance as Political Insurance: Firm-Level Institutional Creation in Emerging Markets and Beyond, *Socio-Economic Review,* pp. 69–98.

Massoud, Mark F., and Cecily A. Raiborn, Sep/Oct 2003, Managing Risk in Global Operations, *The Journal of Corporate Accounting & Finance,* pp. 41–49.

Purda, Lynnette D., Oct/Nov 2008, Risk Perception and the Financial System, *Journal of International Business Studies,* pp. 1178–1196.

Final Self-Exam

FINAL REVIEW

This self-exam focuses on the managerial chapters (Chapters 9 through 21). Here is a brief summary of some of the key points in those chapters. Chapter 9 describes various methods that are used to forecast exchange rates. Chapter 10 explains how transaction exposure is based on transactions involving different currencies, while economic exposure is any form of exposure that can affect the value of the MNC, and translation exposure is due to the existence of foreign subsidiaries whose earnings are translated to consolidated income statements. Chapter 11 explains how transaction exposure in payables can be managed by purchasing forward or futures contracts, purchasing call options, or using a money market hedge that involves investing in the foreign currency. Transaction exposure in receivables can be managed by selling forward or futures contracts, purchasing put options, or using a money market hedge that involves borrowing the foreign currency. Chapter 12 explains how economic exposure can be hedged by restructuring operations to match foreign currency inflows and outflows. The translation exposure can be hedged by selling a forward contract on the foreign currency of the foreign subsidiary. However, while this hedge may reduce translation exposure, it may result in a cash loss.

Chapter 13 explains how direct foreign investment can be motivated by foreign market conditions that may increase demand and revenue or conditions that reflect lower costs of production. Chapter 14 explains how the net present value of a multinational project is enhanced when the foreign currency to be received in the future is expected to appreciate and reduced when that currency is expected to depreciate. It explains how financing with a foreign currency can offset inflows and reduce exchange rate risk. Chapter 15 explains how the net present value framework can be applied to acquisitions, divestitures, or other forms of restructuring. Chapter 16 explains how the net present value framework can be used to incorporate country risk conditions when assessing a project's feasibility. Chapter 17 explains how an MNC's cost of capital is influenced by its home country's risk-free interest rate and its risk premium. The MNC's capital structure decision will likely result in a heavier emphasis toward debt if it has stable cash flows, has less retained earnings available, and has more assets that it can use as collateral.

Chapter 18 explains how the cost of long-term financing with foreign currency–denominated debt is subject to exchange rate movements. If the debt payments are not offset by cash inflows in the same currency, the cost of financing increases if the foreign currency denominating the debt increases over time.

Chapter 19 explains how international trade can be facilitated by various forms of payment and financing. Chapter 20 explains how an MNC's short-term financing in foreign currencies can reduce exchange rate risk if it is offset by foreign currency inflows at the end of the financing period. When there are not offsetting currency inflows, the effective financing rate of a foreign currency is more favorable (lower) when its interest rate is low and when the currency depreciates over the financing period.

Chapter 21 explains how an MNC's short-term investment in foreign currencies can reduce exchange rate risk if the proceeds can be used at the end of the period to cover foreign currency outflows. When there are not offsetting currency outflows, the effective yield from investing in a foreign currency is more favorable (higher) when its interest rate is high and when the currency appreciates over the investment period.

This self-exam allows you to test your understanding of some of the key concepts covered in the managerial chapters. This is a good opportunity to assess your understanding of the managerial concepts. This final self-exam does not replace all the end-of-chapter self-tests, nor does it cover all the concepts. It is simply intended to let you test yourself on a general overview of key concepts. Try to simulate taking an exam by answering all questions without using your book and your notes. The answers to this exam are provided just after the exam questions. If you have any wrong answers, you should reread the related material and then redo any exam questions that you had wrong.

This exam may not necessarily match the level of rigor in your course. Your instructor may offer you specific information about how this final self-exam relates to the coverage and rigor of the final exam in your course.

FINAL SELF-EXAM

1. New Hampshire Co. expects that monthly capital flows between the United States and Japan will be the major factor that affects the monthly exchange rate movements of the Japanese yen in the future, as money will flow to whichever country has the higher nominal interest rate. At the beginning of each month, New Hampshire Co. will use either the spot rate or the forward rate to forecast the future spot rate that will exist at the end of the month. Will the spot rate result in smaller, larger, or the same mean absolute forecast error as the forward rate when forecasting the future spot rate of the yen on a monthly basis? Explain.

2. California Co. will need 1 million Polish zloty in 2 years to purchase imports. Assume interest rate parity holds. Assume that the spot rate of the Polish zloty is $.30. The 2-year annualized interest rate in the United States is 5 percent, and the 2-year annualized interest rate in Poland is 11 percent. If California Co. uses a forward contract to hedge its payables, how many dollars will it need in 2 years?

3. Minnesota Co. uses regression analysis to assess its economic exposure to fluctuations in the Canadian dollar, whereby the dependent variable is the monthly percentage change in its stock price, and the independent variable is the monthly percentage change in the Canadian dollar. The analysis estimated the intercept to be zero and the coefficient of the monthly percentage change in the Canadian dollar to be –0.6. Assume the interest rate in Canada is consistently higher than the interest rate in the United States. Assume that interest rate parity exists. You use the forward rate to forecast future exchange rates of the Canadian dollar. Do you think Minnesota's stock price will be (a) favorably affected, (b) adversely affected, or (c) not affected by the expected movement in the Canadian dollar? Explain the logic behind your answer.

4. Iowa Co. has most of its business in the United States, except that it exports to Portugal. Its exports were invoiced in euros (Portugal's currency) last year. It has no other economic exposure to exchange rate risk. Its main competition when selling to Portugal's customers is a company in Portugal that sells similar products, denominated in euros. Starting today, it plans to adjust its pricing strategy to invoice its exports in U.S. dollars instead of euros. Based on the new strategy, will Iowa Co. be subject to economic exposure to exchange rate risk in the future? Briefly explain.

5. Maine Co. has a facility that produces basic clothing in Indonesia (where labor costs are very low), and the clothes produced there are sold in the United States. Its facility is subject to a tax in Indonesia because it is not owned by local citizens. This tax increases its cost of production by 20 percent, but its cost is still 40 percent less than what it would be if it produced the clothing in the United States (because of the low cost of labor there). Maine wants to achieve geographical diversification and decides to sell its clothing in Indonesia. Its competition would be from several existing local firms in Indonesia. Briefly explain whether you think Maine's strategy for direct foreign investment is feasible.

6. Assume that interest rate parity exists and it will continue to exist in the future. The U.S. and Mexican interest rates are the same regardless of the maturity of the interest rate, and they will continue to be the same in the future. Tucson Co. and Phoenix Co. will each receive 1 million Mexican pesos in 1 year and will receive 1 million Mexican pesos in 2 years. Today, Tucson uses a 1-year forward contract to hedge its receivables that will arrive in 1 year. Today it also uses a 2-year forward contract to hedge its receivables that will arrive in 2 years.

Phoenix uses a 1-year forward contract to hedge the receivables that will arrive in 1 year. A year from today, Phoenix will use a 1-year forward contract to hedge the receivables that will arrive 2 years from today. The Mexican peso is expected to consistently depreciate substantially over the next 2 years.

Will Tucson receive more, less, or the same amount of dollars as Phoenix? Explain.

7. Assume that Jarret Co. (a U.S. firm) expects to receive 1 million euros in 1 year. The existing spot rate of the euro is $1.20. The 1-year forward rate of the euro is $1.21. Jarret expects the spot rate of the euro to be $1.22 in 1 year.

Assume that 1-year put options on euros are available, with an exercise price of $1.23 and a premium of $.04 per unit. Assume the following money market rates:

	UNITED STATES	EUROZONE
Deposit rate	8%	5%
Borrowing rate	9%	6%

a. Determine the dollar cash flows to be received if Jarret uses a money market hedge. (Assume Jarret does not have any cash on hand when answering this question.)

b. Determine the dollar cash flows to be received if Jarret uses a put option hedge.

8. **a.** Portland Co. is a U.S. firm with no foreign subsidiaries. In addition to much business in the United States, its exporting business results in annual cash inflows of 20 million euros. Briefly explain how Portland Co. is subject to translation exposure (if at all).

b. Topeka Co. is a U.S. firm with no exports or imports. It has a subsidiary in Germany that typically generates earnings of 10 million euros each year, and none of the earnings are remitted to the United States. Briefly explain how Topeka Co. is subject to translation exposure (if at all).

9. Lexington Co. is a U.S. firm. It has a subsidiary in India that produces computer chips and sells them to European countries. The chips are invoiced in dollars. The subsidiary pays wages, rent, and other operating costs in India's currency (rupee). Every month, the subsidiary remits a large amount of earnings to the U.S. parent. This is the only international business that Lexington Co. has. The subsidiary wants to borrow funds to expand its facilities, and can borrow dollars at 9 percent annually or borrow rupee at 9 percent annually. Which currency should the parent tell the subsidiary to borrow, if the parent's main goal is to minimize exchange rate risk? Explain.

10. Illinois Co. (of the United States) and Franco Co. (based in France) are separately considering the acquisition of Podansk Co. (of Poland). Illinois Co. and Franco Co. have similar estimates of cash flows (in the Polish currency, the zloty) to be generated by Podansk in the future. The U.S. long-term risk-free interest rate is presently 8 percent, while the long-term risk-free rate of the euro is presently 3 percent. Illinois Co. and Franco Co. expect that the return of the U.S. stock market will be much better than the return of the French market. Illinois Co. has about the same amount of risk as a typical firm in the United States. Franco Co. has about the same amount of risk as a typical firm in France. The zloty is expected to depreciate against the euro by 1.2 percent per year, and against the dollar by 1.4 percent per year. Which firm will likely have a higher valuation of the target Podansk? Explain.

11. A year ago, the spot exchange rate of the euro was $1.20. At that time, Talen Co. (a U.S. firm) invested $4 million to establish a project in the Netherlands. It expected that this project would generate cash flows of 3 million euros at the end of the first and second years.

Talen Co. always uses the spot rate as its forecast of future exchange rates. It uses a required rate of return of 20 percent on international projects.

Because conditions in the Netherlands are weaker than expected, the cash flows in the first year of the project were 2 million euros, and Talen now believes the expected cash flows for next year will be 1 million euros. A company offers to buy the project from Talen today for $1.25 million. Assume no tax effects. Today, the spot rate of the euro is $1.30. Should Talen accept the offer? Show your work.

12. Everhart, Inc., is a U.S. firm with no international business. It issues debt in the United States at an interest rate of 10 percent per year. The risk-free rate in the United States is 8 percent. The stock market return in the United States is expected to be 14 percent annually. Everhart's beta is 1.2. Its target capital structure is 30 percent debt and 70 percent equity. Everhart is subject to a 25 percent corporate tax rate. Everhart plans a project in the Philippines in which it would receive net cash flows in Philippine pesos on an annual basis. The risk of the project would be similar to the risk of its other businesses. The existing risk-free rate in the Philippines is 21 percent and the stock market return there is expected to be 28 percent annually. Everhart plans to finance this project with either its existing equity or by borrowing Philippine pesos.

a. Estimate the cost to Everhart if it uses dollar-denominated equity. Show your work.

b. Assume that Everhart believes that the Philippine peso will appreciate substantially each year against the dollar. Do you think it should finance this project with its dollar-denominated equity or by borrowing Philippine pesos? Explain.

c. Assume that Everhart receives an offer from a Philippine investor who is willing to provide equity financing in Philippine pesos to Everhart. Do you think this form of financing would be more preferable to Everhart than financing with debt denominated in Philippine pesos? Explain.

13. Assume that a euro is equal to $1.00 today. A U.S. firm could engage in a parallel loan today in which it borrows 1 million euros from a firm in Belgium and provides a $1 million loan to the Belgian firm. The loans will be repaid in 1 year with interest. Which of the following U.S. firms could most effectively use this parallel loan in order to reduce its exposure to exchange rate risk? (Assume that these U.S. firms have no other international business than what is described here.) Explain.

Sacramento Co. will receive a payment of 1 million euros from a French company in 1 year.

Stanislaus Co. needs to make a payment of 1 million euros to a German supplier in 1 year.

Los Angele Co. will receive 1 million euros from the Netherlands government in 1 year. It just engaged in a forward contract in which it sold 1 million euros 1 year forward.

San Mateo Co. will receive a payment of 1 million euros today and will owe a supplier 1 million euros in 1 year.

San Francisco Co. will make a payment of 1 million euros to a firm in Spain today and will receive $1 million from a firm in Spain for some consulting work in 1 year.

14. Assume the following direct exchange rate of the Swiss franc and Argentine peso at the beginning of each of the last 7 years.

BEGINNING OF YEAR	SWISS FRANC (SF)	ARGENTINE PESO (AP)
1	$.60	$.35
2	$.64	$.36
3	$.60	$.38
4	$.66	$.40
5	$.68	$.39
6	$.72	$.37
7	$.76	$.36

a. Assume that you forecast that the Swiss franc will appreciate by 3 percent over the next year, but you realize that there is much uncertainty surrounding your forecast. Use the value-at-risk method to estimate (based on a 95 percent confidence level) the maximum level of depreciation in the Swiss franc over the next year, based on the data you were provided.

b. Assume that you forecast that the Argentine peso will depreciate by 2 percent over the next year, but you realize that there is much uncertainty surrounding your forecast. Use the value-at-risk method to estimate (based on a 95 percent confidence level) the maximum level of depreciation in the Argentine peso over the next year, based on the data you were provided.

15. Brooks Co. (a U.S. firm) considers a project in which it will have computer software developed. It would sell the software to Razon Co., an Australian company, and would receive payment of 10 million Australian dollars (A$) at the end of 1 year. To obtain the software, Brooks would have to pay a local software producer $4 million today.

Brooks Co. might also receive an order for the same software from Zug Co. in Australia. It would receive A$4 million at the end of this year if it receives this order, and it would not incur any additional costs because it is the same software that would be created for Razon Co.

The spot rate of the Australian dollar is $.50, and the spot rate is expected to depreciate by 8 percent over the next year. The 1-year forward rate of the Australian dollar is $.47.

If Brooks decides to pursue this project (have the software developed), it would hedge the expected receivables due to the order from Razon Co. with a 1-year forward contract, but it would not hedge the order from Zug Co. Brooks would require a 24 percent rate of return in order to accept the project.

a. Determine the net present value of this project under the conditions that Brooks receives the order from Zug and from Razon, and that it receives payments from these orders in 1 year.

b. Brooks recognizes there are some country risk conditions that could cause Razon Co. to go bankrupt. Determine the net present value of this project under the conditions that Brooks receives both orders, but that Razon goes bankrupt and defaults on its payment to Brooks.

16. Austin Co. needs to borrow $10 million for the next year to support its U.S. operations. It can borrow U.S. dollars at 7 percent or Japanese yen at 1 percent. It has no other cash flows in Japanese yen. Assume that interest rate parity holds, so the 1-year forward rate of the yen exhibits a premium in this case. Austin expects that the spot rate of the yen will appreciate but not as much as suggested by the 1-year forward rate of the yen.

a. Should Austin consider financing with yen and simultaneously purchasing yen 1 year forward to cover its position? Explain.

b. If Austin finances with yen without covering this position, is the effective financing rate expected to be above, below, or equal to the Japanese interest rate of 1 percent? Is the effective financing rate expected to be above, below, or equal to the U.S. interest rate of 7 percent?

c. Explain the implications if Austin finances with yen without covering its position, and the future spot rate of the yen in 1 year turns out to be higher than today's 1-year forward rate on the yen.

17. Provo Co. has $15 million that it will not need until 1 year from now. It can invest the funds in U.S. dollar–denominated securities and earn 6 percent or in New Zealand dollars (NZ$) at 11 percent. It has no other cash flows in New Zealand dollars. Assume that interest rate parity holds, so the 1-year forward rate of the NZ$ exhibits a discount in this case. Provo expects that the spot rate of the NZ$ will depreciate but not as much as suggested by the 1-year forward rate of the NZ$.

a. Should Provo consider investing in NZ$ and simultaneously selling NZ$ 1 year forward to cover its position? Explain.

b. If Provo invests in NZ$ without covering this position, is the effective yield expected to be above, below, or equal to the U.S. interest rate of 6 percent? Is the effective yield expected to be above, below, or equal to the New Zealand interest rate of 11 percent?

c. Explain the implications if Provo invests in NZ$ without covering its position, and the future spot rate of the NZ$ in 1 year turns out to be lower than today's 1-year forward rate on the NZ$.

ANSWERS TO FINAL SELF-EXAM

1. The accuracy from forecasting with the spot rate will be better. The forward rate is higher than the spot rate (it has a premium) when the interest rate is lower. So if the forward rate is used as a forecast, it would suggest that a currency with the lower interest rate will appreciate (in accordance with the international Fisher effect). Yet, since money is assumed to flow where interest rates are higher, this implies that the spot rate will rise when a currency has a relatively high interest rate. This relationship is in contrast to the IFE. Thus, a forward rate will suggest depreciation of the currencies that should appreciate (and vice versa) based on the info in the question. The spot rate as a forecast reflects a forecast of no change in the exchange rate. The forecast of no change in a currency value (when the spot rate is used as the forecast) is better than a forecast of depreciation for a currency that appreciates. The spot rate forecast results in a smaller mean absolute forecast error.

2. The 2-year forward premium is $1.1025/1.2321 - 1 = -.10518$. The 2-year forward rate is $\$.30 \times (1 - .10518) = \$.26844$. The amount of dollars needed is $\$.26844 \times 1,000,000$ zloty $= \$268,440$.

3. Minnesota's stock price will be favorably affected. When the U.S. interest rate is higher, the forward rate of the Canadian dollar will exhibit a discount, which implies depreciation of the C$. The negative coefficient in the regression model suggests that the firm's stock price will be inversely related to the forecast. Thus, the expected depreciation of the C$ will result in a higher stock price.

4. Iowa will still be subject to economic exposure because Portugal's demand for its products would decline if the euro weakens against the dollar. Thus, Iowa's cash flows are still affected by exchange rate movements.

5. Maine Co. does not have an advantage over the other producers in Indonesia because the competitors also capitalize on cheap land and labor.

6. Tucson will receive more cash flows. The 1-year and 2-year forward rates today are equal to today's spot rate. Thus, it hedges receivables at the same exchange rate as today's spot rate. Phoenix also hedges the receivables 1 year from now at that same exchange rate. But 1 year from now, it will hedge the receivables in the following year. In 1 year, the spot rate will be lower, so the 1-year forward rate at that time will be lower than today's forward rate. Thus, the receivables in 2 years will convert to a smaller amount of dollars for Phoenix than for Tucson.

7. a. Money market hedge:

Borrow euros:

$$1,000,000/(1.06) = 943,396 \text{ euros to be borrowed}$$

Convert the euros to dollars:

$$943,396 \text{ euros} \times \$1.20 = \$1,132,075$$

Invest the dollars:

$$\$1,132,075 \times (1.08) = \$1,222,641$$

b. Put option: Pay premium of

$$\$.04 \times 1,000,000 = \$40,000$$

If the spot rate in 1 year = $1.22 as expected, then the put option would be exercised at the strike price of $1.23. The cash flows would be

$$1,000,000 \times (1.23 - \$.04 \text{ premium}) = \$1,190,000$$

Thus, the money market hedge would be most appropriate.

8. a. Portland Co. is not subject to translation exposure since it has no foreign subsidiaries.

b. Topeka's consolidated earnings will increase if the euro appreciates against the dollar over the reporting period.

9. The subsidiary should borrow dollars because it already has a new cash outflow position in rupee so borrowing rupee would increase its exposure.

10. Franco Co. will offer a higher bid because its existing valuation of Podansk should be higher (since its risk-free rate is much lower).

11. As of today, the *NPV* from selling the project is

Proceeds received from selling the project – Present value of the forgone cash flows.

Proceeds = $1.25 million.

PV of forgone cash flows = $(1,000,000 \times \$1.30)/1.2 = \$1,083,333$.

The *NPV* from selling the project is $1,250,000 – $1,083,333 = $166,667. Therefore, selling the project is feasible.

12. a. Based on the CAPM, Everhart's cost of equity = 8% + 1.2(14% – 8%) = 15.2%.

b. Philippine debt has a high interest rate. Also, the peso will appreciate so the debt is even more expensive. Everhart should finance with dollar-denominated debt.

c. Philippine debt is cheaper than Philippine equity. The Philippine investor would require a higher return than if Everhart uses debt. Also, there is no tax advantage if Everhart accepted an equity investment.

13. Sacramento could benefit from the parallel loan because its receivables in 1 year could be used to pay off the loan principal in euros.

14. a. The standard deviation of the annual movements in the Swiss franc is .0557, or 5.57 percent. It is necessary to focus on the volatility of the movements, not the actual values.

The maximum level of annual depreciation of the Swiss franc is:

$$3\% - (1.65 \times .0557) = -.0619, \text{ or } -6.19\%$$

b. The standard deviation of the annual movements in the Argentine peso is .0458, or 4.58 percent.

The maximum level of annual depreciation of the Argentine peso is:

$$-.02 - (1.65 \times .0458) = -.0956, \text{ or } -9.56\%$$

15. a. Order from Razon:

$$\$.47 \times A\$10 \text{ million} = \$4,700,000$$

Order from Zug:

$$\$.46 \times A\$4 \text{ million} = \$1,840,000$$
$$\text{Present value} = \$6,540,000/1.24 = \$5,274,193$$
$$NPV = \$5,274,193 - \$4,000,000 = \$1,274,193$$

b. Order from Zug is $1,840,000 as shown above.

The expected cost of offsetting the hedged cash flows is $100,000 as shown below:

Brooks sold A$1 million forward. It will purchase them in the spot market and then will fulfill its forward contract. The expected future spot rate in 1 year is ($.46), so it would be expected to pay $.46 and sell A$ at the forward rate ($.47) for a $.01 profit per unit. For A$10 million, the profit is $.01 × 10 million = $100,000.

$$\text{Cash flows in 1 year} = \$1,840,000 + \$100,000 \quad = \$1,940,000$$
$$\text{Present value} = \$1,940,000/1.24 \qquad = \$1,564,516$$
$$NPV = \$1,564,516 - \$4,000,000 = -\$2,435,484$$

(An alternative method would be to apply the $.47 to Zug for A$4 million, which would leave a net of A$6 million to fulfill on the forward contract. The answer will be the same for either method.)

16. a. Austin should not consider financing with yen and simultaneously purchasing yen 1 year forward since the effective financing rate would be 7 percent, the same as the financing rate in the United States.

b. If Austin finances with yen without covering this position, its effective financing rate is expected to exceed the interest rate on the yen because of the expected appreciation of the yen over the financing period. However, the effective financing rate is not expected to be as high as the interest rate on the dollar.

c. If the yen's spot rate in 1 year is higher than today's forward rate, the effective financing rate will be higher than the U.S. interest rate of 7 percent.

17. a. Provo should not consider investing in NZ$ and simultaneously selling NZ$ 1 year forward since the effective yield would be 6 percent, the same as the yield in the United States.

b. If Provo invests in NZ$, its yield is expected to exceed the U.S. interest rate but be less than the NZ$ interest rate.

c. If the NZ$ spot rate in 1 year is lower than today's forward rate, the effective yield will be lower than the U.S. interest rate of 6 percent.

Answers to Self-Test Questions

CHAPTER 1

1. MNCs can capitalize on comparative advantages (such as a technology or cost of labor) that they have relative to firms in other countries, which allows them to penetrate those other countries' markets. Given a world of imperfect markets, comparative advantages across countries are not freely transferable. Therefore, MNCs may be able to capitalize on comparative advantages. Many MNCs initially penetrate markets by exporting but ultimately establish a subsidiary in foreign markets and attempt to differentiate their products as other firms enter those markets (product cycle theory).

2. Weak economic conditions or unstable political conditions in a foreign country can reduce cash flows received by the MNC, or they can result in a higher required rate of return for the MNC. Either of these effects results in a lower valuation of the MNC.

3. First, there is the risk of poor economic conditions in the foreign country. Second, there is country risk, which reflects the risk of changing government or public attitudes toward the MNC. Third, there is exchange rate risk, which can affect the performance of the MNC in the foreign country.

CHAPTER 2

1. Each of the economic factors is described, holding other factors constant.

a. *Inflation.* A relatively high U.S. inflation rate relative to other countries can make U.S. goods less attractive to U.S. and non-U.S. consumers, which results in fewer U.S. exports, more U.S. imports, and a lower (or more negative) current account balance. A relatively low U.S. inflation rate would have the opposite effect.

b. *National income.* A relatively high increase in the U.S. national income (compared to other countries) tends to cause a large increase in demand for imports and can cause a lower (or more negative) current account balance. A relatively low increase in the U.S. national income would have the opposite effect.

c. *Exchange rates.* A weaker dollar tends to make U.S. products cheaper to non-U.S. firms and makes non-U.S. products expensive to U.S. firms. Thus, U.S. exports are expected to increase, while U.S. imports are expected to decrease. However, some conditions can prevent these effects from occurring, as explained in the chapter. Normally, a stronger dollar causes U.S. exports to decrease and U.S. imports to increase because it

635

makes U.S. goods more expensive to non-U.S. firms and makes non-U.S. goods less expensive to U.S. firms.

d. *Government restrictions.* When the U.S. government imposes new barriers on imports, U.S. imports decline, causing the U.S. balance of trade to increase (or be less negative). When non-U.S. governments impose new barriers on imports from the United States, the U.S. balance of trade may decrease (or be more negative). When governments remove trade barriers, the opposite effects are expected.

2. When the United States imposes tariffs on imported goods, foreign countries may retaliate by imposing tariffs on goods exported by the United States. Thus, there is a decline in U.S. exports that may offset any decline in U.S. imports.

3. A global recession might cause governments to impose trade restrictions so that they can protect local firms from intense competition and prevent additional layoffs within the country. However, if other countries impose more barriers in retaliation, this strategy could backfire.

CHAPTER 3

1. ($.80 – $.784)/$.80 = .02, or 2%

2. ($.19 – $.188)/$.19 = .0105, or 1.05%

3. MNCs use the spot foreign exchange market to exchange currencies for immediate delivery. They use the forward foreign exchange market and the currency futures market to lock in the exchange rate at which currencies will be exchanged at a future point in time. They use the currency options market when they wish to lock in the maximum (minimum) amount to be paid (received) in a future currency transaction but maintain flexibility in the event of favorable exchange rate movements.

MNCs use the Eurocurrency market to engage in short-term investing or financing or the Eurocredit market to engage in medium-term financing. They can obtain long-term financing by issuing bonds in the Eurobond market or by issuing stock in the international markets.

CHAPTER 4

1. Economic factors affect the yen's value as follows:

a. If U.S. inflation is higher than Japanese inflation, the U.S. demand for Japanese goods may increase (to avoid the higher U.S. prices), and the Japanese demand for U.S. goods may decrease (to avoid the higher U.S. prices). Consequently, there is upward pressure on the value of the yen.

b. If U.S. interest rates increase and exceed Japanese interest rates, the U.S. demand for Japanese interest-bearing securities may decline (since U.S. interest-bearing securities are more attractive), while the Japanese demand for U.S. interest-bearing securities may rise. Both forces place downward pressure on the yen's value.

c. If U.S. national income increases more than Japanese national income, the U.S. demand for Japanese goods may increase more than the Japanese demand for U.S. goods. Assuming that the change in national income levels does not affect exchange rates indirectly through effects on relative interest rates, the forces should place upward pressure on the yen's value.

d. If government controls reduce the U.S. demand for Japanese goods, they place downward pressure on the yen's value. If the controls reduce the Japanese demand for U.S. goods, they place upward pressure on the yen's value.

The opposite scenarios of those described here would cause the expected pressure to be in the opposite direction.

2. U.S. capital flows with Country A may be larger than U.S. capital flows with Country B. Therefore, the change in the interest rate differential has a larger effect on the capital flows with Country A, causing the exchange rate to change. If the capital flows with Country B are nonexistent, interest rate changes do not change the capital flows and therefore do not change the demand and supply conditions in the foreign exchange market.

3. Smart Banking Corp. should not pursue the strategy because a loss would result, as shown here.

a. Borrow $5 million.
b. Convert $5 million to C$5,263,158 (based on the spot exchange rate of $.95 per C$).
c. Invest the C$ at 9 percent annualized, which represents a return of .15 percent over 6 days, so the C$ received after 6 days = C$5,271,053 (computed as C$5,263,158 × [1 + .0015]).
d. Convert the C$ received back to U.S. dollars after 6 days: C$5,271,053 = $4,954,789 (based on anticipated exchange rate of $.94 per C$ after 6 days).
e. The interest rate owed on the U.S. dollar loan is .10 percent over the 6-day period. Thus, the amount owed as a result of the loan is $5,005,000 [computed as $5,000,000 × (1 + .001)].
f. The strategy is expected to cause a gain of $4,954,789 − $5,005,000 = −$50,211.

CHAPTER 5

1. The net profit to the speculator is −$.01 per unit.

The net profit to the speculator for one contract is −$500 (computed as −$.01 × 50,000 units).

The spot rate would need to be $.66 for the speculator to break even.

The net profit to the seller of the call option is $.01 per unit.

2. The speculator should exercise the option.

The net profit to the speculator is $.04 per unit.

The net profit to the seller of the put option is −$.04 per unit.

3. The premium paid is higher for options with longer expiration dates (other things being equal). Firms may prefer not to pay such high premiums.

CHAPTER 6

1. Market forces cause the demand and supply of yen in the foreign exchange market to change, which causes a change in the equilibrium exchange rate. The central banks could intervene to affect the demand or supply conditions in the foreign exchange market, but they would not always be able to offset the changing market forces. For example, if there were a large increase in the U.S. demand for yen and no increase in the supply of yen for sale, the central banks would have to increase the supply of yen in the foreign exchange market to offset the increased demand.

2. The Fed could use direct intervention by selling some of its dollar reserves in exchange for pesos in the foreign exchange market. It could also use indirect intervention by attempting to reduce U.S. interest rates through monetary policy. Specifically, it could increase the U.S. money supply, which places downward pressure on U.S. interest rates (assuming that inflationary expectations do not change). The lower U.S. interest rates should discourage foreign investment in the United States and encourage increased investment by U.S. investors in foreign securities. Both forces tend to weaken the dollar's value.

3. A weaker dollar tends to increase the demand for U.S. goods because the price paid for a specified amount in dollars by non-U.S. firms is reduced. In addition, the U.S. demand for foreign goods is reduced because it takes more dollars to obtain a specified amount in foreign currency once the dollar weakens. Both forces tend to stimulate the U.S. economy and therefore improve productivity and reduce unemployment in the United States.

CHAPTER 7

1. No. The cross exchange rate between the pound and the C$ is appropriate, based on the other exchange rates. There is no discrepancy to capitalize on.

2. No. Covered interest arbitrage involves the exchange of dollars for pounds. Assuming that the investors begin with $1 million (the starting amount will not affect the final conclusion), the dollars would be converted to pounds as shown here:

$$\$1 \text{ million}/\$1.60 \text{ per } £ = £625,000$$

The British investment would accumulate interest over the 180-day period, resulting in

$$£625,000 \times 1.04 = £650,000$$

After 180 days, the pounds would be converted to dollars:

$$£650,000 \times \$1.56 \text{ per pound} = \$1,014,000$$

This amount reflects a return of 1.4 percent above the amount with which U.S. investors initially started. The investors could simply invest the funds in the United States at 3 percent. Thus, U.S. investors would earn less using the covered interest arbitrage strategy than investing in the United States.

3. No. The forward rate discount on the pound does not perfectly offset the interest rate differential. In fact, the discount is 2.5 percent, which is larger than the interest rate differential. U.S. investors do worse when attempting covered interest arbitrage than when investing their funds in the United States because the interest rate advantage on the British investment is more than offset by the forward discount.

Further clarification may be helpful here. While the U.S. investors could not benefit from covered interest arbitrage, British investors could capitalize on covered interest arbitrage. While British investors would earn 1 percent interest less on the U.S. investment, they would be purchasing pounds forward at a discount of 2.5 percent at the end of the investment period. When interest rate parity does not exist, investors from only one of the two countries of concern could benefit from using covered interest arbitrage.

4. If there is a discrepancy in the pricing of a currency, one may capitalize on it by using the various forms of arbitrage described in the chapter. As arbitrage occurs, the exchange rates will be pushed toward their appropriate levels because arbitrageurs will buy an underpriced currency in the foreign exchange market (increase in demand for currency places upward pressure on its value) and will sell an overpriced currency in the foreign exchange market (increase in the supply of currency for sale places downward pressure on its value).

5. The 1-year forward discount on pounds would become more pronounced (by about 1 percentage point more than before) because the spread between the British interest rates and U.S. interest rates would increase.

CHAPTER 8

1. If the Japanese prices rise because of Japanese inflation, the value of the yen should decline. Thus, even though the importer might need to pay more yen, it would benefit from a weaker yen value (it would pay fewer dollars for a given amount in yen). Thus, there could be an offsetting effect if PPP holds.

2. Purchasing power parity does not necessarily hold. In our example, Japanese inflation could rise (causing the importer to pay more yen), and yet the Japanese yen would not necessarily depreciate by an offsetting amount, or at all. Therefore, the dollar amount to be paid for Japanese supplies could increase over time.

3. High inflation will cause a balance-of-trade adjustment, whereby the United States will reduce its purchases of goods in these countries, while the demand for U.S. goods by these countries should increase (according to PPP). Consequently, there will be downward pressure on the values of these currencies.

4.
$$e_f = I_h - I_f$$
$$= 3\% - 4\%$$
$$= -.01, \text{ or} - 1\%$$
$$S_{t+1} = S(1 + e_f)$$
$$= \$.85[1 + (-.01)]$$
$$= \$.8415$$

5.
$$e_f = \frac{1 + i_h}{1 + i_f} - 1$$
$$= \frac{1 + .06}{1 + .11} - 1$$
$$\cong -.045, \text{ or} - 4.5\%$$
$$S_{t+1} = S(1 + e_f)$$
$$= \$.90[1 + (-.045)]$$
$$= \$.8595$$

6. According to the IFE, the increase in interest rates by 5 percentage points reflects an increase in expected inflation by 5 percentage points.

If the inflation adjustment occurs, the balance of trade should be affected, as Australian demand for U.S. goods rises while the U.S. demand for Australian goods declines. Thus, the Australian dollar should weaken.

If U.S. investors believed in the IFE, they would not attempt to capitalize on higher Australian interest rates because they would expect the Australian dollar to depreciate over time.

CHAPTER 9

1. U.S. 4-year interest rate = $(1 + .07)^4$ = 131.08%, or 1.3108. Mexican 4-year interest rate = $(1 + .20)^4$ = 207.36%, or 2.0736.

$$p = \frac{1 + i_b}{1 + i_f} - 1 = \frac{1.3108}{2.0736} - 1$$
$$= -.3679, \text{ or } -36.79\%$$

2. Canadian dollar $\dfrac{|\$.80 - \$.82|}{\$.82} = 2.44\%$

Japanese yen $\dfrac{|\$0.12 - \$.011|}{\$.011} = 9.09\%$

The forecast error was larger for the Japanese yen.

3. The forward rate of the peso would have overestimated the future spot rate because the spot rate would have declined by the end of each month.

4. Semistrong-form efficiency would be refuted since the currency values do not adjust immediately to useful public information.

5. The peso would be expected to depreciate because the forward rate of the peso would exhibit a discount (be less than the spot rate). Thus, the forecast derived from the forward rate is less than the spot rate, which implies anticipated depreciation of the peso.

6. As the chapter suggests, forecasts of currencies are subject to a high degree of error. Thus, if a project's success is very sensitive to the future value of the bolivar, there is much uncertainty. This project could easily backfire because the future value of the bolivar is very uncertain.

Chapter 10

1. Managers have more information about the firm's exposure to exchange rate risk than do shareholders and may be able to hedge it more easily than shareholders could. Shareholders may prefer that the managers hedge for them. Also, cash flows may be stabilized as a result of hedging, which can reduce the firm's cost of financing.

2. The Canadian supplies would have less exposure to exchange rate risk because the Canadian dollar is less volatile than the Mexican peso.

3. The Mexican source would be preferable because the firm could use peso inflows to make payments for material that is imported.

4. No. If exports are priced in dollars, the dollar cash flows received from exporting will depend on Mexico's demand, which will be influenced by the peso's value. If the peso depreciates, Mexican demand for the exports would likely decrease.

5. The earnings generated by the European subsidiaries will be translated to a smaller amount in dollar earnings if the dollar strengthens. Thus, the consolidated earnings of the U.S.-based MNCs will be reduced.

Chapter 11

1. Amount of A\$ to be invested today = A\$3,000,000/(1 + .12)

= A\$2,678,571

Amount of U.S.\$ to be borrowed to convert to A\$ = A\$2,678,571 × \$.85

= \$2,276,785

Amount of U.S.\$ needed in 1 year to pay off loan = \$2,276,785 × (1 + .07)

= \$2,436,160

2. The forward hedge would be more appropriate. Given a forward rate of $.81, Montclair would need $2,430,000 in 1 year (computed as A$3,000,000 × $.81) when using a forward hedge.

3. Montclair could purchase currency call options in Australian dollars. The option could hedge against the possible appreciation of the Australian dollar. Yet, if the Australian dollar depreciates, Montclair could let the option expire and purchase the Australian dollars at the spot rate at the time it needs to send payment. A disadvantage of the currency call option is that a premium must be paid for it. Thus, if Montclair expects the Australian dollar to appreciate over the year, the money market hedge would probably be a better choice since the flexibility provided by the option would not be useful in this case.

4. Even though Sanibel Co. is insulated from the beginning of a month to the end of the month, the forward rate will become higher each month because the forward rate moves with the spot rate. Thus, the firm will pay more dollars each month, even though it is hedged during the month. Sanibel will be adversely affected by the consistent appreciation of the pound.

5. Sanibel Co. could engage in a series of forward contracts today to cover the payments in each successive month. In this way, it locks in the future payments today and does not have to agree to the higher forward rates that may exist in future months.

6. A put option on SF2 million would cost $60,000. If the spot rate of the SF reached $.68 as expected, the put option would be exercised, which would yield $1,380,000 (computed as SF2,000,000 × $.69). Accounting for the premium costs of $60,000, the receivables amount would convert to $1,320,000. If Hopkins remains unhedged, it expects to receive $1,360,000 (computed as SF2,000,000 × $.68). Thus, the unhedged strategy is preferable.

CHAPTER 12

1. Salem could attempt to purchase its chemicals from Canadian sources. Then, if the C$ depreciates, the reduction in dollar inflows resulting from its exports to Canada will be partially offset by a reduction in dollar outflows needed to pay for the Canadian imports.

An alternative possibility for Salem is to finance its business with Canadian dollars, but this would probably be a less efficient solution.

2. A possible disadvantage is that Salem would forgo some of the benefits if the C$ appreciated over time.

3. The consolidated earnings of Coastal Corp. will be adversely affected if the pound depreciates because the British earnings will be translated into dollar earnings for the consolidated income statement at a lower exchange rate. Coastal could attempt to hedge its translation exposure by selling pounds forward. If the pound depreciates, it will benefit from its forward position, which could help offset the translation effect.

4. This argument has no perfect solution. It appears that shareholders penalize the firm for poor earnings even when the reason for poor earnings is a weak euro that has adverse translation effects. It is possible that translation effects could be hedged to stabilize earnings, but Arlington may consider informing the shareholders that the major earnings changes have been due to translation effects and not to changes in consumer demand or other factors. Perhaps shareholders would not respond so strongly to earnings changes if they were well aware that the changes were primarily caused by translation effects.

5. Lincolnshire has no translation exposure since it has no foreign subsidiaries. Kalafa has translation exposure resulting from its subsidiary in Spain.

Chapter 13

1. Possible reasons may include

   - More demand for the product (depending on the product)

   - Better technology in Canada

   - Fewer restrictions (less political interference)

2. Possible reasons may include

   - More demand for the product (depending on the product)

   - Greater probability of earning superior profits (since many goods have not been marketed in Mexico in the past)

   - Cheaper factors of production (such as land and labor)

   - Possible exploitation of monopolistic advantages

3. U.S. firms prefer to enter a country when the foreign country's currency is weak. U.S. firms normally would prefer that the foreign currency appreciate after they invest their dollars to develop the subsidiary. The executive's comment suggests that the euro is too strong, so any U.S. investment of dollars into Europe will not convert into enough euros to make the investment worthwhile.

4. It may be easier to engage in a joint venture with a Chinese firm, which is already well established in China, to circumvent barriers.

5. The government may attempt to stimulate the economy in this way.

Chapter 14

1. In addition to earnings generated in Jamaica, the *NPV* is based on some factors not controlled by the firm, such as the expected host government tax on profits, the withholding tax imposed by the host government, and the salvage value to be received when the project is terminated. Furthermore, the exchange rate projections will affect the estimates of dollar cash flows received by the parent as earnings are remitted.

2. The most obvious effect is on the cash flows that will be generated by the sales distribution center in Ireland. These cash flow estimates will likely be revised downward (due to lower sales estimates). It is also possible that the estimated salvage value could be reduced. Exchange rate estimates could be revised as a result of revised economic conditions. Estimated tax rates imposed on the center by the Irish government could also be affected by the revised economic conditions.

3. New Orleans Exporting Co. must account for the cash flows that will be forgone as a result of the plant because some of the cash flows that used to be received by the parent through its exporting operation will be eliminated. The *NPV* estimate will be reduced after this factor is accounted for.

4.   a. An increase in the risk will cause an increase in the required rate of return on the subsidiary, which results in a lower discounted value of the subsidiary's salvage value.

   b. If the rupiah depreciates over time, the subsidiary's salvage value will be reduced because the proceeds will convert to fewer dollars.

5. The dollar cash flows of Wilmette Co. would be affected more because the periodic remitted earnings from Thailand to be converted to dollars would be larger. The dollar cash flows of Niles would not be affected so much because interest payments would

be made on the Thai loans before earnings could be remitted to the United States. Thus, a smaller amount in earnings would be remitted.

6. The demand for the product in the foreign country may be very uncertain, causing the total revenue to be uncertain. The exchange rates can be very uncertain, creating uncertainty about the dollar cash flows received by the U.S. parent. The salvage value may be very uncertain; this will have a larger effect if the lifetime of the project is short (for projects with a very long life, the discounted value of the salvage value is small anyway).

CHAPTER 15

1. Acquisitions have increased in Europe to capitalize on the inception of the euro, which created a single European currency for many European countries. This has not only eliminated the exchange rate risk on transactions between the participating European countries, but it has also made it easier to compare valuations among European countries to determine where targets are undervalued.

2. Common restrictions include government regulations, such as antitrust restrictions, environmental restrictions, and red tape.

3. The establishment of a new subsidiary allows an MNC to create the subsidiary it desires without assuming existing facilities or employees. However, the process of building a new subsidiary and hiring employees will normally take longer than the process of acquiring an existing foreign firm.

4. The divestiture is now more feasible because the dollar cash flows to be received by the U.S. parent are reduced as a result of the revised projections of the krona's value.

CHAPTER 16

1. First, consumers on the islands could develop a philosophy of purchasing home-made goods. Second, they could discontinue their purchases of exports by Key West Co. as a form of protest against specific U.S. government actions. Third, the host governments could impose severe restrictions on the subsidiary shops owned by Key West Co. (including the blockage of funds to be remitted to the U.S. parent).

2. First, the islands could experience poor economic conditions, which would cause lower income for some residents. Second, residents could be subject to higher inflation or higher interest rates, which would reduce the income that they could allocate toward exports. Depreciation of the local currencies could also raise the local prices to be paid for goods exported from the United States. All factors described here could reduce the demand for goods exported by Key West Co.

3. Financial risk is probably a bigger concern. The political risk factors are unlikely, based on the product produced by Key West Co. and the absence of substitute products available in other countries. The financial risk factors deserve serious consideration.

4. This event has heightened the perceived country risk for any firms that have offices in populated areas (especially next to government or military offices). It has also heightened the risk for firms whose employees commonly travel to other countries and for firms that provide office services or travel services.

5. Rockford Co. could estimate the net present value (*NPV*) of the project under three scenarios: (1) include a special tax when estimating cash flows back to the parent (probability of scenario = 15%), (2) assume the project ends in 2 years and include a salvage value when estimating the *NPV* (probability of scenario = 15%), and (3) assume no

Canadian government intervention (probability = 70%). This results in three estimates of *NPV,* one for each scenario. This method is less arbitrary than the one considered by Rockford's executives.

CHAPTER 17

1.   Growth may have caused Goshen to require a large amount for financing that could not be completely provided by retained earnings. In addition, the interest rates may have been low in these foreign countries to make debt financing an attractive alternative. Finally, the use of foreign debt can reduce the exchange rate risk since the amount in periodic remitted earnings is reduced when interest payments are required on foreign debt.

2.   If country risk has increased, Lynde can attempt to reduce its exposure to that risk by removing its equity investment from the subsidiary. When the subsidiary is financed with local funds, the local creditors have more to lose than the parent if the host government imposes any severe restrictions on the subsidiary.

3.   Not necessarily. German and Japanese firms tend to have more support from other firms or from the government if they experience cash flow problems and can therefore afford to use a higher degree of financial leverage than firms from the same industry in the United States.

4.   Local debt financing is favorable because it can reduce the MNC's exposure to country risk and exchange rate risk. However, the high interest rates will make the local debt very expensive. If the parent makes an equity investment in the subsidiary to avoid the high cost of local debt, it will be more exposed to country risk and exchange rate risk.

5.   The answer to this question is dependent on whether you believe unsystematic risk is relevant. If the CAPM is used as a framework for measuring the risk of a project, the risk of the foreign project is determined to be low, because the systematic risk is low. That is, the risk is specific to the host country and is not related to U.S. market conditions. However, if the project's unsystematic risk is relevant, the project is considered to have a high degree of risk. The project's cash flows are very uncertain, even though the systematic risk is low.

CHAPTER 18

1.   A firm may be able to obtain a lower coupon rate by issuing bonds denominated in a different currency. The firm converts the proceeds from issuing the bond to its local currency to finance local operations. Yet, there is exchange rate risk because the firm will need to make coupon payments and the principal payment in the currency denominating the bond. If that currency appreciates against the firm's local currency, the financing costs could become larger than expected.

2.   The risk is that the Swiss franc would appreciate against the pound over time since the British subsidiary will periodically convert some of its pound cash flows to francs to make the coupon payments.

The risk here is less than it would be if the proceeds were used to finance U.S. operations. The Swiss franc's movement against the dollar is much more volatile than the Swiss franc's movement against the pound. The Swiss franc and the pound have historically moved in tandem to some degree against the dollar, which means that there is a somewhat stable exchange rate between the two currencies.

3. If these firms borrow U.S. dollars and convert them to finance local projects, they will need to use their own currencies to obtain dollars and make coupon payments. These firms would be highly exposed to exchange rate risk.

4. Paxson Co. is exposed to exchange rate risk. If the yen appreciates, the number of dollars needed for conversion into yen will increase. To the extent that the yen strengthens, Paxson's cost of financing when financing with yen could be higher than when financing with dollars.

5. The nominal interest rate incorporates expected inflation (according to the so-called Fisher effect). Therefore, the high interest rates reflect high expected inflation. Cash flows can be enhanced by inflation because a given profit margin converts into larger profits as a result of inflation, even if costs increase at the same rate as revenues.

CHAPTER 19

1. The exporter may not trust the importer or may be concerned that the government will impose exchange controls that prevent payment to the exporter. Meanwhile, the importer may not trust that the exporter will ship the goods ordered and therefore may not pay until the goods are received. Commercial banks can help by providing guarantees to the exporter in case the importer does not pay.

2. In accounts receivable financing, the bank provides a loan to the exporter secured by the accounts receivable. If the importer fails to pay the exporter, the exporter is still responsible to repay the bank. Factoring involves the sales of accounts receivable by the exporter to a so-called factor, so that the exporter is no longer responsible for the importer's payment.

3. The guarantee programs of the Export-Import Bank provide medium-term protection against the risk of nonpayment by the foreign buyer due to political risk.

CHAPTER 20

1. $$r_f = (1 + i_f)(1 + e_f) - 1$$

If $e_f = -6\%, r_f = (1 + .09)[1 + (-.06)] - 1$

$$= .0246, \text{ or } 2.46\%$$

If $e_f = 3\%, r_f = (1 + .09)(1 + .03) - 1$

$$= .1227, \text{ or } 12.27\%$$

2. $$E(r_f) = 50\%(2.46\%) + 50\%(12.27\%)$$

$$= 1.23\% + 6.135\%$$

$$= 7.365\%$$

3. $$e_f = \frac{1 + r_f}{1 + i} - 1$$

$$= \frac{1 + .08}{1 + .05} - 1$$

$$= .0286, \text{ or } 2.86\%$$

4. $E(e_f) = (\text{Forward rate} - \text{Spot rate})/\text{Spot rate}$

$\qquad\qquad = (\$.60 - \$.62)/\$.62$

$\qquad\qquad = -.0322, \text{or} -3.22\%$

$\qquad E(e_f) = (1 + i_f)[1 + E(e_f)] - 1$

$\qquad\qquad = (1 + .09)[1 + (-.0322)] - 1$

$\qquad\qquad = .0548, \text{or} 5.48\%$

5.   The two-currency portfolio will not exhibit much lower variance than either individual currency because the currencies tend to move together. Thus, the diversification effect is limited.

CHAPTER 21

1.   The subsidiary in Country Y should be more adversely affected because the blocked funds will not earn as much interest over time. In addition, the funds will likely be converted to dollars at an unfavorable exchange rate because the currency is expected to weaken over time.

2. $E(r) = (1 + i_f)[1 + E(e_f)] - 1$

$\qquad\quad = (1 + .14)(1 + .08) - 1$

$\qquad\quad = .2312, \text{or} 23.12\%$

3. $E(e_f) = (\text{Forward rate} - \text{Spot rate})/\text{Spot rate}$

$\qquad\qquad = (\$.19 - \$.20)/\$.20$

$\qquad\qquad = -.05, \text{or} -5\%$

$\qquad E(r) = (1 + i_f)[1 + E(e_f)] - 1$

$\qquad\qquad = (1 + .11)[1 + (-.05)] - 1$

$\qquad\qquad = .0545, \text{or} 5.45\%$

4. $e_f = \dfrac{1 + r}{1 + i_f} - 1$

$\qquad\quad = \dfrac{1 + .06}{1 + .90} - 1$

$\qquad\quad = -.4421, \text{or} -44.21\%$

If the bolivar depreciates by less than 44.21 percent against the dollar over the 1-year period, a 1-year deposit in Venezuela will generate a higher effective yield than a 1-year U.S. deposit.

5.   Yes. Interest rate parity would discourage U.S. firms only from covering their investments in foreign deposits by using forward contracts. As long as the firms believe that the currency will not depreciate to offset the interest rate advantage, they may consider investing in countries with high interest rates.

Supplemental Cases

CHAPTER 1 RANGER SUPPLY COMPANY

Motivation for International Business

Ranger Supply Company is a large manufacturer and distributor of office supplies. It is based in New York but sends supplies to firms throughout the United States. It markets its supplies through periodic mass mailings of catalogues to those firms. Its clients can make orders over the phone, and Ranger ships the supplies upon demand. Ranger has had very high production efficiency in the past. This is attributed partly to low employee turnover and high morale, as employees are guaranteed job security until retirement.

Ranger already holds a large proportion of the market share in distributing office supplies in the United States. Its main competition in the United States comes from one U.S. firm and one Canadian firm. A British firm has a small share of the U.S. market but is at a disadvantage because of its distance. The British firm's marketing and transportation costs in the U.S. market are relatively high.

Although Ranger's office supplies are somewhat similar to those of its competitors, it has been able to capture most of the U.S. market because its high efficiency enables it to charge low prices to retail stores. It expects a decline in the aggregate demand for office supplies in the United States in future years. However, it anticipates strong demand for office supplies in Canada and in Eastern Europe over the next several years. Ranger's executives have begun to consider exporting as a method of offsetting the possible decline in domestic demand for its products.

a. Ranger Supply Company plans to attempt penetrating either the Canadian market or the Eastern European market through exporting. What factors deserve to be considered in deciding which market is more feasible?

b. One financial manager has been responsible for developing a contingency plan in case whichever market is chosen imposes export barriers over time. This manager proposed that Ranger should establish a subsidiary in the country of concern under such conditions. Is this a reasonable strategy? Are there any obvious reasons why this strategy could fail?

CHAPTER 2 MAPLELEAF PAPER COMPANY

Assessing the Effects of Changing Trade Barriers

MapleLeaf Paper Company is a Canadian firm that produces a particular type of paper not produced in the United States. It focuses most of its sales in the United States. In the past year, for example, 180,000 of its 200,000 rolls of paper were sold to the United States, and the remaining 20,000 rolls were sold in Canada. It has a niche in the United States, but because there are some substitutes, the U.S. demand for the product is sensitive to any changes in price. In fact, MapleLeaf has estimated that the U.S. demand rises (declines) 3 percent for every 1 percent decrease (increase) in the price paid by U.S. consumers, other things held constant.

A 12 percent tariff had historically been imposed on exports to the United States. Then on January 2, a free trade agreement between the United States and Canada was implemented, eliminating the tariff. MapleLeaf was ecstatic about the news, as it had been lobbying for the free trade agreement for several years.

At that time, the Canadian dollar was worth $.76. MapleLeaf hired a consulting firm to forecast the value of the Canadian dollar in the future. The firm expects the Canadian dollar to be worth about $.86 by the end of the year and then stabilize after that. The expectations of a stronger Canadian dollar are driven by an anticipation that Canadian firms will capitalize on the free trade agreement more than U.S. firms, which will cause the increase in the U.S. demand for Canadian goods to be much higher than the increase in the Canadian demand for U.S. goods. (However, no other Canadian firms are expected to penetrate the U.S. paper market.) MapleLeaf expects no major changes in the aggregate demand for paper in the U.S. paper industry. It is also confident that its only competition will continue to be two U.S. manufacturers that produce imperfect substitutes for its paper. Its sales in Canada are expected to grow by about 20 percent by the end of the year because of an increase in the overall Canadian demand for paper and then remain level after that. MapleLeaf invoices its exports in Canadian dollars and plans to maintain its present pricing schedule, since its costs of production are relatively stable. Its U.S. competitors will also continue their pricing schedule. MapleLeaf is confident that the free trade agreement will be permanent. It immediately begins to assess its long-run prospects in the United States.

a. Based on the information provided, develop a forecast of MapleLeaf's annual production (in rolls) needed to accommodate demand in the future. Since orders for this year have already occurred, focus on the years following this year.

b. Explain the underlying reasons for the change in the demand and the implications.

c. Will the general effects on MapleLeaf be similar to the effects on a U.S. paper producer that exports paper to Canada? Explain.

Chapter 3 Gretz Tool Company
Using International Financial Markets

Gretz Tool Company is a large U.S.-based multinational corporation with subsidiaries in eight different countries. The parent of Gretz provided an initial cash infusion to establish each subsidiary. However, each subsidiary has had to finance its own growth since then. The parent and subsidiaries of Gretz typically use Citigroup (with branches in numerous countries) when possible to facilitate any flow of funds necessary.

a. Explain the various ways in which Citigroup could facilitate Gretz's flow of funds, and identify the type of financial market where that flow of funds occurs. For each type of financing transaction, specify whether Citigroup would serve as the creditor or would simply be facilitating the flow of funds to Gretz.

b. Recently, the British subsidiary called on Citigroup for a medium-term loan and was offered the following alternatives:

LOAN DENOMINATED IN	ANNUALIZED RATE
British pounds	13%
U.S. dollars	11%
Canadian dollars	10%
Japanese yen	8%

What characteristics do you think would help the British subsidiary determine which currency to borrow?

Chapter 4 Bruin Aircraft, Inc.

Factors Affecting Exchange Rates

Bruin Aircraft, Inc., is a designer and manufacturer of airplane parts. Its production plant is based in California. About one-third of its sales are exports to the United Kingdom. Though Bruin invoices its exports in dollars, the demand for its exports is highly sensitive to the value of the British pound. In order to maintain its parts inventory at a proper level, it must forecast the total demand for its parts, which is somewhat dependent on the forecasted value of the pound. The treasurer of Bruin was assigned the task of forecasting the value of the pound (against the dollar) for each of the next 5 years. He was planning to request from the firm's chief economist forecasts on all the relevant factors that could affect the pound's future exchange rate. He decided to organize his worksheet by separating demand-related factors from the supply-related factors, as illustrated by the headings below:

Factors that can affect the value of the pound	Check (✓) here if the factor influences the U.S. demand for pounds	Check (✓) here if the factor influences the supply of pounds for sale

Help the treasurer by identifying the factors in the first column and then checking the second or third (or both) columns. Include any possible government-related factors and be specific (tie your description to the specific case background provided here).

Chapter 5 Capital Crystal, Inc.

Using Currency Futures and Options

Capital Crystal, Inc., is a major importer of crystal from the United Kingdom. The crystal is sold to prestigious retail stores throughout the United States. The imports are denominated in British pounds (£). Every quarter, Capital needs £500 million. It is currently attempting to determine whether it should use currency futures or currency options to hedge imports 3 months from now, if it will hedge at all. The spot rate of the pound is $1.60. A 3-month futures contract on the pound is available for $1.59 per unit. A call option on the pound is available with a 3-month expiration date and an exercise price of $1.60. The premium to be paid on the call option is $.01 per unit.

Capital is very confident that the value of the pound will rise to at least $1.62 in 3 months. Its previous forecasts of the pound's value have been very accurate. The management style of Capital is very risk averse. Managers receive a bonus at the end of the year if they satisfy minimal performance standards. The bonus is fixed, regardless of how high above the minimum level one's performance is. If performance is below the minimum, there is no bonus, and future advancement within the company is unlikely.

a. As a financial manager of Capital, you have been assigned the task of choosing among three possible strategies: (1) hedge the pound's position by purchasing futures, (2) hedge the pound's position by purchasing call options, or (3) do not hedge. Offer your recommendation and justify it.

b. Assume the previous information that was provided, except for this difference: Capital has revised its forecast of the pound to be worth $1.57 3 months from now. Given this revision, recommend whether Capital should (1) hedge the pound's position by purchasing futures, (2) hedge the pound's position by purchasing call options, or (3) not hedge. Justify your recommendation. Is your recommendation consistent with maximizing shareholder wealth?

Chapter 6 Hull Importing Company
Effects of Intervention on Import Expenses

Hull Importing Company is a U.S.-based firm that imports small gift items and sells them to retail gift shops across the United States. About half of the value of Hull's purchases comes from the United Kingdom, while the remaining purchases are from Mexico. The imported goods are denominated in the currency of the country where they are produced. Hull normally does not hedge its purchases.

In previous years, the Mexican peso and pound fluctuated substantially against the dollar (although not by the same degree). Hull's expenses are directly tied to these currency values because all of its products are imported. It has been successful because the imported gift items are somewhat unique and are attractive to U.S. consumers. However, Hull has been unable to pass on higher costs (due to a weaker dollar) to its consumers, because consumers would then switch to different gift items sold at other stores.

a. Hull expects that Mexico's central bank will increase interest rates and that Mexico's inflation will not be affected. Offer any insight on how the peso's value may change and how Hull's profits would be affected as a result.

b. Hull used to closely monitor government intervention by the Bank of England (the British central bank) on the value of the pound. Assume that the Bank of England intervenes to strengthen the pound's value with respect to the dollar by 5 percent. Would this have a favorable or unfavorable effect on Hull's business?

Chapter 7 Zuber, Inc.
Using Covered Interest Arbitrage

Zuber, Inc., is a U.S.-based MNC that has been aggressively pursuing business in Eastern Europe since the Iron Curtain was lifted in 1989. Poland has allowed its currency's value to be market determined. The spot rate of the Polish zloty is $.40. Poland also has begun to allow investments by foreign investors as a method of attracting funds to help build its economy. Its interest rate on 1-year securities issued by the federal government is 14 percent, which is substantially higher than the 9 percent rate currently offered on 1-year U.S. Treasury securities.

A local bank has begun to create a forward market for the zloty. This bank was recently privatized and has been trying to make a name for itself in international business. The bank has quoted a 1-year forward rate of $.39 for the zloty. As an employee in Zuber's international money market division, you have been asked to assess the possibility of investing short-term funds in Poland. You are in charge of investing $10 million over the next year. Your objective is to earn the highest return possible while maintaining safety (since the firm will need the funds next year).

Since the exchange rate has just become market determined, there is a high probability that the zloty's value will be very volatile for several years as it seeks its true equilibrium value. The expected value of the zloty in 1 year is $.40, but there is a high degree of uncertainty about this. The actual value in 1 year may be as much as 40 percent above or below this expected value.

a. Would you be willing to invest the funds in Poland without covering your position? Explain.

b. Suggest how you could attempt covered interest arbitrage. What is the expected return from using covered interest arbitrage?

c. What risks are involved in using covered interest arbitrage here?

d. If you had to choose between investing your funds in U.S. Treasury bills at 9 percent or using covered interest arbitrage, what would be your choice? Defend your answer.

CHAPTER 8 FLAME FIXTURES, INC.
Business Application of Purchasing Power Parity

Flame Fixtures, Inc., is a small U.S. business in Arizona that produces and sells lamp fixtures. Its costs and revenues have been very stable over time. Its profits have been adequate, but Flame has been searching for means of increasing profits in the future. It has recently been negotiating with a Mexican firm called Corón Company, from which it will purchase some of the necessary parts. Every 3 months, Corón Company will send a specified number of parts with the bill invoiced in Mexican pesos. By having the parts produced by Corón, Flame expects to save about 20 percent on production costs. Corón is only willing to work out a deal if it is assured that it will receive a minimum specified amount of orders every 3 months over the next 10 years, for a minimum specified amount. Flame will be required to use its assets to serve as collateral in case it does not fulfill its obligation.

The price of the parts will change over time in response to the costs of production. Flame recognizes that the cost to Corón will increase substantially over time as a result of the very high inflation rate in Mexico. Therefore, the price charged in pesos likely will rise substantially every 3 months. However, Flame feels that, because of the concept of purchasing power parity (PPP), its dollar payments to Corón will be very stable. According to PPP, if Mexican inflation is much higher than U.S. inflation, the peso will weaken against the dollar by that difference. Since Flame does not have much liquidity, it could experience a severe cash shortage if its expenses are much higher than anticipated.

The demand for Flame's product has been very stable and is expected to continue that way. Since the U.S. inflation rate is expected to be very low, Flame likely will continue pricing its lamps at today's prices (in dollars). It believes that by saving 20 percent on production costs it will substantially increase its profits. It is about ready to sign a contract with Corón Company.

a. Describe a scenario that could cause Flame to save even more than 20 percent on production costs.

b. Describe a scenario that could cause Flame to actually incur higher production costs than if it simply had the parts produced in the United States.

c. Do you think that Flame will experience stable dollar outflow payments to Corón over time? Explain. (Assume that the number of parts ordered is constant over time.)

d. Do you think that Flame's risk changes at all as a result of its new relationship with Corón Company? Explain.

CHAPTER 9 WHALER PUBLISHING COMPANY
Forecasting Exchange Rates

Whaler Publishing Company specializes in producing textbooks in the United States and marketing these books in foreign universities where the English language is used. Its sales are invoiced in the currency of the country where the textbooks are sold. The expected revenues from textbooks sold to university bookstores are shown in Exhibit B.1.

Whaler is comfortable with the estimated foreign currency revenues in each country. However, it is very uncertain about the U.S. dollar revenues to be received from each country. At this time (which is the beginning of Year 16), Whaler is using today's spot rate as its best guess of the exchange rate at which the revenues from each country will be converted into U.S. dollars at the end of this year (which implies a zero percentage change in the value of each currency). Yet, it recognizes the potential error associated with this type of forecast. Therefore, it desires to incorporate the risk surrounding each currency forecast by creating confidence intervals for each currency. First, it must derive the annual percentage change in the exchange rate over each of the last 15 years for each currency to derive a standard deviation in the percentage change of each foreign currency. By assuming that the percentage changes in exchange rates are normally distributed, it plans to develop two ranges of forecasts for the annual percentage change in each currency: (1) one standard deviation in each direction from its best guess to develop a 68 percent confidence interval, and (2) two standard deviations in each direction from its best guess to develop a 95 percent confidence interval. These confidence intervals can then be applied to today's spot rates to develop confidence intervals for the future spot rate 1 year from today.

Exhibit B.1 Expected Revenues from Textbooks Sold to University Bookstores

UNIVERSITY BOOKSTORES IN	LOCAL CURRENCY	TODAY'S SPOT EXCHANGE RATE	EXPECTED REVENUES FROM BOOKSTORES THIS YEAR
Australia	Australian dollars (A$)	$ .7671	A$38,000,000
Canada	Canadian dollars (C$)	.8625	C$35,000,000
New Zealand	New Zealand dollars (NZ$)	.5985	NZ$33,000,000
United Kingdom	Pounds (£)	1.9382	£34,000,000

The exchange rates at the beginning of each of the last 16 years for each currency (with respect to the U.S. dollar) are shown here:

BEGINNING OF YEAR	AUSTRALIAN $	CANADIAN $	NEW ZEALAND $	BRITISH POUND
1	$1.2571	$.9839	$1.0437	£2.0235
2	1.0864	.9908	.9500	1.7024
3	1.1414	.9137	1.0197	1.9060
4	1.1505	.8432	1.0666	2.0345
5	1.1055	.8561	.9862	2.2240
6	1.1807	.8370	.9623	2.3850
7	1.1279	.8432	.8244	1.9080
8	.9806	.8137	.7325	1.6145
9	.9020	.8038	.6546	1.4506
10	.8278	.7570	.4776	1.1565
11	.6809	.7153	.4985	1.4445
12	.6648	.7241	.5235	1.4745
13	.7225	.8130	.6575	1.8715
14	.8555	.8382	.6283	1.8095
15	.7831	.8518	.5876	1.5772
16	.7671	.8625	.5985	1.9382

The confidence intervals for each currency can be applied to the expected book revenues to derive confidence intervals in U.S. dollars to be received from each country. Complete this assignment for Whaler Publishing Company, and also rank the currencies in terms of uncertainty (degree of volatility). Since the exchange rate data provided are real, the analysis will indicate (1) how volatile currencies can be, (2) how much more volatile some currencies are than others, and (3) how estimated revenues can be subject to a high degree of uncertainty as a result of uncertain exchange rates. (If you use a spreadsheet to do this case, you may want to retain it since the case in the following chapter is an extension of this case.)

Chapter 10 Whaler Publishing Company

Measuring Exposure to Exchange Rate Risk

Recall the situation of Whaler Publishing Company from the previous chapter. Whaler needed to develop confidence intervals of four exchange rates in order to derive confidence intervals for U.S. dollar cash flows to be received from four different countries. Each confidence interval was isolated on a particular country.

Assume that Whaler would like to estimate the range of its aggregate dollar cash flows to be generated from other countries. A computer spreadsheet should be developed to facilitate this exercise. Whaler plans to simulate the conversion of the expected currency cash flows to dollars, using each of the previous years as a possible scenario (recall that exchange rate data are provided in the original case in Chapter 9). Specifically, Whaler will determine the annual percentage change in the spot rate of each currency for a given year. Then, it will apply that percentage to the respective existing spot rates to determine a possible spot rate in 1 year for each currency. Recall that today's spot rates are assumed to be as follows:

- Australian dollar = $.7671
- Canadian dollar = $.8625
- New Zealand dollar = $.5985
- British pound = £1.9382

Once the spot rate is forecasted for 1 year ahead for each currency, the U.S. dollar revenues received from each country can be forecasted. For example, from Year 1 to Year 2, the Australian dollar declined by about 13.6 percent. If this percentage change occurs this year, the spot rate of the Australian dollar will decline from today's rate of $.7671 to about $.6629. In this case, the A$38 million to be received would convert to $25,190,200. The same tasks must be done for the other three currencies as well in order to estimate the aggregate dollar cash flows under this scenario.

This process can be repeated, using each of the previous years as a possible future scenario. There will be 15 possible scenarios, or 15 forecasts of the aggregate U.S. dollar cash flows. Each of these scenarios is expected to have an equal probability of occurring. By assuming that these cash flows are normally distributed, Whaler uses the standard deviation of the possible aggregate cash flows for all 15 scenarios to develop 68 and 95 percent confidence intervals surrounding the "expected value" of the aggregate level of U.S. dollar cash flows to be received in 1 year.

a. Perform these tasks for Whaler in order to determine these confidence intervals on the aggregate level of U.S. dollar cash flows to be received. Whaler uses the methodology described here, rather than simply combining the results for individual countries (from the previous chapter) because exchange rate movements may be correlated.

b. Review the annual percentage changes in the four exchange rates. Do they appear to be positively correlated? Estimate the correlation coefficient between exchange rate movements with either a calculator or a spreadsheet package. Based on this analysis, you can fill out the following correlation coefficient matrix:

	A$	C$	NZ$	£
A$	1.00			
C$		1.00		
NZ$			1.00	
£				1.00

Would aggregate dollar cash flows to be received by Whaler be more risky than they would if the exchange rate movements were completely independent? Explain.

c. One Whaler executive has suggested that a more efficient way of deriving the confidence intervals would be to use the exchange rates instead of the percentage changes as the scenarios and derive U.S. dollar cash flow estimates directly from them. Do you think this method would be as accurate as the method now used by Whaler? Explain.

CHAPTER 11 BLACKHAWK COMPANY

Forecasting Exchange Rates and the Hedging Decision

This case is intended to illustrate how forecasting exchange rates and hedging decisions are related. Blackhawk Company imports goods from New Zealand and plans to purchase NZ$800,000 1 quarter from now to pay for imports. As the treasurer of Blackhawk, you are responsible for determining whether and how to hedge this payables position. Several tasks will need to be completed before you can make these decisions. The entire analysis can be performed using LOTUS or Excel spreadsheets. Your first goal is to assess three different models for forecasting the value of NZ$ at the end of the quarter (also called the future spot rate, or FSR).

- Using the forward rate (FR) at the beginning of the quarter.

- Using the spot rate (SR) at the beginning of the quarter.

- Estimating the historical influence of the inflation differential during each quarter on the percentage change in the NZ$ (which leads to a forecast of the FSR of the NZ$).

The historical data to be used for this analysis are provided in Exhibit B.2.

a. Use regression analysis to determine whether the forward rate is an unbiased estimator of the spot rate at the end of the quarter.

b. Use the simplified approach of assessing the signs of forecast errors over time. Do you detect any bias when using the FR to forecast? Explain.

c. Determine the average absolute forecast error when using the forward rate to forecast.

d. Determine whether the spot rate of the NZ$ at the beginning of the quarter is an unbiased estimator of the spot rate at the end of the quarter using regression analysis.

e. Use the simplified approach of assessing the signs of forecast errors over time. Do you detect any bias when using the SR to forecast? Explain.

f. Determine the average absolute forecast error when using the spot rate to forecast. Is the spot rate or the forward rate a more accurate forecast of the future spot rate (FSR)? Explain.

g. Use the following regression model to determine the relationship between the inflation differential (called *DIFF* and defined as the U.S. inflation minus New Zealand inflation) and the percentage change in the NZ$ (called *PNZ$*):

$$PNZ\$ = b_0 + b_1 DIFF$$

Once you have determined the coefficients b_0 and b_1, use them to forecast *PNZ$* based on a forecast of 2 percent for *DIFF* in the upcoming quarter. Then, apply your forecast for *PNZ$* to the prevailing spot rate (which is $.589) to derive the expected FSR of the NZ$.

h. Blackhawk plans to develop a probability distribution for the FSR. First, it will assign a 40 percent probability to the forecast of FSR derived from the regression analysis in the previous question. Second, it will assign a 40 percent probability to the forecast of FSR based on either the forward rate or the spot rate (whichever was more accurate according to your earlier analysis). Third, it will assign a 20 percent probability to the forecast of FSR based on either the forward rate or the spot rate (whichever was less accurate according to your earlier analysis).

Exhibit B.2 Historical Data for Analysis

QUARTER	SPOT RATE OF NZ$ AT BEGINNING OF QUARTER	90-DAY FORWARD RATE OF NZ$ AT BEGINNING OF QUARTER	SPOT RATE OF NZ$ AT END OF QUARTER	LAST QUARTER'S INFLATION DIFFERENTIAL	PERCENTAGE CHANGE IN NZ$ OVER QUARTER
1	$.3177	$.3250	$.3233	−.05%	1.76%
2	.3233	.3272	.3267	−.46	1.05
3	.3267	.3285	.3746	.66	14.66
4	.3746	.3778	.4063	.94	8.46
5	.4063	.4093	.4315	.58	6.20
6	.4315	.4344	.4548	.23	5.40
7	.4548	.4572	.4949	.02	8.82
8	.4949	.4966	.5153	1.26	4.12
9	.5153	.5169	.5540	.86	7.51
10	.5540	.5574	.5465	.54	−1.35
11	.5465	.5510	.5440	1.00	−.46
12	.5440	.5488	.6309	1.09	15.97
13	.6309	.6365	.6027	.78	−4.47
14	.6027	.6081	.5409	.23	−10.25
15	.5491	.5538	.5320	.71	−3.11
16	.5320	.5365	.5617	1.18	5.58
17	.5617	.5667	.5283	.70	−5.95
18	.5283	.5334	.5122	−.31	−3.05
19	.5122	.5149	.5352	.62	4.49
20	.5352	.5372	.5890	.87	10.05
21 (Now)	.5890	.5878	(to be forecasted)	.28	(to be forecasted)

Fill in the table that follows:

PROBABILITY	FSR
40%	
40	
20	

i. Assuming that Blackhawk does not hedge, fill in the following table:

PROBABILITY	FORECASTED DOLLAR AMOUNT NEEDED TO PAY FOR IMPORTS IN 90 DAYS
40%	
40	
20	
6	

j. Based on the probability distribution for the FSR, use the table that follows to determine the probability distribution for the real cost of hedging if a forward contract is used for hedging (recall that the prevailing 90-day forward rate is $.5878).

PROBABILITY	FORECASTED DOLLAR AMOUNT NEEDED IF HEDGED WITH A FORWARD CONTRACT	FORECASTED AMOUNT NEEDED IF UNHEDGED	FORECASTED REAL COST OF HEDGING PAYABLES
40%			
40			
20			

k. If Blackhawk hedges its position, it will use either a 90-day forward rate, a money market hedge, or a call option. The following data are available at the time of its decision.

- Spot rate = $.589.
- 90-day forward rate = $.5878.
- 90-day U.S. borrowing rate = 2.5%.
- 90-day U.S. investing rate = 2.3%.
- 90-day New Zealand borrowing rate = 2.4%.
- 90-day New Zealand investing rate = 2.1%.
- Call option on NZ$ has a premium of $.01 per unit.
- Call option on NZ$ has an exercise price of $.60.

Determine the probability distribution of dollars needed for a call option if used (include the premium paid) by filling out the following table:

PROBABILITY	FSR	DOLLARS NEEDED TO PAY FOR PAYABLES
40%		
40		
20		

l.   Compare the forward hedge to the money market hedge. Which is superior? Why?

m. Compare either the forward hedge or the money market hedge (whichever is better) to the call option hedge. If you hedge, which technique should you use? Why?

n. Compare the hedge you believe is the best to an unhedged strategy. Should you hedge or remain unhedged? Explain.

CHAPTER 12 MADISON, INC.

Assessing Economic Exposure

The situation for Madison, Inc., was described in this chapter to illustrate how alternative operational structures could affect economic exposure to exchange rate movements. Ken Moore, the vice president of finance at Madison, Inc., was seriously considering a shift to the proposed operational structure described in the text. He was determined to stabilize the earnings before taxes and believed that the proposed approach would achieve this objective. The firm expected that the Canadian dollar would consistently depreciate over the next several years. Over time, its forecasts have been very accurate. Moore paid little attention to the forecasts, stating that regardless of how the Canadian dollar changed, future earnings would be more stable under the proposed operational structure. He also was constantly reminded of how the strengthened Canadian dollar in some years had adversely affected the firm's earnings. In fact, he was somewhat concerned that he might even lose his job if the adverse effects from economic exposure continued.

a. Would a revised operational structure at this time be in the best interests of the shareholders? Would it be in the best interests of the vice president?

b. How could a revised operational structure possibly be feasible from the vice president's perspective but not from the shareholders' perspective? Explain how the firm might be able to ensure that the vice president will make decisions related to economic exposure that are in the best interests of the shareholders.

CHAPTER 13 BLUES CORPORATION

Capitalizing on the Opening of Eastern European Borders

Having done business in the United States for over 50 years, Blues Corporation has an established reputation. Most of Blues' business is in the United States. It has a subsidiary in the western section of Germany, which produces goods and exports them to other European countries. Blues Corporation produces many consumer goods that could possibly be produced or marketed in Eastern European countries. The following issues were raised at a recent executive meeting. Offer your comments about each issue.

a. Blues Corporation is considering shifting its European production facility from western Germany to eastern Germany. There are two key factors motivating this shift. First, the labor cost is lower in eastern Germany. Second, there is an existing facility (currently government owned) in the former East Germany that is for sale. Blues would like to transform the facility and use its technology to increase production efficiency. It estimates that it would need only one-fourth of the workers in that facility. What other factors deserve to be considered before the decision is made?

b. Blues Corporation believes that it could penetrate the Eastern European markets. It would need to invest considerable funds in promoting its consumer goods in Eastern Europe, since its goods are not well known in that area. Yet, it believes that this strategy could pay off in the long run because Blues could underprice the competition. At the current time, the main competition consists of businesses that are perceived to be inefficiently run. The lack of competitive pricing in this market is the primary reason for Blues Corporation to consider marketing its product in Eastern Europe. What other factors deserve to be considered before a decision is made?

c. Blues Corporation is currently experiencing a cash squeeze because of a reduced demand for its goods in the United States (although management expects the demand in the United States to increase soon). It is currently near its debt capacity and prefers not to issue stock at this time. Blues Corporation will purchase a facility in Eastern Europe or implement a heavy promotion program in Eastern Europe only if it can raise funds by divesting a significant amount of its U.S. assets. The market values of its assets are temporarily depressed, but some of the executives think an immediate move is necessary to fully capitalize on the Eastern European market. Would you recommend that Blues Corporation divest some of its U.S. assets? Explain.

CHAPTER 14 NORTH STAR COMPANY

Capital Budgeting

This case is intended to illustrate that the value of an international project is sensitive to various types of input. It also is intended to show how a computer spreadsheet format can facilitate capital budgeting decisions that involve uncertainty.

This case can be performed using an electronic spreadsheet such as Excel. The following present value factors may be helpful input for discounting cash flows:

YEARS FROM NOW	PRESENT VALUE INTEREST FACTOR AT 18%
1	8475
2	.7182
3	.6086
4	.5158
5	.4371
6	.3704

For consistency in discussion of this case, you should develop your computer spreadsheet in a format somewhat similar to that in Chapter 14, with each year representing a column across the top. The use of a computer spreadsheet will significantly reduce the time needed to complete this case.

North Star Company is considering establishing a subsidiary to manufacture clothing in Singapore. Its sales would be invoiced in Singapore dollars (S$). It has forecasted net cash flows to the subsidiary as follows:

YEAR	NET CASH FLOWS TO SUBSIDIARY
1	S$ 8,000,000
2	10,000,000
3	14,000,000
4	16,000,000
5	16,000,000
6	16,000,000

These cash flows do not include financing costs (interest expenses) on any funds borrowed in Singapore. North Star Company also expects to receive S$30 million after taxes as a result of selling the subsidiary at the end of Year 6. Assume that there will not be any withholding taxes imposed on this amount.

The exchange rate of the Singapore dollar is forecasted in Exhibit B.3 based on three possible scenarios of economic conditions.

The probability of each scenario is shown below:

	SOMEWHAT STABLE S$	WEAK S$	STRONG S$
Probability	60%	30%	10%

Fifty percent of the net cash flows to the subsidiary would be remitted to the parent, while the remaining 50 percent would be reinvested to support ongoing operations at the subsidiary. North Star Company anticipates a 10 percent withholding tax on funds remitted to the United States.

The initial investment (including investment in working capital) by North Star in the subsidiary would be S$40 million. Any investment in working capital (such as accounts receivable, inventory, etc.) is to be assumed by the buyer in Year 6. The expected salvage value has already accounted for this transfer of working capital to the buyer in Year 6. The initial investment could be financed completely by the parent ($20 million, converted at the present exchange rate of $.50 per Singapore dollar to achieve S$40 million).

Exhibit B.3 Three Scenarios of Economic Conditions

END OF YEAR	SCENARIO I: SOMEWHAT STABLE S$	SCENARIO II: WEAK S$	SCENARIO III: STRONG S$
1	.50	.49	.52
2	.51	.46	.55
3	.48	.45	.59
4	.50	.43	.64
5	.52	.43	.67
6	.48	.41	.71

North Star Company will go forward with its intentions to build the subsidiary only if it expects to achieve a return on its capital of 18 percent or more.

The parent is considering an alternative financing arrangement. With this arrangement, the parent would provide $10 million (S$20 million), which means that the subsidiary would need to borrow S$20 million. Under this scenario, the subsidiary would obtain a 20-year loan and pay interest on the loan each year. The interest payments are S$1.6 million per year. In addition, the forecasted proceeds to be received from selling the subsidiary (after taxes) at the end of 6 years would be S$20 million (the forecast of proceeds is revised downward here because the equity investment of the subsidiary is less; the buyer would be assuming more debt if part of the initial investment in the subsidiary were supported by local bank loans). Assume the parent's required rate of return would still be 18 percent.

a. Which of the two financing arrangements would you recommend for the parent? Assess the forecasted *NPV* for each exchange rate scenario to compare the two financing arrangements and substantiate your recommendation.

b. In the first question, an alternative financing arrangement of partial financing by the subsidiary was considered, with an assumption that the required rate of return by the parent would not be affected. Is there any reason why the parent's required rate of return might increase when using this financing arrangement? Explain. How would you revise the analysis in the previous question under this situation? (This question requires discussion, not analysis.)

c. Would you recommend that North Star Company establish the subsidiary even if the withholding tax is 20 percent?

d. Assume that there is some concern about the economic conditions in Singapore, which could cause a reduction in the net cash flows to the subsidiary. Explain how Excel could be used to reevaluate the project based on alternative cash flow scenarios. That is, how can this form of country risk be incorporated into the capital budgeting decision? (This question requires discussion, not analysis.)

e. Assume that North Star Company does implement the project, investing $10 million of its own funds with the remainder borrowed by the subsidiary. Two years later, a U.S.-based corporation notifies North Star that it would like to purchase the subsidiary. Assume that the exchange rate forecasts for the somewhat stable scenario are appropriate for Years 3 through 6. Also assume that the other information already provided on net cash flows, financing costs, the 10 percent withholding tax, the salvage value, and the parent's required rate of return is still appropriate. What would be the minimum dollar price (after taxes) that North Star should receive to divest the subsidiary? Substantiate your opinion.

CHAPTER 15 REDWING TECHNOLOGY COMPANY
Assessing Subsidiary Performance

Redwing Technology Company is a U.S.-based firm that makes a variety of high-tech components. Five years ago, it established subsidiaries in Canada, South Africa, and Japan. The earnings generated by each subsidiary as translated (at the average annual exchange rate) into U.S. dollars per year are shown in Exhibit B.4.

Each subsidiary had an equivalent amount in resources with which to conduct operations. The wage rates for the labor needed were similar across countries. The inflation rates, economic growth, and degree of competition were somewhat similar across

Exhibit B.4 Translated Dollar Value of Annual Earnings in Each Subsidiary (in millions of $)

YEARS AGO	CANADA	SOUTH AFRICA	JAPAN
5	$20	$21	$30
4	24	24	32
3	28	24	35
2	32	36	41
1	36	42	46

countries. The average exchange rates of the respective currencies over the last 5 years are disclosed below:

YEARS AGO	CANADIAN DOLLAR	SOUTH AFRICAN RAND	JAPANESE YEN
5	$.84	$.10	$.0040
4	.83	.12	.0043
3	.81	.16	.0046
2	.81	.20	.0055
1	.79	.24	.0064

The earnings generated by each country were reinvested rather than remitted. There were no plans to remit any future earnings either.

A committee of vice presidents met to determine the performance of each subsidiary in the last 5 years. The assessment was to be used to determine whether Redwing should be restructured to focus future growth on any particular subsidiary or to divest any subsidiaries that might experience poor performance. Since exchange rates of the related currencies were affected by so many different factors, the treasurer acknowledged that there was much uncertainty about their future direction. The treasurer did suggest, however, that last year's average exchange rate would probably serve as at least a reasonable guess of exchange rates in future years. He did not anticipate that any of the currencies would experience consistent appreciation or depreciation.

a. Use whatever means you think are appropriate to rank the performance of each subsidiary. That is, which subsidiary did the best job over the 5-year period, in your opinion? Justify your opinion.

b. Use whatever means you think are appropriate to determine which subsidiary deserves additional funds from the parent to push for additional growth. (Assume no constraint on potential growth in any country.) Where would you recommend the parent's excess funds be invested, based on the information available? Justify your opinion.

c. Repeat question (b), but assume that all earnings generated from the parent's investment will be remitted to the parent every year. Would your recommendation change? Explain.

d. A final task of the committee was to recommend whether any of the subsidiaries should be divested. One vice president suggested that a review of the earnings translated into dollars shows that the performances of the Canadian and South African subsidiaries are very highly correlated. She concluded that having both of these subsidiaries did not achieve much in diversification benefits and suggested that either the Canadian or the South African subsidiary could be sold without forgoing any diversification benefits. Do you agree? Explain.

CHAPTER 16 KING, INC.

Country Risk Analysis

King, Inc., a U.S. firm, is considering the establishment of a small subsidiary in Bulgaria that would produce food products. All ingredients can be obtained or produced in Bulgaria. The final products to be produced by the subsidiary would be sold in Bulgaria and other Eastern European countries. King, Inc., is very interested in this project, as there is little competition in that area. Three high-level managers of King, Inc., have been assigned the task of assessing the country risk of Bulgaria. Specifically, the managers were asked to list all characteristics of Bulgaria that could adversely affect the performance of this project. The decision as to whether to undertake this project will be made only after this country risk analysis is completed and accounted for in the capital budgeting analysis. Since King, Inc., has focused exclusively on domestic business in the past, it is not accustomed to country risk analysis.

a. What factors related to Bulgaria's government deserve to be considered?

b. What country-related factors can affect the demand for the food products to be produced by King, Inc.?

c. What country-related factors can affect the cost of production?

Using Excel to Conduct Analysis

COMPUTING WITH EXCEL

Excel spreadsheets are useful for organizing numerical data. In addition, they can execute computations for you. Excel not only allows you to compute general statistics such as average and standard deviation of cells but also can be used to conduct regression analysis. First, the use of Excel to compute general statistics is described. Then, a background of regression analysis is provided, followed by the application of Excel to run regression analysis.

General Statistics

Some of the more popular computations are discussed here.

Creating a COMPUTE Statement. If you want to determine the percentage change in a value from one period to the next, type the COMPUTE statement in a cell where you want to see the result. For example, assume that you have months listed in column A and the corresponding exchange rate of the euro (with respect to the dollar) at the beginning of that month in column B. Assume you want to insert the monthly percentage change in the exchange rate for each month in column C. In cell C2 (the second row of column C), you want to determine the percentage change in the exchange rate as of the month in cell B2 from the previous month B1. Thus, you would type the COMPUTE statement in C2 that reflects the computation you want. A COMPUTE statement begins with an = sign. The proper COMPUTE statement to compute a percentage change for cell C2 is =(B2-B1)/B1. Assume that in cell C3, you want to derive the percentage change in the exchange rate as of the month in cell B3 from the previous month B2. Type the COMPUTE statement =(B3-B2)/B2 in cell C3.

Using the COPY Command. If you need to repeat a particular COMPUTE statement for several different cells, you can use the COPY command, as follows:

1. Place the cursor in the cell with the COMPUTE statement that you want to copy to other cells.
2. Click Edit on your menu bar.
3. Highlight the cells where you want that COMPUTE statement copied.
4. Hit the Enter key.

For example, suppose that you have 30 monthly exchange rates of the euro in column B and you already calculated the percentage change in the exchange rate in cell C2 as explained above. [You did not have a percentage change in cell C1 since you needed two dates (cells B1 and B2) to derive your first percentage change.] You could then place the cursor on cell C2, click Edit on your menu bar, highlight cells C3 to C30, and then hit the Enter key.

Computing an Average. You can compute the average of a set of cells as follows. Assume that you wanted to determine the average exchange rate of the 30 monthly exchange rates of the euro that you have listed from cell B1 to cell B30. In cell B31 (or in any blank cell where you want to see the result), type the COMPUTE statement =AVERAGE(B1:B30). Alternatively, if you wanted to determine the average of the monthly percentage changes in the euro, go to column C where you have monthly percentage changes in the euro from cell C2 down to C30. In cell C31 (or in any blank cell where you want to see the result), type the COMPUTE statement =AVERAGE(C2:C30).

Computing a Standard Deviation. You can compute the standard deviation of a set of cells as follows. Assume that you wanted to determine the standard deviation of the 30 monthly exchange rates of the euro that you have listed from cell B1 to cell B30. In cell B31 (or in any blank cell where you want to see the result), type the COMPUTE statement =STDEV(B1:B30). Alternatively, if you wanted to determine the standard deviation of the monthly percentage changes in the euro, go to column C where you have monthly percentage changes in the euro from cell C2 down to C30. In cell C31 (or in any blank cell where you want to see the result), type the COMPUTE statement =STDEV(C2:C30).

FUNDAMENTALS OF REGRESSION ANALYSIS

Businesses often use **regression analysis** to measure relationships between variables when establishing policies. For example, a firm may measure the historical relationship between its sales and its accounts receivable. Using the relationship detected, it can then forecast the future level of accounts receivable based on a forecast of sales. Alternatively, it may measure the sensitivity of its sales to economic growth and interest rates so that it can assess how susceptible its sales are to future changes in these economic variables. In international financial management, regression analysis can be used to measure the sensitivity of a firm's performance (using sales or earnings or stock price as a proxy) to currency movements or economic growth of various countries.

Regression analysis can be applied to measure the sensitivity of exports to various economic variables. This example will be used to explain the fundamentals of regression analysis. The main steps involved in regression analysis are

1. Specifying the regression model
2. Compiling the data
3. Estimating the regression coefficients
4. Interpreting the regression results

Specifying the Regression Model

Assume that your main goal is to determine the relationship between percentage changes in U.S. exports to Australia (called *CEXP*) and percentage changes in the value of the Australian dollar (called *CAUS).* The percentage change in the exports to Australia is the **dependent variable** since it is hypothesized to be influenced by another variable. Although you are most concerned with how *CAUS* affects *CEXP*, the regression model should include any other factors (or so-called **independent variables**) that could also affect *CEXP*. Assume that the percentage change in the Australian GDP (called *CGDP)* is also hypothesized to influence *CEXP*. This factor should also be included in the regression model. To simplify the example, assume that *CAUS* and *CGDP* are the only factors expected to influence *CEXP*. Also assume that there is a lagged impact of 1 quarter. In this case, the regression model can be specified as

$$CEXP_t = b_0 + b_1(CAUS_{t-1}) + b_2(CGDP_{t-1}) + \mu_t$$

where

b_0 = a constant

b_1 = regression coefficient that measures the sensitivity of $CEXP_t$ to $CAUS_{t-1}$

b_2 = regression coefficient that measures the sensitivity of $CEXP_t$ to $CGDP_{t-1}$

μ_t = an error term

The *t* subscript represents the time period. Some models, such as this one, specify a lagged impact of an independent variable on the dependent variable and therefore use a *t*–1 subscript.

Compiling the Data

Now that the model has been specified, data on the variables must be compiled. The data are normally input onto a spreadsheet as follows:

PERIOD (*t*)	*CEXP*	*CAUS*	*CGDP*
1	.03	–.01	.04
2	–.01	.02	–.01
3	–.04	.03	–.02
4	.00	.02	–.01
5	.01	–.02	.02
.	...	...	...
.	...	...	...
.	...	...	...

The column specifying the period is not necessary to run the regression model but is normally included in the data set for convenience.

The difference between the number of observations (periods) and the regression coefficients (including the constant) represents the degrees of freedom. For our example, assume that the data covered 40 quarterly periods. The degrees of freedom for this example are 40 – 3 = 37. As a general rule, analysts usually try to have at least 30 degrees of freedom when using regression analysis.

Some regression models involve only a single period. For example, if you desired to determine whether there was a relationship between a firm's degree of international sales (as a percentage of total sales) and earnings per share of MNCs, last year's data on these two variables could be gathered for many MNCs, and regression analysis could be applied. This example is referred to as **cross-sectional analysis**, whereas our original example is referred to as a **time-series analysis**.

Estimating the Regression Coefficients

Once the data have been input into a data file, a regression program can be applied to the data to estimate the **regression coefficients**. There are various packages such as Excel that contain a regression analysis application.

The actual steps conducted to estimate regression coefficients are somewhat complex. For more details on how regression coefficients are estimated, see any econometrics textbook.

Interpreting the Regression Results

Most regression programs provide estimates of the regression coefficients along with additional statistics. For our example, assume that the following information was provided by the regression program:

	ESTIMATED REGRESSION COEFFICIENT	STANDARD ERROR OF REGRESSION COEFFICIENT	t-STATISTIC
Constant	.002		
$CAUS_{t-1}$	.80	.32	2.50
$CGDP_{t-1}$	.36	.50	.72
Coefficient of determination $(R^2) =$	.33		

The independent variable $CAUS_{t-1}$ has an estimated regression coefficient of .80, which suggests that a 1 percent increase in $CAUS$ is associated with an .8 percent increase in the dependent variable $CEXP$ in the following period. This implies a positive relationship between $CAUS_{t-1}$ and $CEXP_t$. The independent variable $CGDP_{t-1}$ has an estimated coefficient of .36, which suggests that a 1 percent increase in the Australian GDP is associated with a .36 percent increase in $CEXP$ one period later.

Many analysts attempt to determine whether a coefficient is statistically different from zero. Regression coefficients may be different from zero simply because of a coincidental relationship between the independent variable of concern and the dependent variable. One can have more confidence that a negative or positive relationship exists by testing the coefficient for significance. A t-test is commonly used for this purpose, as follows:

Test to determine whether $CAUS_{t-1}$ affects $CEXP_t$

$$\text{Calculated } t\text{-statistic} = \frac{\text{Estimated regression coefficient for } CAUS_{t-1}}{\text{Standard error of the regression coefficient}} = \frac{.80}{.32} = 2.50$$

Test to determine whether $CGDP_{t-1}$ affects $CEXP_t$

$$\frac{\text{Calculated}}{t\text{-statistic}} = \frac{\text{Estimated regression coefficient for } CGDP_{t-1}}{\text{Standard error of the regression coefficient}} = \frac{.36}{.50} = .72$$

The calculated t-statistic is sometimes provided within the regression results. It can be compared to the critical t-statistic to determine whether the coefficient is significant. The critical t-statistic is dependent on the degrees of freedom and confidence level chosen. For our example, assume that there are 37 degrees of freedom and that a 95 confidence level is desired. The critical t-statistic would be 2.02, which can be verified by using a t-table from any statistics book. Based on the regression results, the coefficient of $CAUS_{t-1}$ is significantly different from zero, while $CGDP_{t-1}$ is not. This implies that one can be confident of a positive relationship between $CAUS_{t-1}$ and $CEXP_t$, but the positive relationship between $CGDP_{t-1}$ and $CEXP_t$ may have occurred simply by chance.

In some particular cases, one may be interested in determining whether the regression coefficient differs significantly from some value other than zero. In these cases, the t-statistic reported in the regression results would not be appropriate. See an econometrics text for more information on this subject.

The regression results indicate the **coefficient of determination** (called R^2) of a regression model, which measures the percentage of variation in the dependent variable that can be explained by the regression model. R^2 can range from 0 to 100 percent. It is unusual for regression models to generate an R^2 of close to 100 percent, since the movement in a given dependent variable is partially random and not associated with movements in independent variables. In our example, R^2 is 33 percent, suggesting that one-third of the variation in $CEXP$ can be explained by movements in $CAUS_{t-1}$ and $CGDP_{t-1}$.

Some analysts use regression analysis to forecast. For our example, the regression results could be used along with data for $CAUS$ and $CGDP$ to forecast $CEXP$. Assume that $CAUS$ was 5 percent in the most recent period, while $CGDP$ was –1 percent in the most recent period. The forecast of $CEXP$ in the following period is derived from inserting this information into the regression model as follows:

$$\begin{aligned}
CEXP_t &= b_0 + b_1(CAUS_{t-1}) + b_2(CGDP_{t-1}) \\
&= .002 + (.80)(.05) + (.36)(-.01) \\
&= .002 + .0400 - .0036 \\
&= .0420 - .0036 \\
&= .0384
\end{aligned}$$

Thus, the $CEXP$ is forecasted to be 3.84 percent in the following period. Some analysts might eliminate $CGDP_{t-1}$ from the model because its regression coefficient was not significantly different from zero. This would alter the forecasted value of $CEXP$.

When there is not a lagged relationship between independent variables and the dependent variable, the independent variables must be forecasted in order to derive a forecast of the dependent variable. In this case, an analyst might derive a poor forecast of the dependent variable even when the regression model is properly specified, if the forecasts of the independent variables are inaccurate.

As with most statistical techniques, there are some limitations that should be recognized when using regression analysis. These limitations are described in most statistics and econometrics textbooks.

Using Excel to Conduct Regression Analysis

Various software packages are available to run regression analysis. The following example is run on Excel to illustrate the ease with which regression analysis can be run. Assume that a firm wants to assess the influence of changes in the value of the Australian dollar on changes in its exports to Australia based on the following data:

PERIOD	VALUE (IN THOUSANDS OF DOLLARS) OF EXPORTS TO AUSTRALIA	AVERAGE EXCHANGE RATE OF AUSTRALIAN DOLLAR OVER THAT PERIOD
1	110	$.50
2	125	.54
3	130	.57
4	142	.60
5	129	.55
6	113	.49
7	108	.46
8	103	.42
9	109	.43
10	118	.48
11	125	.49
12	130	.50
13	134	.52
14	138	.50
15	144	.53
16	149	.55
17	156	.58
18	160	.62
19	165	.66
20	170	.67
21	160	.62
22	158	.62
23	155	.61
24	167	.66

Assume that the firm applies the following regression model to the data:

$$CEXP = b_0 + b_1 CAUS + \mu$$

where

$CEXP$ = percentage change in the firm's export value from one period to the next

$CAUS$ = percentage change in the average exchange rate from one period to the next

μ = error term

The first step is to input the data for the two variables in two columns on a file using Excel. Then, the data can be converted into percentage changes. This can be easily performed with a COMPUTE statement in the third column (column C) to derive *CEXP* and another COMPUTE statement in the fourth column (column D) to derive *CAUS*. These two columns will have a blank first row since the percentage change cannot be computed without the previous period's data.

Once you have derived *CEXP* and *CAUS* from the raw data, you can perform regression analysis as follows. On the main menu, select Tools. This leads to a new menu, in which you should click on Data Analysis. Next to the Input Y Range, identify the range C2 to C24 for the dependent variable as C2:C24. Next to the Input X Range, identify the range D2 to D24 for the independent variable as D2:D24. The Output Range specifies the location on the screen where the output of the regression analysis should be displayed. In our example, F1 would be an appropriate location, representing the upper-left section of the output. Then, click on OK, and within a few seconds, the regression analysis will be complete. For our example, the output is listed below:

SUMMARY OUTPUT

REGRESSION STATISTICS	
Multiple R	0.8852
R Square	0.7836
Adjusted R Square	0.7733
Standard Error	2.9115
Observations	23.0000

ANOVA

	df	SS	MS	F	SIGNIFICANCE F
Regression	1.0000	644.6262	644.6262	76.0461	0.0000
Residual	21.0000	178.0125	8.4768		
Total	22.0000	822.6387			

	COEFFICIENTS	STANDARD ERROR	t-STAT	P-VALUE
Intercept	0.7951	0.6229	1.2763	0.2158
X Variable 1	0.8678	0.0995	8.7204	0.0000

	LOWER 95%	UPPER 95%	LOWER 95.0%	UPPER 95.0%
Intercept	−0.5004	2.0905	−0.5004	2.0905
X Variable 1	0.6608	1.0747	0.6608	1.0747

The estimate of the so-called slope coefficient is about .8678, which suggests that every 1 percent change in the Australian dollar's exchange rate is associated with a .8678 percent change (in the same direction) in the firm's exports to Australia. The *t*-statistic is also estimated to determine whether the slope coefficient is significantly different than zero. Since the standard error of the slope coefficient is about .0995, the t-statistic is .8678/.0995 = 8.72. This would imply that there is a significant relationship between *CAUS* and *CEXP*. The R-Square statistic suggests that about 78 percent of the variation in *CEXP* is explained by *CAUS*. The correlation between *CEXP* and *CAUS* can also be measured by the correlation coefficient, which is the square root of the R-Square statistic.

If you have more than one independent variable (multiple regression), you should place the independent variables next to each other in the file. Then, for the X-RANGE, identify this block of data. The output for the regression model will display the coefficient, standard error, and t-statistic for each of the independent variables. For multiple regression, the R-Square statistic is interpreted as the percentage of variation in the dependent variable explained by the model as a whole.

International Investing Project

Note to the Professor: You may want to assign this as a project to be completed by the end of the semester. This project helps students to understand the factors that influence the performance of MNCs and foreign stocks. This project can also be done with teams of students and may be used for class presentations near the end of the semester. If you allow students to share their results in class, the students will learn that relationships cannot necessarily be generalized, as some MNCs are more exposed than others to economic conditions and exchange rate movements. The focus in grading this project will be on the explanations provided by the students, not on the movements in the stock prices or exchange rates.

This project allows you to learn more about international investing and about firms that compete in the global arena. You will be asked to create a stock portfolio of at least two U.S.-based multinational corporations (MNCs) and two foreign stocks. You will monitor the performance of your portfolio over the school term and ultimately will attempt to explain why your portfolio performed well or poorly relative to the portfolios created by other students in your class. The explanations will offer insight on what is driving the valuations of the U.S.-based MNCs and the foreign stocks over time.

Select two stocks of U.S.-based MNCs that you want to include in your portfolio. If you want to review a list of possible stocks or do not know the ticker symbol of the stocks you want to invest in, go to the website http://biz.yahoo.com/i/, which lists stocks alphabetically, or to http://biz.yahoo.com/p/, which lists stocks by sectors or industries. Make sure that your firms conduct a substantial amount of international business.

Next, select two foreign stocks that are traded on U.S. stock exchanges and are not from the same foreign country. Many foreign stocks are traded on U.S. stock exchanges as American depository receipts (ADRs), which are certificates that represent ownership of foreign stock. ADRs are denominated in dollars, but reflect the value of a foreign stock, so an increase in the value of the foreign currency can have a favorable effect on the ADR's value. To review a list of ADRs in which you may invest, go to www.adr.com. Go to the website, and click on ADR Universe. Click on any industry listed to see a list of foreign companies within that industry that offer ADRs and the country where each foreign company is based. You should select ADRs of firms that are based in any of the countries shown on the website http://finance.yahoo.com/intlindices. Click on any company listed to review background information, including a description of its business and its stock price trend over the last year. It is assumed that you will invest $10,000 in each stock that you purchase

List your portfolio in the following format:

U.S.-BASED MNCs			
NAME OF FIRM	TICKER SYMBOL	AMOUNT OF YOUR INVESTMENT	PRICE PER SHARE AT WHICH YOU PURCHASED THE STOCK
		$10,000	
		$10,000	

FOREIGN STOCKS (ADRs)				
NAME OF FIRM	TICKER SYMBOL	COUNTRY WHERE FIRM IS BASED	AMOUNT OF YOUR INVESTMENT	PRICE PER SHARE OF ADR AT WHICH YOU PURCHASED THE STOCK
			$10,000	
			$10,000	

You can easily monitor your portfolio using various Internet tools. If you do not already use a specific website for this purpose, go to http://finance.yahoo.com/?u and register for free. Follow the instructions, and in a few minutes you can create your own portfolio tracking system. This system not only updates the values of your stocks, but also provides charts and recent news and other information on the stocks in your portfolio.

Evaluation

At the end of each month during the school term (or a date specified by your professor), you should evaluate the performance and behavior of your stocks.

1. a. Determine the percentage increase or decrease in each of your stocks over the period of your investment and provide that percentage in a table like the one below. In addition, offer the primary reason for this change in the stock price based on news about that stock or your own intuition. To review the recent news about each of your stocks, click on http://finance.yahoo.com/?u and insert the ticker symbol for each firm. Recent news is provided at the bottom of the screen.

NAME OF FIRM	PERCENTAGE CHANGE IN STOCK PRICE	PRIMARY REASON
1.		
2.		
3.		
4.		
Portfolio (average)		

b. How does your portfolio's performance compare to the portfolios of some other students? (Your professor may survey the class on their performances so that you can see how your performance differs from those of other students.) Why do you think your performance was relatively high or low compared to other students' performances? Was it because of the markets where your firms do their business or because of firm-specific conditions?

2. Determine whether the performance of each of your U.S.-based MNCs is driven by the U.S. market. Go to the site http://finance.yahoo.com/?u and insert the symbol for your stock. Once the quote is provided, click on Chart. Click on the box marked S&P (which represents the S&P 500 Index). Then, click on Compare and assess the relationship between the U.S. market index movements and the stock's price movements. Explain whether the stock's price movements appear to be driven by U.S. market conditions. Repeat this task for each U.S.-based MNC in which you invested.

3. a. Determine whether the performance of each of your foreign stocks is driven by the corresponding market where the firm is based. First, go to the site http://finance .yahoo.com/intlindices?u and look up the symbol for the country index of concern. For example, Brazil's index is ^BVSP. Next, go to the site http://finance.yahoo.com/?u and insert the symbol for your stock. Click on Chart; at the bottom of the chart, insert the corresponding market index symbol (make sure you include the ^ if it is part of the index symbol) in the box. Then, click on Compare and assess the relationship between the market index movements and the stock's price movements. Explain whether the stock's price movements appear to be driven by the local market conditions. Repeat this exercise for each foreign stock in which you invested.

b. Determine whether your foreign stock prices are highly correlated. Repeat the process described above, except insert the symbol representing one of the foreign stocks you own in the box below the chart.

c. Determine whether your foreign stock's performance is driven by the U.S. market (using the S&P 500 as a market proxy). Erase the symbol you typed into the box below the chart, and click on S&P just to the right.

4. a. Review annual reports and news about each of your U.S.-based MNCs to determine where it does most of its business and the foreign currency to which it is most exposed. Determine whether your U.S.-based MNC's stock performance is influenced by the exchange rate movements of the foreign currency (against the U.S. dollar) to which it is most exposed. Go to www.oanda.com and click on FXHistory. You can convert the foreign currency to which the MNC is highly exposed to U.S. dollars and determine the exchange rate movements over the period in which you invested in the stock. Provide your assessment of the relationship between the currency's exchange rate movements and the performance of the stock over the investment period. Attempt to explain the relationship that you just found.

b. Repeat the steps in 4a for each U.S.-based MNC in which you invested.

5. a. Determine whether the stock performance of each of your foreign firms is influenced by the exchange rate movements of the firm's local currency against the U.S. dollar. You can obtain this information from www.oanda.com. You can convert the foreign currency of concern to U.S. dollars and determine the exchange rate movements over the period in which you invested in the stock. Provide your assessment of the relationship between the currency's exchange rate movements and the performance of the stock over the investment period. Attempt to explain the relationship that you just found.

b. Repeat the steps in 5a for each of the foreign stocks in which you invested.

Discussion in the Boardroom

This exercise is intended to apply many of the key concepts presented in the text to broad issues that are discussed by managers who make financial decisions. It does not replace the more detailed questions and problems at the end of the chapters. Instead, it focuses on broad financial issues to facilitate class discussion and simulate a boardroom discussion. It serves as a running case in which concepts from every chapter are applied to the same business throughout the school term. The exercise not only enables students to apply concepts to the real world but also develops their intuitive and communication skills.

This exercise can be used in a course in several ways:

1. Apply it on a chapter-by-chapter basis to ensure that the broad chapter concepts are understood before moving to the next chapter.

2. Use it to encourage online discussion for courses taught online.

3. Use it as a review before each exam, covering all chapters assigned for that exam.

4. Use it as a comprehensive case discussion near the end of the semester, as a means of reviewing the key concepts that were described throughout the course.

5. Use it for presentations, in which individuals or teams present their views on the questions that were assigned to them.

This exercise has been placed on the course website so that students can download it and insert their answers after the questions. By the end of the course, students will have applied all the major concepts of the text to a single firm. The focus on a single firm will allow students to recognize how some of their decisions in the earlier chapters interact with decisions to be made in later chapters.

BACKGROUND

One of the best ways to learn the broad concepts presented in this text is to put yourself in the position of an MNC manager or board member and apply the concepts to financial decisions. Although board members normally do not make the decisions discussed here, they must have the conceptual skills to monitor the policies that are implemented by the MNC's managers. Thus, they must frequently consider what they would do if they were making the managerial decisions or setting corporate policies.

This exercise is based on a business that you could easily create: a business that teaches individuals in a non-U.S. country to speak English. Although this business is very basic, it still requires the same types of decisions faced by large MNCs.

Assume that you live in the United States and invest $60,000 to establish a language school called Escuela de Inglés in Mexico City, Mexico. You set up a small subsidiary in Mexico, with an office and an attached classroom that you lease. You hire local individuals in Mexico who can speak English and teach it to others. Your school offers two types of courses: a 1-month structured course in English and a 1-week intensive course for individuals who already know English but want to improve their skills before visiting the United States. You advertise both types of teaching services in the local newspapers.

All revenue and expenses associated with your business are denominated in Mexican pesos. Your subsidiary sends most of the profits from the business in Mexico to you at the end of each month. Although your expenses are somewhat stable, your revenue varies with the number of clients who sign up for the courses in Mexico.

This background is sufficient to enable you to answer the questions that are asked about your business throughout the term. Answer each question as if you were serving on the board or as a manager of the business. The questions in the early chapters force you to assess the firm's opportunities and exposure, while later chapters force you to consider potential strategies that your business might pursue.

CHAPTER 1

a. Discuss the corporate control of your business. Explain why your business in Mexico is exposed to agency problems.

b. How would you attempt to monitor the ongoing operations of the business?

c. Explain how you might be able to use a compensation plan to limit the potential agency problems.

d. Assume that you have been approached by a competitor in Mexico to engage in a joint venture. The competitor would provide the classroom facilities (so you would not need to rent classroom space), while your employees would teach the classes. You and the competitor would split the profits. Discuss how your potential return and your risk would change if you pursue the joint venture.

e. Explain the conditions that would cause your business to be adversely affected by exchange rate movements.

f. Explain how your business could be adversely affected by political risk.

CHAPTER 2

Your business provides CDs for free to customers who pay for the English courses that you offer in Mexico. You are considering mass-producing the CDs in the United States so that you can sell (export) them to distributors or to retail stores throughout Mexico. You would price the CDs in dollars when exporting them. The CDs are less effective without the teaching, but still can be useful to individuals who want to learn the basics of the English language.

a. If you pursue this idea, explain how the factors that affect international trade flows (identified in Chapter 2) could affect the Mexican demand for your CDs. Which of these factors would likely have the largest impact on the Mexican demand for your CDs? What other factors would affect the Mexican demand for the CDs?

b. Suppose that you believe the Mexican government will impose a tariff on the CDs exported to Mexico. How could you still execute this business idea at a relatively low cost while avoiding the tariff? Describe any disadvantages of this idea to avoid the tariff.

CHAPTER 3

Assume that the business in Mexico grows. Explain how financial markets could help to finance the growth of the business.

CHAPTER 4

Given the factors that affect the value of a foreign currency, describe the type of economic or other conditions in Mexico that could cause the Mexican peso to weaken and thereby to adversely affect your business.

CHAPTER 5

Explain how currency futures could be used to hedge your business in Mexico. Explain how currency options could be used to hedge your business in Mexico.

CHAPTER 6

a. Explain how your business will likely be affected (at least in the short run) if the central bank of Mexico intervenes in the foreign exchange market by exchanging Mexican pesos for dollars.

b. Explain how your business will likely be affected if the central bank of Mexico uses indirect intervention by lowering Mexican interest rates (assume inflationary expectations have not changed).

CHAPTER 7

Mexican interest rates are normally substantially higher than U.S. interest rates.

a. What does this imply about the forward premium or discount of the Mexican peso?

b. What does this imply about your business using forward or futures contracts to hedge your periodic profits in pesos that must be converted into dollars?

c. Do you think you would frequently hedge your exposure to Mexican pesos? Explain your answer.

CHAPTER 8

Mexican interest rates are normally substantially higher than U.S. interest rates.

a. What does this imply about the inflation differential (Mexican inflation minus U.S. inflation), assuming that the real interest rate is the same in both countries? Does this imply that the Mexican peso will appreciate or depreciate? Explain.

b. It might be argued that the high Mexican interest rates should entice U.S. investors to invest in Mexican money market securities, which could cause the peso to appreciate. Reconcile this theory with your answer in part (a). If you believe that the high Mexican interest rates will not entice U.S. investors, explain your reasoning.

c. Assume that the difference between Mexican and U.S. interest rates is typically attributed to a difference in expected inflation in the two countries. Also assume that purchasing power parity holds. Do you think that your business cash flows will be adversely affected? In reality, purchasing power parity does not hold consistently. Assume that the inflation differential (Mexican inflation minus U.S. inflation) is not fully offset by the exchange rate movement of the peso. Will this benefit or hurt your business? Now assume that the inflation differential is more than offset by the exchange rate movement of the peso. Will this benefit or hurt your business?

d. Assume that the nominal interest rate in Mexico is currently much higher than the U.S. interest rate and that this difference is due to a high rate of expected inflation in Mexico. You are considering hiring a local firm to promote your business, but you would have to borrow funds to finance this marketing campaign. A consultant advises you to delay the marketing campaign for a year so that you can capitalize on the high nominal interest rate in Mexico. He suggests that you retain the profits that you would normally have remitted to the United States and deposit them in a Mexican bank. The Mexican peso cash flows that your business deposits will grow at a high rate of interest over the year. Should you follow the advice of the consultant?

CHAPTER 9

a. Mexican interest rates are normally substantially higher than U.S. interest rates. What does this imply about the forward rate as a forecast of the future spot rate?

b. Does the forward rate reflect a forecast of appreciation or depreciation of the Mexican peso? Explain how the degree of the expected change implied by the forward rate forecast is tied to the interest rate differential.

c. Do you think that today's forward rate or today's spot rate of the peso provides a better forecast of the future spot rate of the peso?

CHAPTER 10

Recall that your Mexican business invoices in Mexican pesos.

a. You are already aware that a decline in the value of the peso could reduce your dollar cash flows. Yet, according to purchasing power parity, a weak peso should occur only in response to a high level of Mexican inflation, and such high inflation should increase your profits. If this theory holds precisely, your cash flows would not really be exposed. Should you be concerned about your exposure, or not? Explain.

b. If you change your policy and invoice only in dollars, how will your transaction exposure be affected?

c. Why might the demand for your business change if you change your invoice policy? What are the implications for your economic exposure?

CHAPTER 11

Mexican interest rates are normally substantially higher than U.S. interest rates.

a. Assuming that interest rate parity exists, do you think hedging with a forward rate will be beneficial if the spot rate of the Mexican peso is expected to decline slightly over time?

b. Will hedging with a money market hedge be beneficial if the spot rate of the Mexican peso is expected to decline slightly over time (assume zero transaction costs)? Explain.

c. What are some limitations on using currency futures or options that may make it difficult for you to perfectly hedge against exchange rate risk over the next year or so?

d. In general, not many long-term currency futures and options on the Mexican peso are available. A consultant suggests that this is not a problem because you can hedge your position a quarter at a time. In other words, the profits that you remit at any point in the future can be hedged by taking a currency futures or options position 3 months or so before that time. Thus, although the consultant recognizes that the peso could weaken substantially in the long term, she sees no reason why you should worry about its decline as long as you continually create a short-term hedge. Do you agree?

CHAPTER 12

a. Explain how your business is subject to translation exposure.

b. How could you hedge against this translation exposure?

c. Is it worthwhile for your business to hedge the translation exposure?

CHAPTER 13

Assume that you want to expand your English teaching business to other non-U.S. countries where some individuals may want to learn to speak English.

a. Explain why you might be able to stabilize the profits of your total business in this manner. Review the motives for direct foreign investment that are identified in this chapter. Which of these motives are most important?

b. Why would a city such as Montreal be a less desirable site for your business than a city such as Mexico City?

c. Describe the conditions in which your total business would experience weak effects even if the business was spread across three or four countries.

d. What factors affect the probability that the conditions you identified in part (c) might occur? (In other words, explain why the conditions could occur in one set of countries but not another set of countries.)

e. What data would you review to assess the probability that these conditions will occur?

f. Assume that your business has already created some pamphlets and CDs that translate common Spanish terms into English to supplement your primary service of teaching individuals in Mexico to speak English. How could you expand your business in a manner that might allow you to benefit from economies of scale (and perhaps even benefit from your existing business reputation)? When you attempt to benefit from economies of scale, do you forgo diversification benefits? Explain.

g. How would you come to a decision on whether to pursue business expansion that capitalizes on economies of scale even though it would mean forgoing diversification benefits? Do you think economies of scale would be more or less important than diversification for your business?

h. Is there any way to achieve both economies of scale and diversification benefits?

CHAPTER 14

a. Review the different items that are used in the multinational capital budgeting example (Spartan, Inc.). Describe the items that you would include on a spreadsheet if you conducted a multinational capital budgeting analysis of investing dollars to expand your existing language business in a different location.

b. Assume that you recognize your limitations in predicting the future exchange rate of the invoice currency for your expanded business. You think that there are several possible exchange rate scenarios, each with equal probability of occurrence. Explain how you could use this information to estimate the future net present value (*NPV*) and make a decision about whether to accept or reject the project.

c. Now assume that there is also much uncertainty about individuals' demand for your service in the new location. Explain how you can incorporate this uncertainty along with the uncertainty of exchange rate movements so that you can make a decision about whether to accept or reject the project.

d. Explain how you would derive a required rate of return for your capital budgeting analysis. What type of information would you use to derive the required rate of return?

CHAPTER 15

You have an opportunity to purchase a private competitor called Fernand in Mexico. If you decide to purchase the company, you will use only your own funds.

a. When you attempt to determine the value of this company, how will you derive your required rate of return? Specifically, should you use the U.S. or the Mexican risk-free rate as a base when deriving your required rate of return? Why?

b. Another Mexican firm called Vascon is also considering acquiring this firm. Explain why Vascon's required rate of return may be higher than your required rate of return. Is there any reason why Vascon's required rate of return may be lower than your required rate of return?

c. Assume that you and Vascon have the same expectations regarding the Mexican cash flows that will be generated by Fernand. Fernand's owner is willing to sell the company for 2 million Mexican pesos. You and Vascon use a similar process to determine the feasibility of acquiring the target. You both compare the present value of the target's cash flows to the purchase price. Based on your analysis, Fernand would generate a positive net present value (*NPV*) for your firm. Based on Vascon's analysis, Fernand would generate a negative *NPV* for Vascon. How could you determine that the acquisition of Fernand is feasible, while Vascon determines that the acquisition is not feasible?

d. Repeat part (c) but reverse the assumptions. That is, you determine that Fernand would generate a negative *NPV* for your firm, whereas Vascon determines that Fernand would generate a positive *NPV*. How could you determine that the acquisition of Fernand is not feasible, while Vascon determines that the acquisition of Fernand is feasible?

CHAPTER 16

a. Review the political risk factors, and identify those that could possibly affect your business. Explain how your cash flows could be affected.

b. Explain why threats of terrorism due to friction between two countries could possibly affect your business, even though the terrorism has no effect on the relations between the United States and Mexico.

c. Assume that an upcoming election in Mexico may result in a complete change in government. Explain why the election could have significant effects on your cash flows.

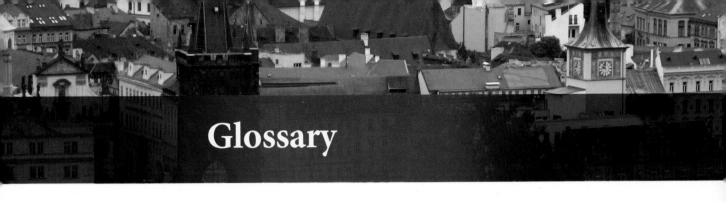

Glossary

A

absolute form of purchasing power parity theory that explains how inflation differentials affect exchange rates. It suggests that prices of two products of different countries should be equal when measured by a common currency.

accounts receivable financing indirect financing provided by an exporter for an importer by exporting goods and allowing for payment to be made at a later date.

advising bank corresponding bank in the beneficiary's country to which the issuing bank sends the letter of credit.

agency problem conflict of goals between a firm's shareholders and its managers.

airway bill receipt for a shipment by air, which includes freight charges and title to the merchandise.

all-in-rate rate used in charging customers for accepting banker's acceptances, consisting of the discount interest rate plus the commission.

American depository receipts (ADRs) certificates representing ownership of foreign stocks, which are traded on stock exchanges in the United States.

appreciation increase in the value of a currency.

arbitrage action to capitalize on a discrepancy in quoted prices; in many cases, there is no investment of funds tied up for any length of time.

Asian dollar market market in Asia in which banks collect deposits and make loans denominated in U.S. dollars.

ask price price at which a trader of foreign exchange (typically a bank) is willing to sell a particular currency.

assignment of proceeds arrangement that allows the original beneficiary of a letter of credit to pledge or assign proceeds to an end supplier.

B

balance of payments statement of inflow and outflow payments for a particular country.

balance of trade difference between the value of merchandise exports and merchandise imports.

balance on goods and services balance of trade, plus the net amount of payments of interest and dividends to foreign investors and from investment, as well as receipts and payments resulting from international tourism and other transactions.

Bank for International Settlements (BIS) institution that facilitates cooperation among countries involved in international transactions and provides assistance to countries experiencing international payment problems.

Bank Letter of Credit Policy policy that enables banks to confirm letters of credit by foreign banks supporting the purchase of U.S. exports.

banker's acceptance bill of exchange drawn on and accepted by a banking institution; it is commonly used to guarantee exporters that they will receive payment on goods delivered to importers.

barter exchange of goods between two parties without the use of any currency as a medium of exchange.

Basel Accord agreement among country representatives in 1988 to establish standardized risk-based capital requirements for banks across countries.

bid price price that a trader of foreign exchange (typically a bank) is willing to pay for a particular currency.

bid/ask spread difference between the price at which a bank is willing to buy a currency and the price at which it will sell that currency.

bilateral netting system netting method used for transactions between two units.

bill of exchange (draft) promise drawn by one party (usually an exporter) to pay a specified amount to another party at a specified future date, or upon presentation of the draft.

bill of lading (B/L) document serving as a receipt for shipment and a summary of freight charges and conveying title to the merchandise.

Bretton Woods Agreement conference held in Bretton Woods, New Hampshire, in 1944, resulting in an agreement to maintain exchange rates of currencies within very narrow boundaries; this agreement lasted until 1971.

C

call see *currency call option.*

call option on real assets project that contains an option of pursuing an additional venture.

capital account account reflecting changes in a country's ownership of long-term and short-term financial assets.

carryforwards tax losses that are applied in a future year to offset income in the future year.

cash management optimization of cash flows and investment of excess cash.

central exchange rate exchange rate established between two European currencies through the European Monetary System arrangement; the exchange rate between the two currencies is allowed to move within bands around that central exchange rate.

centralized cash flow management policy that consolidates cash management decisions for all MNC units, usually at the parent's location.

coefficient of determination measure of the percentage variation in the dependent variable that can be explained by the independent variables when using regression analysis.

cofinancing agreements arrangement in which the World Bank participates along with other agencies or lenders in providing funds to developing countries.

commercial invoice exporter's description of merchandise being sold to the buyer.

commercial letters of credit trade-related letters of credit.

comparative advantage theory suggesting that specialization by countries can increase worldwide production.

compensation arrangement in which the delivery of goods to a party is compensated for by buying back a certain amount of the product from that same party.

compensatory financing facility (CFF) facility that attempts to reduce the impact of export instability on country economies.

consignment arrangement in which the exporter ships goods to the importer while still retaining title to the merchandise.

contingency graph graph showing the net profit to a speculator in currency options under various exchange rate scenarios.

counterpurchase exchange of goods between two parties under two distinct contracts expressed in monetary terms.

countertrade sale of goods to one country that is linked to the purchase or exchange of goods from that same country.

country risk characteristics of the host country, including political and financial conditions, that can affect an MNC's cash flows.

covered interest arbitrage investment in a foreign money market security with a simultaneous forward sale of the currency denominating that security.

cross exchange rate exchange rate between currency A and currency B, given the values of currencies A and B with respect to a third currency.

cross-border factoring factoring by a network of factors across borders. The exporter's factor can contact correspondent factors in other countries to handle the collections of accounts receivable.

cross-hedging hedging an open position in one currency with a hedge on another currency that is highly correlated with the first currency. This occurs when for some reason the common hedging techniques cannot be applied to the first currency. A cross-hedge is not a perfect hedge, but can substantially reduce the exposure.

cross-sectional analysis analysis of relationships among a cross section of firms, countries, or some other variable at a given point in time.

currency board system for maintaining the value of the local currency with respect to some other specified currency.

currency call option contract that grants the right to purchase a specific currency at a specific price (exchange rate) within a specific period of time.

currency futures contract contract specifying a standard volume of a particular currency to be exchanged on a specific settlement date.

currency option combination the use of simultaneous call and put option positions to construct a unique position to suit the hedger's or speculator's needs. Two of the most popular currency option combinations are *straddles* and *strangles*.

currency put option contract granting the right to sell a particular currency at a specified price (exchange rate) within a specified period of time.

currency swap agreement to exchange one currency for another at a specified exchange rate and date. Banks commonly serve as intermediaries between two parties who wish to engage in a currency swap.

current account broad measure of a country's international trade in goods and services.

D

Delphi technique collection of independent opinions without group discussion by the assessors who provide the opinions; used for various types of assessments (such as country risk assessment).

dependent variable term used in regression analysis to represent the variable that is dependent on one or more other variables.

depreciation decrease in the value of a currency.

devaluation a downward adjustment of the exchange rate by a central bank.

devalue to reduce the value of a currency against the value of other currencies.

direct foreign investment (DFI) investment in real assets (such as land, buildings, or even existing plants) in foreign countries.

Direct Loan Program program in which the Ex-Im Bank offers fixed rate loans directly to the foreign buyer to purchase U.S. capital equipment and services.

direct quotations exchange rate quotations representing the value measured by number of dollars per unit.

discount as related to forward rates, represents the percentage amount by which the forward rate is less than the spot rate.

documentary collections trade transactions handled on a draft basis.

documents against acceptance situation in which the buyer's bank does not release shipping documents to the buyer until the buyer has accepted (signed) the draft.

documents against payment shipping documents that are released to the buyer once the buyer has paid for the draft.

dollarization replacement of a foreign currency with U.S. dollars.

double-entry bookkeeping accounting method in which each transaction is recorded as both a credit and a debit.

draft (bill of exchange) unconditional promise drawn by one party (usually the exporter) instructing the buyer to pay the face amount of the draft upon presentation.

dumping selling products overseas at unfairly low prices (a practice perceived to result from subsidies provided to the firm by its government).

dynamic hedging strategy of hedging in those periods when existing currency positions are expected to be adversely affected, and remaining unhedged in other periods when currency positions are expected to be favorably affected.

E

economic exposure degree to which a firm's present value of future cash flows can be influenced by exchange rate fluctuations.

economies of scale achievement of lower average cost per unit by means of increased production.

effective yield yield or return to an MNC on a short-term investment after adjustment for the change in exchange rates over the period of concern.

efficient frontier set of points reflecting risk-return combinations achieved by particular portfolios (so-called efficient portfolios) of assets.

equilibrium exchange rate exchange rate at which demand for a currency is equal to the supply of the currency for sale.

Eurobank commercial bank that participates as a financial intermediary in the Eurocurrency market.

Eurobonds bonds sold in countries other than the country represented by the currency denominating them.

Euro-clear telecommunications network that informs all traders about outstanding issues of Eurobonds for sale.

Euro-commercial paper debt securities issued by MNCs for short-term financing.

Eurocredit loans loans of one year or longer extended by Eurobanks.

Eurocredit market collection of banks that accepts deposits and provides loans in large denominations and in a variety of currencies. The banks that comprise this market are the same banks that comprise the Eurocurrency market; the difference is that the Eurocredit loans are longer term than so-called Eurocurrency loans.

Eurocurrency market collection of banks that accept deposits and provide loans in large denominations and in a variety of currencies.

Eurodollar term used to describe U.S. dollar deposits placed in banks located in Europe.

Euronotes unsecured debt securities issued by MNCs for short-term financing.

European Central Bank (ECB) central bank created to conduct the monetary policy for the countries participating in the single European currency, the euro.

European Currency Unit (ECU) unit of account representing a weighted average of exchange rates of member countries within the European Monetary System.

exchange rate mechanism (ERM) method of linking European currency values with the European Currency Unit (ECU).

exercise price (strike price) price (exchange rate) at which the owner of a currency call option is allowed to buy a specified currency; or the price (exchange rate) at which the owner of a currency put option is allowed to sell a specified currency.

Export-Import Bank (Ex-Im Bank) bank that attempts to strengthen the competitiveness of U.S. industries involved in foreign trade.

F

factor firm specializing in collection on accounts receivable; exporters sometimes sell their accounts receivable to a factor at a discount.

factor income income (interest and dividend payments) received by investors on foreign investments in financial assets (securities).

factoring purchase of receivables of an exporter by a factor without recourse to the exporter.

Financial Institution Buyer Credit Policy policy that provides insurance coverage for loans by banks to foreign buyers of exports.

Fisher effect theory that nominal interest rates are composed of a real interest rate and anticipated inflation.

fixed exchange rate system monetary system in which exchange rates are either held constant or allowed to fluctuate only within very narrow boundaries.

floating rate notes (FRNs) provision of some Eurobonds in which the coupon rate is adjusted over time according to prevailing market rates.

foreign bond bond issued by a borrower foreign to the country where the bond is placed.

foreign exchange dealers dealers who serve as intermediaries in the foreign exchange market by exchanging currencies desired by MNCs or individuals.

foreign exchange market market composed primarily of banks, serving firms and consumers who wish to buy or sell various currencies.

foreign investment risk matrix (FIRM) graph that displays financial and political risk by intervals so that each country can be positioned according to its risk ratings.

forfaiting method of financing international trade of capital goods.

forward contract agreement between a commercial bank and a client about an exchange of two currencies to be made at a future point in time at a specified exchange rate.

forward discount percentage by which the forward rate is less than the spot rate; typically quoted on an annualized basis.

forward market market that facilitates the trading of forward contracts; commercial banks serve as intermediaries in the market by matching up participants who wish to buy a currency forward with other participant who wish to sell the currency forward.

forward premium percentage by which the forward rate exceeds the spot rate; typically quoted on an annualized basis.

forward rate rate at which a bank is willing to exchange one currency for another at some specified date in the future.

franchising agreement by which a firm provides a specialized sales or service strategy, support assistance, and possibly an initial investment in the franchise in exchange for periodic fees.

freely floating exchange rate system   monetary system in which exchange rates are allowed to move due to market forces without intervention by country governments.

full compensation   an arrangement in which the delivery of goods to one party is fully compensated for by buying back more than 100 percent of the value that was originally sold.

fundamental forecasting   forecasting based on fundamental relationships between economic variables and exchange.

futures rate   the exchange rate at which one can purchase or sell a specified currency on the settlement date in accordance with the futures contract.

G

General Agreement on Tariffs and Trade (GATT)   agreement allowing for trade restrictions only in retaliation against illegal trade actions of other countries.

gold standard   era in which each currency was convertible into gold at a specified rate, allowing the exchange rate between two currencies to be determined by their relative convertibility rates per ounce of gold.

H

hedge   to insulate a firm from exposure to exchange rate fluctuations.

hostile takeovers   acquisitions not desired by the target firms.

I

imperfect market   the condition where, due to the costs to transfer labor and other resources used for production, firms may attempt to use foreign factors of production when they are less costly than local factors.

import/export letters of credit   trade-related letters of credit.

independent variable   term used in regression analysis to represent the variable that is expected to influence another (the "dependent") variable.

indirect quotations   exchange rate quotations representing the value measured by number of units per dollar.

interbank market   market that facilitates the exchange of currencies between banks.

Interest Equalization Tax (IET)   tax imposed by the U.S. government in 1963 to discourage U.S. investors from investing in foreign securities.

interest rate parity (IRP)   theory specifying that the forward premium (or discount) is equal to the interest rate differential between the two currencies of concern.

interest rate parity (IRP) line   diagonal line depicting all points on a four-quadrant graph that represent a state of interest rate parity.

interest rate parity theory   theory suggesting that the forward rate differs from the spot rate by an amount that reflects the interest differential between two currencies.

interest rate swap   agreement to swap interest payments, whereby interest payments based on a fixed interest rate are exchanged for interest payments based on a floating interest rate.

International Bank for Reconstruction and Development (IBRD)   bank established in 1944 to enhance economic development by providing loans to countries. Also referred to as the World Bank.

International Development Association (IDA)   association established to stimulate country development; it is especially suited for less prosperous nations, since it provides loans at low interest rates.

International Financial Corporation (IFC)   firm established to promote private enterprise within countries; it can provide loans to and purchase stock of corporations.

international Fisher effect (IFE)   theory specifying that a currency's exchange rate will depreciate against another currency when its interest rate (and therefore expected inflation rate) is higher than that of the other currency.

international Fisher effect (IFE) line   diagonal line on a graph that reflects points at which the interest rate differential between two countries is equal to the percentage change in the exchange rate between their two respective currencies.

International Monetary Fund (IMF)   agency established in 1944 to promote and facilitate international trade and financing.

international mutual funds (IMFs)   mutual funds containing securities of foreign firms.

International Swaps and Derivatives Association (ISDA)   a global trade association representing leading participants in the privately negotiated derivatives industry.

intracompany trade   international trade between subsidiaries that are under the same ownership.

irrevocable letter of credit   letter of credit issued by a bank that cannot be canceled or amended without the beneficiary's approval.

issuing bank   bank that issues a letter of credit.

J

J-curve effect   effect of a weaker dollar on the U.S. trade balance in which the trade balance initially deteriorates; it only improves once U.S. and non-U.S. importers respond to the change in purchasing power that is caused by the weaker dollar.

joint venture   venture between two or more firms in which responsibilities and earnings are shared.

L

lagging   strategy used by a firm to stall payments, normally in response to exchange rate projections.

leading   strategy used by a firm to accelerate payments, normally in response to exchange rate expectations.

letter of credit (L/C)   agreement by a bank to make payments on behalf of a specified party under specified conditions.

licensing   arrangement in which a local firm in the host country produces goods in accordance with another firm's (the licensing firm's) specifications; as the goods are sold, the local firm can retain part of the earnings.

locational arbitrage   action to capitalize on a discrepancy in quoted exchange rates between banks.

lockbox   post office box number to which customers are instructed to send payment.

London Interbank Offer Rate (LIBOR)   interest rate commonly charged for loans between Eurobanks.

long-term forward contracts   contracts that state any exchange rate at which a specified amount of a specified currency can be exchanged at a future date (more than one year from today). Also called long forwards.

M

macroassessment   overall risk assessment of a country without considering the MNC's business.

mail float   mailing time involved in sending payments by mail.

managed float   exchange rate system in which currencies have no explicit boundaries, but central banks may intervene to influence exchange rate movements.

margin requirement   deposit placed on a contract (such as a currency futures contract) to cover the fluctuations in the value of that contract; this minimizes the risk of the contract to the counterparty.

market-based forecasting   use of a market-determined exchange rate (such as the spot rate or forward rate) to forecast the spot rate in the future.

Master Agreement   an agreement that provides participants in the private derivatives markets with the opportunity to establish the legal and credit terms between them for an ongoing business relationship.

Medium-Term Guarantee Program   program conducted by the Ex-Im Bank in which commercial lenders are encouraged to finance the sale of U.S. capital equipment and services to approved foreign buyers; the Ex-Im Bank guarantees the loan's principal and interest on these loans.

microassessment   the risk assessment of a country as related to the MNC's type of business.

mixed forecasting   development of forecasts based on a mixture of forecasting techniques.

money market hedge   use of international money markets to match future cash inflows and outflows in a given currency.

Multibuyer Policy   policy administered by the Ex-Im Bank that provides credit risk insurance on export sales to many different buyers.

Multilateral Investment Guarantee Agency (MIGA)   agency established by the World Bank that offers various forms of political risk insurance to corporations.

multilateral netting system   complex interchange for netting between a parent and several subsidiaries.

multinational restructuring   restructuring of the composition of an MNC's assets or liabilities.

N

negotiable bill of lading   contract that grants title of merchandise to the holder, which allows banks to use the merchandise as collateral.

net operating loss carrybacks   practice of applying losses to offset earnings in previous years.

net operating loss carryforwards   practice of applying losses to offset earnings in future years.

netting   combining of future cash receipts and payments to determine the net amount to be owed by one subsidiary to another.

net transaction exposure   consideration of inflows and out-flows in a given currency to determine the exposure after offsetting inflows against outflows.

non-deliverable forward contract (NDF)   like a forward contract, represents an agreement regarding a position in a specified currency, a specified exchange rate, and a specified future settlement date, but does not result in delivery of cur-rencies. Instead, a payment is made by one party in the agreement to the other party based on the exchange rate at the future date.

nonsterilized intervention   intervention in the foreign ex-change market without adjusting for the change in money supply.

notional value   an amount agreed upon by the parties in an interest rate swap.

O

ocean bill of lading   receipt for a shipment by boat, which includes freight charges and title to the merchandise.

open account transaction   sale in which the exporter ships the merchandise and expects the buyer to remit payment according to agreed-upon terms.

overhedging   hedging an amount in a currency larger than the actual transaction amount.

P

parallel bonds   bonds placed in different countries and de-nominated in the respective currencies of the countries where they are placed.

parallel loan   loan involving an exchange of currencies be-tween two parties, with a promise to reexchange the curren-cies at a specified exchange rate and future date.

partial compensation   an arrangement in which the deliv-ery of goods to one party is partially compensated for by buying back a certain amount of product from the same party.

pegged exchange rate   exchange rate whose value is pegged to another currency's value or to a unit of account.

perfect forecast line   a 45-degree line on a graph that matches the forecast of an exchange rate with the actual ex-change rate.

petrodollars   deposits of dollars by countries that receive dollar revenues due to the sale of petroleum to other coun-tries; the term commonly refers to OPEC deposits of dollars in the Eurocurrency market.

Plaza Accord   agreement among country representatives in 1985 to implement a coordinated program to weaken the dollar.

political risk   political actions taken by the host government or the public that affect the MNC's cash flows.

preauthorized payment   method of accelerating cash in-flows by receiving authorization to charge a customer's bank account.

premium   as related to forward rates, represents the per-centage amount by which the forward rate exceeds the spot rate. As related to currency options, represents the price of a currency option.

prepayment   method that exporter uses to receive payment before shipping goods.

price-elastic   sensitive to price changes.

privatization   conversion of government-owned businesses to ownership by shareholders or individuals.

product cycle theory   theory suggesting that a firm initially establish itself locally and expand into foreign markets in re-sponse to foreign demand for its product; over time, the MNC will grow in foreign markets; after some point, its for-eign business may decline unless it can differentiate its product from competitors.

Project Finance Loan Program   program that allows banks, the Ex-Im Bank, or a combination of both to extend long-term financing for capital equipment and related services for major projects.

purchasing power parity (PPP) line   diagonal line on a graph that reflects points at which the inflation differential between two countries is equal to the percentage change in the exchange rate between the two respective currencies.

purchasing power parity (PPP) theory   theory suggesting that exchange rates will adjust over time to reflect the differ-ential in inflation rates in the two countries; in this way, the purchasing power of consumers when purchasing domestic goods will be the same as that when they purchase foreign goods.

put   see *currency put option.*

put option on real assets   project that contains an option of divesting part or all of the project.

Q

quota   maximum limit imposed by the government on goods allowed to be imported into a country.

R

real cost of hedging the additional cost of hedging when compared to not hedging (a negative real cost would imply that hedging was more favorable than not hedging).

real cost of hedging payables is equal to the cost of hedging payables less the cost of payables if not hedged.

real interest rate nominal (or quoted) interest rate minus the inflation rate.

real options implicit options on real assets.

regression analysis statistical technique used to measure the relationship between variables and the sensitivity of a variable to one or more other variables.

regression coefficient term measured by regression analysis to estimate the sensitivity of the dependent variable to a particular independent variable.

reinvoicing center facility that centralizes payments and charges subsidiaries fees for its function; this can effectively shift profits to subsidiaries where tax rates are low.

relative form of purchasing power parity theory stating that the rate of change in the prices of products should be somewhat similar when measured in a common currency, as long as transportation costs and trade barriers are unchanged.

revaluation an upward adjustment of the exchange rate by a central bank.

revalue to increase the value of a currency against the value of other currencies.

revocable letter of credit letter of credit issued by a bank that can be canceled at any time without prior notification to the beneficiary.

S

semistrong-form efficient description of foreign exchange markets, implying that all relevant public information is already reflected in prevailing spot exchange rates.

sensitivity analysis technique for assessing uncertainty whereby various possibilities are input to determine possible outcomes.

simulation technique for assessing the degree of uncertainty. Probability distributions are developed for the input variables; simulation uses this information to generate possible outcomes.

Single-Buyer Policy policy administered by the Ex-Im Bank that allows the exporter to selectively insure certain transactions.

Single European Act act intended to remove numerous barriers imposed on trade and capital flows between European countries.

Small Business Policy policy providing enhanced coverage to new exporters and small businesses.

Smithsonian Agreement conference between nations in 1971 that resulted in a devaluation of the dollar against major currencies and a widening of boundaries (2 percent in either direction) around the newly established exchange rates.

snake arrangement established in 1972, whereby European currencies were tied to each other within specified limits.

spot market market in which exchange transactions occur for immediate exchange.

spot rate current exchange rate of currency.

standby letter of credit document used to guarantee invoice payments to a supplier; it promises to pay the beneficiary if the buyer fails to pay.

sterilized intervention intervention by the Federal Reserve in the foreign exchange market, with simultaneous intervention in the Treasury securities markets to offset any effects on the dollar money supply; thus, the intervention in the foreign exchange market is achieved without affecting the existing dollar money supply.

straddle combination of a put option and a call option.

strangle a currency option combination; similar to a *straddle.*

strike price see *exercise price.*

strong-form efficient description of foreign exchange markets, implying that all relevant public and private information is already reflected in prevailing spot exchange rates.

Structural Adjustment Loan (SAL) established in 1980 by the World Bank to enhance a country's long-term economic growth through financing projects.

supplier credit credit provided by the supplier to itself to fund its operations.

syndicate group of banks that participate in loans.

syndicated Eurocredit loans loans provided by a group (or syndicate) of banks in the Eurocredit market.

T

target zones   implicit boundaries established by central banks on exchange rates.

tariff   tax imposed by a government on imported goods.

technical forecasting   development of forecasts using historical prices or trends.

tenor   time period of drafts.

time-series analysis   analysis of relationships between two or more variables over periods of time.

time-series models   models that examine series of historical data; sometimes used as a means of technical forecasting by examining moving averages.

trade acceptance   draft that allows the buyer to obtain merchandise prior to paying for it.

transaction exposure   degree to which the value of future cash transactions can be affected by exchange rate fluctuations.

transfer pricing   policy for pricing goods sent by either the parent or a subsidiary to a subsidiary of an MNC.

transferable letter of credit   document that allows the first beneficiary on a standby letter of credit to transfer all or part of the original letter of credit to a third party.

translation exposure   degree to which a firm's consolidated financial statements are exposed to fluctuations in exchange rates.

triangular arbitrage   action to capitalize on a discrepancy where the quoted cross exchange rate is not equal to the rate that should exist at equilibrium.

U

Umbrella Policy   policy issued to a bank or trading company to insure exports of an exporter and handle all administrative requirements.

unilateral transfers   accounting for government and private gifts and grants.

W

weak-form efficient   description of foreign exchange markets, implying that all historical and current exchange rate information is already reflected in prevailing spot exchange rates.

Working Capital Guarantee Program   program conducted by the Ex-Im Bank that encourages commercial banks to extend short-term export financing to eligible exporters; the Ex-Im Bank provides a guarantee of the loan's principal and interest.

World Bank   bank established in 1944 to enhance economic development by providing loans to countries.

World Trade Organization (WTO)   organization established to provide a forum for multilateral trade negotiations and to settle trade disputes related to the GATT accord.

writer   seller of an option.

Y

Yankee stock offerings   offerings of stock by non-U.S. firms in the U.S. markets.

Direct Exchange Rates over Time

Index

International Credit

Feb. 10, 2007 Leaders of major countries meet to discuss recent slowdowns in the economy and weakness in the U.S. housing market.

Spring, 2007 Several subprime mortgage lenders in the U.S. experience financial problems.

July 10, 2007 The Fed announces a major increase in consumer credit debt in the U.S.

Aug. 28, 2007 The National Association of Realtors reports that the supply of homes available is at its highest level in 16 years.

Fall, 2007 Several commercial banks and investment banks experience losses and cut job positions.

Dec. 3, 2007 Moody's says it may cut ratings on debt valued at more than $100 billion.

Jan. 21, 2008 Global stock markets experience the largest one-day loss since September 11, 2001.

Jan. 24, 2008 The U.S. announces a $150 stimulus plan.

Feb. 7, 2008 Leaders of several large countries agree to a plan to deal with the subprime mortgage crisis.

March 17, 2008 Bear Stearns, a large U.S. investment bank, is rescued by an acquisition by J.P. Morgan Chase, partially financed by the Federal Reserve.

Spring, 2008 Liquidity begins to dry up in various financial markets in the U.S. and U.K.

May 12, 2008 HSBC (England), the largest bank in Europe, reports a writedown of $3.2 billion in assets over the first quarter of 2008, due to exposure to subprime mortgages.

July 29, 2008 U.S. housing prices decline 15.8% in May, the largest monthly decline on record. This follows a 15.3% decline in April.

Aug. 4, 2008 HSBC warns that the credit crisis is having adverse effects on Asian countries.

Sept. 7, 2008 Fannie Mae and Freddie Mac, which are agencies that provide liquidity to the mortgage market, are rescued by the government.

Sept. 15, 2008 Lehman Brothers, a large U.S. investment bank, fails, and Merrill Lynch (the largest U.S. investment bank) is acquired by Bank of America (one of the largest commercial banks in the U.S.).

Sept. 16, 2008 The U.S. government bails out American Insurance Group (AIG), as the Fed agrees to lend up to $85 billion to AIG.

Oct. 7, 2008 Russia announces plan to infuse capital into its largest banks.

Oct. 8, 2008 Six central banks reduce their interest rates in an effort to stimulate their economies.

Oct. 13, 2008 Leaders of several industrialized countries establish an agreement to implement a stimulus plan.

Oct. 20, 2008 South Korea announces a stimulus plan of $130 billion for its banks.

Crisis Timeline

Oct. 21, 2008 The French government injects $15 billion of capital into its six largest banks.

Oct. 31, 2008 Japan announces a $50 billion stimulus plan. Hungary is given a $25 billion loan by the IMF, European Union, and World Bank.

Nov. 6, 2008 Italy announces a plan to infuse $40 billion of capital into its banks.

Nov. 9, 2008 China announces a $586 billion stimulus plan.

Nov. 25, 2008 The International Monetary Fund approves a $7.6 billion loan to Pakistan to save it from defaulting on other debt.

Nov. 26, 2008 The European Commission announces a $280 billion stimulus plan.

Dec. 1, 2008 Canada's five largest banks announce major writedowns of their assets, due to a decline in mortgage loan valuations.

Dec. 4, 2008 The central bank of New Zealand reduces its interest rate by 1.5%, the largest cut in its history.

Dec. 8, 2008 India announces a $4 billion stimulus plan while France announces a $40 billion stimulus plan. The European central banks cut its interest rate by .75%, its largest cut in history.

Dec. 11, 2008 The central bank of Korea lowers its interest rate to 1%, its lowest rate in 9 years.

Dec. 12, 2008 Japan doubles the funds dedicated to its existing stimulus plan.

Dec. 15, 2008 The Irish government infuses capital in its major banks.

Dec. 16, 2008 Bernard Madoff's hedge fund investment fraud causes major losses at banks around the world, including HSBC (U.K.), Fortis (Belgium), Royal Bank of Scotland, BNP Paribas (France), Nomura (Japan), and Banco Santander (Spain).

Dec. 17, 2008 The Federal Reserve reduces its interest rate to .25%.

Jan. 1, 2009 The stock market performance over 2008 was -42% for France, -40% for Germany, -42% for Japan, -40%, -41% for the U.S., and -31% for the U.K.

Jan. 8, 2009 The Bank of England reduces its interest rate to 1.5%, the lowest level in its history.

Jan. 19, 2009 Iceland's government collapses.

Jan. 21, 2009 The Bank of England plans to purchase large amounts of corporate bonds in order to improve the liquidity in the corporate bond market. Spain's AAA credit rating is reduced, which is the first time a country's AAA rating is reduced in 8 years.

Jan. 18, 2009 The European Central Bank lowers its interest rate to 2%, as it expects the recession in the Eurozone to get worse.